EX LIBRIS

ARTHUR AND

ELIZABETH BAYNTUN

HISTORY OF BEDFORDSHIRE

Frontispiece: The Ouse navigation near Willington. This picture was bought by the late Isaac Godber from the executors of Rudge's daughter.   B. RUDGE, 1839

JOYCE GODBER

HISTORY OF BEDFORDSHIRE

1066-1888

BEDFORDSHIRE
COUNTY COUNCIL
1984

First published 1969

Second impression 1970

Reprinted 1984

© Joyce Godber

ISBN 0 907041 272

Printed in England by Stanley L. Hunt (Printers) Ltd, Rushden, Northants

CONTENTS

PLATES AND MAPS

Note: Unless a more precise date is given all the above original sketches
      are early 19th cent.

FOREWORD

Among the people of Bedfordshire generally I believe there is today an increasing awareness of their past – and the students who come in large numbers to the County Record Office need an authoritative history of the County to give them the background for their work.

For teachers, especially those who come new to the County, the need is imperative.

The *Victoria County History* issued over the years 1904–1912 has long been out of print, and more than 50 volumes of source material have been printed by the Record Society since 1912.

Many tons of documents have come into the hands of the County Record Office since its foundation in 1913 – the first in the country.

So it was very fortunate that the time when the need had become urgent should have coincided with the culmination of Miss Godber's period of devoted service as County Archivist, and that the Council should have been able to second her to write this book.

It is of course not final or definitive – no such history can pretend to be. Much documentary material still needs exhaustive sifting, and there are problems still engaging the attention of national historians which must reflect on the local history of even a small county such as ours. But the compilation in this volume is the result of team work among the County Record Office staff, three of whom number between them more than 60 years of service.

Miss Godber has the gift of bringing local history to life in a way which the ordinary man and woman will understand and enjoy, while deepening our understanding of our national history, made up as it is of so many strands. To the scholar and historian this work will, I hope, present a base for further study and development.

DENIS W. HYDE,
Chairman of the County Records Committee

May, 1969

Since 1969 8,000 copies of the *History of Bedfordshire* have been sold. Miss Godber aimed to provide the background information needed by anyone interested in the county's past, in particular, by historians, and students and teachers working on local topics. In this she has been successful, and the continuing steady demand for her book warrants a further printing, which is a testament to the foresight of the old County Records Committee.

A. ROY SOLLARS
Chairman of the Leisure Committee

October, 1984

SOME TERMS AND ABBREVIATIONS USED

B.H.R.S.	Bedfordshire Historical Record Society
B. Mag.	Bedfordshire Magazine
B.N. & Q.	Bedfordshire Notes and Queries
B.P.R.	Bedfordshire Parish Registers
C.R.O.	County Record Office
copyhold	tenure of land by copy of court roll
hide	originally land adequate for a household; later an assessment unit
hundred	in Bedfordshire a sub-division of the shire, probably dating from the 10th cent
P.R.O.	Public Record Office
strip	sub-division in the common fields, in mediaeval times approximately 1 acre, and normally ploughed in 4 ridged selions
villein	(in simplest terms) one who holds land by labour service
virgate	area of land of varying measurement, but possibly averaging 30 acres
V.C.H.	Victoria County History (of Bedfordshire unless otherwise state d)
L.R.S.	Lincoln Record Society

ACKNOWLEDGEMENTS

My most grateful thanks are due to historians who kindly read and commented on some parts of this book: Professor Dorothy Whitelock (Saxon period); Professor Kathleen Major (mediaeval section); the Rev. Professor David Knowles (the mediaeval church); Professor A. G. Dickens (Reformation) and Dr. Joan Thirsk (Tudor agriculture). Specific help from others is acknowledged at various points. Dr. John Dony read the later period. I am also indebted to Mr. H. G. Tibbutt (Nonconformity), and the Very Rev. Canon Anthony Hulme (Roman Catholicism). Mr. L. R. Conisbee made useful comments. Three teachers advised on presentation: Mr. J. Wilkins of Mander College, Mr. L. P. Banfield of Dunstable Grammar School, and Mr. D. A. E. Calcott of Toddington Secondary Modern School. To many other local people I owe help and encouragement.

My deep gratitude goes to the County Record Office staff: to Patricia Bell, who "held the fort" while I was seconded, and found time to read every chapter in draft; to Alan Cirket, who brought many points to my notice and who supervised the production of maps and illustrations generally; and to Sheila Holgate, for whom no trouble was too much.

The Clerk, Mr. G. O. Brewis, gave me unfailing support. Among many former colleagues at the Shire Hall, I cannot forbear to single out Mr. G. E. Glazier, formerly County Librarian, and the late O. G. Prudden who gave me election details just before he died.

Unless otherwise stated, practically all photographs were taken by the County Council photographer, Mr. K. Whitbread, who spared no effort. Others were supplied by Mr. E. G. Meadows (13b, 16, 17, 18b, 33a, 69a and b); Dr. J. K. St. Joseph of the Cambridge University Committee for Aerial Photography (8b, 9a and b, 10a and b); the National Portrait Gallery (36b, 54b, 55a); the British Museum (14a, 37b, 65); the Tate Gallery (35b); the National Monuments Record (33b); the London Museum (44b); Mr. A. Chrystal (14b); Mr. G. W. Keep (93b); the *Bedfordshire Times* (78b). Plates 19b, 82a are reproduced from T. Fisher's *Collections*. Blocks were lent by the *Bedfordshire Magazine* (48b, 57a-c, 91b, 92a); by Luton Museum (1b, 42, 43); by White Crescent Press Ltd (22a, 93a); and by the Bedfordshire Historical Record Society (64). In general, however, an attempt has been made to avoid duplicating illustrations, especially buildings in *Bedfordshire Heritage*.

Illustrations in private hands are reproduced by permission of Mr. Noel Page-Turner (30a and b, 50b, 53a and b, 60b, 61a and b, 63a, 67, 70b, 73a and b, 77b); Dr. M. S. Longuet-Higgins (23a, 38a, 62b, 86a and b, 89b); Lady Lucas (35a, 46a and b, 54a, 56a and b, 64 – some from photographs taken before the Wrest portraits were dispersed); the late Mrs. Shuttleworth (22b, 52b, 58a, 71a and b); the Duke of Bedford and the Trustees of the Bedford Settled Estates (68, 74a);

the Hon. H. de B. Lawson Johnston (36a, 66); the Marquess of Ailesbury (37a); Mrs. Casebourne (55b); Frank Godber (frontispiece, 31a); Mrs. Hanbury (89a); the Rev. Gregory Page-Turner (38b); Mr. J. R. Pedley (88b); Mr. Samuel Whitbread (78b). Luton Museum further allowed reproductions (1c, 90b); Cecil Higgins Museum, Bedford (18a, 49a, 49b, 81b – the last by permission of Mr. T. W. Bagshawe); Bedford Museum (1a, 23b, 50a); Bedford Corporation (45a, 70a, 78a, 95b); the Master, Fellows and Scholars of St. John's College, Cambridge (32a); and the Inner Temple Library (72a); the remainder came from the collection in the County Record Office. The photographs for 74b and 91a were supplied by Mr. A. Bullwinkle and Mrs. A. F. Cirket.

Early maps are mainly simplified versions of those prepared by the late G. H. Fowler for the Bedfordshire Historical Record Society (3, 4a, 5a and b, 7, 11a) and *Archaeologia* (4b); one is from the *Victoria County History* (11b); one was prepared by Mr. F. G. Emmison for the Record Society (84); and all were redrawn in the County Planning Office.

I thank the Chairmen of the County Records Committee: Mr. R. B. Hobourn under whom this work was begun; and Mr. D. W. Hyde, under whom it has been completed; and Major Simon Whitbread, Chairman of the County Council 1967–69 for his personal interest and backing throughout.

Both for text and illustrations the personal interest and care of Mr. Harold White and Mr. Peter White have been available at every stage.

JOYCE GODBER

1969

To

Charlotte Priest and Agnes Sandys

Prologue

1 – BEFORE THE CONQUEST
(With archaeological material contributed by James Dyer)

THERE ARE difficulties in recounting the Anglo-Saxon history of the area now known as Bedfordshire. One is that before the 10th cent. the name itself cannot be used, for there was no such unit. Others arise from the scantiness of information. Of the days of the first settlements, we can only piece together evidence from the newcomers' archaeological remains, which can still be seen,[1] but have been discovered partly by chance; and we can add something from the names which they gave to the places where they settled.[2] A complication is that both Angles and Saxons came to our area, and it is now thought almost impossible to demarcate them. Such written accounts as have come down to us were mainly written many years after the events described, and by writers living at some distance from the midlands. Traditions cannot help, for when the Danes invaded in the 9th cent. local organisation was disrupted and traditions were lost. Thus only a tentative reconstruction can be given.[3]

A TROUBLED TIME

The earliest Anglo-Saxon settlements in this country were probably in controlled conditions and mostly of friendly barbarians brought in by late Roman authority. They were brought as protection against Picts and Scots, who raided from the north in spite of the great wall, with forts and ditch, built by the emperor Hadrian; or against the wilder Saxon raids along the southeast coast (which, because of such attacks, was called the Saxon shore, and again was protected by forts). When the Roman army withdrew, conditions worsened. On at least three occasions after 383 Britons appealed to Rome for help, but in 410 the emperor Honorius wrote telling them to defend themselves. Britons then continued to invite and make friends with Saxon settlers, to gain their help against the barbarians from the north, and Saxons and Romanised Britons mixed, intermarried and traded.

Mainly this organised settlement was elsewhere, near existing Romano-

---

[1] There is Saxon material in the Bedford Museum. At Luton Museum the 1925 finds from Argyll Avenue, Luton, and the 1957 finds from Marina Drive, Dunstable, are displayed. Finds before 1904 are listed in *V.C.H.* i, 175, and some illustrated; the most important of these, those from Kempston, are in the British Museum but not on view. For a map of Anglo-Saxon sites in the county, see *Beds. Arch.J.* i, 64.

[2] Place-name explanations in this chapter are taken from A. Mawer and F. M. Stenton, *The place-names of Beds. and Hunts.*; see also E. Ekwall, *Oxford dictionary of English place-names*.

[3] The main fabric of this chapter is taken from F. M. Stenton, *Anglo-Saxon England*, and D. Whitelock, *The beginnings of English society*. See also however H. R. Loyn, *Anglo-Saxon England*, for a recent viewpoint.

I

British towns, but there are in our area Anglo-Saxon finds early enough to make it possible that some settlement began in this way; both at Caembes or Kempston, where the old name survives, and where finds made in 1863 included Romano-Saxon pottery and Roman coins pierced for wearing as ornaments;[4] and also in the south, where one late Roman settlement had been largely abandoned.[5] The newcomers used the British names for the Lea and the Ouse.[6] In some places they buried their dead in the local Romano-British buryingplace.[7]

From about 450 ever-increasing arrivals of Saxons and Angles meant chaos and confusion and uncontrolled land-seizure. The invaders probably came from two directions: from the south up the lower Thames and the Lea; and from the Wash up the Ouse. Finds include the brooches with which the newcomers fastened their mantles; some cruciform, some saucer-shaped, and some equal-armed; also a pottery vessel of a distinctive type.[8] Some early settlements are believed to be those with names ending in "ing", which denote groups of people; Knotting, Pillinge, and Kechinge (Kitchen End in Pulloxhill.)[9] The Gifle people gave their own name to the Ivel, and it survives also in Northill, Southill and Yielden.

Battles raged in which the native British were defeated, till about 490, when the British won a great victory at an unidentified site called Mons Badonicus, and the newcomers were checked for a time. Then in the middle of the 6th cent. the West Saxons began to move northwards, gaining control of much of the south and centre of the country. They moved eastwards along the Chilterns, or north from the upper Thames. At an unidentified place, Cuthwulf fought a battle in 571, and regained the former settlement of Limbury, together with other places not far distant (Aylesbury, Eynsham and Benson).[10]

SETTLEMENT EXTENDS

Following this victory, settlement in our area was expanded and consolidated. In a cemetery near Leighton [Buzzard] some 18 graves were discovered in 1932, with decorated glass beads, hair pins and buckles, knives and spearheads, a small hanging pot, and a drinking cup made of bronze and wood.[11] The graves lay in a haphazard scatter, and no traces of coffins were found, though one skeleton had a turf sod placed under its head as a pillow. Objects buried at about the same time in the Kempston cemetery include a beautiful pale-green glass cone-shaped cup, many beads of glass, amber and crystal – one woman's grave contained 120 beads – amethyst and crystal pendants, as well as a great square-headed brooch and several bronze bracelets. Three small gilt bronze workboxes had been attached by chains

[4] *Proc. Beds. Architect. & Archaeol.Soc.* vii, 269–99.

[5] Runfold Avenue, Luton; *Beds. Archaeologist* i, 21–7.

[6] For river names, see Ekwall, *English river-names*; and Loyn, *op.cit.*, 6–10.

[7] Anglo-Saxon saucer brooches have been found in the Roman cemetery at Shefford; *V.C.H.* i, 187.

[8] A type common in northwest Germany called a *bückelurn*. Besides the Kempston cemetery, there was an early one at Deadman's slade, Leighton

Buzzard, *Proc.S.A.* ix, 29; at Luton, *Ant.J.* viii, 177–92; and at Sandy; *V.C.H.* i, 184; *Ant.J.* xxxiv, 201–8; and xxxvii, 224–5.

[9] This has lately been queried: J. McN. Dodgson and A. Meaney, *Medieval archaeology*.

[10] *B. Mag.* iv, 13. "Bedcanford" is a lost site, not Bedford.

[11] Chamberlain's Barn; *Arch.J.* cxx, 161–200.

to girdles, and contained scraps of linen, thread and wool. The men's graves contained the usual spears, two-edged swords and shields; to the front of one of the latter a silver-plated tin fish-badge had been fixed; presumably it was the personal symbol of the owner.

Many Christian Britons must have been killed, enslaved or driven westwards. Fighting must have been endemic; somewhere about 600 one thriving settlement in the south of our area was completely wiped out: in about 50 graves have since been found two bronze work-boxes, beads, rings, a fine bone comb, and 20 knives.[12] A watch-hill (Warden, Totternhoe) was important; as things grew quieter, one of these became the "old watch-hill" (Old Warden).

Much of our area is low-lying, the highest point being 796 ft. above sea-level, and some of it was then marshland and fen (Marston, Fenlake). Though the newcomers made some settlements on lower ground (denu or valley, as in Stagsden, Wilden), and along the valleys of the Ouse, Lea and Ivel, they tended to prefer higher ground, such as Higham. Some place-names are derived from hoh or hill-spur as in Bletsoe, Keysoe, Silsoe; or from hill as in Clophill, Odell, Pulloxhill, Wroxhill; one hill they jokingly called ant-hill – Ampthill; and two others cliff – Clifton and Hockliffe. Down, often later corrupted, occurs in Battlesden, Billington, Caddington, Dunton, Harlington, Stondon, Sundon, Toddington. Excluding riparian settlements, which average 130 ft. above sea-level, the average height of the remaining two-thirds of our settlements is about 280 ft.[13]

Large stretches were then covered with woods (Wootton; also hurst and grove, as in Bolnhurst, Gravenhurst, Potsgrove). Used to forests in their continental homeland, the new settlers made their clearings (leah, as in Hatley) among the oaks (Oakley, Eggington), the aspens (Aspley), the birches (Little Barford), the willows (Salford, Willington), and the brushwood (Riseley). In the woods and elsewhere were wild boars (Eversholt, Everton). In one place they were struck by the number of cranes (Cranfield); and in another by the crows (Crawley). Good farming land they sought for (Leighton): and good pasture (Astwick, Dilwick, Flitwick, Hinwick, Tilwick); and streams or burns to water their livestock (Tilbrook; Sharnbrook – dung-brook calls up a picture of cattle sheltering on a hot day; Bourne End, Husbourne, Melchbourne, Woburn). Fords were required for crossing the rivers (Barford, Bedford, Girtford, Langford, Salford, Shefford, Stafford, Stratford, Tempsford; and Biggleswade).

A settlement was often fortified – a single-storied wooden hall, with smaller detached buildings, surrounded by an earthwork and stockade (burh, as in Cadbury, Limbury, Medbury, Upbury); or merely enclosed (worth, as in Colworth, Colmworth, Edworth, Kensworth, Tebworth, Tilsworth, Wrestlingworth).

---

[12] On the site of what was afterwards Dunstable; *Beds. Arch.J.* i, 25–47. See also C. L. Matthews, *Ancient Dunstable.*

[13] The church, possibly sometimes on the site of a former heathen shrine, has been taken as the basis, an older church (as at Segenhoe and Birchmore) being preferred to a newer one.

It might be a collection of huts; recently a number of rectangular huts were discovered at Puddle Hill;[14] they measured 10 ft. x 12 ft., were heated by central hearths, and had pitched roofs which spanned from a central ridge-pole to the ground; their floors were sunk between 12 in. and 18 in. into the enclosed ground level, and scattered on them were scraps of pottery, bone and bronze pins, and the bones of sheep, cattle, pigs and fowls. Sometimes a settlement was called home or farmstead (ham, as in Biddenham, Blunham, Bromham, Clapham, Felmersham, Pavenham, Studham); or homestead (Greathampstead, Wilshamstead); or cottages (Biscot, Caldecote, Cotton End, Eastcotts, Fancott, Hulcote, Thorncote); or farm (ton).

The names grew up haphazard, so it is not surprising that there are two "hill-farms" (Houghton), and two "river-farms" (Eaton: ey was used for land in the bend of a river, as at Arlesey, Lewsey, Sandy, Turvey). "Middle farm" seems odd, and we have two of them (Milton), presumably a settlement that came after the surrounding area was occupied: "south-farm" (Sutton) apparently followed Potton to the north; similarly with "east-farm" (Astwick) and "west-farm" (Weston).

In this, their new country, our forebears held rites to the old gods, Woden, Thunor and Tiw. Those who held land provided places for their kinsfolk and dependants to worship, and two such sites are approximately known; the sacred grove at Harrowden; and Woden's hill, Wodneslaw, somewhere near Biggleswade. At certain times in such places they sacrificed with ceremonial feasting; in the ninth month, Halegmonath, after harvest; or in the eleventh month, Blotmonath, when some of the livestock had been killed off to salt down for the winter. In the spring, in Eosturmonath, was the festival of the goddess Eostre.

And who were they, and what manner of men, who gave their names to our settlements: Aelfric, Baedel, Beda, Bida, Biccel, Billa, Blaecc, Bluwa, Cada, Culma, Cocca, Edda, Feolumaer, Golda, Herela, Hocgna, Cen, Caeg, Cnotta, Lytel, Papa, Pearta, Pudda, Pullox, Hroc, Scyttel, Sifel, Steapa, Styfa, Sunna, Tuda, Wibba, Wil, Wraestel and Widmund? We shall never know. A woman Ceolwynne gave her name to Chellington, perhaps an heiress, or a widow whose husband was killed in the fighting, while his men fell close beside him, faithful to their lord.

It is not known what was the earliest organisation in our area. The newcomers were accustomed to open-air meetings, and such meetings were probably held at Tingrith (assembly-brook). Whether there was in these early years a king of the Middle Angles (as of the neighbouring East Angles, whose treasures were found a few years ago at Sutton Hoo) is not recorded. Bede in the early 8th cent. tried to find out what he could, but he lived in Jarrow. Nor did short-lived heathen

---

[14] *Beds. Arch. J.* i, 51–3. An account of only one hut has so far been published. For Eaton Socon finds, see also *Camb. Ant. Proc.* lviii, 38–73.

kingdoms seem to him important. To our north, however, the Angles settled in the valley of the Trent, which rises far westward in what was then British country, and they came to be called the "boundary folk" (Mierce). Among them arose a great line of kings. Thus we became absorbed into the kingdom of Mercia, which by the 7th cent. stretched over most of what may now be called central England.

CHRISTIANITY COMES

How soon Christian teaching filtered into Mercia it is hard to say. One early place for it was perhaps the "cross on a hill" (Maulden). Whence did it come? There were two possible directions: from southern England, deriving from Rome; and from northern England, deriving from Ireland.

In Kent and among the Saxons to the south, St. Augustine and other Christian teachers sent by the Pope had made great headway since 597. Between the various kingdoms of England there must have always been some intercourse. Radiating out from Canterbury, St. Augustine's centre, was a formal church organisation, in touch with that on the continent. It adopted the continental method of calculating the date of the festival which in England was beginning to be called Easter.

But there was also an ancient Christian church in Ireland, which dated from St. Patrick in the 5th cent. When Britain and Gaul relapsed into heathenism, this church had lost contact with the Papacy, but it continued none the less, and it had a strong missionary spirit. Missionaries from this Irish church converted Northumbria, north of Mercia. From Northumbria came the official beginning of the conversion of Mercia, which under King Penda (killed in battle in 654) had been a stronghold of heathenism. Penda's son, on his marriage with a Northumbrian princess, was baptised in his father's lifetime in 653, and with his bride came four priests. These priests, says Bede,[15] for their erudition and good life were deemed proper to instruct and baptise his nation, and he returned home with much joy. They were willingly listened to, and many, as well of the nobility as the common sort, renouncing the abominations of idolatry, were baptised daily. We know that elsewhere such large-scale baptisms sometimes took place by the rivers, and here probably it was so too. (Wells afterwards known as holy wells may have had a pagan significance, for later bishops frowned on them).[16]

One of the four priests of 653, Diuma, was an Irishman, and he soon afterwards became the first bishop of the Mercians. Perhaps something of Irish asceticism, saintliness and learning reached our forefathers through him, from a tradition which went back through Lindisfarne and the Irish monasteries to earlier days of the Christian church. In these early times, what few priests there were normally operated from a monastery or minster church as a centre. The minster church for this area may have been what became St. Paul's church, Bedford. The ford over the Ouse made Bedford a suitable centre; and much later (ch. 5) when more is

---

[15] *Eccles. hist.* iii, ch.24.
[16] Holy wells are known, for instance, at Bromham,

Odell and Stevington; see *B.H.R.S. Survey* ii; and compare *V.C.H. Bucks.* i, 288.

known of St. Paul's, it was served, not by one priest, but by a group of canons. The earliest bishops worked at full pressure – elsewhere one is said to have instructed and baptised from dawn to dusk,[17] and so probably did Diuma. Bede says that in a short time he gained many people to our Lord. It was on tour among the Middle Angles that he died, and a later text says that he lies at Charlbury (Oxon.).

With the coming of Christianity pagan cemeteries fell into disuse, and new ones were started, but it was not easy to discard the old practice of burying gifts and personal possessions with the dead. At Leighton[18] another cemetery was begun with nearly 70 graves orientated approximately east-west; here have been found sets of linked silver pins, some inlaid with garnets; silver rings; a disc brooch in gold set with garnets; a silver quoit brooch; and innumerable beads of glass, silver and amber; all often contained in wooden jewel boxes; there were also a few knives; but the only arms were part of one spearhead and the conical boss of a late 7th cent. shield.

When, near Whitby in 663 or 664, a synod met to consider whether the Christian church in Northumbria should follow continental or Irish ways, and decided for the former, it influenced other churches further south. For the future of England it was important to have a common Christian practice, and it was desirable that this practice should be in harmony with the main stream of Christendom. But in our own area people had so recently had Christian teaching that they were probably little aware of different methods of calculating the date of Easter, and were perhaps still getting used to the fact that Eostre's festival had been transformed into a Christian one. Christianity was now to be the dominant religion in England, but some pagan thoughts and practices lingered or were driven underground (even in Kent in 695 a law forbids "sacrifice to devils");[19] and a few of these showed themselves in various ways for centuries to come (ch. 16).

Besides, at this time the people of our area had other concerns. It was no easy time when Christianity came. King Penda's defeat and death meant for Mercia temporary dismemberment and decline. Troubled conditions meant the undermining of law and order; war with neighbouring states brought loss of life in battle, destruction of villages and crops and consequent scarcity and famine.

KING OFFA OF MERCIA

With Ethelbald (d. 757) and Offa (d. 796) Mercia enlarged her bounds and gained supremacy among the other kingdoms of England. There were interruptions to this, and periodical fighting, both in the more distant areas of Offa's influence in England, and with the British till he constructed the dyke which bears his name. But probably for most of the 8th cent. our area enjoyed comparative peace.

---

[17] *Eccles.hist.* ii, chs. 14, 16.
[18] See n. 11.

[19] *English Historical Documents* (gen.ed. Douglas), i (ed. Whitelock), p.363, the laws of Wihtred.

The widespread Mercian kingdom of this time could no longer be governed on the early simple lines. Its sub-areas were called in Latin *regiones* – we do not know the English term; they seem to have been the old tribal groups, and their area and distribution are hard to identify, except with an entry for the Gifle people of the Ivel valley, found on an old list. A *regio* was in the charge of an ealdorman, or chief officer. Of these there were in Mercia perhaps as many as eight or ten. The ealdorman, when travelling on the king's service, must – like the king – be entertained.

Next of consequence were the thegns, who had usually derived their rank as a reward, by royal grant of services formerly due to the king. Many had by the 8th cent. become lords of villages. The mass of the people were in general still the free peasants of the original migration. They often owned slaves (these could be penal slaves). The normal peasant holding for assessment purposes was called a hide, originally an amount of land considered adequate to maintain a household; but the number of hides continued as the basis for assessing an area long after it had any necessary relation to the actual number of holdings.

Besides the obligation to entertain the king or his representatives, there were three general obligations. A man must serve in the fyrd or fighting force when there was fighting in the neighbourhood; he must help with fortifications (of the earthwork and palisade type) when these were required; and he must work on bridges (there may have been some simple wooden structures over our rivers, though there is no certain reference even to Bedford bridge till much later).

In our area, common field agriculture (though it never spread over all England) was probably by now established, with two fields, of which one at a time was left fallow, with waste and scrubland around them. In these fields the peasants or ceorls had land in scattered strips, while they lived in villages with crofts by their houses. Water-mills were not known to our forefathers when they came – slaves ground their corn; but mills may have come into use in eastern England in the 8th cent., and Millbrook occurs in 931.[20]

How soon boundary lines between townships were drawn is not known. Some (e.g., the river in riparian settlements) would no doubt date almost from the first, but it would be less easy or urgent to define where the boundary ran over waste land between two villages, and in fact at least one boundary was in dispute a millennium later.

One or two descriptions of boundaries exist, and are perhaps relevant here, though they come from the 10th cent.; as at Chalgrave in 926[21] when King Athelstan confirmed to his thegn Ealdred land "where the dyke shoots on to Watling Street [a Roman road], then along Watling Street to the ford, then

---

20 R. Bennett & J. Elton, *History of corn milling*, i, 97-8; Birch, *Cart. Sax.* no. 553, Myllenburne *c.* 880. Reference to a Dover mill in 762 is ambiguous; and supposed reference to a water-mill at Croyland in 833 is a post-conquest forgery.
21 *B.H.R.S.* v, 43.

along the brook to the second ford, then from the ford up to the spring" and so on; or Aspley [Guise] in 969[22] (this document was a grant by King Edgar to his faithful thegn Alfwold) "up to the little knoll, thence to the apple tree where three land boundaries meet, of the men of Woburn, and of the men of Wavendon, and of the men of Aspley; from the deer-gate over the heath" and so on. This same description also refers to another meeting of three boundaries: "of Cranfield men, and of Marston men, and of Hulcote" near an old maple-tree.

We cannot trace in detail the steps by which dependence on the minster church, with its group of clergy, grew into the parochial system. These steps involved personnel, buildings and finance.

How rapidly there developed a sufficient priesthood is uncertain. Even in the 7th cent. Englishmen were sending missions to their former continental homeland, but Bede in 735 thought the supply for the priesthood very inadequate.

Local buildings[23] were required, at this time of wood, and often built by a local thegn, who thus felt it his property. The result was haphazard. In Bedford more churches were built than can have been needed to accommodate the inhabitants; on the other hand at Houghton [Conquest], where the shares of Houghton gildable and Houghton franchise lasted till 1641, there may possibly have been two original builders. A new building was not necessarily at once a parish church. A parish church had a graveyard and font and might serve a wide area. At some distance from it there might be a chapel, where services could be said on Sundays and holy days, provided people visited the parish church four times a year, and took their children to be christened and their dead to be buried. Thus Clapham was a chapelry of Oakley. At a later stage such a chapel might become a parish church.

Then there was the financing of the new religion. It took some time before this was standardised. All dues were first paid to the original minster of the district, and when other churches were built this retained the first claim; as late as the 10th cent. various dues were legally payable to it in preference to local churches. Only slowly did tithe (a tenth of produce) become part of the endowment of the parish priest. As to the origin of glebe, we have no evidence; presumably it was by early gift or bequest.

All in all, because of the differences between one village and another, and between personalities in the same village at different periods, it is likely that there was great variation in the dates when churches were built, in their being recognised as parish churches, in their size, and in the plate and vestments with which they were equipped; yet it seems probable that in our area, more populous and less troubled than the north, parish churches with sufficient revenue to maintain a

---

[22] B.H.R.S. v, 46. If anyone interferes with this gift, "may he be cut off from the fellowship of Holy Church, and be wretchedly punished by the everlasting flames of the pit, along with Judas."

[23] Excavations at a Buckinghamshire church (Wing) near Leighton Buzzard indicate that it was late 7th cent. (J.Brit.Arch.Assoc. xxv, 18–20.)

priest, with part at least of the tithes, and burial fees, were well advanced by the end of the Saxon period (see also ch. 4). We may compare in recent times the building of schools and halls.

Perhaps our divided parishes arose in cases when the thegn who originally built the church had land in more than one place: Bletsoe with a small area in Sharnbrook; Harlington with one in Weston[ing]: Higham (Pulloxhill); Pertenhall (Bolnhurst); Pulloxhill (Flitton); Houghton Regis (Buckwood); and the confusion between Shillington and Holwell. Such a custom, once introduced, continued long after the cause had lapsed and even the reason for it was forgotten – in fact, until the 19th cent.

Probably village priests then, as for centuries to follow, had enough Latin to get through the services. Married clergy were common. It was said by Alfred about 890 that "before everything was ravaged and burnt . . . the churches throughout all England were filled with treasures and books," but he was probably thinking of cathedrals, monasteries and large minsters.

Church organisation developed. In 737 a bishopric was set up at Leicester, to which we probably belonged. Not only this; it was irksome to Offa that the primacy of all England should be seated at Canterbury in the sub-kingdom of Kent, which was restive under his influence. In 788 he persuaded the Pope to elevate Lichfield into an archbishopric. Tradition claims that he founded the great abbey of St. Albans in 791, and in the following year granted it land at Biscot.[24]

Offa was of European standing: he corresponded with Charlemagne, and in 786 the Pope sent legates to him. But with his death in 796 the great days of Mercia were over, for his successors were not of his calibre. The archbishopric of Lichfield, unpopular with the English church, was suppressed by the Pope in 803 at the request of the Mercian King Cenwulf himself. In 829 Mercia was defeated by Wessex. The heathen Danish invasions began in 835.

THE DANES

During the next 30 years several Danish descents on the north and east of England are known, and at least twice a Danish army wintered in England. Some local earthworks – that at Etonbury in Arlesey near the Hiz, that at Beeston near the Ivel, that at Water End, Renhold, near the Ouse, and probably also one at Willington are believed to be Danish.[25] In each case the settlement is beside a river, with a D-shaped earthwork in front. The Danish method was to come up the rivers, to seize a defensible position and fortify it, laying up their boats; and, commandeering local horses, to ravage the country round as a mounted force, driving off the cattle for their supplies, and taking the plate from the churches. Their chief weapons were the sword and the axe. Though at first they came as raiders, as time went on they began to settle. The settlement was chiefly in the north of England and in East Anglia, but by 878 a large army had also settled

---

[24] *V.C.H.* ii, 361.　　　　　　[25] *V.C.H.* i, 278, 280; *B. Mag.*, viii, 235.

in part of what had been Mercia. The bishop had to leave Leicester for the south. The names Carlton (Danish carl corresponds to Saxon ceorl) and Toft in Sharnbrook (like the Saxon croft) bear witness to the Danes in our midst; and the term "Danish axe" passed into local idiom, and was still in use 400 years later.[26]. The suffering must have been great; it may have been worse in our border area than to the north and east of us, where perhaps some harsh order prevailed.

Wessex was now the hope of England, and Wessex was saved by King Alfred. A boundary was agreed with a main force of the Danes (that of Guthrum of East Anglia) probably in 886: up the Thames; up the Lea to its source; then to Bedford and along the Ouse to Watling Street. In our area it seems an awkward boundary, and in fact soon after Alfred's death in 899 the Danes came south and west of Bedford, making of Bedford a centre. The ford over the Ouse, which seems to have caused the choice of Bedford as a mission centre, was probably the reason for its being chosen as a stronghold. This was under a local leader, perhaps the jarl Thurcetel who later appears in command at Bedford. Chalgrave, mentioned above as confirmed to Ealdred the thegn by the king in 926, had actually been bought by Ealdred "from the heathen" no later than 911 and by King Edward's orders. Thus at the beginning of the 10th cent. our area was border territory in the Danelaw (by which is meant that part of England in Danish occupation).

The Danelaw, however, was not a unit. It was a collection of areas under semi-military occupation, the local army-leader being sometimes called king, sometimes jarl. In our area the Danish jarl was Thurcetel, and it was at Bedford that the local Danish settlers concentrated in war, or met for deliberation in peace.

When some time had elapsed since the Danes settled and began to accept Christianity, Alfred's son Edward began to move cautiously against them, with the help of his sister, Aethelflaed, Lady of the Mercians (whose husband had been caldorman of that part of Mercia which remained English). First Edward built a double defensive earthwork, or burh, on the Lea at Hertford, one north and one south of the river. Next he moved against the Danes of Essex. The English gained confidence: when in 913 a Danish raiding band "rode out against Luton . . . the people of the district became aware of it, and fought against them and reduced them to full flight, and rescued all that they had captured and also a great part of their horses and weapons."[27]

In October 914 King Edward built a burh at Buckingham. "And Earl Thurcetel came and accepted him as his lord, and so did all the earls and principal men who belonged to Bedford."[28] The king followed up this submission by occupying Bedford. He "went with his army to Bedford before Martinmas [11 Nov. 915]

---

[26] "Striking him to the heart with a 'denesch' axe"; Eaton Socon, 1275; B.H.R.S. xli, 75.

[27] *Anglo-Saxon chronicle*, ed. Whitelock, p.63. All quotations from this chronicle are taken from this

revised translation of 1961, where the vexed question of differing dates is most clearly dealt with.

[28] *Op.cit.*, p.64.

and obtained the borough . . . and he stayed there four weeks, and before he went away he ordered the borough on the south side of the river to be built."[29] Already there must have been fortifications on the north, probably following a semicircle or rectangle from the Severn ditch on the west, through St. Peter's church on the north, and St. Cuthbert's on the east. Now, to protect the area south of the Ouse, about 45 acres, he had a moat constructed in a semicircle, the "king's ditch". Though on a larger scale, it was similar to the Danish fortifications referred to above. The king's ditch is still clearly marked as such on an 1841 map of Bedford, and at that date it still almost contained south Bedford. Though now nearly completely built over, it added to the flooding of Bedford in 1947.

Thus, in case of future trouble, the king had made Bedford an English centre for defence. These new fortifications made it a safe place for a market. Men came to settle here to trade; they hired plots from the king, and the rent they paid him was called the hagable, *haga* being the hedge or fence round each new plot. (Centuries later this hagable rent was still paid). The king's port-reeve administered the borough, which was now in a special relationship to the king.

The Danes of Huntingdon and East Anglia took alarm, expecting their turn next, and they advanced against Bedford in 917. "The army [i.e. the Danish army] came from Huntingdon and East Anglia, and made the fortress at Tempsford, and took up quarters in it and built it . . . thinking that from Tempsford they would reach [recover?] more of the land with strife and hostility. And they went till they reached Bedford; and the men who were inside went out against them and fought against them, and put them to flight and killed a good part of them."[30]

The northward advance of the king and his sister against the other Danish headquarters, Derby, Leicester, Stamford, Nottingham, continued. When Edward died in 924, his son was recognised not only as King of Wessex but also of the old Mercia. The Danes were treated with a good deal of tolerance. King Edgar said "It is my will that among the Danes such good laws shall be valid as they best appoint."

SHIRE AND HUNDRED

Some form of local administration was now necessary in the reoccupied area of midland England. The original groupings or tribal divisions of Mercia, the old *regiones*, had been lost when the Danish armies imposed their own areas. It was simplest therefore to transform each Danish area into a new-style English unit. Thus arose the midland shires (though it is not till 1011 that the word Bedfordshire actually occurs in the Anglo-Saxon chronicle). The county boundary (if indeed it was the same then as we find it more than a century later) was not to modern eyes altogether rational. On the borders with Northamptonshire, Huntingdonshire and Hertfordshire, it divided various parishes; while two inland areas (Swineshead and part of Meppershall) belonged respectively to Hunting-

[29] *Loc.cit.*   [30] *Op.cit.*, p.65.

donshire and Hertfordshire.[31] Again the explanation may be due to some long-forgotten estate-ownership.

During the 10th cent. there also arose a new officer. The ealdorman, or earl as he began to be called, remained for larger areas, but the officer for the shire was the shire-reeve or sheriff.

The midland shires were sub-divided (probably during the 10th cent.) into smaller areas, the hundreds. Unlike the hundreds of southern England, which appear to be older and which vary in size, the midland hundreds (including those of Bedfordshire) are roughly comparable. In Bedfordshire there were nine whole hundreds (Stodden, Willey, Barford, Redbornstoke, Wixamtree, Biggleswade, Clifton, Flitt and Manshead); and three half-hundreds (Buckley, Stanbridge and Wensley, later merged in the others). A century later, when we have hidage for the hundreds, the whole hundreds are found to range from 98 to 123 hides, and the half-hundreds from 50 to 62 hides.[32]

Each hundred had a court which met every four weeks in the open air. Some of these meeting-places are known or surmised. Thus Manshead probably met at the old meeting-place at Tingrith. Two other hundreds met at particular trees; Willey near some special willow-tree; Wixamtree at "Wihstan's tree", thought to be a forerunner of Deadman's Oak at the centre of the hundred.[33] Biggleswade, Clifton and Flitt probably met in the parishes from which each hundred took its name; so also Barford, perhaps in a field where there was a stone cross.[34] Stodden seems to have met in a field at Pertenhall, and Redbornstoke somewhere in Marston.[35]

When, during the fighting of the previous century, the bishop took refuge in the south, he made Dorchester-on-Thames his seat; and Dorchester remained the seat for the vast midland diocese when the midland Danes had become Christian and were absorbed into the southern kingdom.

Now came a revival of church-building. The English had learnt to build in stone. How many stone churches there were in Bedfordshire in the 10th and 11th cents. it is impossible to say, because most early building was swept away in subsequent centuries in the constant process of enlarging and rebuilding. But along the course of the Ouse (perhaps the stone was brought by river) some Saxon work remains in the towers of Clapham, Stevington, Bedford St. Mary and St. Peter,[36] and a carved stone cross base was recently found at Elstow.

The monastic movement made some progress. There was in the 10th cent. a

---

[31] *Guide* to Bedford R.O., pp.28–9.
[32] *B.H.R.S.* Qto., i.
[33] *B.H.R.S.* xxv, 1.
[34] Cf. C.R.O., BC 140; "una roda apud ston' crosse", 1472. What appears to be the base of a stone cross is now in the village at the corner of Silver Street; it may have been moved there (cf. *V.C.H. Hunts.*,

iii, 1).
[35] *B.H.R.S.* xii, 93, 95.
[36] E. H. Fisher, *The greater Anglo-Saxon churches*, pp. 151–5; also H. M. & J. Taylor, *Anglo-Saxon architecture*, i, 58–9, 158; ii, 571, 626; also *Beds. Arch.J.* iii, 7–14.

monastery at Bedford, though a small one.[37] Here, though it would hardly aspire to copy classical works, or, like Peterborough, to keep a version of the Anglo-Saxon chronicle, it may be that Bibles and service-books were written and illuminated, and perhaps some other books, such as the works of Bede, the life of Alfred, and the popular story of St. Guthlac, who was born and brought up "in the region of the Middle Angles". [38]Astwick church is dedicated to him.

An important monastery in Huntingdonshire had extensive land in Bedfordshire: Ramsey Abbey. Lay lords made gifts to it: Athelstan Mannesunu (d. 986) gave Clapham;[39] Alwyn (d. 998) gave Cranfield;[40] and Edgiva Little Barford;[41] while other estates were bestowed on this Abbey by successive bishops of Dorchester: Shillington in the early 11th cent. by bishop Aethelric (he had bought it from a Dane who felt ill at ease among his English neighbours); and Barton a little later by bishop Eadnoth.[42] To Thorney Abbey Aelfleda gave Bolnhurst.[43] But before this much trouble had again fallen on the county, as must shortly be related.

Englishmen began the long process of Christianising the stubborn heathenism of the Scandinavian homelands. But as the names of these missionaries are not known, we cannot tell whether any went from Bedfordshire.

Trade grew in the 10th cent., and Bedford, still administered by the king's port-reeve, developed further as a trading-place. The standard coin in England was now a silver penny. The dies for this were produced from one centre, but the minting was carried out locally. Such minting was naturally entrusted to fortified places already possessing markets. The king appointed a moneyer in Bedford and supplied him with dies, and he minted coins for local use, adding (for identification) his own name and that of Bedford. Bedford coins can thus be traced. Among the known Bedford moneyers are three with Danish names, Grim, Gunni and Ulcetel.[44]

The comparative peace was not to last. A fresh wave of Danish invasion broke on the country in 980 and gathered increasing force. Neither fighting nor money payments availed. This time there was no national hero to lead and plan. For Bedfordshire the climax came in the years 1009–10. This is probably when the Bedford monastery came to an end. The northern Danes came from the northwest "along the Ouse until they reached Bedford, and so on as far as Tempsford,

---

37 The only known abbot bore the same name as the Danish jarl of the previous generation, Thurcetel. He was a kinsman of the then Archbishop of York, who died at Thame in 971, and he brought the body to Bedford; *Anglo-Saxon chronicle*, p. 76. "In the first decades of the revival under Dunstan [d. 988] . . . the writing of manuscripts must have occupied . . . a very large fraction of the total monastic population;" D. Knowles, *The monastic order in England*, 519.

38 *English Historical Documents*, i. 709. St. Guthlac, who died in 714, understood the Britons' speech,

for "in former vicissitudes . . . he had been an exile among them", p.711.
39 *V.C.H.* iii, 128.
40 *V.C.H.* iii, 276.
41 *V.C.H.* ii, 207.
42 *V.C.H.* ii, 21, 294; 309.
43 *V.C.H.* iii, 124.
44 *Anglo-Saxon coins*, ed. R. H. M. Dolley, pp.122–35; *Catalogue of English coins in the British Museum*, Anglo-Saxon series, ii, 158–461. There are also Bedford coins in Scandinavian museums, and some in Bedford and Luton Museums.

and ever they burnt as they went. Then they turned back to the ships with their booty. And when . . . the English army should have come out . . . the English army went home. . . . In the end no shire would even help the next."[45] In 1016 there came a restoration of order when the able Dane Cnut became king of England. Not till 1042 was there again an English king, Edward, whose youth had been spent in exile with his mother's people in Normandy; and he had no son to be his heir. His continental friends began to come to England. Count Eustace of Boulogne married his sister. Albert of Lorraine acquired land at Chalgrave. However, under King Edward there was peace for about 20 years, and we can gain an impression of Bedfordshire at this time.[46]

ON THE EVE OF THE CONQUEST

The king held, besides Bedford, the ancient royal lands of Leighton, Luton and Houghton Regis (70 hides). These manors paid gold annually to the queen: 2 oz. each from Houghton Regis and Leighton, and 4 oz. from Luton; and they also paid considerable sums for the king's dogs for hunting.

The earl seems at first to have been Tostig, who was also Earl of Northumbria and apparently of Huntingdonshire and Northamptonshire, though he had only 29 hides in this county, mainly Potton. Tostig the trouble-maker was outlawed in 1065, when Waltheof was given an earldom of Bedfordshire, Cambridgeshire, Huntingdonshire and Northamptonshire;[47] but though men of Waltheof held land in this county he himself held none in demesne. Other men of note elsewhere who had some land here included Harold, the future king, (Weston [Ing] and Arlesey; he gave the latter to his foundation, Waltham Abbey). His brother Gyrth held Kempston. The sheriff was Godric.

Thegns held 38% of the land; Aschil or Anschil had the most (69 hides scattered over the county); next was Ulmar (57 hides, mainly Eaton Socon and Sandy); Levenot (40 hides in the northwest and south); and Borred (31 hides, mainly Melchbourne and Yielden). Some thegns had land in other counties also, for instance Aschil at Ware in Hertfordshire; and they would live now at one estate, now at another, their scattered lands being managed by local reeves. All these thegns had their "men", that is, smaller men, who looked to them for protection, but were not necessarily bound to them; thus Aluin and Aluric of Sharnbrook, Godwin of Milton [Ernest], Leuric of Wymington, and Ulueva of Shelton were all "men of Borred", as also were 23 socmen in the neighbourhood. The number of landholders is hard to assess; when a name occurs twice in the

[45] *Anglo-Saxon chronicle*, p.90. There is at Tempsford only a small earthwork, and for this reason it has been suggested (*B.Mag.* viii, 236–8) that the site may have been Beeston, Eaton Socon or Shillington. It has also been suggested that an earthwork at Biggleswade was, in its earlier phase, like the 11th cent. earthwork at Trelleborg in Denmark (Dyer-Stygall-Dony,*Luton*,42; and cf. J. Brondsted,

The Vikings, 162–7. All await excavation.

[46] The Anglo-Saxon set-up in Bedfordshire on the eve of the conquest has been analysed in *B.H.R.S.* Qto. i, 53, 81–9, 102–6, with maps of thegns' estates and of the distribution of socland. See also O. von Feilitzen, *The pre-conquest personal names of Domesday Book*.

[47] *B.H.R.S. Qto.* i, 81–2, 105; Stenton, p.591 & n.

later Domesday survey which records Saxon holders, it may mean two men, or one man with two pieces of land.

Socmen,[48] most of whom "could do what they would with their land" (i.e., it was not tied to a particular lord) accounted for 29% of the land, chiefly in the north and east, with very little socland in the south.

As to men of lower status, it is impossible to say how numerous they were. They would often owe agricultural work in return for what land they held. There were some slaves, about 12% of the population, some perhaps enslaved as punishment or because they could not pay fines. Even as late as about 1200 there is a reference to the fact that formerly men were sold at Luton.[49]

Craftsmen must have existed. Most esteemed would be workers in metal, such as the earlier goldsmith Leofsige, who was rewarded by Aelfhelm with half a hide at Potton;[50] and armourers, for armour was highly prized; thus Atheling Athelstan in 1015: "to Siferth I grant the estate at Hockliffe, and a sword and a horse and my curved shield."[51]

There would be "blacksmith, who makes ploughshare and coulter, goad and fish-hook, awl and needle" (our iron probably came from Northamptonshire); and "carpenter, responsible not only for various tools and utensils, but for houses" and boats. There were millers for just over a hundred water-mills,[52] of which more than half were on the Ouse, Lea and Ivel, the remainder being on lesser streams, some of which could probably only be worked in winter. There would be fishermen, especially in marshy areas such as Fenlake. Perhaps there were gleemen who sang in the alehouses old songs such as that of Beowulf. And someone must have sewn and embroidered the vestments used in our churches.

In January 1066 King Edward died, and Harold was chosen king. In September the King of Norway invaded England in alliance with Earl Tostig, the exile. It is not certain how many Bedfordshire thegns marched north with King Harold to defeat the Norwegian invader; and then turned south to meet the attack of the Norman Duke William. The battle of Hastings changed the history of England and of Bedfordshire. But in the misty centuries before it, nearly all our villages had been settled, the parochial system had largely evolved, the shire and hundreds were marked out, the county town (though not yet self-governing) recognised. The framework for subsequent development was there.

48 "The liability to suit of court, which was the special mark of the sokeman;" Loyn, p. 344-5. "All socmen had this in common, that they owed soke to some lord, that they must 'seek' him or his court for certain purposes;" *B.H.R.S. Qto.* i, 84; "we shall not err far in regarding the socman as holder of a small estate in which was inherent a fixed soke of some kind; who might be a free man as able to dispose of his land, or unfree in so far as he could not do so; who incidentally might be the 'man of' someone else, or might not be

such;" *ibid.*, 85. Cf. Eaton Socon, which at one time was a separate jurisdiction from the hundred; *B.H.R.S.* xxi, 150-1: "on Eaton because it does not share with the hundred," 1247.
49 *V.C.H.* ii, 350; Dyer-Stygall-Dony, 59-60.
50 *B.H.R.S.* v, 48; and *Anglo-Saxon charters*, ed. A. J. Robertson, 144-5.
51 D. Whitelock, *Anglo-Saxon wills*, p.61.
52 The number is that of mill-wheels; thus two wheels under one roof ranked as two mills; *B.H.R.S. Qto.* i, 72.

The Conquest and After

2 – BARONS AND KNIGHTS, 1066–1200

WHEN NEWS of King Harold's defeat and death at Hastings on 14 October 1066 reached Bedfordshire, it was a disaster not yet felt as final. London was not taken, and the northern Earls could still act. There were still leading Englishmen alive, such as the young Earl Waltheof. Though local men had been killed, and probably there had been difficulty in getting in the harvest, many must have thought that the storm could be weathered, as Danish attacks had been weathered in the past.[1]

THE NORMANS ARRIVE

The Norman army approached up the Icknield way,[2] seized the royal manors of Luton, Leighton and Houghton Regis, Harold's property at Weston[ing], and the town of Bedford. As it came, it levied supplies; quantities of meat and corn for the men and fodder for horses would be required; and resistance met with severe reprisal. The food requirements of such a number probably meant the confiscation of plough oxen and seed corn, with disastrous results for the following season. Valuations show that a year later villages on the Norman line of march were less than half their former value: Streatley, Sundon, Harlington, Tingrith, Flitwick, Steppingley, Ampthill, Millbrook, Clophill, Campton, Wilstead, Elstow. Those that fared worst were Clophill, Wilstead and Elstow (18%, 21% and 20% respectively of their previous value); perhaps they had resisted and been punished accordingly. From Bedford the Norman army turned southeast – Willington, Roxton and Potton suffering in the same way – and marched to Hertford. Soon news came that London had surrendered; perhaps the news came via Biscot, where Edwin, man of Asgar, sheriff of Middlesex (who had been wounded at Hastings) might know that his lord had been carried in a litter to Berkhamsted to head the delegation from London which surrendered to the Conqueror. Next men would hear that in London a castle was being built – the Tower; pending its completion the Conqueror stayed at Barking Abbey. That news may have come via Lidlington, where the Abbey had property. Then came reports of the coronation and of disturbances in London on that day.

It would soon be known in Bedford that there was fighting in the north, and that in punishment the Normans had laid waste wide areas there. It would

---

[1] The background of this chapter is taken from D. M. Stenton, *English society in the early middle ages*, with reference also to A. L. Poole, *Domesday book to Magna Carta*. The main fabric is taken from the late Dr G. H. Fowler's microscopic analysis of Domesday Book (*B.H.R.S.* Qto. 1), and page references to this are given only for a few specific points.

[2] *Archaeologia*, xlii, 41–50.

transpire, too, that Norman castles were being made at Cambridge and Huntingdon. It is probable that there now began the making of Bedford castle.[3] Hitherto the object of Bedford's fortifications had been to protect the town, but the castle was meant to hold down the town on either bank, and to dominate the river (with ford or bridge), protecting the line of communication. Local men would be made to work on clearing away a network of little streets and houses, raising the great mound or motte, and protecting with a stockade the courtyard or bailey round it, adding (on the side away from the river) a ditch and drawbridge. As yet there would be no buildings on the mound. Its height (either now or later) was 25 ft. and its diameter 160 ft.; and the eventual moat round the bailey was 50 ft. wide by 8–9 ft. deep. Half-timbered huts in the bailey would provide living quarters for the garrison. Here probably came Ralf Tallebosc to live and to hold the castle as castellan for the king; he had been given the lands of the chief local thegn, Anschil of Ware.

It was perhaps almost at once that men on the estates of other English thegns who had been killed or fled found a Norman owner coming to take possession. In the northwest of the county the men of Borred discovered that he had been superseded by the Bishop of Coutances, a cleric who "knew better how to train mailed warriors to fight than cowled clerks to chant."[4] At Eaton Socon and Sandy the men of Ulmar had to receive Lisois de Moutiers,[5] a bold soldier who, in William's advance northwards, found and forced a ford over the River Aire. Some who had not previously acknowledged an overlord must have had a rude surprise, as when socmen in Bolnhurst and Wilden were given orders by representatives of the Bishop of Bayeux, who is said to have fought at Hastings with his mace; or when a Breton, Gozelin, arrived in Potsgrove where there had been small thegns. The new estates which thus resulted were not compact, any more than English ones had been; and since they were nearly always bigger (a Norman often received more than one estate and perhaps those of several small men) they were still more scattered. At first a Norman's main object would be to hold what he had received; a little later a man in a strong position like Ralf Tallebosc could make adjustments and perhaps get the better of others. Thus the first change, painfully accepted by local Englishmen, might later be followed by a second.

The people of Bedfordshire learned to know the heavy hand of Ralf Tallebosc, for he became sheriff (the former sheriff, Godric, was killed at Hastings). Before long he exchanged Ware in order to add to his Bedfordshire estate land at Goldington (over 5 hides), Renhold, Salph End (5 hides), and Cople (9 hides). He was high-handed, even with Normans, for he disseised de Caron of 60 acres at Little Staughton "as the men of the hundred say".[6] At Sandy too he annexed

---

[3] V.C.H. i, 285.
[4] B.H.R.S. Qto. I, 92.

[5] Op.cit., 94–5; B.H.R.S. i, 69.
[6] V.C.H. i, 226.

3 acres from another Norman lord;[7] and it was said later that there were 30 acres at Houghton [Conquest] which "Ralf took possession of unjustly when he was sheriff";[8] besides some land at Clophill.[9] He took upon himself to enlarge the royal lands also: Leighton by 10 hides and 7 hides which had belonged respectively to Wlnesi and Starcher;[10] Houghton Regis by 3 hides at Sewell;[11] and Luton by 5 hides at Biscot "and separated it from the hundred".[12]

ENGLISH SURVIVORS

One leading English survivor with Bedfordshire connections was allowed to retain his rank and reluctantly accepted William: Waltheof, Earl of Huntingdon. Such English adhesion helped William's claim to be the rightful heir of his cousin, the late King Edward, and therefore he married Waltheof, who was quite a young man, tall and strong, to his niece Judith. To Judith he had given large property elsewhere, and a Bedfordshire estate of 85 hides comprising Elstow, Kempston, Potton, Maulden and Harrold. In spite of Waltheof's standing under the new régime, the Earl was unhappy. When Yorkshire rose against William, he could not resist joining, and as fire drove the Normans from York in 1069, he stood at one of the city gates hewing them down: "he burnt in the hot fire a hundred of the king's henchmen"[13] said a contemporary Norse poet. This time he was pardoned. When a few years later, during William's absence in Normandy, there was a plot by two of the Norman earls, Waltheof was at first drawn in, then repented and confessed, first to the archbishop, then to the king. How far Judith knew of the plot is uncertain. Waltheof was arrested, imprisoned and beheaded at Winchester; and the monks of Crowland brought his body back to their abbey, where he was regarded as a martyr. No doubt the people of Bedfordshire thought him so. It was said then that Judith betrayed him; what part, if any, she took is not entirely clear, but her life can have been no easy one. (For her foundation of Elstow Abbey, see ch. 4). They had daughters only; one of these married King David of Scotland, bringing the honour (see below) of Huntingdon to him, and a Scottish connection to Bedfordshire.

Of lesser English thegns who survived Hastings, very little trace is found. Their lands were wanted, and they themselves were not important to the king. A few lived on in obscurity. Such was Levenot, nearly all whose estate (the north-west and Totternhoe) went to Flemings, adventurers who had joined William's force. Levenot had had land in Northamptonshire as well as in this county, and in 1086 he was left with a single hide in the former.[14] One of Levenot's men, Lant of Wymington, was only commended to his lord, and had had the right to assign and sell his 4 hides of land; but most of it went to swell the estate of the Flemings, and Lant's widow and five sons had to manage on less than one hide,

[7] Op.cit., 235.
[8] Op.cit., 260.
[9] Op.cit., 244.
[10] Op.cit., 222.
[11] Op.cit., 223.
[12] Loc.cit.
[13] D.N.B.
[14] B.H.R.S. Qto. i, 105.

without a plough. Alwin, a thegn who held mainly at Flitton, Flitwick and Maul-den, but also had a few acres of Keysoe, retained only the latter, where in 1086 he was farming with two oxen.[15]

At night, as opportunity offered, solitary Normans were killed. For this, William imposed the "murdrum fine", that is, unless it could be shown that a murdered man was English, the whole hundred was held responsible and must pay accordingly. (The English machinery of hundred court and shire court continued – see ch. 6). The Normans were comparatively few. This was no mass migration; only one new place-name was added: Ridgmont (rouge mont); and even here the old name of Segenhoe lingered. It has been estimated that in William's army his chief followers scarcely numbered 200, with about 4,000 supporting knights. Though 54 tenants-in-chief for Bedfordshire are listed, less than half of these are of the baronial class, and most did not live here. Their under-tenants were about 200. Even allowing for attendant knights living in the households, the numbers were small to hold down a population estimated as between 3,000 and 4,000 adult males; i.e., the Normans were not more than 5-6%. Their strength was in their leadership and in the efficiency of their military methods and military organisation.

THE EARLY MILITARY ORGANISATION

The organisation was through their estates. The estates were held of the king by military service, a very large estate being called an honour. Some of these ran into many counties – about a quarter of Bedfordshire formed small parts of great honours elsewhere. A few estates were almost entirely in this county, and their holders made their homes here; thus we have three or four Bedfordshire baronies, and these account for nearly half the county. The remainder was either royal land, or held by ecclesiastics or religious houses, or by smaller men.

Each Norman lord kept part of his estate for his own use, and allotted others to his followers as reward for their service and to enable him to meet the king's requirements. For in return for land the king demanded knights to fight for him if need be – for convenience the numbers required were reckoned in multiples of five or ten. By knight (in Latin *miles*) at this date was meant merely a man who could fight on horseback; the English called them *cnihtas*, meaning serving youths or retainers. The knights wore leather tunics covered with metal rings, and helmet; and their arms were lance, sword and shield (the markings, if any, were for decoration). They were often rough adventurers, younger sons, seeking to establish themselves by prowess or by marriage.

When Norman lords of lands here had their main seat outside Bedfordshire, their knights or tenants had to wait on them at the head of their estate, wherever it might be. Some of these lords were colourful personalities, still restless and ready to take on a new adventure. Such was Ernulf de Hesding, whose land at Todding-

---

[15] *Op.cit.*, 103.

ton was a tiny fraction of his estate in 11 counties; when the call came in 1095 to drive the infidels from the Holy Land and retake Jerusalem, he went on crusade, and, like other knights wearing armour under the hot eastern sun, he fell ill at Antioch and died there. It was, however, a son of Count Eustace of Boulogne (who held Stevington and Pavenham), Godfrey, who became Christian king of Jerusalem. William d'Eu, who had received the lands in several counties of Alestan of Boscombe (here Arlesey, Edworth and Sundon), opposed the king, and in punishment for his offences was blinded and mutilated in 1095. But in the main the greater Norman estates concern this county only so far as the subsequent history of the property is concerned. Thus Stevington was held by a tenant of the barony or honour of Boulogne for at least 200 years; while Toddington was forfeit to the crown by Ernulf de Hesding's descendant in 1205 (he was actually living in Normandy when Normandy was lost to England).

The military organisation as it stood in 1086 can be seen in Domesday Book, the result of the great enquiry ordered by the Conqueror at the end of his reign. By this time young people were growing up who had only known a Norman king. News came that at Christmas 1085 at a council at Gloucester the king had resolved on a great enquiry into all land. To men of the time it seemed an un-warrantable intrusion, and it would be received, here as elsewhere, with distrust and resentment. Commissioners came into Bedfordshire. Each village had to answer, among other questions, how much land is there?, who held it in the time of King Edward? who holds it now? There must have been racking of memories among the older men who had to recall what happened twenty years ago, and old wrongs must have rankled. The information required was probably taken to the hundred court by representatives of the villages, (priest, reeve and six men), but there seems also to have been an enlarged meeting of the shire court.[16]

Tenants-in-chief of the king and their under-tenants had also to make returns. When the king's clerks had the details, they re-arranged them under the holders of land: first the king; next ecclesiastics, both those who had Bedfordshire estates in their private capacity, like the Bishops of Bayeux and Coutances; and those who held by virtue of their position, like the Abbot of Ramsey; then laymen from the biggest, with all their tenants named, down to quite modest men.

The extent of estates is given in Domesday Book in hides of arable land. The hide, it will be remembered (see ch. 1) was a unit of assessment, not an area measurement.[17] Roughly a hide is land sufficient for the cultivation of one plough in the year (a plough drawn by a team of eight oxen).[18] While over the rest of England there is much variation, in Bedfordshire it seems that a very rough estimate for a teamland is 120 acres. But it must be remembered that it is centuries before measurements are exact; a perch in Bedfordshire might be anything from 15 to

[16] F. Stenton, *Anglo-Saxon England*, 644.
[17] B.H.R.S., Qto. i 59-60.
[18] *Op.cit.*, 61.

18 ft.;[19] and as late as 1800 documents may be found which describe land as thought to be of such-and-such an area, but now by admeasurement found to be more (or less as the case may be).

THE BEDFORDSHIRE BARONIES

After the king's own estate, the largest in the Bedfordshire Domesday, and also the largest Bedfordshire barony, is that of Hugh de Beauchamp. It seems to have come to him by marriage with Matilda Tallebosc.[20] Ralf Tallebosc had died before this, leaving a widow Azelina. They had no son, but they had a daughter who was a considerable heiresss. Marriage with an heiress was an opportunity for some of the younger able men who had come over with William or subsequently, but were not in 1066 of sufficient standing to qualify for large grants of land. Such apparently was Hugh de Beauchamp. Of his origin almost nothing is known. The name, meaning "fair field", was common in Normandy, and it is not clear that he was connected with other Beauchamps settled in England. Outside this county he had lands in Buckinghamshire at Linslade, Lathbury and Soulbury, and also some in Hertfordshire. Probably he had married Matilda sometime previously, and was of middle age when he was established as the leading Norman lord in Bedfordshire, and apparently also sheriff in succession to his father-in-law. His land was distributed over the county from Keysoe in the north to Streatley in the south, and further property would come to him later from his mother-in-law, Azelina Tallebosc, who was an heiress, from her estate at Hockliffe and Hatley [Cockayne]. Presumably his holding of Bedford castle and barony was confirmed by William II in 1087. This coronation seems to have been the first at which the baron of Bedford acted as almoner. No description of the occasion survives – times were still dangerous; but 150 years later, when more attention could be paid to ceremony, it was stated that the duties of the Beauchamp of the day were to lay the cloth on which the king walked (afterwards he gave that part of it which was in Westminster Abbey to the sacristan, and that which was outside to the poor); to distribute to beggars and lepers alms from a silver alms-dish which stood before the king, and to have jurisdiction over them in case of disorder arising; and after the coronation feast he was allowed to keep the silver dish and to have also a tun of wine.[21] Some such state was probably observed at the coronation of William II.

As has been said, the greater part of the Beauchamp fee came (through Ralf and Azelina Tallebosc) from the lands of the thegn Anschil or his men; that is, Bletsoe, Colmworth, Goldington (including Putnoe), Haynes, Hockliffe, Keysoe, Ravensden (Chainhalle), Stotfold, Streatley and Willington. There were also

---

[19] B.H.R.S. xxii. Cf. also V.C.H. ii, 77.
[20] B.H.R.S. i, 2, 266–7.
[21] Red Book of the Exchequer, ii, 756, 759; V.C.H. iii, 12, 14. Long after the death of the last male Beauchamp in 1265 and after the fragmentation of the

barony, the claim to act as almoner at coronations was made; e.g. in 1685 by Sir John Carteret, Thomas Snagge and Sir George Blundell; it was then however allowed to the Earl of Exeter, and thereafter remained with this family.

lands from other thegns; from Alsi came Bromham; from Auti, Milton [Bryan]; from Leveva, Aspley; and from Turchil, Eversholt and Salford. Stagsden had formerly been held by two unnamed men of King Edward. The other main places on the Beauchamp estate had been held by socmen in numbers varying from 3 to 13: Cardington, Cople, Gt. Barford, Astwick, Houghton [Conquest], Gravenhurst, and Higham [Gobion]. Hatley [Cockayne] had a different source, as probably part of Azelina's dower.

Of these, Hugh de Beauchamp kept a large proportion in his own hand, probably to support a numerous retinue at Bedford castle. These lands which he retained were mostly near Bedford; Bromham, Cardington, Putnoe, Ravensden (Chainhalle), Willington and Stagsden; and some a little farther away, such as Haynes, Houghton [Conquest], Salford and Stotfold. To William de Locels he or his predecessor Ralf granted his holdings at Higham [Gobion] and Streatley; to William Froissart, Gravenhurst and Milton [Bryan]; to Serlo de Ros, Bromham; to Osbert de Broilg, Bletsoe; to Acard de Ivri, Aspley; to Wimund de Taissel, Colmworth; and to Ralf, Eversholt.

The considerable estate of Nigel d'Albini was not transferred to him as a unit, but had previously been held by 25 thegns and 117 socmen. From Aluric he took over Cainhoe in Clophill, and Silsoe; from Godwin, Millbrook; from Suglo, Marston; from Lewin, Streatley; and from Alward, Wyboston in Eaton Socon. Clophill itself, Husborne Crawley, Tingrith and Harlington had previously been held by small thegns, Tingrith by as few as two, Husborne Crawley by as many as nine. The other main places on the d'Albini estate had belonged to socmen in numbers varying from 7 to 21: Marston, Ampthill, Westcotes in Wilstead, Pulloxhill, Radwell in Felmersham, Wyboston in Eaton Socon, Henlow and Harrowden in Cardington. Socmen, too, had been his predecessors in various small pieces of land elsewhere.

Nigel d'Albini may have come from Aubigny near Coutances, or from Aubin St. Vast in Artois. (For the family's connection with St. Albans Abbey, see ch. 4). He made his headquarters at Cainhoe in Clophill, and here either he or later members of his family made a fortified dwelling[22] on a spur of high ground, protected on the north by a small stream, which probably at this time was marshy. The central mound is comparatively small, and is surrounded on the sides away from the stream by a deep ditch about 40 ft. wide. To the east and south are wards, and the entrance seems to have been on the west. It was no doubt at this time fortified with a stockade.

The obligation of the d'Albini barony was to produce 25 knights. For his own use, Nigel retained Cainhoe, Clophill, Harlington, Harrowden and Westcotes. To his chief follower, Nigel de Wast, he granted Ampthill, Millbrook and Radwell; to Pirot, Streatley and Wyboston; to Turgis, Tingrith and

22 *V.C.H.* i, 291–2.

part of Husborne Crawley. Erfast received Marston; and Roger and Ruallon, Pulloxhill. Silsoe was allotted to his concubine.

A smaller estate established itself as the third of the Bedfordshire baronies. This is connected with a family of Flemish adventurers. It seems that there were with the original Norman force two brothers, Seier and Walter, the younger still living in 1086, but the elder having died leaving two sons, Walter and Hugh; thus the younger Walter was head of the barony, and since he made his headquarters at Odell, his family came to be known as Wahull (an old form of Odell).

The nucleus of this estate was that of the former thegn Levenot. Levenot had held Odell, Podington, Thurleigh, Segenhoe or Ridgmont, part of Silsoe, and also Totternhoe; while one of his men held Wymington. To this was added Langford, which had been held by another thegn, Lewin. The Flemings too had other small pieces of land, of which one at Henlow had been held by 6 socmen, one at Podington by 4 socmen; and pieces at Milton [Ernest] and Holme in Biggleswade, each of which had been held by 2 socmen.

Walter de Wahull's headquarters were at Odell on a strong defensive site overlooking the river, the site of Lord Luke's present house. An 18th century writer says of it that it "must have been an impregnable fortress from its advantageous situation near the river and on a rock of considerable height and steep ascent."[23] Impressive, too, was his brother Hugh's stronghold at Thurleigh – Hugh's descendants took their name from the old form of Thurleigh, and were known as Lega. Here is a mound in two levels, rising 23 ft. above the bottom of the ditch or fosse, which is about 25 ft. across and 8–10 ft. deep. The outer rampart encloses a very wide area, and the entrance seems to have been on the northeast.[24] The family had another stronghold on the Ridgmont holding, perhaps built later.[25]

In 1086 nearly all the holding was in the hands of members of the family. Walter de Wahull kept in his own hands Odell and Langford. Hugh (later de Lega) had Podington and Thurleigh. The senior Walter had Segenhoe and some land at Silsoe. To a man called Osbert had been granted Wymington and the outlying Totternhoe.

With this barony went also the duty of sharing castle-guard in the royal castle at Rockingham – it was later commuted for a money payment.[26]

These three baronies, Beauchamp of Bedford, d'Albini of Cainhoe, and Wahull of Odell, were to remain for 200 years or more. But fortunes of some families fluctuated, and this gave rise to two smaller baronies.

The Eaton Socon and Sandy estate, which had first gone to Lisois de Moutiers, was by 1086 in the hands of Eudo, William I's steward, whose father had helped William in his early struggles in Normandy; he himself helped to secure the

---

23 *V.C.H.* iii, 69, citing O. St. J. Cooper.
24 *V.C.H.* i, 287.
25 *V.C.H.* iii, 321.
26 *V.C.H.* iii, 70, 82.

accession of William II by swift action in securing the southeastern castles. He had lands in Essex, and his own seat was at Colchester, where Roman masonry had made it possible at once to build a stone castle. It was in Normandy, however, that he died, blind, in 1120, leaving no direct heir. The Bedfordshire part of his estate then went, either by royal grant or by some marriage connection not certainly known, to a Beauchamp, probably a younger relative of Hugh de Beauchamp of Bedford. Thus arose the lesser barony of Beauchamp of Eaton,[27] and these Beauchamps also used the name Hugh. At their seat, the Hillings, overlooking the river, recent excavations showed that, though there was earlier occupation of the site, the castle assumed its present form in the 12th century. Hugh de Beauchamp of Eaton went on crusade and was killed at the great battle of Tiberias, at which Saladin captured the true cross, in 1187, the year in which Jerusalem fell once more to the infidels. (For his grandson's foundation of Bushmead Priory, see ch. 4).

The lesser barony of Trailly arose through a known marriage connection. In the family of Spech or Espec the male line also failed. William Espec was succeeded by his son or nephew Walter (for Walter's foundation of Warden Abbey, see ch. 4). When Walter died in 1153 he was succeeded by three sisters. To one of these, who married Geoffrey de Trailly, went his lands in Northill, Southill, Roxton and Biddenham. The Traillys in 1086 held Yielden from the Bishop of Coutances, and thus the Traillys, with this accession, became also lesser barons. The Trailly stronghold at Yielden has a great mound about 130 ft. x 90 ft. in area, and 40 ft. high, with an inner and outer bailey, and a moat from 30 ft. to 100 ft. wide, connected with the Till. Here excavation has shown that there was at one time a stone building.[28]

These, then, were the main baronial estates in Bedfordshire. They, together with the smaller tenants-in-chief in the county, and the greater ones elsewhere, all had the obligation to provide the king with knights for military service. They provided it partly from their tenants; and partly from the retainers in their castles, young men and boys, sons of other magnates, who came there for training. The knights, in addition to serving in the field when required by the king – perhaps against Hereward the Wake in the fens in the rising of 1070-1, or the Norman rising of 1075, or when there was trouble on the Welsh border – had to guard their lord's castle, and do escort duty when he was travelling. Gradually there came the need to define the amount of service due from those to whom the lord had allotted lands, as distinct from the retainers in the castle; one instance outside the county early in the next century laid down that the service due for one knight in peace time was 40 days a year, and in case of war two months.

THE CIVIL WAR AND AFTER

During the 11th cent. the king often had to call on his barons and knights.

[27] B.H.R.S. ii, 61–8; Camb. Ant. Soc., xlv, 48–60.   [28] V.C.H. i, 289.

By the reign of Henry I, 1100–35, who had married an English queen, the English had accepted the monarchy, and the families of the original Norman knights had settled down. But in 1135 the succession was disputed, the military machine was at odds with itself; and between the two claimants, Henry's daughter, Matilda, and her rival Stephen, there was something like a baronial free-for-all, neither side sparing ordinary folk. It was the question of the custody of the royal castle at Bedford which mainly drew fighting here, for the castle was now of masonry; there was a "strong and unshakable keep" and a strong and high wall.[29]

Stephen, who had succeeded in establishing at Luton one of his own followers, Robert de Waudari, called on Miles de Beauchamp, grandson of Hugh, to give up Bedford castle to his nominee Hugh le Poer, whom he declared to be Earl of Bedford, and who married Miles' cousin. Miles at first was prepared to recognise Stephen "provided that the king did not try to remove him from what was the hereditary possession of himself and his family", otherwise he would never get the castle until Miles was reduced to the last extremity. Stephen approached with an army, and Miles prepared for a siege. "He forcibly took from everyone and carried away with him any food on which he could lay hands, and shamelessly robbing the townsmen and their neighbours, whom hitherto he had humanely spared as his own dependants, he gathered in the castle everything that met his eyes." Stephen ordered the "construction of different sorts of engines" (probably battering rams and mangonels), but could not take the castle by storm. He and his nominee therefore blockaded it for some weeks at Christmas, 1137. The supplies Miles had hastily collected gave out, and he had to surrender. At the same time Stephen was besieging a fortified stronghold at Meppershall;[30] this was presumably that of William de Meppershall, who was a small tenant who held direct of the king by the office of king's larderer, and was apparently supporting Matilda.

Then Stephen's reverses elsewhere turned the scale, and in 1141 Miles de Beauchamp and his followers, "as triumphant and fierce as they had once been humble and downcast" recovered Bedford castle from that "dissolute and effeminate man", Stephen's nominee, the so-called Earl of Bedford. Sometime later, probably after Miles' death, Stephen's supporters again secured the castle, and in 1153 the young prince Henry "suddenly arrived at the town of Bedford, where the king's supporters had taken refuge in a very strong castle, and, after heavily plundering the town, delivered it to the flames".[31]

At Luton Robert de Waudari had constructed a castle in the heart of the

---

[29] *Gesta Stephani*, trans. K. R. Potter; the references to fighting at Bedford are pp.31–3, 77, 155; see also *B.H.R.S.* i, 6–7; and *V.C.H.* iii, 9. Generally the castle seems to have been kept in repair by the Beauchamps, but in 1180 and 1183 the sheriff accounted for £4 10s. 1s. and £12 respectively for repairs; and in 1188 for work on the bridge and the postern towards the river, amounting to £4 6s.; R. A. Brown, H. M. Colvin, A. J. Taylor, *History of the king's works*, ii, 558.

[30] *V.C.H.* i, 296, ii, 288.

[31] *Gesta Stephani*, loc.cit.; see also *B.H.R.S.* xliii, 33.

township – a motte or mound, surrounded by a yard or bailey and a ditch 10 ft. wide.[32] Here no siege is recorded; and with the accession of Henry II in 1154 the former lord regained possession of Luton, and the castle was probably dismantled. Its memory is preserved in the name of Castle Street, and its site revealed by recent excavation.

LATER CHANGES

At the Conquest the sub-tenants were all knights of fighting age. As time went on, some would be too old to fight; there might be illness; or death, leaving an heiress. It must soon have been necessary to allow money payment in lieu of service. Thus arose scutage or shield-money. Once this principle was admitted, it was no longer necessary to equate a holding exactly with numbers of knights, when this was not convenient in terms of the land; and thus arose fractions of knight service.

In 1166 Henry II required each baron to state in a letter authenticated by his seal how many knights were enfeoffed on his lands in 1135, how many he had enfeoffed since, and how many he was providing from his private resources. Simon de Beauchamp, nephew of Miles, owed 36 knights from the old feoffment; he had enfeoffed 8 more; and would supply 9 from his demesne (for his foundation of Newnham Priory see ch. 4). Robert d'Albini, grandson of Nigel, had enfeoffed 13 knights and would supply 12 from his demesne. Walter de Wahull (grandson of the Walter de Wahull of 1086) replied as follows.[33] "To his well-beloved lord, the king of the English, greeting and faithful service from Walter de Wahull. I inform you that, in the year when King Henry [I] was alive and dead, my father and I had enfeoffed 27 knights of the old feoffment, and I supplied 3 from my demesne." He then gives a list for 1166 beginning with his relative, Hugh de Lega, who is responsible for 10 knights, and 18 other names, of whom 7 are responsible for from one to three knights, and the others for one half, one third, one quarter, one fifth and even one tenth, which account for 27 knights; and explains that he still supplies the remaining three from his demesne.

There were other obligations due from the sub-tenants to their lords. They must attend the court for the honour. Tenants, for instance, of the honours of Huntingdon, Boulogne or Gloucester (the last was the former estate of Walter Giffard), had a journey outside the county. The knights on the Beauchamp estate, however, had only to come to Bedford; thus Simon de Beauchamp about 1180 executed a document "before me and my barons in my court at Bedford".[34]

As the king, when need was, could take an aid from his barons, so could the baron from his tenants. By the time these conditions were defined, knighthood as a status had risen; it had come to be distinct from the tenure of land by knight-service, and a young man would become a knight by a formal ceremony. Thus the

[32] Dyer-Stygall-Dony, *Story of Luton*, 54–5.   [34] *B.H.R.S.* xiii, 135–6.
[33] *Red Book of the Excheq.*, i, 319–24.

lord was entitled to take an aid when his eldest son was knighted, or when his eldest daughter was married, or if he himself should be taken prisoner in war and have to be ransomed.

When a tenant died, his son paid a relief or fine for permission to enter on the land, and did homage to the lord. The position might be complicated if he held of more than one lord. Even in 1086 William de Caron, who was a substantial tenant at Clifton of Eudo the steward, also held land in Tempsford of the Bishop of Lincoln, and such instances multiplied later.

SETTLING DOWN

Just as the family fortunes of some barons fluctuated, so no doubt did those of the original Norman knights of 1066. Most of these cannot be traced, partly because the general adoption of surnames was gradual, partly because record references to this lower rank in the first century after the Conquest are even fewer than for the barons. But some families who appear in 1086 can still be found more than a century later. Sometimes this is in connection with founding or endowing a monastery, sometimes they are acting on presenting juries or in other public capacities, sometimes simply making trouble. Such are the Bolebecs of Woburn, the Passelews of Biddenham, the Burnards of Arlesey, the Blossevilles of Harrold, the Broilgs or Broys of Bletsoe, and the Carons of Tempsford.

Language caused some difficulties in the new England. Before the Conquest English had been used for official purposes, and after the Conquest Latin took its place for this. The baronial and knightly class spoke Norman–French; and since England's connection with the continent lasted for 400 years, French continued to be spoken or understood by those of high rank. But the knights or tenants, in dealing with the men on their estates, and in taking part in hundred and shire courts, must soon have learnt some English, and so probably did their children growing up in the country. An early 12th century piece of evidence comes from a family connected with the Beauchamps. Beatrice de Beauchamp, sister of Miles, married Hugh de Morville of Cumberland. It was a lady of this family (probably not Beatrice herself) who warned her husband of danger in the words "Ware, ware, ware! Lithulf heth his swerd adrage!"[35] If English could be used in a family connected with the Beauchamps, there seems no reason why it should not be understood anywhere in Bedfordshire.

Feudal Bedfordshire in the first century after 1066 may be summed up as follows. There had been a wholesale redistribution of land, and this had gone to a comparatively small number of Normans, who held it by military service. The main Bedfordshire baronies were those of Beauchamp of Bedford, d'Albini of Cainhoe, and Wahull of Odell; two lesser ones were those of Beauchamp of Eaton and Trailly of Yielden; and some parts of Bedfordshire were held of great honours elsewhere. Under a strong king the system provided order; under a weak

[35] A. L. Poole, *Domesday Book to Magna Carta*, p.252; see also *B.H.R.S.* i, 8.

one the disturbances could be worse than before. The "knights" whom the barons had settled as tenants on part of their land were taking part in local affairs. The king controlled Bedford, Leighton, Luton and Houghton Regis; for the first three and for the newly-founded town of Dunstable, see ch. 5. A monastic revival had begun (see ch. 4). For many, life was hard; they were at the mercy, not only of bad harvests, but of fighting among their superiors. The position of these ordinary folk after the Conquest is discussed in ch. 3.

3 – COUNTRYSIDE AND VILLAGERS, 1066–1200

THE BEDFORDSHIRE of 1086 had a population far less than that of today. Leighton and Luton, with their adult men of 129 and 145 respectively, may have been about 700; Bedford perhaps nearer 1,000. Few other places can have had more than 200 inhabitants, the chief being Eaton Socon, Toddington and Biggleswade; the general average would have been nearer 100. The relative positions were not always those of today; Stagsden and Stevington were more populous than Flitwick.

THE COUNTRYSIDE

Much of the land was uncultivated. Some of it, perhaps about 25,000 acres, is described in Domesday Book as woodland. By wood is not meant the close-planted wood of today, but a more open, grassy and sometimes marshy area, with some trees and not much undergrowth. A belt of this woodland ran across the county from Cranfield to Haynes; and south of it were similar stretches at Weston[ing], Harlington and Luton; but there was less round Leighton Buzzard, and not much along the Ouse and in the north on the colder land. In these woods droves of pigs under swineherds fed on acorns and nuts from the trees and such food as snails in the marshy areas. The extensive Luton area was reckoned to support as many as 2,000 pigs and Cranfield 1,000; but 100 was a more usual number, with only 20 at Podington and none listed for Biddenham.

Of actual forest (that is, areas reserved by the king for hunting deer, and under special forest law, as was the New Forest) there seems to have been none in Bedfordshire in the 11th cent. Early in the 12th cent. an area was afforested, but as it was unpopular with barons as well as everyone else, they redeemed it by a heavy payment in 1190–1, and it is not certain where it was.[1] However, Bedfordshire men were sometimes involved in forest cases over the border, as was Gervase of Dean in 1251, when foresters at Weybridge in Brampton, Huntingdonshire, recognised him as one of 12 men with greyhounds and bows and arrows "who entered the wood, and on account of the thickness of the wood and the darkness of the night, the foresters know not what became of them", but they said that Gervase "is wont to do evil in the forest".[2]

In 1086 there were normally in a Bedfordshire parish two open fields, cropped and fallow in alternate years; and when gradually additional land was cleared from the waste, it was at first still worked on the 2-field system. In the fields men held scattered strips of about an acre (it will be remembered that

---

[1] *B.H.R.S.* vii, 52, 61, 69, 225.   [2] D. M. Stenton, *English Society*, 117–8.

measurements were still imprecise); the strips were normally a furlong – "furrow-long" (220 yards) in length, a length which the oxen could draw without stopping.[3] Partly for drainage purposes, a strip was ploughed in four ridged selions of about a rood width; the ploughman began on the crest of the ridge, and, by always turning to the right, the sods were turned inward toward the centre, and the whole selion became arched and formed a ridge and furrow. (This conformation of land formerly ploughed in ridge and furrow, but since grassed over, was to be seen in several places in the county till the extensive tractor ploughing of the 1939–45 war, and even after that aerial photography often reveals it, as for instance at Chellington and Stanbridge.) In addition the method made it easier to demarcate one man's strip from another; even so, the attempt, while ploughing, to filch a furrow from a neighbour's strip was often made.

Meadow was chiefly found in the valleys of the Ouse and the Ivel, and in the southwest, though there would always be some on the banks of brooks or small streams.[4] It was grazed after the hay was carried, but beasts were also grazed on fallow and stubble. It is probable that now, as later, meadow was normally held in severalty, i.e. by separate holders in proportion to their arable holdings; but later references to doles or to lot-meadow show that it could be subject to yearly re-allotment.

Of the hundred or so mills (Luton had no less than seven) the more important ones on the main rivers paid annual dues of eels to the lord – sometimes 200 or more along the Ouse, as at Harrold; a smaller number along the Ivel (150 at Clifton). Other fresh-water fish were no doubt caught in the rivers and fenlike areas.

Along the rutted or muddy roads, barons and knights rode on horseback; ladies (if they had to travel) went in a litter; others walked; and goods were carried by packhorse. According to the season, the traveller would see the slow-moving plough-teams of 8 oxen; or the villagers harvesting with sickles; and hear the splash of the mill-wheel as he passed near some stream. If it was the right date, he might see a meeting of the hundred court in progress in the open air; or be passed on the road by the sheriff's men, with a strong guard, taking the king's dues in bullion up to Winchester; and he would hurry at dusk through overgrown areas where "evil-doers unknown" might lurk. If he were an elderly man, who had recently had to answer the questions of the Domesday commissioners, he might be sad at heart as he thought of the changes time had wrought for him, for almost certainly he was reduced in status.

THE RISE OF THE MANOR

Looked at from above (see ch. 2) the military organisation was simple. Regarded from below as a social-economic framework it was more complex. A new term was introduced by the Normans: manor; in over a hundred cases

---

[3] *B.H.R.S.* Qto. ii, 4–6. Fn.1 (ch. 2) applies also to   [4] *Op.cit.*, 5.
this chapter.

entries in Domesday Book are prefixed by "M" for manor, or it is said "this land is held as a manor". But though the term was new, there had been before the Conquest a trend to consolidate estates; nor was this process completed by the Conquest's agency. It has been said: "Later in the middle ages there were three features that one would expect in every manor: a consolidated estate, the lord's rights of jurisdiction, a peasantry bound to labour service. It is impossible to prove that these elements preponderated in our Domesday *maneria*."[5] What the Conquest did was to give the process an impetus.

There is another new term, villein. This term, too, in 1086 is not as precise as it became when the manor was fully developed. The Norman clerks who compiled Domesday Book did not find it easy to understand the variations among English villagers, who did not easily fit their neat categories. Roughly speaking, however, the villein is the villager of the better class, but in general he could no longer change his lord.[6] About half the population of Bedfordshire in 1086 were listed as villeins (49·7%). Taking an average over the whole county, the villein has been described as a work-paying tenant holding up to about 120 acres, generally about 60 acres, probably not less than 20 acres; and owning half a plough-team.[7] The villeins of Bedfordshire were on the whole more prosperous (with larger holdings and more oxen) than those of many other parts of England.[8]

Less than half the population are listed in Domesday Book as men of lower status; they are described as bordars and serfs. The bordar (30·7%) might have 15–30 acres and two oxen.[9] The serf (12·7%), who was a slave or near-slave, might perhaps have 5 acres and occasionally an ox.[10]

But to take the county as a whole, and to make an average, does not allow for the differences in Bedfordshire in 1066. In southwest Bedfordshire the pre-Conquest tendency for the thegns to become lords of villages was marked; but in northeast Bedfordshire it had been disrupted by an influx of free peasant settlers in the Danish invasions. In this respect Bedfordshire reproduces on a small scale the pattern of the whole of England.[11] Thus in 1086 the impetus to manorialisation is strongest in the southwest (where also are the largest holdings, Leighton and Luton with their attendant hamlets, in the king's hands); but more hesitant in the north and east.

A simple instance comes from the southwest. In 1066 the whole of Aspley was held by a lady, Leveva, who was commended to Earl Waltheof. Aspley (perhaps on Waltheof's execution) was allotted to Hugh de Beauchamp or his father-in-law, who entrusted it to his knight, Acard de Ivri. At Aspley there were in 1086 16 villeins and 9 men of lower status. Here was a consolidated estate, probably with the villeins doing labour service for their land. They were not

[5] Loyn, *Anglo-Saxon England*, 339.
[6] *B.H.R.S.* Qto. i, 77.
[7] *Op.cit.*, 73.
[8] Loyn, 346.

[9] *B.H.R.S.* Qto. i, 75.
[10] *Loc.cit.*
[11] Loyn, 339–43.

necessarily badly off; they had 8 teams between them. Over 30 single holdings, mainly in southwest and central Bedfordshire, are in 1086 of similar pattern. Here the Norman take-over must have gone comparatively smoothly, with no great change.

A little further north was a slightly different pattern. In 15 places the land had been held by anything from 4 to 15 socmen or a few thegns, and was transferred entirely or almost entirely to one lord; thus Ampthill had been held by 7 socmen, Pulloxhill by 8 socmen, Harlington by 4 thegns. Here by 1086 the Norman lord had imposed some consolidation. Sometimes he kept the land in his own hands, as Nigel d'Albini kept Harlington, where the former 4 thegns (if still alive) were probably among the 12 villeins listed for this village; they may not have been poverty-stricken – they had 5 teams between them – but they were no doubt of less status than before. In other places the baron had entrusted the holding to a single tenant; thus Nigel d'Albini entrusted Ampthill to his tenant, Nigel de Wast; and the former 7 socmen have to be sought among 6 villeins, 2 bordars and a serf.

In many parishes transferred, not to one lord, but to two or more, there were similar results. Thus at Houghton [Conquest] Hugh de Beauchamp kept in his own hands the 5 hides formerly held by 7 socmen; while Adeliza de Grentmesnil, who had $4\frac{1}{2}$ hides formerly held by 3 socmen, had in 1086 only one socman and one other tenant; there were in the parish 19 villeins who had only $3\frac{1}{2}$ teams, and there were 20 men of lower status. At Marston again there were two lords: Walter Giffard entrusted the hide formerly held by 2 thegns to Hugh de Bolebec; and Nigel d'Albini, on his holding of 8 hides once farmed by 21 socmen, had only one tenant, Erfast; the population included 20 villeins with 10 teams, and 11 men of lower status. In at least thirty similar instances the new lord combined a number of small holdings. Consolidation, then, was the preponderant trend; and in all these cases there must have been friction and painful adaptation to new ways.

In parts of the east, however, the trend to consolidate was less marked. The position was diverse to start with, and had not been much simplified by 1086. In Sutton in 1086 there were 17 socmen, and there were 6 other holders of land, most of whom had lords (among the lords named are Levegar and Ederic), and may have been tenants. The greater part of Sutton (7 hides) went to the Countess Judith. In 1086 she had among her tenants the Englishmen named above, Levegar and Ederic, each subsisting on half a hide formerly held by his "man"; and 6 others. Here most of the men had been depressed in status, and, if still living, must be sought among the 2 villeins and 18 bordars (there was no serf in Sutton). On the other hand, Countess Judith had not found it practicable to combine her 7 hides into a single holding. Her 8 tenants had nearly 4 teams, and 4 of the bordars had a team between them. Similarly at Gt. Barford Hugh de Beauchamp, who had taken over the lands of 11 socmen, had reduced the holdings to 4; at Cople from

▲ *1a Saxon urns (in Bedford Museum), found at Kempston.*

▼ *1b Saxon brooch (in Luton Museum), found at Luton.*

▼ *1c Pair of Saxon brooches (in Luton Museum), found at Dunstable.*

D

2b Saxon cross base (in Elstow Moot Hall),
found at Elstow.

2a Saxon arch in Stevington church.

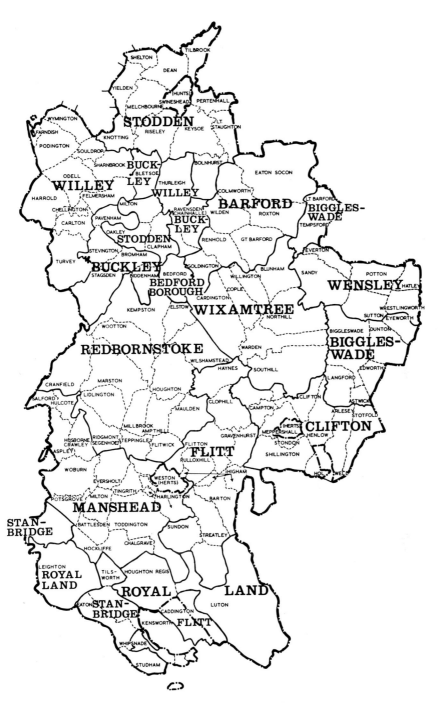

3   *Map showing hundred boundaries in the 11th cent.*

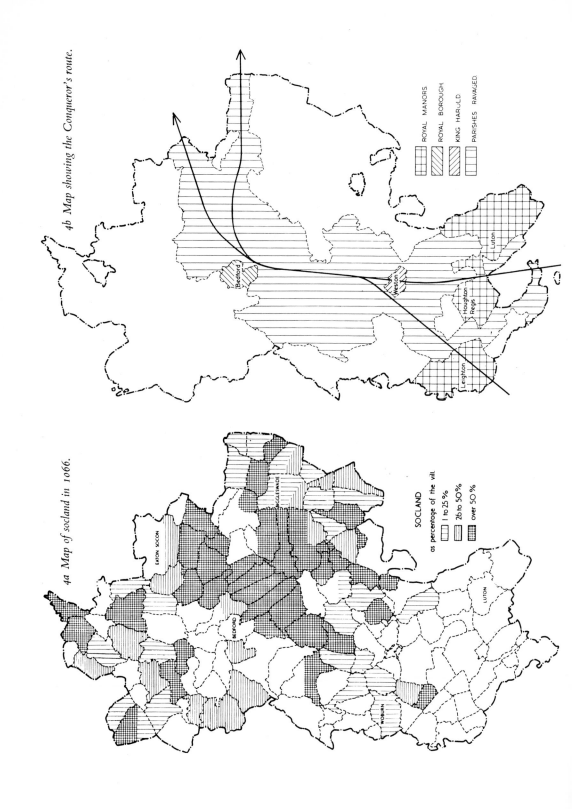

4b Map showing the Conqueror's route.

ROYAL MANORS
ROYAL BOROUGH
KING HAROLD
PARISHES RAVAGED.

Bedford
Weston
Houghton Regis
Leighton
Luton

4a Map of socland in 1066.

SOCLAND
as percentage of the vill.
1 to 25 %
26 to 50 %
over 50 %

EATON SOCON
BIGGLESWADE
BEDFORD
WOBURN
LUTON

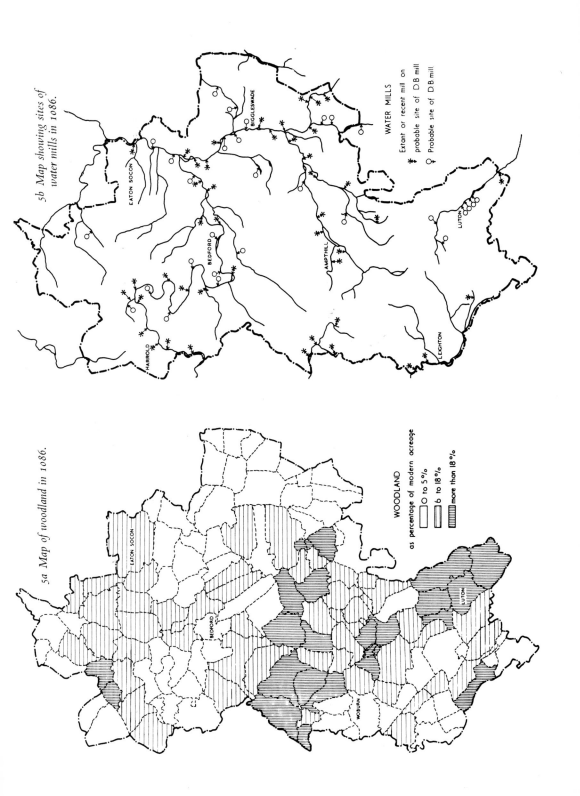

5a Map of woodland in 1086.

WOODLAND
as percentage of modern acreage

☐ 0 to 5%
▨ 6 to 18%
▥ more than 18%

5b Map showing sites of water mills in 1086.

WATER MILLS

✳ Extant or recent mill on probable site of D.B. mill
○ Probable site of D.B. mill

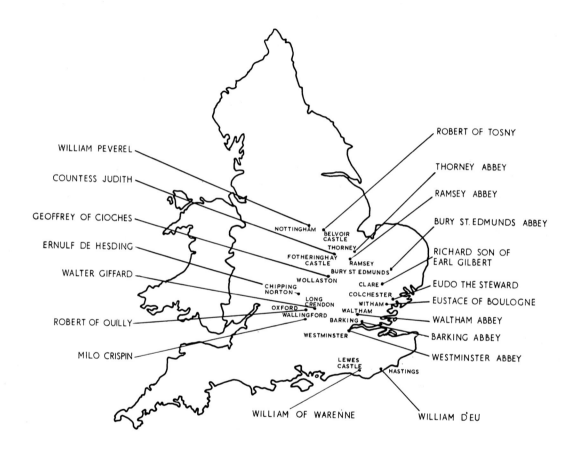

WILLIAM PEVEREL

COUNTESS JUDITH

GEOFFREY OF CIOCHES

ERNULF DE HESDING

WALTER GIFFARD

ROBERT OF OUILLY

MILO CRISPIN

ROBERT OF TOSNY

THORNEY ABBEY

RAMSEY ABBEY

BURY ST. EDMUNDS ABBEY

RICHARD SON OF EARL GILBERT

EUDO THE STEWARD

EUSTACE OF BOULOGNE

WALTHAM ABBEY

BARKING ABBEY

WESTMINSTER ABBEY

NOTTINGHAM
BELVOIR CASTLE
THORNEY
FOTHERINGHAY CASTLE
RAMSEY
BURY ST EDMUNDS
WOLLASTON
CHIPPING NORTON
CLARE
COLCHESTER
LONG CRENDON
WITHAM
OXFORD
WALTHAM
WALLINGFORD
BARKING
WESTMINSTER
LEWES CASTLE
HASTINGS

WILLIAM OF WARENNE

WILLIAM D'EU

6 *Map showing seats of the main non-Bedfordshire overlords, 1086.*

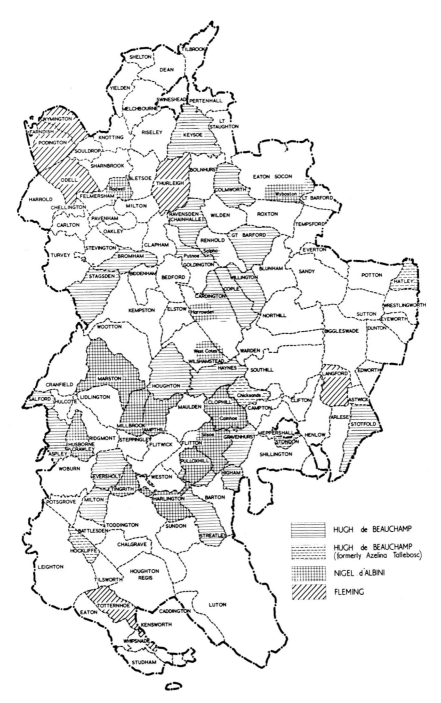

7 *Map showing approximate areas of Bedfordshire baronies, 1086.*

▲ *8a Bedford castle mound.*

▼ *8b Cainhoe castle site from the air.*

▲ 9a *Thurleigh castle site from the air.*

▼ 9b *Yielden castle site from the air.*

10b *Surviving traces of ridge and furrow cultivation at Stanbridge.*

10a *Surviving traces of ridge and furrow cultivation at Chellington.*

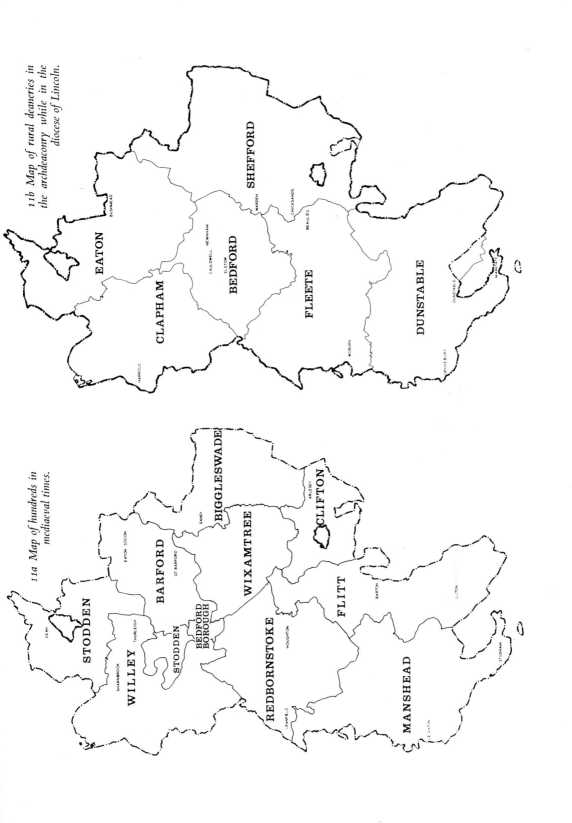

11b Map of rural deaneries in the archdeaconry while in the diocese of Lincoln.

EATON

BUSHMEAD

CLAPHAM

HARROLD

NEWNHAM
CAULDWELL
ELSTOW
BEDFORD

SHEFFORD

MARDEN

CHICKSANDS

BEAULIEU

FLEETE

WOBURN

DUNSTABLE

DUNSTABLE

MARKYATE

GROVEBURY

11a Map of hundreds in mediaeval times.

STODDEN

DEAN

WILLEY

SHARNBROOK

THURLEIGH

STODDEN

BARFORD

EATON SOCON

GT BARFORD

BEDFORD BOROUGH

BIGGLESWADE

SANDY

WIXAMTREE

CLIFTON

ARLESEY

REDBORNSTOKE

CRANFIELD

HOUGHTON

FLITT

BARTON

LUTON

MANSHEAD

LEIGHTON

STUDHAM

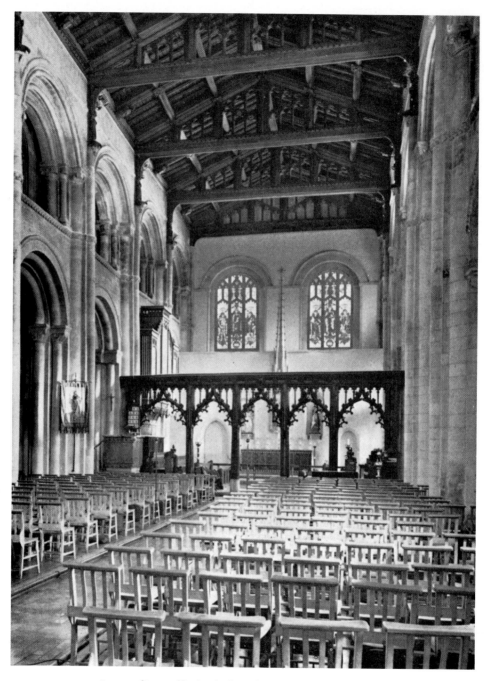

12   *Interior of Dunstable church, formerly part of priory church, 12th cent.*

▲ *13a Interior of parish church at Knotting, 12th cent.*

► *13b Doorway of
St. Thomas' chapel,
Meppershall,
12th cent.*

▲ *14a Crozier-head, c. 1160, found in a stone coffin at Warden Abbey.*

▼ *14b Tiles, 14th cent., found in recent excavations at Warden Abbey.*

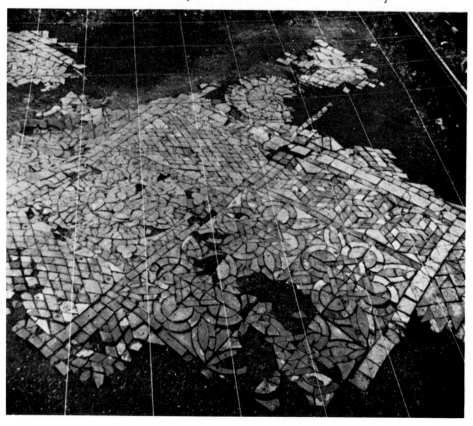

15 *Ironwork on Eaton Bray Church door, attributed to Thomas of Leighton, 13th cent.*

16　Felmersham church, 13th cent.

15 to 7; and at Goldington only from 13 to 10.

In parts of north Bedfordshire there were some similar cases, as at Sharnbrook on the holding of the Bishop of Coutances. Here in 1066 on 4½ hides allotted to him there were 7 socmen and 3 other holders. In 1086 the same 7 socmen were still there, nor had the Bishop amalgamated the other 3 holdings, though he kept one himself, and one was held by Turgis "Englishman"; there were 1 villein and 6 bordars, no serf. Here the English pattern seems not to have been disturbed at all. The socmen had 3 teams between them, and the other two tenants a team each. At Tillbrook also, held by William of Warenne, were 20 socmen still on the land, who were said to be the same who held it before the Conquest; they had only 6 teams. At Salpho in Renhold, held by Hugh de Beauchamp, the pre-Conquest 11 socmen were still there – they had 8 teams.

The fact that a consolidated estate had not emerged by 1086 does not necessarily mean a permanent difference from the rest of Bedfordshire, but can mean a slower process. Small holdings in the same village held of one overlord tended to coalesce. In the next century at Sutton[12] Countess Judith's land had become the manor of Sutton held by the family of Foliot. In Sharnbrook the Bishop's land had become the manor of Temple Hills, held by the Templars[13] (the order founded in the first Crusade to protect the Holy Land). But this consolidation was not invariable. In Cople a direct connection cannot be traced between the 7 tenants of Hugh de Beauchamp in 1086 and the later six manors of Cople, but it is noticeable that these holdings never did coalesce into a single manor[14], nor did Gt. Barford.

Where a parish was divided between two or more lords, as time went on the larger holdings usually became manors. In Sharnbrook where, in addition to the Bishop of Coutances' 4½ hides, Albert Lorraine had 2 hides and Count Eustace of Boulogne had 2 hides, the former became Lorings manor and the latter Toft manor. At Marston Nigel d'Albini's 8 hides became the main manor of Marston: and Walter Giffard's 2 hides became Wroxhill manor. Thus the first cause of there being more than one manor in a parish is that shares were originally allotted to more than one Norman lord. Other causes for the multiplication of manors came later (see ch. 7).

Thus the centre of village life tended to be the manor or manors. The term thegn had disappeared. The term socman was on the way out; for 1066 as many as 600 are mentioned, but in 1086 only about 100. Yet later indications (ch. 8) seem to be that, by the time we get a legal approach to the question of free or unfree (i.e., those who could, and those who could not bring their cases before the king's judges), a number of men had established a position as freemen or as free tenants of the manor. It is in economic terms that Domesday Book is couched. Economically the socman of 1086 did not necessarily have an advantage over a

[12] *V.C.H.* ii, 247.
[13] *V.C.H.* iii, 90.
[14] *V.C.H.* iii, 238.

villein, just as a 20th cent. owner of a small farm may work harder and have a lower living-standard than a tenant farmer. The socmen of Sharnbrook and Till-brook, though they were direct tenants of their Norman overlord, were not as well off for plough-teams as the villeins of Aspley, and far less so than those of Clapham, where 18 villeins had no less than 20 teams. Besides, there may have been scope for an able man in becoming the reeve of a progressive lord.

The next stage of manorialisation cannot be worked out in detail over the county. Domesday Book provides a brief glimpse of a continuing process; it is like a still picture from a silent film of which the next sequence is missing. Manorial records appear not to have been kept as early as the late 11th and early 12th centuries; and when they were kept, few survive before the 13th century. By then the manor was fully developed (see ch. 8). But there is an exception to the paucity of records in the great and ancient abbey of Ramsey with its important estate at Barton, Cranfield and Shillington.

THE RAMSEY ABBEY ESTATE

At Ramsey was recorded, apparently about 1140,[15] the stock on the demesne at Barton (the demesne is the equivalent of the home farm – the land reserved for the abbey's own use, in this case $1\frac{1}{2}$ hides). The stock consisted of 2 plough-teams, a horse for harrowing, 200 sheep, 11 cows, 1 bull, 1 sow and 8 young pigs. The reeve, William, held 2 virgates, for which he paid 6s. rent.

For Cranfield[16] c. 1140 the monks of Ramsey recorded the following. "John son of Adam holds $\frac{1}{2}$ hide, for which his father in the days of King Henry [1] attended the shire and hundred courts and was free from service; and the same John now holds it and does likewise, and renders 5s. for the increase which he has from his assart [land newly cleared from the waste]. Richard son of Ailric holds $\frac{1}{2}$ hide free, and he attends the shire and hundred courts. Thurkil holds a virgate free, and he attends the shire and hundred courts; and for another which he has he renders 5s. Ralf, steward, has $\frac{1}{2}$ hide free, of the demesne assart, by gift of Abbot Reynold [1114–33], and must be at the abbot's pleas through all Bedfordshire. Ailwin son of Athelstane had 2 virgates in the days of King Henry; for one he then rendered 3s. rent, now 4s.; and the other is at service. [Here free and unfree tenure are united in one man.] Except the above lands, there were in the days of King Henry 23 virgates, with that of the said Ailwin, at service; and also 8 cotlands at service.

This is the service of a virgate. He works 3 days in the week, and ploughs a fourth day; this he does from Michaelmas to the beginning of August, except Christmas, Easter and Whitsuntide. And from the beginning of August to Michaelmas he works 5 days a week without ploughing. And each month he does

---

[15] *Ramsey Cart.* iii, 274. It has been suggested (R. Lennard, *Rural England* 384n) that these surveys are late 12th cent., partly on the ground that "King Henry" may mean Henry II instead of Henry I. But it is usually only the first king of a series who is named without a number.

[16] *Op.cit.*, 301–4.

carrying service to London, Ramsey, or Cambridge; or else he pays 7½d. at Martinmas and a seam of oats and 4 hens.

This is the service of a cotland. He works 2 days a week and does carrying service on foot."

There seems at this time to have been an extensive clearance from the waste in Cranfield, and this land or assart is described as never having been subject to service. About 30 men are listed as paying rents from 4d. to 6s., most of which seem to be for assart. Among them however appear two men, each paying 6s. for a virgate "which virgate was formerly at service"; and 3 men similarly paying rent for cotlands "which cotlands were formerly at service".

It will be seen that there are some free tenants in Cranfield, and three of these, with the priest, represent Cranfield on the abbey's behalf at the shire and hundred courts. Five men who formerly did service are paying rent. At Barton are similar indications. Richard holds apparently 4 virgates at rent. "But if he has a virgate at service, he works Monday and Wednesday and ploughs Friday." At Shillington[17] at the same date there were three free tenants, Ebroinus, Silvester and John. Here 35 virgates were held at rent, most of them paying 22d. each; and 32 virgates were at service. The service due from Shillington villeins and cottagers was much the same as at Cranfield.

The earlier part of this chapter shows how impossible it is to argue from one village to another or to the county as a whole. These three parishes are in the south of the county; moreover they are all held of a religious house, whose practice may differ from that of a lay lord. But the differences they show from the neat categories of Domesday Book, after the lapse of only two generations, are a reminder of the variety of human circumstances and of the continual process of change.

Incidentally, the men's names may be noted. There are Alfred, Athelstane, Ailwin, Edward, Edwin and Godwin. There are also Thurkil and Sweyn. But there are two Roberts, two Geoffreys and five Williams, for a new fashion has set in.

---

[17] Op.cit., 307–8.

4 – CHURCH AND MONASTERIES, 1066–1200

THE NORMAN newcomers in 1066 were unlike the Danes – "the heathen" – in that they had the same Christian background as the English. They too accepted unquestioningly the Christian faith; to them the after-life (be it heaven, purgatory or hell) was inevitable; the saints were real; and God must be worshipped in the finest buildings they could raise. They might often behave in a way that seemed to belie this; but to a practical man there was the possibility of repentance, even on his death-bed; of making good by endowing a monastery or giving alms, or having prayers said for his soul after death.[1]

Thus at the Conquest English ecclesiastics were less vulnerable than English earls and thegns. Though their sympathies were with Harold, they could not be deliberately displaced by a good son of the church, even though they were important landholders. Seven of the 35 English monasteries had lands in Bedford-shire. However there were a few losses and uncertainties. Ramsey Abbey lost Clapham. Apparently it was taken from the tenant, Bricxtric, on the assumption that it was his: "the abbot and monks of Ramsey claim this . . . and the whole hundred bears witness."[2] They could not recover Clapham, but their estate in the county still amounted to 51 hides. St. Albans Abbey, which apparently had already lost Biscot during the Danish period, suffered losses at Stotfold and Streatley,[3] and this seems due to the uncertainties of the time. Harold's foundation of Waltham Abbey temporarily lost its hold on land at Arlesey. Abbess Aelgifu of Barking Abbey (where William stayed in 1066) retained Lidlington. The late King Edward's new Abbey at Westminster kept Holwell. Thorney Abbey retained Bolnhurst. At the Abbey of Bury St. Edmunds (which had land at Biddenham, Blunham and Sandy) there was already a Norman abbot; for King Edward, with his Norman affiliations, had appointed him in 1065. St. Paul's cathedral kept its recently acquired estate at Caddington.

EPISCOPAL ORGANISATION

But there was a change, a spirit of energy and of practical organisation, which became felt in the diocese. Already the view had gained ground that a bishop's see should be at an important centre. Bishop Wulfwig died in 1067 or 1068, still at Dorchester-on-Thames. A Norman, Remigius, was then appointed, who came from Fécamp Abbey, and he moved the see to Lincoln. A fitting

---

[1] For the national background for this chapter, see D. M. Stenton, *English Society in the Early Middle Ages*; and for religious houses, D. Knowles, *The monastic order in England.*
[2] *V.C.H.*, i, 234.
[3] *Op.cit.*, 198.

cathedral must be built; the first stage of this, on a commanding height, was consecrated three days after Remigius died, on 6 May 1092. A suitable residence for the bishop would come later; Bishop Robert even lived, by the king's permission, in one of the gates to the city.

The Normans separated ecclesiastical and lay cases. Whereas in English times, bishop and earl had sat together in the hundred courts, William decreed that the bishop should hold a separate court for ecclesiastical cases. Such cases would often relate to the large number of assistant clergy in lesser orders. Cases concerning advowsons were not included, for they were real property, dealt with in the king's courts.

Till now, the bishop had normally had one archdeacon as his chief administrative officer. It was Bishop Remigius who divided his large diocese into seven districts and put an archdeacon in charge of each. In Bedfordshire it was a simple matter to make the archdeaconry of Bedford co-terminous with the shire. (In adjoining Hertfordshire, where St. Albans Abbey had a wide sphere of influence, the position was less simple; and in 1163 a later bishop came to a common-sense agreement with the abbot by recognising the area round St. Albans as in the abbot's jurisdiction.)

The first archdeacon of Bedford was Osbert. He was followed by Ralf, who was "miserably killed" (how is not recorded); then came Hugh; whose successor, Nicholas, was archdeacon for about 40 years and whom we shall meet again. The archdeacon by his visitation of parishes in his archdeaconry saw that churches were equipped with books and vestments and that they were kept in repair. Before his court also were brought drunkards and scolds, adulterers and witches. He went on horseback with attendants. When the bishop likewise made a visitation at longer intervals, he had a considerable retinue. To proffer hospitality would have been difficult for a poor priest, and payment known as procurations was made in lieu. By the middle of the 12th cent. the archdeaconry had been sub-divided into six rural deaneries (Bedford, Eaton, Clapham, Fleet, Shefford, Dunstable) – areas rather larger than the hundreds, and therefore bearing only a loose relation to these; and the rural deans held deanery chapters.

Meanwhile, the cathedral services at Lincoln must be maintained in their stately round by cathedral clergy. The archdeacons were members of the chapter, but they were much occupied with their archdeaconries. The chief dignitaries were the dean, precentor, chancellor and treasurer; gradually there were added a number of canons. Each canon had an estate or church assigned to him as a prebend for his support. Bishop Remigius established several prebends, among which may have been Bedford Major and Minor; by about 1200 two more have appeared; their names still appear, with that of the archdeacon of Bedford, on the stalls in Lincoln cathedral. One was Biggleswade. Biggleswade was granted by Henry I to Bishop Alexander in 1132, and either he or a later Bishop made it into a prebend (this perhaps was not till after 1163).[4] The other was Leighton, which was in the Bishop's hands at an earlier date – it was the Conqueror himself who gave the church of this royal manor, with accompanying land which became the prebendal manor, to Bishop Remigius; but it seems to have been a much later Bishop, Bishop Hugh (1186–1200) who made it into a prebend. Apparently the first prebendary was Theobald de Busar. Some years later, a scribe at Lincoln (to avoid confusion with the prebend of Leighton, Hunts.) added "Busar" to his entry; and the name stuck.[5] The prebendaries were members of the cathedral chapter equally with the archdeacon; and thus their areas were removed from his jurisdiction. Thus arose the Peculiars (or exempt jurisdictions) of Biggleswade and Leighton Buzzard. Continuous residence was of course not practicable for these prebendaries, either on their benefice or at the cathedral; but there were many unbeneficed assistant clergy all through the Middle Ages; and a prebendary could arrange for a vicar choral to undertake his share of the cathedral services. Thus the Bishop had at call responsible men, without having to be concerned with minor arrangements.

It had been an early custom at Whitsuntide for clergy and laity to come in procession to their cathedral with offerings. To visualise this at Lincoln cathedral on its commanding site, the visitor should not drive through thronging traffic up the curving main street with its smooth gradient, but should slowly climb the steep straight narrow path up the hill, where no cars come. In those days many went on pilgrimage to one shrine or another, even to the Holy Land. Nevertheless, the Whitsuntide procession as a regular matter offered some difficulties to the more distant parts of the diocese, and in time these sent a money payment instead, originally assessed at a farthing per house. Northill churchwardens' accounts in 1563 still record the paying of "Lincoln farthings".[6]

CHURCH–BUILDING

The rebuilding of parish churches in stone, begun before the Conquest, continued. Totternhoe stone was quarried in Norman times. If there were still places without churches it is probable that a Norman baron or knight provided one before long. He had, after all, become rich by the Conquest, and it might be well to employ some of his gains in this way. Since a new church began as the chapelry of an existing church, the fact that Pavenham was for long a chapelry of Felmersham may mean that its first place of worship was of late date; but it does not follow that it was post-Conquest; for Clapham was a chapelry of Oakley, and its surviving tower is pre-Conquest. Upper Gravenhurst was a chapelry of Shillington, and Knotting of Melchbourne.

Many churches still show traces of Norman work which have survived later enlargement and rebuilding. Sometimes it is the lower part of the tower, as at

[4] C.R.O. Guide, p.23.
[5] B.H.R.S., xxi, 88.
[6] B.H.R.S., xxxiii, 7.

Blunham, Kempston, Meppershall, Oakley, Thurleigh, Old Warden; sometimes part of the nave, as at Everton, Knotting, Riseley and Shelton; or the chancel arch as at Milton [Bryan]; or part of the chancel, as at Milton [Ernest]; or rarely a font, as at Renhold. There are fine Norman doorways at Bedford St. Peter (this was built for another church of St. Peter which stood opposite St. Mary), Caddington and Farndish. The usual church plan at this date was an aisleless nave and chancel, both smaller than at present. The addition of aisles, when it came, was protracted, and did little more than begin in this period; thus at Pertenhall and Tillbrook a north aisle was added by the end of the 12th century; at Riseley a new nave was built, and the former nave became a south aisle. One special chapel was built at Meppershall, when Henry II's fateful quarrel with Archbishop Thomas Becket ended in the murder of the archbishop in his own cathedral, and all England looked on him as a martyr. It was dedicated to St. Thomas the Martyr, and those who could not make the pilgrimage to Canterbury went here.[7] Becket had stayed at Chicksands in 1164 on his way south.[8]

It is not till much later that documents enable us to reconstruct the internal appearance of parish churches, or that fragments of wall-paintings survive; but it cannot be doubted that the 12th cent. church was full of colour and brightness. People went to church on Sundays and holy days and on the patronal festival; for most, these were the only respite from a long round of work. Coming from their stud-and-plaster cottages, with only a living-room or hall, and any livestock they had partitioned off under the same roof, with wooden shutters and with only rush lights, they thought the church large, the candles on the various altars dazzling, the wall-paintings colourful and rich. Here, crowded together (the weakest going to the wall), and listening to a service imperfectly understood, they briefly glimpsed eternal verities. And if they were overtaken by trouble (for since Adam man is prone to sin), if a man in a violent dispute in the fields ran on another with a pitchfork, or killed him with his dagger in a drunken brawl at the inn, the church, if he could reach it before the hue and cry was raised, offered sanctuary; he could confess and be shriven; and he could stay there at least till declared an outlaw and he left home to try life elsewhere.

THE MONASTIC MOVEMENT

In 1066 there was no monastery in Bedfordshire. There were however secular canons serving St. Paul's church in Bedford – two of them were called Osmund and Ansfrid; they lived independently, i.e. not as a community, each having some land for his maintenance. They may have been the successors of the priests serving the original 7th cent. minster church (see ch. 1). In the mid-12th cent. there were six of them, William, Gilbert, Philip, Ralf, Richard and Nicholas (who was also Archdeacon of Bedford); it is possible their numbers had been increased, for laymen such as Ralf Tallebosc and Payn de Beauchamp had added

---

[7] V.C.H., ii, 293   [8] V.C.H. ii, 27.

to their endowments. There was also a school under their direction.[9]

A monastery was soon founded by Countess Judith, niece of the Conqueror and widow of Waltheof, probably soon after her husband's death in 1076 (see ch. 2).[10] Later it was said that Waltheof had been betrayed by her, and a tradition arose that she founded Elstow Abbey in expiation.[11] But the chronicler, Orderic, who says that Waltheof was condemned "on the testimony of his wife Judith"[12] writes in the next generation when English people had crowded in great numbers to Waltheof's tomb at Crowland. It seems more likely that the young widow founded it in her grief. This Abbey belonged to the old Benedictine (black-robed) order, with its emphasis on stately services. Judith endowed it with $3\frac{1}{2}$ hides at Elstow, 10 hides at Kempston, 3 hides at Wilstead, and 5 hides at Maulden. The first known Abbess was Cecily, and later ones bear such names as Balliol and Morteyne, for it tended to be an aristocratic house. Part of the Norman nave remains in the present parish church.

For about 50 years the monastic movement went no further in Bedfordshire, though in monasteries elsewhere Norman abbots, influenced by the new learning at Bec in Normandy, were building up libraries and increasing proficiency in Latin, as well as tightening discipline. But a widespread monastic ferment was working. Sometimes it reached a layman here through a monastic relative overseas (for ties with the continent were still close), as Samson le Fort of Harrold was prompted by a kinsman who was a canon of Arrouaise; sometimes through a connection in an important monastery here, as Henry d'Albini through his uncle who was abbot of St. Albans. Perhaps the uncertainties of Stephen's reign (1135–54) led men to reflect on the need to serve God; and the peace of the next reign gave new monasteries a chance to develop. Many individual decisions combined to bring about new foundations. A single holy man or woman sparked off consequences. Trouble among secular canons brought the suggestion that they should live under a rule. The individual founder might be moved by grief at a loss, by a wish to promote in others the life he himself could not aspire to, or even by a feeling that a monastic foundation was due from his position; and if he had no direct heir, any of these promptings would be strengthened; indeed, subsequent owners might feel he had gone too far. The founder's grant by itself would seldom have been sufficient; small benefactors rallied round when a lead had been given. Then there were the individual men and women who entered the cloister.

In the sixty years 1132–95 came eleven more monasteries, if we include Markyate on the then boundary with Hertfordshire. Two of these, like Elstow, were of the ancient Benedictine order (Beaulieu, 1140–6, and Markyate, 1145). Only two were Cistercian, the new order of white monks, with their austere devotion to simplicity and to remote places (Warden by 1135, Woburn in 1145).

---

[9] B.H.R.S. xliii, 127.
[10] V.C.H. i, 353; B. Arch.J., iii, 22–30.

[11] Wigram, Chronicles of Elstow.
[12] Orderic, ed. Forester, ii, 84.

The most popular order in Bedfordshire was the Augustinian, a comparatively late order, under which canons, following the example of monks, began to live as a community (Dunstable, 1132; Caldwell by 1153; Newnham, c. 1166; Bushmead, c. 1195). There was one house of the only English order, the Gilbertine (Chicksands, 1150). There were two cells of overseas monasteries: the nuns at Harrold, connected with Arrouaise, 1140–50; and a small priory at Grovebury, after 1164, a cell of the Abbey of Fontevrault. In addition, two Northamptonshire monasteries, Canons Ashby and Pipewell, owe their foundation to men of Bedfordshire. The circumstances in which the various Bedfordshire houses arose vary in nearly every case; the climate of the time was favourable; sometimes one combination, sometimes another, brought about a new foundation.

HOLY MEN AND WOMEN

To an individual holy man or woman, three of these seem to owe their beginning. Of hermits there were in Bedfordshire quite a number. A recluse worked out his own conception of a life pleasing to God. Such a life was not out of touch with the community. People came to ask advice or bring offerings, and young devotees came to live near the master to learn how to follow in his steps. The life of St. Wulfric, a hermit in the southwest of England, c. 1125, tells how he taught a boy to become a scribe, and how he knew when a woman in the village doing church embroidery had made mistakes in the work.[13] At Cardington in the late 12th cent. there was a recluse called Isabel.[14] There was one at Wilden in 1195.[15] In the early 13th cent. at Renhold, at a place called Welbury (whose identification has been lost), there was a hermit, Simon, who had round him young men learning to be hermits; Simon, as he grew older, was anxious about these, and bequeathed the charge of them and of his hermitage to the Prior of Newnham.[16] Milton [Ernest] had a hermitage, but the name of the hermit is not known;[17] there was also one at Sudbury in Eaton Socon;[18] at Bletsoe;[19] there seems to have been one at Luton on the site of what became the Hospital of St. Mary Magdalene;[20] and one is mentioned at Barton.[21] As late as 1442 there was one at Dunstable.[22]

At Moddry in Clophill Henry d'Albini granted a site to Ralf the hermit. A little later, this developed to a small cell of St. Albans Abbey (where Richard d'Albini was abbot 1097–1119). Robert d'Albini, son of Henry, about 1140–6 endowed it as a Benedictine priory of 4–5 monks, and it took the name of Beaulieu.[23]

Much later, at the end of the 12th cent. William of Colmworth gathered

---

[13] Stenton, 214–5.
[14] B.H.R.S. xliii, 18, 25, 75.
[15] B.H.R.S. vii, 102.
[16] B.H.R.S. xliii, 196; see also V.C.H. iii, 147.
[17] B.H.R.S. xliii, 208.
[18] B.H.R.S. xxii, 171.
[19] V.C.H. iii, 43.
[20] C.R.O., DW 8, 10–16.
[21] Ramsey cart., i, 480.
[22] B.H.R.S. xiv, 108.
[23] V.C.H. i, 351; B. Arch. J., iii, 31–4; B. Mag. viii, 244, 281.

round him some brothers who did not belong to any of the recognised orders. About 1195 Hugh de Beauchamp of Eaton (grandson of the Crusader) endowed them with the site of Bushmead and 28 acres. However the trend was towards conformity with the established orders, and after William's death about 1215 the house became an Augustinian priory.[24]

But the recluse of whom we know most, and who became the first prioress of Markyate, was St. Christina. [25] Her biographer was impressed with a beautiful girl's resolution to achieve celibacy, and tends to neglect her more positive qualities, but she was a remarkable woman. Today she would have become a headmistress or the principal of a women's college, and her career would have met throughout with sympathetic encouragement and parental pride. Christina, faced with continual misunderstanding and opposition, had to work out a career which she herself did not at first envisage. She was born at Huntingdon of a family which before the Conquest seems to have had thegn rank, and apparently her father was a merchant. When she was about 14, the family visited St. Albans Abbey (staying a night at Shillington on the way). Had the visit been to Elstow Abbey, she might already have seen her destiny clear; but as it was, the abbey church, where the great Norman nave was already in position, made such an impression on her that after mass she approached the altar with a penny, saying in her heart "O Lord God, to thee as a surrender of myself I offer this penny." It might have been the passing whim of an impressionable girl, but when a year or two later a young man, Burhred, wished to marry her, she would not consent, to the annoyance of her puzzled and irate parents. At a feast of the gild merchant (see ch. 5), at which her parents presided, she had to serve the wine, but secretly managed herself to drink water. After a year of pressure, in a moment of exhaustion, she agreed to the betrothal, apparently in a youthful belief that it would be practicable to live with her young husband without the normal relationship. This betrothal, considered as binding as marriage, was a stumbling-block for those who might have helped her, and equally so was the fact that it was difficult not to think of her as an attractive young woman. Burhred had a thin time between Christina, who talked to him of the saints, and her family, who voted him "a spineless and useless fellow" because he did not achieve his purpose willy-nilly. At last, with the help of a servant boy who procured a horse for her, Christina escaped in men's clothes and took refuge with a recluse, Alwen, at Flamstead.

Between Flamstead and Dunstable was an old hermit, Roger, of still greater repute. It is not surprising that Roger, when threatened with responsibility for a beautiful girl, sighed and went fasting into his chapel. After two years he did accept the charge; but to test her he had her walled into a small cell where she could hardly move, and from which she was released for a short walk once a day. The strict confinement affected her health "What was more unbearable was that

[24] V.C.H. i, 385; B.H.R.S. xxii.   [25] Christina of Markyate, ed. & trans. C. H. Talbot.

42

she could not go out until the evening to satisfy the demands of nature." There she remained four years; her personality matured and her purpose deepened; she won Roger's trust; and the old hermit began to call her his Sunday daughter "myn sunendaege dohter". At last Burhred in Roger's presence released her from her promise; and when Roger died she inherited his cell.

Already she had become a woman of note. She was the trusted adviser of Abbot Geoffrey of St. Albans (he was that Geoffrey who had taught in Dunstable (see ch. 5). She was invited to take charge of a community of nuns at York, but refused. At last, by arrangement between the dean and chapter of St. Paul's, London, and Abbot Geoffrey of St. Albans, Markyate Priory for Benedictine nuns was founded in 1145 with her as the first prioress.[26] She must therefore have been able to organise and to administer, as well as to pray and teach. "The lady Christina of the wood" received recognition from the king.[27] She was also skilled in the considerable art of church embroidery, for she sent embroidered mitres of exquisite workmanship of her own making to the English Pope, Adrian IV.[28]

THE CISTERCIANS

Quite other circumstances gave rise to the two Cistercian monasteries in Bedfordshire. This new order came from Citeaux, where an Englishman, Stephen Harding, was abbot 1109–22, and drew up its rules; but it was St. Bernard, abbot of the first daughter house, that of Clairvaux, who spread it far and wide. Coming to England in 1128, it was most readily accepted in Yorkshire, which, so often devastated in the past, had scarcely any surviving monastery. Here Walter Espec, son or nephew of the William Espec of 1087, the lord of Warden, and itinerant justice in the north for Henry I (see ch. 2, 5) had lands, his chief seat being Helmsley castle, and here he founded Rievaulx Abbey. Two miles from Helmsley the Cistercian monks set up their huts in 1132. A young Englishman, Ailred, coming to York in 1134 in the service of the Scottish king, heard how "certain monks had come to England from across the sea, wonderful men, famous adepts in the religious life, white monks by name and white also in vesture . . . They venerate poverty, not the penury of the idle and negligent, but a poverty directed by a necessity of the will and sustained by the thoroughness of faith, and approved by divine love."[29] They had no personal property; bread, cabbages and beans were all their food; personal standing was merged in the equality of each and all. Ailred longed to see them. He spent two nights at Helmsley castle with Walter Espec, and Walter rode over with him and introduced him to the monks. The result was that Ailred entered Rievaulx as a novice under the novice-master Simon. From the elderly Simon's account of his saintly young novice Ailred, we get some idea of the teacher who could elicit and appreciate such qualities in a novice. "In truth, he was my companion, not my pupil, and by his

[26] *V.C.H.*, i, 358.
[27] *Op.cit.*, 359n.
[28] *Loc.cit.*
[29] *Life of Ailred*, ed. F. M. Powicke, 11–14.

assiduity he excelled his teacher in that school, in the days of his young manhood, when the heat of the blood so often erases the mind and clouds the feelings and burns away the energy, and in the testing place of his noviciate, where a man finds it so hard to stamp out the old and endure the present and make precaution against future vices . . . I watched him attentively wait upon all the novices with whom he lived, abase himself utterly in their ranks, and above human measure in his humanity to the rest. The most remarkable thing in one who exceeded all in the other virtues was a charity, which won the victory over himself. Every time he submitted the preference of his own will to the need of another he won this victory."[30] The man who thus trained the saintly Ailred was the first abbot of Warden Abbey. For Walter Espec, who had only sisters to succeed him, had no need to stint his generosity, and next invited the Cistercians to Warden.[31] A Cistercian Abbey, in founding a daughter house, usually sent out twelve monks with an abbot, and the new house thus founded became independent. Warden was founded by 1135. As Rievaulx is distant from Helmsley, so Warden Abbey is some distance from the village of Old Warden, and in early times was called St. Mary de Sartis (i.e. of the assart, or newly-cleared land). Another Warden monk was a friend of Ailred's and figures in one of his books, De spirituali amicitia, by name Ivo.[32] Ailred, when abbot of Rievaulx, must often have come to Warden, probably on his way south to Citeaux, for every Cistercian abbot had to visit each year not only Citeaux but all daughter-houses of his abbey: the Cistercian order was self-governing under the Pope. Incidentally, Walter Espec was one of the leaders in the great battle of the Standard, 1138, when the Scots invaded England to oppose Stephen, and many consecrated banners were carried with the English army, which won a complete victory.

Perhaps it was Walter Espec's example which inspired Hugh de Bolebec. He was the grandson of Hugh de Bolebec who held land at Woburn, Marston and Maulden as a knight of Walter Giffard (see ch. 2), and he had only a daughter to succeed him.[33] In 1145 he invited from Fountains Abbey a party of Cistercian monks, who came with their first abbot, Alan. These settled far from both the parish church of Birchmore[34] and the hamlet of Woburn. Woburn Abbey would have been visited regularly by the abbot of Fountains.

Warden and Woburn are not quite the same as a Yorkshire valley; but perhaps we can get from the life of Ailred some idea of the feeling of early Cistercians: "High hills surround the valley, encircling it like a crown. These are clothed by trees of various sorts and maintain in pleasant retreats the privacy of the vale, providing for the monks a kind of second paradise of wooded delight. From the loftiest rocks the waters wind and tumble down to the valley below."[35] But the

---

[30] Op.cit., 16–17.
[31] V.C.H., i, 361; B.H.R.S., xiii.
[32] Life of Ailred, p.lviii, lxix.

[33] B.H.R.S., vii, 194.
[34] V.C.H., i, 366.
[35] Life of Ailred, 12–13.

monks of Warden and Woburn did not spend their time in poetic contemplation – they worked hard to reduce the land around them to cultivation. Warden pears were famous. As the monks acquired land elsewhere, they built granges on it and cultivated that too, so that their abbeys became widespread economic units. Warden had 12 granges by 1190.[36] A grange had a chapel and refectory, with some lay brothers in charge of a monk; these stayed for short periods and then returned to the mother house. Insistence on seclusion from the world could mean that, where there were existing dwellings near a proposed grange, these were cleared away.[37] This may have happened, for instance, at Putnoe.

THE AUGUSTINIANS

Different again were the circumstances which gave rise to the houses of Augustinian canons. Monasticism is in essence a life apart from the world. Canons, who were in full priests' orders, lived at centres of population, as in Bedford, at first independently. But as monasticism spread, it began to be thought, first on the continent and then in the 12th cent. in England, that it was an advantage for the canons at any one place to live as a community, and for this purpose general directions for a godly life laid down centuries before by St. Augustine of Hippo were adapted as the Augustinian rule. Two canons went from England to Chartres and Beauvais to see the Augustinian rule in action. For Henry I's new town at Dunstable (see ch. 5), a priory of Augustinian canons was the appropriate choice in 1132.[38] The loss by drowning of his son William was heavy on his heart. "Henry, king of the English, greeting to his Archbishops, Bishops, Abbots, Earls, Barons, sheriffs, and all faithful ministers, French and English. Know that, for God, and for my health, and for the soul of my son William and of Queen Matilda my wife, I have given to the church of St. Peter of Dunstable (which I founded in honour of God and of his apostle,) and to the regular canons serving God there, all the manor and borough of Dunstable."[39] He goes on to mention the land, the market (all who come there are to have his peace), a school, and rights of jurisdiction, using the old English terms of "thol et theam et infangenethef"; but explains that he is retaining his house and garden in the town, where he is wont to stay. The first prior was Bernard, one of the two canons mentioned above. The church of St. Peter, of which the great Norman nave remains, was begun almost at once, but the king's death and the troubled time which followed held up building, and it was not consecrated till 1213. The main part of this was for the canons' own services; the north aisle was used for parish purposes, and here an altar to St. John the Baptist was consecrated in 1219.[40]

Dunstable was a deliberate and appropriate royal foundation. On the other hand, the origin of the little Augustinian priory of Caldwell is obscure. It was

[36] B.H.R.S. xiii, 289.
[37] D. Knowles, *The religious orders*, 73–4.
[38] V.C.H. i, 371; B.H.R.S. x, 240.

[39] B.H.R.S. x, 240.
[40] V.C.H., iii, 364–5.

there by 1153[41], and the name of Simon Barescote or Barscot is connected with it. In Bedford in the 13th cent. are found no less than seven men bearing this surname in various forms, one of them, Simon, having a house in High Street; and the name is also found in the 14th cent. It seems very possible that the original Simon Barscot was a leading Bedford merchant in the early days of the gild merchant (see ch. 5) and before the mayoralty had become established.

Unusual circumstances gave rise to the other Augustinian Priory at Bedford, that of Newnham, c. 1166, by Simon de Beauchamp.[42] It is also noteworthy that a foundation by the leading family came so late. But the Beauchamps had not the monastic connections of the d'Albinis; Bedford castle had been a storm centre while Cainhoe castle had not; and so (though his mother had already founded Chicksands – see below) it was not till the young Simon was coming of age that the moment arrived. In fact it was outside events and not Simon's initiative that precipitated matters. One of the canons of St. Paul, Bedford, Philip de Broy, in 1164 in circumstances which are not fully known killed a man. The de Broys were Simon's own tenants at Bletsoe; the canons those of his nearest church. Both the young man and Archdeacon Nicholas (himself a canon) must have felt that some forward step was needed, and that it would be better if in future the Bedford canons, like those of Dunstable, lived as a community under a rule with a prior. The first steps were taken in conjunction with Simon's mother, the Countess Rose, who herself contributed to the endowment. By the time the approval of Bishop, Archbishop and King had been gained, she had died. At a solemn service in St. Paul's church in 1166 Simon de Beauchamp granted the church, with its prebends and possessions, to the regular canons. One of them, William, became the first prior; and some advice was obtained from Merton Priory in Surrey. Buildings at Bedford were a problem, for there was neither peace nor space for a cloister in the busy maze of streets and alleys round St. Paul's church. When William died or resigned, by 1170, the new prior, Auger (who perhaps came from Merton), planned new buildings outside the town of Newnham, and organised the move there by 1178. Probably the canons, whose own services after the move were held at Newnham, still in the main took the services at St. Paul's, Bedford, also; though they may have appointed a resident chaplain.[43] Archdeacon Nicholas at first retained control of the school, but later resigned it to Newnham Priory.[44] In the Augustinian order there was no hier-archial system, as with the Cistercians; and they, like the Benedictines, came under the bishop's control. However periodic general chapters were held, and in the 13th cent. more than one of these met at Dunstable.[45]

---

[41] V.C.H. i, 382.
[42] Op.cit., 377; B.H.R.S. xliii.
[43] A vicar was appointed in 1528; Linc.R.O., Reg.27, f.263 v; the vicarage was, till the present century, a little house on the south side of the square. For the relations of Augustinian canons with their parishes, see J. C. Dickinson, The origins of the Austin canons, 214–41.
[44] B.H.R.S., xliii, 127.
[45] Ann. Mon. iii, 179, 341 (1249 and 1288).

OTHER MONASTIC ORDERS

There was another Beauchamp foundation, but this was mainly the work of Simon's mother, Countess Rose: Chicksands.[46] Rose had led an eventful life. She had previously married that stormy petrel, Geoffrey de Mandeville, Earl of Essex, whose career is more turbulent that that of any other baron in Stephen's reign. When he died in 1144 she married Payn de Beauchamp. Her first husband had founded an abbey at Walden, and she now, with her second husband, about 1150 founded Chicksands Priory for nuns of the Gilbertine order. She was a masterful woman, and when her son Geoffrey de Mandeville died, she sent armed retainers to fetch the body to be buried at Chicksands; however, his servants managed to elude her and to take it to Walden Abbey. She herself was buried at Chicksands.

Two small Bedfordshire religious houses had overseas connections. At this time ties with the continent were close, but such connections later gave rise to trouble. The little priory for nuns at Harrold was founded by Samson le Fort.[47] He was not himself of a Bedfordshire family, but in right of his wife, Albreda de Blosseville, held Harrold as a life-tenant (for the honour of Huntingdon) till the succession of her son.[48] Samson was prompted to found Harrold by his kinsman, Hilbert Pelice, a canon of Arrouaise, and so Harrold Priory was at first a cell of Arrouaise, c. 1145.[49] (The Arrouaise rule was an adaptation of the Augustinian). The distance made the connection difficult, and in 1177 Arrouaise seems to have ceded its rights to Missenden Abbey; and this too made friction, and in 1188 Harrold's independence from Arrouaise was acknowledged and it became an Augustinian priory under the bishop.

The other alien house had a royal origin. The royal manor of Leighton was granted by Henry II to Fontevrault Abbey in 1164, and soon afterwards a cell of this abbey seems to have been established at Grovebury. But this was to run into trouble in the Hundred Years War.[50]

At Melchbourne there was a preceptory of knights Hospitallers (an order formed for service in the Holy Land).

THE ORDINARY MAN AND THE MONASTERY

The founder of a monastery was only one of many benefactors, both great and small, who came forward with gifts, both in the early days while the monastic buildings were rising (now, alas! almost completely swept away), and continuing later for many years as those around knew and respected the monks and nuns who lived among them.

Sometimes the gifts were ear-marked for the building fund: William of Broom in the 12th cent. gave $\frac{1}{2}$ acre "to St. Paul of Newnham for the building of

46 V.C.H., i, 390.
47 V.C.H., i, 387; B.H.R.S., xvii.
48 B.H.R.S., xi, 69–71.

49 B.H.R.S., xvii, 9.
50 V.C.H., i, 403.

the church"[51]; or again for the services: thus Ambrose of Dunstable about 1190 gave 12d. rent in Houghton Regis for a light before the altar at Dunstable Priory.[52] One practical Carlton donor to Harrold Priory a good deal later specified that part of his gift of rent was to repair and maintain as needed the leaden channels of the cloister called "goteris" (gutters);[53] perhaps he knew that the nuns had had trouble there. At other times the gifts were for some aspect of monastic life or work. William Lenveise about 1175 gave to Warden Abbey an acre "for the use of the hospice of the poor";[54] in the next cent. William Goldsmith of Dunstable gave the Dunstable almonry a rent of 3s. from a house in South Street.[55] In the 13th cent. Robert Byssop of Pertenhall gave a rent of 15d. for a lamp in the infirmary at Bushmead Priory,[56] and Robert son of Ralf gave to Newnham Priory 4s. rent in Bedford for a light in the infirmary chapel.[57] Sometimes the donor coupled his gift with a request to be prayed for, or received into fraternity and mentioned in the daily orisons, as did William of Eyeworth to Warden Abbey about 1200;[58] he might even ask to be buried at the monastery, as did Henry de Braybrook before 1234 when he left a bequest for five sick poor to be cared for by the canons of Bushmead.[59] Occasionally a donor, impressed perhaps with the monks' austerity, made a gift for an occasional treat or pittance, as did William Carbonel of Wyboston to Bushmead Priory on 7 November, when they were to celebrate an obit or memorial service for his mother Heloise and himself.[60] Walter de Kyrkebi in 1234 asked Dunstable Priory to keep his two sons in food and clothing till they were 20, and to give them an education (lay or clerical as seemed best).[61]

But the great majority of gifts were made in simple faith without conditions. As time went on, the monks copied out the documents concerning them into books of charters called cartularies; and for five of the twelve monasteries these cartularies have survived and are in print.[62] The number of individual donors is between one and two thousand; and if the other religious houses had a corresponding proportion there must have been about three thousand donors, even allowing for the fact that some donors made gifts to more than one religious house, as William le Eyr of Cople, c. 1200 gave both to Warden Abbey and to Bushmead Priory. Sometimes several members of one family gave, as did the Passelews to Dunstable Priory or the Morins to Harrold Priory. The Wahulls founded no monastery of their own, but Walter de Wahull (d. c. 1173, and see ch. 2), his son Simon (d. 1191), and others of the family made grants both to Dunstable and to Harrold Priories. Often an individual donor continued giving, till his successors thought that he had gone too far, and at a later stage made difficulties

[51] B.H.R.S., xliii, 364.
[52] B.H.R.S., x, 78.
[53] B.H.R.S., xvii, 171.
[54] B.H.R.S., xiii, 229–30.
[55] B.H.R.S., x, 146.
[56] B.H.R.S., xxii, 125.
[57] B.H.R.S., xliii, 137.
[58] B.H.R.S., xiii, 64.
[59] B.H.R.S., xxii, 57.
[60] B.H.R.S., xxii, 97.
[61] B.H.R.S., x, 150.
[62] B.H.R.S., x, xiii, xvii, xxii, xliii.

with the recipient. Some benefactors lived outside the county. The donor's status and the amount he or she gave could vary greatly, as with Newnham Priory, from the Triket family, lords of Toft manor, Sharnbrook,[63] to Alan of Stotfold, who gave $1\frac{1}{2}$ roods in Brook Mead, Stotfold, and of whom nothing more is known.[64]

And what of the individual men and women who made their vows and entered the cloister? Later on, through entries in the cartularies, and through episcopal visitations, we get to know a little about some of them; but in the 12th cent. there is no one of whom we know so much as of St. Christina. It may be supposed that the first, or sometimes the second abbot or prior, abbess or prioress, was a man or woman of high character, striking personality and organising ability, as Auger at Newnham and Simon at Warden; sometimes perhaps an outstanding man was to come later, as Richard de Morin at Dunstable (1202–42). But in the 12th cent., though we have so little personal detail, there was a vitality and a confidence in monasticism. The monastic life was widely held to be the best and the most pleasing to God, though not all could aspire to it. The monasteries were the repositories of learning; they cared for the poor; an outstanding prior might be sent on a royal mission. It was their greatest time.

---

[63] B.H.R.S., xliii, 292–302.

[64] B.H.R.S., xliii, 380.

F

5 – MARKETS, FAIRS AND TOWNS, 1066–1300

MARKETS

From very early times[1] weekly markets were needed to dispose locally of surplus goods and make up deficiencies. They were in safe and recognised places, so that transactions could take place before witnesses, the sale of stolen goods would be more difficult, and the lord's tolls could be collected. They were normally held on Sunday. In 1066[2] there were four. Bedford must have been the most important, though it no doubt suffered temporarily from the clearance of houses to make way for the castle. It was held then, as later, in the High Street. That at Leighton, held – as it still is – in the main street, was worth £7 p.a. in tolls; that at Luton £5. There was also a small one for the east of the county at Arlesey, but its yearly tolls brought in only 10s.

The right to hold markets was granted by the king, so that he could control their distribution and exact payment for his grant. For more than a century after the conquest, records for such grants have not survived (except Dunstable – see below); Biggleswade was granted by King John and confirmed 1227;[3] and Potton in the east[4] and Melchbourne[5] in the north may date from this time. In the 13th cent. weekdays began to be chosen (it was at first illegal to change the day without royal licence); Luton altered its day to Monday[6] and Potton to Saturday[7] in 1203, and Arlesey to Wednesday in 1270.[8] Gradually week-day markets became general. Now and in the early 14th cent. several more markets were added: 1218 Toddington and Warden; 1219 Ampthill; 1222 Odell; 1242 Woburn; 1267 Aspley; 1304 Weston[ing]; 1314 Blunham; 1315 Sundon; 1319 Silsoe; 1324 Marston.[9] When a new market was proposed, enquiry was usually first made as to whether it would injure an existing one; thus it was asked in 1222 whether Odell market would interfere with that of Olney;[10] and in 1225 the sheriff was ordered to enquire whether a Shefford market was harmful to Bedford.[11] By 1324 the county was well supplied with markets, except in the northeast, where people probably went to St. Neots and Kimbolton. Probably the larger centres drew most custom and the others remained small.

---

[1] For the background to this chapter, see A. L. Poole, *From Domesday Book to Magna Carta*, 63–95; D. M. Stenton, *English Society in the Early Middle Ages*, 160–207; J. Tait, *The mediaeval English borough*; A. Ballard, *British borough charters*. See also *V.C.H.* ii, 88.

[2] *V.C.H.* i, 222, 234. Bedford is not given.

[3] *V.C.H.* ii, 212.

[4] *V.C.H.* ii, 268.

[5] *V.C.H.* iii, 142. Harrold is thought to be 17th cent.: *V.C.H.* iii, 64.

[6] *V.C.H.* ii, 349.

[7] *V.C.H.* ii, 239.

[8] *V.C.H.* ii, 263.

[9] For most of these, see *V.C.H.* ii, 88; Sundon, *V.C.H.* ii, 385; Marston, *V.C.H.* iii, 311.

[10] *V.C.H.* iii, 69.

[11] *V.C.H.* ii, 268.

FAIRS

A fair was a bigger occasion. An important fair brought traders from London and elsewhere with goods not easy to get locally, such as iron, gold, silver and brass;[12] it was an occasion for trading in horses and other livestock; and it drew purchasers from a wide area. It was held on the date of a church festival, often lasting 3 days (i.e., including the eve and morrow). On such a day all would be free to attend; and jugglers and beer would not be lacking.

Here again there must be a grant from the king, and for several the date of this is not known. Those at Bedford,[13] Biggleswade,[14] and Luton,[15] seem to have been early. Elstow Abbey[16] had from Henry I the right to hold a fair on the green (the stump of a cross still marks the site), and this fair provoked the traders of Bedford, so that the king ordered the reeve and burgesses of Bedford to see that no harm came to those attending it. Dunstable fair dates from 1203.[17] Potton fair was confirmed to its lord in 1227;[18] the right to hold a fair at Leighton was granted to Fontevrault Abbey in 1254;[19] at Melchbourne to its lord in 1264;[20] Arlesey 1270;[21] Shefford 1312;[22] Blunham 1314;[23] Silsoe 1318;[24] Ampthill 1330;[25] and others are uncertain.[26] In larger places, such as Bedford, Leighton and Luton, the right was gradually obtained to have several.

The season for fairs ran from the spring to the autumn. Thus Elstow (Holy Cross) and Leighton (St. Dunstan) fell in May; Arlesey (Saints Peter and Paul) in June; Potton (St. James) in July; in August both Luton and Biggleswade fell at the Assumption till in 1228 Biggleswade changed to the other Holy Cross Day in September;[27] Shefford was at Michaelmas; and Ampthill in November (St. Andrew). Probably at this time, as they did later, some people went regularly to every fair within reach.

TOWNS

Towns in Bedfordshire in the 12th and 13th centuries are of three kinds. There is first the county town, Bedford, with its mint, numerous churches, privileges obtained from the king by charter, a settlement of Jewish financiers, it had a high standard of living, and it eventually sent members to parliament. There are two other towns of old standing, Leighton and Luton, without privileges as important as those of Bedford, but yet developing and distinct from the

12 A London merchant, William de St. Briavells, had a brass ewer and spoon stolen from his booth at Elstow in 1294; *V.C.H.* iii, 281.
13 *V.C.H.* iii, 21.
14 *V.C.H.* ii, 212.
15 *V.C.H.* ii, 349–50, 351n. See also *B.H.R.S.* ii, 157–82.
16 *V.C.H.* iii, 381; S. R. Wigram, *Chronicles of the abbey of Elstow*, 42–3.
17 *V.C.H.* iii, 362–3.
18 *V.C.H.* ii, 239.
19 *Cal. Pat. R.* 1247–58, p.383.
20 *V.C.H.* ii, 88; iii, 142.

21 *V.C.H.* ii, 263.
22 *Op.cit.*, 268.
23 *V.C.H.* iii, 229.
24 *V.C.H.* ii, 330.
25 *V.C.H.* iii, 272. In 1542 the profits were only 13s 6d. (P.R.O.: S.C. 6, Hen. VII, 6070, f.10).
26 Woburn was by 1334 (*B.H.R.S.* xxix, 97). Harrold is uncertain. Ickwell was in 1676 (*V.C.H.* iii, 246). Toddington was in 1692 (C.R.O., X 95/390). Sometimes, as at Shefford, a fair declined and was revived by a later grant.
27 *V.C.H.* ii, 212.

villages. And there are two instances of town-planning: a new settlement at Dunstable planned by the king; and the Bishop of Lincoln's attempt to develop Biggleswade.

BEDFORD

A mint was found only in Bedford (see ch. 1). Local mints continued after the Conquest, and though before this there were sometimes several moneyers in Bedford, after 1066 there seem to have been at first two, later one. Sibrand and Sigod were moneyers in the time of William II.[28] They were leading merchants, who fetched the royal die from London and employed "hammermen" to strike the coins at a forge. A moneyer was tempted to have the coins made of debased silver and short in weight; but his name on the coin made it possible to check up on him. When such malpractice had become wide-spread, Henry I summoned the moneyers at Christmas 1125 to Winchester, and they were deprived of their right hands and emasculated as a dire warning.[29] The Bedford one seems to have been Edric. The coin in which the revenue was paid was carefully checked; when the sheriff annually took his barrels of silver pennies to the exchequer, a sample of 240 pennies was melted down to test its fineness. There were also offenders who collected silver by clipping money; and so even at ordinary times money was counted by weight rather than by number. Gradually the number of local mints was curtailed. In Stephen's reign there was a moneyer called Tomas. In 1279 Edward I issued a new coinage which included halfpennies and farthings; and, though some local mints continued for a time in large towns, one officer in London was responsible.

A gild was a form of association even before the conquest. Bedford was administered by the king's reeve, and early in the 12th cent. the traders probably felt that a gild merchant could promote their interests. Strictly speaking, it could not be formed without the king's licence. Elsewhere it was often formed first and obtained its licence when it was well established. Perhaps there was such a gild merchant at Bedford years before it was formally recognised, and it would help to build up a corporate spirit. Details of the Bedford gild have not survived, but it was probably something like that of Leicester.[30] The gild charged an entrance fee, and a gildsman was bound by its rules for maintaining standards, for buying and selling, and for the payment of wages. A stranger coming to the town could deal only with a gildsman, and that after he had paid toll.

The gild also had social functions. It may well be that c. 1115 at Bedford as at Huntingdon the gild would have an all-day festival, with "a great throng of nobles gathered together", and the merchants' comely daughters, with mantles laid aside and sleeves rolled up, would "courteously offer drinks", and that few would be sober. At Huntingdon this was held in a hall with several entrances.[31]

[28] G. C. Brooke, *English coins*, 61–3, 70, 83, 89, 97.
[29] D. M. Stenton, *op.cit.*, 165.
[30] Stenton, *op.cit.*, 180–5.
[31] *Life of St. Christina*, p.49.

There was later at Bedford a small gildhall or moothall with stalls under it, on what is now St. Paul's Square, but it is unlikely that it was built before the late 12th cent., perhaps replacing an earlier one.

The main object of the gild merchant was to regulate trade, and a burgess was not necessarily a gildsman. Nevertheless the gild probably included the most active and prosperous burgesses. These began to seek privileges from the king. It is likely that they obtained a charter from King Henry I (d. 1135) when some other county towns were beginning to do so; this charter is lost; it was probably only brief and couched in somewhat general terms.

The charter, according to a later statement by Bedford burgesses,[32] was kept in St. Paul's church, probably with the charters of the canons (see ch. 4). But St. Paul's church suffered from its nearness to Bedford castle, which was besieged in 1137 and 1153 (see ch. 2). On the latter occasion the town was set on fire, and St. Paul's church suffered severely, so that Henry (then Duke of Acquitaine, afterwards Henry II) promised St. Paul's £8 from the hagable to repair the destruction he had caused.[33] It was on this occasion that the canons' own early charters were lost,[34] and it seems reasonable to accept the burgesses' statement that a charter from Henry I to Bedford was burnt at the same time.

The enterprising burgesses of the early 12th cent. had little chance to make headway in the 19 years' anarchy of Stephen's reign, when they suffered exactions from both sides and the town was seriously damaged in the two sieges. Under the steady rule of Henry II (1154–89), prospects were better, and they again applied for a charter. It cost them 40 marks[35] and was granted while the king was at Rouen in 1166. It confirmed "the liberties and free customs which they had in the time of King Henry my grandfather, as they have been recognised in the county of Bedford."[36] In case of doubt as to what these were, they were to be "as the burgesses of Oxford have them". Oxford had obtained a charter in 1156;[37] the rights in this were: to have a gild merchant; to have their own court and not plead outside the borough; and to be quit of toll when they traded elsewhere. It was the claim to be quit of toll which caused the dispute of 1226[38] when Bedford burgesses would not pay toll at Yaxley; such grants by the king to many boroughs

---

[32] *Curia Regis rolls,* xii, 513: "combuste fuerunt in ecclesia sancti Pauli apud Bedeford' in obsidione ducis Henrici." This claim was made in 1226, when the burgesses' right to exemption from toll at Yaxley market was contested; and for good measure the burgesses stated also that at the same time they lost charters from William I and II. It is much less likely that they had charters of so early a date; but 70 years later they might well not be quite clear how many charters there were. The siege they refer to must be that of 1153. Had the destruction of Henry I's charter taken place later, the 1166 charter would have been destroyed also. St. Paul's church suffered again under King John, who is said to have destroyed it (*Cal. Pat. R.* 1216-

25, p.29); and it probably suffered also in the siege of 1224; but by this time the canons' charters were stored at Newnham Priory (see ch. 4), and the town charters may have been at the moot hall. Incidentally, it is hardly surprising that the surviving fabric of St. Paul's church is of late date.
[33] *B.H.R.S.* xliii, 33.
[34] *Op.cit.,* 53.
[35] *V.C.H.* iii, 17.
[36] *Corporation records,* ftispiece; *Schedule of ancient charters,* 4.
[37] A. Ballard, *Brit. Bor. ch.,* i, 7, 13, 99, 113, 117, 182, 204, 209.
[38] See n. 32.

eventually broke down trade barriers all over the country.

It must have been unsatisfactory that Bedford's 1166 charter was not more explicit. The chance to get rights like those of Oxford stated came with a new reign in 1189, when Richard I, eager to go on the Third Crusade, was ready to be generous to boroughs offering cash down. The new charter stated these rights,[39] but did not include financial control. This, in the king's hands, must have been increasingly irksome to a growing and prospering community. Till now the tolls of the market, the profits of the court, the hagable and other rents were all collected by the reeve and accounted for at the exchequer by the sheriff. Yet from 1190 the burgesses, perhaps on a temporary basis, did in fact pay a lump sum (or fee-farm) of £40 for their financial dues.[40] The sum was large, but the right to pay it meant a great step forward. It did not necessarily and at once imply that the town could choose its own reeve or bailiffs, but this would follow before long.

Soon after 1200 the centre of Bedford had probably taken the shape which it was to have till about 1800. Whatever primitive bridge there may have been previously over the river, there certainly was a stone one by about 1185, with a chapel on it where passers-by made offerings for its upkeep.[41] The county gaol is mentioned in the sheriff's accounts.[42] In addition to the six older churches (St. Paul, the two St. Peters, St. Mary, St. Cuthbert, All Hallows), there was also the little chapel of St. Mary in the Herne (or corner of what is now St. Paul's Square) and there was now the church of St. John for its hospital and tiny parish (see ch. 9). There was a house of Franciscan friars (see ch. 9); the school under the aegis of Newnham Priory; and St. Leonard's hospital away in the fields. Most houses were of stud and plaster, but there were a few of stone: Thomas Aket had a stone house by the bridge about 1150,[43] and it probably looked much like the two 12th cent. stone houses surviving at Lincoln in Steep Hill, with an undercroft for storage, and living quarters above.

After the third and last siege of the castle in 1224 (see ch. 7), it must have been with satisfaction that the burgesses heard of the king's order that what was left of it was to be pulled down and that the Beauchamps would in future only have a house on the site, which was not to be fortified. Some of the stone was given by the king to Newnham and Caldwell priories, but a good deal found its way into the repair and rebuilding of little streets round about. This time when the burgesses repaired or rebuilt Butcher Row, Fish Row, Pudding Lane and the Poultry Market,[44] they had hope that there would be quieter times henceforth. A way through what had been the outer bailey of the castle became Castle Lane. The

---

[39] Corporation records, 5.
[40] B.H.R.S. vii, 44, 55, 64 etc.
[41] B.H.R.S. ix, 180.
[42] B.H.R.S. vii, 36; there were repairs to the extent of £2 15s. 2d. in 1189.

[43] B.H.R.S. xiii, 110.
[44] B.H.R.S. xxv, 15–81 and plan. The Bedford of 1506 can be approximately plotted, and it is probable that the streets then were much the same as in the 13th century.

Moot Hall, whether now built for the first time or rebuilt, was on the west of High Street, backing on to Fish Row;[45] there were shops on the ground floor; and stairs at the east end led to a hall on the first floor.[46] A later plan shows that it measured 45 ft. x 29 ft.

When in 1227 the cautious burgesses got their fee-farm (or composition for financial dues) recognised in a charter from Henry III,[47] it is probable that they chose their own officers if they had not already done so. When the judges came in 1247, Bedford was represented before them by Simon Barscot (who is described as alderman) by two bailiffs, William de Leyc' and Robert de Stiveton, and by twelve burgesses. Through overseas trade, English burgesses had already become aware of what was happening on the continent, where central government was much weaker, and many towns secured complete independence, calling themselves communes. The word "commune" is even used of Bedford c. 1185,[48] but here probably it meant only community. London had in Stephen's reign tried to be a commune in the continental sense but did not succeed. However, the continental word, "maire," for chief burgess began to be used in Bedford in the 13th cent.;[49] and the first mayor for whom a definite date can be given is John Cullebere in 1297. "Alderman" came to be used for those who had served their turn as mayor.

A community developing in all these ways was unlike the rigidifying organisation on the manors. A burgess, if he did not own his tenement, paid money rent for it, and had no obligation to regular manual service. Indeed, it became established that, if a villein lived for a year and a day in a borough without being recovered by his lord, he thereby became free. Moreover, while a villein's son succeeded to his father's holding on paying a heriot (or death duty) at the manor court, and a knight's son succeeded on paying a relief, a burgess could bequeath his tenement as he wished. Burgage tenure was free tenure; and must have in general obtained in Bedford from quite early times. But hard and fast rules rarely apply in the middle ages any more than at any other time, and there were one or two cases, such as Elstow Abbey's manor of Aldermanbury, where some manorial organisation seems to have existed.[50]

A sign of an active business centre was a Jewry. Christians were not supposed to lend money on usury; and lords, knights and even religious houses who were embarrassed for money, besides merchants who wanted to expand their trade, applied to Jews.[51] The Jews' position was insecure, and they naturally charged high rates of interest. Isaac of Bedford occurs as early as 1192 and Bonefand in 1202;[52] and in 1251 Boniface and his son are mentioned.[53] In 1261 the king made a

45 Speed's map, V.C.H. iii, 2. For plan, see C.R.O., R (uncat.).
46 P.R.O., KB 9/230 B,m. 214.
47 Corporation Records, 5; Schedule of ancient charters, 4.
48 B.H.R.S. ix, 177–80.
49 Cal. Cl. R. 1261–4, p.364 (1264 – no name given).
50 V.C.H. iii, 23.
51 See for instance B.H.R.S. x, 84, 101, 103, 124.
52 B.H.R.S. vii, 70; i, 231.
53 B.H.R.S. xiii, 207.

general enquiry, and in Bedford Simon Passelew was appointed to open the Jews' chests and enrol all the debts he found there, and enquire how much each had in gold, silver and jewels.[54] One called Peitevin (i.e., of Poitou), was heavily fined: 735 marks; and his widow Belia, after paying 400 marks, had leave to pay off the rest at 40 marks annually.[55] His son Jacob was later hanged.[56] In the disturbances of 1264 (see ch. 7) a wave of anti-Semitism devastated local Jewries, and their chests of mortgages were burnt by angry creditors and others.[57] This time the king tried to protect them, and 11 Bedford Jews are named in 1266.[58] But in 1290 they were expelled from the country; and King Edward I gave to Newnham Priory two houses which had formerly belonged to Jacob and Benedict, sons of Peitevin.[59] It is an unhappy aspect of 13th cent. Bedford.

The taxation returns of 1297 tell something of the Bedford burgesses of the day. Those with goods worth less than 9s. were not taxed; this leaves 98 who were. Often the nature of their merchandise is not given, but there were 11 tanners; there were butchers, fisher, spicer and salter; there were drapers, blanket-maker, dyer, tailor and shoemaker; and there were smiths, carpenters and wheelwrights, probably more skilled than those in the villages. Forty of them had houses sufficiently comfortable to be assessed for extra taxation, having a good bedroom or chamber in addition to the hall or living-room. Sixty-six had household utensils of brass, pewter or wood sufficient to qualify for tax; six had mazers, which were prized bowls of maplewood inlaid with silver. Two had silver spoons; one was John Cullebere, the mayor of 1297, and borough representative in parliament in 1295[60] (see ch. 7); he had also a cart, 2 horses and 4 oxen;[61] the other was John Wymund, who had a stock of iron worth 20s., salt 10s., sea coal 10s., and oil 10s; he had also a cart and 3 horses.[62] There were ten burgesses whose goods were worth £2 and over; 37 worth £1 or over; and 51 under £1. The wealthiest, John super Muro, worth £6 14s. 8d., was not as rich as the Dunstable tycoon John Durant (see below), but the general standard of living in Bedford was higher than anywhere else.[63]

LEIGHTON AND LUTON

In Leighton and Luton the atmosphere was altogether more placid. They were bigger than the villages round about, but allowance must be made for all their surrounding hamlets (Billington, Eggington, Heath and Stanbridge for Leighton; Biscot, Hyde, Leagrave, Limbury and Stopsley for Luton). In general in the early days one church sufficed for the population of each (there was soon a chapel at Limbury).[64] There probably simply were not enough people to develop

---

[54] *Cal. Pat. R. 1258–66*, p.186.
[55] *Op.cit.*, p.192.
[56] *Cal. Pat. R. 1281–92*, p.183.
[57] *Cal. Pat. R. 1266–72*, p.21.
[58] *Loc.cit.*
[59] *B.H.R.S.* xliii, 34.

[60] *V.C.H.* iii, 20.
[61] *B.H.R.S.* xxxix, 97.
[62] *Loc.cit.*
[63] *B.H.R.S.* viii, 119–31; xxxix, 96–101.
[64] *B.H.R.S.* xxi, 148.

an active corporate spirit like that at Bedford.

If they sought, as Bedford did, to gain privileges by charter, there is little surviving evidence of it. Had they done so, they would have found it difficult. Though English kings had no intention of letting English towns become as independent as continental ones, yet towns were a useful counterweight to the barons, and when a king was in need of money, as Richard I was in 1189, he was forthcoming. But Leighton and Luton soon passed out of the king's hands. In the early 12th cent. the king granted Luton to Robert, Earl of Gloucester; and when the next Earl died without issue in 1182, the king granted it to Baldwin de Bethune, through whose daughter it went to her husband, William Marshal, Earl of Pembroke, in 1214. Leighton the king granted to Fontevrault Abbey in 1164. Neither of these was a hopeful prospect for aspiring townsmen. A lay lord was apt to keep tight control; and an abbey was not likely to act on impulse.

Leighton, though at first the judges were in doubt whether it should not answer with the half-hundred of Stanbridge, appeared separately at the eyre (i.e., before the judges) in 1247.[65] (Incidentally its 12 representatives were fined for falsely presenting Englishry; the murdrum fine for dead Normans had never been abolished, for it brought in some money to the king; in this case John Ordwy had been accidentally killed by the overturn of a cart; and the men of Leighton saw no reason why they should have to pay a fine for a pure accident, just because Ordwy happened to have some Norman blood, so they declared him English.) They then went on to testify that "the prior [of Grovebury] and bailiffs of Leighton do not allow the bailiffs of the lord king to enter their liberty for any distraint or summons" – here Leighton seems to have been trying to follow Dunstable (see below).

The tax assessors of 1297[66] also treated Leighton separately as a town. There were in Leighton two glovers, a dyer and a spicer; out at Billington there was a bowyer; and in the town itself were 8 merchants for whom no details are given. No one had a mazer, or silver spoons, nor were their houses worthy of special notice; but 8 had household utensils of copper, brass, pewter or wood which qualified for tax. Three men were worth £2 and over; 15 £1 and over; and 31 under £1. The wealthiest was Ralf of Olney (£3 10s. od.). Leighton seems to have been a small but flourishing trading centre.

Incidentally, Thomas of Leighton, who in 1293-4 made ironwork for Queen Eleanor's tomb in Westminster Abbey[67], does not appear in the 1297 return – perhaps he was dead. He was almost certainly of Leighton Buzzard, and

[65] B.H.R.S. xxi, 185–6, 202–3.
[66] B.H.R.S. xxxix, 83.
[67] R. Richmond, *Leighton Buzzard*, p.91: £13 "to master Thomas de Leghton, smith, for ironwork about the tomb of the queen at Westminster, and for the carriage of the same from Leghton to London and the expenses of the said Thomas and his men dwelling in London to place the said ironwork about the tomb aforesaid." His contemporary, Thomas of Houghton, king's carpenter, was almost certainly a Bedfordshire man, in view of the Bedfordshire provenance of his fellow-workers; *Ant.Jnal.* xxx, 28–33.

the fine ironwork on the church door there, as elsewhere in Bedfordshire (see ch. 9), is attributed to him.

Luton is more difficult to assess. Like Bedford, it fell in King John's reign into the hands of his mercenary, de Breauté, who built a castle there in 1221 between the church and the river[68] (see ch. 7); but it did not suffer from fighting as much as Bedford did. Nor – in case of siege – would it be likely to do so, for the actual township was small; unlike Bedford, much of its value lay in the flourishing agriculture in the hamlets in its wide area. However its market was important, and its fair was disputed between the lord of Luton (Baldwin de Bethune) and the powerful abbey of St. Albans which held the advowson. The abbey succeeded in establishing its claim to the profits of the fair, except for the sale of gold, of horses, and of tanned hides, "and of men who of old were sold."[69] In 1221 its trade was sufficient for the archdeacon to think of it as a borough, for when arbitrating in Dunstable (see below) about tithes arising from trade, he laid down that in case of doubt the "custom of Luton, Berkhamsted or other neighbouring borough" should be followed.[70] From Luton, by the way, Henry III took his head carpenter, Peter of Luton,[71] and his queen took Prince Edward's nurse, Alice of Luton, who accompanied her when she went to Provence.[72]

Luton was represented before the judges in 1247 by its bailiff and 12 representatives.[73] The tax assessors of 1297 also treated it as a town; here, however, there is a complication, for the township was not listed separately from the hamlets, and the whole vast mainly agricultural neighbourhood appeared in one return. However, 2 tanners, 2 turners, a ploughmaker, 2 butchers, a tailor, a dyer and a cooper were listed; and 7 merchants whose trade was not specified. No house qualified for special notice, nor had any man silver or mazer, but two had wooden vessels of quality sufficient to carry tax. Of the merchants, the most well-to-do was Roger Heved (£3 4s. 8d.).[74]

TOWN-DEVELOPMENT AND TOWN-PLANNING

In the 12th cent. both king and lords made various attempts at town-development. They parcelled out areas into little building plots, charged a small standard rent of 1s. or so for each, and if the venture prospered (which did not necessarily follow) they made a better profit than with purely agricultural land. Sometimes it was done by expanding an existing manor; sometimes by deducting an area and making a completely new start. Biggleswade and perhaps Toddington are examples of the first; Dunstable of the second. Biggleswade was only moderately successful; Toddington still less; Dunstable much more.

Biggleswade in 1086 was only small (34 adult men, even with Stratton and Holme) and there was no market. Henry I gave the manor to the Bishop of

[68] Dyer-Stygall-Dony, 63.
[69] V.C.H. ii, 349–50; Dyer-Stygall-Dony, 59–60.
[70] B.H.R.S. x, 143.
[71] Cal. Cl. R. 1231–4, p.56.
[72] Cal. Pat. R. 1247–58, p.376; 1258–66, p.220.
[73] B.H.R.S. xxi, 202.
[74] B.H.R.S. xxxix, 74–83.

Lincoln in 1132 and the bishop endowed a prebend with part of the property, including the church (see ch. 4), perhaps after 1163. At least some bishops seem to have visited Biggleswade annually.[75] Its position on the Great North road seemed to indicate that it was suitable for development, and it may be that the laying-out of small plots at an annual rent of 1s., of whose existence we have later evidence,[76] came at the end of the 12th cent., or shortly before the acquisition of a market and fair (see above). The word "burgage" is used of a transfer of property in 1247.[77] In 1294 the men of Biggleswade claimed the right to leave their burgages by will.[78] But development during the 13th cent. seems to have been only small. When the judges came round in 1247 they did not look on Biggleswade as a town; it was represented before them with the rest of the hundred.[79] Nor did the tax assessors of 1297 treat it separately from the rural manors or in a different manner; no merchandise was listed, nor household goods.[80] Dunstable on the Watling Street had had the start of Biggleswade, and there seems not to have been room for both.

Of an attempt at town-planning in Toddington, almost nothing is known. The initiative may have been taken by Paulinus Pever (ch. 7) in the 13th cent. The earliest surviving court-rolls (1423) refer to holdings inside and outside the borough.[81] But far more than Biggleswade Toddington was overshadowed by Dunstable.

Dunstable become the other important medieval urban centre. It was a new[82] settlement on an area of only about 450 a. deducted by Henry I from his manor of Houghton Regis. He chose the site well, for the south of the parish, where the old Roman Watling Street crosses the still older Icknield Way, was overgrown, and a convenient hide-out for bad characters.[83] The story of robber Dun, who infested these parts, later got embroidered out of all recognition,[84] but he is first briefly noted in the 13th cent. tractatus written at the priory,[85] and he may have some foundation in fact.

The burgage plots at Dunstable must have been very readily taken up, for sometime before 1119 Geoffrey of Gorham, who had been delayed in coming to take charge of a school at St. Albans, found enough scope at Dunstable to teach there instead, and also enough support to produce a miracle play of St. Katherine.[86] (This was that Geoffrey who afterwards, as Abbot of St. Albans, was the friend of

---

[75] Bishop Sutton was frequently there in the 1290's: L.R.S. lii, lx.

[76] A Lincoln compotus of 1509/10 mentions 123 burgages paying 1s. p.a. rent: Linc. R.O., B.P. ministers' accounts 8, mm. 5, 5vo; and also refers to profits of courts, both borough and foreign (i.e., inside and outside the borough). The surviving court rolls from 1651 are similarly headed: C.R.O., X 338.

[77] V.C.H. ii, 212; B.H.R.S. vi, 135; xxi, 99.

[78] L.R.S. lii, 184.

[79] B.H.R.S. xxi, 200.

[80] B.H.R.S. xxxix, 49.

[81] C.R.O., X 21/395.

[82] There had been a Roman posting-station at Durocobrivae; and later a Saxon settlement which did not last; Henry I's foundation was thus a new beginning, though on an old site.

[83] V.C.H. iii, 350.

[84] C. Lamborn, Dunstaplelogia.

[85] B.H.R.S. xix.

[86] V.C.H. iii, 350.

St. Christina – see ch. 4; and a fire which destroyed St. Albans' copes borrowed for the play was the occasion of his entering the abbey as a monk.) The school continued after this, and a century later its then master, Richard of Stanford, became a canon at the priory.[87] This was just after there had been a fight between the scholars and the townsmen, in which one of the latter was killed. There was not much agricultural land in Dunstable; those who farmed seem to have done so in the surrounding villages; but the town was well placed for carrying on trade with London and even overseas.

Royal visits to Dunstable, when reigning monarchs stayed at the royal residence of Kingsbury[88] (built by Henry I on 9 acres reserved by him, and looked after in his absence by a housekeeper who was paid a penny a day) must have brought visitors of note. Once at Christmas he received there the envoys of the Count of Anjou.[89] Stephen kept Christmas there in 1137.[90] Even after King John gave it to the priory in 1204, the royal family still came to Dunstable, now staying at the priory. Henry III came several times; in 1247 the priory presented his children, Prince Edward and Princess Margaret, with gold buckles. Edward I stayed there in 1275; and after the death of his beloved queen Eleanor in 1290 the sad funeral procession spent the night at the priory, and a cross was built in the marketplace where the coffin had rested. Perhaps both because knights got to know Dunstable well on these occasions, and because of its easy access, it became a favourite place for tournaments, gatherings at which men might not only joust but plot (see ch. 7). Dunstable therefore, visited by royalty, well placed for distant trade, was developed perhaps to some extent by thrusting men.

It also had a small Jewry. About 1185 the priory had been involved in transactions with the famous Jew, Aaron of Lincoln;[91] and some twenty years later a corrody-holder at the priory, in difficulties, had pledged his corrody to several Jews, Flemengus, Bendinus, Jacob and Leo.[92] Flemengus and his son Leo about 1210, for a payment of two silver spoons annually, had permission to come and go or stay.[93]

But Dunstable had to deal, not with the king, but with the prior. About 1132, when King Henry I founded Dunstable Priory (see ch. 4), he endowed it with his "manor and borough" of Dunstable. The priory became important, and kings were willing to concede rights (at a price) to this royal foundation. From that needy king, Richard I, it gained wide rights.[94] When the king's judges came to try cases at Bedford, the prior expected them to make a special visit to Dunstable.[95] As the chronicle says in 1219: "the same year we proved our right to hold a court at Dunstable for all pleas of the king . . . the justices of the

---

[87] *Ann. Mon.* iii, 85–6.
[88] R. A. Brown, H. M. Colvin, A. J. Taylor, *The history of the king's works*, ii, 924–5.
[89] *Loc.cit.*
[90] *V.C.H.* iii, 352.
[91] *B.H.R.S.* x, 84.
[92] *Op.cit.*, 124, 103.
[93] *Op.cit.*, 101.
[94] *Op.cit.*, 242.
[95] *V.C.H.* iii, 356; *Ann. Mon.* iii, 54–5.

lord king sat there, and the form of the oath sworn was as follows: 'You hear this, Lord prior justice of St. Peter de Dunstable.' " The Dunstable session of 1224 was the occasion of the *cause célèbre* which led to the last siege of Bedford castle (see ch. 7). The judges disliked the extra visit, and tried in 1259, 1276 and 1286 to avoid it.

The priory was notable in other ways. From 1202–42 it had as prior a remarkable man of affairs, Richard de Morin, and it was probably he who caused the chronicle to be kept – the only one in Bedfordshire. He was visitor for religious houses in the diocese of Lincoln, and later for Augustinian canons even in the province of York. He went on overseas missions for the king, drew up reports for the pope, attended the Lateran Council of 1215, and was appointed to preach the next Crusade in Bedfordshire and adjoining counties. With all this he was a scholar who had studied for a year at the university of Paris.[96] Thus there were yoked in uneasy association a priory concerned with high affairs in church and state, and a new town with active enterprising men determined to get ahead. Thirteenth cent. Dunstable was not unlike 20th cent. Luton.

Up to a point, priory and townsmen were in harmony in upholding the status and good order of Dunstable. Some customs drawn up in 1221[97] are early rules for town management: shopkeepers must not have pigsties outside their doors, and butchers must not cast blood and filth into the street, though a burgess might have a dunghill so long as it did not obstruct the king's highway; market booths must be cleared away on the day of the market; and victuals must not be sold before 1 o'clock.

It was money matters that caused trouble. Tithe, or giving a tenth of produce to the church, had arisen in an agricultural society. As later centuries were to show elsewhere, it was difficult to apply tithe to trade. However, the archdeacon of Bedford was able to get a settlement in 1221 which "was read out in the church in the presence of all the people of Dunstable, and was approved by all, and was confirmed by judges delegated by the pope, that is to say, that all will give a tithe of their trade."[98]

A later dispute was more acute. It began in 1227 with various claims by the burgesses, including one that fines in the prior's court should be limited to 4d. for each offence. The prior got his charter confirmed by Henry III for the large sum of £100, and since this did after all maintain Dunstable's special position, the burgesses paid an aid of 100 marks towards it; but when distraint was made on a defaulter, it was only after an affray in the streets that the prior's servants were able to get the cart of wheat through the priory gate. In annoyance at this, the people withheld their offerings. Offenders who were excommunicated persisted in coming to church, so that the canons retreated to celebrate mass in the infirmary

[96] *V.C.H.* i, 371–2.
[97] *V.C.H.* iii, 360; *B.H.R.S.* x, 236–7.
[98] *Ann. Mon.* iii, 65.

chapel. Again it took the archdeacon to smooth things over. The burgesses even said that they would rather go to hell than give way, and they negotiated with William de Cantilupe of Eaton Bray "that he would grant them 40 acres in a field near ... where, transferring their houses, they could live quit of toll and tallage."[99] Once more in 1230 the archdeacon negotiated a settlement by which, for a down payment of £60, the prior renounced his right to tallage (or tax) the town, and agreed to limit fines to 4d.[100] The archdeacon must have found Dunstable the most troublesome place in his archdeaconry; and perhaps the canons sometimes envied the monks of Warden and Woburn their peaceful seclusion.

How was it that the burgesses were so assured and pugnacious in contending, though with meagre success, with an important monastery enjoying royal favour? Whether or not this was so early in the 13th cent, certainly later their wealth in part depended on the growing trade by which England exported wool to the continent to be made up into cloth. When in 1270–8 there was an embargo on the export of wool to Flanders, and there survive lists of merchants who had conditional export licences[101], though there are on these lists no other Bedfordshire names, there are several Dunstable merchants. The chief is John Durant; others are Robert Brian, Richard le Jevene, Richard le Keu, Stephen Aungevill, William le Pessoner, John de Wootton, Henry Chadde. Some merchants also dealt in corn from the fertile area around.[102]

John Durant was dead by 1297, but the tax assessors then rated his goods at £20 16s. 8d., three times as high as any other Bedfordshire merchant. In Dunstable in 1297 there were 15 merchants worth £2 and over; 17 worth £1 and over; and 16 under £1. They were not listed as having any of the conveniences of civilised living found at Bedford, and to a lesser extent at Leighton; but there were more well-to-do men in Dunstable than in Bedford.[103] By this time things seem more settled in Dunstable. Perhaps the Dominican friars who came in 1259 (see ch. 9) had a good influence.

[99] *Ann. Mon.* iii, 122. See also *B.H.R.S.* iii, 121–6.
[100] *Loc.cit.*; *V.C.H.* iii, 358–9.
[101] *Cal. Pat. R. 1266–72*, pp.554, 595, 689, 699, 704, 713.
[102] *B.H.R.S.* xxxix, pp. xxi–xxii.
[103] *Op.cit.*, 90–6.

6 – ADMINISTRATION, JUSTICE, AND LIFE IN GENERAL, 1066–1300

THE SHERIFF

The sheriff[1] after the conquest was the high-handed Ralf Tallebosc. At that time the sheriff needed to be a leading Norman baron in order to cope with his fellows and with the recalcitrant English. Often a son followed his father, and in Bedfordshire Ralf seems to have been followed by his son-in-law, Hugh de Beauchamp.[2] But by 1100 the king began to find that this practice was giving some barons too much power, and that he could better control the sheriff if he appointed new men, trained in the royal household in his service. Such were Hugh of Buckland and Maenfinin Brito.[3] After this period came the anarchy of Stephen's reign, and then once more a strong king determined to appoint his own men as soon as he had sufficient to do so. In 1170 Henry II held an inquest of sheriffs, investigating all complaints; most sheriffs were dismissed (the Bedfordshire sheriff was Hugh de Lega), and men in the king's service appointed. Even after this a local baron occasionally held the office, as Simon de Beauchamp did in 1194 and William d'Albini in 1198. By this time, incidentally, it had become customary for one sheriff to hold both Bedfordshire and Buckinghamshire, and this practice continued till 1574.

The office of sheriff was at its peak under the early Norman kings, when the sheriff was for almost all matters the king's representative in the shire; and through the 12th cent. it continued to be important.

In case of need, it was the sheriff who called out the men of the shire to fight, in what used to be known as the fyrd but was now called the posse. Though at first the king mainly relied on barons and on the knights they sent, he might need the sheriff in time of emergency for home defence. This was more apt to happen on the Welsh or Scottish border than in Bedfordshire (cf. the battle of the Standard, ch. 3). The sheriff might also have to produce military supplies for local sieges, as sheriffs of nearby counties were called on to do for the last siege of Bedford castle (see ch. 7).

The sheriff's financial responsibilities included the king's lands, where he had to see that the royal manors were properly stocked, collect the market tolls and so on. Thus at first he had to account for Leighton, Luton, Houghton Regis, Weston[ing], and for the borough of Bedford. During the 12th cent. one by one

---

[1] For the background to this chapter, see D. M. Stenton, op.cit., 93–9; A. L. Poole, *Domesday Book to Magna Carta*, 385–424; W. A. Morris, *The medieval English sheriff*.
[2] *B.H.R.S.* i, 2.
[3] Morris, 77, 82.

the king granted away these manors,[4] and from 1190 the burgesses of Bedford (see ch. 5) paid a composition to the exchequer. But the sheriff still accounted for any lands escheated (forfeited for some offence or in default of heirs), or in wardship because the heir was a minor. He had also to account for judicial fines, for justice was an important source of revenue. At first this meant only his own court and the hundred courts; but during the 12th cent., when the king began to send round judges, the sheriff was responsible also for fines imposed by them. When the king had not required knights from the barons, or when money payments began to be made instead of knight service, the sheriff collected the scutage money due.

Thus in 1198 the sheriff, William d'Albini, accounted as follows.[5] He first listed payments he had made at the king's direction. From the Bedfordshire revenues the king allowed the Templars a mark a year to maintain their work in the Holy Land, although a few years since Jerusalem had fallen to the Saracens. He had also directed the sheriff to pay to John Piedefer 1d. a day; John Piedefer may have been a pensioner; or this may have been his wage for some special service such as musician or wolf-taker. Then the sheriff noted that the royal lands of Leighton, Luton and Houghton had been granted out, and so he was not to account for them, nor for the borough of Bedford. Expenses such as repair of the gaol (from 1166 county gaols had to be built where they did not already exist) normally follow, but there were none in 1198.

After these deductions, the sheriff accounted for the money he was paying in. Among fines imposed by the judges when they came round was one on Clifton hundred for concealment; it was 9s., but only 2s. had so far been paid. For the two counties, Bedfordshire and Buckinghamshire, the fines in all amounted to between £30 and £40, with a still larger sum for forest cases which was due only from Buckinghamshire, for Bedfordshire was disforested (see ch. 3). There was scutage from the barons; thus Robert d'Albini (the sheriff's brother) owed £9 9s. od., but it was still outstanding. In most counties there would have followed the proceeds of royal lands, but this no longer applied for Bedfordshire.

For justice the sheriff was responsible for the holding of shire and hundred courts. The hundred court was normally held by a subordinate, called sergeant or bailiff. It met once a month, and dealt with minor cases like village brawls, obstructing the highway, breaking the assize of bread and ale (which provided that these staple foods should be of sufficient quality and sold at the proper rates, varying with the price of corn). From each township came a reeve and four men to report such matters; and also more serious ones which would go on to the county court.

Since there were no police, it was necessary to have some other means of bringing offenders to justice. Everyone was supposed to seize offenders; when anyone raised the hue and cry (called out for help), all within earshot were sup-

[4] V.C.H. ii, 350; iii, 390, 403, 451.   [5] B.H.R.S. vii, 133.

posed to come to his aid and secure the felon or felons, or at least pursue him or them to the parish boundary, when the responsibility would devolve on the next township. But this was not always effective; in 1247 when evildoers unknown burgled a house in Biggleswade "the hue and cry was raised and Biggleswade did not pursue".[6] Even before the Conquest there had been some attempt to bolster up this sytem with another: men had begun to group themselves in tithings of ten men with one man at the head of each tithing. If a member of the tithing committed an offence, the others must bring him to justice; if they did not or could not, they themselves would be held responsible. This system now became general, and was known as frankpledge (i.e., the members of a tithing were pledges for each other). Thus when Richard le Monner in 1267 was suspected of stealing from and killing Henry Ailwit at Renhold, and fled, it was stated that "he was in the tithing of Hugh le Bedel", and his tithing was fined for not producing him.[7] More rarely it could happen that a tithing secured the release of an innocent man from prison, as in 1247 when John of Little Barford was framed by a gang of toughs.[8] All men over twelve had to be in a tithing. Twice a year the sheriff made a round of the hundred courts to see that they were; this was called view of frankpledge; and this periodic tour by the sheriff was known as the sheriff's tourn. If a man managed to evade being in a tithing (and there must have been some men for whom no one was anxious to be responsible), the village was fined when it was discovered, as happened when a Henlow murderer in 1202 escaped after killing William son of Ailbricht.[9]

In the shire court or county court, the sheriff always presided. This also met monthly. At its meetings would be announced any messages or orders from the king. Here were tried more important cases, breaches of the peace, which were an offence against the king. It is probable that from quite early times representatives of the hundreds reported serious offences here, but from 1166 it was laid down that twelve men from each hundred should do so. These twelve are the origin of the jury of presentment, later called grand jury, which eventually became a pure formality and was abolished in the present century.

ITINERANT JUDGES

But serious crime was not the sphere of the sheriff alone. Early in the 12th cent. the king had begun to send round judges. In 1194 the king directed the election in each county of coroners (chosen in the county court), who would hold inquests on deaths in case there was need for the matter to be brought before the judge, keep the pleas of the crown, and deal with treasure trove. Bedford and Dunstable had their own coroners. The earliest known by name is a Dunstable one, Ellis of Woburn, 1228; the earliest county coroner known is Hugh of Salford

[6] B.H.R.S. xxi, 171.
[7] B.H.R.S. xli, 8.

[8] B.H.R.S. xxi, 176-7.
[9] B.H.R.S. i, 229.

G

who died in 1230.[10]

For this early period few court records are available. At first they were probably not even written down. It is not till the late 13th cent. that some brief records begin to survive for the manor courts (ch. 8), which were the most immediate in the life of the ordinary man. It may be that in the 12th cent. records for the hundred and shire courts began to be written down, but there was a new sheriff every year and no continuity in keeping the series. So rare are sheriff's judicial records that only one roll for Bedfordshire has survived, and that is for the 14th cent. (ch. 11). It was naturally with the central government that the first effective record-keeping in these matters began. From 1202 records of actual cases before the king's judges on circuit (the records of central courts are a little earlier) begin to survive, supplemented from 1265 by the coroner's records, and give a picture of justice in Bedfordshire in the 13th cent.

The chief civil cases in the courts related to land – the great necessity. In the anarchy of Stephen's reign, and also later when times were at all uncertain, it was easy for the well-armed and strong to evict the weak, whose only chance then was to sue at law. Henry II evolved a procedure to deal with this question: had there been disseisin (forcible eviction)? At this stage it made no difference if the man who had used force happened to be the rightful owner. The question was put to a jury of twelve men, who answered yes or no. If they said yes, eviction had taken place, the man in possession had to give up the land, or the sheriff would forcibly evict him. Only after the disseisin had been rectified could the question of right to the land be discussed.

A case from 1202 is as follows.[11] The question put to the jury was: did Ralf de Tivill unjustly and without a judgement disseise Roger de Argentoin and his wife Matilda of their free tenement in Meppershall? The jury said that he thus disseised him. Judgement: let Roger and Matilda have their seisin (possession) and Ralf be in mercy (fined). Or again: did Nicholas de Parco unjustly and without a judgement disseise Gerald son of John of his free tenement in Cranfield?[12] The jury said that he thus disseised him. Judgement: let Gerald have seisin and Nicholas be in mercy. Sometimes however a claim of disseisin could be wrongly made. Roger claimed that his father was seised (i.e., possessed) of a virgate in Chawston on the day that he took the road of his pilgrimage to Jerusalem on which he died, and this land was now in the possession of Walter son of Amfrid.[13] But the jury said the father never had the land. Let Walter hold and Roger be in mercy for a false claim; but Roger was pardoned, probably because he was too poor to pay a fine. All these cases come from the troubled reign of King John.

The question of right could now be raised. Formerly it was dealt with in a baron's court; that is, men on Simon de Beauchamp's estate would bring their

---

[10] *B.H.R.S.* xli, pp. xxxviii, xliii.
[11] *B.H.R.S.* i, 207.
[12] *B.H.R.S.* i, 199.
[13] *B.H.R.S.* i, 185.

case before his court. There it would be settled by duel – the claimants would fight it out. But people were beginning to look to the king's judges for decisions. At first here too the old method of the duel was used. The claimant need not necessarily fight himself, but could put in someone to fight for him. Thus in 1202 Gilbert claimed against Simon 3 virgates in Whipsnade, and this he offered to prove by a certain freeman of his, Ralf forester.[14] But in this instance there were certain complications, which caused the case to be referred to Westminster. Or in 1247 fishery in the Ouse at Carlton was disputed between Ralf Morin and Henry de Lega.[15] Ralf Morin offered to defend his right by the body of his freeman, Adam Wagestef, who was present and offered defence by his body as the court should consider. (It seems possible that Henry de Lega did not like the look of Adam Wagestef.) And because plaintiff brings no proof but his bare word, it is considered that defendant may hold in peace.

But there was now another method of settling disputes before the king's judges. A litigant could use the king's procedure. Thus in 1202 the Ralf de Tivill referred to above was concerned in another case, this time with his tenant Gilbert who held of him in Ickwell.[16] Ralf said the rent was 4s. annually, and Gilbert said it was a pound of pepper. So Gilbert "put himself on the grand assise of our lord the king," that is, he asked for a jury. This case shows how the jury was formed. There was no elaborate machinery, such as there is to-day, for compiling lists of those liable for jury service. Four knights (two from each side) chose twelve suitable men. They were: Hugh de Budna, William Wischard, John de Carun, Stephen de Holwell, William Brito, William de Faldo, Robert de Buelles, William de Bretteville, Hugh de Richespaud, Simon Mallore, Adam de Port and Richard Gobion. From the names it is clear that several were from villages roundabout. But Gilbert lost the case. The jurors, when sworn, said that Gilbert owed Ralf for that land 4s.

In cases brought before the judges at Bedford in 1240[17] many jurors' names are given. It seems that there were several men scattered over the county who were of good reputation in public affairs and were constantly chosen for jury service. Such, among others, were Peter Loring of Chalgrave, Simon Pertesoil of Riseley, Ralf Pirot of Harlington, and Jordan Lenveise of Gt. Barford.

The chief criminal cases were violence and theft. Sometimes the incident is fully described. On a June evening in 1272, John of Chellington was going to Simon Pattishall's house at Cainhoe.[18] He was perhaps unwise to be out after sunset. Robert Atewater of Gravenhurst jumped out from the hedge, struck him with a Danish axe, took his hood of perse (bluish-grey), his red belt with latten bars (metal alloy), his purse of white sheepskin with $3\frac{1}{2}$d. in it, his gloves, his

---

[14] B.H.R.S. i, 187.
[15] B.H.R.S. xxi, 122.
[16] B.H.R.S. i, 192–3.

[17] B.H.R.S. ix.
[18] B.H.R.S. xli, 57.

cowskin shoes, and his knife and trencher-knife. At Putnoe at twilight in 1275 a felon hiding among blackthorns stole from a man and boy; but the hue and cry was raised so quickly that, though he defended himself with bow and arrows, he was slain in flight.[19] Violence could arise out of a peaceful occasion, as when the whole countryside met at Limbury for sports in 1247, and after a scuffle, William shot Roger le Keu with an arrow and fled (Biscot, Bramblehanger and Limbury were all fined because they did not seize him).[20] Similarly, Gilbert carter in 1247 wounded John le Messager in the stomach with an arrow so that he died at once – the whole vill of Stevington was present, and did not seize Gilbert.[21] In 1247 Warin smote William Hogge with a knife in the stomach in the fields between Henlow and Arlesey – he died on the tenth day;[22] and that same year Stephen of Sutton smote Nigel Wigein at Cople with his coulter (iron blade of plough share);[23] and Ralf of Lavendon killed William Pekke at Harrold with an iron fork.[24] Violence could on occasion turn into a general melee, as in a dispute over Souldrop advowson, when one claimant with his men took possession of the church, and the other attacked the church with crossbows and brought fire to burn the door, while those inside shot arrows – one man was killed;[25] this was in 1270. When the victim was not killed but merely wounded, he was apt to make extravagant claims about the wounds he had received: Roger Marchys at Houghton (unspecified) in 1247 said that Robert Caterin gave him two wounds on the head with a pickaxe, one six thumbs long and a thumb deep.[26]

The difficulty was to apprehend the criminals. A man who had been overtaken by his hasty temper, or who had local sympathy, would almost certainly be able to take sanctuary. In 1247[27] sanctuary had been taken in the churches of Bedford, Dunstable, Leighton, Luton, Biggleswade and 11 villages, some of them more than once. There a felon could remain 40 days; then or earlier, in the presence of the coroner, he abjured the realm, and had to go, in sackcloth and carrying a wooden cross, to the port indicated by the coroner, where he was to take ship overseas. The coroner saw him off on this journey to the coast; it is anybody's guess what happened after that.

If a known offender had escaped, the chance of getting him was small. All that could be done was to outlaw him. Still less was there a chance of securing those ubiquitous men "evildoers known", who beset travellers at night and broke into houses. Hanging, when it took place after sentence by the judges, was probably at Gallows Corner on the Biddenham road where all might see (the gallows there was taken down in 1802; for gallows elsewhere, see ch. 11).

When an offender was brought to justice, old methods of proof still some-

[19] *B.H.R.S.* xli, 78.
[20] *B.H.R.S.* xxi, 148.
[21] *B.H.R.S.* xxi, 163.
[22] *B.H.R.S.* xxi, 168.
[23] *B.H.R.S.* xxi, 179.
[24] *B.H.R.S.* xxi, 162.
[25] *B.H.R.S.* xli, 52.
[26] *B.H.R.S.* xxi, 189.
[27] *B.H.R.S.* xxi.

times applied. When Robert Fale of Shelton was accused of burglary in 1202, it was said: "Let him purge himself by water."[28] He would be trussed and lowered into a pool of hallowed water; if he sank he was innocent; if he floated he was guilty. The result in Robert's case is not given. Another old method was to clear oneself by oath-helpers. Thus in 1202 a purchaser of ale at Bedford said that Clarice had sold him 3 gallons for a penny by false measure, and Clarice, who declared her innocence on oath, brought eleven oath-helpers to maintain that her oath was to be relied on.[29] But in a criminal case also it was possible to have a jury. Bonefand, a Bedford Jew, accused in 1202 of wounding and killing Richard, offered $\frac{1}{2}$ mark to have a jury, and the jury declared him innocent.[30] In 1247 William of Stanbridge, accused of horse-stealing, "put himself on the country", and the jury said they did not suspect him of any ill-doing; "he is therefore quit".[31] (Sometimes sheep and pigs were stolen as well as horses, but thefts of livestock are not numerous, probably because they were difficult to conceal.)[32]

LIFE IN GENERAL

The records of judge and coroner also give many sidelights on 13th cent. life in Bedfordshire, and from these some sort of picture can be reconstructed.[33] Clothes, for instance, are mentioned in other cases besides that of John of Chellington given above. The king's bailiff, Robert Pippard, attacked in 1273 near St. Neots, was wearing a robe worth 2s. 6d.[34] Surcoats are of burnet or russet. A haqueton, or protective jerkin, was not amiss if a man had to go out at night; and John Dreu of Beeston, going to look for a delayed corn cart, took also a helmet and lance;[35] this was in 1271.

Houses of stud and plaster were often flimsy; it was as easy to break through the wall as to force the door. Inside there were few possessions; when thieves broke the wall of Henry Ailwit's house at Renhold in 1267 they "took away all the goods of the house".[36] The goods of Adam of Elstow in 1272 were: a chest, a basket, some wooden utensils, 2 ewers, a basin, a gallon pot and a small pot, and 2 posnets (small metal pots for boiling).[37] The only table mentioned is a trestle table. The staple foods were ale and bread. The oven seems to have been outside in the courtyard; and Emma Sagar of Sutton in 1276 heated hers with straw.[38] If the supply of ale ran out, it was not advisable to go out at night to get more; when Henry Colburn of Gt. Barford in 1266 went and did not return, his mother sought next day at dawn and found his body with eleven wounds in it.[39] Where possible, bread and ale were supplemented by bacon; if the family possessed pigs, they hung the hams from the beams. Utensils were few; a sma"

[28] B.H.R.S. i, 223.
[29] B.H.R.S. i, 245.
[30] B.H.R.S. i, 231.
[31] B.H.R.S. xxi, 184.
[32] B.H.R.S. xxi, 170, 175.
[33] B.H.R.S. i, iii, ix, xxi give the eyres for 1202, 1227, 1240, 1247; and B.H.R.S. xli the coroners' rolls from

1265.
[34] B.H.R.S. xli, 76.
[35] B.H.R.S. xli, 48.
[36] B.H.R.S. xli, 8.
[37] B.H.R.S. xli, 39.
[38] B.H.R.S. xli, 93.
[39] B.H.R.S. xli, 3.

trencher-knife was carried in the belt; this could be dangerous with boys at play, for when John and Henry at Duloe in 1266 fell into a pit, John's knife, protruding from its broken sheath, fatally wounded his playmate.[40]

Windows were apertures fastened with shutters, and if they were broken into it was with an axe. Livestock (if any) were under the same roof, probably partitioned off; Ailbricht of Willington in 1202 accused men of coming to his house by night, breaking open the door and taking his fowls.[41] Water was heated in a cauldron on a trivet on the open hearth, and a child could knock it over, as 1-year old Alice Bercher did at Cople in 1273.[42] Tools were also kept in the house; when in 1247 John Blechelie desired to beat his wife and she fled, he threw the stick at her, and it knocked down a mattock which fell on their 6-month old son in his cradle.[43] Beds were normally straw pallets rolled up in the daytime; when Nicholas le Swon of Bedford in 1300 told his wife to make his bed, she unrolled the pallet.[44] By the end of the century, however, at least some houses had a chamber – a separate room for sleeping – or a loft; John Clarice of Houghton Regis in 1276 had a chamber; and in 1317 there seems to have been a loft in Maud Bolle's house at Dean, for a thief got a ladder to the roof to steal a ham, and fell from the ladder with it, breaking his neck.[45]

Outside the house, wells were a hazard. For convenience they were nearly always close to houses, and as they were in constant use they were often left uncovered. Old people could easily fall into them, as did feeble old Mariot, wife of the Pertenhall reeve, in 1270 when she went to get some water.[46] It was a gruesome thought of Richard of Staploe in 1269 to put the murdered body of his wife into the village well, where the shepherd found it next morning.[47] Wells were an especial danger to children; little 2-year old Alice Wigein in 1267 wandered on to Goldington green and fell down the well there;[48] and 2-year old William Mustard of Renhold in 1268, "looking for other boys" to play with while the household was at church, fell down the well.[49] Even if help came at once it was almost impossible to get anyone out quickly.

Other dangers beset children. A deep ditch near the house was not necessarily fenced off, and 2-year old Cicely of Wilstead in 1270, toddling out of the house with a piece of bread in her hand, was followed by a small pig, which in trying to take it from her pushed her into the ditch, where she was drowned.[50] When a cart stuck in a ditch at Turvey in 1275, and the carter pushed from behind, 6-year old Hugh in front was run over.[51]

Horses and carts often involved men in accidents. When the barley cart

[40] B.H.R.S. xli, 3.
[41] B.H.R.S. i, 239.
[42] B.H.R.S. xli, 73.
[43] B.H.R.S. xxi, 159.
[44] B.H.R.S. xli, 105.
[45] B.H.R.S. xli, 116.
[46] B.H.R.S. xli, 33.
[47] B.H.R.S. xli, 11.
[48] B.H.R.S. xli, 6.
[49] B.H.R.S. xli, 9.
[50] B.H.R.S. xli, 35.
[51] B.H.R.S. xli, 90.

stuck in 1275 in Robert's yard at Bolnhurst, and Richard tried to push it, the cart fell on him and crushed him.[52] Henry Costentin's feet slipped in 1267 at Eaton Socon and he was impaled on the cart's pole.[53] At Bromham a horse in 1272 pursued a filly and upset the cart it was drawing, killing William Passelew's carter.[54] William le Wylur, struck with the palsy, in 1271 fell from his horse at Leighton Buzzard and lay speechless.[55] To carry a sack of flour on horseback was ill-advised; John Madur of Wyboston, fetching his flour from the mill in 1274, attempted it and fell and broke his neck.[56]

Bridges and boats were sources of disaster. Such bridges as there were, whether over brook or river, were usually of wood, and seem often to have been flimsy and without guard rails. Thus Joan, a poor child, in 1274 was drowned crossing "Fordebrugge" in Riseley; this was in May, and the bridge may have been defective.[57] In December 1270 Blunham bridge over the Ivel was slippery with frost, and Hugh the cobbler fell on to the ice below and was drowned.[58] In 1281 a severe frost caused Bromham (or, as it was then called, Biddenham) bridge to give way, and a woman was carried away on an ice floe.[59] The only other bridges over the Ouse known at this time, besides Bedford bridge, were those at Harrold and St. Neots. Boats were much in use and necessary repairs and replacements seem often to have been left too long. Five people at Little Barford in 1267 rashly tried to cross the Ouse with a load of flour from the mill in December when the river was high – only one got safely to land.[60] The crossing by Little Barford mill was something of an accident black-spot; Robert in 1271 kindly agreed to take four paupers across, but through the fierceness of the wind and current the boat sank, and though the passengers escaped Robert was drowned.[61] Drowning could also happen to a man while fishing, as to John Dreu at Sandy mill on the Ivel in 1271;[62] or while setting hooks for eels like Richard Newnham of Stevington in 1273;[63] or while bathing, as to 12-year old John Wyte of Wilden in April 1269 when he was supposed to be watching his father's lambs.[64]

Mills were dangerous. At Husborne Crawley in 1269, Thomas' arm was broken while greasing the mill-wheel;[65] and at Eyeworth windmill in 1276 (the knowledge of windmills is believed to have been brought home by crusaders) an impatient customer interfered with the boy in charge, went too near the mill-wheel and was caught by the cogs.[66]

Life was hard. In the 1250's there were some bad harvests, and the price of

[52] B.H.R.S. xli, 84.
[53] B.H.R.S. xli, 6.
[54] B.H.R.S. xli, 58.
[55] B.H.R.S. xli, 42.
[56] B.H.R.S. xli, 76.
[57] B.H.R.S. xli, 82.
[58] B.H.R.S. xli, 28.
[59] V.C.H. iii, 44. Biddenham (or Bromham) bridge existed by 1227–8 (B.H.R.S. vi, 74). Till 1813 it was over the river only, not the flood area (B. Mag. viii, 129).
[60] B.H.R.S. xli, 8.
[61] B.H.R.S. xli, 47.
[62] B.H.R.S. xli, 48.
[63] B.H.R.S. xli, 87.
[64] B.H.R.S. xli, 11.
[65] B.H.R.S. xli, 40.
[66] B.H.R.S. xli, 103.

corn rose high.[67] Old Sabinia in 1267 begged for bread in Colmworth, and at twilight – probably faint with hunger – fell into a stream and was drowned.[68] Emma of Hatch in 1264 begged in Beeston from door to door, and was overcome by cold as the January night drew on.[69] In Turvey Beatrice Bone collapsed in the road in 1273 "because she was weak and infirm", and was not found for two days.[70] Such a fate could happen also to a child or a man, as to Arnulf Argent of Ravensden in November 1275,[71] but probably a man in want more often took to bad ways. None the less there was a toughness and a resilience not always found in a more affluent age: suicide was almost unknown, – it was mortal sin.

[67] Ann. Mon. iii, 189, 207–8, 210–1.
[68] B.H.R.S. xli, 4.
[69] B.H.R.S. xli, 74.

[70] B.H.R.S. xli, 87.
[71] B.H.R.S. xli, 89.

The Manor at its Height

7 – BARONS AND KNIGHTS, 1200–1400

IN 1200 the barons and knights had recognisable links with the Bedfordshire of 1086.[1] The Beauchamps were still at Bedford castle; Simon de Beauchamp (founder of Newnham Priory) was nearing 60; he may have made improvements there, for the science of castle-building was continually advancing, and Richard I's Château Gaillard in Normandy was the finest of its day; but Simon's young manhood had been spent in the ordered reign of Henry II and he is not known as a soldier. Robert d'Albini was at Cainhoe; this was a more peaceful site, and it is not certain that there was ever a masonry castle here. At Odell there was John de Wahull; at Yielden, Walter de Trailly. At Eaton Socon, the representative of the lesser line of Beauchamp bore the well-known name of Hugh (founder of Bush-mead Priory). On some manors knights came of families which went back to the conquest, such as Burnard, Caron, Loring and Passelew.

KING VERSUS BARONS

Already Richard I's crusade and capture had meant a less firm hand at home than in the days of his father. In 1199 he was succeeded by his able but arbitrary and erratic brother John, who lost Normandy and quarrelled with the Pope. North-country barons objected to overseas service to regain the king's continental possessions; and in fact kings now made increasing use of paid soldiers or mercenaries, some recruited overseas, such as the able Fawkes de Breauté from Poitou, who had a successful campaign in Wales in 1211. The strong administration built up by recent kings irked the barons still more when the king in 1213 appointed as justiciar a foreigner, Peter des Roches, Bishop of Winchester; this man for a time held Toddington (which had escheated, or fallen into the king's hands, because its owner lived in Normandy).[2] When in 1214 John was finally defeated in France, and returned to demand a high rate of scutage from barons who had not sent their service, opposition spread to the south to adventurous hot-headed spirits among the younger barons, including Simon's son, William de Beauchamp, who succeeded 1206/7. The northern barons assembled at Stamford and on their way south in the spring of 1215 were received by William de Beauchamp at Bedford castle. In London they were joined by William de Cantilupe of Eaton

---

[1] The background for this chapter is taken from D. M. Stenton, *English Society in the early middle ages*, 46–59, 91–9; A. R. Myers, *England in the late middle ages*, 1–22; A. L. Poole, *From Domesday Book to Magna Carta*, 459–86; F. M. Powicke,

The thirteenth century; M. McKisack, *The fourteenth century*.
[2] *V.C.H.* iii, 439. He held it only a short time, and it was soon in the hands of Paulinus Pever, an able man in the king's service.

[Bray], who now constructed Eaton [Bray] castle[3] and by Henry de Braybrook, who later had Bedfordshire connections through his wife. In this emergency most older barons stood by the king. Charters of rights had previously been issued by kings. Though the movement against King John was to some extent partisan, Archbishop Stephen Langton's influence helped to produce, not a partisan, but a national document, Magna Carta, which was accepted by the king on 15 June.[4]

William de Beauchamp paid for his support by losing his home for nine years. The confrontation of king and barons continued. Troops under Fawkes de Breauté attacked Bedford, which surrendered on 2 December; and King John bestowed the castle on Fawkes and "caused the castle of Bedford to be strengthened"[5], using stone from St. Paul's church. Thus it was in 1216 and by a leading soldier of his day that Bedford castle was modernised. The old keep seems to have been kept, but the walls of the inner and outer baileys (or yards) were much improved.

Fawkes de Breauté[6] was a professional soldier, loyal to the king who had engaged him, and proficient at his job. During nearly all the years he spent in England, the monarchy, whose servant he was, was on the defensive. At the same time he looked out for his own advantage without scruple as to means; moreover in his home country he had not been used to as high a degree of order as normally prevailed in England. Fawkes was left by King John partly in command at London, while he went north to confront the opposition and died.

Fawkes remained loyal to John's 9-year old son. He was a member of the council to advise him, and was in command of the midland castles from Oxford to Cambridge. He relieved the siege of Lincoln castle in 1217, where he took William de Beauchamp prisoner. In this year he became sheriff of Bedfordshire and Buckinghamshire. During the baronial war he acquired Luton[7], and he built a castle here in 1221 (ch. 5). His widespread evictions may have been partly to make room for his castle, but they were more than was needed for this purpose, for they amounted to about 150 a. The names of about 20 victims are known from their later pleas, from Alice de Linleg' and her sons William and Robert who bore the chief loss, and the Master of Farley Hospital (for hospitals see ch. 9) who lost 10 a., down to three poor men, Ralf, Richard and Ralf, who lost common of pasture. The jury told also how Fawkes' dam damaged the property of the abbot of St. Albans. "By the raising of the dam the water of Luton flooded two houses and a meadow of the abbot, and a tenement which his tenants held from him, whereby he lost his yearly rent; and besides, when the water is held up the mill of the abbot in Luton cannot grind."

---

[3] V.C.H. iii, 370; Ann. Mon. iii, 66.
[4] Poole, op.cit.
[5] Cal.Pat.R., 1216–25, p.29.
[6] The chroniclers do not see Fawkes de Breauté objectively; see Poole, op.cit., 299, 471, 480; Powicke, op.cit., 3–4, 9, 11, 22, 25–7.
[7] Ann. Mon. iii, 66. For Fawkes at Luton, see W. Austin, Luton, i, 96–105; B.H.R.S. ix, 51–9.

By Fawkes' help and that of others who stood by the monarchy, gradually the position of the boy king was established; and it was other councillors who saw that Magna Carta was confirmed in 1217 and 1225. Now Fawkes' position began to be anachronistic. As a faithful supporter, he could not be discarded; but he could not adapt himself to times of peace. He brought about his own undoing by acts of violence over a wide area. He killed a monk of Warden Abbey and carried off others to Bedford castle; and he oppressed the monks of St. Albans; though in both cases he afterwards submitted to be disciplined by them – in the latter case to soothe his wife, who was alarmed by a dream.[8] When the judges came to Dunstable in 1224 he was found guilty of over 30 charges and heavily fined. As if the baronial war were still in progress, he had one of the judges – Henry de Braybrook – seized and brought in chains to Bedford castle.

Despite Fawkes' past service, the young king Henry III had now to act. In June he came in person[9], collecting forces, and summoning the sheriffs far and wide to send skilled men, such as smiths, carpenters, stone-workers; tools such as pick-axes, hammers and mallets; military supplies, such as iron and cords; and personal requirements such as wine and spices. No less than six mangonels (large catapults for throwing stones) were used to break the outer walls, while other workers undermined them. From two high wooden towers archers shot into the interior. First to go was the barbican or entrance, and the men of Dunstable led the way into the outer bailey, where were horses and livestock, and outhouses with corn and hay – which were burnt. Next the miners secured the collapse of the inner wall and tower, and gained access to the inner bailey. On 14 August the miners, who had undermined the old tower or keep, fired the props, and the walls began to crack. The garrison, under the command of Fawkes' brother, surrendered. Eighty were hanged. Fawkes himself surrendered to the king – the list of his armour has survived; it includes a hauberk (or shirt of mail), with additional back and breast pieces, a pair of "iron hose", iron cap and helmet; to wear under it there was a linen tunic, probably wadded, and a coif or skull-cap.[10] He was exiled and died soon afterwards.

This was the end of Bedford castle. The sheriff was ordered to fill up the trenches and break down the walls. Some stone was given to Caldwell and Newnham Priories; and some to William de Beauchamp[11], who was given back the inner bailey and allowed to build a dwellinghouse there, which must not be crenellated. It was hard for William de Beauchamp to see the castle come down; and he made some difficulties for those supervising the work.[12] By the destruction

---

[8] *D.N.B.* gives a full life of Fawkes.
[9] The chronicle sources are: Mat. Paris, iii, 84–8; *Ann. Mon.* ii, 299; iii, 86–9; Rog.Wend. ii, 116, 163, 217. See also *Rot.Lit.Claus.* i, *passim.* The best description of the siege is V.C.H. iii, 10–11. There are various other accounts, including A. R.

Goddard, *The great siege of Bedford castle*; B.Mag. iv, 183–90; C. F. Farrar, *Old Bedford*, 46–50.
[10] *B.H.R.S.* ix, 60.
[11] *Rot.Lit.Claus.* i, 632a.
[12] *Royal and hist. letters*, i, 236.

of the castle a big step was taken towards hamstringing any baron of Bedford who might oppose the king. Luton was regained by William Marshal, Earl of Pembroke; but he died in 1231, and his widow married Simon de Montfort, Earl of Leicester.

William de Beauchamp, who made his peace with the young king after his capture at Lincoln in 1217, lived to a good old age, and was henceforward on the side of the administration. He was one of the barons of the exchequer – that office which derives its name from the early 12th cent., when there was introduced an oblong table covered with a chequered cloth, the barons at the head, clerks on either side, the sheriff at the foot, to do the accounts. On the chequered cloth were put counters which could be added up more quickly than could roman numerals (for arabic numerals were not yet in use). William de Beauchamp himself served as sheriff 1235-6, though it was now becoming rare for a baron to do so.

KNIGHTS AND ARCHERS

Either William de Beauchamp or his son of the same name served in 1244-5[13] in one of the wars to preserve peace on the Welsh border; so did his namesake of Eaton Socon, and four others; while John of Pavenham, who owed only the service of one-fifth of a knight, was represented by Ralf of Wilden with bow and arrows. Seven men is a small number compared with the large liabilities for knight service acknowledged by Bedfordshire barons a century previously (see ch. 2), but the system was changing.[14] King John in 1205 had demanded that one knight in ten should do actual service, being paid by the other nine; this was to ensure that the knight should remain for the whole campaign, not just for 40 days. Though archers were hired, knights were still needed for cavalry or as officers. It was difficult to get enough knights, for, in spite of the social status now attaching to knighthood, many mature men found sufficient interest and occupation on their estates with their families or in county affairs, and thought armour an unnecessary expense and overseas service a nuisance.

To ensure a sufficiency of knights, in 1234 the king directed the sheriff to see that all men of a certain standing procured arms and caused themselves to be knighted. This was not fully effective, and the order had constantly to be repeated. A list of 1255 gives nearly 50 men "who have £15 worth of land in Bedfordshire and Buckinghamshire and are not knights".[15] Among the Bedfordshire ones are a Bretteville from Gt. Barford, a Burnard from Arlesey, a Caron from Tempsford, a Flamville from Renhold, a Pertesoil of Riseley, and that Ralf de Tivill whose litigation has been noted (ch. 6). It was possible to buy exemption from the king; or for a smaller sum to bribe the sheriff or his deputy "not to be made a knight", as did Walter of Steppingley and James Grim, in both cases for 20s.[16]

---

[13] B.H.R.S. ii, 246.
[14] For the reductions in Bedfordshire, see B.H.R.S. ii, 185-218.
[15] B.H.R.S. ii, 250.
[16] Rot.Hund. i, 2-3.

However, the attitude of mature men was not shared by restless young ones. That physical fitness and skill which young men now acquire in sport was then attained in the use of arms; and adventurous spirits, who now go speeding or pot-holing, then flocked to tournaments to test their prowess. Tournaments had a useful side in keeping men in training, but they also gave an opportunity for disgruntled young barons to grumble about the king's methods. The barons felt that they, in the king's council, were not summoned as often and consulted as fully as they should be; that the king tended to rely too much on centralised administration by such men as Paulinus Pever, his steward, an able administrator and soldier, who obtained Toddington.[17] They also disliked the fact that the king's servants were often foreigners. Grumbling might lead to plots; so Henry III, artistic, devout, and no lover of fighting as such, tried to prevent tournaments taking place. Dunstable was a convenient place for them; and continually in the 1250's, as baronial discontent grew, tournaments planned to take place there were forbidden, as was also one at Bedford in 1255.[18]

At last it came to war. Among knights captured by the king early in 1264 were Simon de Pateshull of Bletsoe, Ralf Pirot of Harlington, and Hugh Gobion of Higham Gobion.[19] The discontented baronial party won the next success in May. Again a tournament was planned at Dunstable for February 1265; once more it was cancelled because feeling was running high and the baronial party itself was divided.[20] In August at Evesham the rival armies met. Again there was a young Beauchamp, John, in his first battle, the youngest but only surviving son of William de Beauchamp (d. 1260); in manly bearing he was said to surpass the young men of his time. At this battle the baronial leader, Simon de Montfort, was defeated and killed, and with him John de Beauchamp, the last male of the Bedford line. "Who", said the chronicler, "could keep from tears at the death of John de Beauchamp?"[21]

The victory was chiefly due to the young prince Edward, and it made the monarchy in the main secure for his father's time and his own. A soldier as well as a lawgiver, he loved tournaments, and one was held at Bedford in 1268,[22] which the king attended, lodging at Elstow. Edward I as king appointed commissioners of array to raise troops for him. In 1282 he ordered all men with £30 worth of land at least to provide themselves with horse and armour, even if they were not knighted. He also tried to ensure a supply of knights by investing knighthood with glamour. At the end of his reign in 1306, when the Prince of Wales was knighted in London with great splendour, 267 young men from all over the country were knighted with him, and two swans decked with golden chains were brought into

---

[17] *V.C.H.* iii, 439–40; *B.H.R.S.* x, 316–8.
[18] Dunstable, 1253, 1255, 1257, 1258; *Cal.Pat.R.* 1247–58, pp.229, 508, 594; *Cal.Pat.R.* 1258–66, p.5. Bedford, 1255; *Cal.Pat.R.* 1247–58, p.506.
[19] *V.C.H.* ii 30, or *Ann. Mon.* iii, 229. Later (1294)

Hugh Gobion's son was knight of the shire: *B.H.R.S.* xxix, 44.
[20] *V.C.H.* ii, 30–1.
[21] *Ann. Mon.* iv, 174.
[22] *V.C.H.* ii, 33.

the hall. Incidentally a swan pendant was recently found at Dunstable.

Patterns on shields had developed into coats of arms. The Beauchamp[23] arms had been simple (quarterly or and gules, a bend gules). Those of the more recent family of Grey[24] of Wrest (barry argent and azure with three roundels gules in chief) were a little more developed. Later families had to have ever more complicated patterns in order to differentiate their arms; and it was the function of a herald to know them all. When a tournament was held, a roll of arms was made out, depicting the arms of participants. Two such rolls have survived for Dunstable tournaments in 1308 and 1334;[25] in the former, nearly 20 Bedfordshire knights took part, including Sir John de Morteyn, Sir David de Flitwick, Sir Ralf de Goldington, and Sir Ralf Pirot of Harlington.[26]

PARLIAMENT

The baronial movement against Henry III had one notable feature, the parliament of January, 1265. It was not unique. Throughout the 13th cent. the word had come to be used for various assemblies which had occasionally included men of the shires or of the boroughs as well as barons and clergy. That of 1265 at which there were both men of the shires and of the boroughs was merely a parliamentary assembly of the supporters of Simon de Montfort and of the barons who sided with him. Edward I continued to summon parliamentary assemblies at which some representatives of the commons were present. The first known knight of the shire for Bedfordshire is Robert de Crevecoeur of Gt. Barford in 1275. The parliament of 1295 was the most complete; in this the county was represented by Robert de Hoo of Luton Hoo and Ralf of Goldington, both of whom served in several parliaments.[27]

As yet the commons' role was mainly to listen and to answer questions. But their support was beginning to be of use, especially in taxation. It had formerly been thought that the king should govern the country from his own private income. Very soon this did not suffice, and he had gradually to dispose of his lands, the Bedfordshire ones going quite early (see ch. 5); and this diminution of the royal estate made taxation even more necessary. Assent by the commons to taxes helped collection. Legislation was not strictly a function of the commons, but the enunciation of a law during a session of parliament gave it publicity. The commons also presented petitions; from these petitions legislation later evolved.

The county representatives in the 14th cent. were usually knights, and of middle age, mainly between 30 and 50. Many of them served in several parliaments, so that they became experienced. Several were at one time or another sheriff, for it was now usual to appoint a lesser landowner to this post; and often

[23] B.Mag. i, 137.
[24] B.Mag. iii, 120.
[25] A. R. Wagner, *Catalogue of English medieval rolls of arms*, 39, 56; *Antiq. Jnal.*, xxxii, 202.
[26] *Beds. N. & Q.*, i, 33–4. For an analysis of baronial

groupings at this tournament, see *E.H.R.* lxxiv, 70–89.
[27] *B.H.R.S.* xxix. Sir David de Flitwick also attended the parliament of 1295.

they had held other local office. Such was Sir John de Morteyn,[28] who was frequently knight of the shire from 1306 to 1330. His family had acquired Marston by marriage, and were to give the parish their name. He had done military service in 1297; he had been constable of Rockingham castle, commissioner of array, and justice of the peace (ch. 11); and it was he who obtained the grant of Marston market (ch. 5). Sir Baldwin Pigot[29] of Cardington served in three parliaments from 1389 to 1401. From his will we get some idea of the kind of man he was – attached to his family, his servants and his tenants. He mentions his sister Margaret, a nun at Elstow Abbey, and two sisters "in religion at Sempringham". He refers to six servants by name, one of whom was to have a cow; and to all servants unnamed he left 40d. each; to the poor 40s.; and to the fabric of Cardington church 40s.; while his tenants were to be excused rent for one term.[30] A few knights of the shire were of wider influence. Sir John Trailly (1376, 1381) of the Yielden family had interests overseas in Aquitaine, and was mayor of Bordeaux for at least ten years (1390–1400).[31] Thomas de Hoo of Luton Hoo, knight of the shire in 1376, was chosen speaker, and had a prophetic dream of the role of the commons, in which he received on their behalf the seven gifts of the spirit (represented by seven gold coins).[32]

THE HUNDRED YEARS WAR

Now that the commons had appeared, though in a small way, in politics, the barons would eventually try to make use of them; but at first this scarcely appears. For one thing they were as yet of little account; for another there was in Bedfordshire no outstanding baron; and lastly, in the 14th cent. Edward III distracted the national attention by a French war. It was a policy of sowing dragon's teeth; it produced a bitter harvest in the 15th cent.; but for the moment there was euphoria. A hundred years previously the chroniclers had grievously lamented violence and destruction in England by King John's mercenaries – "vile filthy Brabanters under a blood-thirsty cut-throat". Now Froissart arose to sing the age of chivalry and "encourage all valorous hearts", and the devastation and suffering took place out of sight and hearing – in France. However at an early battle in this very war, as yet ineffectual but soon to develop, appeared that very gunpowder which was eventually to eliminate from war much of the attraction of personal prowess.

Of those who went with the "noble King Edward" and were "accounted right valiant", who fought at Sluys, Crecy and Poitiers, most important were the archers, for it was by the English bowmen that these battles, even the naval battle of Sluys, were mainly won. In this century archery was the national sport. It needed long training, but skill could be acquired by the ordinary man by steady practice at the village butts. References to butts occur in medieval deeds, for

---

[28] *B.H.R.S.* ix, 5–22; xxix, 66.
[29] *B.H.R.S.* xxix, 78.
[30] C.R.O., W.41.

[31] *B.H.R.S.* xxix, 92–3.
[32] *V.C.H.* ii, 35. See also a full discussion in *Bull.I.H.R.* xli, 139–49.

instance at Biddenham in 1307.[33] An arrow shot from a 6 ft. yew bow could penetrate chain mail. Under Edward III men from 15 to 60 were bound to possess arms – if they were knights, helmet, hauberk and sword; if a poor man, bow and arrows.

The names of Bedfordshire archers who fought in the Hundred Years War are not known, but there is a list made by the sheriff just before the Crecy campaign which gives over 50 men holding £5 worth of land who were supplying one bowman each; it includes names like Thomas Conquest (this family's name was now being added to the northern Houghton to distinguish it from that near Dunstable), Sir John Guise (whose name was being attached to Aspley), William Launcelyn of the Cople area, and John Pever of Toddington. [34] Another list gives those owning £10 worth of land who were to provide a light horseman (hobeler); and a third those with £20 worth who were to provide men-at-arms.

There was not as a rule difficulty in recruitment. The king's fame as a commander and the chance of booty made the service popular with many, though not with all. Some preferred to stay at home discharging some public office in the county, and arranging advantageous marriages for their children. Thus Esmond de Morteyn in 1358 arranged that one of his three daughters – to be chosen by himself – should marry the grandson of Roger de Goldington, John; little John was to go to Marston when he was 7 years old and be brought up with his prospective bride(s).[35]

The most noted name in the war is that of Nigel Loring of Chalgrave.[36] He was with the small English fleet which in 1340, with wind and tide in their favour and the sun on their enemy's faces, steered full sail into the harbour at Sluys on the much larger French fleet at its moorings – "so great a number of ships that their masts seemed to be like a great wood". The English ships were in threes, one with men-at arms between two ships of archers, who sent a deadly hail of arrows on the congested enemy. Nigel Loring was knighted for bravery. Crecy followed in 1346 and Poitiers in 1356, and he was sent home to announce the victory.

When Edward III created a knightly order of 26 knights, including himself, in imitation of King Arthur's Round Table, Nigel Loring was one. All the knights were to be equal in friendship and honour. Garters and robes were issued for the victory tournaments in England. The Order of the Garter was initiated with a state banquet in the tower of Windsor castle, then newly reconstructed, probably on St. George's day, 1348.[37] In St. George's chapel his was the tenth stall on the Black Prince's side. In 1351 the Black Prince made Sir Nigel Loring his chamber-

---

[33] C.R.O., TW 9. References are sometimes found much later, e.g. at Gt. Barford in 1661 "the common butts"; C.R.O., WW. 141.
[34] B.H.R.S. ii, 261-2.
[35] C.R.O., L 409.

[36] D.N.B. Sir Nigel is mentioned by name only in the Amiens MS. of Froissart: see the edition by Simeon Luce, Paris, 1870, ii, 223.
[37] McKisack, op.cit., 251.
[38] B.H.R.S. xxviii, p.xviii.

lain; and when for a time the war ceased with the Treaty of Bretigny in 1360, Sir Nigel was one of the commissioners to enforce its terms, being allowed 13s 4d. a day from August to December, and two sea voyages for himself, his men, and 9 horses.[38] When war broke out again, he served with the Black Prince; was sent home by him to get royal instructions; and was with the Prince in his Spanish expedition. He continued to serve till 1370.

A KNIGHT'S HOME

When Sir Nigel died in 1386, his property was divided between his daughters. There is a description of his house,[39] and this, with some other descriptions of manor-houses in 1376,[40] helps to build up a picture of the domestic arrangements of a 14th cent. knight.

It may be compared with what we know of the best 13th cent. manor-houses. At Luton William of Someries (d. 1231) had a fortified manor-house surrounded by a rampart.[41] At Toddington Paulinus Pever's house had "state rooms, bed-chambers and other apartments, of stone covered with lead, and was environed with orchards and parks."[42] At Eaton Bray William Cantilupe's fortified dwelling in 1273 had a moat and two drawbridges;[43] in other respects his group of buildings represents an earlier version of the following.

The late 14th cent. descriptions indicate a fair-sized compound, surrounded with a mud wall, with a watch-tower at the principal gate. Inside this was not only the original hall (sometimes with cellar under, sometimes the cellar was under the domestic offices), which at Haynes is said to have been "built long ago," and at Willington to be "of ancient fashion;" but also all the additions made to meet rising standards of living: a chamber for the lord; a chamber for the lady with small chambers annexed and a passage leading to the "noricerie". At Willington there was a separate building called "garite" for clothes. At Chalgrave latrines are mentioned. The hall was connected by a passage with the kitchen. At Haynes a separate building was called the "lardehous"; at Chalgrave there were two larders and pantry and buttery; also bakehouse and brewhouse, woodhouse, malthouse, kilnhouse and well-house. All three had a chapel, and Haynes had also a "presteshous". At Chalgrave there was a garden; Sir Nigel had also in 1365 had leave to make a park. Stotfold manor-house was similar to the above but on a smaller scale. The materials of these houses were either stone or timber, and they were roofed with shingles, tiles, slates or thatch.

Light on the running of such houses, with many servants, comes from accidents recorded in the coroners' rolls. At Lady Christine de Furnivall's house in Eaton Socon in 1267, water was boiled in a big lead vat; the washerwoman, drawing hot water in a bowl, missed her footing and fell in, and a man who tried

---

[39] Op.cit., p.xxxi.
[40] Cal.inq.misc. iii, 392–3 (3 manor-houses on the Mowbray estate).

[41] Dyer-Stygall-Dony, op.cit., 66–7.
[42] V.C.H. iii, 439.
[43] V.C.H. iii, 370; B.H.R.S. xix, 116–7.

to save her slipped and fell in likewise.[44]. Brewing too was dangerous; in Lady Juliana de Beauchamp's house in the same village in 1270 Amice and Sibyl were pouring a tub of grout into a boiling lead vat, when Amice slipped and fell in, followed by the tub.[45] It was from gentry's households that there came the stolen sheets sometimes found in a felon's possession. By 1380 a lord of a manor (William Pykard of Goldington) had a chair in which he sat by the fire in his hall.[46]

BREAK-UP OF ESTATES

While parliament was developing, and while the Hundred Years War was being waged overseas, changes were taking place in Bedfordshire estates and manors. Several Bedfordshire estates had broken up, and manors had multiplied by division among co-heiresses. Even in the 12th cent. this had occurred (see ch. 2: Spech in 1153). In the 13th cent. it was extensive. On the Huntingdon estate (descendants of Countess Judith) there was in 1237 a division among the late Earl's sisters, which split manors. Thus at Kempston[47] one third of the manor went to Devorgilla Balliol, and when William Daubeny bought it in 1337 it acquired the name of Daubeny; one third went to Isabel Bruce and was called Brucebury; and one third to Ada Hastings, from whom it was at first called Hastingsbury, and when the Greys secured it in 1389 it became Greys. The Potton manor[48] was similarly divided, but as the new manors got into other hands they acquired different names; thus one third which went to Ada Hastings took the name of its tenants, Burdett.

The battle of Evesham of 1265 broke up the barony of Bedford.[49] John de Beauchamp's estates were divided among his three sisters. Nationally speaking, the Beauchamps had been comparatively small figures, but henceforward there was in Bedfordshire no baron even of their status, until the Greys reached that stature. Each of the three Beauchamp sisters took a share of the estate, and again three of the larger manors (Bromham, Cardington and Wootton) were split into thirds. The eldest sister, Maud, took her third of the estate to the Mowbrays, later Earls of Nottingham and Dukes of Norfolk; while the other two Beauchamp heiresses had daughters, and this resulted in further complications for the property.

The line of the d'Albinis of Cainhoe also ended with heiresses a few years later in 1272; at the death of Simon d'Albini no castle is mentioned – only a capital messuage, or large house, garden and dovecote. The three co-heiresses further divided an inheritance which had been partly broken up in 1233, though marriage and purchase reunited some of it in the 14th cent. in the families of St. Amand and Dakeney.[50]

At Luton the failure of the Marshal line in 1274 resulted in the division of this large manor into sixths.[51] Three of these, the shares of Isabel, Maud and

[44] *B.H.R.S.* xli, 5.
[45] *Op.cit.*, 13.
[46] *Op.cit.*, 127.
[47] *V.C.H.* iii, 297.
[48] *V.C.H.* ii, 237.

[49] *V.C.H.* iii, 12–15.
[50] *V.C.H.* ii, 321–2; iii, 271–2. *B.H.R.S.* ii, 211, 256; xix, 115, 143.
[51] *V.C.H.* ii, 351–4. Cf. *Cal.inq.p.m.* vii, no. 142, where Reginald son of Reginald held a half of

Agatha, eventually became reunited as the main manor of Luton in the hands of the Wenlock family, who first appear as having part of it in 1389; one-sixth in 1387 went to Dunstable Priory; and the other two-sixths of the former Marshal estate became respectively the manors of Halyard and Woodcroft.

In other ways the baronial overlordship was weakening. By one means or another, sometimes perhaps helped by an advantageous marriage, men were building up small properties and beginning to call them manors. In early days there is little record of transfers of land: it was done on the spot by handing over a clod in the presence of witnesses; the recipient held the land from the grantor, who remained in the same position as previously towards his own lord; so that there arose a complicated mesh of feudal relationships. In 1290 a law was passed by which in future the buyer held of the seller's lord. Henceforward transactions were increasingly put into writing.

SMALL MANORS

It is not often that the process of lay manor-building can be traced in detail, because an even smaller proportion of documents has survived than for monastic estates; but an instance is Washingleys manor, Cranfield.[52] Here the main manor belonged to Ramsey Abbey. William may have come to Cranfield in the mid-13th cent. in the abbot's service. He prospered, acquiring 3 selions from Richer of Bourne, 7 selions from Adam son of Geoffrey, 8 selions from John of Olney, and 27 selions from Ralf Mareschal. His son, William of Washingley, was the abbot's steward;[53] and in the 1270's acquired 11 a. and 43 selions by about fifteen transactions. In 1287 he obtained what seems to be a large compact holding next the meadow called Heweneyerd near the abbot's pasture, extending to Robert of Bourne's garden, and so by the land of Philip Richer; and the annual rent of £2 which he was to pay he gradually compounded within the next few years. By 1301 he had also obtained the rents of over 30 free tenants. It is not surprising that the property began to be known as Washingleys manor, and that a 3-weekly court was held for it. Rodlaunds manor in the same parish almost certainly had a similar derivation; perhaps it was built up by the 13th cent. coroner, Geoffrey Rodlaund or Rouland.[54]

The emergent lay manors seem, as would be expected, usually to be single holdings. Often such a manor took the name of its lord, as Lovell (Lovellsbury, Potsgrove); Morin (Morinsbury, Ravensden); Rous (Rousberry, Wootton); Drayton (Draytons, Tempsford); Flamville (Flamwells, Renhold); Faldo (Faldo, Higham Gobion); Parentine (Parentines, Sharnbrook). Sometimes they complicate investigation by simply being known as a second manor of the same name as the main manor; like the Croxtons' manor at Shelton, the Tirells' at Wilden, or the Chanu manor at Colmworth, or one at Whipsnade held by a family called

one-sixth of Luton manor.
[52] B.H.R.S. xxv, 4–9; V.C.H. iii, 276.

[53] W.O. Ault, *Court rolls of the abbey of Ramsey*, 233.
[54] B.H.R.S. xxv, 8–9, V.C.H. iii, 277.

"de Whipsnade". Sometimes they acquired intriguing names, like Dame Ellensbury (the Malherbe manor at Houghton Conquest). Occasionally the family held more than one manor; the Bosom family of Roxton manor is found in the 13th cent. with a manor called Bosoms at Stagsden and in the 15th cent. with another called Bosoms at Wootton. But generally the family seems resident on its one manor, like the Cauz family at Sharpenhoe, who in 1234 were allowed their own chapel there.[55]

The multiplication of manors continued. A 14th cent. example comes from Wootton.[56] Thomas de Stodley began by marrying an heiress, Joan St. Edward, sometime before 1318. From this time till 1340, by about 30 transactions, he steadily added to his holding anything from a rood to a virgate, and began to hold a court; hence, Stodleys manor.

About 50 such manors had emerged by 1400, and the process went on. When it was complete, there were to be between 400 and 500 manors (including lay and monastic) in Bedfordshire (county area just under 300,000 a.). Luton with its hamlets provided more than 30. Only about 20 parishes (one in six) remained single-manor parishes; and these were mainly smaller ones, such as Stevington, Little Staughton, Ampthill, Milton Bryan, Tilsworth, Cockayne Hatley; though there were one or two large ones such as Eaton Bray. The single-manor parishes – about 10% of the county's area – averaged 1,500 a. In multiple-manor parishes – about 90% of the county's area, even supposing all land to be part of some manor, and including the lands held by free and customary tenants as well as the demesne, the average manor cannot have been much more than 600 a. If we take a particular area in 1279 for which an unusual amount of information is available, and where we can separate the demesne from the tenant land, that is to say, the hundreds of Stodden and Willey in the north (area 20,500 a.), the average size of 53 lay estates was then 390 a.;[57] this was the area of Danish settlement (chs. 1-3); and these small northern manors are comparable with those in adjoining Cambridgeshire and Huntingdonshire. Bedfordshire shows a different picture from the great manors covering several parishes in some other parts of England.[58]

THE GREYS

One new estate was being built up. In the 13th cent. John Grey, son of an Essex man and apparently connected with the Wahulls, is found on their estate at Silsoe, and was sheriff in 1233. His son, Sir Reynold de Grey, rose in the king's service, was granted in 1282 the Ruthin estate on the Welsh marches, and in 1290 received a personal summons to parliament, whereby he is held to have become Lord Grey. When Reynold died in 1308 he left a scattered estate, including

---

[55] V.C.H. ii, 382.
[56] B.H.R.S. xliii, 234-8; V.C.H. iii, 331.
[57] E. A. Kosminsky, *Studies in the agrarian history of England*, 110-1. This is based on the hundred rolls. See also his p.90-1, where he calculates that the

demesne arable was 33%, villein land 21% and free holdings 46%.

[58] In Devon as late as 1635 there were in the Hundred of Lifton (area 79,500 a.) only 40 manors (inf. Mr. P. Kennedy, County Archivist).

Wrest, Thurleigh and Brogborough; and when in 1323 Roger, Lord Grey of Ruthin, succeeded, the Bedfordshire estate included also Harrold manor and property elsewhere in the county.[59] Roger married Elizabeth Hastings; their son Reynold died in 1388; and their grandson, also Reynold, through failure of the Hastings male line, inherited Blunham, Kempston Greys, and properties in six other counties.[60] The Greys were becoming, by Bedfordshire standards, great lords. Incidentally, the Wahull estate was declining; John Wahull, who died in 1336, held only Odell and Langford, and a little property outside the county.

[59] *Cal.inq.p.m.* vi, no. 517. Bedfordshire shows a very different picture from that painted by a recent study of the noble family's estate as a centre from which much of the life of the 14th cent. was directed; G. A. Holmes, *The estates of the higher nobility in 14th cent. England.*

[60] *B.H.R.S.* xlvi, 6.

8 – COUNTRYSIDE AND MANOR, 1200–1400

BY THE 13th cent., though the number of manors had not arrived at its maximum, the manorial organisation in Bedfordshire had reached its peak.[1] But not all men nor all land came within its scope. Small freemen have already been noticed among benefactors to monasteries (ch. 4). As a further indication, two parishes may be taken as examples: Cranfield from the west and Eaton Socon from the north-east.

AREA OUTSIDE MANORS

Cranfield[2] was up to the early 13th cent. a single-manor parish, the manor belonging to Ramsey Abbey; and in 1244 the Abbey had several free tenants, who paid money rents or attended shire and hundred courts in lieu. But in this century there are a number of free men who cannot be identified among Ramsey tenants. Thus three successfully resisted disseisin (eviction): Gerald son of John in 1202, Muriel in 1227, and William Culpyn for 8 a. in 1247. Others bought or sold land: a woman called Cesaria in 1202; Peter de More and Robert le Megre in 1240; John of Olney in 1284 (in this instance over 60 a. were involved); while the deeds of Adam son of Geoffrey (7 selions), William son of William (3 a.), Gilbert son of Walter (1 a.) and Stephen of Souldrop are not dated but appear to be mid-13th cent. Perhaps John of Olney lived at Olney and Stephen of Souldrop at Souldrop, but probably not; perhaps some of the others are too early or too late to tie up with the Ramsey extent of 1244; but it is to be noted that in all the above records appear also men bearing names of Ramsey free tenants (the families of Bourne, Mareschal, de la Rode and Rodlaund). Since probably the surviving records of disseisin and of transfers of land do not provide an exhaustive list of Cranfield free men, there were presumably more than these.

Eaton Socon[3] even by 1200 had more than one manor. Here there is no surviving 13th cent. extent (or list of tenants) to act as check-list. Several cases of disseisin were successfully resisted: in 1247 a woman, Jocea Crofte, recovered 3 a. which had been wrongfully withheld; Richard son of Robert got back his $1\frac{1}{2}$ a.; widow Beatrice received her dower of one third messuage and an acre; William de Newton recovered an acre; and Richard son of Hugh retrieved a piece as small as 2 ft. wide by nearly 2 r. long. Many land transactions are recorded for the 13th

---

[1] The background for this chapter is taken from M. McKisack, *The fourteenth century;* and A. R. Myers, *England in the late middle ages.*

[2] *B.H.R.S.* i, 199; iii, 12; vi, 23, 118; xii, 15, 31, 77; xxi, 39. C.R.O., WN 1–25.

[3] *B.H.R.S.* iii, 49, 199; vi, 50, 73, 78, 80, 91, 101, 104, 109, 112, 124, 126, 139, 141, 151–2, 159, 188; ix, 94; xii, 8, 11, 32, 36, 41, 43, 50, 52–4; xxi, 43, 52, 54, 62, 64, 79, 83, 91, 135; xxii, 73–4, 77, 80, 82, 88–95.

cent.; when names such as Beauchamp have been eliminated, there remain small ones such as holders of 8 a. (Simon Bastard to Ralf Noreis, 1228); 9 a. (William son of Nicholas to Nicholas Borard, 1247); a messuage and 1 a. (Warin Puttock to Elias Aylbright in 1296). Among gifts to Bushmead Priory are several small ones, such as half a croft from Hugh Heluin; 1 a. assart from Richard Costentin; 2 selions from Robert Brussel; 3 a. from Albin son of Bernard, ½ a. from Simon son of Ralf. Probably (as indeed might be expected, since manorialisation was later in the north) there were rather more free men in Eaton Socon than in Cranfield.

The existence of free men outside the manor sometimes made complications, as at Knotting in 1247.[4] The lord of the manor, John Buszard, summoned 9 men and a woman to show by what right they claimed common in his land, as he claimed no common in theirs, nor did they do him service. However, these ten people needed common right for their beasts; and so a formal agreement was made. They would of their own free will accord him certain services (3 days ploughing and 3 days spent respectively in hoeing, reaping and fencing); and would give him 2 hens at Christmas and 12 eggs at Easter; and in return he allowed them common the whole year in a specified area, in the lands of his villeins and in fallow lands after the crop was carried; but not in his demesne. The ploughing was to be shared; a man with a complete team would do a full 3 days; the others would co-operate according to the beasts they had. Perhaps one or two had only an elderly ox liable to be carried off by the murrain, for if anyone had no beast he would not be expected to plough. To be free was not necessarily to be well off.

Who were these free men? Some were perhaps of Norman origin, like John Ordwy of Leighton (ch. 5), as murdrum fines show. Many were probably Englishmen, descendants of sokemen or others who had managed to preserve their free legal standing (ch. 2). A certain number may have been emancipated villeins (see below).

THE MANORIAL ORGANISATION

Though not universal, the manor was the most important agrarian organisation in the county in the 13th cent. By manor is meant a consolidated estate run at least in part by labour service, and under the jurisdiction of its lord. (For its administrative and legal functions, see ch. 11).

One difficulty here is that there is most information for the least typical. It is precisely for the three manors[5] (Barton, n.d., Cranfield, 1244, Shillington, 1255) which had for centuries been held by the great abbey of Ramsey that there is earliest and fullest evidence. It is as if there survived for the future full information on Vauxhall works but on little else at Luton, and as if a future historian were to think he had all the answers because he knew something about Vauxhall. For what it is worth, however, the Ramsey manors must be discussed; and then

---

[4] B.H.R.S. vi, 139.   [5] Ramsey cart. i, 437–86.

the meagre other evidence; and a balance struck.

In all three cases the information comes from an inquisition attended by the chief villagers at which the steward wrote down for future reference the name of each tenant, the size of his holding, and the rent or service he owed; this was called an extent. First come the free tenants, their number varying from 4 to 9; their holdings in size up to 2 hides or more and down to a few acres – in the latter case probably it supplemented other land elsewhere. Some of the free holdings carry the obligation to attend shire and hundred courts, and these owe no rent. Then come the villeins owing labour service; at Barton and Shillington about half the men of servile status hold 1 virgate; at Cranfield $\frac{1}{2}$ virgate is the usual holding; but the difference is apparent rather than real, for though all jurors agree that there are 4 virgates to a hide, at Barton they say that a virgate is 23–28 a.; at Cranfield they don't know, but they think it is 48 a. After these come the cottagers, holding cotlands of 10–20 a., about a sixth of the population at Barton and Cranfield; then those with only a small croft or pightle by their cottages, about one-third of the population; these include people like Richard the smith and Lambert the miller and probably other specialised workers like carpenters.

On none of these three manors are the duties entirely standard, but the most typical case is Herbert son of Gregory at Barton. He held a virgate (which at Barton meant 23–28a), and also a croft of 2 a. which no doubt was by his house and for which he paid 9d. p.a. rent. On St. Andrew's day he also paid 4d. for the heusire (customary payment).[6] From Michaelmas to August he worked each Monday and Wednesday. For most of the year he also ploughed on Friday; and shared with the rest of the vill the provision of seed corn for 3 a. of the abbey's demesne. Exactly how much work he was expected to do in a day had been established no doubt in a centuries-old tussle between abbey and villagers. When ditching, he should do $2\frac{1}{2}$ p. a "spadegraft" deep; when threshing (with a flail) he must thresh 24 sheaves of wheat or 30 of barley or oats. When carrying dung he must take 6 cart-loads. When doing carrying-duty (3 duties between Michaelmas and the Purification – 2 Feb.), if he had to go to Ramsey he received a pasty and forage for his horse; if to London 1d.; if to the neighbouring market (Luton or Hitchin?) he got no such allowance, but the short trip counted as one day's work. He was not expected to carry on Saturday.

Harvest was the "rush" period of the year, when he did extra work or boon-work. To the first boonwork all his family except his wife accompanied him, and also two tenants (tenentes); this was something of a festive occasion, and followed by a special meal provided by the abbey, consisting of a loaf, ale, meat and cheese (a better meal than he could normally afford, and no doubt meant to encourage a good turn-out at a time when every virgator would be itching to get on with his

---

[6] It was usual to make a payment to the lord for the holding of the court, and this was called by different names in different places.

own harvest). The second boonwork was similar, but on that occasion there might be fish instead of meat. For the third only one of his family had to go, but this was called the "hungerbedrype", for no food was given. After that, if the harvest still was not in, there might be extra works called "lovebones", but no more food was provided.

Limited sick leave was allowed. If he was so ill that he had the sacraments, he was quit for 15 days (his testament should be made in the bailiff's presence). If he died, for 30 days his widow would not have to provide labour service; and she might keep the land as long as she wished; but she would have to surrender the best beast and pay a heriot (or death duty) of 5s.

The other Barton virgators had similar duties, one man with 2 virgates doing more, and 7 men with $\frac{1}{2}$ virgate doing less in proportion. All of these had crofts varying from 1 r. to 8 a., and a few had a little extra land as well which in two cases is said to be "formerly demesne".

The cotlanders, with their smaller holdings of 10–12 a. naturally did less work. Thus Simon Church worked on Monday; shared a carrying-duty, carrying on his back 5 capons or 6 chickens or 3 ducks or 100 eggs; drove pigs, sheep and oxen; and had the ticklish duty of guarding thieves if caught.

With Lambert son of Rawnilda we seem to come down to the lowest level. His croft was only a rood, though most of his fellows had bigger crofts, one as much as 5 a. He paid 3s. annually for rent, and 4d. for heusire; he did a day's weeding, a day's haymaking, and came to the "hungry" day at harvest. He may have worked for the bailiff or the virgators for wages. But Richard the miller, who also had to discharge 3 days' labour by his own work or by someone connected with him, was presumably normally occupied at the mill he worked; as was no doubt Lambert the miller (there were 3 water-mills, two of them let out and one in the abbot's hands); and some, no doubt, were other specialised workmen.

In considering the amount of work to be done, it must be remembered that a full day's work was only expected when a meal was provided; otherwise, at least at Shillington, and apparently often, but not always, elsewhere, it seems to have stopped at noon, and a man could work on his own land for the rest of the day.[7] At Shillington, if a man worked also from noon to vespers, the day counted as two works. There was provision, however, against any man doing fencing near the yard knocking off early, even if he had done his stint; he must work from when the ploughs were yoked to when they were unyoked. Again, Herbert son of Gregory did not necessarily or even probably discharge all these duties himself, except at harvest; at other times he probably sent one of his sons if he had sons, or even perhaps Lambert son of Rawnilda.

On the other two Ramsey manors the provisions are similar. At Shillington the width of a hedge after hedging is noted: it must be trimmed so that a plough-

[7] H. S. Bennett, *Life on the English manor* (1965 ed.), 104–5; *Ramsey cart.* i, 461.

share will not project from it. If all carrying-duties are not taken up in one year, they cannot be carried forward to the next. At the harvest meal, the meat is to be beef, and the fish herring; and pottage is thrown in. Sick leave provisions include the possibility (disregarded at Barton) that an illness may last more than 15 days; in this case (unless at harvest) sick leave may be extended to 3 weeks. Holidays (i.e., church-festivals other than the main festivals) were counted to the abbey or the worker in turn; these would include in each parish the festival of the saint to whom its church was dedicated; and 12 days were allowed for Christmas, at least at Shillington.

There were occasions for humour in the annual round. One was at Barton when hay was mown. A sheep was let loose "in the meadow in the midst of them, and if they can take it they have it, and if it escapes they lose it for that year."[8] Perhaps there was originally a genuine stray sheep and a good-humoured bailiff, anticipating a good crop (though he would have to account for the sheep later); and the incident crystallised into custom. At Shillington a custom may have arisen from a wager: each man could claim as much hay as he could carry on the haft of his scythe; but if he was greedy or over-estimated his skill and dropped the hay, he lost it.

Hay and harvest provided their moments of good fellowship and rejoicing. But there were irksome obligations: paying merchet on a daughter's marriage, or leyrwite for adultery, and needing to have the lord's consent to make one's son a clerk. Also the interest of a man holding land would be in his own land but not in the work he had to put in for the lord. This is brought out at Shillington, where it is stipulated that one who sends 3 men to work at harvest (presumably an older man no longer able to work) must walk behind them and admonish them that they work well. The terms "go slow" and "work to rule" are modern, but the possibility is as old as the employment of labour.[9] When customs began to be written down, this would have some stabilising effect, but a written document can be a dead letter. That skirmishing was still in progress on the Ramsey manors is shown by Cranfield's refusal to pronounce offhand on merchet; and their statement that there is a mistake in the "great roll" about carrying duty to Ramsey; "they never did more than one carrying-duty per fortnight to those remote parts".

There is little or no mention of commutation of services.

Caddington also was an old manor, held by the dean and chapter of St. Paul's cathedral, and usually leased by them to one of their canons. An extent of Caddington in 1297[10] shows that there were as many as 50 free tenants, holding a virgate, half a virgate or less. The customary tenants were fewer than 20: John de

---

8 *Ramsey cart.* i, 476.

9 In 19th cent. Russia centuries of serfdom had made the peasants past masters in the art of obstruction; cf. Tolstoy, *Anna Karenina*, where Levin's relations

with his peasants are Tolstoy's own.

10 St. Paul's cathedral library, Lib. 1 (W.D. 16), f. 113d–116. I am indebted for the transcript of this extent to Mr. P. E. N. Butt.

Godrichesputte had ½ virgate; he owed 96 works a year, which were valued at ½d. each; and he could either produce 3 quarters of malt or pay 3d. maltsilver; at Christmas he carried 5 capons or 10 chickens to London, though William Waryn had to carry 2 quarters of corn and 2 quarters of oats. Of cottagers there were only three, a shepherd and two women.

Chalgrave too was an old manor, held by the Lorings since just before the conquest, but reduced in size by grants to Dunstable Priory (from which grants arose Wingfield manor). At Chalgrave there is no detailed extent for the 13th cent., but some evidence is provided by the court rolls which survive from 1278.[11] Here is a feeling of a simpler community. The lord, Sir Peter Loring, sometimes himself sat in the court, as in 1288 when he excused a man for non-attendance; and sometimes a decision is postponed "till conference be had with the lord". The demesne seems to have been about 200 a.; and in 1279 it was said that 29½ virgates (the size of the virgate is not given) were held by 15 freemen, and 10 virgates by an unspecified number of customary tenants. The normal size of holding apparently was ½ virgate; and the policy was to maintain this standard size; when Walter of Leagrave in 1294 got an extra acre he had to give it up. The duties[12] are only very briefly indicated. In 1287 only the ploughing and harrowing are mentioned; each customary tenant must plough an acre three times a year and harrow twice a year. In 1303 a price-list is given, varying from 1d. for two days' weeding to 12d. for 8 days' work in harvest; evidently sometimes at least commutation was practised; but not as a regular thing; for John Saly in 1293 ploughed with another man's ox; and Reginald Pycot in 1305 was fined 1d. for working on his own holding instead of coming to the great boonday. A widow's rights were upheld in 1279 when Richard Ballard was allowed to take over his father's holding only when his mother Avice agreed, and he promised to give her a regular annual supply of corn and beans. In 1280 the heriot caused dispute, for Reginald, the vagrant son of a villein, died; his only animal was a cow, which he had wished to go to his sister Juliana, a leper; the vicar wrongfully took it for a mortuary; whereas in fact it was legally due to the lord, who in the end secured it. The straying cattle, sheep and geese in the corn often gave trouble, and when they were impounded the owner was tempted to break into the pound and get them out. The lord's rights of multure (use of his mill) were enforced against Ellis the carpenter, who in 1297 was using a handmill. Many specialised occupational names occur; probably these occupations were practised by some of those with very small amounts of land: baker, carpenter, cobbler, cooper, gooseherd, hayward, miller, shepherd, smith, swineherd, tailor; and Andrew Pycot was evidently a wheelwright, for he charged Roger 2s. 2d. for an unsatisfactory wheel-

---

11 *B.H.R.S.* xxviii.
12 The services valued in late 13th cent. inquisitions generally give a light impression, especially for

Almaric de St. Amand at Cotes in 1285; *B.H.R.S.* xix, 113–41.

repair. In short, though sometimes the lord's rights appear to be enforced severely, there seems an element of paternalism; there does not appear to exist an exhaustive list of duties (a surviving one of 1376 is quite short), and these duties are at least sometimes commuted.

In so far as any general conclusion can be drawn, it seems that there must have been great diversity on Bedfordshire manors about 1300. On some manors there seem to have been many free tenants: at Stanbridge in 1259 there were 20;[13] at Eaton [Bray] in 1274 the rents of free tenants amounted to £20;[14] on one-sixth of the manor of Luton in 1299 there were 18 free tenants "called soke-men" and only 4 villeins.[15] On those comparatively few old manors which formed part of estates outside the county, there was an approach to efficient standardisa-tion. On the great majority of manors, which were either part of small estates or were units in themselves, and many of which were of recent origin, conditions must have varied as widely as human nature varies. Commutation of services was practised, but how widespread and how regular it was is impossible to say.[16]

On the many small manors the human element would have more play than in a large impersonal organisation. When Sir Peter Loring accepted Thomas le Nunneman's excuse for non-attendance at court, he probably did not think of him as a villein but as Thomas le Nunneman, and perhaps knew all his circum-stances. There may often have been mutual respect between lord and villagers, based on their common feeling for the land and understanding of its problems.

VILLEIN STATUS

Gradually, but with gathering force, the need was felt to outgrow villeinage. The payment of rent in kind by service was reasonable in an economy where money was not plentiful. When litigation in the king's courts became common, it was harmful to the villein to find that he could not plead: Walter of Husborne Crawley in 1202, attempting to dispute a virgate with Turold, had to admit that he held in villeinage and was not entitled to plead.[17] In a similar case in 1227 the man was able to establish his freedom; "it is clear that he is free, because Ralf the day before in that court granted him certain land."[18] In 1247 such cases of disputed status had greatly multiplied.[19] Again, a villein family could be divided between co-heiresses, as was that of Thomas Colles much later (1386).[20] This

---

[13] B.H.R.S. v, 222.
[14] B.H.R.S. xix, 117.
[15] P.R.O., Ch. inq. p.m., C. 133/88.
[16] About 1230 15 people on one of the small Luton manors paid a mark and increased rent to be quit of merchet and of certain services; B.H.R.S. ii, 239. At Whipsnade in 1247 Simon le Jovene ob-tained from the lady of the manor commutation during her life for 3s. annually for the service of his virgate; B.H.R.S. xxi, 47. Inquisitions post mortem (B.H.R.S. v and xix) give the value of services, but do not normally show whether they were in fact commuted. However at Eyeworth in 1284, half-virgators paid 8s. 5d. for all service; and at Renhold

in 1286 virgators paid 30s. for all service: B.H.R.S. xix, 135, 139. It could vary on the same estate. Thus on that part of the Beauchamp estate which went to the descendants of Beatrice, in 1286 the small number of customary tenants were rendering 30s. each for all service, apparently as a regular thing; but at Cardington the works of 11 customary tenants were valued at 12s. each, and thus apparently were still sometimes required; B.H.R.S. xix, 139, 141.
[17] B.H.R.S. i, 207.
[18] B.H.R.S. iii, 115; cf. also 119.
[19] B.H.R.S. xxi, passim.
[20] B.H.R.S. xxviii, p.xxii.

lack of status before the law, which did not apply to a free neighbour who perhaps had fewer oxen and less land, must have been increasingly resented.

In daily life the line between free and unfree was often blurred. Villeins were sometimes tenants of free land,[21] just as freemen occasionally held villein land. It was not always easy for the courts to decide cases. Alexander of Sharnbrook in 1247 was considered to hold freely because his service was fixed and known.[22] In the same year, 22 men on the prebendal manor at Leighton were upheld in their free status by a jury, which declared that their service was limited only.[23] Marriages occurred between free and unfree, complicating questions of inheritance.[24]

What chance had the 13th cent. villein of emancipation? If he managed to spend a year and a day within a borough, it would establish his freedom; William of Ampthill is reported in 1227 to have "lived for several years in Bedford, and there has land and house and wife".[25] He might be formally freed by his lay lord, as Walter was at Wyboston; it was said in 1227 that "in truth he was at one time a villein, but Osbert de Meisy freed him and gave him that land";[26] or as Arnulf de Flora was by Ralf de Neville about 1250.[27] He might also be freed by a monastery, as were William and Simon by Dunstable Priory a little earlier.[28] But on St. Paul's cathedral estate at Caddington it was a condition of the lease that no villein should be freed – actually there were only few.[29] Buying freedom is believed to have been one method; but instances in this county are not readily traced, though in the above cases some unrecorded payment may have passed. He might leave the manor, though not necessarily to go to a borough; and it was difficult for the lord to get him back. Robert son of John, who only went 3 miles from Chalgrave to Milton Bryan, was in 1278–9 three times ordered to return; but after that his name appears no more.[30] At Shillington in 1288 four men had left: William Wyldeful, Walter Horkel and his son, and William of Barton.[31] How many villeins had by 1300 become free by any or all of these ways it is impossible to say; but it could be done, and some did it.

ECONOMIC POSITION OF THE VILLAGER

The economic position of the villager, whether lord of the manor, free or unfree, is shown for the hundreds of Barford, Biggleswade and Flitt in 1297 by taxation returns.[32] These returns omit ploughs, farm equipment and poultry; and where the figures can be compared with other information they are always lower; they must therefore be taken as an understatement. They cover 77 manors and 1,051 holdings of villagers; the former account for £479 of the total assess-

---

21 B.H.R.S. xiii, 254–5, 260, 350.
22 B.H.R.S. xxi, 85.
23 B.H.R.S. xxi, 87.
24 For instance, B.H.R.S. iii, 38.
25 B.H.R.S. iii, 139. In the 14–15th cents. more than one mayor of Bedford bore a village name, though this does not necessarily imply villein ancestry: Astwood (1324), Kempston (1358), Stotfold (1471), Chicheley (1475).

26 B.H.R.S. iii, 37–8.
27 B.H.R.S. xvii, 114.
28 B.H.R.S. x, 160.
29 B.H.R.S. i, 81.
30 B.H.R.S. xxviii, 3–9.
31 Ault, op.cit., 191.
32 B.H.R.S. xxxix.

ment for tax, and the latter for £882. Of the lay manors, only three were worth more than £10; in the £5–10 group was for instance Higham Gobion with 18 oxen, 2 cattle and 12 sheep; the group below £5 comprised more than half the lay manors.

Very few villagers were worth as much as £3 (this it will be remembered was the mayor of Bedford's assessment); the majority of those assessed – i.e., those having goods worth 9s. or more – were worth from 9s. to £1. Thus villagers do not compare unfavourably with townsmen (ch. 5). The village where most peasants owned sheep was Barton on the downs (40 out of 57 taxed); but in the Biggleswade area there were 3 villages with an average of more than 5 sheep to each man taxed. Two examples of the assessments are taken at random: William Patric of Sundon had 2 cows and 5 sheep and was worth 27s. 2d.; Robert de la Haye of Wilden had a heifer, a hive of bees, and 2 piglets, and was worth 9s. But how many men were below the tax level there is no means of knowing.

AGRICULTURAL BOOM

The comparative welfare of the better-class villagers partly reflects the agricultural boom of the 13th cent. Rising production was needed for the growing population. Population cannot be closely estimated, but is believed to have doubled between 1086 and 1300.[33] For instance, in Pulloxhill in 1086 there were 26 men; in 1297 there were 41 men paying tax, plus an unknown number of men below the tax level.[34] The towns as well as the enlarged village population needed food; and the county was in reach of the London market. During the 13th cent. on a big estate it paid well to organise production for this purpose; hence the carrying-duties to London on the Ramsey manors. Small estates probably dealt with the Dunstable corn merchants at the Luton and Dunstable markets.[35] In the southeast of England generally it was a time of high farming.[36]

The medieval yield was very low. It has been estimated that the average 13th cent. yield of wheat would not exceed a fourfold increase. Unfortunately there is not evidence to calculate an average Bedfordshire yield for any medieval years, nor for a single manor over a period. At Higham Gobion in 1381–3 the increase was 3·4, but there is no means of knowing what the season was like.[37] On the same farm in 1966 the increase was 25·3.[38]

Thus it was necessary to take in uncultivated land from the waste (assart or forlond). In the south marginal land on the downs seems to have been cultivated.[39] At first the new land would have a higher yield than the old. Modern experiments

[33] McKisack, *op.cit.*, 313.
[34] *B.H.R.S.* xxxix, 61–3.
[35] *B.H.R.S.* xxxix, p. xxi.
[36] McKisack, *op.cit.*, 315; Myres, *op.cit.*, 43–4.
[37] The size of the former Bedfordshire bushel is thought to have been 2 pints more than the Winchester bushel, which was 2218·19 cubic inches (Museum of English Rural Life). On this particular manor at this date 2 bush. per acre were sown and

the yield was 6·72 and 6·77 bush.; C.R.O., BS. 1175. Cf. Bennett, *op.cit.*, 86.
[38] Manor Farm, Higham Gobion (by kind information of Messrs. Parrish Bros.): 1½ cwt. wheat sown per acre; yield 38 cwt. On the same farm in 1961 in exceptional conditions one field yielded 65¼ cwt. per acre. In each case 6 cwt. of fertiliser were used.
[39] *Inq. Non.* (R.C.), 11–22.

show that the yield from new land, if not fertilised, at first drops, and then stabilises at a low level.[40] Thus without the aids known to modern agriculture, and with a limited amount of land, the period of expansion could last only for a time.

With the new land there usually came a change-over to a 3-course rotation. At first the new land was worked into the existing 2-field system, cropped in alternate years; thus Houghton Regis about 1230 had North and South Fields;[41] and it is said at Stanbridge in 1259 of a man's holding of 92 a. that 48 a. could be sown in one year, 44 a. in another.[42] But in the 13th cent. there begin to be references to a third field and a 3-course rotation; thus in 1247 at Honeydon "they were wont to common every third year",[43] and at Knotting there is mention of "the year when the field lies fallow . . . but in the other years when it is sown."[44] The new land was rarely a compact field, but consisted of irregular areas filling in between the original fields and the parish boundary; thus in practice there might be several fields. At Renhold in the 13th cent. there were North Field, South Field, West Field, Bradefeld, Litelfeld and Wynmulnefeld.[45] At Luton Bromfeld and Hofeld are mentioned in 1252,[46] and there were probably many more. However many there were, normally they were henceforward worked on a triennial system.[47]

Milling facilities had improved by the 13th cent., for the windmill had come into use, supplementing the water-mill. In 1212 at Leighton Buzzard the inhabitants complained that the prior had set up a windmill and charged excessive toll.[48] At Dunstable in 1221 the amount of tithe due for the windmill was in dispute.[49] At Colmworth in 1227 the mortgagee foreclosed on the mill by removing it.[50] At Studham in 1230 a widow claimed one-third of the windmill as her dower.[51] There was a windmill at Eyeworth in 1276 (ch. 6).

COMMON

Extension of the arable area reduced the waste that was available for livestock. Selection for breeding does not seem to have been attempted with cattle and

---

[40] An area continually sown with wheat from 1844 produced a diminishing crop for 30 years and then stabilised at 6·7 cwt. to the acre. Recently part has been left fallow every fifth year, and on this part the mean yield has been 8·8 cwt. to the acre.

   1st year after fallow 16·3 cwt. per acre
   2nd year after fallow 9·3 cwt. per acre
   3rd year after fallow 9·3 cwt. per acre
   4th year after fallow 9·1 cwt. per acre.

There has been trouble with fungus disease. This revised experiment does not quite correspond with medieval methods, for in the fallow (or third) year, weeds grew, and the field was grazed by stock, so that some plant nutrients accumulated. I am indebted for this information to Mr. G. V. Dyke, Head of the Field Experiments Section at Rothamsted. See also Bennett, op.cit., 78–9, citing R. Lennard and A. D. Hall. The yield per acre has greatly increased in the present century:

Bedfordshire:
   1929–39 average yield 17·7 cwt. per acre
   1941–50 average yield 19·7 cwt. per acre
   1951–60 average yield 25·5 cwt. per acre.
The Bedfordshire average for 1964 was 35·2 cwt. to the acre. I am indebted for these figures to the N.A.A.S.
[41] B.H.R.S. x, 196.
[42] B.H.R.S. v, 221.
[43] B.H.R.S. xxi, 43.
[44] B.H.R.S. vi, 139.
[45] B.H.R.S. xliii.
[46] B.H.R.S. vi, 149.
[47] The system is discussed in B.H.R.S. Qto. series, ii, 5–6.
[48] B.H.R.S. xiv, 23.
[49] Op.cit., 16.
[50] Op.cit., 11.
[51] Op.cit., 37.

sheep, and would scarcely be possible while the animals pastured together. They were no doubt very small. (For the wool trade see chs. 10, 12–13). For horses some selective breeding must have taken place, for heavy horses were required as war-horses to carry knights in armour.

Common rights were of two kinds: pasture on the waste; and pasture on the arable fields after the crop was gathered and on the meadows after the hay was mown. Grants of common in the 12th cent. are in general terms, as at Flitwick about 1175;[52] or if specific are generous, as at Herne in Toddington about 1170: for a ploughteam, 6 cows, 100 sheep, 30 swine, and the necessary horses.[53] Even in the 13th cent. there are some fair-sized grants; for instance 120 sheep at Studham about 1230.[54] But disputes about common began to arise. At Luton in 1227 27 men overthrew a hedge: "they were wont formerly to have common in the wood of that vill, and Simon put up that hedge, so that they were unable to come at their common".[55] At Arlesey in 1227 the jury said that "in truth Roger was wont to have his common there after the corn was carried, but now they deprive him of it".[56] By 1247 questions of common are acute. At Cople Robert Picot challenged the right of Simon le Rus to build a house for himself on his own land because it was subject to common right;[57] and at Sutton claims were made on Adam le Waleys for common on his separate holding of 3 a., but the jury upheld his claim that "no one ever commoned there save by grace and permission".[58] Sometimes men tried to share in the common of adjoining vills, as a Souldrop man at Knotting and a Stanbridge man at Eaton [Bray], but were debarred. By long custom intercommoning might continue, as on the great moor between Eaton Bray, Totternhoe and Houghton Regis as late as 1475 "from time that no mind is and yet do," but extension was firmly resisted.[59]

AGRICULTURAL SLUMP

The boom period began to fail. Some few accounts survive, for instance those of Swanton manor, Harrold, belonging to the Templars.[60] This small manor was said some years earlier to be about 200 a., of which only 3 virgates were in demesne. In the first quarter of 1308 10 bondsmen did 96 days' work (the reeve was excused while in office), and 144 works were sold at $\frac{1}{2}$d. each. There were regular servants who were paid small wages and had a corn allowance: a cook, a carter, 2 shepherds, a cowherd, and 7 other herdsmen for horses and oxen. The crops grown were wheat, barley, oats, dredge (mixed barley and oats), and peas or beans; some were consumed; some kept for seed; and some sold (wheat for 3s. 6d. a quarter, oats 2s. a quarter, dredge 2s. 4d. a quarter). Threshing was done on piece-rates (1d. or 2d. a quarter). Also sold were underwood, eggs,

[52] B.H.R.S. x, 40–1.
[53] B.H.R.S. x, 68.
[54] B.H.R.S. x, 182.
[55] B.H.R.S. iii, 13.
[56] B.H.R.S. iii, 84.

[57] B.H.R.S. xxi, 44.
[58] B.H.R.S. xxi, 61.
[59] B.H.R.S. xxi, 32, 41–2; viii, 165–7.
[60] P.R.O., S.C. 6/741, no. 29. Rot. Hund. ii, 329.

an elderly cow, and some pigs and poultry; and 139 hoggets (young sheep), though there was some question whether they did not belong to a neighbouring manor of the Templars. Two ewes, 9 lambs and 2 horses died of the murrain.

A few years of bad harvests round about 1316 made widespread famine conditions. This loss of life and setback no doubt contributed to the fall in the number of taxpayers and in tax returns between 1309 and 1332. In 1309 a tax of one twenty-fifth produced in Bedfordshire £687; in 1332 a heavier tax (one fifteenth on the county and one tenth on the town) brought only £615.[61] Some owners of manors began to evade difficulties by leasing the demesne, as Warden Abbey did to John de Grey in 1323.[62]

In 1333-4 there are accounts for Clapham Bayeux.[63] This again was a small manor. If the set-up was still the same as in 1279, there were 168 a. in demesne; 10 free tenants holding a virgate or less; and 12 customary tenants with ½ virgate each, owing services whose commutation value was 20s. annually. In 1333-4 the list of servants of the manor includes reaper, shepherd, swineherd, keeper of calves, carter and 4 ploughmen. At Christmas these had presents costing 2d. in all; and their Christmas dinners amounted to 4½d. ("victual and drink on the day of the birth of Our Lord"). The lamp-oil for the cowshed cost 2s. 1½d., and 1½ bushels of salt 7½d. But there are two changes from the Swanton account. The price of corn had ceased to rise; in fact it had fallen to 3s. 4d. a quarter. And no works were sold, so that presumably the services were exacted. The exaction of services instead of commuting them was one way in which lords tried to reduce production costs in a falling market.

How widespread the increased exaction of services was on the small Bedfordshire manors cannot be ascertained owing to lack of evidence. At a larger manor,[64] Kempston Hastingsbury in 1341, all services were evaluated in cash terms, which implies some commutation. This manor was an outlying part on a large estate; it was that third of the original manor of Countess Judith which in 1341 was held by the Earl of Pembroke and was shortly to pass by marriage to the Greys. Its total arable area was about 960 a., of which 302 a. were in demesne. There were 18 free tenants, one of whom held as little as a rood and one as much as 46 a.; one also kept a shop in Bedford. Of the customary tenants, 21 held either a virgate or ½ virgate (size of virgate not given). Their services were typified in those of William Godwyne. His rent was 19d.; in addition he paid 1s. for some few services – unspecified – which had been allowed to lapse. The services still expected (unless commuted, usually for 1d.) were as follows. From Michaelmas to 1 August he worked Monday, Tuesday, Wednesday from sunrise to vespers, and on Friday he ploughed; and from 1 August to Michaelmas he worked every weekday but Saturday. Harrowing, weeding and similar duties are set out; but

---

61 *Two Beds. subsidies*, 102, 188.
62 P.R.O., S.C. 6/119/2.
63 *B.H.R.S.* xiv, 135-45.
64 *B.H.R.S.* xxxii, 71-9.

carrying-duty involved only carrying hay or corn to the lord's barn or carrying wood. When ditching the required length for a day was 1 r. 15½ ft. After William Godwyne and his fellows come six people holding a virgate or ½ virgate in bondage, but paying rents of 5s. 7d. or 3s. 8d. and owing very few services. There were 15 cottagers: Richard Ravening had an acre for which he paid 4d.; his duties included spreading dung, making hay, and coming to one autumn boonwork without food; but he had no carrying duties.

In 1340 some more information on the difficulties of agriculture comes from tax assessments.[65] These were made by parishioners on oath, and it was natural that they should make them as low as they reasonably could, and should justify themselves with all the arguments they could devise. Thus Bolnhurst, Pertenhall, Keysoe and Riseley all complained that agriculture was suffering from over-taxation. Again, too much emphasis must not be placed on a single season, especially when it was a bad one, a summer drought with failure of several crops being followed by a severe winter when many sheep died at lambing time. Further, there seems to have recently been an epidemic in the south – many houses at Studham and Eversholt were empty.[66] Farming must have been affected, too, by the absence of men serving in the army in France; in March 1339 a further 112 had been called up for home defence.[67] Several parishes complained of falling prices for both corn and wool. In over 30 parishes there was some land left uncultivated, mainly on the downs, as at Eaton [Bray], Totternhoe and Barton, but also in isolated places further north; for instance there were said to be 200 a. at Odell and 110 a. at Wilden. It was often stated that this was because of the parish's poverty. At Houghton Regis the reasons alleged were the barrenness of the land and the poverty of the people, who had neither animals to plough nor seed to sow. The total amount said to be out of cultivation was over 2,000 a. (a good deal less than the 5,000 a. reported in Cambridgeshire),[68] but these figures are rough estimates, almost certainly exaggerated.

THE BLACK DEATH

In the mid-14th cent. slump came a disaster. A new form of bubonic plague from the East was carried across Europe by black rats and reached England in 1348. It got to London in November and spread north during 1349. Its peak in Bedfordshire was from March to August of that year. Its effect was worst in towns (ch. 10), where small houses were crowded together in little streets, for it was pneumonic, and transmitted by coughing and sneezing (compare the nursery rhyme: "Tishoo, Tishoo! All fall down together.") However it affected the country also. In those days before the keeping of registers it is not possible to tell exactly how many ordinary people died; but out of 123 benefices, the incum-

---

[65] *Inq. Non.* (R.C.), 11–22.
[66] The numbers are given as: Studham, 60; Eversholt "many"; but these seem typical medieval random estimates. At Studham in 1671 there were less than 50 houses.
[67] *Cal.Cl.R. 1339–41*, p.55.
[68] *V.C.H. Cambs.*, ii, 71.

bents of at least 54 died; and 18 clergy resigned, probably because they were offered elsewhere better livings to replace dead clergy.[69] At Chalgrave, Dunton and Wymington, perhaps also at Thurleigh, two incumbents died in quick succession. Chantry priests died at Eaton Socon, Silsoe and Toddington; and also at Sandy where the chantry had only been founded the previous year (ch. 9). Bushmead Priory lost its prior, and Markyate Priory lost one prioress after another. The distribution of clergy deaths suggests that, though individual villages here and there may have escaped the plague, no area of the county was entirely free, and some places had worse epidemics than others.

Probably (as on the continent) country people died in their cottages or on the roadside, or among their crops; and made little attempt to reap or to care for their animals, which browsed at will, and at night through force of habit came home untended.[70]

Usually the lord of the manor escaped – there were better living conditions at the manor-house than in the village; but at Clophill Peter de St. Croix died on 16 March, his son Robert on 25 May, and there were no rents of bondmen or cottagers "because they are all dead through the pestilence"; and the same thing happened on his property at Ampthill.[71] At Stevington the dovecote stood in ruins, the garden was worth nothing, and the fulling-mill was worth less, because of the pestilence.[72] The water-mill at Pavenham was not running because there was no miller.[73] In 1351 at Riseley on Harvies manor 300 a. of arable land were uncultivated because "no one wants to occupy them".[74]

In 1361-2 there was a further outbreak, but this was felt less in Bedfordshire. There were only 12 clergy deaths. There was however a bad epidemic at Toddington; Nicholas Pever died on 17 July, and a little later the manor was said to be "worth only £12 because the tenants are dead".[75] Again in 1369 the plague broke out, but this time, so far as is known, Bedfordshire seems to have escaped. Over the whole of England during the period 1349-69 it is thought that from one-third to one-half of the population may have died; perhaps one-third may be true for Bedfordshire.[76] For a long while the effects were to be seen in land out of cultivation and buildings out of repair. At Haynes in 1376 the windmill lacked sails and axle, and both there and at Willington the total cost of repair to put the

---

[69] Details given below of clergy deaths from plague are taken from clergy lists in C.R.O. extracted from the episcopal registers at Lincoln.

[70] G. G. Coulton, *The Death Death*, p.19 (citing Boccaccio).

[71] *Cal.inq.p.m.* ix, no. 230.

[72] *V.C.H.* iii, 100.

[73] *Op.cit.*, 78.

[74] *Op.cit.*, 158.

[75] *Cal.inq.p.m.* xi, no. 177.

[76] McKisack, *op.cit.*, 332; Myres, *op.cit.*, 9. The following calculations have been made for Bedfordshire, and census returns are given for comparison.

1086 15,000 *B.H.R.S.* Qto. i, 77. Increase till the Black Death, when perhaps one-third died.

1377 20,239 *V.C.H.* ii, 90, excluding children and paupers.

1563 23,741 Based on Harl. M.S. 618, which gives number of families, except for the Peculiar of Leighton. The number has been multiplied by 4·25, the method used in *B.H.R.S.* xvi below, and a conjectural 800 added for Leighton.

1671 39,874 *B.H.R.S.* xvi, 13.

1801 63,393 census.

1831 95,483 census.

manorial buildings in a good state was estimated to be £100.[77] These 14th cent. plague outbreaks were the worst, but the pestilence was to erupt periodically until the late 17th cent. One reason for its disappearance was that the black rat, whose fleas were plague carriers, gave place to the brown rat.[78] Improved living conditions helped.

Already times had been difficult for the bigger estates; and now, with scarcity of labour and rising wage demands, they were more so. The government appointed justices (ch. 11) to deal with labour questions and to enforce a maximum for wage rates. The Bedfordshire proceedings of these special justices (who functioned only till 1359) have not survived, except for a case of 6 villeins from Sharpenhoe in 1352, who took jobs in Caddington, Streatley, Luton and St. Albans at high rates (John atte Well was to get no less than 10s. a month at St. Albans), but were made to return to Sharpenhoe.[79] A few cases in 1363 occur before the ordinary justices of the peace.[80] At Birchmore the servants of Alexander Conditt tried forcibly to detain a shepherd who had sworn to serve another master. Six other men at Northill, Southill and Wootton took excessive wages; the sheriff was not able to seize them and eventually they were outlawed. Perhaps three of them were immigrants taking advantage of the labour situation – their names were Adam Irrysheman, and John and Laurence Welsheman. In general, Bedfordshire's smaller units may have been in a better position than bigger ones elsewhere; the small man with fewer labourers could better adapt himself.

THE LATE 14TH CENTURY

The surviving evidence seems to show that the lords of the manor reacted in different ways to changing conditions. On the small manor of Higham Gobion the lord seems to be trying to carry on in the old way.[81] The heiress, Hawise Gobion, had married a Butler, and the lord was Sir Edward Butler. There were formerly 21 customary holdings, but those of John Holewell, John Wilgod, Thomas Neweman, John Smyth, Walter Aleyn and Robert Bonde were in the lord's hand – apparently he had not been able to find occupants for them; five other holdings were at farm; and he received only 100 eggs instead of the former 210. "Works" were sold to the extent of 297 at prices from $\frac{3}{4}$d. for boonworks to 6d. for carrying-duties. Wages had advanced considerably. Whereas at Swanton in 1308 they had ranged from 2s. 8d. to 7s., at Higham Gobion in 1380 the carter was paid 14s. 4d. a year; 4 plough servants, a shepherd and a warrener 10s. each;

---

[77] Cal.inq.misc. iii, 392–3.
[78] Dr. A. J. Duggan, Director of the Wellcome Museum of Medical Science, writes that the flea vector of the plague was probably Xenopsylla cheopsis, a parasite of the black rat, and believed now to be extinct in this country. The flea associated with the brown rat, Nosopsyllus fasciatus, is a less efficient plague-carrier, and the brown rat is less in contact with people than was the black rat. The flea which attacks human beings, Pulex, can in some circum-

stances transmit plague. Dust and dirt in human dwellings provided breeding-places for fleas, and the gradual improvement in standards of cleanliness helped to eliminate them. However, plague has declined all over the world, and is now very rare; and its disappearance in a relatively short period cannot yet be fully explained.
[79] V.C.H. ii, 89.
[80] B.H.R.S. xlviii.
[81] C.R.O., BS 1175.

and a dairyman 8s. 6d. The price of wheat had not advanced proportionally; it was 4s. 8d. a quarter locally, though in London it was fetching 7s. 4d.

A different line was taken by John de Mowbray, Earl of Nottingham, who had 3 Bedfordshire manors as part of his Beauchamp inheritance. Willington, near Bedford, had probably suffered badly from the plague. However, by 1382 the holdings had been rearranged, a new extent prepared, and all tenure was free. Half-virgators, acre-men, cottagers, molmen, all who lately held of the lord in bondage now held freely by rent at the rate of 13s. 4d. for each messuage and half-virgate.[82]

On the Wrest estate, Eleanor widow of Reginald, Lord Grey of Ruthin, leased the demesne. In 1390 she leased Thurleigh manor for 12 marks (£8) a year. She was to repair the hall, chapel, barns, granary, sheep-pen, dairy-house and kilnhouse before the tenant entered, but thenceforward he was to do repairs. She would retain the rents of her bond and free tenants and the profits of courts.[83]

Monastic estates tended to be run on conservative lines, but the main change was a new type of money rent which included commutation of services: on the manor of Arlesey Bury in 1378 Waltham Abbey let to William Spencer a messuage and 4 a. at 10s. p.a., of which 9s. 7½d. was for services commuted.[84] Other methods tried by this Abbey on the same manor were the lease for years; in 1378 a messuage and ½ virgate which for over 16 years had been without a tenant were let on a 10-year lease to J. Jurdon; and leases "at will" (i.e., not protected by the custom of the manor either as regards amount of rent or security of tenure) "because no heir wished to take it at the old rent and custom" (1379; cf. also 1390).

More villeins left the manors. Nine left Podington between 1384 and 1394; Richard Wyteby was at Berkhamsted; but the whereabouts of others was not known.[85] John Wilden of Kempston in 1399 was living at Luton with several children.[86] James Quarrer and John Syward in 1397 had left Arlesey for London, and were working as pewterers in Candellwyk street[87], and Quarrer did well enough to get himself and his son formally manumitted. The majority however stayed on (for their future, see ch. 13).

Nationally it was an uneasy time. The slow drain of the French war continued, without the compensation of famous victories. The old king lost his grip and sank into his grave in 1377, to be succeeded by the boy Richard II. In 1380 a poll-tax was imposed, especially unpopular in the towns, where men were gathered together and their discontent fomented. There was an outbreak in Essex. Old soldiers returning from France through Kent took fire, and when they and the

[82] C.R.O., R iii, 166.
[83] C.R.O., C 1252.
[84] C.R.O., IN 58. See also *V.C.H.* ii, 90; and J. A. Raftis, *Estates of Ramsey Abbey*, 281, a detailed study of Ramsey estates, dealing mainly with the Huntingdonshire manors.
[85] C.R.O., OR 798, mm. 1–7.
[86] C.R.O., PE 466/1.
[87] C.R.O., IN 58.

townsmen collected in bands, discontented villagers joined them in a march on London in 1381.[88] The men of Hertfordshire rose, especially the townsmen of St. Albans, and the men on the manors of St. Albans Abbey joined in.[89]

At Dunstable a Hertfordshire landowner, Sir William Croyser[90] who also had land at Pavenham and Riseley, took refuge in the priory. His Bedfordshire estates are the only ones on which violence is reported.[91] William Bateman, probably of Therfield,[92] also took refuge at Dunstable. But, though there were other disturbances in some counties, the Bedfordshire villages were surprisingly quiet, as were those of Buckinghamshire. Dunstable was (apart from the isolated trouble in north Bedfordshire) the only place in the county where there was an actual outbreak (ch. 10), but it was an outbreak not of normal villeins but of townsmen. These townsmen are said to have been joined by a few men from the surrounding villages; but even some of these may have come from Hertfordshire. Perhaps it was the lord, rather than the customary tenant, who was getting the worst of things on the many small Bedfordshire manors, and the poll-tax alone was not sufficient to incite the freemen to rise.

[88] For a general account, see McKisack, op.cit., 407–22.

[89] V.C.H. Herts., iv, 198–206.

[90] V.C.H. ii, 90.

[91] Ann.Mon. iii, 418; V.C.H. iii, 77–8, 158; V.C.H. Herts. ii, 156; iii, 10–11.

[92] V.C.H. Herts. iii, 283–4.

9 – THE CHURCH, 1200–1400

IN 1200 St. Hugh, bishop of Lincoln, died, and he was followed by eminent bishops, the greatest Robert Grosseteste (1235–53).[1] The archdeaconry of Bedford was by 1200 well established: John Houghton (1218–31) was a notable archdeacon (ch. 5);[2] and the rural deaneries were functioning. By this time there were presumably churchwardens; churchwardens are mentioned at a London Council in 1127, but the first local ones whose names are known are those of Bedford St. Peter in 1379, Thomas Roket and John Balle.[3] The monasteries were all founded. The medieval Catholic church was perhaps at its peak with the Lateran Council of 1215 (where, among England's representatives, was prior Richard of Dunstable). In the 13th cent. parish churches were enlarged and beautified, and religious houses were extended to provide hospitals for at least lepers and some of the aged. But any advance often brings unsuspected problems; with the monasteries, it was the care of the estates which had been given to them, and their relation with parishes. Moreover, the human spirit is always moving on to new endeavour; and thus arose the friars, the furtherance of learning in universities, and the writings of the mystics; and a search by the laity for a more personal religious expression, which took the form of chantries.

CHURCHES

The enlarging of churches went on apace. Though developments in church building show a general trend, each church is different, having been altered or rebuilt at various times by many people, who sought to provide the best building they could for the worship of God. The chancel was the responsibility of the rector; the nave that of the parish.

Where a church was rebuilt, the date of its reconsecration is sometimes known, as happened with two churches in 1220: Pulloxhill[4] (unfortunately again rebuilt in 1846) and Studham.[5] Most of Studham church is still extant, and the change from the stiffer scalloped capitals to graceful foliation shows developing style as the work progressed. Sometimes such rebuilding is probably due to a notable lord of the manor, as when the general plan of the stately church at

---

[1] For the background to this chapter, see D. M. Stenton, *English Society in the early Middle Ages*, 219–46; A. R. Myers, *England in the late Middle Ages*, 60–81; M. Powicke, *The thirteenth century*, 445–510; M. McKisack, *The fourteenth century*, 272–311, 499–532; also D. Knowles, *The monastic order in England*, and *The religious orders in England*; and J. R. H. Moorman, *Church life in England in the 13th century*. See also *V.C.H.* i, 309–48. *V.C.H.* ii and iii give architectural descriptions of all churches.

[2] See also *V.C.H.* i, 320.

[3] C.R.O., DDP 100/6/4.

[4] Not 1219, as in *V.C.H.* ii, 379, see *Ann. Mon.* iii, 56.

[5] *V.C.H.* iii, 430.

Toddington dates from the time of Paulinus Pever (ch. 7); and in spite of later alterations some masonry of his time survives in the tower. But at Felmersham in the early 13th cent., where the manor was held by two families and Radwell by a third, there must have been notable co-operation to produce a church "of quite unusual scale and richness". Yielden was probably rebuilt by the Traillys. At Leighton Buzzard in the late 13th cent. perhaps it was the prebendary who instigated rebuilding. This was in the time of the noted iron-worker, Thomas of Leighton, whose foliate wrought-iron hinges appear on the west door: and also at Eaton [Bray] and Turvey.

More often, alterations to churches were carried out piecemeal. Eaton [Bray] and Turvey show a main feature of the 13th cent., enlargement by building arcades and adding north and south aisles. This was done also at Barton, Harrold, Kempston and Sharnbrook. Sometimes the parish could manage only one aisle at a time, as at Campton, Carlton, Husborne Crawley, Ravensden and Sutton. Eversholt and Henlow merely lengthened the nave to the west; while Battlesden and Tilsworth simply rebuilt their naves without adding aisles. In other parishes the chancel was enlarged, as at Arlesey, Blunham, Caddington, Meppershall, Oakley, Potton, Shelton and Warden. Milton Ernest and Podington concentrated on a new tower. Sometimes small details of this period remain, as at Wilden a piscina; and at Tilsworth a group of little carved stone figures, perhaps representing St. Thomas Becket.

In the early 14th cent. the process continued, was checked by the Black Death,[6] then gathered force again. A wholesale rebuilding at Weston[ing] was probably due to the new family of Inge, soon to give the parish their name; and at Sundon, "a perfect and well-designed example", to Giles de Badlesmere, who died in 1338 leaving three sisters. At Shillington in 1333 the bishop had to stir up the parishioners, and the result was the present commanding church on its hilltop site. The little church of Lower Gravenhurst was built by Sir Robert de Bilhemore (d. 1361) – "Robert de Bilhemore, chiualer, qe fist faire cette eglyse de nouele, gist icy"[7] (Sir Robert de Bilhemore, who rebuilt this church, lies here). Dunton, Harlington, Houghton Conquest, Langford, Northill and Tempsford, too, are mainly of this century; and Wymington owes its rebuilding to the wool merchant, John Curteys (ch. 10).

Many parishes which had already enlarged the nave with one aisle added another in the 14th cent. Some, like Ampthill, built the two aisles at once. Oakley went so far as to take the next step: raise the roof of the nave and add a clerestory. In many parishes the chancel was enlarged. Several built towers, and at Houghton Conquest in 1392 the details of the contract have survived: the masons were William Farele of Dunstable and Philip Lessy of Totternhoe, and they were to complete it in 3 years; it was expected to cost £40 (10s. a foot for the foundations,

---

[6] E.g., *V.C.H.* ii, 278; iii, 93.　　　　　[7] *V.C.H.* ii, 338, and plate.

and 13s. 4d. and 6 quarts of frumenty for every foot above ground).[8] In some parishes where the main structure was now established, small chapels were added – at Luton by the Hoo family. Some other details of this period survive, such as fonts at Arlesey and Keysoe (the latter given by Warel, who asked for the prayers of passers-by); at Edworth fragments of the wall-painting which once existed in all churches; and at Tilsworth a coffin-lid inscribed "Adam de Tulles-worthe gist yci, dieu de sa alme eyt mercii" (Adam of Tilsworth lies here – God have mercy on his soul!).

Of the equipment of the churches we can get some idea from a Kensworth (then in Hertfordshire) list of 1297.[9] There were 4 surplices; vestments both for Sunday and for festivals (chasuble, maniple, stole), sometimes embroidered with gold or trimmed with gold fringe; towels; various altar frontals and chalice covers (some embroidered); 2 chalices (one of silver); 3 pyxes (casket for the host), two of them wooden and one ivory; 2 pewter candlesticks; a bell; and two figures of the Virgin Mary. The service-books included 2 missals (one good, one old), manual, 2 grails (one old), 4 antiphoners, 3 psalters (one in bad condition), ordinal, book of tropes, and 2 temporals (books dealing with seasons and movable festivals). In these days before printing, service-books were not uniform, and different areas of the country followed the practice of one or other of the great cathedrals. Such fragments of Bedfordshire service-books as have survived conform to the Salisbury practice (known as Sarum use).

Church festivals were simple and dramatic to bring home spiritual truths to ordinary people. Thus on Ash Wednesday ashes were sprinkled on the congregation in token of mourning and penitence. With some festivals the agricultural round was linked; thus from Candlemas (2 February, Purification of the Virgin), when candles were carried in procession, there was no more common on the open fields till harvest; at Rogation processions the crops were blessed; and Lammas (1 August) was loaf-mass from the first ripe corn. A new festival in the 13th cent. was Corpus Christi, established in 1264, when the whole parish walked in procession. Mystery plays were performed, showing spiritual feeling, simple humour and a lack of respect for rank: they certainly took place at Dunstable (ch. 5); and probably simple ones were acted even in small villages; for much later, when church vestments were listed, there were noted at Eversholt 6 curtains of dornix (Tournai work) "whereof is made 4 playing coats", and an early 16th cent. will refers to "my playbooks and garments".*

In some scattered parishes, where the inhabitants had to come to church from a distance, there was a chapel of ease, such as Chalgrave (Tebworth), Flitton (Silsoe), Flitwick (Ruxox), Haynes (St. Mark), Leighton Buzzard (Heath and

---

[8] *V.C.H.* iii, 294n.
[9] St. Paul's cathedral library, WD 16, f.58d.
* F. C. Eeles & J. E. Brown, *Edward inventories for*

Beds., p.2 (Alcuin Club Coll. vi); and C.R.O., ABP/R 2, f.192d.

Stanbridge), Meppershall (St. Thomas), Marston (Wroxhill), and Toddington (Chalton). Ruxox was given to Dunstable Priory by Philip de Sanvill about 1150; his son Gilbert challenged the gift and bullied the chaplain; when Gilbert developed leprosy, it was thought by himself and others to be a judgement on him, and he made restitution.[10]

Often the lord of the manor liked to have a private chapel on his own premises, as William de Bretteville did at Gt. Barford in the 12th cent., and several families did in the 13th cent.[11] When permission was given for this, the bishop always stipulated that the dues of the parish church should not suffer.

HOSPITALS

Medical knowledge at this time was almost non-existent, and little care was available even for the wealthiest. It was equally impossible to make general provision for the old, though sometimes a benefactor endowed a corrody at a monastery, by which he, and later his descendants, could nominate one or two aged retainers to be fed and cared for; or he could even provide for his own old age in this way. Thus a corrody-holder at Dunstable in 1234 received 7 white loaves, 7 gallons of ale, and pottage such as the canons and lay-brothers had.[12] But compassion was aroused by the very worst cases, and the obvious way, if a benefactor could afford it, was to set up a hospital,[13] where a few brothers in minor orders, under a master and sharing dormitory and refectory, could care for a few old or sick people, maintain the usual services, and pray for benefactors.

Such provision for sickness was not directed against the plague, which, when it came, was sudden and general, but against leprosy, which was fostered by bad living conditions. A lepers' hospital had to be outside a town; thus that of St. Leonard at Bedford, in existence by 1207, was at the junction of the roads to Luton and London – an awkward position from the point of view of Elstow Abbey and Elstow inhabitants, for it blocked their path to Bedford and obliged them to make a detour. It had a master and five brothers, who went out to seek alms for their sick. For Dunstable the hospital of St. Mary Magdalene seems to have been founded about the same time. For Luton, that of St. John the Baptist, founded a little later, was at Spital Hill in north Leagrave. There may have been more. One at Sudbury in Eaton Socon is known from an attack on visitors in 1265:[14] Margery, with her son John and her sister, was on her way from St. Neots market to the leper hospital at Sudbury (apparently to visit her husband Thomas), when a gang of four set on them; the hue and cry was raised; and the attackers fled to Hail bridge, so as to escape into Huntingdonshire; on the bridge, one of them

---

[10] B.H.R.S. x, 40, 43, 271.
[11] B.H.R.S. x, 147, 173 (Alan of Hyde at Hyde; William de Eltesdon at Barworth in Studham); B.H.R.S. xliii, 137 (Gt. Barford); V.C.H. ii, 382–4 (Cauz family at Sharpenhoe); V.C.H. iii, 374 (Eaton Bray), 446 (Pever family at Toddington;

see also C.R.O., CRT 130/7).
[12] B.H.R.S. x, 149.
[13] V.C.H. i, 396–403.
[14] B.H.R.S. xli, 1. Centuries later the site was known as Hospital close – see award.

turned, and with his sword killed William the shepherd, but was himself seized by the men of Sudbury.

One hospital was set up for the sick and not merely for lepers: that of St. Thomas and St. Mary Magdalene at Luton by 1349;[15] it seems to have been precarious, for more than one donor specified that if the hospital declined and the clergy left it, his gift should revert to him until such time as the hospital should be once more filled with clergy.

For the very poor also some provision was made at Bedford, Luton, and in two villages, all these hospitals being dedicated to St. John the Baptist. At Bedford the hospital was founded by the late 12th cent. for needy Bedford people who had become poor through misfortune rather than by fault. At Luton, Farley hospital was founded in 1156 by Henry II on land granted by him to the Norman hospital of St. Inglevert near the port of Wissant, perhaps after a rough Channel crossing. At Hockliffe the hospital seems to date from the early 13th cent.; in 1290 there was a fire there, and in 1310 there was trouble between the brothers and their master, Luke of Nutley, which resulted in an appeal to the bishop and in Luke's resignation.[16] At Toddington the hospital was much later – 1433; this was very small, and provided only for three poor men living with a chaplain.

MONASTIC ESTATES

The monasteries were now securely established. Details of the monks' daily life, their rising at 2 a.m., their round of services, their studies, are hard to come by for Bedfordshire in the 13–14th cents., and must be taken from their general historian.[17] Of their numbers in the late 14th cent. some indication is given by tax returns.[18] Warden Abbey was the largest, with 24 monks and 6 lay brothers; the next were Woburn Abbey and Dunstable Priory with 17 each; and the smallest Beaulieu with only two.

Their security raised some problems for themselves and others. For themselves there was the care of their estates. If an abbot or prior was an inspiring religious leader, he was not necessarily good at estate management.[19] Yet if he did not exercise care in this respect, especially if he was enlarging or rebuilding the monastic church to the glory of God, the house could easily get into financial difficulties and become indebted to Italian merchants, as Newnham Priory did. When Woburn was in debt in 1234, abbot Richard was removed, and a new abbot, Roger, sent from Fountains to replace him.[20] At Dunstable in 1280 Bishop Sutton found the priory in debt, and deposed the prior, William le Breton (who was

---

15 C.R.O., DW 10-16.
16 L.R.S. xlviii, 4; V.C.H. i, 401.
17 Knowles, Monastic order, 448 – 560.
18 B.H.R.S. i, 27–61.
19 The election of the new head of a religious house was a tricky matter, apart from his or her religious and administrative capacity. The patron sometimes tried to intervene. There could also be division in

the house; H. Johnstone describes a disputed election at Elstow Abbey in 1315, where the minority made great efforts to secure the election of Elizabeth Beauchamp, "a most religious woman, honourable in spiritual matters and circumspect in temporal" (Church Quarterly Review, 1941, pp.46–54).
20 V.C.H. i, 366; Ann. Mon. iii, 140.

pensioned off at the priory's cell at Ruxox, Flitwick, with a small regular allowance for himself and a servant, and 14 loaves, 14 gallons of beer, and 8d. for relish), and the bishop advised the new prior to keep the priory's expenses within a fixed sum; the chronicler apologises for the new prior dining with the tycoon John Durant in 1283; "this was quite against the custom observed in our monastery, but it may be excused, because he owed John so much money and dared not offend him".[21]

There was sometimes also a problem of getting title recognized, when a disgruntled heir made difficulties about his father's gifts to a religious house. The little priory of Bushmead had trouble for years with the Pateshull family about a rent of £8 which Simon de Pateshull remitted about 1260. Simon's great-grandson, John, seized the priory's cattle, and when one of the canons, Richard of Little Staughton, went with the bailiff to redeem them, John's men seized him "sitting on his horse, and led him to the manor of Bletsoe, and impounded him; and he was impounded there; and would not get down from his horse" till forcibly dismounted.[22] This particular dispute was brought to an end by a "love-day" (negotiation). But sometimes litigation was necessary to maintain or regain possession; then a monk or canon had to put the house's case in the courts.

The estates of the Bedfordshire monasteries were not comparable in size or antiquity with the great religious estates of England. In 1200 they were almost all quite recent. In assessments for tax purposes in 1291, none is rated at more than £200, as compared with Ramsey Abbey's £1,310. Their closest analogy is with the small lay manors (ch. 8). Where a monastery received a sizeable grant in a parish, and this was augmented by small supplementary gifts from humbler donors, it might by judicious exchange form a demesne or home-farm, use the services of the villeins given to it,[23] buy additional villeins,[24] and hold a court. At Sharnbrook in the 12–13th cents. three generations of the Triket family of Toft manor gave Newnham Priory various amounts of land and rent.[25] Over the same period there were several other benefactions in the same parish, including grants of villeins – Robert Slyngboter and his family, William Clauehog and William Manipeny. From about 1166 to 1300 the priory made exchanges in Sharnbrook, probably to make a more convenient demesne. Thus emerged Ouse manor. However it had been formed partly from the honour of Bedford and partly from that of Boulogne. The Beauchamps, overlords of the Druels at Colworth, made no demur; but from the honour of Boulogne (of which Toft manor was held) there was an attempt to make representatives of the priory attend the honour court at Wyham in Lincolnshire, which attempt the priory successfully resisted. In seven cases elsewhere the priory's property came to be known as a

---

21 *V.C.H.* i, 375. For Ruxox, see also J. L. Ward Petley, *Flitwick*, 118–21.
22 *B.H.R.S.* xxii, 58–67.
23 E.g., *B.H.R.S.* xvii, *passim*.

24 Dunstable Priory bought several villeins: *B.H.R.S.* x, 77, 117, 154–5, 224; in at least two cases they were allowed to serve freely: x, 160.
25 *B.H.R.S.* xliii, 286–311.

manor. Cartularies have not survived for all Bedfordshire monasteries (ch. 4), and where they have the relevant entries are not always easy to follow; however, some manor-building can be disentangled.[26] The king in 1279 regulated the acquisition of land by monasteries, but the effect was that a monastery had to pay for a permit to acquire lands from a would-be donor. Something similar happened with Bedfordshire estates of over a dozen monasteries outside the county.[27]

While it is known that in the 13th cent. the Ramsey Abbey manors were exploited for markets both distant and local (ch. 8), there is little firsthand information for the smaller estates of the Bedfordshire monasteries. It is probable that they were managed by bailiffs supervised by the monks,[28] like the Templars' small manor of Swanton (ch. 8). Sheepfarming was carried on by religious houses as by other landowners (Dunstable Priory's heavy losses in sheep in a bad season in the Peak district, where the priory had some property, are mentioned in 1243);[29] and was successfully practised by the Cistercians, whose newly-cleared lands came into full production as the wool trade was expanding. The problems of 14th cent. agriculture hit the monastic estates as much as those of the laymen; and reduced the supply of lay brothers; and it is probable that the monasteries too eventually turned to leasing their estates.

Building extensions, the difficulties of estate management, and inefficient administration within the religious house were not the only causes of occasional financial troubles. The duty of giving hospitality was a burden to a monastery near a road, as the nuns of Harrold found (they suffered also in flood-time from their proximity to the Ouse).[30] Guests could be very inconsiderate, as at Dunstable in 1276, when the king's falconers came back to the priory one evening, having had rather too much to drink, beat up the porter, and in the resulting scuffle killed a chaplain, so that the prior rang the great bell to summon the townsfolk to help.[31]

MONASTERIES AND VICARAGES

Another form of monastic endowment was advowsons. These were con-

---

[26] Cf. Dunstable Priory at Segenhoe in Ridgmont (*B.H.R.S.* x, 70–2, 110, 125, 138, 153, 186, 199, 212–3; *V.C.H.* iii, 321–2). After the lord of the manor, Simon de Wahull, had given a lead, there were grants from many other persons, and thus arose the priory's manor of Segenhoe. Something of the kind lies behind this priory's small manors at Flitwick, Wingfield, Caldecote in Houghton Regis, Barworth in Studham, Wadlowes in Toddington and Upbury in Pulloxhill. Cf. also Warden Abbey: Putnoe, Warden, Southill, Henlow and Meppershall. Probably those monasteries for which we have no cartularies built up their manors in like manner: Chicksands at Keysoe, Cople, Hasells in Sandy, Campton and Stotfold; Woburn Abbey at Herne in Toddington; Caldwell Priory at Girtford; Bushmead Priory at Bushmead;

and little Beaulieu Priory at St. Mark's in Haynes.
[27] The Lanthony manors in Arlesey and Henlow belonging to Lanthony Priory, Mon.; Notley manor in Sundon belonging to Notley Priory in Bucks.; a Dunton manor belonging to Holywell Priory, Middlesex; an Eyeworth one to St. Helen's Priory, London; and Mosbury in Everton belonging to Stratford Langthorne Abbey in Essex. The order of Knights Templar had Swanton manor in Harrold; Temple Hills in Sharnbrook; Covington fee in Pertenhall; and a manor in Millbrook; the Hospitallers had Polehanger manor, Meppershall and manors in Kempston and Langford.
[28] Knowles, *Religious orders*. 37.
[29] *V.C.H.* i, 372.
[30] *V.C.H.* iii, 65–6.
[31] *V.C.H.* i, 374.

sidered the patron's property; and perhaps it was natural for him to entrust a parish to a religious house in which he was interested, especially as it was an inexpensive gift for him. Perhaps for this reason the Augustinian priories, which were later than other houses, received most advowsons; besides the gift might seem appropriate to an order of canons. Newnham Priory had 15 advowsons, and Dunstable Priory 12. Dunstable did in fact appoint canons to at least some livings; thus canon Richard of Caudewell was presented to Flitwick in 1263;[32] but there were arguments against such practice. The austere Cistercian houses, on the other hand, were not supposed to accept advowsons, and in fact Warden Abbey had only one – Warden; and Woburn Abbey one – Woburn (or Birchmore). In all, nearly half the benefices in Bedfordshire (55) were handed over to local monasteries, and most of the rest to monasteries outside the county, leaving only just over 20 in lay hands.

These grants of advowsons were not always securely held. St. Albans Abbey had a long struggle to make good its claim to Luton; this powerful abbey not only desired Luton church and its 5 hides, but was also uneasy that they were after the conquest in the hands of a layman; it succeeded by 1154.[33] The nuns of Harrold took years to make good their claim to Stevington, given them by Baldwin of Ardres about 1140.[34] Two advowsons given by Simon de Beauchamp to Newnham Priory were disputed; and letters he wrote to the bishop on the subject show how a baron conducted his correspondence. "Simon de Beauchamp to his most holy father Hugh, Bishop of Lincoln, greeting! Be it known to your holiness that, when I founded the church of St. Paul of Newnham, I also gave the canons among others Aspley church. I did temporarily grant my vill of Aspley to my knight, Roger of Salford, until I could assign him for his service land elsewhere, but not the advowson; from which your holiness will know that no one but the canons of Newnham has ever had from me or my ancestors any right to Aspley church. Farewell!"[35] Or again: "Be it known to your holiness that I am very much surprised that Henry de Port calls himself patron of Hatley church and presents a parson to it. That church belongs to my canons of Newnham by ancient right. I ask your holiness to see that nothing is done contrary to my right and that of my canons, whose right of patronage I neither can nor will see diminished."[36]

However, apart from these struggles to keep hold of an advowson once given, the system had the drawback that there was no safeguarding of the needs of the parish or of the parish priest; and that a greater or smaller amount of the income might be deflected to the monastery, while the parish was left with a poorly paid chaplain. After the Lateran Council of 1215 the bishops of Lincoln were among the earliest to put matters on a better footing in one parish after

---

[32] L.R.S. xx, 191.
[33] V.C.H. ii, 356, from Gesta Abbatum; told in more detail by Dyer-Stygall-Dony, op.cit., 56–8. The 5 hides became Dallow manor.
[34] B.H.R.S. xxxii, 1–26. See also Thorney Abbey's suit about Bolnhurst, 1113–51, V.C.H. i, 314.
[35] B.H.R.S. xliii, 20.
[36] B.H.R.S. xliii, 393.

another. The process seems to have extended throughout the 13th century. They obliged monasteries, as rectors of the living, to appoint a deputy (or vicar), who must receive a minimum provision.[37]

The details of early vicarages are much briefer than later ones. Thus the value of Cople, ordained by Bishop Hugh of Welles early in the 13th cent., was only 4 marks; the vicar was to have all altar dues, and the prioress of Chicksands was to find him a suitable house by the church.[38] Much more information is given for Wootton, ordained by Bishop Gravesend in 1273; besides his house and the altar dues, the vicar was to have all tithes except those of corn and hay (i.e., he was to have the small or vicarial tithes of lambs, poultry, fruit etc.); 12a. of land (4 in each field), and $1\frac{1}{2}$ a. meadow in Smethemade; he was however to be responsible for paying the usual 7s. 6d. in lieu of hospitality to the archdeacon on his visitation.[39]

There were far more clergy in proportion to people than to-day, though many of them were only in minor orders, and probably these were paid little and carried out very minor functions. Bishop Grosseteste in 1238 said that each church, in addition to its incumbent, ought to have a deacon and sub-deacon where funds permitted; and if funds did not permit this, at least one clerk to assist in the divine office. Whether or not he achieved this in his time, later the practice was different. In the late 14th cent. a clergy list[40] shows that about 20 parishes had a single priest; these included Aspley Guise, Bromham, Eyeworth and Keysoe. At Luton there were the vicar, 8 chaplains and 5 clerks; and at Biggleswade the vicar, 8 chaplains and 6 clerks. Other parishes had anything from one to ten assistant clergy. The distribution does not seem to go by population, for Roxton, which had 10 assistant clergy (and another on the list but suspended for complicity in murder) had before the Black Death only 36 taxpayers to Bromham's 68.[41]

Only occasionally do we get some personal details of a cleric. Thomas Hervy of Thurleigh,[42] who died 1382/3, was not typical. Thurleigh was a rectory worth £10 p.a. (most vicarages were about half this); but he was not the rector – he was a distinguished man who held various important posts. He left his red vestment and great missal to Thurleigh, his green and white vestments to two other parishes. He possessed a mazer, silver plate, brass vessels, a blue bed and a green bed; and he left £4 for the poor of Thurleigh, and 100 marks to build a chapel in honour of the Holy Trinity in the churchyard above the bodies of his mother and himself. Sometimes there are references to priests in trouble – in any large group of people there must be an occasional unsatisfactory character. Adam, vicar of Oakley, chased a parishioner into the church with a drawn knife in 1361; and Robert Ouseflet, rector of Eversholt, in 1356 from his rectory shot arrows at men coming to arrest him.[43] Perhaps a more typical priest was John Lother, chaplain of

[37] R. A. R. Hartridge, *Vicarages. V.C.H.* i, 315–7.
[38] Rot. Welles (*Cant. & York Soc.*), 185.
[39] *L.R.S.* xx, 197.
[40] *B.H.R.S.* i, 27–61.

[41] *Two Beds. subsidies*, 120, 126.
[42] *B.H.R.S.* xiv, 94–5.
[43] *B.H.R.S.* xlviii.

Leighton Buzzard, who was set upon in 1314 when carrying the consecrated wafer to a sick woman.[44]

FRIARS AND UNIVERSITIES

In spite of the responsibilities which devolved on abbots and priors, men and women anxious to devote their lives to God still entered the cloister. Monasteries also continued to be centres of learning. Some MS. books formerly in the libraries of Bedfordshire religious houses still survive,[45] and show that the religious studied the early fathers, such as Origen, Jerome and Augustine; from Woburn Abbey a Cicero and a Boethius survive; and Warden Abbey had Bede and Ailred. Some education was provided for others. So far as is known, the school at Bedford connected with Newnham Priory continued; and also that at Dunstable.[46] The small Bushmead Priory planned to set up a school in 1332, but the energetic canon, Richard of Little Staughton, who applied to the bishop for the requisite licence (and who incidentally was probably responsible for the writing of the cartulary) died in the Black Death just after he had become prior.

Two more recent developments now challenged the dominance of the old monastic ideal – the friars and the universities. To some the monastery seemed too secure, too ordered, too divorced from the people. "He has shown me the way of simplicity," said St. Francis, "and I do not want you to mention to me any other rule." Why not renounce all, and go out into the centres of population as Christ had done? St. Dominic, an Augustinian canon, wished to give the people more advanced teaching, since so many parish priests were little better instructed than their flocks. The Dominicans or black friars landed in England in 1221; the Franciscans or grey friars in 1224.

A few years later the Franciscans reached Bedford. Their fame preceded them, and in 1232 two young canons escaped from Dunstable Priory through a window to join the Franciscans at Oxford, where the chief settlement was. They were brought back and did penance, but were promised that, if after a year they remained of the same mind, they would be allowed to go.

To explain the Franciscan position at Oxford, it must be recalled that in the previous century Oxford had become a centre of study or university; and it may be noted here that, when in the 13th cent. the earliest halls of residence emerged, it was Devorgilla Balliol, lady of Kempston manor, who in her widowhood drew up in 1282 statutes for Balliol College, which had been founded by herself and her husband John.[47] In 1284 the sons of John Durant, the Dunstable merchant, were at Oxford;[48] they must of course have taken minor orders and have had interests different from those of their father. At Oxford the work of the Franciscans developed in a way not foreseen by St. Francis, for they made notable contributions to

---

[44] B.H.R.S. xxxii, 49.
[45] N. R. Ker, *Medieval libraries*, 51, 60, 77, 129, 193, 205.
[46] Knowles, *Monastic order*, p.492

[47] C. E. Mallet, *History of the university*, i, 99; V.C.H. ii, 30.
[48] *Ann.Mon.* iii, 313.

intellectual life and thought. The Franciscan friaries in England were eventually grouped under seven custodies, of which Oxford was one, and Bedford came under Oxford.

Elsewhere in the country, however, the work of the Franciscans consisted of humble preaching and teaching on the lines of their master. They were in Bedford by 1238 when the king gave them 10 oak stumps for fuel.[49] Friaries, like leper hospitals, were built outside towns because land was cheaper there, and a small friary was built to the west of the then town. Later, about 1280, Edward I at Biggleswade discussed with the Provincial, Robert Cross, how best he could help the friars in general, and Cross made some request for the Oxford friary;[50] the king's gift in 1280 to the Bedford Franciscans of 3 oaks from Weybridge forest in Huntingdonshire for the building of their church may have been another result of this conversation.[51] The Bedford church was consecrated in 1295.[52] The Franciscans' numbers grew, and when in 1300 14 Bedford friars were presented to the Bishop when he was at Elstow to be licensed to hear confessions, he thought it was too many, and would license only four, Simon de Witton the Guardian (or prior) and three others.[53]

Extension of the Bedford premises followed in 1310 and 1353.[54] It is possible that there was a Provincial Chapter at Bedford in 1324.[55] More than one Provincial of the order seems to have come from Bedfordshire, since they chose to be buried at Bedford: John de Rodyngton in 1348 and William Tichemerch c. 1371.[56]

The modification of the original rule of poverty to allow even very poor huts and the simplest wooden church caused some heart-searching among friars. Abroad some resisted, and two were condemned and burnt at Avignon in 1354. A fragment of a document about their trial has been preserved in the binding of a Bedfordshire register.[57] Did the Bedford Franciscans have heart-searching too? At all events their standing must have been high, for when in 1375 the Minister General of the Franciscan Order came to England, it was at Bedford that he held the Provincial Chapter on Passion Sunday, and he stayed three days in Bedford.[58] The work of the Franciscans seems to have been still expanding, for a few years later in 1397 the Bedford site was enlarged by over 2 acres.[59] Bedford was not the county's only Franciscan link, for the Aldgate friars in 1392 obtained Potton rectory for a small annual rent.[60]

---

[49] *Cal.Cl.R. 1237–42*, p.62. See also *V.C.H.* i, 395; iii, 22; and A. R. Martin, *Franciscan architecture*, 154–9. I am much indebted to the Fr. Commissary Provincial, the Rev. Justin McLoughlin, O.F.M., for help with this section. The statement by Leland (*Itin.*, ii, 165) that the Bedford friary was founded by Mabel Pateshull seems probably due to a misreading of a tomb inscription; the only Mabel Pateshull known is 14th cent.

[50] A. G. Little, *Studies in English Franciscan history*, 14, 223.

[51] *Cal.Cl.R.. 1279–88*, p.51.
[52] *V.C.H.* i, 395.
[53] Little, *Franciscan papers*, 230–5.
[54] *V.C.H.* iii, 22.
[55] Little, *op.cit.*, 213.
[56] Emden, *Biographical register of the university of Oxford to 1500*, iii, 1584, 1875.
[57] *B.H.R.S.* xxxviii, 1–11.
[58] *E.H.R.* lxxii, 170–8.
[59] *V.C.H.* iii, 22.
[60] *V.C.H.* ii, 239.

The Dominicans or black friars arrived in Dunstable in 1259[61], and the king directed the priory to help them settle there. It was rather unwillingly that the canons did so, for it seemed a challenge to their own ability to provide for Dunstable. Later the king gave them timber for their church. By now, both orders of friars were finding it necessary to have a house, however small and poor, and a church, as headquarters. The Dunstable friary was on the west side of South Street. While they were building their church at Dunstable, the prioress of Markyate, Agnes Gobion, made them a daily allowance of bread. The rule of absolute poverty brought its own dangers of absolute privation; and when the prioress thought the immediate occasion had passed with the completion of the church, and was withdrawing the allowance, the Dominicans begged the Pope to order its continuance, and he complied.

On the whole, canons and friars at Dunstable co-operated; prior William visited the Dominicans in 1277; and in 1282, when a parishioner desired to be buried in the Dominican church, the occasion passed off without trouble. However, in 1287 the canons uneasily took the precaution of getting their porter to buy the next house to the friary, lest the friars should want to extend. Adam of Biscot, vicar of Luton, joined the black friars.[62] They seem to have been popular in Dunstable – friars were both expert and even entertaining preachers – and in 1298 many were making their confessions to them; however in 1311 the bishop himself thought, when 10 additional friars were presented to him to be licensed to hear confession, there were rather too many.

A Dominican provincial chapter was held at Dunstable in 1332, when the king gave the friars £15 to help with the commissariat for the 3-day event. Dominican priories were grouped in visitations, and Dunstable came under Cambridge.

CHANTRIES

The founding of chantries[63] – i.e., the provision for daily or weekly masses for a private intention, usually the souls of particular individuals – began in the 13th cent. and became increasingly popular. It was something the small man could do, and it could be personal to himself or his family, or to a revered friend; thus a late 14th cent. prior of Dunstable, Thomas Marshall, arranged for one for his parents.[64] The founder could draw up his own rules for the chantry. A special building was not needed (though he could provide this if he could afford it); when in 1325 Simon Wulston founded a chantry for the soul of Geoffrey le Smyth, he arranged for it to be celebrated in the chapel which had been built in 1295 on Biddenham bridge.[65]

The earliest steps in this direction were to ask a religious house to celebrate

---

[61] The best account is by A. R. Martin, *Jnal.Brit. Archaeolog.Ass.*, n.s., xxxiii, 321–33, followed by an account of the 1924 excavations, 334–42 by T. W. Bagshawe. See also *V.C.H.* i, 359, 374 n, 395–6.
[62] H. Cobbe, *Luton church*, 122.

[63] Earlier the word was used for any service performed by a private chaplain; K. L. Wood-Legh, *Perpetual chantries in Britain*, 1–2.
[64] *V.C.H.* i, 325.
[65] C.R.O.: TW 103.

such services, as at Dunstable in 1234, 1236 and 1272;[66] or at St. Leonard's Hospital, Bedford, in 1288.[67] At Elstow in 1272 Ivota built a chapel to St. Helen in the abbey churchyard.[68] It became customary to appoint a special priest for a chantry. When the last of the Eaton Socon Beauchamps, Roger, founded two chantries at Eaton Socon and at Sandy in the mid-14th cent., he provided the following equipment for the services: "one suitable chalice, price 13s. 4d., one set of vestments, price 10s., 2 pairs of towels for the altar, price 18d., one towel, price 6d., one missal, price 20s." For the priest's domestic arrangements he provided a brass pot and a saucepan, price 5s.; and he did not neglect the farming outfit which the priest would need to till the land with which the founder had endowed the chantry: "1 horse, price 6s. 8d.; 1 ox, price 8s.; 1 waggon and 1 plough with all the harness, price 5s."[69] If the priest became ill, he was to be maintained for the rest of his life, but to make what prayers and devout intercessions he could. Edmund Bulstrode of Flitwick in 1355 laid down that the priest must give 6 months' notice of his intention to resign.[70] At Segenhoe, Ridgmont, a chantry for various members of the Grey family was founded in 1323.[71] Religious houses were still sometimes asked to undertake or to supervise chantries; Newnham Priory in 1349 agreed that a canon should say mass daily for Henry Arnold in St. Paul's church, Bedford, while he lived, and after his death, within the priory; if by chance the mass was omitted, two should be said the next day.[72] In all, about 17 Bedfordshire chantries are known to have been founded in the 14th cent.

THE MYSTICS

If we seek direct contact with religious thought in the 14th cent., it is most readily found in the writings of the English medieval mystics between 1330 and 1400: Richard Rolle of Yorkshire; the anonymous author of *The Cloud of Unknowing*, who may have come from the north midlands; Walter Hilton of Nottinghamshire; and others. In the days of handwritten books, new writings spread slowly, and how soon or how widely they were read in Bedfordshire is not known. Walter Hilton's *Scale of Perfection* was in the next century often in the hands of Margaret Beaufort,[73] and may have been known to her step-brother, John St. John of Bletsoe. Walter Hilton comments thus on the parable of the woman and the lost coin: "This groat will not be found so easily as it is thought, for this work is not of one hour, nor of one day, but many days and years, with much sweat and swink of body and travail of soul. If thou cease not, but seek busily, sigh and sorrow deeply, mourn stilly, and stoop low, till thine eyes water for anguish and for pain, for that thou hast lost thy treasure Jesus, at the last (when his will is) well shalt thou find thy groat Jesus."[74]

[66] *V.C.H.* i, 325–6; *Ann.Mon.* iii, 141, 144, 255.
[67] F. A. Page-Turner, *Chantry Certificates*, 68.
[68] *V.C.H.* iii, 283.
[69] Wood-Legh, *op.cit.*, 51, 53, 217.
[70] *Op.cit.*, 72.
[71] Page-Turner, *op.cit.*, 78.
[71] Wood-Legh, *op.cit.*, 130, 280.
[73] Knowles, *The English mystical tradition*, 118.
[74] *Ibid.*, 117.

Perhaps Margaret and John also read the *Cloud of Unknowing*. "Lift up thine heart unto God with a meek stirring of love . . . At the first time when thou dost it, thou findest but a darkness and as it were a cloud of unknowing, thou knowest not what, saving that thou feelest in thy will a naked intent unto God . . . If ever thou shalt see him or feel him as it may be here, it must always be in this cloud and in this darkness."[75]

[75] *Ibid.*, 77.

10 – TOWNS AND TRADE, 1300–1400

BEDFORD

Bedford in 1300, with its charters from the king and its elected officer or mayor, seemed set for development. It was desirable to get the town's charters confirmed by each new king – they were suspended in the time of Edward III until a fine was paid in 1331 for the restoration of liberties. In future the charters were inspected and confirmed by each new king except Henry V.

But in fact Bedford was not expanding. The lack of a resident baronial family probably diminished trade, but the causes went deeper. The depression which was affecting agriculture influenced the town as well. Taxation returns show 116 taxpayers in 1309 but only 72 in 1332; and though tax was heavier in the latter year it produced less return than in the former.[1]

Whether townsmen went to the Hundred Years War is not known. In 1346 (the year of Crecy) Bedford paid £12 to furnish three substitute men-at-arms.[2]

Bedford was now represented in parliament by burgesses – in that of 1295 by John Cullebere (see ch. 5) and Simon de Holland. Surnames of some later burgesses call to mind the trades carried on in the town. There was Simon le Tanner, 1302; Reginald Spycer, 1348; John Spycer, 1365; Roger Peyntour, 1368; William Brasiere, 1371; John Glover, 1378; and Robert Baker, 1379. Other tradesmen's names found in tax returns are Taylour, Roper, Drapere, Parchiminer, Scriptor (scrivener) and Aurifaber (goldsmith); Gilbert the goldsmith had brooches and rings stolen in 1314.[3] Many townsmen bear names which indicate that they had come to Bedford from surrounding villages (Blunham, Stevington, Wilden, Wootton, Stagsden, Keysoe, Radwell, Mogerhanger, Ravensden, Bletsoe, Budna, Rowney); and even from places outside the county, such as Yardley, Ely, Catworth, Wollaston, Gamlingay, Amersham and Leicester. Often a past or future mayor acted as one of the town's representatives in parliament: John atte Wal (see John super Muro, ch. 5) was mayor 1313 and 1319, and represented Bedford in 1307 and 1313; Simon Cullebere, mayor 1327 and 1330, represented Bedford in 1327 and 1337; Henry Arnold, who represented Bedford in 1336, was mayor several times.[4]

For a reason which is not clear, there was in this period a brush between

---

[1] S. A. H[ervey], *Two Beds. subsidies*, 54, 187. It must be remembered however that tax assessments must be treated with caution – the natural tendency of local assessors being to lower rather than to raise the assessment.

[2] *Schedule of ancient charters*, 6.

[3] *B.H.R.S.* xxxii, 49.

[4] *Corporation yearbook*.

the mayor and the sheriff.[5] The mayor appointed a chaplain to the chapel on Bedford bridge, and the sheriff, claiming to act in the king's name, ejected him and put in another. The town bell was rung, and there was a free fight. The dispute went on for twelve years – the bridge getting steadily worse – till it was settled that the appointment rested with the king, and the pontage, or contributions for bridge upkeep, with the goodmen of Bedford.

In the Black Death in 1349 the town seems to have suffered very severely, as might be expected from its little close-packed streets round St. Paul's church. All the clergy died, except the priest at All Hallows, and he resigned; the priors of Newnham and Caldwell died; and so did the master of St. Leonard's hospital. Perhaps the contemporary description of a continental town is true of Bedford; many died in the open streets by day or night; sometimes it was by the stench that neighbours were first aware of death in the next house, and dragged the corpses to the threshold and fetched boards to carry them on. Often as a priest walked with a cross in front of a corpse, three or four processions with biers fell in behind. Great pits were dug, where the dead were packed in layers like bales in a ship's hold, and covered thinly with earth.[6] The effect of the pestilence in Bedford and the surrounding villages must have diminished trade in the following years.

However, one trade that was expanding was that in wool. The Henry Arnold mentioned above founded a chantry in 1349 (ch. 9), perhaps fearing that he would not survive the pestilence; but he did, for he was subsequently both mayor and M.P. He was a wool merchant, and was one of six in Bedfordshire and adjacent counties who negotiated a large purchase of wool for the king in 1337.[7] In the 14th cent. weavers are known in many Bedfordshire villages; fullers at Barton, Biggleswade, Eaton Socon, Leighton Buzzard and Pulloxhill; fulling-mills (a new invention) at Gt. Barford as early as 1228 and at Stevington in the next century; and dyers at Bedford, Cranfield and Leighton; but these were probably all supplying local demand for cloth. Henry Arnold apparently bought up surplus wool for export (the national export was at this time over 30,000 sacks p.a.); as did John Curteys of Wymington (d. 1391).[8] The wool trade went through a prescribed depot or centre of distribution, called a staple; here toll was collected and quality enforced; and through it the government could control the trade when it wished to do so for purposes of foreign policy. After 1363 the staple was normally at Calais, and John Curteys was at one time mayor of the Calais staple.

In the mid-14th cent. there are known to have been one or two embroiderers. There was a demand for embroidery, especially for church purposes; probably the best work was obtained from London; but an embroiderer called John de

---

[5] V.C.H. iii, 30.
[6] G. Coulton, Black Death, 17–18, citing Boccaccio.
[7] V.C.H. ii, 91.
[8] V.C.H. iii, 118.

Maydenbury is known at Ford End 1338–51; and others in 1351 and 1361.[9]

The confirmation of Bedford's charters by Richard II in 1396[10] seems to have been obtained economically as a reward for Bedford's stability in the revolt of 1381 – "the good demeanour of mayor and burgesses who have manfully resisted the malefactors, late insurgents against our peace" (ch. 8 and below). It gives more detail than do previous charters. With the mayor it links the bailiffs; how early this office began is uncertain; it may have carried on from the days of the king's bailiff, the number being increased to two as the town grew. From early in the 14th cent. the names of many bailiffs are known, such as John Koc and John Knotting in 1336,[11] for it was usual for any transaction relating to property in the town to be witnessed by mayor and bailiffs. Richard II's charter states that there must be no interference with the market, unless the mayor and bailiffs are remiss in executing the office of the market, in which case they could be fined by the king. No one not of the merchant gild should sell retail in Bedford (wine is especially mentioned); and no one even of the gild should expose goods for sale till toll had been paid, under pain of forfeiture. Perhaps some members had evaded toll by going out to meet other merchants coming with merchandise by land or water, for this evasion is expressly forbidden. Twice a year the mayor and bailiffs could hold view of frankpledge (ch. 6, 11); this supervision, which had originally been carried out by the sheriff, was now frequently exercised in country districts by lords of manors.

By 1400 the town was divided into twelve wards, each with its constable.

DUNSTABLE

The 14th cent. trade recession was slower in hitting Dunstable. In 1309 Dunstable paid more in tax than Bedford (£22 as against £20), and there were 170 taxpayers. But by 1332 these had shrunk to 114, and the product of the tax to £13.[12] At Dunstable too the tax returns yield names like Markaunt, Barbour, Taylour, Glovere, Tannere, Whittawer, Spicer, Fruttere, Ropere, Coupere, Masoun, Tylere, Peyntour, Parcheminer; while besides miller, carpenter, shepherd and sawyer, there are fowler and falconer. Some Dunstable men are called Battlesden, Chalton, Hockliffe, Hulcote, Kensworth, Marston, Sewell, Crawley, Toddington, Stanbridge, Pilling, Shefford, Stotfold, Wilstead and Wootton; while others have come from outside the county, from Cheddington and Dagnall.

One favourable factor Dunstable had which Bedford lacked: its continued visits from royalty. Edward II's queen, Isabella, stayed there in 1326. Edward III came for two tournaments. For that in 1329, some of his retinue stayed at the premises of the late John Durant (ch. 5), which presumably were on a scale to match the status of that wealthy merchant, but now needed a good deal of repair

9 C.R.O., TW 64, 74, 254. For English secular embroidery, see M. Jourdain's *History*.
10 *Schedule of records*, 7–15.
11 C.R.O., TW 63.
12 *Two Beds. subsidies*, 19, 149.

to be brought up to a standard to accommodate the royal train; for 7 carpenters, 6 tilers and 2 plasterers worked for 9 days, using 1,000 tiles, 1000 laths and over 4,000 nails;[13] the house had its own well.[14] At the tournament of 1341 "the more part of the lords and ladies of the land were present" for "a great juste . . . with other counterfeited feats of warre".[15]

From the Black Death Dunstable seems to have suffered surprisingly little. The chronicle refers to it in passing as "the time of the pestilence". Prior John of London resigned in 1348; prior Roger of Gravenhurst, then elected, died in 1351, but not apparently of the epidemic.

The priors of Dunstable continued to uphold the priory's privileged position when it was queried by the king's judges. Thus in 1330 such an enquiry produced an account of the exercise of special rights over many years.[16] These included the hanging of offenders in the previous reign; and the taking over for a year and a day the houses of convicted felons. Such houses are listed as being in the East End, the North End, or the South End. Once a Coventry merchant is mentioned – William le Mercere. The jury who reported on the matter said that neither sheriff nor escheator had intermeddled in Dunstable, only the prior's bailiffs. However the prior's special position continued to be questioned at intervals, in 1341, 1366 and 1375.[17] Undesirable vagrants and squatters tended to settle on the town's outskirts, resulting in a high rate of crime (so it was alleged in 1366).[18]

Neither did the prior yield ground to the burgesses, who made no further progress towards self-government, notwithstanding that to one parliament (1311) they sent representatives, and that Dunstable had its own coroner (ch. 6). Perhaps one reason why Dunstable did not again send burgesses to parliament was that to this right they did not attach importance; few 14th cent. towns valued it, for burgesses' expenses had to be paid. But they were always on the defensive against the priory. When in 1366 there was a query as to the interpretation of the arbitration award of 1230 (ch. 5), which limited the rate of fine which the prior could exact, the king's council removed the limitation, which even in those days of slowly-changing values was somewhat out-of-date;[19] and this rankled.

It was in 1381, when news came of outbreaks in southern England that active trouble broke out. Near at hand there were risings at Berkhamsted and Hemel Hempstead; and at St. Albans the abbot was forced to grant a charter. Some Dunstable merchants who were at St. Albans market on the Saturday thought their chance had come. That evening they held a council at Dunstable, and chose Thomas Hobbes as spokesman. Since rumour had it that the young king, Richard II, was in sympathy with the rebels, Hobbes resolved to take a high line and represent himself as the king's emissary.

---

[13] V.C.H. iii, 354.
[14] Ann.Mon. iii, 297–8. Dunstable wells were very deep; see B.H.R.S. Survey ii, 9.
[15] V.C.H. iii, 354.

[16] Cal.Excheq.R. (in press), no. 932.
[17] V.C.H. iii, 357.
[18] Op.cit., 352.
[19] Op.cit., 359.

The prior, Thomas Marshall, who also had heard what was happening elsewhere, and with whom two landowners (Croyser and Bateman: see ch. 8) had taken refuge, thought it best to be diplomatic, and bowed to Hobbes as if he were in fact the king's emissary. "The king commands that you make a charter of liberties for his burgesses of Dunstable, as they had in the time of Henry I", said Hobbes. At first the prior could not bring himself to give way so far. But considering what had taken place in London and St. Albans, and influenced by the timorous Croyser and Bateman, he caused a charter to be prepared. Its exact contents are not known. One suggested clause was that butchers and fishmongers from neighbouring villages should not be allowed to sell in Dunstable. This caused some outcry in the mob, among whom were apparently some Luton men, who felt that this was aimed at them. However, the men of Dunstable would not give way on the point. At last the charter was completed and sealed.

But already elsewhere the rebellion was being put down with severity. Almost at once Dunstable was obliged to give up its charter, which was cancelled. The prior showed magnanimity, and made great efforts in time and money to secure from the king's judges lenience for the Dunstable ringleaders, none of whom was executed.[20]

Just as Dunstable, in spite of vying with Bedford in economic importance, was never to secure self-government from the priory, so its religious services too were subordinate to the priory's observances. The parishioners had their altar to St. John the Baptist in the north aisle of the nave; and in the late 14th cent. they wanted to have another altar to the Holy Trinity. This the prior found an obstruction to his services. Again in 1392 there was recourse to arbitration. It was ruled that the priory was to have processions as usual in the lower part of the church, and if there was a parish service at the same time, it must cease till the canons had returned to the choir. The parishioners were to have all normal services in their part of the church, but at the six chief feasts they were to attend in the chancel.[21]

MARKET TOWNS

The market towns, Leighton, Luton and Biggleswade, show a decline in the number of taxpayers between 1309 and 1332 comparable with that in Bedford and Dunstable: Leighton, 145–136; Luton, 163–114; Biggleswade, 37–19.[22] Similarly in Leighton and Biggleswade the higher rate of tax at the latter date produced a smaller return: Leighton, £18–£15; Biggleswade, £6–£5; only in Luton was there a slight rise, £19–£21; but at Luton an extensive fire in 1336 reduced the town considerably.[23] There is difficulty in making an overall comparison of these urban centres, for the Leighton return includes what were then the hamlets of Billington, Eggington and Heath, though not Stanbridge; and the

[20] Op.cit., 359–60.
[21] Op.cit., 360.
[22] Two Beds. subsidies, 22, 32, 68; 112, 151, 162.
[23] Cal.Cl.R., 1333–7, p.691; Inq.Non., 11–22. The

number of houses stated in 1340 to be vacant was 200; but in 1671 there were only 228 in the township and about 200 in the hamlets; B.H.R.S. xvi.

Luton return includes all its hamlets (Limbury, Leagrave, Stopsley, Hyde etc.); so that in both cases a good deal of agricultural land is included, and neither town is as near Bedford and Dunstable as a trading centre as the figures seem to imply. On the other hand, in the tax returns Biggleswade is entered separately from Stratton and Holme, which makes its entry small; even allowing for this, it must have been much more modest than Leighton and Luton.

All three were still under the influence of their lords. As the main manor of Leighton was held by Fontevrault Abbey, while there was war with France during the 14th cent. it was taken over by the king, or was temporarily granted out by him; the prebendal manor was still held by the prebendary; and various smaller manors were in other hands. At Luton the main manor had been much divided; of the many smaller manors, that of Luton Hoo had been held for many years by the Hoo family (who had sometimes represented the county in parliament – ch. 7); and that of Someries by a family of that name. Biggleswade was still held by the bishop of Lincoln. Bishop Dalderby in 1302 granted an indulgence to those contributing towards Biggleswade bridge, so the first bridge here over the Ivel seems to have been built then.[24]

The Black Death was worst in the two bigger towns. Luton and Leighton lost more than one vicar in that year; and Biggleswade lost another vicar in a later plague year, 1369. The shortage of labour caused such demands that two Streatley villeins, Geoffrey and Stephen atte Well, took jobs as ploughman and harvester in Luton at inflated wages, and were prosecuted before the labour justices (ch. 8).[25]

There is no record of disturbances at Leighton or Biggleswade in 1381, nor in Luton itself, though some Luton men joined in the agitation at Dunstable (see above). Six Luton men, including a tailor and a weaver, forfeited goods for the part they played.[26]

Of all three, the only manorial records which survive for the 14th cent. are the court rolls of the main manor of Leighton Buzzard from 1393. These show more cases than in the normal rural manor, as would be expected from the extra population; and several cases of debt arising in a trading community.[27]

At Toddington in 1386 Thomas Pever obtained the grant of a 3-day fair.[28]

[24] E. Gervoise, *Ancient bridges.*
[25] *V.C.H.* ii, 89.
[26] *Loc.cit.*

[27] C.R.O., KK 619.
[28] J. H. Blundell, *Toddington*, pp.180–1. See also C.R.O., X 95/390.

II – ADMINISTRATION AND JUSTICE, 1300–1400

MANOR COURT

The court most familiar to the majority of people for most of the middle ages was the manor court, meeting every few weeks and presided over normally by the lord's steward. At Chalgrave in the 13th cent. it was summoned by the bailiff, and in 1279 one tenant, William, objected that a summons on Saturday night was not sufficient notice for attendance on Monday morning. The place of meeting is sometimes given as in the church.[1]

Today's clear distinction between private and public affairs did not apply, and the business dealt with covered a wide range. It cannot be thoroughly illustrated from the surviving records: it was a long while before records of manor courts were written down at all. At first what was committed to writing was very brief indeed (one court of the little manor of Eggington[2] at the beginning of the 14th cent. covers parchment measuring less than 5 x 5 in.), and not till the 15th cent., when the long slow decline of the manor has definitely begun, are manor court rolls really detailed (ch. 13).

Matters of straightforward estate administration arising between the lord and his tenants, such as repairs, are dealt with. Usually the lord supplied the timber and the tenant the labour: thus at Podington in 1383[3] it was reported that John Barker's barn had collapsed; he was to mend it within six months' time (All Saints' day), or he would be fined 20s. Changes of tenancy are recorded, giving the names of outgoing and incoming tenants, but seldom much information on the terms of tenure, which are at most described as "at the lord's will and according to the custom of the manor", thus safeguarding both parties. Usually the incoming tenant is the son or widow of a deceased one; as at Podington, when Agnes Milner took over a toft and $\frac{1}{2}$ virgate on the death of her husband William, for which she was to pay 16s. 6d. p.a.; but if the late tenant had no heir the holding could go to another, as when John Baker junior took a house and 9 a., rent 9s. p.a., formerly held by Richard Wright; or again the holding might go with a spinster or widow to her (new) husband: as at Blunham in 1318 when William Dybeman "entered a cottage which Sarah Cole formerly had, and has her to wife by the lord's licence, and gives the lord annually for the said cottage a capon at Christmas"; in this case an entry fine of 8s. is noted.[4]

The manor court also dealt with what might be called the agricultural

---

[1] *B.H.R.S.* xxviii, 40.
[2] C.R.O., X 310.

[3] C.R.O., OR 798.
[4] C.R.O., L 26/50.

discipline necessary for semi-communal agriculture. Thus at the same court at Podington, Simon Wedon was fined 2d. for letting a ditch overflow on to the highway; if he did not clean it out in a specified time he would incur a further fine of 40d. John Say and many others had allowed their cattle to stray in the lord's corn, and were fined sums from 2d. upwards, according to the damage done. Straying cattle were liable to be impounded by the bailiff, and John Whiteby had released his from the pound.

Most of the more important manor courts by the 13th or 14th cent. supervised the arrangements for frankpledge formerly supervised by the sheriff (the system by which men were pledged in groups or tithings to keep the peace – ch. 6). In fact, the chief men of the manor, sometimes called homage or jury, were often the chief tithingmen; thus at Podington at the court mentioned the 10 chief tithingmen pointed out that a youth, Robert Roos, was not yet in a tithing, and he was assigned to one and sworn. The assize of ale (ch. 6) was also operated by the chief manor courts, and tasters of ale were appointed to enforce it; on the same occasion at Podington the tasters reported four breaches of this assize, and the offenders were fined sums from 2d. to 2s. 4d. Poaching in the lord's warren was also presented.

Private jurisdiction sometimes went further than this. Prompt public punishment was a great aid in keeping order. There was probably constant recourse to pillory, cucking-stool and stocks, and these get into the record only when a bigger crime is involved. Thus in 1275 Thomas Kek of Oxford, a cut-purse at Shefford market, cut the purse of Walter Sparuwe of Meppershall which contained 7s., and was put in the stocks by the bailiff; afterwards his ear was cut off and he was led outside Shefford – he was found later some miles further along the road murdered.[5] In 1375 William Palmere of Leighton Buzzard escaped from the stocks there, but we hear of it only because he was wanted for the murder of Thomas Wydeshall at Wrestlingworth; he took sanctuary in the church for 13 days, was then outlawed, asked to be given the port of Chester, but the coroner assigned him Dover.[6] In 1368 no less a man than the cellarer of St. Albans Abbey was put in the pillory at Luton market by Philip of Limbury, but the abbot brought proceedings for assault.[7]

In times of national uncertainty and disorder in the 12–13th cents. it had probably been necessary that a lord should go further still. Thus in 1247 there is a reference to "the Earl's prison at Luton" (i.e., Simon de Montfort, Earl of Leicester, then holding Luton manor in right of his wife).[8] Some lords of the more important manors claimed the right to hang thieves caught red-handed; they might not have an actual gallows – the sentence could be carried out on the king's gallows – but sometimes they had; thus in 1247 the abbess of Barking had recently put up a

---

[5] B.H.R.S. xli, 79.
[6] B.H.R.S. xli, 122.

[7] W. Austin, *Luton*, i, 155.
[8] B.H.R.S. xxi, 144.

new gallows at Lidlington.[9] There could be trouble when such rights were claimed by lords of adjoining manors; when Houghton Regis manor changed hands, the new lord in 1273 claimed that they could be exercised only by the lord of the main manor, and his bailiff forcibly removed a felon from the prison of the prior of Dunstable (who held the subsidiary manor of Caldecote), and threw down the prior's gallows.[10]

In 1274 there was a general enquiry as to who was exercising such powers and with what justification. Claims were made by religious houses, such as Dunstable Priory, Elstow Abbey and Ramsey Abbey; and by lay lords, such as Almeric de St. Amand and Baldwin Wake.[11] The practice was usually allowed to continue on payment of a fine, but future encroachment was made more difficult. Centuries later such names linger as Gallows close, corner, field, furlong, hill, way (Cranfield, Harlington, Hulcote, Keysoe, Luton, Pertenhall, Sandy, Shillington, Southill).[12]

THE SHERIFF

The sheriff still continued. As he operated from his own house and held office for a year only, his records have scarcely ever survived, except for 1323-4, when the sheriff was a Buckinghamshire man, Ralf de Wedon, member of an old Amersham family.[13] Ralf was not well, and had to be represented at the exchequer by a deputy; he was "detained by such infirmity that he cannot travel". However, since the disappearance of royal lands in Beds., his financial duties were less than they had once been.

The sheriff's staff consisted of clerks whom he employed to deliver writs (in this particular case the clerks, like the sheriff, were not Bedfordshire men – e.g., William of Berkhamsted); and of a bailiff in each hundred in either county. Sometimes the same bailiff carried on for some years; sometimes a new sheriff appointed a fresh man. They were of modest status; thus the bailiff of Flitt hundred was John of Limbersey, perhaps the man who in 1332 was paying the fairly large sum of 4s. in subsidy (tax) for Houghton Conquest.[14] For Manshead the bailiff was Walter Sporoun, probably of Harlington.[15] For Wixamtree it was John of Budna, perhaps the Beeston man who paid 1s. in subsidy in 1332.[16] Sometimes the king granted or farmed the profits of the hundred court in a particular hundred (Willey was farmed at £2 p.a.), but still the bailiff was accountable to the sheriff. Bedford however had its own two bailiffs; and Dunstable had one bailiff (at this time Giles of Marston, who was paying 1s. 4d. in subsidy).[17]

[9] *B.H.R.S.* xxi, 189.

[10] *V.C.H.* iii, 392; *Ann. Mon.* iii, 261-3. The new Lord of Houghton and of Eaton Bray was Eudo la Zouche of Harringworth, Northants., who had married Millicent, sister of the last male Cantilupe. There seems to have been another gallows on the Kensworth side of the town; cf. C.R.O. DW 289-90 "the alfacre by the galewes".

[11] *Hund. R.*, i, 2-3.

[12] C.R.O., field-names index.

[13] *B.H.R.S.* Qto, iii.

[14] *Two Bedfordshire subsidies*, 171.

[15] *Op.cit.*, 148-9.

[16] *Op.cit.*, 137.

[17] *Op.cit.*, 150.

The bailiff of the hundred was not paid for his office; he paid a fixed sum to the sheriff, and hoped to recoup himself by perquisites and "sheaves, hay and the like."[18] It is not surprising that an enquiry in 1274 brought the response that "the bailiffs oppress the people in many ways". He had many opportunities, as he summoned people to court, distrained on their goods at the sheriff's order, or arranged for carrying duty in the king's service. Thus in 1314, when Edward II was marching to Scotland to fight the battle of Bannockburn, John Graundyn, bailiff of Wixamtree, pretended to commandeer baggage carts in Shefford, and then, on a payment to himself, released them.[19]

The sheriff held the county court. Here he had to fit in both Bedfordshire and Buckinghamshire, so the latter was held the last Wednesday in the month, the former on the following Monday. It was both a court of law and a county meeting. As a court of law it dealt with debt, or with cases brought by men who could not get justice in their lord's court, so long as the value involved did not exceed 40s. Thus in 1332 Henry le Taillour of Ampthill brought a case of debt against Michael le Warde of Bolnoe, but Michael was not there, and order was given for him to be distrained to appear. For the next 3 months there is a similar entry. At last the bailiff reported that Michael had no goods on which he could distrain.[20] In another case of debt brought by Simon of Cranfield against Ralf Bronewyne, the latter's cow was seized.[21]

The county meeting had other functions. Here outlawry was declared. Here the election of coroners took place. Here also took place the election of knights to represent the shire in parliament; it was in no sense like a modern election. It was probably settled by leading people unofficially among themselves, sometimes amicably, sometimes after a trial of strength (cf. ch. 12). Thus there was probably seldom a contest on the day; but if there was, it was decided either by "voices" (i.e. by the candidates' supporters shouting his name, when the sheriff judged the volume of noise); or by show of hands; or if it was a near thing by "view", by the supporters of each candidate collecting in separate groups. From 1430 electors were limited to 40s. freeholders, and the sheriff was entitled to enquire into a voter's qualification.

THE JUSTICE OF THE PEACE

There were now justices of the peace. At first, in times of disturbance, as a special measure a few country gentry were appointed to have particular responsibility for seeing that the peace was kept. This happened more and more often. Thus in 1314, the year of the final campaign against Scotland, three were appointed for Bedfordshire and Buckinghamshire, one of whom was Nicholas Fermbaud (who had married a Passelew). He and his fellows had the usual difficulty in bringing offenders to justice, especially a gang of unknown men from Hertford-

---

[18] B.H.R.S. Qto, iii, 6.
[19] B.H.R.S. xxxii, 43.

[20] B.H.R.S. Qto, iii, 55 et seq.
[21] B.H.R.S. Qto, iii, 56 et seq.

shire who had made a raid on Aspley.[22] They succeeded in hanging 6 offenders and fining over 20 others, such as Robert in the Hale, who had seized William Dalroun's cart in the fields of Bramblehanger, and was fined 1 mark;[23] and 2 men who had beaten the gaoler at Bedford, John Walecoks.[24] Sibyl de Merdele of Bedford, who had stolen poultry, was imprisoned for 6 days "and afterwards let her be set free on account of the smallness of the theft."[25] John of Barton was found guilty of receiving 20 sheep which had been stolen from Nicholas Fermbaud himself.[26]

In 1360 the justices of the peace were directed to hold sessions quarterly each year, and by 1380 they had a clerk of the peace. He, like the sheriff, operated from his own house; and quarter sessions were held at the Bedford moot hall (see ch. 12) which belonged to the borough; so that there was no place for the records to accumulate; and almost always they were discarded by him or his family when reference was no longer made to them, or when a new clerk took over. Occasionally however a case from quarter sessions was referred to the court of king's bench at Westminster, and thus very rarely a Bedfordshire sessions roll, like the 1314 roll mentioned above, was sent up to London and preserved; this happened to one of 1355–9 and one of 1363–4.

The few rolls thus preserved deal only with judicial matters, though gradually the king's council began to look to the justices of the peace to deal with some matters of administration. They were minor county gentry who had no real power of their own; so that their being able to do this depended on the government being strong. For most of the 14th cent. Edward III was a firm ruler, and the only important Bedfordshire magnate was Lord Grey; so that, apart from the perennial problem of catching the offender, the new system began to work satisfactorily.

The justices of the peace in 1355 were only 9 – the chief being the Wrest magnate, Reynold, Lord Grey of Ruthin (son of Roger, ch. 7). There were with him one or two lawyers; and gentry like Sir Gerard de Braybrook, who had often been returned to parliament, and Sir Peter de Salford, who had been sheriff; besides more modest men, such as John Marshall of Wootton and John de Rokesdon, both of whom had been among the special justices 1351–9 to deal with labour cases (ch. 8). These two last, Marshall and Rokesdon, are known actually to have sat – it does not necessarily follow that a man whose name appears on the commission did in fact officiate.

The procedure in judicial matters was as follows. The local juries made presentments; then those who were indicted were summoned to appear at the next session; if they then appeared and pleaded guilty, they were usually fined; if they

---

[22] B.H.R.S. xxxii, 48.
[23] Op.cit., 57.
[24] Op.cit., 50.
[25] Loc.cit.
[26] Op.cit., 65.

pleaded not guilty they were given a trial by jury. If five attempts to secure their appearance failed, they were outlawed by the county court.

By far the greater number of cases were of violence. A particularly difficult character was Edmund Pulter of Caddington. He seems to have had a feud with Thomas Bredon, driving him out of his own close, assaulting his herdsman, and abducting his servant. From another Caddington man, whom he beat, he took a cart; he beat another, Michael Pursele; and he extended his operations to Luton, where he assaulted William Arderne; he also attacked a brother of Farley hospital, drew blood from the master's servant, John Hyche, and threatened the master himself so that he dare not remain in the hospital. Eventually Pulter was outlawed.[27]

A wholesale case of violence and theft occurred at Flitwick in 1356. The servants of the prior of Dunstable had just branded 100 oxen and put them out to pasture, when two men armed with bows and arrows drove away the cattle, and the frightened servants fled to Ruxox, whence they dared not stir forth.[28] Fraud entered into a large-scale theft at Wootton; three strangers calling themselves royal purveyors (agents) took 10 sheep from Thomas Drewe, 20 from Roger Marchant, 18 from Thomas Taillour and John Croude, and 13 from Thomas Sternehull.[29]

As by the time of the latter roll the special justices for labour cases were no longer operating, one or two economic cases occur in it. Three Biggleswade tanners were fined for selling hides in Shefford market at an excessive price.[30] A Carlton shepherd, John Campioun, who had changed his job and become a slater, was summoned; as he did not appear he was finally outlawed.[31]

Only two men were hanged out of about 250; 170 were fined; and 45 did not appear.

The constable is frequently mentioned in the surviving sessions rolls, and so must have been well established in the 14th cent. How far back this office goes is not certainly known. Nor is it clear how he was chosen; sometimes the appointment appears on the manor court rolls, sometimes not. He was a local man, chosen for the time being, and responsible for calling out the hue and cry when an offence was committed; but when the offender escaped into the next parish his responsibility ended.

OTHER OFFICERS

Besides those of sheriff, bailiff, and justice of the peace, there were many other offices which fell to be discharged by local people, and they covered wider or smaller areas. The coroner (ch. 6) must hold an inquest in cases where it was suspected that a death was from unnatural causes. The escheator had temporary

[27] B.H.R.S. xlviii, 53–5.
[28] Op.cit.
[29] Op.cit.
[30] Op.cit.
[31] Op.cit.

17 *Interior of Eaton Bray church, 13th cent.*

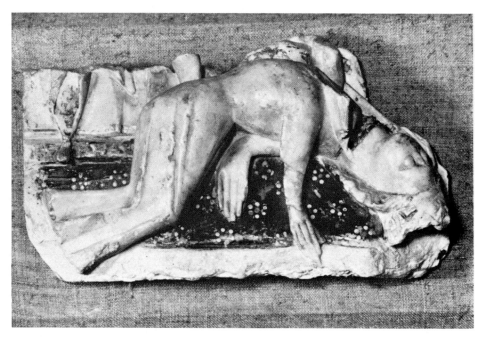

▲ *18a Alabaster figurine of St. Catherine, 15th cent., (in Cecil Higgins Museum), found at Westoning.*

▼ *18b Church screen at Oakley, 15th cent.*

▲ *19a Stall-ends in Luton parish church.*

▼ *19b Stained glass window, formerly in Ampthill church, depicting Lord Fanhope (d. 1444) and his wife.*

▲ *20a Wymington church, 14th cent.*
▼ *20b Interior of Marston Moretaine church, 15th cent.*

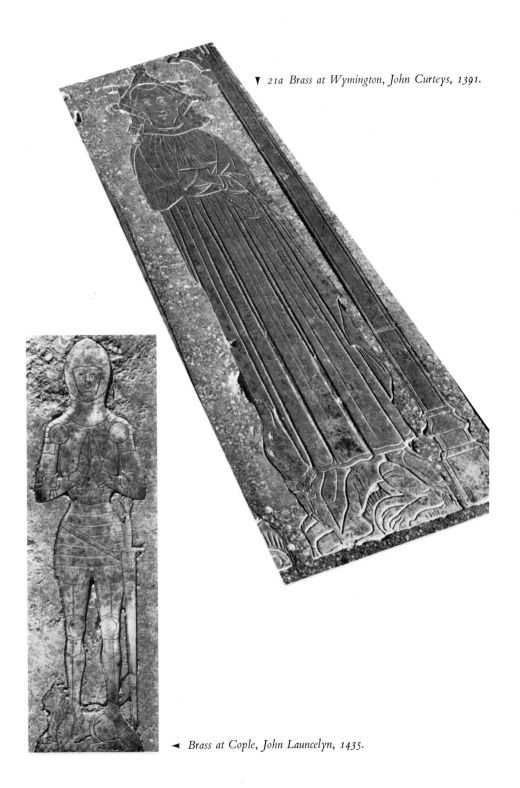

21a Brass at Wymington, John Curteys, 1391.

◀ *Brass at Cople, John Launcelyn, 1435.*

▲ *22a Farley farm, Luton, showing remains of old hospital.*

▼ *22b Herne chapel, formerly at Bedford.*

▲ *23a Remains of Bushmead priory.*

▼ *23b Remains of Franciscan friary, Bedford.*

24 *Odell church, 15th cent.*

25   *Colmworth church, 15th cent.*

26   *Gatehouse at Tilsworth, 15th cent.*

27   *Gatehouse at Someries castle, 15th cent.*

▲ *28a Sutton packhorse bridge.*

▼ *28b Harrold bridge.*

29a *Stevington cross.*   29b *Leighton Buzzard market-cross, 15th cent.*

▲ 30a Farmhouse at Tebworth, Chalgrave.

▼ 30b Farmhouse at Totternhoe, now the Old Farm Inn.

▲ *31a Houghton House.*

▼ *31b Hillersdon House, Elstow (modern reconstruction).*

▲ 32a Margaret Beaufort, 1443–1509.
▼ 32b Pall in Dunstable church, formerly belonging to the Fayrey family.

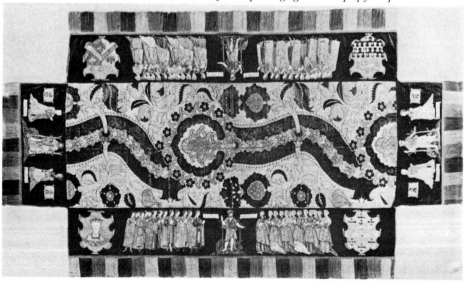

charge of the lands of a dead tenant-in-chief of the king, till an enquiry was held into the terms on which the land was held and the identity of the rightful heir. Commissioners of array were charged with raising men for military service. Tax assessors assessed or collected taxes. A public-spirited man (or it might be a busy-body) might hold many offices.

Thus the son of Nicholas Fermbaud mentioned previously, Sir Thomas Fermbaud, began his career badly by being concerned in a brawl at Woburn fair in 1334. However, he was six times M.P. for Bedfordshire; he collected taxes between 1338 and 1348; he served in the French wars and was present at Crecy; from 1347 he was a justice of the peace; from 1349–50 he was both sheriff and escheator. After that he was committed to the Fleet prison for debt, having apparently never recovered from the large fine he incurred in his youth.[32] Sir Thomas Pever of Toddington (who married Margaret Loring) was M.P. 1377–85, sheriff 1378, escheator 1380, alnager (wool agent) 1395; he was also justice of the peace, commissioner of array and tax collector. His last commission in 1414 was to arrest all Lollards (ch. 14) hiding in Bedfordshire, and he was finally buried with a stately tomb in Toddington church.[33] More modest duties were discharged by lesser men. Thus Richard Whitbread of Shillington was a tax assessor in his neighbourhood in 1301,[34] and John Whitbread was a collector in Biggleswade Hundred in 1330.[35]

No local officer received a salary, but took what fees and perquisites he could with his office. The system was bad, but at this date it was scarcely possible to organise a better one. Centuries were to elapse before there could be a professional local government service. Many instances of bribery are quoted at an enquiry of 1274.[36] Robert Travers, imprisoned on suspicion, was not freed till his friends gave the sheriff 20s. and Roger le Rider and Robert Trone (apparently the sheriff's men) 5s. John Florence, though the jury declared him innocent, had to pay ½ mark to the sheriff before he was released, and again Roger le Rider took 2s. from him and Peter of Northwood his horse. The escheator, Richard Clifford, took venison in the park at Eaton [Bray] and fished in the fishpond while the estate of the deceased George Cantilupe was in his charge. Worst of all, perhaps, was the coroner – for it was not possible to keep the body of a dead man indefinitely. Geoffrey Rodlaund of Cranfield took 2s. from Beeston before he would view a dead man; 6s. from Warden for 4 dead men; and 4s. from Southill for 2 dead men; in fact 2s. a corpse seems to have been his standard charge, with a reduction to 1s. 6d. for quantity.

To modern eyes much seems strange about 13–14th cent. arrangements. Private matters are confused with public ones; but in a developing society it is

---

[32] *B.H.R.S.* xxix, 38.
[33] *B.H.R.S.* xxix, 76–7.
[34] *B.H.R.S.* xxxix, 109.

[35] *B.H.R.S.* xliii, 46.
[36] *Hund.R.*, 2–3.

M

important that justice should be taken care of at all; once there is public jurisdiction it will gradually drive out its private equivalent.

Again, there is little co-ordination; but practical experience is much more widespread than in the days when nearly all power under the king was in the hands of the sheriff, and this was a good omen for the future.

Corruption was rife, but the government enquired into it from time to time and people protested. The concept of public service has to be painfully learnt by trial and error.

The Later Middle Ages

12 – BARONS AND KNIGHTS, 1400–1530

BEDFORDSHIRE in the 15th cent. must be seen against the national background: the last and worst of the baronial struggles, struggles which eventually involved rival kings of the houses of York and Lancaster. The kings of the Lancastrian line had obtained the throne by deposing Richard II and hence were insecure. There were powerful nobles with bands of paid retainers, nobles who were concerned with their own position and with rivalries among themselves. To occupy them, the soldier king Henry V knew only of the old bad remedy: war with France; his victory at Agincourt in 1415 brought temporary éclat, but his infant son Henry VI inherited a losing war, and grew up kindly and weak. Against such a background local administration had no secure basis.

GREY VERSUS FANHOPE

For some years the leading family had been that of Lord Grey of Ruthin at Wrest. As long as the Greys' influence was generally acknowledged in Bedfordshire things seem to have functioned smoothly. Families like the Braybrooks, who often served as M.P., were used to working with Reynold, Lord Grey (d. 1388). In the 15th cent. M.P.s like Sir Thomas Wauton of Eaton Socon and John Enderby of Biggleswade, and justices of the peace like Harry Etwell of Putnoe and John Fitz of Westhey, seem to have looked to his son, also Reynold, Lord Grey (d. 1440), whose position was strengthened by his Hastings inheritance (ch. 7). The younger Reynold, when he succeeded, had been a prominent supporter of Henry IV, and was involved in the king's struggle with Owen Glendower (Glendower twice sacked Ruthin and in 1402 even captured Grey himself, but he was soon ransomed). He had been a member of Henry IV's council. By the 1430's he was growing old; his son predeceased him, and his grandson Edmund was young.

A new note was struck when in 1425 one of the M.P.s for Bedfordshire was Sir Thomas Wenlock of Luton. The Wenlocks' connection with Bedfordshire probably began about 1377, when William Wenlock of Shropshire acquired land in Luton;[1] though his uncle, a former canon of St. Paul's cathedral, may already have become master of Farley hospital. Sir Thomas, elder son of William, had served in the French wars. When he died, one of the M.P.s from 1433 onwards was his younger brother John Wenlock, afterwards to rise high. This family made common cause with another new man with Shropshire connections – Sir John

---

[1] B.H.R.S. xxxviii, 14.

Cornwall; in fact, Sir Thomas' war service had been in Cornwall's retinue.

Sir John Cornwall was descended, though illegitimately, from the royal line (from Richard, Earl of Cornwall, younger son of King John), and had made his own fortune. He had ability, ambition and pride; and skill at arms. At a tournament at York in 1400 he won the heart of Elizabeth, sister of the new Lancastrian king, Henry IV. He became constable of Sheppey castle, and knight of the shire for Salop. He decided to make his main seat in Bedfordshire, and acquired Ampthill manor from Ralf St. Amand's widow. His royal connection was probably the cause of his being made a knight of the Garter about 1409 – his arms are still on the 25th stall-plate on the sovereign's side in St. George's chapel, Windsor.

When Henry IV died, and the young Henry V (Cornwall's nephew by marriage) renewed the Hundred Years War, he served in the army and distinguished himself at Agincourt in 1415. He collected ransoms from important French prisoners (among them the Count of Vendôme). He was left in high command when the king returned to England; and took part in the siege of Rouen. His only son, John, joined his father at the wars; and now Cornwall had his first setback; John the younger was killed at the age of 17 in 1421, a year before Henry V's own death. A few years later Cornwall's wife died.

The situation had changed drastically; and French resistance was growing. Cornwall returned to England, perhaps somewhat embittered. He built the Dominican friars a chapel in London at Ludgate. For himself he built a castle at Ampthill, only 4 miles from Wrest.[2] Later plans show that its area was about 220 sq. ft., with two projecting towers in front, and nine others at intervals, the courtyard being about 115 x 120 ft. He consoled himself for the loss of his heir with another love, apparently at Ampthill, who bore him two illegitimate children, John and Thomas. In 1432 he was created Baron Fanhope. He also, with the help of his protégés, the Wenlocks, began to throw his weight about in Bedfordshire, and some rallied to him. The elderly Lord Grey was suspicious and resentful, and most who had accepted Grey's leadership were not prepared to change their allegiance. An atmosphere of mutual distrust impeded local administration. Today a distinguished newcomer would be welcomed and his co-operation invited, but that was not the approach of a 15th cent. baron.

Thus in 1437, when four justices were appointed to make some special enquiries, they appointed a rendezvous at Silsoe as a comparatively central point. The old Lord Grey bestirred himself to come out of his house with 50–60 men, supported by John Enderby, who came up with over 100 men, to ask why they had chosen his church – he would not obstruct the sessions, but had come to see what was going on. Lord Fanhope appeared with 60 men, asserting that the choice of rendezvous was a move by Lord Grey. Reinforcements arrived for both sides. Sir Thomas Wauton, who seems to have been a man of sense and courage,

---

[2] *V.C.H.* iii, 270; *Walpole Society* xl, pls. 120–1.

persuaded each to withdraw to opposite sides of the village, and the session was postponed.

Lord Grey was failing. In January 1439 Lord Fanhope (though he too was growing older) thought fit to come with his retainers to Bedford for Epiphany sessions. Sir Thomas Wauton, John Enderby, John Fitz and Harry Etwell were already in the Moot Hall. When they heard that Fanhope was in the town, with 60 men with thick doublets and swords and bucklers, some of whom began to come into the hall (the rest jostling on the stairs and in High Street and Fish Row), they delayed beginning the sessions. Fanhope entered the hall – the others stood up to greet him, but Wauton, though he doffed his hood, remained seated. Fanhope sat down, apparently to take the chair; the clerk took his seat by him; and he called Fitz and Peck to him. Fitz pointed out that Wauton and Enderby were above him in the commission; Fanhope answered "Nay, come an ye will, the one shall be welcome, the tother may choose." They sat down.

A dispute arose between John FitzGeffrey of Thurleigh and one of Fanhope's servants, who seems to have been insolent. Wauton, a former speaker of the House of Commons, had both spirit and experience, and exclaimed "It is the unruliest sessions that I have ever seen in Bedford; and if it be not otherwise ruled, I will complain to the king's council." Fanhope returned "Complain as you will – I defy thy menacing and all thine evil will." Wauton seems to have lost his temper: "I set little of thy defiance." Rumour and noise arose in the hall. All rose. Fanhope stood upon the checker-board which stood afore the bench (perhaps, as at the exchequer, a board marked out for calculating money, in this case, fines); he had a dagger in his hand, but laboured to stint the noise. On the narrow entrance stair, many men crowded together – some fell in the burly-burly and could not rise. A later account says that the stairs collapsed. At last the tumult was quelled.[3]

The sessions were not held. The dead at the entrance, who had been suffocated or trampled on in the press, numbered 18. Fanhope went to his inn, and "fellowshipped" the other justices of the peace to their lodgings for their more surety, even inviting Wauton and Enderby to drink with him. He said to Wauton "You shall be welcome, for I give him drink which I have less cause to love than some" (meaning Enderby). Wauton however was not to be cajoled; public proprieties had been flouted and lives lost; and he and his fellow justices, as they had threatened, sent an account of the day's events to the king's council.

But on the king's council was not only Fanhope himself, but lords like the Duke of Gloucester and the Earl of Northumberland, who had far greater retinues; civil servants representing a gentle and not very able king; and prelates who could not unaided ensure a strong line. An enquiry was made, but the upshot was that Fanhope and his supporters were exonerated. The list of the latter is revealing; there were 55 men, of whom 19 came from Ampthill, the majority known to have

---

[3] *Selden Soc.*, xxxv, 104–7; P.R.O., KB 9/230 B.

been Fanhope's paid servants or retainers, and including Patrick Irisshman, Matthew Welshman, and Peter Frenshman. Six men came from outside the county. The rest were drawn from 16 scattered parishes. The only justice of the peace seems to have been William Pekke of Cople; the only recognisable gentry, Thomas Hasilden of Goldington and John Wenlock of Luton.[4]

Sir Thomas Wauton was not going to take this sitting down. He organised further representations to the king's council.[5] This second list comprises nearly 100 people from 35 places; there were 9 from Silsoe and 8 from Biggleswade (the home town both of John Enderby and of Thomas Stratton, clerk of the peace), but this does not seem excessive. The king's council were in a quandary; they exonerated these also. They uneasily charged the assize judges in 1442 to send to London the names of any who impeded justice at Bedford.[6]

The most arresting figure in all this is Sir Thomas Wauton. He was not a man of substance, but he had character and experience. Yet he could not secure the proper conduct of county business, and the government could not back him up.

In 1440 old Lord Grey died, and he was succeeded by his grandson Edmund. In January 1444 at Ampthill castle Lord Fanhope also died. Staying with him at the time were no less men than the bishop of Lincoln and the new archbishop of Canterbury (he was after all the king's great-uncle). As these prelates were sitting in the west window of the great and principal chamber of the castle on 5 January, a member of the staff brought the bishop his late master's will, together with his silver armorial seal (kept in a linen bag which was sealed with his gold signet). The bishop directed that seal and signet should be defaced with a hammer, that they might not again be used; and he opened and read the will.[7]

Lord Fanhope's wish was that he should be buried in the Dominican chapel at Ludgate. To the little boys, John and Thomas, he left about £300 and £200 respectively. Over 120 named people in his service were remembered with sums from £10 to 13s. 4d. These included apparently four chaplains (one had a university degree); those who waited on him personally (barber, or "of the wardrobe", or "of the chamber") domestic staff (baker, cook, caterer, laundress). Of the remaining hundred, probably about half were other administrative or domestic staff. Perhaps the other half were those retainers who had served in his retinue; among them are thirteen who were with him a few years previously at the troubled sessions at Bedford. Ampthill (to the annoyance of Lord Edmund Grey) passed to his stepson.

LORD WENLOCK

In Bedfordshire there was still John Wenlock,[8] able, ambitious, and not over-scrupulous in an age when principle was hard to discern. Perhaps fortunately for

[4] Cal.Pat.R.,1436–41, p.246.
[5] Op.cit., p.282.
[6] V.C.H. ii, 37.

[7] B.H.R.S. xiv, 111–2.
[8] B.H.R.S. xxxviii, 12–48.

this county, his energies sought a national outlet. A prominent M.P. (speaker 1455–6), he was sent on overseas missions by the king several times, and at last in 1442 to treat with France for an end to the disastrous war. He held various offices, and by 1448 was the queen's chamberlain, when on her behalf he laid the foundation-stone of Queens' College, Cambridge. He added the Wenlock chapel to Luton church.[9] He lent the king money, and when the wars of the roses finally broke out in 1455, he was wounded at the battle of St. Albans and "carried home in a cart sore hurt" – it must have been a painful jolting journey to Luton.

So far he had been loyal to the Lancastrian king, but now he became involved in the fortunes of that more powerful and dangerous baron, the Earl of Warwick. With Warwick he went over to the Yorkist side; with him he besieged and captured the Tower; and by Edward IV he was made knight of the garter, Lord Wenlock, and given several offices. Once more he often went abroad on diplomatic negotiations. He became lieutenant of Calais. To replace the old castle of the Someries family at Luton, he began to build in brick a great manorhouse, of which the gatehouse remains.[10] (Tiles were known at Dunstable in 1297; Warden Abbey had inlaid, stamped and embossed floor tiles; and roof tiles were used for Felmersham tithe barn and at Luton; but the use of brick in construction was comparatively new.)[11]

But it was an uneasy time. The discontented Earl of Warwick began to think that he could make king whom he pleased; Wenlock at first objected, then went along with Warwick. In 1471, with his former lady, Queen Margaret, fighting at Tewkesbury for the Lancastrian side, he was killed. Thus ended the Wenlock line in Bedfordshire. His Luton property, forfeited to the king, was granted to Thomas Rotherham, bishop of Lincoln, shortly to become chancellor.[12] Bishop Rotherham, who is known to have built elsewhere in brick, probably continued the building at Someries with a fine chapel.[13]

EDMUND GREY, EARL OF KENT

Wenlock was not the only man to change sides in 1460. Edmund, now Lord Grey of Ruthin, at the battle of Northampton where heavy rain immobilised the royal guns, was in charge of the Lancastrian vanguard, and changed sides as the battle was actually joined – his conduct may have decided the issue. Thus he too had become a Yorkist, and so he remained. He bought Ampthill in 1455.[14] When Edward IV married a family connection of his (the widow of his cousin, Sir

[9] V.C.H. ii, 368, 372.
[10] Dyer-Stygall-Dony, op.cit., 95–9; B. Mag., v, 157–62; see also W. Austin, Luton, i, 188; G. Davis, Luton, 23–4; N. Pevsner, Beds., Huntingdon, Peterborough, pp.118–9.
[11] Adam le Cous at Dunstable in 1297 had 13s. 4d. in stock of tiles and lime; B.H.R.S. xxxix, 90. The Warden tiles were excavated in 1960–1; Beds.Arch.J. ii, Figs. 3–5, Pl. V. Tiles were used for roofing at Radwell in 1419; C.R.O., LL 1/220.

The accounts for Felmersham tithe barn include 7,500 tiles and carting, and 7 score ridge-tiles; Trinity Coll. MSS. Luton fraternity accounts mention 10,000 tiles in 1526–7, and payment to the tiler and his man for 12 days; Gough, Luton gild accounts, pp.189–91.
[12] V.C.H. ii, 352.
[13] For an archaeological report on Someries, see Beds.Arch.J., iii, 36–46; see also Pevsner, op.cit.
[14] B.H.R.S. xlvi, 5, 34–5.

John Grey), the Grey fortunes were set fair. In 1463 he was made treasurer; in 1465 Earl of Kent. He was a sword-bearer at Richard III's coronation in 1483.

His style of dress and his domestic surroundings were probably like those of Sir Gerard Braybrook of Colmworth (d. 1429)[15] but they would be on a grander scale. Sir Gerard had a colourful wardrobe – 3 scarlet gowns, one of murrey or purple-red, one green and 2 black; the winter ones were furred with marten, miniver or grey squirrel; and the summer ones were lined with buckram. His 4-poster bedsteads were hung with silk in black or red, with cushions to match; the hangings to his rooms were of arras or tapestry; and among his cherished possessions was a covered cup of silver-gilt enamelled with greyhounds. His private chapel was well equipped with vestments of green silk and of blue and black "bawdekyn" (rich silk with gold thread), and of white striped silk; and for Lent there were altar-cloths painted with a "pity" (weeping Mother of Christ). He had also many service books (antiphoner, breviary, grail, missal), most of which he bequeathed to Colmworth church, with an iron-bound coffer to keep them in.

For information on the estate of a 15th cent. lord there is much in the surviving MSS. of Edmund Grey, Earl of Kent, himself, especially a published valuation of his English estates in 1467–8.[16] His gross income from these (the Ruthin estate is not included) was £1,212, of which Bedfordshire brought in just over one-third (£421). Only a small amount of land was kept in his own hands, and valued at £8. Wood sales brought in £28. Profits of courts produced £6. Thus the greater part of his income was derived from rents, as was now usual for a magnate.

The Bedfordshire rents amounted to £360, whether from leases or from any other form of rent. They would have been slightly higher than this, but some holdings were vacant, probably because tenants were still scarce; and in some cases the Earl had made a special grant, as at Harrold "my lord hath granted the cottage to William Saltere without any rent, 4s." In general, the valuation summarises the position on each manor and does not go into detail.

Some other surviving MSS. give a close-up view of individual manors on the Grey estate and illustrate the kind of problem a 15th cent. lord had to consider. Blunham may serve as an instance, but an instance only, for it is not possible to argue from one manor to another, even on the same estate. A 1457 rental[17] shows three groups of tenants. The demesne arable, pasture and meadow were divided into many small parcels and let out, with the site of the manor, to tenants, bringing in altogether £17 12s. 8d. Another group consists of about 40 free tenancies of ancient standing; some of the properties being as little as a rood or $\frac{1}{2}$ acre; two brought in only $\frac{1}{2}$d. annually; several only 1d.; only one or two larger holdings brought in bigger sums (chiefly the mill, 18s.); clearly most of these rents had

[15] *Reg. Hen. Chichele* (ed. E. F. Jacob), ii, 409–14. [17] C.R.O., L 26/154.
[16] *B.H.R.S.* xlvi.

been stabilised for years and become quite uneconomic; they brought in £2 12s. 0½d. The third group comprises what had at one time been villein properties and were now held by copy of court roll (see ch. 13); they are largely standard holdings with more realistic rents, most being ½ virgate at 8s. 4d. p.a., or ¼ virgate at 4s. 2d. p.a.; here again there are about 40, bringing in £15 6s. od. With a few capons, the total amounts to £37 3s. 2½d., to be collected and entered in over a hundred small sums. By 1467 the Earl of Kent had decided that this was simply not worth while; he had farmed Blunham, lock, stock and barrel, to John Worsley and William Smyth for £38.

On the small amount of land which he did keep in his own hand, he took steps to keep his wage bill as low as possible. The current way to do this was by enclosure for sheep-farming, which employed fewer men. Though elsewhere in England a native cloth industry was growing up, Bedfordshire's surplus wool was still being exported; William Hicchecok (d. 1450), a mayor of the Calais staple. was an Ampthill man.[18] At Broybury in 1467 the "cost of closure" was 13s. 6d.; at Harrold £4 4s. 6d.; and it may be that there had been some enclosure at Blunham before Worsley and Smyth took over, for there is an entry of 2s. 6d. for a rood of underwood "for the closure at the manor", probably for fencing.[19]

Thus in the management of his estate the Earl of Kent seems to have been shrewd and practical. In maintaining his position as a great magnate he also avoided excess. His retinue consisted of about 40 men, whose fees (as was usual) were charged against individual properties on his estate. Walter Stotfold, whose family had long been in the Greys' service, received £5 p.a.; the rest, on average, rather more than £2 p.a. each. The retainers cost about one-tenth of his income, a modest proportion for a 15th cent. lord (the Percys' retainers are reckoned to have cost them one-third of their income). He lived within his means. When the Countess and elder children moved, only 38 horses were required; and the babies and nurse in a horse-litter were accompanied by 16 men and women and 17 horses. In hunting he perhaps did indulge himself, for he added 9 a. to the park at Ampthill castle, and had another park at Norwood.[20]

LATER EARLS OF KENT

Now that the hazards of the wars of the roses were over, and in the confused political game of "spot the winner" a winner had at last been found, the position of the Earls of Kent seemed assured. George Grey, 2nd Earl of Kent, who succeeded in 1490, held various offices under Henry VII. He is described as appearing at court wearing cloth of gold and crimson velvet pearled, and riding on a sorel horse, with harness of Venetian gold and fringes half a yard deep.[21] But as he lay dying

---

[18] V.C.H. iii, 273. The prosperity of a Calais merchant at this time is illustrated by an inventory of the goods of John Saunders, whose widow married Sir William Boteler; his woollen goods at Calais amounted to £461, his ready money to £100, and "good debts" in Bruges, Holland and Brabant to £203; C.R.O., TW 1094.
[19] B.H.R.S. xlvi, 83, 90, 97.
[20] Op.cit., 103, 107.
[21] V.C.H. ii, 37.

in 1503 he was troubled by foreboding that his son Richard "will not thrive but will be a waster."[22] So it proved. One man can destroy what several generations have built up.

Richard Grey, 3rd Earl of Kent, though he also held office, was a gambler, and soon in debt, among others to that careful king, Henry VII. He had to give up Ampthill to the king in 1508. He alleged that the king's advisers tricked him out of the Ruthin estate. It must have galled his pride when in the next reign he humbly and unsuccessfully besought the butcher's son, his right reverend father-in-God, Cardinal Wolsey, chancellor, to help him regain Ruthin.[23] Most of the Hastings inheritance outside Bedfordshire went also. He continued to cut a figure at Henry VIII's court, and attended him in 1520 at the field of the cloth of gold, while his finances became ever more tangled. When he died in 1523, his impoverished son did not use the title of 4th Earl of Kent, but called himself plain Sir Henry Grey.

Even Wrest seems to have been alienated and in danger of being pulled down and sold for building material, till Sir Henry, having no convenient house of his own, and for pity that the house wherein many of his ancestors had dwelt should be so utterly destroyed, managed to buy back Wrest manor by selling some remaining land elsewhere.[24] The Greys survived, but they were brought low. By 1530 the power structure in Bedfordshire had reverted to that at the end of the 13th cent.; for practical purposes there was no great family.

KNIGHTS AND GENTRY

Of some knights or gentry mention has already been made, as involved in the affairs of Fanhope or of Grey. This applied to others too. William Ludsopp of Odell, M.P. in 1427, had been at Agincourt with Sir Thomas Wenlock, and Thomas Reynes of Marston (M.P. 1441) was another of Fanhope's men. Others were in the Grey camp. Two M.P.s were the sons of Grey mothers, Henry Cockayne of [Cockayne] Hatley, 1421, and Sir William Lucy, 1467 (the latter's main interest was in Warwickshire). Richard Carlisle, 1477/8, was almost certainly the Earl of Kent's receiver-general of that name – in 1472 he bought from Walter Stotfold, another Grey man, what became known as Carlisle's manor in Roxton.

The gentry were continuing to gain experience in various capacities, as in the preceding century (ch. 11). Roger Hunt of Roxton, M.P. 1414, 1420, was speaker of the commons, and so was Sir John Mordaunt of Turvey in 1487.[25] Sir Thomas Hoo of Luton Hoo was made Lord Hoo in 1447 for his war service (but was succeeded in 1454 by a half-brother and by daughters). At the end of the century in 1490 an important newcomer to the county was Sir Reginald Bray, to whom the king granted Eaton [Bray]; he was treasurer, and was also concerned in the building of Henry VII's beautiful chapel in Westminster Abbey. His nephew Edmund

22 *Complete peerage.*
23 C.R.O., L 24/453.
24 C.R.O., L 24/16.
25 *D.N.B.: V.C.H.* iii, 220.

became Lord Bray, but Eaton remained with the family only till 1574. A family which was to become notable was that of Oliver St. John, who married the heiress of Bletsoe, to which their son John succeeded in 1483. The St. Johns were an old family elsewhere,[26] and this marriage connected them with the descendants of one of the Beauchamp heiresses of 1265. The Bletsoe heiress married twice, and her daughter by her second marriage, Margaret Beaufort, was the mother of Henry VII.

On their lands the knights had problems like those of the lords, and they met them in similar ways. In general they seemed to keep only a small amount of land in their own hands, and live on rents. Their methods of doing this took various forms. Some went over to leases for years. At Kempston Draytons,[27] after the heiress Elizabeth Drayton married Sir John Wenlock, there seems to be a whole-sale system of 20-year leases, from sizeable holdings (Hugh Horle's rent amounted to 27s. 4d.) down to quite small ones. About 40 such tenancies are entered on the court roll for 1434; thus William Hunte did fealty and acknowledged that he held from the lord by charter for 20 years half a cottage at Mill End at 19d., a croft in Box End at 2s., 1 a. pasture in Holesdole at 10d., $\frac{1}{2}$ a. land in Thornfurlong at 4d., and $1\frac{1}{2}$ a. in Church Field at 9d., with suit of court. The phrase "by charter" seems to imply that the lease was the effective document, and that the court roll merely noted it.

Another method was tenancy "at will", perhaps where the lord had to offer it for an indefinite period at an advantageous rent because he could not dispose of it on other terms. Thus at Tilsworth in 1472[28] on Richard Chamberlain's manor there were 16 tenants at will (as compared with 15 free tenants); one had only 1 a.; most had from 10 to 39 a.; and the biggest holders were Robert Fuller with 55a. arable, 4 a. meadow; John Hebbes with 92 a. arable, 8 a. meadow; and William Huette with 102 a. arable, 7 a. meadow.

It is probable that, like Lord Grey, some Bedfordshire gentry were stepping up their sheep-farming. Sheep were prominent in the south of the county in the late 15th and early 16th cents. (ch. 15); there was a figure of St. Blase in Luton church; and Richard Fermor of Luton Hoo was a wool merchant c.1530.[29] The small parish of Higham Gobion was enclosed by the Butler family (cf. ch. 8), probably for sheep-farming; there was but one parishioner in 1518.[30] Another process which often went with, but did not necessarily involve enclosure, was the amalgamation of holdings to make larger units capable of paying more rent; thus at Battlesden Edmund Bray (nephew of Sir Reginald and afterwards Lord Bray) in 1513 pulled down a house and amalgamated its 30 a. with another holding; in 1501 at Eversholt John Lee of Wakes manor pulled down a house and amalgama-

[26] B. Mag. vi, 120–1.
[27] C.R.O., PE 466.
[28] C.R.O., CH 4.

[29] C.R.O., DW 6, 29–30.
[30] L.R.S. xxxiii, 103.

ted its 30 a. with another holding; at Westoning in 1504 John Rufford of Aynels manor did the same with a house attached to 80 a.[31] This might also be done by the rising yeoman on his own account (ch. 13).

In 1517, anxious for the effect of these developments on the poorer dwellers in the countryside, the government set up a commission to investigate. For Bedfordshire only supplementary returns have survived. From these and from subsidiary papers it has been calculated that about 4,317 a. (about 1% of the county area) were affected in 36 parishes, but that the complaint with regard to 3,153 a. of this was of amalgamation.[32]

Two 15th cent. links with London instance the two-way traffic which was to grow with security and with better communications. Sir William Stocker of Eaton Socon was a member of the Drapers' Company; he was knighted on the field of battle (probably Tewkesbury), and was Lord Mayor in 1484, but died within a few days of the sweating sickness.[33] Another Lord Mayor came from Biddenham: Richard Boteler married Grace Kirton, heiress of Kirtons manor, and their son William was master of the Grocers' Company and Lord Mayor in 1515–16.[34] Similarly it sometimes happened that a London merchant bought an estate in Bedfordshire. George Monoux, a master of the Drapers' Company, and Lord Mayor in 1514, bought property at Wootton in the same year and so founded a line of Bedfordshire squires.[35] (For further London connections, see Dunstable, ch. 15).

---

[31] I. S. Leadam, *Domesday of inclosures*, ii, 462–5.
[32] Leadam, *op.cit.*, i, 38–40, reprinted in *Agrarian Hist.* iv, 241 (ed. J. Thirsk); see also *R. Hist.Soc.Trans.*, xviii. Parishes mentioned in the supplementary returns are Battlesden, Biddenham Bromham, Eversholt, Maulden, Northill, Streatley, Sutton, Westoning, Wrestlingworth. The largest area mentioned is 80 a. If the original returns were at all like those of 1607 (see ch. 17) it is probable that they covered similar small adjustments in the greater part of the county.
[33] *B. Mag.* iii, 183.
[34] C.R.O., TW catalogue; and Boteler wills, P.C.C. More 23, Godyn 9.
[35] *Walthamstow Ant.Soc.*, iii.

FOR THE ordinary villager the period covered by this chapter was one of opportunity – opportunity to rise or to sink.[1] It saw the emergence of the yeoman and (it might almost be said) of the pauper.

FREEHOLD AND COPYHOLD

It may be as well to recall what classes of villager there were (ch. 8). There were a number of freemen, who might either be freeholders or free tenants of the manor; and there were men (villeins and cottagers) with larger or smaller holdings, personally unfree, and until recently owing service to the lord. It would be more correct to speak, not of classes of men, but of kinds of tenancy, for it will be remembered that the dividing lines were blurred, that the same man might hold land by both free and unfree tenure, and that inter-marriage took place.

Able freeholders continued to make their way as before. They can often be seen in a collection of 15th cent. deeds building up a little holding by small amounts, like Edmund Wryghte of Wilden, acquiring for instance 10 selions in 1407 and 4 selions in 1409;[2] or Nicholas Davy at Maulden, who in 1416 had 18 a. land and 3 a. meadow;[3] or the Hawes family of Tempsford about 1450,[4] and later (see ch. 16). Some had begun the process in the 14th cent., like the Goffes of West Hyde.[5] Sometimes the series covers a few years only. Sometimes, as with the Milwards of Fielden, it carries on till well into the 16th cent.; Thomas Milward the elder handed over his goods to his son in 1542, stipulating that he should provide the old folks with 2 cows, a horse, a sow, 8 steers, a goose, and their clothing, bedding in their chamber, and sufficient meat, drink and fire.[6]

Now those who had hitherto held by unfree tenure had also more scope. This period saw the end of any attempt by the lord, lay or ecclesiastic, to exact service from the former villein for his holding. The memory of service lingered for some time; it continued to be referred to in the new type of commuted rent (ch. 8), as on Waltham Abbey's manor of Arlesey Bury, where in 1415 J. Smyth took over 28 a. at 10s. $1\frac{1}{2}$d. for rent and all services; and in 1424 J. Bryd took over $3\frac{1}{2}$ a. at 1s. 6d. for rent and all services.[7] There are surprisingly late references to service; at Toddington in 1483, on the manor of John Broughton (son of Mary Pever) Alice Gobyons was said to hold a tenement and 40 a. by "one whole

[1] For general background, see A. R. Myers, *England in the late Middle Ages*, 134–49, 208–20; and E. F. Jacob, *The fifteenth century*, 346–84.
[2] C.R.O., BD 1024–5.
[3] C.R.O., LL 1/155, 166–7.
[4] C.R.O., BS 651–2, 1279.
[5] C.R.O., DW 213–9.
[6] C.R.O., BS 42–6, 55–7, 68.
[7] C.R.O., IN 59.

customary service", ploughing in spring, "in le Steering", and at sowing; 1 harrowing duty; 1 carrying-duty at haytime and one in autumn; and 2 "bedrips"; but it seems most unlikely that she carried these out.[8] In 1485 on the same manor 5 tenants paid fines of 4d. or 8d. for not doing their customary service – such a small fine for non-performance was cheaper than an agreed commutation.[9] Service simply could not be enforced, and for all practical purposes it was obsolete.

By and large the former villein became a copyholder. Changes of tenancy were entered in the court roll; the tenant received a copy of the entry, recording his admission to the holding (the earliest surviving Bedfordshire example is in 1402 at Gravenhurst);[10] and so he came to be called a copyholder. Copyhold became an inferior kind of property, which in some cases remained until the 20th cent. It might continue to descend from father to son; thus at Arlesey Bury in 1464 Richard Body, sick to death, surrendered his half-virgate to Adam Body, and the death duty or heriot of a horse was paid (or rather, its value, for at this date it was usual to redeem the heriot by a money payment.)[11] Alternatively it might change hands by payment from one copyholder to another, provided the change was entered in the court roll, and the entry fine paid to the lord; at the same court it was recorded that Robert Tyllys had surrendered a house and an acre to William Fann, and William Fann paid an entry fine of 3s. 4d.

A Cranfield custumal of 1484 states the copyholders' position, which has become so established that they say it has been so "time out of mind".[12] At a copyholder's death, there is a heriot to the lord (who must allow it to be redeemed), and the widow is entitled to keep the holding for her life; afterwards it goes to the heir. A copyholder may alienate his holding either in court, or through a representative, such as the bailiff, who will present it at the next court; and he that taketh shall pay to the lord an entry fine, but the fine must be "never above one whole year's rent".

Where procedure like this became smoothly established, especially on a large manor where the ownership remained stable, it continued for centuries. But on small manors, especially if the ownership changed frequently, copyhold tenure tended to disappear. In the County Record Office copies of court roll survive for only about 60 manors, though there were over 400.[13]

The abler men, whether freeholders or copyholders, now had increased opportunities. Even in the past the appointment to act as bailiff for the lord had offered useful experience in coping with a larger unit. Thus Richard Bulmer of Little Staughton sometime before 1383 had been bailiff for the Hospitallers; and

---

[8] C.R.O., X 21/395.
[9] Loc.cit.
[10] C.R.O., L 450.
[11] C.R.O., IN 61.
[12] C.R.O., AD 341.
[13] It must be remembered that it was as important to preserve a copy of court roll as a deed; that in the 18th cent. the growth of great estates swallowed up many small ones; and that copies of court roll can – and do – appear as evidence of title even in the Duke of Bedford's collection.

the Bulmer family, with those of Crowe and Dean, was rising in Little Staughton in the 15th cent.[14]

The rising man might well, if he could get away with it, put fences round his area, as the lord did. At Kempston in 1476 Thomas Cok was presented at the manor court for not allowing others to common in winter on his close called the Brade; in 1480 he was told to make a gap in the hedge; next year he was fined 12d. for not doing so.[15] He might succeed in obtaining another holding for the sake of its land, letting the house get into disrepair, as Richard Lantowe did at Maulden in 1505 with a house attached to 24 a.[16] (For the government enquiry in 1517 into such matters, see ch. 12).

The lords' policy of leasing the demesne gave further scope. If a small man undertook this, he needed to be prosperous to undertake initially to pay the larger rent; and at Cockayne Hatley in 1406 Richard Aleyn, the farmer of the manor and the manorial enclosures, let the farm buildings get in bad repair.[17] After the first effort however he probably did well. At Tilsworth in 1472 the demesne (302 a. arable, 54 a. meadow) was let to Thomas Monte for £13 6s. 8d.[18]

These men, where they were able and energetic, were able to cope with the situation because their holdings were normally not big enough to give rise to labour problems. They and their families worked hard. Some exceptional ones rose to be gentry. Robert Gostwick of Willington was bailiff for the Mowbrays in the 1380's, and his descendant John, who went to school at Potton, was able to buy the manor from them in 1529[19] and build a new manorhouse in the new material of brick. At Bolnhurst in 1493 the canons of Canons Ashby leased Glyntils manor to Thomas Francklin;[20] this family also rose. But in the main the 16th cent. was to be the heyday of the smaller man – the yeoman.

THE LESS FORTUNATE

All did not rise; some fell. The change to copyhold made a difference to the size of holdings. While the lord needed the service of his tenants, he had·in general prevented one man from having a very large holding, or another's holding from becoming too small when he got into difficulties in a bad year. At such times the latter perhaps lost his few animals; in 1461 at Arlesey Bury Richard Bound's heriot was a cow; but when the next year his wife Katherine died "she had no animal when she died" and the heriot had to be barley. Now there was in general no restriction on the alienation of copyhold land, the inefficient and un-lucky man's holding declined; as the better-off villagers prospered, the poor grew poorer still. The Earl of Kent's charter of 1471 to his Blunham men, witnessed by over 30 of them, seems to be exceptional; it stated that though they could buy and sell, a half-yardland holding (normally 14 a. land, 2 a. meadow) must not be

[14] C.R.O., PR 35-191.
[15] *Kempston History*, ed. H. A. Carnell, T. Booth, H. G. Tibbutt, 21.
[16] I. S. Leadam, *Domesday of inclosures*, ii, 463.
[17] C.R.O., BW 1248.
[18] C.R.O., CH 4.
[19] B.H.R.S. xxxvi, 51, 57, 59-60.
[20] C.R.O., FN 80.

allowed to fall below 6 a.[21]

At the same time, to the extent that sheep-farming was increasing, the poorer man found less demand for his labour. The extent of this is hard to assess (chs. 12, 14, 15). In 1510 at Toddington sheep seem to be multiplying,[22] for tenants are directed to adjust the size of their flocks according to their lands (unfortunately the ratio is not given); but at this time commons in general are in danger of being over-stocked by animals of all kinds, and offences of overstocking the common by "beasts" are brought up at the same court. Higham Gobion was presumably almost entirely given over to sheep-farming; (ch. 12). At Old Warden Richard Merywether in 1518 had a considerable flock.[23]

There was another drawback for the man who had been unfree. Though his land had lost its vexatious obligations, he had not necessarily won free from his personal restrictions (ch. 8), such as inability to sue at law, restriction on leaving the manor, liability to pay merchet on his daughter's marriage. The successful man could pay for a formal manumission, as Thomas and William Colman of Shillington did in 1457 and 1464.[24] Another way was to chance your arm and leave the manor. Thus in 1452 it was reported at Arlesey Bury that Giles Rangedich, villein by birth, had without leave apprenticed his son Thomas to a Dunstable mercer, and it was ordered that Thomas be brought to court; but there is no evidence that he was.[25] At Kempston in 1462 the roll states that John, Thomas and William Aylmer, villeins by birth, were at Maulden, Woburn and Bedford respectively, and the bailiff was told to get them; but in 1463 they were still away; and in 1487 Thomas Aylmer was at Raunds.[26] By whatever means, personal servitude disappeared from view for practical purposes in the 15th and early 16th cents.

The last indication of serfdom appears, as might be expected, at Barton, Cranfield and Shillington, which until the dissolution of the monasteries were estates of Ramsey Abbey (ch. 8). An enquiry of 1577 rounded up about 50 people, mainly the families of Frost and Burrell (deriving from Cranfield), Howson and Colman (Shillington), Priour and Child (Barton). Several of them claimed that they had in fact been manumitted. One or two of them had done well, such as Matthew Howson who left as much as £42; but most were very poor, one blind, and one "a poor simple man".[27] It was in fact people like the Burrells and the Childs, men with less capacity, bad luck, poor health, a large family (Thomas Priour had 9 children), who experienced the drawbacks of the changed conditions of the 15th cent.

THE 15TH CENT. MANOR

How did the manor stand after these changes? The lord was still the chief

[21] C.R.O., L 26/229.
[22] C.R.O., X 21/395.
[23] B.H.R.S. xxxvii, 74.
[24] C.R.O., PE 35–6.

[25] C.R.O., IN 60.
[26] C.R.O., PE 466.
[27] B.H.R.S. ix, 61–74.

landowner; he still had rights on the waste; he still had the profits of courts. On the larger manors courts still met; in fact for the 15–16th cents. court rolls are fuller than at any other time. It was not only for changes of copyhold tenancy that they met. They put youths into tithings, enforced the assizes of bread and ale, fined those who had committed small offences, appointed officers, and so on. The rolls of the manor of Willington, 1463–9 (one of the few single-manor parishes) provide some examples.[28]

Thus officers were appointed: John Flawndrys and Robert Cooke were chosen constables; John Myton and John Sterlyng tasters of ale; and there were 12 chief tithingmen.

Estate administration was a main item. The buildings of several tenants were defective; either they reported this themselves, and were allotted wood from Sheerhatch by the bailiff; thus John Morborne asked for two oaks to rebuild his barn, and John Yerwey a smaller quantity to repair his stable; or they were reported as having defective buildings (such as Ralf Bawdewyn's "hoggiscote") and were directed to repair them by a certain date under pain of fine; the dam and causeway at the mill also needed repair. When the necessary repairs had been provided for, the bailiff sold the remaining amount of underwood (10 a.).

Matters of agricultural practice were regulated. John Morborne was to clean out his ditch, and three others were given the like directions. John Warnere and some other tenants had put up fences enclosing some of the roadside verge, and this, besides being an encroachment, impeded the carts of others; the fences must be taken down within a week. Margaret Ussher had seized her stray animal in the bailiff's hands. John Fage of Cople had encroached with his plough on Willington land in a stretch 20 ft. long. This regulation of matters of common farming concern was an important function of the court, and in time long and detailed agricultural "Orders" would be drafted at the court and re-enacted or amended from time to time.

Small offences were dealt with. There were cases of poaching: John Kyng fished in the lord's water without licence. The assize of ale had been broken several times. No one must play at tennis till 12 years old, and not then except at Christmas (men were supposed to get their amusement in practising archery). John Osberne had attacked John Malton with a dagger and drawn blood. Alice Dylerton went for John Roper with her fist. John Odyll or Wodehyll used a staff against the wife of William Rydy.

John Wodehyll was the miller, and seems to have been an awkward customer, for he was told to grind the tenants' corn properly or he would be fined 40d. (Millers, perhaps from their solitary occupation, tended to develop idiosyncrasies, like the miller in the song who cared for nobody.)

Incidentally, a lease of Cardington mill in 1469[29] is one of the earliest sur-

[28] Brit.Mus., Add.Ch, 26813. [29] C.R.O., W 2/44.

N

viving Bedfordshire documents in English. The miller, Thomas Wytston, was to pay about £5 a year rent, and a new house 60 x 16 ft. was to be built for him by Christmas; he was also to have a "gown competent and able for a yeoman to wear", (the word yeoman was now coming into use). The landlord was responsible for the repair of "water whelys, water yates, millstones, cogge wheles, trendels, cogges, rowngges, reynddes, spyndeles, hoppes". Over the use of water the miller was to co-operate with the miller at Castle Mills.

The movement to enlarge and beautify Bedfordshire churches continued. Some were entirely rebuilt in the new perpendicular style, a native English development; such were Cople, Dunton, Odell and Tingrith. Colmworth, of rare scale and dignity, probably owes its rebuilding to the Braybrooks, a family who had given the county much service; and Flitton to Edmund Grey, 1st Earl of Kent (ch. 12). At Luton the beautiful double-arched Wenlock chapel was built by Lord Wenlock (ch. 12).

The new style was lofty, and the tendency was towards admitting more light, so several churches heightened the nave roof, added clerestory windows and built on aisles, as at Eaton [Bray]. Sometimes the new timbered roofs were fine, as at Wilstead with its carved apostles, or Leighton Buzzard with figures of angels and carved leaf bosses.

The most frequent alteration to a church was a more impressive tower, as at Caddington, Gt. Barford, Eversholt, Harlington, Houghton Regis, Potton, Roxton, Sharnbrook and a number of others; and often also a porch, as at Husborne Crawley.

Some roodscreens of the period have survived. That at Pertenhall, once coloured and gilded, seems to have had as finial a group of the transfiguration; that at Tilbrook had figures of saints; Felmersham's was the gift of Richard Kyng and his wife Agnes. At Shelton the pulpit is probably of this time; and some of the pews which were now coming into use. Traces of wall-painting in a more formal style remain at Houghton Conquest and Langford. Milton Ernest's font is an octagonal traceried bowl.

There now begin to be more personal reminders of our Bedfordshire forebears of 500 years ago, in brasses where either figure or inscription may be lost, but which sometimes show us what they looked like, and ask disarmingly for our prayers. Sometimes the brass is to a priest, like John Waleys, once vicar of Houghton Regis; or to an abbess, as to Elizabeth Harvy at Elstow; or to an archdeacon, as to John Ruding at Biggleswade, 1481. At other times it is to the lord of a manor as at Marston to Thomas Reynes, 1451, his wife Elizabeth and 9 children. At Eaton Bray the inscription for Jane Bray reads:

> I, Jane the daughter of Edmund, Lord Bray,
> Under this stone lieth closed in clay.
> All ye my friends, I pray you, pray for me,

Perhaps most appealing is an anonymous one at Ampthill:

> Maker of man, O God in Trinity,
> That has alone all things in ordinance,
> Forgive the trespass of my "juvente" [youth],
> Nor think not, Lord, upon my ignorance.
> Forgive my soul all my misgovernance.

These churches, bright with colour as they had always been, and now possessing larger windows and beginning to have the comfort of pews, were lighted by great candles called "torches". Often around the church were figures of saints, before which small oil lamps burned. Usually such a lamp was kept burning before the rood or cross above the carved screen which separated nave from chancel; and another before a model of the holy sepulchre; while nearly every church had a figure of the Virgin, sometimes more than one. But some churches went much further than others.

Perhaps the church most adorned was Houghton Regis. There were figures of Saints Anne, Anthony, Christopher, Clement, John, Katherine, Margaret, Mary Magdalen, Michael, Nicholas, Swithin and Thomas.[1] Eaton Bray had several of these, and also St. George.[2] Luton had Saints Christopher, Clement and Katherine, and some more unusual ones; St. Blase, a 4th cent. martyr who was the patron saint of wool-combers; St. Armel, a 6th cent. Briton; St. Osith, a Saxon princess; and St. Roch, a 14th cent. Frenchman who had devoted his life to the plague-stricken.[3] Houghton Conquest, Sandy and Shillington were other churches peopled in this way.[4] Totternhoe honoured St. Agatha, a patient 11th cent. matron, and St. Giles, a 7th cent. hermit.[5]

But in other churches much greater austerity prevailed. In some, like Barton and Wilstead no images are referred to at all about 1500.[6] At Dunstable there is mention only of the rood-light, and a light before the eucharist.[7] It was not due to parsimony, for John Pettit in 1521 left money to repair the church roof;[8] was it the influence of earlier Lollardy (see below)? At Bedford there is a similar outlook. In St. Paul's church we know only of lights for the sepulchre, for Our Lady of Pity, and for St. Andrew;[9] and in the other Bedford churches of one light or none; if more lights existed, Bedfordians did not feel impelled to bequeath money for their upkeep. Poverty was not the cause, for William Joye in 1503 left money to St. Paul's for the north porch and for the making of seats;[10] and John Stow the same year to the building of St. John's steeple.[11] The same is true for some village parishes, such as Sutton, where Thomas Hobson in 1519 left money

---

[1] B.H.R.S. xxxvii, 12.
[2] Op.cit., 53.
[3] Op.cit., 43.
[4] Op.cit., 65, 41, 59.
[5] B.H.R.S. xlv, 66.
[6] B.H.R.S. xxxvii, 51, 53.

[7] B.H.R.S. xxxvii, and xlv, passim.
[8] C.R.O., A.B.P./R. 2, f.102d.
[9] B.H.R.S. xxxvii, 12, 16; xlv, 37.
[10] B.H.R.S. xxxvii, 13.
[11] Op.cit., 12.

to repair the windows;[12] Riseley, where William Gamman in 1509 left £4 to buy a cope of white damask;[13] and Souldrop, where John Lane in 1505 was interested in the paving of the aisle.[14]

Repairs to the fabric, as they still do, needed constant attention. At the visitations of 1518 and 1530,[15] churches in bad repair were Chellington, Cople, Farndish, Flitwick, Gravenhurst, Pulloxhill, Roxton, Sundon, Tingrith, Weston-ing and Willington; while at Cranfield, Haynes and Ridgmont, the roof was leaking above the high altar; and at Biddenham, Harlington, Kempston and Wootton, windows were broken. The bishop also found that in several parishes where the advowson belonged to religious houses there had not been a recent distribution of alms. There were cases of immorality at Bedford, Cranfield and Dunstable. At Studham Robert Bemund did not attend divine service.

The founding of chantries (ch. 9) continued to be popular. There were new ones at Biggleswade, Chalgrave, Shillington, Tempsford and several other places. That at Houghton Regis, founded by a mercer, William Dyve, in 1515, provided that the chantry priest was to keep a school for 6 poor children.[16]

Northill church became collegiate in 1405, there being four fellows besides the rector.

Like the towns (ch. 15), but in a smaller way, many villages had religious fraternities. Blunham's, dedicated to the Trinity, was very flourishing;[17] so was that of Eaton Socon, dedicated to Corpus Christi.[18] They arose alike in places like Houghton Regis[19] and Shillington[20], where the churches were filled with side-altars and figures of saints, as in those where greater plainness prevailed, as at Potton[21] and Riseley.[22] The Sharnbrook one seems to have petered out, for in 1522 a parishioner left money "if the parish will begin the brotherhood of the Trinity again", while at Eaton Bray in 1521 a fraternity priest was under considera-tion, for a parishioner left money "to the brotherhood priest if the parish have one".[23]

MONKS AND FRIARS

Of 15th cent. monasteries we have some details from visitations. The Cister-cian abbeys of Warden and Woburn were visited only by their own order. About 1492 there seem to have been incompatible temperaments at Warden; investiga-tion by other abbots of a supposed plot brought to light only hastily spoken words; and the offender, after a year's penance in another house, was recommen-ded for reinstatement.[24] For other orders we have episcopal visitations. The bishop's aim was not to write an objective report, but to make a confidential

12 Op.cit., 76.
13 Op.cit., 21.
14 Op.cit., 27.
15 L.R.S., xxxiii, 102–7; xxxv, 1–7.
16 V.C.H. ii, 150.
17 Ch.Cert., 6–7.
18 Op.cit., 22–3.

19 C.R.O., ABP/R 2, f.57.
20 B.H.R.S. xlv, 16 etc.
21 Op.cit., 11.
22 Op.cit., 42.
23 C.R.O., ABP/R 2, f.89.
24 Camden Soc., 4th ser., iv, 162–5.

investigation of defects; thus these records bear a relation to monastic life somewhat like that of 20th cent. law-reports to the life of to-day.

The level of education in the monasteries was one which caused the bishops concern, for the main centres of learning were now the universities of Oxford and Cambridge, and the monasteries had been to some extent reduced. However they tried to keep in touch with the latest developments. As early as 1379 prior Thomas Marshall at Dunstable set aside for the support of a scholar at the university the profits of a chantry which he founded for his parents;[25] and when a century later Erasmus met at Oxford prior Richard Charnock he found him a man after his own heart.[26] About 1434 St. Albans Abbey closed down its cell at Beaulieu Priory; this monastery had always had rather a struggle, and the patron, Lord Grey, agreed to the closure. The funds so freed were applied to the support of St. Albans' monks studying at Oxford.[27] A canon from Newnham, John Lidlington, was at the University in 1432.[28] But brother John Kempston at Newnham was said to be almost unlettered and, "understands not what he reads".[29] Both Dunstable and Newnham were told by the bishop in 1432 to provide themselves with a teacher to improve their standards;[30] and Elstow Abbey, which tended to be a home for better-off spinsters, was directed to receive teachable girls, whether or not these could make a financial contribution to the abbey (the nuns were not to wear silver pins or silken gowns).[31] With Cambridge Bedfordshire seems to have had less connection to begin with than with Oxford, but Lady Margaret Beaufort, daughter of a Bletsoe heiress, founded there Christ's College, 1505, and St. John's College, 1508.

Unbusiness-like management was found in some cases, full accounts not being regularly supplied to the chapter (or general meeting of the monks). A rough-and-ready cook at Newnham, who apparently served up unattractive canteen meals, made an excuse for the canons to visit the kitchen independently.[32] The bishops also felt that the religious were making too much of their need for a personal social life and even for recreation. The nuns of Markyate, when going home, sometimes stayed 7 or 8 days, not counting the journey.[33] At Elstow secular visitors disturbed meditation in the cloister.[34] The canons of Dunstable were directed not to invite parents, brothers, sisters or kinsfolk to have refreshment without the prior's leave;[35] and at Newnham the canons were reminded that such visitors must feed separately, so that the reading of a sacred book in the frater at mealtimes should not be interrupted.[36] There was some slackness in rising early for services. Several houses were told that silence must be kept in church and cloister,

---

[25] *V.C.H.* ii, 178.
[26] Knowles, *Religious Orders*, iii, p.152.
[27] *V.C.H.* i, 352.
[28] *L.R.S.* vii, 91.
[29] *L.R.S.* xxi, 233.
[30] *L.R.S.* vii, 47, 89.
[31] *L.R.S.* vii, 52–3.
[32] *L.R.S.* xxi, 239.
[33] *Op.cit.*, 228.
[34] *L.R.S.* vii, 51.
[35] *Op.cit.*, 46.
[36] *Op.cit.*, 88.

frater and dorter. At Cauldwell and Newnham the canons kept pet dogs;[37] those at Dunstable had gone hawking, probably on the downs;[38] and dice was not unknown.[39]

In religious houses in or near towns the inmates had been rather apt to mix with the townsfolk, which was forbidden by the bishop without special leave from the prior. At times a monk or nun temporarily quitted the cloister; at Caldwell the prior did not want to receive back the repentant brother, Thomas Goldington, and was sternly told to do so and treat him with brotherly love;[40] sister Katherine Titsbury likewise made a return to Markyate;[41] and sister Pernell, who left Elstow, was to be sought out and corrected with motherly pity.[42]

A few more serious allegations of immorality were made, especially at Newnham and Markyate, but these seem to have been unfounded. Newnham discipline about 1440 was definitely weak, partly because of the great age of prior William Wootton,[43] who, after a vigorous manhood, had become senile. The bishop ordered that his venerable old age should be treated with reverence and courtesy. His successor as prior, John Bromham, was not of stern enough calibre for his uphill task, and the bishop tried to encourage him to "take a stout and manly heart".[44] At Dunstable in 1444 there was a regrettable incident between the canons at the priory and some townsmen on one side, and the Dominican friars on the other – one friar, Peter Hobard, is said to have been thrown into a pool of water. Medieval allegations are usually exaggerated, and without the result of the enquiry it is impossible to assess what happened; but clearly there was some violence, probably from the townsmen; and it seems likely that neither canons nor friars were entirely free from blame.[45]

It is important to remember that minor irregularities and more serious faults were in fact reproved by the bishop; and that when he reprimands one religious house and reminds its inmates that they should diffuse a calm brightness of holiness, like the light on a candlestick, it is implied that this holiness is what he found in other houses. Again, there was hardship in some houses, shortage of both victual and raiment; the nuns of Markyate had no laundress, nor had they a light in the dorter for getting up at night to sing their offices.[46] In more than one house numbers had declined; there was no longer so strong a feeling that the cloistered life was superior; Walter Hilton had written "Such as lead in the world active life suffer many tribulations and temptations . . . and they have full mickle travail and dis-ease for their own and other men's sustenance . . . and they do many good deeds."[47] (By the end of the 15th cent., the *Scale of Perfection*, hitherto circulating

[37] *Op.cit.*, 27; *L.R.S.* xxi, 234.
[38] *L.R.S.* vii, 47.
[39] *Op.cit.*, 46.
[40] *Op.cit.*, 29.
[41] *Op.cit.*, 83; and cf. xxi, 229.
[42] *L.R.S.* vii, 54.

[43] *Op.cit.*, 91.
[44] *L.R.S.* xxi, 235.
[45] *Cal.Pat.R. 1441–6*, p.287.
[46] *L.R.S.* xxi, 230.
[47] *Scale of perfection* bk. i, ch. 17.

in MS. copies, was printed). In 1530, when the bishop came round, all was well at Newnham, except that they would have been glad to have some more young canons; and he dismissed them in peace, exhorting them to the perfect observance of religion.[48]

As to the Franciscans of Bedford and the Dominicans of Dunstable, many people, not only in Bedford and Dunstable but also in the villages round, left money for the friars to pray for them, or left them small donations outright. The grounds of the Bedford Friary had been enlarged about 1460 by a coney croft with a dovecote on it[49], and must now have comprised about 8 acres. A letter of 1531 mentions many kindnesses which Sir John Dyve of Biddenham had done to the brethren. There is however an adverse comment on a Dunstable Dominican in 1530, Thomas Pett, who was rather apt to frequent taverns.[50]

LOLLARDS

What is hard to assess is how far new ways of thought were coming. In some parts of England these had begun in the late 14th cent. with the Lollards. Lollardy has been described as a set of more or less consistent attitudes rather than of carefully worked-out doctrines, with tendencies towards a scriptural fundamentalism and a common-sense rationalism; it was anti-sacerdotal and anti-authoritarian.[51] For instance, Wyclif and his followers objected to the veneration of the saints, as this might lead to taking symbols for realities. There must always be new ways of thought; the testing-time comes when the new insight must be fused with the old, as was that of the monastic orders, the friars, and the universities in their time; or estrangement and conflict will ensue. This time it came to conflict.

Lollardy, though it began with an Oxford intellectual, had spread mainly among craftsmen in towns in many areas. The Lollard area which affected Bedfordshire was that of the mid-Thames valley, covering Woodstock, Wycombe, Gt. Gaddesden and Hitchin.[52] From north Hertfordshire it spread to Dunstable, where its chief supporter was a brewer, Robert or William Morley.

In 1406 the government passed a law to assist the bishops in putting down heresy. The Lollards rose in 1414 and their rising was put down. A commission was issued to the sheriff and to Lord Grey, Sir John Cornwall, and Thomas Pever to arrest all Lollards hiding in Bedfordshire.[53] Morley, who had been implicated in the rising, was hanged at Harringay.[54] He seems to have been personally ambitious, and the fact that he was hanged and not burnt indicates that the case against him was more political than religious.

A new insight is not necessarily superior; it may have defects, and it brings

[48] L.R.S. xxxvii, 28.
[49] Cal.Pat.R., 1452–61, p.581.
[50] L.R.S. xxxv, 7.
[51] J. A. F. Thomson, The later Lollards, pp.239–50. Some of these points had been made previously; on the veneration of saints, compare the Cloud of Unknowing: "Surely he that seeketh God perfectly,

he will not rest him finally in the remembrance of any angel or saint" (ch. 9).
[52] Op.cit., pp.53–94.
[53] Cal.Pat.R. 1413–16, p.177.
[54] Thomson, op.cit., p.55; Worthington Smith, Dunstable, p.183; V.C.H. iii, 363; see also K. B. McFarlane, John Wycliffe.

the danger of spiritual pride. So thought Walter Hilton when he wrote that heretics "deem and despise and set at nought other men that will not do as they do and teach . . . therefore lift they themselves upon high in their own sight above all others, weening that they live better than other and that they have only the sooth-fastness of good living and singular grace of God . . . they have neither meekness in will nor in feeling".[55] Such an attitude did not appeal to one whose main teaching was "Shape thee for to be arrayed in His likeness, that is in meekness and charity."[56] What was unfortunate was that a rift had been established. Lollardy lingered for another century over much of England, but in obscurity, with occasional arrests and executions. Though no further arrest in Bedfordshire is known, some Lollard ideas probably continued at Dunstable, and perhaps something of the same outlook became established also at Bedford (see above).

THE BIBLE

There were others who desired to make the Bible generally available. Much of the Bible was in fact known through the teaching of friars and through quotations in devotional works, such as "If I had full knowing of all thing, yea! and knew all privities and I had no charity, I am right nought", or "Whoso high himself, he shall be lowed, and whoso low himself, he shall be highed", or "What manner of deed that ye do, all do in the name of our Lord Jesus Christ, forsaking yourself and offer it up to him." But many desired to have the whole Bible. Here again there are two points of view. Modern Biblical scholarship has amply confirmed that for a proper understanding of the *whole* Bible much study is needed, though simple faith, concentrating on the gospels, can avoid pitfalls. One of those who wanted the whole Bible, and who in some other ways had developed an attitude of his own, was George Joye of Renhold, fellow of Peterhouse, Cambridge.[57] It seems that he discussed these with the prior of Newnham, John Ashwell, perhaps when paying a courtesy call at the priory on some occasion when he was visiting his relatives at Renhold. But John Ashwell was a conservative, and was worried, and expressed his anxiety to the bishop. Joye took alarm, and fled to Antwerp, where his translation of the psalter appeared in 1530, the same year as Tyndale's Pentateuch. His language has not the music of Coverdale's; nor had he "meekness in will nor in feeling" – he quarrelled with Tyndale. But he was true to his insights; and since the rift was now widening, all parties had at least to be that, whatever damage they might inflict or receive, until the passage of time should enable them to come together again.

All in all, the Bedfordshire evidence shows that in the early 16th cent. many people felt esteem and affection for their parish priest, for the monks of their nearest religious house, and for the friars of Bedford and Dunstable, left them bequests, and desired their prayers. Many followed practices which the next cen-

---

[55] *Scale of perfection*, bk. i, ch. 20.
[56] *Op.cit.*, bk. i, ch. 51.

[57] C. C. Butterworth and A. G. Chester, *George Joye*; B. *Mag.* viii, 351.

tury was to discard, such as masses for the dead (a trental, 30 successive daily masses, cost 10s., and a half-trental 5s.). There was variety throughout the county, and one surmises more simple faith and conservatism at Luton and Houghton Regis, more interest in new attitudes at Dunstable and Bedford. Joye no doubt had some friends in this county as well as at Cambridge. One would hazard a guess that the majority of people were satisfied with the old ways, if not passionately devoted to them, but that changing ways of thought were gaining ground in some places, and at Dunstable went back a long way.

BEDFORD

Since the 12th cent., Bedford's affairs had been run by the leading townsmen or burgesses. Though there is not at this date evidence as to what constituted a burgess, burgessdom probably, as it did later, descended from father to son, or could be obtained by paying a fee. Burgesses were members of the merchant gild (chs. 5, 10) and ran the town's trade. Probably a newcomer to the town, if he prospered, might be able to buy membership of the gild and become a burgess. In effect, Bedford was an oligarchy, and there would be many men who served the burgesses as journeymen, or who were too poor to rank as burgesses.

An incident of 1425 first draws attention to these townsmen of lesser status. Bedford continued to be represented in parliament by two burgesses, a representation which, as in other boroughs, was looked on rather as a burden than a privilege, because the M.P.s' expenses had to be paid. These expenses for 1423–4 (apparently a long session) amounted to £11 3s., which was felt to be very heavy. The non-burgesses, led by Thomas Blithe, John Southwode, Robert Belasys, John Crosse, John Smythe and Nicholas Taverner, refused to pay: they had no say in the town's affairs, and thought the expense should devolve on those who had. Feeling was so high that the prior of Newnham had to mediate, and eventually an award was pronounced by two judges in St. Sepulchre's church, Farringdon ward, London, in 1425. The judges awarded that the £11 3s. should be paid by all men, as well burgesses as non-burgesses.[1] The mayor, bailiffs and burgesses (the oligarchy) were to choose 4 representatives; and the non-burgesses 2 representatives; and these six were to apportion the payment according to every man's rank and standing. If, when it was collected, there was a balance, the balance should be deposited in the common chest to meet future liabilities in the town; and if at any time there was sufficient in the common chest to pay the M.P.s' expenses without an *ad hoc* levy, this should be done.

It is noticeable in the 15th cent. that borough elections were still a matter for the town only. Elsewhere in several boroughs local lords brought influence to bear. But the Greys of Wrest never seem to have had a footing in Bedford, still less the Wenlocks of Luton. The time for outside influence in Bedford's politics had not yet come.

Perhaps one reason for the financial dispute of 1425 was that Bedford was still not prospering. When a bridge was built over the Ouse at Gt. Barford, this

[1] Corporation MSS.

seems to some extent to have increased Bedford's difficulties by causing some trade to bypass the town. The townsfolk in 1447 complained that it was so great a thoroughfare to the other market towns of the county, for people who formerly came to Bedford, that tolls due to the mayor and commonalty were entirely lost. They even said that the greater part of the inhabitants were ready to abandon Bedford, unless the king provided some remedy (medieval people were good at "telling the tale"). They added that the town had come into excessive decay and ruin on account of great burthens and paucity of inhabitants, and that the fee-farm rent of £46 due to the crown could not be levied.[2] Bedford was not the only town suffering a regression at this time. There must have been substance in the account of their distress, for £22 of the annual fee-farm rent was remitted for 60 years.

When Bedford's fraternity, dedicated to the Holy Trinity, was founded is not clear. It held property which in 1547 was worth about £8 p.a., besides plate, probably used at the fraternity's special services, and maintained its own priest.[3]

Shortly after 1500 there is sufficient evidence to reconstruct the town.[4] It consisted of a small built-up area surrounded by a few closes and by open-field land and meadow. The chief congestion was round St. Paul's church and the Moot Hall, where were Butcher Row, Fish Row, Poultry Market and Pudding Lane; and of course High Street where the Saturday market was held. Here were most of the inns, the Bell, Christopher, Cock, Crown, Falcon, George and Swan. Also in the High Street stood the pillory; just off it the county gaol; and Cuckingstole lane led to a pond in St. Peter's parish. The castle mound stood green and bare, and the castle-ditch was clear for all to see (a site on the river still bore the name of Fawkes' arbour). West of the bridge was a ford called Abel's ford, probably after an earlier townsman, Abel Atewater. From various wells the townsfolk got their water; St. Laurence well was near St. Paul's church; there was one in Well Street (later Midland Road); and other wells were out in the agricultural land (Hawkewell, Hertwell and Yrenwell).

Several mills ground the corn grown by burgesses and townsmen; on the north bank of the river was Portmill; on the south bank Joel's mill (later Duck mill); and there was a horse-mill near St. Cuthbert's church. On the way to this last was the schoolhouse, and the street was called School Street. For having dung-heaps in this street five men were fined 6d. each in 1508, and it was not unknown to put dung in the Ouse.[5]

Holydays lane (the road to Goldington) was perhaps a favourite walk when at Eastertide or Maytime the townsfolk gladly left their small dark houses and confined streets.[6] Procession way probably indicated the path taken by the Rogation procession.

[2] Schedule of records, 15–16.
[3] Ch.Cert., 8–10.
[4] B.H.R.S. xxv, 19–81.

[5] Court of pleas, 1508/9, Corporation MSS.
[6] There was a family Haliday, but their known connections are with Biddenham.

The open fields north of the river (Conduit, Middle, Bury, Oak and East Fields) came close up to the edge of the built-up area, and to the Franciscan priory and the outlying churches (All Hallows, St. Peter Merton and St. Cuthbert). Stonyland and Stonypiece witness that some was not good land, but Larkslade has a pleasant sound. Between the river and Forth Street was Trumpington mead. South of the river, though the field names have not survived, the fields probably reached the king's ditch. The former hospital of St. Leonard, which was well out of the town, seems to have become a farm, for leprosy had practically died out, and though there was still a master he held it with another benefice. Both north and south of the river were butts for archery practice.[7]

By 1500 another office had appeared, that of two chamberlains, changed every year. Some of their accounts for 1507–11 have survived.[8] Their annual turnover ranged from £4–£6. Out of this they paid fees to the recorder and the steward. They dealt with the upkeep of the Moot Hall – paying for mats (10½d.), for hooks and hinges, repairs to the door or the paving beneath the hall, and having a bench made (18d.). They repaired the cucking-stool or had a new one made (5s. 3d.). They also seem to have been responsible for the chapel on the bridge, where they maintained a lamp before the Blessed Mary. Fees for becoming a burgess appear in their accounts; Henry Smith paid 26s. 8d., and William Duffyn (who was paying his by instalments) 7s. 11d. in part payment. Sometimes they paid for wine for the judges or other important people, and for minstrels. They saw that the town's armour was kept in good repair: the furbisher received 3s. 4d. for furbishing it up; they bought arrows (3s. 4d.) and a sword. When a tax was levied they spent 1d. on paper to make out the list. When there was a parliamentary election, the sheriff's warrant cost 1s.; however, the parliamentary session in 1511 seems to have been short, for the M.P.s were paid only £2 13s. 8d. The chamberlains did not deal with the hagable – the ancient rents formerly paid to the king; this came in the bailiffs' province (as did profits of the court of pleas) and in fact the chamberlains paid the bailiffs 2d. hagable for 2 acres bequeathed to the borough.

DUNSTABLE

By the 15th cent. the Dunstable chronicle had ceased. Perhaps relations between priory and town had settled down, for no more is heard of attempts by the townsmen to achieve self-government. It seems possible that Dunstable, like Bedford, was going through a recession. The overseas wool trade, so important to John Durant in the late 13th cent., was declining as the cloth industry expanded at home; nor does a Dunstable man seem to have held the office of mayor of the Calais staple, as did John Curteys of Wymington or William Hicchecok of Ampthill. Tournaments were less frequent. Traffic still passed along Watling Street – some of it not desirable, as in 1415 when some Shropshire men

[7] C.R.O. TW 362–3; A 8, p.62; A 26, p.225.   [8] Corporation MSS.

waylaid at Dunstable and maltreated there the Salop tax-collectors on their way to London to render their account.[9]

There were still occasional visits from royalty; Henry VI in 1459 during the wars of the roses issued a proclamation at Dunstable against the private armies of lords: "The king commandeth that no manner of man of this township, of what craft or mystery he be of, be adherent or drawing to any lord, to aid or go with him".[10]

Like Bedford, Dunstable had a religious fraternity (dedicated to St. John the Baptist), founded in 1442, the endowment of which in 1547 brought in about £9, and which maintained a priest.[11] Its illuminated register for some years between 1506 and 1541 shows that it drew members from the neighbourhood in both Bedfordshire and Hertfordshire.[12] A pall of brocaded Florentine velvet with a fringed border of satin, embroidered with figures of St. John the Baptist, is thought to have belonged to the fraternity.[13]

Some Dunstable men sought their fortunes further afield. John of Dunstable (d. 1453), the head of the English school of composers of his day, was musician to the Duke of Bedford (Henry V's brother). Much of his music for the mass, or motets for liturgical occasions, has been published.[14] Sir Thomas Chalton became a member of the Mercers' Company of London, where he was Lord Mayor in 1449.[15] Another family of London merchants was that of Fayrey: John was a mercer, and his son Henry (d. 1516) a haberdasher; on the velvet pall mentioned above, besides St. John the Baptist, are embroidered 27 figures of the Fayrey family, and the family may have presented or bequeathed the pall to the fraternity.

There seem to have been a number of well-to-do residents. Richard Anable or Anlaby (d. 1453) had 3 dozen silver spoons and 4 mazers, and his descendant Thomas was one of the wealthiest residents in 1524.[16] Both Joan Russell (d. 1513)[17] and Richard Welsh (d. 1519)[18] lived in South Street; and Joan's house was separated only by a close from the open fields – she left to the church enough oil to keep the lamps going for a year. Helen Church (d. 1517)[19] possessed two blue gowns, a russet gown, beads, girdles and pursells (hanging purses); her kitchen contained a cauldron, a number of brass pots and pans, chafing-dish, skillet and colander. The furniture of Richard Mone (d. 1506)[20] included two bedsteads (one with a featherbed), table, form, turned stool, and ambry (food-cupboard). The host of the Bull Inn, John Awoode (d. 1518),[21] could afford to leave £10 for works of charity in the town. Most parishioners left money to the high altar of the priory church, the parish (Trinity) altar, the Dominican friars and the fraternity;

---

[9] E. F. Jacob, *The fifteenth century*, 134.
[10] *V.C.H.* ii, 37.
[11] *Ch.Cert.*, 46.
[12] *B.H.R.S.* xxv, 1.
[13] Worthington Smith, *Dunstable*, 91–4.
[14] *Musica Britannica*, viii.
[15] *B. Mag*, iii, 183.

[16] *B.H.R.S.* xiv, 113; C.R.O., ABP/R 2, f.76 d. Cf. also ch. 16.
[17] *B.H.R.S.* xlv, 86.
[18] *B.H.R.S.* xxxvii, 71.
[19] *Op.cit.*, 68.
[20] *B.H.R.S.* xlv, 54.
[21] *B.H.R.S.* xxxvii, 73.

sometimes for repairs or running expenses, sometimes for masses for their souls. It seems that the school was still in being, for William Newton, the fraternity chaplain who died in 1500,[22] left 1d. to each poor scholar, and Richard Mone wanted his grandson kept to school. The hospital also was still in existence, though probably not now used for lepers.[23]

LUTON

The trading importance of Luton in the 15th cent. seems less than its function as a collection of agricultural estates, great and small, raising grain and rearing sheep. The Hoo family of Luton Hoo ended with four co-heiresses in 1486.[24] The many smaller manors were in different hands – the little manor of Plenties belonged to John Crawley by 1519.[25] Lord Wenlock, who held the main manor and Someries, had risen high in the wars of the roses, only to fall at Tewkesbury in 1471 (ch. 12). His estate was then granted to Thomas Rotherham, bishop of Lincoln; and the descendants of the bishop's brother, John, were to hold it for more than a century.

Thomas Rotherham was a remarkable man. He became chancellor in 1474, and his sermon to parliament in 1477 on the text "The Lord reigns over me and I nothing lack"[26] foreshadows the powerful monarchy which the Yorkists were striving for and the Tudors were to achieve. He was more than once employed on diplomatic service overseas by Edward IV. In 1480 he became archbishop of York. He was not afraid to take the difficult line, and lost his chancellorship at the accession of Richard III. He promoted learning, being one of the benefactors of Lincoln College, Oxford.[27] He began the rebuilding of his southern residence in the diocese, Buckden palace, which is in brick, and not unlike Someries[28] (Someries was probably in part his work – see ch. 12).

He also concerned himself with Luton. He left to Luton church some grey-green vestments embroidered with pheasants.[29] He and his brother in 1475 founded the Luton fraternity dedicated to the Holy Trinity, which had an endowment more than double those of the Bedford and Dunstable fraternities, and which has left records showing how a rich fraternity worked.[30]

Luton's illuminated register of members was kept continuously from the foundation, instead of sporadically, as at Dunstable. It is not a fraternity merely of small-town tradesmen. It includes Edmund Grey, Earl of Kent, his countess and his son; the prior of Dunstable and the abbot of St. Albans; and clergy and gentry from much of Bedfordshire and a wide area in Hertfordshire, its range being roughly as far as Cople, Langford and Barnet. Its endowments in 1547

---

[22] B.H.R.S. xlv, 18.
[23] B.H.R.S. xxxiii, 62: "when we went to Dunstable spitle".
[24] V.C.H. ii, 355.
[25] B.H.R.S. xxxvii, 45.
[26] Jacob, op.cit., 318.
[27] D.N.B.

[28] N. Pevsner, Bedfordshire, Huntingdonshire and Peterborough, pp.118, 215.
[29] H. L. Bennett, Archbishop Rotherham, 154; "unam sectam de glauco bawdkin", Surtees Soc., liii.
[30] H. Gough, Luton church gild register; list, pp.17–180; accounts, pp.181–237. See also Ch.Cert., 39–40.

brought in £23 p.a. For its charter legal advice in London was obtained; its constitutions were written, both in English and in Latin, in a book bought in London; and these and the deeds of its property were kept in a great coffer, probably in the Brotherhood House[31] (the cost of repairs to this house appears in the accounts). It owned a silver cope and silk banner, probably used at its special services; and at every church festival there was a good deal of expenditure on wax tapers for the altar.

How it first functioned is not clear, but nearly 50 years later the surviving accounts show that its income was spent partly on the upkeep of its property, partly on "dirges of casualties", i.e., dirges for deceased members; and the rest on a magnificent feast. The feast presumably took place in the hall of the Brotherhood House (the hall windows are mentioned in repairs); and probably on this occasion the diaper table-cloth 7 ells long and the parcel-gilt silver salt came into use at the high table, canvas cloths being used at the other tables. At this time too would be used its 12 dozen trenchers (wooden platters), and 11 dozen spoons (forks were not yet known, and each member would have his or her own knife), its pots and pans, jelly-bag and strainer, and its 14 forms; but it was also necessary to hire 26 dozen pewter plates or dishes from St. Albans for 4s. 10d. (carriage 10d.). In 1521 there were bought 61 geese, 47 pigs, 61 capons, 74 chickens, 7 dozen rabbits, 20 lambs, 600 eggs, 27 gallons of milk; besides beef, mutton, cloves, mace, citron, cinnamon, raisins, ginger, prunes, almonds, dates, saffron and comfits. Special brewing was done; there were 4 cooks (John Koke of Dunstable with 3 assistants); and also 2 men to watch the meat turning on the spits. The "whole sum of the dinner" was £20 7s. 0½d. The scale of the feast seems daunting. The 15th cent. was nearer than we are to the primitive society in which it is sensible to eat what food is available, for years of bad harvest and scarcity will surely come. Even today a festive occasion is often celebrated with a large meal.

Notwithstanding the lavish expenditure above, no Luton testator round about 1500 seems as well off in clothes or furniture as his Dunstable contemporary. Thomas Wynche (d. 1516) had two houses, one in Church Street and one in Castle Street;[32] and Alice Briggs (d. 1500) had a blue gown as well as her best gown.[33] Sheep are often mentioned; John Penthlyn, vicar (d. 1444), a Glamorgan man, who wanted mass celebrated for him in his Welsh home town, left his friend a breviary and "other books as he shall please", and to each godchild a sheep.[34] Edward Colyn (d. 1509) left each of his five children 16 sheep;[35] and Valentine Lawrence (d. 1500) left each child 20 sheep.[36] The number of sheep in 1513 bequeathed in legacies by John Sylam of Bramingham manor was 750.[37]

---

[31] Afterwards the site of the Red Lion, Market Hill; W. Austin, *Luton*, i, 208.
[32] *B.H.R.S.* xxxvii, 67.
[33] *Op.cit.*, 48.
[34] *B.H.R.S.* xiv, 112.
[35] *B.H.R.S.* xlv, 50.
[36] *Op.cit.*, 30.
[37] Austin, *op.cit.*, i, 230.

LEIGHTON BUZZARD

Leighton Buzzard still preserves its beautiful 15th cent. cross. This was probably a replacement of an earlier one. Wayside crosses and shrines were found in villages too, as at Eaton Bray and Totternhoe,[38] though only Stevington has preserved its cross intact. Almost certainly the Moot Hall must have been in existence (there was probably one at Luton too), though the earliest reference so far found to it is 1585.[39] Neither wills[40] nor fraternity records have survived for this period, though Leighton had a fraternity comparable with that of Bedford, founded in the mid-15th cent.[41] But another aspect of small-town life can be illustrated – the manorial one, for court rolls have survived for Leighton[42] for this date, though they have not for Biggleswade, Dunstable or Luton. The manor changed hands more than once during this century, for the long French wars at last in 1414 brought the precarious existence of Grovebury Priory (with its dependence on Fontevrault Abbey) to a close. In 1480 the manor went to the dean and canons of St. George's chapel, Windsor, with whom it remained for nearly four centuries. The court rolls show how close was the life of a small town to that of a village (ch. 13).

At the court, Billington, Eggington, Heath and Leighton each made separate presentments, each having its own officers (constables, chief tithingmen and ale-tasters). Attendance at court tended to be better from Leighton than from the hamlets; in March 1464 there was only one absentee from Leighton without a reasonable excuse, but nine from the hamlets.[43] However, offenders of all kinds were much more numerous in Leighton than in the hamlets.

In 1468[44] there seems to have been a drive for a price-freeze; the traders fined 4d. each for overcharging include 4 butchers, 2 bakers, 4 tanners, 2 leather-dressers, a chandler and a glover; and at most courts there are several breaches of the assize of ale and occasionally of that of bread. Sometimes there are several instances of petty brawls with dagger or staff; the fine was usually 2d. each if no blood was drawn, 4d. if it was. In November 1469 three men set on William Smith with dagger, sword, buckler and staff, and drew blood from him, but he gave a good account of himself and drew blood with his staff from one.[45] Occasionally there was violence in the hamlets; at Heath in 1468 William Harnell attacked the wife of Patrick Irysheman with a sickle.[46] One entry in 1469 seems to imply that night-watches were regularly kept in Leighton. These were ordered by Edward I, but an enquiry in 1314 revealed that in most villages "the watches are not kept".[47] Apparently by the 15th cent. they were kept in towns, for Edward Wallyngton

[38] B.H.R.S. viii, 165.
[39] C.R.O., KK 319.
[40] As Leighton was a peculiar, wills were proved locally and few survived.
[41] Ch.Cert., 49.
[42] C.R.O., KK 622.
[43] Loc.cit., m.1.
[44] Loc.cit., m.14.
[45] Loc.cit., m.16.
[46] Loc.cit., m.14.
[47] B.H.R.S. xxxii, 49.

o

and Richard Doget were fined 3s. 4d. each for refusing to obey the constable to keep watch at night, to the great harm of the whole town, and they were warned that the next offence would cost them 6s. 8d.[48]

After matters relating to law and order comes the "small court" dealing with tenancies. Thus in March 1464[49] William Straunge and his wife surrendered a house, a close, 34 acres of arable land and 3 roods of meadow; and these were taken over by John Morell the younger – very conveniently for him, for the house was next to that of his father. The arable land was described strip by strip; in each case specifying the man who held land on either side, and the field and furlong, such as East Field, Alde Field, Bidwell Field; Middlesand furlong; and other helpful landmarks, such as Salters well; or field ways (North way and Ridge way); or when the strip was a headland. The meadow was in Bridge mead, and the close at Town's End. The new tenant paid an entry fine of 13s. 4d., and was to hold the land to himself and his heirs.

An admission of 1467 records that the house of Richard Whyteman had its own well, but there were also public wells.[50]

BIGGLESWADE

Biggleswade seems to have remained small. An account of the Bishop of Lincoln's estates in 1509/10[51] shows rent from 123 burgages paying 1s. each. The greater part of the income came from rents of assize (over £36); and though 12 cotlands are noted on the roll, no sum is entered against them. This account shows that separate courts were held for borough and "foreign", i.e. inside and outside the borough; and it is noticeable that the common fine, or customary payment made when the court met, was considerably less for Biggleswade itself than for the agricultural land at Stratton.

TODDINGTON

The 15th cent. court rolls of Toddington[52], though they use the expressions "borough" and "outside the borough", appear to show only a large village (cf. ch. 5). Among the free tenants in 1510 were Richard Clockmaker and John Colermaker; and there was a butcher, William Scot.

From the patchy records of 15th cent. towns in Bedfordshire, some sort of picture emerges. All towns are small, especially Biggleswade. All have open fields and closes coming close in to the built-up area, and most townsmen have some connection with the land; this is least true of Dunstable, most of Luton. All but Bedford are towns only in the sense that they have more specialised occupations than do the villages (though this is a matter only of degree; most villages have their blacksmith, carpenter and miller, if not weaver); and also in the sense that their markets and fairs tend to be bigger and attract more custom than do those of the

[48] C.R.O., KK 622, m.16.
[49] Loc.cit., m.1.
[50] C.R.O., X 126/3; see also B.H.R.S. Survey, ii, 16.
[51] Linc. R.O., B.P. ministers' accounts 8, mm.5, 5vo.
[52] C.R.O., X 21/395.

villages. Their inhabitants still owe suit at the manorial courts of their lords – only Bedford has no lord but the king, and holds its own court. But the rights of Bedfordians are limited; a minority chooses the mayor, bailiffs and chamberlains; and the majority are beginning to be conscious of this and resent it. And Bedford is vulnerable; up to now it (or rather the burgess minority) has been unhampered in choosing representatives for parliament; but as parliament gains more standing, Bedford will have difficulty in withstanding interference from outside.

16 – LIFE IN GENERAL, 1400–1530

The machinery of local government continued much as it had in the 14th cent. The sheriff still functioned. The office was still shared with Buckinghamshire, and one sheriff used for his official seal a design with buck's horns for that county, and a lantern – for going to bed – for this.[1] Bedfordshire holders of it included Thomas Pever (1406), Thomas Wauton (1428), John Wenlock (1444), John Rotherham (1476), Edmund Cockayne (1492), John St. John (1501), John Dyve (1510), William Gascoigne (1517). But the sheriff was losing ground. In 1461 he lost what was left of his criminal jurisdiction by an act which gave legal effect to what seems for some time to have been the practice (ch. 11); though indictments and presentments were still made to him on his "tourn" of the county, he no longer had authority to decide the cases.

These were to go to the next sessions held by the justices of the peace. On 15th cent. commissions of the peace are names like those on the list of sheriffs; Thomas Pever, John Cockayne, John Rotherham and so on. This office (held for life, while the sheriff acted only for a year) was that in which local gentry got their main experience, though there were still many other offices to hold as in the previous century (ch. 11). In the troubled years of the wars of the roses they were caught up in baronial rivalries (ch. 12). More than one justice was of doubtful character: Hugh Haselden of Goldington was summoned before the Privy Council in 1427 for acts of violence;[2] and John Lawrence of Wyboston was charged with cattle-lifting in 1454.[3] Many of them had to take special oaths not to maintain breakers of the peace.[4] But, as under Henry VII and Henry VIII a strong monarchy emerged, the justices of the peace settled down as the main framework of county administration.

At the parish level things were less clear. The parish was scarcely as yet a civil institution. When in 1532–3 the government passed an act promoting the destruction of rooks and crows, responsibility for providing a net for this purpose was laid on the churchwardens. It was still the manor, or chief manor, that appointed constables. How far the constable was effective is another matter. In 1470 one at Wrestlingworth seems to have been passive: a gang of ten men with swords and bows and arrows entered John Cockayne's premises and seized John Wareyn. Cockayne brought an action against them for intimidating four of his servants.

[1] C.R.O., AD 2294 (1463).
[2] B.H.R.S. xxix, 48.
[3] Op.cit., 56.
[4] Op.cit., 37, 39, 47, 57, 59–60, 64, 75, 81.

Their version was that John Wareyn had stolen 2 silver shillings; and they only "placed their hands gently on the said servants and pushed them quietly to one side"; they then took Wareyn to Wrestlingworth and delivered him to the constable, John Balky, for transfer to Bedford gaol.[5]

LIVING CONDITIONS

Of the manner of living of Bedfordshire gentry about 1500 little detail has survived. No doubt at Wrest Park under Richard Grey, Earl of Kent (d. 1523), there was lavish display; and in 1520 when he, and John Mordaunt of Turvey, and John Gostwick of Willington (a new man), and possibly others were at the Field of the Cloth of Gold, they and their attendants were certainly resplendent. However, the Earl of Kent was to die heavily in debt, and no family was outstandingly well-to-do at this time. A few details have come down to us. Astwick manor-house in 1479 was small and simple.[6] The hangings in Joan Poley's house at Biddenham were of red say (fine woollen cloth).[7] Robert Percell, of Pertesoils manor in Riseley, had a doublet of tawny satin.[8] Rosaries were sometimes of coral, or coral and silver; and purses of damask.

For the moderately well-do-do, that is to say the better-off townsman, the agriculturalist who was beginning to be called a yeoman, and the most prosperous craftsmen among the many crafts of all kinds (cf. ch. 18), there is a good deal of information. This was their heydey. But it must be remembered that their style of living was very different from the extreme simplicity and even hardship (by modern standards) which was the lot of many in town and village. They were the upper middle-class; the living conditions of the richer among them verged on those of the lesser gentry; while the poorer approached those of their cottage neighbours.

The houses in which they lived were still as a rule half-timbered. Recently the structure of one such, a farmhouse at Tyrrells End, Eversholt, has been analysed as 15th cent. pre-fabrication:[9] a dimensional code must have been in the mind of every house-wright; minor timbers were tenoned at each end and interlocked with main members, and could not be inserted at a late stage. Main members had to be assembled together to stop the building falling over while building; thus at least one structural bay would have all members fabricated before building began.

On the walls of their hall or living-room some people had hangings or hall-ings, of coarse material on which simple designs were painted. William Wodill of Marston had one of the crucifix and another of the story of Job; and William Gold of Bedford, (who was a priest) had a cloth of St. Jerome.[10] A few, such as William Moore of Blunham,[11] possessed chairs as well as forms, and Thomas Joy of

---

[5] *Selden Soc.*, xlvii, 158–60.
[6] *V.C.H.* ii, 205: only hall, buttery, pantry and kitchen are mentioned.
[7] *B.H.R.S.* xlv, 51.
[8] *B.H.R.S.* xxxvii, 46.
[9] *Architectural Review*, cxliv, 139.
[10] *B.H.R.S.* xxxvii, 16, 29.
[11] *Op.cit.*, 65.

Bedford[12] had a settle. Several had masers, which were still prized. Quite a number, like William Core,[13] the Potton butcher, owned silver spoons – Helen Church of Dunstable[14] had 8 of them; and more than one, like Henry Davy of Ampthill,[15] had a silver dish with cover, called a "piece;" while Simon Sakewyle of Riseley[16] had a silver salt-cellar. In general however their table-ware (apart from wooden trenchers too cheap and simple for mention) consisted of pewter platters and chargers (dishes). Rarities were table-cloths, perhaps even of diaper, and board-cloths – John Edwards of Houghton Conquest[17] had more than one.

Cooking apparatus was still that appropriate for an open fire. For roasting there was a spit (William Taylor at Northill mentions his "greatest spit").[18] For boiling there were brass pans (saucepans); when Agnes Smith of Houghton Regis[19] put her stew on the table, she probably transferred it from the pan to her great brass pot. (Copper pots were not unknown but they were unusual). For heating water there were specially big pans or cauldrons (then called kettles), with a cubic capacity of anything from 2 to 10 gallons. The best-equipped household had also skillets (long-handled pots), chafing-dishes, posnets and trivets; perhaps even a colander. A few possessed an ambry, or ventilated wooden food-cupboard.

Some of the better-off slept on bedsteads with feather-beds, like John Hawes of Tempsford,[20] a thriving yeoman (ch. 13). Alice Grey of Goldington[21] had hangings to her bed, which must have been a 4-poster. Others slept on mattresses (probably filled with straw). Quite a number had pillows or bolsters; and several had at least one pair of sheets (Roger Bunker of Tingrith had 3 pairs, and Thomas Frystone of Toddington had 11 sheets in all); for best, the richest might have a pair or two of flaxen sheets; but hempen or harden sheets were more usual among the minority who could afford them at all.[22] A few had a blanket, perhaps a coverlet or quilt; Thomas Rame of Sandy[23] had a coverlet of yellow and green. At the bed's head usually stood the coffer, as did Thomas Boynon's or Bunyan's at Elstow;[24] or, if there was more than one, the best coffer. It probably held, besides best clothes, any valuables and cash. Sometimes the coffers were of spruce: sometimes painted. Harry Goditot of Wootton[25] had a red one; and that of Margery Norman at Tempsford[26] was iron-bound. John Stevens of Westoning[27] had two coffers in his chamber (bedroom) and another in the loft. Only William Arnold of Elstow[28] is known to have had a press; he must have made it himself, for he was a master-carpenter.

For washing, the better-off had a latten basin or laver, and ewer, but a towel

[12] Op.cit., 32.
[13] Op.cit., 27.
[14] Op.cit., 68.
[15] B.H.R.S. xlv, 88.
[16] B.H.R.S. xxxvii, 48.
[17] Op.cit., 65.
[18] B.H.R.S. xlv, 44.
[19] B.H.R.S. xxxvii, 12.
[20] Op.cit., 14.

[21] Op.cit., 40.
[22] Op.cit., 47; B.H.R.S. xlv, 45.
[23] B.H.R.S. xxxvii, 53.
[24] B.H.R.S. xlv, 97.
[25] B.H.R.S. xxxvii, 79.
[26] B.H.R.S. xlv, 15.
[27] B.H.R.S. xxxvii, 23.
[28] B.H.R.S. xxxvii, 78.

was a luxury. Candlesticks (as distinct from a simple iron rushlight-holder) might also be of latten or pewter. Books were owned by clergy; almost certainly some gentry had them too, since quite a number were now printed. The yeoman and townsman seem not yet to have reached this point, though they might leave money to buy a book for the church – Cecily Hopkyn of Dunton[29] left £5 to buy for the church a new copy of *Nova Legenda*.

DRESS

For clothes, men's wear for the older or more conservative still included the long or full-length gown, which might be of black or blue (Thomas Cyne of Houghton Regis[30] had a violet one), but was usually of russet or tawny. If the wearer could afford it, it was furred, perhaps with black lamb. Probably originally it was worn for warmth in draughty halls; and now that houses were better built it was giving place to a short gown, tunic or doublet, which generally was of fustian, worsted or buckskin, and for gay wear might (like John Lord's of Millbrook[31]) be of murrey or purple-red. John Rudde of Eaton Bray[32] – possibly a gay young man – had violet hose.

Better-off women also had fur on their gowns; Kathleen Vincent of Elstow[33] wore one furred with fox; Joan Porte of Bedford,[34] for defence against the cold, had to be content with lining hers with thick frieze. One of the best-dressed women in the neighbourhood must have been Elizabeth Mason of Renhold,[35] who, besides her everyday gown of mustredevilliars (grey woollen cloth), had gowns of sanguine, blue and violet, girdles of blue and green, and kirtles of russet, violet and red. Most women, however, like the men wore russet or black, protected with an apron, and also wore a kerchief. Some extravagance might be allowed with the girdle; Matilda Bath of Henlow[36] even had one of silver; and with beads or rosary. The rosary belonging to Kathleen Vincent[37] had an *agnus dei* (wax stamped with the figure of a lamb, blessed by the Pope). When they needed to carry money, women wore pursells or hanging purses. Money, however, was still of limited use – most people thought in terms of crops and stock. A legacy to a godchild would more often take the form of a calf or a lamb than of cash; and even a bequest for a public purpose would quite often be a measure of barley or a cow (perhaps specifying the red, the black or the brindled heifer, as the case might be).

ROADS AND BRIDGES

After the church, the public purpose next the heart of respectable folk was the upkeep of roads and bridges. Since before the Conquest this had been a public liability, but there was no satisfactory machinery for enforcing it. Bedford streets

29 *B.H.R.S.* xlv, 83.
30 *B.H.R.S.* xxxvii, 22.
31 *B.H.R.S.* xlv, 80.
32 *B.H.R.S.* xxxvii, 53.
33 *Op.cit.*, 17.

34 *Op.cit.*, 38.
35 *Op.cit.*, 28.
36 *B.H.R.S.* xlv, 14.
37 See 33.

were bad; in 1505 Joan Studdeley[38] left 40s. to repair the worst roads and streets there; and John Cowper[39] a like sum in 1502 for ways near Bedford. In the county it must have been much worse, even though the traffic was mainly horse traffic, packhorses (for whom Sutton packhorse bridge was built), waggons and those on foot. Even 50 years later in 1549 the people of Gravenhurst[40] said that between them and Shillington were "two several waters, and the same waters at divers and many times of the year do use to rise with land floods so high that the people cannot pass over the same without danger of drowning and cannot pass by the highway in the winter season for dirt and mire". Some public-spirited people left money, even if only 12d., for roads in their parish "where most need is". Others were precise: John Maynard[41] wanted the work to be done on the road from his house in Broom to the gate of Southill church. Puddle Hill was what worried Thomas Anlaby of Dunstable.[42] One of the worst places in the county was Tempsford. Twenty loads of stone and gravel were left for roads here by John Fisher;[43] and according to John Hawes[44] the road from Tempsford to Biggleswade was called the Soul Slough. The bridge most often needing repair was Stafford bridge between Oakley and Pavenham; those over the Ouse at Barford, Biddenham, Turvey and Harrold, and over the Ivel at Girtford also required attention, as did many small bridges over local brooks, such as Tymsyll bridge in Stagsden.

LEISURE PURSUITS

Amusements for the gentry were mainly hawking (in which the Dunstable canons were tempted to indulge on the downs), or hunting deer, as the Earl of Kent did in Ampthill park, till he lost it in 1508 to the king. Ampthill then became one of Henry VIII's favourite hunting seats; he enlarged the park and in 1532 he took Anne Boleyn there, and she gave him a hunting frock and hat, with a horn and a greyhound.[45] Many gentry who could not rise to a deer park had a coney warren (under royal licence perhaps going back to the 13th or 14th cent.).[46] In 1515 Clophill warren was let for as much as £3 p.a.[47] Humbler people no doubt went poaching, especially for conies. Cockfighting, certainly practised later in Bedfordshire, probably took place at this date. There were also bull-baiting and bear-baiting; in Bedford these took place in St. Paul's churchyard at the east end where a path still runs.[48]

Holidays at the main church festivals gave ordinary folk an outlet for their energies; and probably in the 15th cent. too there were occasions such as that in 1247[49] when "the whole countryside met at the chapel of Limbury for sports";

[38] B.H.R.S. xlv, 2.
[39] Op.cit., 33.
[40] C.R.O., P 17/25/14.
[41] B.H.R.S. xxxvii, 60.
[42] C.R.O., ABP/R 2, f.76d.
[43] B.H.R.S. xlv, 14.
[44] B.H.R.S. xxxvii, 14.
[45] V.C.H. ii, 38.
[46] Flitton, 1319: Priestley, 1336; C.R.O., L 682, 827.
[47] C.R.O., L 343.
[48] V.C.H. iii, 139; B.H.R.S. xxxvi, 18.
[49] B.H.R.S. xxi, 148.

or wrestling-matches, as at Goldington in 1267 or Hockliffe in 1283.[50] Though we have no specific Bedfordshire references for them, some form of cricket and of football existed in the 14th cent. and presumably were played here. Indulgence in many games was forbidden by law, and this finds its echo in manor court rolls. When these merely give a general prohibition, as in Leighton Buzzard in 1469[51] when tennis, quoits and dice were forbidden, there is a suspicion that such games were in fact being played; but there is no doubt about it at Ampthill in 1502 when 11 men were fined 20d. each for playing bowls and 12 (some of them the same) for playing tennis;[52] and in Bedford in 1508 men were fined for playing cards.[53] The object of such restrictions was to encourage all youths and men to spend their leisure practising archery, but as all these games were simpler in form than at present probably young men often managed to play in a quiet spot unobserved by constable or tithingman. There was certainly music sometimes, for we hear of Beatrice "le fitheler" in 1305, William "le taborer" in 1294, and William Leche, minstrel, in 1468.[54]

A festive occasion which also had a public purpose was a church ale, when, in aid of church funds, the churchwardens organised a special brewing to which the parish came. Refreshment was also called for at the beating of bounds in Rogation week, and more than one parish had an endowment to provide for a "drinking" then; at Potton it had been bequeathed by Robert Whyttesyde.[55]

Some celebrations went back to pre-Christian days (ch. 1), even though their origin was no longer remembered or understood. They are found later, and so must have continued through the Middle Ages. One such for which we have Bedfordshire evidence was Plough Monday, following the mid-winter solstice, the death of the old season and the birth of the new. In Christian times it was celebrated on the Monday after the twelve days of Christmas recess. With blackened faces for anonymity, the ploughboys toured the village with a dummy plough, singing, and demanding gifts.[56]

Another survival was a spring fertility rite which continued till the summer solstice. The maypole, 100 ft. high, the tallest and straightest tree in the wood, brought in with the may and with a special song, was a phallic symbol, and the Morris dancers stamped to awaken the earth-goddess and jumped high for growing corn. (The term Morris came into use in the 15th cent. from the continent, probably from ancient combative dances of Christians and Moors, but the dance is older.) This festival had been largely converted to church uses. The Bedford-

---

[50] *B.H.R.S.* xli, 7; *V.C.H.* iii, 383.
[51] C.R.O., KK 622.
[52] C.R.O., L 26/48.
[53] Court of pleas (Corporation MSS.).
[54] C.R.O., TW 19, 46, and see also LL 1/9. Corporation MSS X 67/68.
[55] *B.H.R.S.* xxxvii, 31.
[56] Mr F. Hamer kindly informs me that Plough Monday was observed in the present century in several villages in the north of the county – Harrold as late as 1937 (cf. Harrold school logbook 9 Jan. 1888) and in Stevington and Little Staughton. If money was refused, the boys would make a feint of ploughing up the ground before the door. Elsewhere a play was performed; see E. O. James, *Seasonal feasts and festivals*, 297.

shire practice seems to have been that some villages were special centres, as was Northill.[57] The churchwardens provided the funds for the Morris dancers' bells, shoes and coats; and between Whitsuntide and Midsummer Day the dancers toured the neighbourhood, bringing luck and collecting money. The proceedings ended with a substantial feast (3 calves, spice, fruit, and "hops to brew the beer withal") on Midsummer Day, and with a bonfire for the summer solstice. On the occasion for which we have most details, the churchwardens' outlay nearly doubled itself in the return brought in for church funds.

One more pagan survival was witchcraft. Though no medieval instances in Bedfordshire are recorded, yet they occur in the 17th cent., and witchcraft must have lingered throughout the middle ages.

Bedfordshire in 1530 was a county of small estates. It had no great lord or figure of national importance. There were one or two energetic men among the new gentry. There were also many agriculturalists of moderate status, who were beginning to be called yeomen; and these and the craftsmen were thriving. There were also in the county poorer men who had not succeeded in profiting by the new opportunities. It had two sizeable towns (by national standards they were small), one self-governing, the other not; and some smaller market-towns. It had ties with London trade. Its churches were nearly all built in the form in which they have come down to us now; its religious houses seem to have been conservative and respected; and it had links with new thought at Cambridge. It had at least four schools, and printed books were beginning to circulate. So far as we know. local administration by justices of the peace in quarter sessions functioned smoothly, for, like the rest of England, it was thankfully at peace under the rule of a firm king. It seemed set for peaceful development. Like the rest of England it was now to receive a shock – the Reformation.

---

[57] *B.H.R.S.* xxxiii. For the May song in Bedfordshire see *Jnal.E.F.D.S.*, ix, 81–5. The geographical distribution of English ceremonial dance traditions was recently plotted by J. Needham (*Jnal.E.F.D.S.* iii, 1–39). In Bedfordshire the season (Whitsuntide) and the use of bells show affinity with "Cotswold Morris" practised in the area described by Needham as Saxon Mercia (northwest Morris is in August, and East Anglian Morris had no bells). For the Midsummer bonfire, see James, *op.cit.*, 314–6.

The Reformation and After

17 – LORDS AND SQUIRES, 1530–1603

SIGNS OF CHANGE

The movement known as the Reformation had economic and religious consequences. The economic ones will be taken first. This is because the economic effect of the dissolution of religious houses in Bedfordshire was felt at once. The religious effect of Henry VIII's changes came as delayed action. New ways of religious thought had not left Bedfordshire untouched; people did not rush (as they did in the north) to the defence of the old order; neither, on the other hand, were many anxious for a new order – it was to be a hundred years before puritanism began to grip the county. It is important to see the changes through contemporary eyes. The king himself, in his own view, was making no fundamental change in doctrine, though in fact he was releasing more than he knew. Kings and Popes had disagreed before now, and things had righted themselves after a time, so many probably thought that they would do so again. Religious houses had been dissolved before now (the alien houses during the Hundred Years War, as with Grovebury in 1414 or Farley hospital in 1447; and some years later Beaulieu Priory was closed because of poverty – ch. 14). Our forebears can be imagined in the 1530's as for the most part looking on with slight puzzlement; not saying too much, because, with a king like Henry VIII, this was unwise; but waiting to see which way the cat would jump; and with some exceptions (ch. 18) not at first feeling deeply involved.

To most people in Bedfordshire the first impact of events was probably late in 1532 or early in 1533 when Queen Catherine was brought for a few months to Ampthill castle; while on 10 May in the church of Dunstable Priory the new Archbishop, Thomas Cranmer, accompanied by four bishops, opened a court to adjudicate on the validity of her marriage to the king (that question which Henry VIII had for years been trying to resolve by existing means). Sentence was pronounced against Catherine on 23 May in her absence, for she refused to appear, and would not relinquish the title of Queen. When in July at Ampthill her chamberlain remonstrated with her, unwell as she then was and lying on her couch, and addressed her as Princess Dowager, she objected, and with her own hand struck out the words from his draft report to the king. Soon afterwards she was transferred to Buckden palace and then to Kimbolton castle, where she died in 1536. It may well be the general sympathy for her locally that later in central Bedfordshire caused her name to be (erroneously) associated with pillow-lace;

and in north Bedfordshire a confused tradition survived of her journey to Buckden.[1]

To shrewd men possibilities began to appear ahead. Henry VIII had now disbursed most of the full treasury to which he had succeeded. An act of parliament in 1534 declared him supreme head of the church; and another appropriated to him the first-fruits of benefices. In 1536 he dissolved the smaller religious houses; and a few years later the larger ones; and confiscated their property. Thus he re-established a royal estate which had almost disappeared since 1066; and provided himself with ready cash by sales of surplus land. In the first place, the sequence of events gave opportunities in the royal service for at least a short term; and secondly those who were quick off the mark would have first chance to purchase, for investment or speculation, land. Once again there was land hunger, for nearly two centuries had restored the population, and recurrences of the plague were mainly limited to London (there was one in 1534–5) and to towns. There was a great difference in outlook between the 15th and 16th cents. Then the openings were for warlike supporters of great lords, and treason was an admissible political counter. Now the opportunities were for peaceful investment in land, and treason was the worst of all crimes.

The county representatives in the reformation parliament, 1529–36, were George Acworth and Sir William Gascoigne. Acworth was son of John Acworth, a founder-member of the Luton gild; he owned the manor of Limbury-cum-Biscot. Gascoigne was descended from the famous judge – the family had acquired Cardington manor by a Pigot marriage; a later writer describes him as "a rough gentleman, preferring rather to profit than please his master", but valued by Wolsey for his shrewdness. He had been controller of the household for that magnificent prelate, who rose to power and riches without equal in the kingdom, and fell and died in 1529. A connection of Gascoigne's, John Gostwick of Willington (ch. 13), had also been in Wolsey's service, and both managed to side-step their master's fall; later in this reign he too was to become M.P., as were John and Oliver St. John of the Bletsoe family (ch. 12).

A MAN OF HIS TIME

Gostwick's career[2] illustrates his age. In his earlier years he had found time to carry on some trade; he had obtained a grant of arms; and had built a new manorhouse on the manor where his ancestors had been bailiffs. By 1530 he was already well-to-do. He was on good terms with Thomas Cromwell, to whom on one occasion he sent a calf and pigeons. In 1534 he became a justice of the peace. He was now appointed treasurer of the first-fruits at a salary of £100 p.a. He served as commissioner for the dissolution of the Franciscan friary at Bedford, of Elstow Abbey, and of Dunstable and Newnham Priories. With building stone which may have come from the last, he erected new farm buildings at Willington

---

[1] Evidence in the 1967 footpath survey. [2] B.H.R.S. xxxvi, 57–75.

(a stable and dovecote completely of stone, but the stone did not quite suffice for the third, a barn). In 1540 he was knighted. In 1541 he received the king at Willington, and the room the king occupied was remembered afterwards: "King Henry VIII of famous memory of late lay therein." The furniture of the manorhouse included a Turkey carpet, tapestries, a cypress chest, and (in his own room) a bed with a yellow and black tester embroidered J.G.

When Gostwick died in 1545 he left written advice for his 20–year old son.[3] After practical hints on household and estate management, he continued "I charge you of my blessing to get the goodwill and favour of all your neighbours, as well in Willington as in all the whole shire, and to do for them and help them in all other causes according to your power. And in your so doing you shall please God and also have the love of them ... And be true to God, the king and your friend." He and his like realised how their prosperity depended on the mystique of kingship which had grown up in the last 50 years. If anyone should talk treason to young Gostwick, "then I charge you not to keep his counsel, but open it to two or three of the next justices of peace which dwelleth next unto you, or else to one or two of the king's most honourable [Privy] Council if you may get unto them. But in any wise, utter it as soon as is possible, for the longer you keep it the worse it is for you, and the more danger toward God and the king's majesty."

REDISTRIBUTION OF PROPERTY

The ex-monastic property in Bedfordshire was not only that of the 9 abbeys and priories, 2 friaries and a preceptory. Religious houses in surrounding counties also had Bedfordshire property: Berkshire (Reading Abbey); Bucks. (Notley Priory); Cambs. (Thorney Abbey); Essex (Waltham Abbey); Glos. (Lanthony Priory); Herts. (St. Albans Abbey and Sopwell Priory); Hunts. (Ramsey and Sawtry Abbeys and St. Neots and Stonely Priories); Leics. (St. Mary's Abbey); Middlesex (Holywell Priory); Northants. (Pipewell Abbey and Canons Ashby Priory).

Besides land there were tithes and advowsons. Though tithes were originally offerings for the clergy and church, when transferred to religious houses the great tithes (or tithes of corn – ch. 1) were looked on as property like any other; and it was not thought incongruous that they should now come into lay hands. With the great tithes, or rectory, usually went the advowson; advowsons had always been thought of as private property.

What were the economic consequences for Bedfordshire of the re-distribution of monastic property? One was that again the crown had a considerable estate in the county, though it lacked cohesion and before long dwindled. For centuries there had been no royal land here till a debt owed to that careful king, Henry VII, prised Ampthill from the grasp of the careless Earl of Kent. Ampthill therefore

[3] B.H.R.S. xxxvi, 38–45.

would be the head of the royal estate. Harking back to the term honour, used centuries earlier for large baronial estates and still in use elsewhere, an honour of Ampthill was set up by act of parliament in 1542.[4] In it were included extensive ex-monastic lands in this county and some in Bucks. The rents of these properties now went to the king. Special privileges often went with an honour, and that of Ampthill had its own coroner. From the royal estate provision could now be made when needed for members of the royal family; thus in 1550 the young Edward VI granted to his sister, the princess Elizabeth, the ex-Ramsey manors of Barton, Cranfield and Shillington, and property at Eversholt and Warden.

Part of the available wealth went for public purposes, but it was a small part. (For the abortive proposal for a bishopric at Dunstable see ch. 18). Trinity College, Henry VIII's foundation at Cambridge, received property at Roxton and Stotfold, and several rectories and advowsons, such as Gt. Barford, Cardington, Eaton Bray, Keysoe and Felmersham. Eton College acquired some property of Caldwell Priory in Bromham and also the advowson; Christ Church, Oxford, that of Cople (formerly Chicksands).

Who got the remainder? A general acquisitiveness prevailed.[5] Thus Bushmead Priory "lay so near his [Sir John St. John's] house that if he should be driven to remove he could find no place so meet . . . but I hear Mr Gascoigne labours for the same".[6] Or the Franciscan friary at Bedford would be a convenient second residence for John Gostwick; "if sickness should happen in his house, he has no other to resort to".[7] Those who were in a position to do so bought what they could get, with the idea of later disposing of or exchanging what they did not want. In this game of "catch as catch can", property changed hands as a rule not only once but many times. So much became available at once that it unbalanced the market for years. In most cases it was not until two generations had passed that a stable pattern began to emerge. By this time only a small fraction remained with the families of the original grantees (some of whom seem to have been simply speculators); and in some cases it had disintegrated into very small holdings, and become lost to view among the most modest holders of land (ch. 20).

By 1603 it can be seen that some existing families have been strengthened, whether of lords or squires. For there were now a few lords. Sir Henry Grey (d. 1562) had lived circumspectly, had managed to acquire the manor of Tewelsbury in Gravenhurst (Ramsey Abbey) and that of St. Thomas chapel in Meppershall (Chicksands Priory); and his grandson, Henry Grey (d. 1615) was able to hold up his head as 6th Earl of Kent. The Mordaunts of Turvey (John Mordaunt was created Baron Mordaunt in 1533) secured St. Neots Priory's land in Turvey. The St. Johns, established at Bletsoe in the 15th cent. (Oliver was created Lord St.

[4] *V.C.H.* iii, 271.
[5] Particular references are not given for acquisitions of monastic land; they are easily traced in the

V.C.H.
[6] *V.C.H.* iii, 197.
[7] *B.H.R.S.* xxxvi, 69.

John in 1559), obtained the manors of Bolnhurst (Thorney Abbey) and of Keysoe Grange (Chicksands Priory). Thomas Cheney, who married the Toddington heiress, Anne Broughton, secured land in the neighbourhood and his son became Lord Cheney.[8]

Several squires had also improved their position. Incidentally the term esquire, which at one time meant an attendant on a knight, now stood for the holder of a moderate-sized estate and member of a family bearing arms. Arms, originally a device for recognising a man in armour, were now a status symbol; and their use was supervised by the College of Arms (whose heralds made visitations of the county in 1566 and 1582).[9]

Thus the Boteler family, who had established themselves as gentry in Biddenham by the 16th cent., acquired in 1540 the Biddenham property of Newnham, Caldwell and Harrold priories, which they still retained.[10] The Gostwick family, represented by the descendants of Sir John's brother, still had Newnham Priory's Renhold and Ravensden lands. The Crawley family of Luton had in 1586 secured Dallow manor (St. Albans Abbey) from the original grantee, and were extending their holdings in the area. The Luke family, where two generations had already made fortunate marriages (with a Launcelyn[11] heiress in Cople and a Wauton heiress in Eaton Socon) had by marriage with Anne Hemmyng, whose father purchased for £709 the manor of Arleseybury (Waltham Abbey), secured that property.

Some families had used their acquisitions as bargaining counters. The Burgoyne family had come to Sutton about 1500. They secured various ex-monastic properties: Millo manor, Dunton (Waltham Abbey) in 1541; a Girtford manor (Caldwell priory) in the same year; Hasells manor, Sandy (Chicksands priory) in 1542; Higham Gobion advowson (Markyate priory) about the same time; and some Sawtry Abbey land in Everton. Most of these outlying properties they had disposed of by 1603, and had extended their holdings in Potton, which lay more conveniently for their Sutton seat. To some extent a similar policy was practised by the St. Johns.

Some families who appeared to start in a good position had obtained little or no enhancement. Thus though George Acworth got Lewsey manor (Markyate priory) in 1545, he soon sold it, nor did he fare better in the north. Though Sir William Gascoigne got the Bushmead site by exchange with St. John, it did not long remain with his family.

Sometimes the steward did well (monasteries often had as steward a local gentleman), as did Edward Staunton at Woburn[12]; by the end of the century this family was well established. (Yeomen who were monastic tenants were also well

---

[8] J. H. Blundell, *Toddington*, 48–9.
[9] Printed in *Harl. Soc.* xix.
[10] C.R.O., WW 243.
[11] Ann Launcelyn was nurse to Henry VIII; *Harl. Soc.*

xix, 39.
[12] *V.C.H.* iii, 461; and cf *V.C.H.* ii, 40, 44; iii, 418; also *B.H.R.S.* xvi, 59.

placed – see ch. 20, which also deals with fragmentation of ex-monastic lands among men of humble standing.)

There were some families new to the county. Thus Harrold Priory had been obtained by a London grocer, Ralph Farrar or Farrer. Elstow Abbey, by the marriage of the grantee's heiress, had gone to the Radcliffe family, and was soon to be sold by them to Thomas Hillersdon, a family which was to remain. In the north Bushmead Priory and much of its estate had finally gone in 1562 to the Gerys of Cambridgeshire origin; while in the east in 1578 the Osborn family had established themselves at Chicksands (Richard Osborn was another London grocer); these two were to stay for centuries. A more distant family, Payne from Worcestershire, had in 1545 secured Podington rectory and advowson (Canons Ashby Priory); William Payne, who built up a Podington estate, was an able man, and at the turn of the century was both clerk of the peace for the county and town clerk for Bedford.

One new family could in 1603 hardly be said as yet to be of Bedfordshire. Henry VIII, in making John Russell a trustee of his will, had stipulated that a gift should be made to him, and in 1547 Russell received the manor and site of Woburn; he purchased the preceptory of Melchbourne; and in 1550 was created Earl of Bedford. The family's main interests were elsewhere, and it was reluctantly that the then Earl temporarily opened up the dilapidated abbey for Queen Elizabeth in 1572, when he asked Burleigh to "help that her Majesty's tarrying be not above two nights and a day – for so long time do I prepare".[13]

LAND USE

Turning from the ownership of land to its use, it will be remembered that in the 15th cent. (ch. 12) there were occasional parks for hunting, that the trend was for owners to lease out lands and live on rents, and that there was a little enclosure, apparently mainly for sheep-farming.

Some parks were enlarged in this century. Henry VIII, not satisfied with Ampthill park, enlarged the small park nearby at Houghton Conquest by 1542, reducing the holdings of over a dozen tenants by 66 a. in all; a note in the rental says "the rents have not been paid because the bailiff does not know where the property is and who holds it."[14] The Earl of Kent enlarged Wrest park, then to the north of the house, taking in land from Flitton and Clophill.[15] The parks at Harrold and Steppingley may be one reason for the comparatively small population of these parishes in relation to their area, though there were other factors; that at Harrold contained about 100 deer, which the keeper was to maintain to his uttermost power, delivering at Wrest such venison as the Earl required, and being allowed annually for himself a buck and a doe.[16] The Harrold deer

[13] V.C.H. iii, 459.
[14] P.R.O., S.C. 6 Hen. VIII, 6070.
[15] C.R.O., L 153 and cf. L 4/296-9.
[16] C.R.O., L 7/51-68.

attracted poachers from Olney.[17]

Where the estate was of sufficient size, or where it belonged to an institution, owners continued to let the demesne of outlying manors. The Earl of Kent still let Thurleigh; St. Paul's cathedral let Zouches in Caddington; a Kentish owner let Rowney; there was usually a yeoman or husbandman ready to act as tenant (ch. 20). As for the copyhold tenants, where the manor was of sufficient size, it was worth while to see that the steward held regular courts to enforce copyhold tenure; and where there was steady ownership this policy could be maintained. Sometimes the coalescence of parts of manors helped to form more sizeable units; courts continued to be held at Potton and Kempston, at Stevington and Podington; and in general on the Wrest estate; but at Thurleigh leases for terms of years with an entry fine were used even for very small holdings;[18] these leases usually allowed the tenant to lop willows and maples; but any oaks or ashes in pightle or close (as distinct from open field land) were listed for preservation. Where manorial courts were held they were gradually becoming irregular. In many small so-called "manors" they must have been either obsolescent or extinct.

ENCLOSURE

There remains the question of enclosure, whether for sheep-farming or for other purposes. It was by no means merely a concern of lord or squire, but for the most part it may conveniently be discussed in this chapter. It was carried out piecemeal over a long period: by exchange a man could collect together some of his strips in the open fields; after that it was a question whether he could get away with putting up fences; thus at Arlesey in 1592 Newcomen enclosed a balk, but was ordered to allow inhabitants to pass along it with their cattle, and it was agreed there should be a gate.[19] If he could exclude his neighbours from common right he could do as he wished with the land.

In the early Tudor period the booming cloth trade elsewhere increased the drive for sheep-farming, but after about 1547, when there were risings in Norfolk and the west, for various reasons the demand for wool slackened.[20] In Bedfordshire, after William Boteler of Biddenham (d. 1554), merchant of the Calais staple, the only wool-merchant or woolman of whom we hear is William Fanne of Langford (d. 1591).[21] Very few shepherds are known (only 3 wills survive). Where there are records of stints, they usually allow 2 sheep to 1 a. of cultivated land,[22] though at Luton in 1551 Thomas Crawley grossly exceeded his allowance; and stints of cattle are discussed at least as often as stints of sheep. The numbers engaged in the clothing trades are those required to supply local demand (ch. 19). At Harrold, where enclosure for sheep was known previously, the Earl of Kent let

---

[17] C.R.O., L 24/189–204.
[18] C.R.O., L 15.
[19] C.R.O., IN 66.
[20] S. T. Bindoff, *Tudor England*, 112–46; *Agrarian*

History of England, iv (ed. J. Thirsk) 211.
[21] C.R.O., ABP/R 23, f.67d.
[22] C.R.O., CRT 160/45. Gostwick in 1545 kept 400 ewes; *B.H.R.S.*, xxxvi, 43.

P

his sheepwalk for £22 in 1584.[23] In south Bedfordshire the developing trade at this time was in malt (ch. 19); while in east Bedfordshire the gardener and in central Bedfordshire the dairyman and grazier are about to appear.

But enclosure might also be made for other purposes, and there are some parishes where it can be traced, apart from the vanished or unsatisfactory returns made to government commissions. The main initiative seems to come from the squire, sometimes acting with his tenant, and with a varying amount of local agreement.

At Dunton in 1593 John Burgoyne made sufficient exchanges to let Chamberlainsbury with land, meadow and pasture "now altogether enclosed".[24] At Rowney in 1569, where the tenant was Nicholas Thoroughgood, yeoman, the manor included two arable fields called Shefford Field, 300 a., and Pond Field, 107 a., besides various closes and woods;[25] one cannot be sure how much was due to owner, how much to tenant.

At Bromham about 1560 Sir Lewis Dyve (according to his son's later statement)[26] used persuasion when enclosing a meadow. He pointed out that everyone lost by the method of setting forth, measuring, allotting and carrying of the grass and hay by lots and doles in small pieces far distant one from the other, and induced his tenants and others to exchange and amalgamate their holdings. Other owners agreed, and Latimer's tenant "for his better satisfaction therein carried the one end of the line wherewith the land was measured". At Bromham too (again probably instigated by Dyve) there are references in 1595 to enclosure of arable land in East and North Fields.

Persuasion did not always prevent trouble. At Blunham, with the agreement of the most part of the better sort, the Earl of Kent agreed to forgo his right of pasture on the common (said to be about 300 a.), in return for enclosing about 10 a. near his house, where he often spent some part of the summer.[27] But Blunham was a ticklish place. There had already in 1581 been a fight with Tempsford about inter-commoning, when 17 Tempsford men (4 yeomen and 13 labourers or cottagers), drove out the men of Blunham with horses and carts, although Blunham men deposed that they had "continually time out of mind eaten [i.e. grazed] the grass there as parcel of the waste ground". On this later occasion, which appears to have been in April 1604, the discontented met in the church and

[23] C.R.O., L 7/51.
[24] C.R.O., FN 534-5.
[25] C.R.O., X 95/133.
[26] C.R.O., TW 1031; also TW 1019.
[27] P.R.O., St.Ch. 8, 156/32 is an undated petition by the Earl of Kent, in which he makes the surprising statement that the enclosure was carried out 16-17 years previously; he also says that about three score persons took part in the riot, though the names given number only about 20, of whom half are women and several of Robert Ball's own household. Ball's will (ABP/R 29, f.57) shows that he was able to

leave £10 to each of seven children. Laurence Wootton, whom he appointed deputy constable during his absence in St. Neots, was a yeoman (ABP/R 26, f.88); he died in the spring of 1605 leaving young daughters, which seems to indicate that the riot was in April 1604. The agreement is C.R.O. L 1/2. For the earlier trouble at Blunham, see C.R.O., BS 1380; and for the general background L 24/618-46; L 24/643 states that some Blunham men were claiming right of common for 6 cattle to every half-yardland, though some half-yardlands had shrunk from 16 a to 6 a.

"to the intent to give the more full and absolute assurance the one to the other of their persisting and holding together . . . they bound themselves in the sum of 40s. apiece"; they broke down the fence, cut the quick hedge; and drove in their own cattle. The Earl's servants tried to drive out the intruding cattle and repair the fence, but about 20 men and women with staves and pitchforks withstood them, while a "dissolute rogue", Thomas Reyner, shouted "Now for King James and the commons of Blunham!" The leading spirit seems to have been, not Reyner, but Robert Ball, who was one of the constables for that year, and was not a poor man (having a mercer's business in St. Neots); the other constable did his best endeavour to cause the peace to be kept. However in October 1604 a formal agreement was made by which about 40 men released their rights in the pasture in question; most were yeomen or husbandmen; there were also the mercer, Robert Ball, a glover, 2 tailors, carpenter, smith and 5 labourers (or cottagers).

On the other hand there sometimes was general tacit agreement. For Caddington (which belonged to St. Paul's cathedral) there exists a list dated 1569 of enclosures carried out at intervals during the last 30 years, made by 25 men and totalling 367 a.[28] The chief enclosure was made by the tenant of Zouches manor, about 150 a., Richard Mershe; Thomas Mershe had also enclosed 26 a. and his son Henry 23 a. The other men had enclosed anything from 1 to 31 a., several of them taking more than one bite at the cherry (ch. 20).

Maps can show the results, though not the process; but early Bedfordshire maps are rare. One for Toddington in 1581 shows a certain amount of enclosure and the rest of the parish in strips; some for Salford in 1595–6 show (by comparison with an earlier rental) that about 50 a. of arable land had been enclosed during the preceding century, yet most of the area still lay in common fields.[29]

LARGER UNITS

Connected with, but not necessarily involving enclosure, was the formation of larger units. Rising prices and demand from London and other towns for agricultural products offered a reward for the man who could farm a bigger area than his neighbours; so that, on a much smaller scale, there was a tendency at work like that of to-day. For a bigger holding the lord could charge more rent. Where farms were amalgamated, the lesser farmhouse was either let to a cottager or labourer, and so down-graded, as happened about 1600 with one at Houghton Conquest, when Francis Clerke gentleman took its 30–40 a. to work in with other land; or it might actually be pulled down, as was done about the same time by Thomas Cheney esquire at Sundon with a house which had accompanied about 40 a.[30] It was part of a trend towards more efficient agriculture, but at the time it was called engrossing, because (according to the old idea of land

---

[28] C.R.O., CRT 130/1.
[29] M. Beresford, *History on the ground*, 87, 179; see
also J. H. Blundell, *Toddington*, 36–47.
[30] P.R.O., C 205/5/3.

serving the community) one man was getting an undue share. Enclosure made this amalgamation easier, but it was possible for two holdings to be worked by one man without their being enclosed. This forming of larger units was also done by the yeoman (ch. 20).

As to the whole extent of engrossing in Bedfordshire, calculations which have been attempted are thought to be uncertain.[31] Any attempts to reconstruct statistics for the past are like groping in a dark room, yet it is better to grope than stand still. For what it is worth, the estimate from returns made in 1607 is that during the previous 30 years 6,687 a. had been amalgamated with larger units, and over 100 houses downgraded or pulled down. Even taking twice or thrice this figure to make a guess at the period 1530–1607, clearly what is involved in a county of 300,000 a. is merely a gradual trend.

As to the whole extent of enclosure (i.e., including engrossing), this estimate reckons that in the same 30 years 10,004 a. were enclosed in 69 parishes, or just over 3% of the county area. This is small compared with far greater enclosure much earlier in a number of other counties like Essex; and it is also smaller than that estimated for the more comparable counties of Northamptonshire (where however there was an area of forest) and Leicestershire. The returns of 1607 for Bedfordshire show no large-scale action, but a multiplicity of small adjustments constantly being made in parish after parish by men of differing status, some quite modest (ch. 20). Almost certainly this had been going on for most of the century (cf. chs. 12–13). Again, though in Bromham (see above) and Hockliffe[32] it may have been extensive, in relation to the whole county the net result was small, as maps nearer the time of parliamentary enclosure over a century later confirm. (For disturbances in 1607 see ch. 21.)

The significance is not in the area involved, but in its relation to population. A high proportion of population needed a larger number of livestock, and therefore (since the land available was limited) meant pressure on the common and on grazing rights in the open fields. Such pressure was noted as far back as the 13th cent. (ch. 8); pestilence removed it; now population growth was made good and pressure renewed. Population must not be overstressed; there was no spectacular 16th cent. rise in this county.[33] But any enclosure, however small,

---

31 R.Hist.Soc.Trans., n.s., xviii, 212; Agrarian Hist. of England, iv (ed. J. Thirsk), 242.

32 Some enclosure in Hockliffe was reported at the 1607 enquiry; and a number of 17th cent. references seem to imply recent enclosure; e.g. "closes in South Field"; and "6 a. in a place called Hitch Field,"; C.R.O., CH 244–5; X 116/6, 9, 15, 20.

33 A striking population rise for Leicestershire in this century is claimed in V.C.H. Leics. iii, 137–40; the calculations are based on communicants and on 9 parish registers. Of 24 Bedfordshire parish registers which have been investigated:
    3 show a fairly marked rise (Caddington, Woburn, Wootton);

9 show a slight rise (Chalgrave, Cople, Henlow, Houghton Regis, Pavenham, Salford, Sandy, Southill, Sutton);

12 show a fluctuation due to epidemics, or a decline. Another source of information is the ecclesiastical return of families in 1563 (Harl. MS. 618). If this is compared with the hearth tax of 1671 (B.H.R.S. xvi) it seems to show that in the period 1563–1671 more than half the county had a varying population increase of up to 50%; more than a quarter of the county (including Bedford and 6 market towns) had a larger increase; of the remaining parishes, some were stationary, some decreased, and in some cases it was not possible to make a comparison.

curtailed grazing rights. Hence, if in any one parish there was sufficient pasture for the inhabitants' livestock, things might go easily; but where it was insufficient there might be disturbances such as that at Blunham. Common right was guarded, not only against the encroaching squire and yeoman, but against the squatter and new cottager; before long we get references to old cottages having common right and new cottages having none, but how early this distinction was made it is impossible to say.

Another significance is in the changing outlook, giving greater scope to the individual and looking ahead to what could be achieved. Thomas Reyner may or may not have been a dissolute rogue, but perhaps in a confused way he sensed that the old order based on the community was being eroded.

THE GENTRY AT HOME

Of the domestic surroundings of a squire earlier in the century something has been gleaned from John Gostwick. His advice for running a house in 1545 was as follows.[34] The lady of the house should have but one woman to wait upon her, who should be sad [serious] and discreet, "else she may do you and your wife much harm and displeasure"; but this waiting-woman should have honest wages. The dairy, which should include 16–20 cows, would require two women; the linen, one – it should be "delivered her by an inventory". There should be a man baker or cook, who should have the women's help as required. Three score sheep would be sufficient to kill for the household.

The establishment at Wrest which the 6th Earl of Kent took over in 1573 was not much more ambitious.[35] There were Venice carpets, and coverings from Tournai, and my lord's bed had curtains of crimson velvet and yellow satin with dolphins, while those for my lady were of white satin and green cloth of gold. There were some carved cupboards, and cushions of knotted work or embroidered with roses. The hangings were of say (fine cloth) in red, blue or green; and the curtains of sarsenet or buckram. There were cloths, towels and napkins, often of diaper; and about 30 pr. of sheets, one of cambric, some flaxen, some holland. But there was very little plate, and what there was was parcel-gilt. Most of the table-ware was pewter, some of it old and bad; and there were some wooden trenchers, probably for the servants' hall. Kitchen appointments included 7 spits, gridiron, skillet, pothooks and pothangers, skimmer, chafing-dishes, pestle and mortar; and here again some of the brass ware was very old. In the brewhouse was brewing apparatus, vat, cooler, and some great old troughs. In one or two little-used rooms upstairs were some "coverings of imagery, very old".

Henry Cheney's house at Toddington, presumably the one in which he entertained Queen Elizabeth in 1563, is illustrated on a Toddington map of 1581; it had three stories and was built round four sides of an inner court, while outside

---

[34] *B.H.R.S.* xxxvi, 38–45.   [35] C.R.O., L 31/169.

were great garden, little garden, great court and back court.[36] Warden pear trees were still cherished; leases of 1566 and 1574 reserve to the landlord half the crop of warden pears.[37]

[36] Blundell, op.cit., p.49 and pl.   [37] C.R.O., TW 606, 674.

18 – THE CHURCH, 1530–1603

OPPOSITION TO THE KING

It is only slowly and rarely that we find indications as to what the people of Bedfordshire thought of the ecclesiastical changes of the 16th cent. The first evidence comes from the victims. Shortly before Cranmer's court was to open at Dunstable to pronounce on the validity of Henry VIII's marriage with Catherine of Aragon, a friar in the Franciscan church at Greenwich had the moral courage to preach on the story of Ahab and the lying prophets. The following Sunday another preacher was more diplomatic, but "one Elstow, a fellow friar" interrupted the sermon and would not be silenced: "Even unto thee I speak, who art one of the 400 prophets into whom the spirit of lying is entered, and seekest by adultery to establish succession, betraying the king unto endless perdition." Next day both the original speaker and Friar Elstow were brought before the Council and threatened with being thrown in the Thames. Friar Elstow answered "We know the way to heaven to be as ready by water as by land, and therefore we care not which way we go."[1] As yet, these were early days; Friar Elstow escaped with being rusticated to the Bedford friary; and the friars at Greenwich wrote anxiously to know how he was treated, "whether friends may resort to him or write", and offering to contribute to his needs.[2]

As the violence of the king's wrath at any opposition reached its height, as Sir Thomas More was beheaded and the Carthusians brutally executed, fewer were found to stand against him. A visitation of the monasteries began in 1535 under Thomas Cromwell, with their suppression in mind. How much credence is to be given to accusations of immorality against the nuns of Chicksands and Harrold is uncertain; the former is only on the evidence of "an old beldame". The prosecution was also judge. But if most monks and nuns in Bedfordshire were respectable, they were not of the stuff of which martyrs are made. The nearest candidates are the monks of Woburn. The abbot, Robert Hobbes, was apparently a normally honourable man, made unhappy by the circumstances in which he found himself, but not quite able to take a firm line and keep to it; moreover he was not well. It worried him to see the pope's name erased from service books, "considering the long continuance of the Bishop of Rome"; his conscience was uneasy at taking the oath of supremacy, and he expressed his uneasiness to many people. The new treason act caught him, the sub-prior (Ralph Barnes of Woburn) and

---

[1] E. Hutton, *The Franciscans in England*, 239–41.   [2] *B. Notes & Queries*, i, 191.

another monk (Laurence Peck of Blunham). At the last they hesitated, and submitted to the king's mercy. But they were hanged – tradition says it was on an oak at the abbey gate.

MEN'S BELIEFS

There is little evidence of the doctrinal views of those who were active in carrying through the king's measures. Probably, like Henry VIII, they thought of themselves as true sons of the church, and did not see to what his measures might ultimately lead. One far-reaching step was the order in 1539 that there should be a translation of the Bible in all churches; thus Houghton Conquest "for a Bible when the parish were commanded to have one in the church, 24s".[3] The great days of church-building in Bedfordshire were now over; but the north aisle of the old church at Lidlington was built by the Taylor family about this time;[4] there is some early 16th cent. work at Cople and Oakley; and it was almost certainly Sir John Gostwick who rebuilt Willington church (Willington was that rarity in Bedfordshire, a single-manor parish; till now it had had an absentee lord, and probably the old church was small and in bad repair). In 1539 Gostwick drew attention in parliament to a sermon recently preached by the Archbishop, Thomas Cranmer, which seemed to question the still accepted doctrine of transubstantiation. The prompt result was a message from the king to "that varlet Gostwick" to "acknowledge his fault unto my lord of Canterbury".[5] Gostwick made his peace with the Archbishop, but the incident shows that he held to the old doctrines.

A somewhat uncertain figure is that of the first Lord Mordaunt. (By this time the family were living mainly at Drayton in Northamptonshire, and used Turvey Park chiefly as a dower house).[6] He was at Harrold Priory just before the visitation, to the indignation of the commissioners, but what he was trying to do is not clear. At all events the Mordaunts for many years were to continue a fluctuating adherence to the old faith.

SETTLING DOWN

At first it was a time of settling down after the recent changes. Hope that a bishopric might be established at Dunstable was short-lived. The diocese of Lincoln was very large, and such a new diocese might well have covered the area represented by the present diocese of St. Albans. There were to be a dean and 6 prebendaries; 6 canons; 6 singing-men in the choir; a reader in divinity; 2 students each at Oxford and Cambridge; a schoolmaster for a [Latin] grammar school, where 20 scholars were to be taught; and there were even to be pensions for 6 "old serving-men decayed by wars or by the king's service". The whole endowment was to be £800.[7] But this seemed to the king a good deal too much. New bishoprics for Oxford and Peterborough were carved out of the old Lincoln

[3] F. C. Eeles & J. E. Brown, *Edwardian inventories*, 28.
[4] *Harl. Soc.* xix, 144.
[5] *B.H.R.S.* xxxvi, 74. For the date 1539 see *Camden Soc.* lxxvii, 251–4; and P.R.O. E 159/319.

[6] Northants. R. O., Stopford Sackville, 222. *Centenary souvenir of Northampton diocese*, p.22.
[7] H. Cole, *Henry King VIII's scheme of bishopricks*, 60–2.

diocese, but Bedfordshire remained part of it. Dunstable's magnificent priory church, reduced in size, was at least partly saved by becoming a parish church for Dunstable; there was a similar result for Elstow abbey church; and perhaps in part for that of Harrold Priory; but of the other monastic churches not a wrack remains. Not only did they go, but in Bedford the church of St. Peter Dunstable was soon declared redundant (its Norman doorway was transferred to St. Peter Merton), and All Hallows may have disappeared at this time. In nearly all cases the domestic buildings of the religious houses continued for sometime in the occupation of purchaser or lessee; sometimes with rebuilding, as at Warden; sometimes neglected, as at Woburn. Humphrey Bourchier, lessee of Markyate in 1539, had "much cost in translating of the priory into a manor-place",[8] and Newnham was leased as a residence from 1559 by Sir Robert Catlin, chief justice of the queen's bench.[9]

EX-MONKS AND EX-FRIARS

Most of the ex-monks quietly accepted their pensions. For an abbot or prior these were good. That of John Burne, last prior of Newnham (which was surrendered 1541), was £60 p.a.; he soon died (1542), when he asked to be buried in St. Paul's church, Bedford, near Simon de Beauchamp "sometime founder of Newnham"; and he left to this church "all such ornaments as I have to the honour of God".[10]

For the rank and file, pensions were much smaller, and friars had none. Some of the older men soon died. Thus a Franciscan, Richard Elmer, died in 1543; he had two sisters in Bedford, who probably cared for him; he left directions that his books should be sold "to some honest priest for 4 nobles," and the money used "to hire a priest for to sing for me and my good friends a quarter of a year"; his best gown was to be sold for 16s., and 12 dozen of bread given at his burial to "poor folks".[11] If a younger or middle-aged ex-monk could supplement his pension by obtaining a benefice, he was reasonably well-to-do, but in some circumstances the pension was lost on obtaining preferment. There were now many candidates for benefices, and he might have to wait years and not succeed at all. The canons of Dunstable were comparatively fortunate.[12] Out of a total (with the prior) of 13 canons, 10 sooner or later secured benefices, 3 of them in Bedfordshire. Thus canon George Edwards became curate of Hockliffe, but not till 1548; ten years later he became rector of Milton Bryan, where he died in 1561. The other seven eventually got benefices in other counties; perhaps they were younger, for three of them married. Five ex-monks from outside the county were incumbents of Bedfordshire livings in 1548.[13]

[8] *V.C.H.* ii, 317.
[9] M. E. Finch, *Five Northants. families*, 50–1.
[10] C.R.O., ABP/R 6, f.136.
[11] C.R.O., ABP/R 11, f.6.
[12] G. Baskerville, *English monks and the suppression of*

the monasteries, App.
[13] *L.R.S.* liii, 88–92; at Harrold, Knotting, Souldrop, Stotfold and Yielden. Ex-canons of Newnham held Carlton and Cockayne Hatley, and an ex-canon of Chicksands held Haynes.

Perhaps adjustment was most difficult for the nuns. A little group of ex-nuns from Elstow Abbey settled in St. Mary's parish, Bedford.[14] The abbess, Elizabeth Boyvill, took a house in Potter Street;[15] perhaps some of the other nuns lived with her, Alice Boyvill, Elizabeth Foxe, Elizabeth Napton, Ann and Margery Preston, and Elizabeth Stanysmore; if so, it was probably both happier and more economical for them. Years later Henry Goodall, son of the miller of Duck Mill, prized a mazer lipped with silver that Margery Preston had given him.[16]

FURTHER CHANGE

The accession of the boy king, Edward VI, gave his advisers a chance to take things further, with an English prayerbook, with the removal from the churches of ornaments deemed superfluous, and with the dissolution of the chantries. Incidentally Protector Somerset's amanuensis was Thomas Norton, grandson of a Sharpenhoe yeoman and translator of Calvin.[17]

The removal of church ornaments was not purely for religious reasons. The Privy Council minutes on 3 March 1551 noted candidly that "the King's majesty had need presently of a mass of money".[18] Commissioners were directed to make the necessary inventories. The chief emphasis was on plate; chalices and patens were usually of silver, parcel gilt; crosses were sometime of copper and gilt, as at Battlesden.[19] Cranfield had 4 brass candlesticks and 2 censers.[20] Later it was collected by Nicholas Luke, baron of the exchequer, and two assistants, leaving the churches only with essentials. The weight of plate collected was 2,867 oz., of which nearly half was defaced – that is, it had probably borne some representation of a saint, and this had been excised.[21] It was handed in to the Tower, where it was melted down.

Vestments too were listed, but usually disposed of locally. Westoning had vestments of blue, white and red satin, of red and black say, of green velvet and green sarsenet.[22] Houghton Regis, which had recently lost some church goods "when the church was robbed" still had 13 vestments.[23] At Houghton Conquest Edmund Conquest bought a "crimson velvet coat with jewels, called Our Lady's coat", probably for love of the old ways.[24] At Meppershall it was later alleged that one of the churchwardens, Thomas Stringer, yeoman, had the vestments to make beds and painted hangings for private use.[25] Bells, though often listed, were not as a rule taken over. At Harlington "a pair of organs" was sold.[26]

The closing down of the chantries and the fraternities (ch. 14) came home also to nearly every parish.[27] No more were there to be at Luton convivial dinners of

---

[14] They died there; see *B.P.R.* xxxv.

[15] C.R.O., ABP/W 1574/45.

[16] *Loc.cit.*

[17] *D.N.B.*; *B. Mag.* v, 113–8. For his active parliamentary career, see J. E. Neale, *Elizabeth and her parliaments, passim*; also the *History of Parliament*. For his Streatley connection, see the will of his uncle Robert, C.R.O., ABP/R 15, f.52.

[18] Eeles, p.iii.

[19] *Op.cit.*, p.1.

[20] *Op.cit.*, p.13.

[21] *Op.cit.*, p.41.

[22] *Op.cit.*, p.9.

[23] *Op.cit.*, p.4.

[24] *Op.cit.*, p.24.

[25] *Op.cit.*, p.17.

[26] *Op.cit.*, p.26.

[27] For chantry priests pensioned in 1548, see *L.R.S.*

the Trinity gild; no more "drinkings" at Potton and Stevington; nor parish beadrolls for prayers for the departed. Where a chantry was solely for one or more individuals, perhaps the only one who much regretted its closure was the then incumbent, who was probably an elderly and not very erudite priest; but sometimes another purpose was served by the chantry, for example for the upkeep of a bridge, as at Biddenham. At Houghton Regis the chantry priest kept a school; John Couper, who was 40 and had an annual stipend of 26s. 8d., taught 6 poor children; and though he was only "meanly learned" his teaching was better than nothing.[28] Sometimes with the chantry was swept away a chapel-of-ease for a distant hamlet, as at Wroxhill in Marston.[29]

While probably most people were merely confused by the continued changes, there begin now to be indications that some are forming their own views. George Joye (ch. 14) had returned from exile; and in 1549 Sir Henry Grey of Wrest presented him to the rectory of Blunham. A Sandy miller in 1553, Robert Webster, seems to have known of Calvin's teaching about the predestination of the elect; he trusted that he would "rise again at the coming of my lord Jesus Christ and be set on his right hand among his elect";[30] and similar hopes were expressed by John West and Thomas Knight of Bedford.[31] They were early converts, for it was not until 1559 that Thomas Norton translated Calvin's *Institutes* into English. When the boy king died, Sir Thomas Palmer of Pulloxhill was anxious for the current trend in church affairs to continue, and supported Lady Jane Grey – when the attempt to enthrone her failed he was attainted.[32]

REVERSAL TO ROMAN CATHOLICISM

Queen Mary came to the throne, and one who came to assure her of his loyalty, and to tell her that, though he was an old man, he would pray for her preservation, was Lord Mordaunt. That the daughter of Catherine of Aragon would try to reverse the trend of her brother's reign was a foregone conclusion. That trend was strongest in London and the southeast of England. The Marian fires did not burn in Bedfordshire, though Thomas Rose, afterwards vicar of Luton, had a narrow escape.[33] Incidentally his predecessor as vicar of Luton, John Gwyneth, 1537–58, was a composer of church music, but his music has unfortunately been lost.[34]

But there were enquiries about church ornaments. Accusation and counter-accusation make it hard to distinguish the truth. Thomas Stringer of Meppershall, "an old man and not used to journey", was perplexed by the aspersions cast on the way he had discharged his duty as churchwarden; and his neighbour, Thomas

---

liii, 10.
[28] *Chan.cert.*, p.45.
[29] *Chan.cert.*, pp.35–6.
[30] C.R.O., ABP/W 1553/268.
[31] C.R.O., ABP/W 1557/241; 1558/71.
[32] *V.C.H.* ii, 377.

[33] Foxe, *Acts and Monuments*, viii, 581–90. The nearest martyrs were John Hullier, a minister at Cambridge, 1556; and John Kyrde, a shoemaker at Northampton, 1557; *ibid.*, viii, 131, 423.
[34] *B. Mag.* i, 257.

Hemmyng of Arleseybury manor, took his statement and wrote up to the commissioners on his behalf.[35] Joan Conquest, widow of Edmund, refitted out Houghton Conquest with a silver chalice, a very fair cope of white damask powdered with spread eagles of gold, worth £10, two great standing candlesticks, and a frontal of red branched damask.[36] John Crawley, executor of Edward Crawley, formerly churchwarden of Luton, bestowed on Luton church a cope, a vestment of blue velvet and a chalice.[37] A puzzled contingent of inhabitants of Sandy said there had been two bells placed in their churchyard by Robert Burgoyne; after his death his widow removed them, as far as they knew, to London to pay Burgoyne's debts; "and further we cannot say, as knoweth God."[38]

A check-up in 1556 revealed that over 70 ex-religious from Bedfordshire religious houses were still drawing their pensions.[39]

Married clergy were deprived of their livings. This happened, for instance, to John Nyxe, former canon of Dunstable, and now vicar of Offley, Herts.[40] Gervase Markham, the last prior of Dunstable, still living in the town, must have hoped that the old days were really coming again, for in his will he left his chalice and vestments "if they may at any time hereafter be occupied in the church again";[41] but before he died in 1561 Queen Elizabeth's act of uniformity of 1559 had laid down a Protestant pattern for many years to come.

To draw up a balance-sheet of the unfortunate period 1530–58 would be difficult. On the debit side would be the Henrician and Edwardian spoliation, and the Marian persecution; on the credit side the Bible and the prayerbook.

THE CHURCH OF ENGLAND

To the young queen Elizabeth George Acworth the younger, of the Luton family and now studying at Padua, wrote, "When all hope of good had become extinguished and as it were twisted and torn from our hands, nevertheless by the divine blessing both your highness has become possessed of rule, and we seem from the miseries amongst which we were tossed to be snatched back and re-stored."[42] This was the language of hope rather than of expectation, for no one knew for certain what lay ahead.

Morale must have been low in 1558. For the clergy some of the uncertainties of the preceding years are reflected in the career of John Rogers, vicar of Potton.[43] He began life as a vicar choral at St. Stephen's College, Westminster. He later became a chantry priest at Ashwell, Herts. At some stage after the chantries were dissolved, he married, but he does not seem to have felt at home as a married man; not every woman would marry an ex-monk, and she may have found problems of her own. In his last few years he became vicar of Potton. When in 1562 he

[35] Eeles, p.21–2.
[36] Eeles, p.28.
[37] Op.cit., p.27.
[38] Op.cit., p.29.
[39] P.R.O. Excheq. Misc. books, 31, f.23.
[40] Baskerville, loc.cit.
[41] C.R.O., ABP/W 1561/140.
[42] L. G. H. Horton-Smith. George Acworth, p.23.
[43] C.R.O., ABP/R 16, f.69; L.R.S. liii, 95.

died, though he left his wife Margaret most of his estate, it was to be hers only if she continued "in all honesty and godly behaviour; or else, if the contrary be evidently perceived" it was to be divided among his kinsfolk. Incidentally he had many books, books of English service and books of divinity, and he still cherished his Latin Bible, his "songbooks of the old sort" and his virginals (musical instrument).

Marriage for the clergy was in fact frowned on in Elizabeth's reign, and her injunctions stipulated that the bride's honest and sober living should be certified by two justices of the peace; this was done when Margaret Gibson of Sandy married John Havering (vicar of Roxton 1562–1602).[44]

To build up an Anglican church, its outlook must be formulated; and personnel, buildings and equipment all mattered. The process was national; in Bedfordshire we see the local application.

It was a bishop, not of Lincoln but of Salisbury, John Jewel in his *Apology*, 1562, who made the first notable statement of Anglican thinking: "We have planted no new religion, but only have renewed the old that was undoubtedly founded and used by the apostles of Christ."[45] In 1564 his work was ordered to be placed in every church. Another book which had a great vogue was Fox's *Book of Martyrs*, 1563; at Woburn Joan Ball left money to buy a copy for the "public benefit" in 1587.[46] A century and a half later Jewel at least was still to be found in many Bedfordshire churches (Wootton's copy survives today) and sometimes also Fox; thus Eaton Bray in 1708: "one Bible, two prayerbooks, The book of martyrs, Paraphrase on the New Testament by Erasmus, Bishop Jewel."[47]

Most important were the men who were to reanimate the church under the wise and scholarly leadership of Archbishop Parker. The new bishop of Lincoln was Nicholas Bullingham. He had been chaplain to Cranmer; then he spent the years of Mary's reign in exile; now he returned and became Parker's chaplain, and in 1560 Bishop of Lincoln. The new archdeacon of Bedford in 1560 was William Forde. It is not surprising that the new bishop set his face against the old semi-pagan celebrations from May to Midsummer Day. In 1562 in Northill the Morris dancing, the feast and the bonfire still took place; in 1565 Morris bells were still bought by the churchwardens;[48] but after that these festivities disappear from view. At Shillington there was a May men's dinner as late as 1575;[49] but the rest is silence, as far as churchwardens are concerned. (May festivities did not, however, die out – see ch. 26.)

The work of building up an informed ministry animated by a new spirit was probably slow; some Bedfordshire men in fact were active elsewhere – George Acworth in 1561 became vicar-general to the reforming bishop of Winchester.[50]

[44] *B.P.R.* xiii, A 94.
[45] J. B. Black, *Reign of Elizabeth*, p.28.
[46] C.R.O., ABP/W 1587/116.
[47] C.R.O., ABE 2, vol. ii, f.392.

[48] *B.H.R.S.* xxxiii, 6–12.
[49] *Op.cit.*, 64.
[50] *D.N.B.*

A *Book of Homilies* was issued in 1562, but the clergy did not always use it; in 1578 Barton complained that they had "no sermons but those made up by the parson",[51] and Farndish said they had only one sermon that year.[52] Sometimes we get a glimpse of a Bedfordshire incumbent. There is the occasional unsatisfactory one, like the vicar of Milton Ernest, who at the bishop's visitation in 1585 was said to rail with his neighbours and to be at the alehouse at an unlawful time in the night;[53] or the rector of Cranfield, who in 1602 struck Hugh Bradley in church "and did spurn his hat up and down the church and miscalled him".[54]

Of another stamp however were such men as Francis Woodmansey, who was vicar of Podington 1561–1607, and directed in his will that Bullinger's *Decades* should "be laid by Mr. Jewel's book upon a like desk for every man to read during the pleasure of God, and to be made fast by one chain"[55] (Heinrich Bullinger, who died in 1575, was a Zwinglian or moderate).[56] An attractive figure was Thomas Archer, rector of Houghton Conquest from 1589;[57] he noted down epitaphs, accounts of notable events, descriptions of church property and the trees he planted, and even proverbs, some of which must have had an old-fashioned sound by his time: "A young priest shall never be rich nor wise till he hath heard an old priest's confession." At the episcopal visitation of 1603 practically all clergy in the archdeaconry were noted as being of good behaviour, and only about one in five was not a graduate.[58]

As for the fabric of Bedfordshire churches, no longer was every other village improving its church. An exception was Hulcote, which was rebuilt by the Charnock family, and has been described as Gothic in form but with renaissance feeling. It was however necessary to keep existing buildings in repair. At the visitation of 1578 there seems to be a determined drive to get repairs done; a number of churches required attention, and at Pavenham the chancel was "ready to fall down" – at the fault, the churchwardens hastened to add, of Trinity College.[59] Evidence of the whitewashing of church interiors is rare, but Robert Norton of Streatley, yeoman, evidently thought that completely plain walls were dull, and in 1559 he left 20s. to new paint the church "with texts of scripture in English, if it by the laws of England may be suffered".[60]

Because of the scarcity both of visitation records and of early churchwardens' accounts, there is not so much information about equipment as might be wished. Houghton Regis, Barton and Harlington in 1562 were given a date by which they must destroy their "superstitious monuments" such as the roodloft.[61] Northill, perhaps cautious and certainly thrifty, kept the roodloft (in store?) till 1564, and then sold it for 13s. 4d., the sepulchre for 14d., and various latten articles, including

[51] C.R.O., ABC 3, f.3.
[52] C.R.O., ABC 3, f.1.
[53] Linc. R.O., Vj. 16.
[54] Linc. R.O., Cj 13, f.31.
[55] C.R.O., ABP/R 27, f.69d.
[56] See also *B.H.R.S.* xxxiii, pp.xxvi, 21.

[57] C.R.O., P 11/28/1.
[58] *L.R.S.* xxiii, 256–64.
[59] *B.N.Q.* iii, 16–18.
[60] C.R.O., ABP/R 15, f.52.
[61] Linc. R.O., Cj 3, f.138d.

a cross, two candlesticks and a pyx.[62] Now that communion was received by the laity in both kinds, new plate, different in shape and size, was needed, and the Archbishop himself instituted enquiries as to whether any profane cups were still in use. Nearly one out of every six old churches in the archdeaconry still has plate dating from about 1570.

One extraneous factor which helped to build up the Anglican church was the thread of nationalism woven into it. The old faith was associated with the fear of Spain; and after the defeat of the Armada in 1588 (when the churchwardens of Shillington paid 5d. for "drink for the ringers" of the church-bells),[63] the Anglican church was associated with national pride. At this time there probably prevailed in the county a greater degree of religious unity than there has ever as yet been since.

Even in Bedfordshire there were a few who adhered to the old faith. This faith also was animated by a new spirit, but the new spirit had come to both in their division, so with it was intolerance and fear; and fear bred persecution. Thomas Norton, now practising law in London and a prominent member of parliament, was in 1581 appointed official censor of Roman Catholics; he examined many under torture, and acquired the unenviable nickname of "rack-master-general".[64] Roman Catholic priests came on the English mission, and in 1585 one, Thomas Freeman, was arrested in this county, while about 1590 another, Francis Tillotson, was taken at the house of Robert Willowes of Gt. Barford.[65] But Bedfordshire offered an unpromising field. On the recusant roll of 1593-4, which accounts for confiscation of Roman Catholic property, only one land-owner appears under Bedfordshire, and he was a Northamptonshire man, Lord Vaux, who had property at Eaton Socon.[66]

Bedfordshire recusants are hard to trace. Both the bishop's visitations of 1571 and 1585 and the archdeacons' visitation of 1578 record a sprinkling of people who did not come to church or did not receive the sacrament, but some of these may be merely negligent. At Chellington "Henry Tucke and the most part of his household doth come to the church very seldom, that is once in the month", and they had not received communion for a year;[67] and at Ridgmont Arthur Cordon "doth not observe the holy days but laboureth in them",[68] while at Sandy John Waller "keeps unlawful rule in his house in service-time".[69] Usually a court sentence was effective, as with William Bemond of Studham in 1598 – the incumbent wrote "I do now find him very conformable, in that he

---

[62] C.R.O., P 10/5/1.
[63] B.H.R.S. xxxiii, 85.
[64] See n.17.
His purpose was honest if misguided; see his prayer quoted in the *History of Parliament*. [God] "bless me and my poor hod upon my back, among the mortar-bearers in the work of God . . . in cleansing and reparation . . . of the church of England."
[65] V.C.H. i, 335; *Northampton diocese centenary souvenir*, 1950.
[66] Cath. Rec. Soc., lvii, 1.
[67] Linc. R.O., Vj 16, f.103d-121.
[68] Loc.cit.
[69] Loc.cit.

voluntarily came unto me to have it effected."[70] Returns sent in to the bishop in 1603 list 27 persons in 9 parishes as recusants.[71]

In general the picture of the local community reflected by late Elizabethan visitations is probably much the same as its medieval forerunner (ch. 4). There were a few scolds, like Helen Sturmound of Eversholt in 1571;[72] and at Bedford in 1585 two women were "sowers of discord among their neighbours".[73] There was the occasional drunkard, like William Atkinson at Dunstable.[74] Some matrimonial differences occur, such as husband and wife living apart, as at Millbrook;[75] and a fierce dispute at Cranfield between William Young and his wife Isabel, who said she had been forced into marriage.[76] A number of cases of immorality were alleged; at Little Staughton in 1599 the incumbent interceded for Agnes Halle;[77] she had not been able to do her penance, as he himself was ill when she was excommunicated; but she was very penitent, and was utterly undone with trying to bring up her child, her seducer having left her. Sometimes a legacy was withheld, such as a charitable bequest to the parish, as at Wootton.[78] Schools provided some problems; at Colmworth in 1585 Alexander Cox was teaching school without licence from the bishop;[79] and at Eaton Bray in 1578 the schoolmaster was misused in the church by an irate parent "for beating of the children of the said John Buckmaster."[80] In short, pastoral care for the general well-being of the flock continued.

PURITANS

But there were also a few signs that views gaining ground in London and elsewhere had not left Bedfordshire untouched. Partly these views related to practice in worship; if vestments were superfluous, why wear a surplice and not an ordinary black gown? and was not musical liturgy a distraction? Partly they related to church government; if a man could himself interpret the Bible, why not dispense with bishops? Partly they related to doctrine, to a belief that some were pre-destined to salvation.

Of the existence of such views, one sign is the matter (in itself small) of not wearing a surplice. It seems that an incumbent might either be soon called to account or might continue unchecked for years. In 1578 at the archdeacon's visitation the churchwardens of St. John's church, Bedford, said that their minister did not wear a surplice.[81] In 1585 at the bishop's visitation it was presented that Linford, rector of St. Peter's church, Bedford, "doth never wear the surplice but toward the time of the visitation".[82] At Northill Anthony Hoggett seems not to have worn a surplice for twenty years, for during this period there is no entry in

[70] Linc. R.O., Ch.P. 1598–9, f.3.
[71] L.R.S. xxiii, 256–64.
[72] Linc. R.O., Vj 14, ff.30–49.
[73] See n.67.
[74] See n.67.
[75] See n.67.
[76] See n.67.
[77] Linc. R.O., Ch.P. 1598–9, f.13.
[78] C.R.O., ABC 3, f.1.
[79] See n.67.
[80] C.R.O., ABC 3, f.102, wrongly given as Eyeworth in B.N. & Q., iii, 18.
[81] B.N.Q. iii, 16–18.
[82] L.R.S. xxiii, p.xxx.

the churchwardens' accounts for its washing (usually 2d.); and in 1590 Northill sold its organ for 40s.[83]

Another indication of puritan views is an "exercise";[84] in September 1603 John Bostock, vicar of Southill, invited four colleagues for this purpose: the two Dillinghams (ch. 22); Andrew Dennis, vicar of St. Paul's, Bedford; and Thomas Brightman, the scholarly and "angelical" vicar of Haynes, whose works were later published. The exercise lasted from 9 a.m. to 5 p.m.; the confession was said, a lesson from Daniel read; and each cleric present preached a sermon of an hour or more – the sermons being interspersed with psalms. Brightman's discourse dealt with matters that he thought called for reform: the church hierarchy; and defects among the clergy – ignorance, sloth and misbehaviour.

In the following year some disciplinary action was taken.[85] Several clergy were charged before the bishop for not wearing the surplice. It is noticeable that the offenders were pretty well scattered over the county: in the north, William Ford at Thurleigh, and John Orme (friend of Bulkeley – see ch. 22)[86] at Bletsoe, and Henry Lee at Colmworth; in the south, John Richardson at Dunstable; in the west, Thomas Dutton at Eversholt, Humphrey Hill at Tingrith, and Caesar Walpoole at Woburn; in the east, Thomas Norton (son of the lawyer?) at Blunham, and John Henlow at Holwell. When it came to the point, nearly all conformed; and in due course the churchwardens certified "he is very conformable" or "he doth wear the surplice orderly and well". Only at Northill Hoggett would not conform and was suspended.

All the above are clergy. Some Bedford laymen seem to have held Calvin's views on predestination, such as Harry Field, who hoped to be numbered among the "blessed company of the elect saints in heaven", and Henry Cartwright, who aspired to be among the "number of God his elect children".[87] It is possible that seven men at Sandy who refused to contribute to church repair and to the recasting of the bells had an objection in principle.[88] At all events, where clergy had preached on puritan lines, it is probable that some at least of their congregation shared their views. Puritanism in Bedfordshire had begun.

[83] *B.H.R.S.* xxxiii, 23–49, surplice not mentioned; 48, organ sold.
[84] *L.R.S.* xxiii, pp.cxvi–cxviii.
[85] *Loc.cit.*
[86] C.R.O., ABP/R 32, f.99d. The Bulkeleys were overseers of Orme's will.
[87] C.R.O., ABP/W 1564/56 and 1578/99.
[88] L.R.O., Ch.P. 1601–3, f.8.

Q

BEDFORD

Bedford, like the county, lost its religious houses, chantries and gilds, and most fringe benefits associated with them. It lost Caldwell Priory, the Franciscan friary outside the built-up area, and Newnham Priory just over the boundary. As for the hospitals, St. Leonard's had, since leprosy was now rare, for sometime been merely a farm, held with another living; and St. John's, in the corporation's gift, continued with its tiny parish. Some churches and chapels went. One of these was the church of St. Peter Dunstable; since 1448 it had been held with St. Mary, the services alternating between the two, and the books and ornaments being carried backwards and forwards across the street. This at the chief festivals gave rise to strife and contention, worst (according to the incumbent in 1546, John Neygott[1]) "at the holy feast of Easter when all Christian men should be in most ardent love and charity"; and he was weary thereof, and resigned. However, the patron of both livings was now the Bishop of Lincoln, and the bishop said "Well, take it again for my sake! I have told these honest men your neighbours my mind, which is that you and they shall take down one of the churches and maintain the other," so the church of St. Peter Dunstable came down. Herne chapel, near St. Paul's church, probably stood neglected, until in the course of time secular uses were found for it. All Hallows is not heard of again, nor St. Loyes chapel.[2]

When a chaplain in the chapel on the bridge no longer took alms for the bridge's repair, the bridge walls soon decayed so much that children and cattle were in danger of falling into the river. The walls were repaired with stone from St. Peter Dunstable, and 20 loads of stone from this church were kept as reserve for future needs. By 1569 bridgewardens were appointed.[3] Eventually (1589)[4] the chapel became the town lock-up (the county gaol of course remained in Gaol Lane); there had been a previous town lock-up called the Stonehouse, but it was noisome.

In Bedford as well as in the county much ex-monastic property was soon on the market, affording to far-seeing business men an opportunity for speculation. John Williams alias Scott in November 1545 for £256 obtained a large grant of such property in Bedford, and with it the school-house in School Lane.[5] The school was obviously in danger of being another casualty to the dissolution,

---

1 *B.H.R.S.* xxxvi, 15–19.
2 Recently there came to light in the Ship Inn in St. Cuthbert's Street a painted capital which may have come from one of these.
3 Corp. MSS., X 67/80.
4 *B.H.R.S.* xxxvi, 20n.
5 *Letters & Papers of Henry VIII*, xx, pt.2, p.446.

but after over 20 years of uncertainty it emerged with an endowment of its own.

By some means the school was kept going till 1545, when Williams, mayor 1545–6, had the north door from St. Peter Dunstable to "make a door" for it. Williams does not seem to have had himself the makings of a public benefactor, but he was shrewd, and not averse from doing a good stroke for the town, while at the same time relieving himself of an encumbrance. In London was a successful merchant-tailor, William Harpur, from the Bedford and Biddenham family – perhaps Williams and Harpur had been at school together. It may have been the death or retirement of the old schoolmaster which brought matters to a head. At all events in 1548 Edmund Green came from New College, Oxford, to teach at Bedford.[6] Probably Harpur paid the stipend. Soon after this Harpur acquired (almost certainly from Williams) a site near St. Paul's church – a piece of land which had formerly belonged to the Trinity gild,[7] and built a new schoolhouse on it. Williams was thus free to dispose of the old schoolhouse. There was still the future. Williams was mayor again in 1549 and 1551; and in 1552 the corporation obtained from Edward VI letters patent authorising them to accept an endowment for the school.

Meanwhile Harpur's career was reaching its peak[8] – and he had no family. The house leased by him in London was said to be the "largest and stateliest in this city". In 1552–3 Harpur was master of the Merchant Taylors' company; and in 1561 Lord Mayor, when the Lord Mayor's show represented harpers in history and legend. "The new mayor took his barge towards Westminster, my new lord mayor, Master Harpur, with the aldermen in their scarlet, and all the crafts of London in their livery and their barges . . . and landed at Paul's wharf and so to Paul's churchyard, and there met them a pageant gorgeously made with children with divers instruments playing and singing, "in the midst David with his story about him, on the right side Orpheus with his story before". In 1562 Harpur was knighted. By now he felt in a position to put the school on a permanent footing. In 1564 he bought 13 a. of farmland in Holborn – he was shrewd enough to be aware that it should appreciate; and in 1566 he conveyed it to the corporation as an endowment for the school. The income was not large, but it was enough to keep the little school going, with some to spare for charity.

Bedford was prospering and recovering from the recession of the last century. Peace was favourable for its expansion as the county's main market centre. At the time of the 1550 subsidy about a dozen people were in the upper income bracket, contributing £1 and over.[9] In 1554 Bedford obtained a grant of another

---

[6] C. Farrar, *Harper's Bedford Charity*, 2. There was a Green family at Biddenham, which had some connection with the Harpers, but this seems to be a coincidence; see C.R.O., CRT 130/47.

[7] Corp. MSS., X 67/70.

[8] *V.C.H.* ii, 158.

[9] C.R.O., TW 875. Occupations in this subsidy list show the usual "mixed bag" of general trades – no special new developments. Bedford's prosperity seems almost entirely due to the advantages of being a main marketing centre in a long period of peace. For markets in general at this time, see *Agrarian Hist. of England* iv (ed. J. Thirsk), 467–592.

market, to be held on a Tuesday, and of two more fairs.[10] There was dispute about the site of these, till in 1557 on the arbitration of Sir Humphrey Radcliffe and Nicholas Luke it was ordered that, while the fairs should be held north of the river, the Tuesday market should be held according to the grant (i.e., in St. Mary's parish, where conveniently the site of St. Mary's square was now vacant). A few years later, in 1556, Bedford addressed to Oxford queries on the proper management of town affairs (ch. 5).[11] How far did the mayor's authority go? Could he, for instance, cause the corporation to be taxed? Could he punish by imprisonment his brethren, late mayors? Who appointed court days? Did a coroner rank above or below the bailiffs? Could notorious transgressors be disfranchised? Could the bailiffs hold a court without the mayor? Most of the answers tended to raise the position of the mayor. Bailiffs were said to rank below the coroner but above the town clerk.

In Elizabethan Bedford the mayor was the most important inhabitant.[12] He must be a burgess. Failure to serve when elected meant a fine of £10. When he took office on Michaelmas day, having received his predecessor's accounts and the mace, he entertained the aldermen and burgesses to dinner at his house. When Bedford first had a mace is uncertain, but probably by the 15th cent.; and now the rule was that when the mayor went to church to hear divine service, he must always be preceded by the sergeant with gown and mace. The mayor summoned aldermen and burgesses to the council chamber in the Guildhall. He fixed the price of victuals and some other commodities; and appointed some minor officers. He could commit offenders to prison at his pleasure for contempt. Incidentally it may be noted that relations between the mayor and the vicar of St. Paul's were not always good. Alexander Hunt, mayor 1581–2, caused St. Paul's church bells to be rung immoderately on saints' days and at inconvenient times; and when the vicar, Ralph Jones, objected, replied that he would cause ringing as pleased him, and that the devil was in Jones' preaching.[13]

Of the other offices, the most ancient was that of the two bailiffs, and here again a fine of £10 followed refusal to serve. At Michaelmas they too gave an election dinner, but theirs was given to non-burgesses. Next to them ranked the chamberlains. By this time the income of which they disposed was higher than at the beginning of the century; thus in 1578–9[14] they started with a comfortable balance of £31 from the previous year, and they collected £37 in rents, £18 in fees (from new burgesses and from "setters-up" in trade), and some small sums in fines and in sale of willows. At Sir William Harpur's burial they spent 6s. on 3 gallons of Gascony wine. The bridgewardens were responsible for the bridge. The offices of steward (comparable to the steward on a manor) and town clerk

---

[10] *B.H.R.S.* xxxvi, 13.
[11] Corp. MSS.
[12] Unless otherwise stated, the following is taken from the Black Book (*B.H.R.S.* xxxvi, 20–37). Begun

in 1562, it contains many, but not all, rules laid down at the court leet over a period of years.
[13] L.R.O., Ct. papers 69/1/77.
[14] Corp. MSS.

were usually held by the same individual. There was now also a recorder, a London lawyer who came down from time to time to settle cases of particular difficulty. Minor officers were constables for each of the twelve wards, wood and bucket-searchers, fieldsmen and herdsmen, and sergeants. The wards were from about 1590 known by name.[15]

Burgessdom came by inheritance or election. In theory a burgess should at the next leet present the name of such man-child as God shall send him, paying a fee of 2d., but it is not certain that this was done. An elected burgess paid a fee of 2s. 8d. A foreign burgess (one not living in the town) must have there chattels worth 40s. as security for paying his rates, but this was not always enforced. A burgess must attend the council chamber when summoned by the mayor; and unless he had come direct from his place of business he must then wear his gown; when there he should not speak malicious or unseemly words, or lay his hand on his weapon, or he might be imprisoned till he had paid 20s. He must pay his proper share for the renewing of the town's charter when necessary, or be disfranchised. He must serve as bailiff when required; but after that he would be eligible to share in burgess land and mead (the land was about 34 a. in Newnham Field and the meadow was at Goldington); and he could have one additional common right as well as his own.

Freemen or commoners had few rights, beyond being represented on the assessment committee, which consisted of 3 aldermen, 6 burgesses and 3 freemen. At Michaelmas when the new bailiffs took office, they resorted to the bailiffs there to receive and take freely their dinner, but so also did foreigners. They served as constables and held other minor offices.

The population is difficult to estimate, but is seems probable that more than half was concentrated in St. Paul's parish, and about one-fifth in that of St. Mary, with a sprinkling in the other parishes. In 1603 there were said to be 1,033 communicants.[16] St Peter's parish had an outbreak of the plague in 1575–6 when 30 died: "all these were buried in the time of the plague";[17] and a little later in 1578–9 there was a worse epidemic apparently in St. Paul's parish, when the chamberlains distributed £10 "to the people of this town in the time of God's visitation of sickness".[18] Rules relating to public health were almost nil. Butchers should in the evening, or at least early in the morning, carry away all the inwards and entrails of beasts slaughtered in the shambles or Butcher Row, so that these did not annoy the inhabitants with corrupt savour or smell, but this garbage was only to be taken to nearby Offal Lane (later the Broadway). Riverside dwellers were required to clean and scour their brinks, and the fine for throwing dung,

---

[15] The wards were: (south of the river) St. John's, High Street = St. Mary's, Potter Street, Cauldwell Street; (north of the river) East of High Street, West of High Street, St. Peter's, St. Cuthbert's, Mill Lane, Well Street, Prebend, St. Loyes otherwise All Hallows.
[16] L.R.S. xxiii, 256.
[17] B.P.R. xl.
[18] Corp. MSS.

carrion or other noisome thing into the Ouse was 20s. One glover, Richard Pearce, washed his limed skins in the river.[19]

Fire was a recognised risk, and householders had to provide leather buckets containing water. Two wood-searchers went about the town once a month to see that no inhabitant had laid faggots within 10 ft. of a chimney. Chimneys must be sufficient, and of stone or brick; and roofs must be of tile or slate – not thatch (evidence of the greater availability of tiles: see ch. 20).

Trade was strictly controlled. Foreigners were under special restrictions; in particular they must not buy before the market bell; hides and tallow must be sold only to Bedford tanners, glovers and chandlers; and foreign butchers must have their standings below those of Bedford butchers. The market bell was rung at 11. Toll on the sale of grain was taken in kind: $\frac{1}{2}$ peck for 4 quarters, or 1 pint for 4 bushels.

No one, whether a Bedford inhabitant or foreigner, might "set up" in trade without permission. An apprentice who had served 7 years in Bedford came to the mayor and did him to understand that he was ready; the mayor then summoned bailiffs, chamberlains, bridgewardens and burgesses to consider whether the applicant be a meet man; he would normally be allowed to set up on giving the council a gallon of wine (the chamberlains' accounts show that he often paid a varying fee as well). Other applicants, if allowed to set up, paid a fee assessed in each case, plus 4d. to the sergeant. A currier who set up, apparently without being authorised, was presented in 1593 at the court leet for "occupying the trade of currying to the impoverishment of Robert Cooke, a poor man of that trade".[20]

Perhaps the clothing trades accounted for the largest number. There were weavers, dyers and fullers; mercers, drapers and tailors; glovers and shoemakers. A tailor's bill in 1592 for making a jerkin was 20d.; the cloth cost 8d., 3 doz. buttons 3d., and $\frac{1}{2}$ yd. of watchet or light blue taffeta, apparently for trimming, 6d.[21] Gowns for William Broughe's daughters in 1597 seem rather dull, for they were of black woollen material, trimmed with black silk lace and with russet wrought velvet; the hooks and eyes for them cost 1d.[22] One of the many shoemakers mentions in his will his "lasts, boot-trees, knives and other tools."[23]

Craftsmen included several pewterers, for most household utensils in common use were of pewter; there were also cutlers, saddlers, smiths, coopers and joiners; and at least one potter in St. Mary's parish who presumably lived in Potter Street. Building trades were represented by masons, tilers, carpenters and painters; one tiler, Thomas Cockman, was marched off to Tilbury during the Armada scare and did not appear at the court leet, but in the circumstances his fine was waived.[24]

[19] Court leet, 1592.
[20] Corp. MSS.
[21] Court of pleas.

[22] Loc.cit.
[23] Thomas Rechford, 1600: CRO, ABP/R 24, f.45.
[24] Corp. MSS.

Special rules applied to some occupations. Tallow-chandling was not allowed in High Street, and tallow must not be kept untried above 14 days. Brewers must produce 12 gallons of ale from a quarter of malt. Bakers must sell to hucksters by the baker's dozen: 13 loaves as 12. Butchers must sell tallow to the chandlers within 14 days after the flesh be killed. The raw hides required by tanners might be bought and sold only by the well in High Street or in St. Mary's churchyard; a dicker of leather was 10 hides.[25]

Sometimes there is information on the contents of house or shop. When Robert Stapulton's furniture was distrained on in 1592,[26] it consisted of a great settle, a form, 4 tables of varying kinds (one a trestle-table), 3 chests, 2 cupboards, 6 pieces of pewter, a candlestick, a salt, and 6 bedsteads. A barber, Percival Hudson, who bequeathed to his apprentice the tools of his trade, had in his shop a great chest and a coffer, 2 chairs, 6 shaving cloths, 5 basins, 2 ewers, 8 knives, 2 pairs of scissors, and hanging candlesticks.[27]

Some Bedford inhabitants were yeomen or husbandmen, but often they combined farming with other occupations, and many rules were made for agricultural matters. For arable farming the main provision was that stubble in the open fields must not be entered upon by animals before St. Luke's day. The common rights of others could not be acquired except by burgesses, and even a burgess could have only one additional common right. The keeping of livestock was regulated. For each acre of land a man could keep 1 sheep; for 20 acres a cow or ox; he paid the common herdsman $\frac{1}{2}$d. a week for each animal, and the herdsman every morning blew his horn in three places in the town to give warning to inhabitants to bring him their cattle; and in the evening likewise to collect them again. Cottagers however could stake cattle on the common balks between Candlemas and Lammas (the old names were still used). A horse must not be allowed loose in the fields from All Saints' Day to harvest. Pigs were a problem; they must be ringed, and must not be allowed to wander in streets, churchyards and gardens; and if the mayor was so lax as to remit the fine, he made himself liable to one of 20s.; it was he incidentally who appointed the swineherd or hoggerd. Nets must not be used when catching fish in the river. Wood or bushes growing on the balks or at the roadside, or willows in Trumpington mead, were sold by the chamberlains.

Legal cases in Bedford[28] at this time throw some light on the town. There were three courts; the court leet for minor offences (like a manorial court elsewhere); the court of pleas for civil cases; and sessions (from at least the time of Queen Mary Bedford had its own court of quarter sessions). Most of the cases are modest and indicate a town still small. Thus cases of debt might be for as little as 4s.; security for a loan might be a silver goblet or a feather-bed; a cloak

---

[25] Court of pleas, 1597–8.
[26] Court of pleas.
[27] C.R.O., ABP/W 1575/76.
[28] Corp. MSS.

is stolen; an unsound horse sold; cattle are driven out of another man's close. In a case of slander, whereby a man was brought into shame and discredit among his neighbours, the words spoken were "Thou art a thief and didst steal a hen of mine", and a similar case ran "Thou stolest my purse and my money". A poor old woman, Agnes Jeffes, was accused of bewitching Nicholas Beacham, who languished under grave sickness as a result; at the first offence in 1591 she was imprisoned for a year, and once a quarter she was made to stand for 6 hours in the pillory in High Street. When in 1594 a third case was brought against her, she was hanged, although not one of her 3 alleged victims had died.

Amusements still included bull and bear-baiting; in fact John Williams made for this very purpose a large and pleasant place before his house, with rubble from St. Peter Dunstable.[29] Gambling included a game called "passage"; Robert Paradine lost great sums at this game to William Peacock, who, he alleged, was using false dice subtly made.[30]

At the end of the century there are two pointers towards the future. One is that a change had come about in Bedford's parliamentary representation; in general, burgesses seem to have given up representing the borough in parliament. Names of local gentry appear; George Gascoigne, 1558; Oliver St. John, 1563; John Burgoyne, 1563; William Boteler, 1586; Thomas Snagge, 1586; Humphrey Winch, 1593; Oliver Luke, 1597. Some of these, like Winch, were legally qualified and of standing in their profession, and held the office of recorder or deputy recorder. The office of recorder carried only a small fee; and if at the same time the holder represented the borough in parliament, the connection was more worth his while, and he could also on occasion be a useful friend. But the fact that burgesses were prepared to relinquish the office of M.P. was to have later consequences.

The other is that again there are signs of restiveness among the freemen or commoners. Already by 1597 there was a proposal at the court leet that they should share in the election of mayor and bailiffs.[31] It was unsuccessful, but the more enterprising freemen would not always be content to be constables and bucket-searchers. It is the burgess minority in Bedford which catches the eye; but the majority included many humble people; some hardworking and reliable; some inefficient, ill and unlucky, living on the poverty line. The supposed witch, Agnes Jeffes, who had no chattels, and John Broune the cobbler, who owned only a little coffer, a blanket, a hammer and a hobbing iron,[32] were scarcely exceptional.

THE MARKET TOWNS

The full evidence required for a step-by-step comparison of Bedford with the market towns throughout the century does not survive, but some broad con-

---

[29] *B.H.R.S.* xxxvi, 18.
[30] Court of pleas, 1597–8.

[31] Corp. MSS.
[32] *B.H.R.S.* xx, 112.

clusions can be reached. Dunstable, which must now be treated with the market towns, lost the second place in the county. Leighton and Luton townships or urban centres kept roughly in step, as they probably had done since 1066; and very roughly each was about half the population of Bedford. Thus, in 1603 Luton township and hamlets were estimated to have 1,200 communicants;[33] if these represent 400 in the township and 800 in the hamlets, the township was nearly half Bedford's figure of 1,033. In 1628 a subsidy gives, not absolute figures of economic wealth, but relative figures for comparison, since it would be impossible to favour any place or places unduly (ch. 21). Bedford paid over £31; Leighton over £26, of which the township paid half; Luton £33 of which the township paid one-third; Biggleswade township £10; Dunstable £8. Thus the relevant figures for comparison are Bedford £31; Leighton £13; Luton £11; Biggleswade £10; Dunstable £8.[34]

DUNSTABLE

Any special status Dunstable had was lost at the dissolution; the sheriff at once claimed entry, and when in 1540 the constable tried to restrain him from evicting a tenant, the sheriff put the constable in the stocks and brought back to Bedford gaol others who joined in the affray.[35] Two years later Dunstable was annexed to the royal honour of Ampthill, and was administered by a bailiff who had a lease of his office. Its area was small (453 a.); it was not, like the ancient Saxon royal manors of Leighton and Luton, surrounded with agricultural hamlets; and those of its inhabitants who were much concerned with agriculture had lands in neighbouring parishes. It had no resident family of importance.

At the time of the dissolution,[36] the priory had about 150 tenants; the minority paid rents of assize, or small fixed rents; the majority were tenants at will, whose economic rents brought in a larger sum; altogether, counting the farm of the rectory, the annual value of the priory's estate was just over £100. What proportion this bore to the whole of Dunstable it is not possible to say. For the 1524 subsidy about 60 people were assessed, 7 of whom were in the upper income bracket, paying £1 or over; and Dunstable's tax assessment was nearly £20 (£3 more than the township of Leighton).[37]

There were some well-to-do inhabitants at the time of the dissolution in 1540. John Fensham, a smith, owned silver salts, spoons and cups; and was in a position, when he died a few years later, to leave 10 loads of stone every year for 10 years to repair the road between Dunstable and Houghton Regis.[38] Thomas Bentley owned the White Horse, where Henry VIII himself stayed in 1537 (he was already beginning to dissolve the monasteries and so did not care to stay at the priory); Bentley had an extensive wardrobe, with doublets of black satin and

[33] L.R.S. xxiii, 259.
[34] C.R.O., T 53/10.
[35] V.C.H. iii, 361.

[36] P.R.O., SC 6 Henry VIII, 6070.
[37] P.R.O., E 179/71/114.
[38] C.R.O., ABP/R 11, f.88.

white fustian, a blue jerkin, black hose and white hose, a worsted gown guarded with velvet, and a chamlet one lined with taffeta; he took advantage of the dissolution to lease what had been the Dominican friary.[39] A musician, Robert Foster, had two assistants, Richard Pryor and Hugh Plate, who (if they served out their year with his wife when he died in 1563), were each to have one instrument to get their living withal; among his instruments was a bass-viol.[40]

Had the proposed bishopric materialised, Dunstable might have been midway in importance between Ely and Peterborough. As it was, the dissolution seems to have been a setback. Royalty did not visit; Elizabeth in her royal progresses through the country (local church bells were rung "when the queen's majesty passed by")[41] requisitioned hospitality from the aristocracy. No Lord Mayor of London came forward to endow the school in South Street, the Fayrey family (ch. 15) were just too early; though there probably was from time to time someone who tried to make a living by teaching, for Elizabeth Ameas in 1591 wanted her son brought up at school.[42] The hospital continued at least till 1606. But it seems certain that, at least relatively to other market towns, Dunstable declined during the 16th cent. It has been estimated that in the mid-16th cent. the population was about 1,000, and that a century later it had fallen by about 15%.[43] In 1628 only 28 people were assessed for tax, and Dunstable's total was £5 less than that of Leighton township.[44] Such a drastic revision in Manshead Hundred would not have been accepted unless it had a basis in economic fact.

There was traffic along Watling Street. In 1540 there were many inns; the Angel, Bull, Falcon, George, Lamb, Lion, Peacock, Ram, Saracen's Head, Swan, White Hart and White Horse.[45] Many of these continued to prosper. Edward Carre, innholder, who died in 1589, left to his daughter 6 cushions of tapestry in the chamber over the gatehouse, some tapestry coverlets, a carpet which used to lie on the table in the parlour, and quantities of bedding and linen.[46] But not all travellers were well-to-do people who put up at inns. Some probably brought the plague with them; between 1578 and 1603 there were five outbreaks, the worst being 1593–4 when 63 people died.[47] There came along Watling Street poor people trying to get to London in the hope of improving their lot, or vagrants wandering aimlessly; sometimes their strength gave out at Dunstable and they died there; 20 strangers were buried between 1573 and 1603.[48] A woman on the road in 1599, great with child and so weak and feeble that she could travel no further, was taken in by Alice Willet, herself very old and poor, and Alice found herself in trouble with the church court.[49]

[39] C.R.O., ABP/R 11, f.250.
[40] C.R.O., ABP/R 16, f.57.
[41] B.H.R.S. xxxiii, 13.
[42] C.R.O., ABP/R 22, f.111d.
[43] B.P.R. xlii.
[44] C.R.O., T 53/10.

[45] See n.36.
[46] C.R.O., ABP/R 22, f.71d.
[47] B.P.R. xlii.
[48] Loc.cit.
[49] L.R.O., Ch.P. 1598–9, f.15.

Some tradesmen still flourished. Such was Thomas Finch, draper, who in 1587 left his son Richard a tenement in West Street and an acre in Houghton Regis, and charged him to give, as heretofore it hath been accustomed yearly, 3s. 4d. in bread to the poor on the Monday after the feast of St. Michael; his wife was to have his tenement in South Street, but must not take down the wainscote or the glass windows.[50] Among the yeomen was Henry Bennell (d. 1571), who left to his son Henry land in Houghton Regis, Caddington, Kensworth and Totternhoe; and to his son William all his cart-horses, carts, ploughs and plough-harness.[51] Two men (yeomen?) after an accident in 1599 were excommunicated, Thomas Waters and Edmund Temple; they were driving a loaded cart into Dunstable in the dusk one Saturday evening, when the axletree broke in the way. They were obliged to leave the cart there overnight, and went out early in the morning to bring in the load. Other inhabitants testified for them that they always demeaned themselves in a very good and honest manner, and only apparent necessity forced them to cart upon the Sunday.[52]

LEIGHTON AND LUTON

The economic life of Leighton and Luton was not much affected by the dissolution. The main manor of Leighton remained the possession of St. George's chapel, Windsor; and as it was a big manor and did not change hands, its court records continued to be regularly kept; and its copyhold tenures strictly enforced. In the hamlets the small manors changed hands at various times, apparently becoming less and less manorial in character. At Luton too there was some stability with the more important manors. Some fractions of the main manor which had been reunited remained with the Rotherham family of Someries. The Hoo manor was in the hands of the Fermors – Richard Fermor in the 1530's was a merchant of the Calais staple (for the prominence of sheep in the Luton area in the early 15th cent., see ch. 15).[53] In 1611 these manors coalesced under the Napier family at the Hoo; henceforward this new-style Luton manor descended with whatever family was at the Hoo; and here again copyhold tenures were enforced. Some smaller Luton manors (such as Greathamstead and Haverings) coalesced into the Crawley estate, but there is little manorial evidence for them; and the welter of remaining small "manors", continually changing hands, were probably manorial only in name. Thus both at Leighton and Luton, though much outlying land seems to have grown free from manorial control, there was to remain for centuries one strong manor where copyhold tenures were firmly administered for a resident lessee or owner.

When there was first a market-house or moot hall in either township cannot be established, but probably quite early in the middle ages. It was used both for markets and fairs, and for the holding of courts. The loft of that at Leighton was let

---

[50] C.R.O., ABP/R 22, f.23.
[51] C.R.O., ABP/R 16, f.181d.

[52] L.R.O., Ch.P. 1598-9, f.15.
[53] D.N.B.; see also C.R.O., DW 6, 29-30.

out in 1585 by the dean and chapter's lessee to a local tanner, Edmund Bolsworth, who was restricted in his use of it; he must keep the loft "comely benched" at one side and one end, and the window glazed, and must allow admittance to those attending the courts below.[54]

Both at Leighton and Luton teaching was probably available only when an enterprising local man or woman was willing and able to take pupils. It occurred to one Luton man, John Norris (d. 1537) that it would be desirable to have a (Latin) grammar school in Luton, and he thought of leaving £20 "to build and make a house to keep therein a grammar school, and the house to be near unto the church, and at the advice of the parish where it shall be set", but family feeling prevailed, and the money was left to his brother, the school being conditional on his brother's death – the brother lived.[55]

In both townships were such traders and craftsmen as drapers, glovers, tanners, weavers, shearmen, tailors and chandlers. The better-off inhabitants were used to amenities. Joined furniture was frequent, especially at Leighton; joined bedsteads, tables, forms and stools, for instance, were in the house of Robert Gladwen (d. 1585);[56] there was also in similar houses plenty of bedding, feather-beds, flock beds, mattresses, pillows, bolsters, sheets, blankets, red and green coverlets and occasionally a quilt; Elizabeth Blick of Leighton (d. 1590) had two chamber-pots.[57] Coffers were plentiful; Jelyan Kylbe of Luton (d. 1546) had two painted ones;[58] Joan Marston of Luton (d. 1540) one of spruce;[59] and Elizabeth Blick a carved coffer. Linen occasionally included tablecloths and towels and sometimes even table-napkins – Reynold Hollande of Leighton (d. 1586) had six.[60] On the walls were painted cloths; Jelyan Kylbe wanted those in her hall to remain where they were. Most of the better-off inhabitants were well supplied with clothes. John Evered of Luton (d. 1549) had besides his best and his second gown a violet-sleeved coat, a black fustian doublet and a buff leather jerkin;[61] and Joan Marston had a violet gown with a black pursel, and a russet gown purselled with otter. At Leighton there is more than once mention of a special christening sheet.

Sometimes there is information about a man's occupation. Thomas Godfrey, a Luton weaver (d. 1546), had 3 looms; his hare (flax) loom was left to a friend at Toddington, with 2 combs and slays (spare parts) and a bolt of hare; his woollen loom and two linen gears to another friend; and to his servant, Thomas Ympey, his "bassertt" loom and all his shop gear not bequeathed and all his yarn and his russet gown; various friends received shirts and flaxen sheets; his servant Agnes Fisher got his household utensils of pewter and brass and 2 kerchieves; and 12

54 C.R.O., KK 319.
55 C.R.O., ABP/R 4, f.90d.
56 C.R.O., ABP/R 22, f.2.
57 C.R.O., ABP/R 22, f.97.

58 C.R.O., ABP/R 11, f.183d.
59 C.R.O., ABP/R 6, f.34.
60 C.R.O., ABP/R 22, f.1.
61 C.R.O., ABP/R 12, f.71.

poor women a kirtle each.[62] A carpenter at Leighton left his daughter 50 ashen inch-boards.[63] Apprenticeship was usual: Thomas Leach of Leighton left a nephew 20s. "after that he doth come forth of his prenticeship."[64]

Maltmaking was important at Luton. Probably, though the evidence does not survive, it had been increasing at Luton in the 15th cent; we know at least that from elsewhere in Bedfordshire malt had been sent to London as far back as 1381.[65] A particularly well-to-do Luton maltman was Richard Evered (d. 1556).[66] He left legacies of over £200; his servants had nearly £10 between them, and the poor of Luton £20; and the poor were also to have 10 quarters of malt where most need is; his wardrobe included 4 coats and a buff leather jerkin. William Deane, who also had various gowns and coats and doublets, left 12 bushels of malt to the poor householders of Luton, a peck at every poor house (i.e., about 50 houses).[67] Not all maltmen were so well off; William Stallworth (d. 1564) could only manage 6d. for the poor men's box.[68]

Yeomen and husbandmen were especially numerous in Luton; several of these mention their copyhold land; and probably many of them lived in the hamlets. John Evered (d. 1549) mentions over 60 a. apparently of freehold land, and 14 a. of copyhold, and 4 houses; he left £10 to "the building of the aisle of Luton church where the scaffold doth stand", 40s. for mending the streets where most need is, and ½ bushel of malt to 100 poor householders "unless that I do give it myself before my decease", and 1s. each to 20 poor widows; he had at least 5 horses and a number of sheep; and his wardrobe included a buff leather jerkin, a violet-sleeved coat, and a doublet with satin sleeves.[69] Another Luton yeoman, John Smith (d. 1550) had 5 sons and 2 daughters to whom he left £10 each, dividing his silver spoons among them; he had 3 houses in Church Street, Castle Street and in the North End; and he left 20s. to "building the roof of the aisle when they go about to set it up".[70] Thomas Perat (d. 1550) left his wife his white ambling horse, his black horse and his grey horse, a cow, all his hogs and all his poultry, 25 sheep and £10; while each grandchild was to have a lamb.[71]

As Luton was such an agricultural centre, it is not surprising that it was at Luton in September and October of each year that some of Queen Elizabeth's supplies from Bedfordshire were handed over to her purveyors by an agreement of 1588, namely 120 capons at 4s. a dozen, 360 hens at 2s. a dozen, and 360 chickens at 1s. a dozen (the cattle and sheep from this county for her beef and mutton were driven up and handed over at the court gate on specified dates).[72]

[62] C.R.O., ABP/R 11, f.161d.
[63] C.R.O., ABP/R 22, f.2.
[64] C.R.O., ABP/R 22, f.116d.
[65] C.R.O., BS 1175.
[66] C.R.O., ABP/W 1556/85.
[67] C.R.O., ABP/W 1555/83.

[68] C.R.O., ABP/R 16, f.133d.
[69] C.R.O., ABP/R 12, f.71.
[70] C.R.O., ABP/R 12, f.130.
[71] C.R.O., ABP/R 12, f.97d.
[72] C.R.O. Guide, p.137.

OTHER TOWNS

Biggleswade in 1547 was exchanged by the Bishop of Lincoln with the crown for other lands, and during this century the crown leased it out (it was not attached to the honour of Ampthill). Here, as at Dunstable, innkeeping was prominent, and Walter Fisher (d. 1567) of the Bell had among his possessions a great carved chest wainscoted.[73] A tailor, Thomas Adcocks (d. 1570) drew customers from places as far away as Cardington and Hitchin, but not all of them were good payers.[74] Henry Fynche (d. 1565), yeoman, had managed to get over a dozen burgages into his hands, three of which had formerly belonged to the fraternity, and he left each of his 4 children 20 sheep.[75] Biggleswade (or rather Holme) had a school for 8 poor children, founded in 1557 by Edward Peake.[76]

Ampthill, though nominally the head of the royal estate, was not commercially of much importance. The tolls of the fair in 1542 brought in only 13s. 6d. annually, as compared with £30 for rents of farms, warrens and mills, and £20 for the remainder of the property.[77] Like other small places with markets, it may be more conveniently considered in ch. 20.

Toddington's weekly market was renewed in 1531, and its markethouse is said to have been built with materials from the demolished hospital of St. John the Baptist.[78]

In all the market towns it is the solid and the prosperous inhabitants for whom evidence survives. There were also the many below the tax level, who had too little property to make a will worth while, and who often were servants of their better-off neighbours, or who struggled independently to make a difficult living. They were grateful for a pittance from the poor men's box, or for a distribution of bread or of money at the funeral of a better-off townsman; they were often hungry, cold, and in rags. For them in this century there was little provision (ch. 21). Frequently no doubt some of them stole and were put in the stocks or whipped in the pillory. Only occasionally does one of them get into the record, like Alice Willet of Dunstable, who was very poor (see above). These have no memorial.

---

[73] C.R.O., ABP/R 17, f.12d.
[74] C.R.O., ABP/R 16, f.164d.
[75] C.R.O., ABP/R 17, f.66. See also a well-to-do husbandman in 1575, B.H.R.S. xxxii, 102.

[76] *V.C.H.* ii, 179.
[77] See n.36.
[78] Blundell, *Toddington*, p.179; *V.C.H.* iii, 441, 444.

20 - YEOMEN, CRAFTSMEN AND COTTAGERS, 1530-1603

IN TUDOR Bedfordshire the difference between town and country was small. Bedford had yeomen. Dunstable, Leighton, Luton and Biggleswade had manorial residues like those in the country, and the same parochial machinery (ch. 21). In all of these craftsmen and traders were only slightly more numerous and specialised than those in the villages.

Though many of the village markets set up in the 13–14th cents. (ch. 5) had now died out or become negligible, a few markets outside those of the five main towns were still viable: Ampthill, Harrold, Potton, Shefford, Toddington, Woburn. Thus these smaller market towns were the next largest trading centres. At Ampthill were to be found chandler, draper, tiler, maltman, smith, warrener and wheelwright; at Toddington cooper, glover and mercer; at Shefford glover, mercer, poulterer, scrivener and tanner; at Woburn chandler, draper and joiner.

CRAFTSMEN AND OTHERS

But the distribution of occupations was wider, wider even than can be exactly shown, because not all the evidence has survived, and not all is precise. Because almost everyone had something to do with the land, subsidy lists (ch. 21) for general purposes classified taxpayers into a small number of esquires and gentry and a large number of yeomen and husbandmen (in the early period also wage-earners); and usually ignored such other occupation as a man might follow besides cultivating a small area. This occupation might however be his main source of livelihood; and thus when the small man made a deed, and sometimes when he made his will, or when he was buried and a careful incumbent made up the parish register (which was now a legal obligation), his main occupation was noted. Not all registers were carefully kept or have survived, nor have all deeds; but there is enough evidence to show a diversified economy, even though these crafts served only a local not a national market.[1]

Especially prominent were occupations to do with agricultural service. Carpenters and smiths were almost everywhere. There were ploughwrights, like Richard Assum of Tebworth, William Wylcocks of Gravenhurst, John Day of Wilstead, and others at Colmworth, Tempsford, Odell and Kempston. Tempsford and Odell also had whittawers, who made the collars required for horse and ox. Turvey and Sandy had wheelwrights, Campton and Shillington had joiners; and Maulden a turner, John Wynsly. Clophill had a whipcord-maker.

[1] Unless otherwise stated, occupations are taken either from the occupations index in the County Record Office; or from the indexes to B. Par. Reg.

Equally to be expected are trades concerned with food. Millers were every-where, and there was a millwright at Felmersham. Butchers and bakers naturally were common. Although there was not now quite so much emphasis on eating fish on Fridays as earlier, when there were many fishermen along the river, there were still some fishermen, such as Henry Kemeshedd of Bromham.[2] At Riseley there was a poulterer; at Husborne Crawley an oatmeal-maker; and at Chalgrave a fowler, Henry Howes. Maltmen were not confined to towns; there was one at Elstow, William Forbes. At Pulloxhill there was a badger or licensed dealer in corn.

Occupations to do with clothing were as much to be found in the country as in the town. Weavers were widely distributed; at Houghton Conquest, probably also in all large parishes, there were two. Tailors might be found anywhere from Felmersham to Totternhoe, for all clothes must be individually made, though there would be a difference between making a working jerkin and a satin or chamlet doublet. In between these two numerous groups come some more specialised ones; fullers at Kempston, Oakley, Studham and Blunham, where John Elliott leased the fulling mill with four going "stokkes" and two going wheels; at Stevington also the fulling mill was still working.[3] There were shear-men, like William Elborne and Lancelot Clarke at Henlow. Glovers were to be found at Cranfield, Eaton Socon, Girtford, Segenhoe and Toddington. Even retailers practised in the countryside – there was a mercer at Lidlington. Foot-wear, like clothes, had to be made, so shoemakers were frequent.

As most houses were still half-timbered, the carpenter was the mainstay of the building trades; and connected with him was the sawyer. In the stone areas there were masons, as at Milton Ernest (William Lynford) and at Totternhoe, where were also quarrymen. Tiles, already known to be in local use (ch. 12), were now definitely in local production. The first known reference is in Luton, and is a case of angry intervention by the lord of the manor: in June, 1541, under orders from Sir Thomas Rotherham, several men expelled a tenant, Barnard Spayn, from a close let to him, broke a great number "of new tile brick crests", and took away many "loads of clay ready digged".[4] At Riseley Thomas Heatley (d. 1558) owned a tileyard with pits; and at Marston Claipitt furlong occurs in 1579. At Leighton in 1579 Edmund Bolsworth had license to make brick and tile. There was a tiler at Ampthill as well as those at Bedford (where thatch was now forbidden) and Luton. There were beginning to be more glaziers, as at Silsoe, for though windows in most houses were small, glass was coming into more general use. At Clophill there was a plumber, Robert Whitfield.

The carrying trades were represented by tranters (as at Gt. Barford and Tilsworth), and Margaret Price of Carlton was a peddler.

[2] B.H.R.S. xli, nos. 23, 114, 116, 122, 134, 299.   [4] P.R.O., Star Ch. Pro., 31/96.
[3] B.H.R.S. xxxvii, 25.

Other occupations flourished which have either now disappeared, or have no place in small-scale production today. Thus at Henlow there was a colony of bowstring-makers; no less than five are known between 1553 and 1597, and there was another at Clophill, Martin Allen. Tanners were important; because of the numbers of horses and oxen there was a good supply of leather; and it was used, not only for footwear and gloves, but also for jerkins, for breeches, for buckets, for jugs or jacks, and for harness; such was John Smith of Biddenham; and tanners are known too at Potton and Riseley. Riseley also had a potter. Basket-making probably flourished, though no Tudor reference has come to light. There are other ways of life which would not be expected in the country; Maulden must have had a minstrel, for his widow was buried in 1584; and Wilden a scrivener, Edward Latner. No 16th cent. bell-founders are known, though over 50 bells are of this century: Shillington bells were recast at Hitchin on one occasion;[5] and bells in the Bedford area were probably recast at Bedford by a travelling bell-founder from Leicester.[6]

Almost non-existent was the medical calling; the housewife dispensed traditional herbal remedies or charms. Medical knowledge (ch. 26) was still rudimentary, and its supposed training theoretical; there was a doctor of physic at Wilstead, John Warner, and one at Eaton Socon, Thomas Pooley; and occasionally a barber practised some primitive surgery; such were probably Thomas Musserege of Northill and Philip Davies of Campton.

An apparently new craft practised mainly by women and children had come into existence: the making of lace with bobbins on a pillow, hence called pillow-lace, or bone-lace because some bobbins were made of bone.[7] By 1596 it was being taught at Eacon Socon to poor children by a woman who was paid 2d. a week by the parish; out of this she had to make good the weight of that thread *that shall be wasted or lost under her hands in the working of the lace*; and each child was paid *"so much as they shall earn by their working"*.[8] This is the first surviving description of what was to become widespread, the so-called lace-school, in fact the organised production of lace by children.

YEOMEN AND HUSBANDMEN

Such were the neighbours among whom the yeomen and husbandmen lived, together with cottagers and shepherds, and a few warreners and woodwards. Nationally it is considered that the yeomen were the more substantial farmers, with upwards of 70 a. of land, and in a minority in most villages; and that the husbandmen had on an average 30 a. (though richer ones might have 60 a. and poorer ones 15 a.) and did not need to work for wages. Wills show that in Bedfordshire the number of yeomen was less than half that of husbandmen; possibly

---

[5] B.H.R.S. xxxiii, 86.
[6] T. North, *Church bells of Beds.*, 40.
[7] The tradition associating Catherine of Aragon with pillow-lace is of late growth and unsubstantiated by 16th cent. evidence.
[8] C.R.O. *Guide*, pl. VI.

R

(if a number of poor husbandmen did not make wills) the proportion of yeomen to husbandmen was something like 1:3. On the other hand there were often men calling themselves yeomen who were in fact quite poor. There were also a number of men calling themselves husbandmen who were as well off as any yeoman;[9] and because of their wealth and activity they have left more evidence than their humbler neighbours. The following paragraphs deal with the better-off agriculturalist, whether nominally yeoman or husbandman; he had a holding which might vary considerably in size; and he might or might not cultivate additional land (freehold or copyhold). Such men had seen lords decline and monasteries dissolved and gentry come and go; on balance they had moved less and had found new opportunities. Sometimes they might feel the parish lacked an influential spokesman – a letter to the county subsidy collector reads "desiring you would be pleased, in regard we have nobody to speak for us, to stand our friend so far as shall seem fitting in your wisdom",[10] but in the main they had a new confidence.

Some rose to become gentry. Sometimes ex-monastic land helped, especially where the yeoman had been tenant of a monastery. For 50 years the Francklins had leased Glyntils manor, Bolnhurst, from Canons Ashby priory; in 1546 they were able to buy it; and at the heralds' visitation of 1566 they were bearing arms; by the end of the century George Francklin had built up a moderate estate in north Bedfordshire, which he was rationalising in the 1590's.[11] Nicholas Thurgood, yeoman, in 1569 leased Rowney manor for £66 p.a.; he seems to have been occupying the manorhouse, which he agreed to improve by adding four chimneys, for he undertook to receive his landlord and suite there once a year for a limited stay.[12] He bought Gastlyns manor, Southill, in 1587. Sometimes the family progressed slowly through the 16th cent., like the Reeves of Toddington, husbandmen or yeomen, who also owned the Dolphin inn; they added acre to acre; some of their relatives were cottagers or labourers, like John Reeve of Tilsworth in 1588; but in 1663 George Reeve was able to call himself gentleman.[13] Of the Hanscombes of Shillington, Matthew died a yeoman in 1592; but in the next century the family were gentry.

[9] For Bedfordshire no statistical analysis of the average size of holdings as between yeomen and husbandmen can be made, because for this period of flux scarcely any surveys have survived; nor, for the same reason, can a comprehensive one be made from probate valuations. There is however a chance group of probate valuations for 1617–20 (printed B.H.R.S. xx). This contains 16 yeomen's inventories averaging £150, and 18 husbandmen's inventories averaging £130. If we take it that this sample is more trustworthy as regards yeomen and less so as regards husbandmen (since a smaller proportion of husbandmen was likely to be rich enough to make wills), we may conclude that the true average valuation for a husbandman would almost certainly be below £100. On the other hand, the highest valuation in this sample is that of a husbandman (£577), and the lowest is that of a yeoman (£9). Once more a man's label must be treated with caution.

[10] C.R.O., TW 1102.

[11] C.R.O., FN 80–1; V.C.H. iii, 126; see also P.R.O., C 205/5/3.

[12] C.R.O., X 95/133; V.C.H. iii, 258.

[13] C.R.O., X 86/265–98. Nearly 300 years covered the rise and decline of one family, the Hangers of Souldrop. John Hanger, husbandman, occurs in ABP/R 11, f.231d; and yeomen and husbandmen follow him in the neighbourhood for many years. In 1825 "John Hannah, jintellman born, come to

Sometimes trade helped. Robert Norton, a Sharpenhoe yeoman who died in 1559, was impressed by his brother's prosperity as a citizen of London, and by the already promising career of his nephew Thomas, the future "parliament man"; he asked them to bind his own young son apprentice in London, with a bequest to follow if young Norton "serve his years out honestly and truly without picking, stealing, running away or other notable falsehood and lewdness".[14] William Denis, born in 1597 of a family of husbandmen in Kempston, went to London and became a merchant; be bought two Kempston manors which he bequeathed to his nephew, who thus became a gentleman.[15]

However, sometimes the yeoman or husbandman who became tenant of a whole manor was exceptionally able, and his family were not able to sustain the position to which he had raised them. Thomas Cadwell, husbandman, paid no less than £100 p.a. rent in 1593 for the manor of Thurleigh, with 233 a. in the open fields, 26 a. meadow, and closes totalling over 160 a., in all over 400 a.; and he undertook to build a new barn for which he was allowed timber.[16] William King who died in 1546 had a lease of the manor of Colesden, and had land also in Gt. Barford, Wilden and Tempsford.[17] But these families remained yeomen or husbandmen.

A more representative yeoman is Richard Sampson of Biddenham, who in his notebook in 1540 entered an account of his land.[18] To begin with, there were 28 a. of common field land and 2 a. meadow; then he had bought rather more than that of Richard Lord; and a smaller area from John Smyth; so that his total holding in Biddenham was about 76 a. in the common fields and 8½ a. meadow; and he also had some in Westoning. In this book he noted down when he sent grain to the mill, for malting, or for sale; when he paid the blacksmith; and when he bought and sold livestock; also such useful items of information as that a kilderkin of beer contains 18 gallons; that a thousand of tile covers 12 sq. ft.; and that a mile is 1,000 yards!

At least some yeomen and husbandmen saw the opportunity to improve their holdings by enclosure. This is most easily seen at Caddington;[19] among those who enclosed in the 1560's were Edward Davey (1563, 9 a.; 1565, 4 a.; 1566, 6 a. in Mill Field and another 6 a. in North Field); Thomas Bray (1563, 15 a. in Taylor's Field; 1566, 8 a. in Mill Field); and Thomas Street who in the ten years before 1569 enclosed 21¼ a. by five instalments. At Cranfield Thomas Reade and Richard Wheeler were enclosing small areas about 1600.[20] Engrossing too was practised by them.[21] At Chalgrave Richard Parrat, husbandman, having already a house of husbandry wherewith was about 30 a., about 1601 hired and took into his hands a

work on the road for his living"; *B.H.R.S.* xl, 139.

14 C.R.O., ABP/R 15, f.52.

15 C.R.O., PE 358; *Hist of Kempston* (ed. H. A. Carnell, T. Booth, H. G. Tibbutt), 34–5.

16 C.R.O., L 15/34.

17 C.R.O., ABP/R 11, f.139 d.

18 C.R.O., TW 799.

19 C.R.O., CRT 130/1.

20 P.R.O., C 205/5/3.

21 *Loc.cit.*

tenement and 20 a., and in 1604 another messuage and 50 a., "wherein he now dwelleth, and useth therewith all the above except 3 a. which he letteth to Robert Crawley". At Wilstead Thomas Dickons of Elstow leased a farm of about 80 a., occupied the land himself, and put a cottager in the house.

Some share of former monastic land percolated down to yeomen and husbandmen as the former monastic estate disintegrated. A one-time manor of Caldwell priory in Girtford was sold in 1563 to Edmund Cosyn, who (having no son) divided it between his sisters Elizabeth and Margaret, one of whom divided her share among three sons.[22]

The extent of the yeoman's livestock is not easily assessed, because most probate inventories have been lost. Matthew Woodward of Barton in 1591 had 2 milch cattle, a weaning calf, 3 young pigs, over 40 sheep, and poultry.[23] George Reeve of Toddington, who died in 1581, left his daughter Mary the black cow, Elizabeth the brindled cow, and his son John the pied cow; John was also to have (if father did not live for the wedding) two of the best sheep for his marriage dinner; his son Thomas was to have the shod long cart, the dung cart, and some grain for his children.[24] Sometimes cows are referred to by name; Robert Lord, a Riseley husbandman who died in 1581, called his Goldilocks and Ladieface;[25] and an Eversholt man had a black cow called Jenkyns.[26] Farm implements mentioned at Edworth in 1561 are 2 shod carts, a dung cart, 2 harrows, a roll, 2 iron rakes, scythes, a new plough "with all things that belongeth to a plough for 6 horses".[27]

Of the house of yeoman or husbandman we get the clearest descriptions in a 1604 survey for Thurleigh.[28] Peter Selby, a husbandman paying tax in 1597, occupied a house of 4 bays, 50 x 16 ft., of which the parlour and one other bay were lofted over; he also had a kitchen and kilnhouse in a separate building of 2 bays, 28 x 16 ft.; while his farm buildings comprised 2 barns, a cart-house and a hogscote; his holding included orchard, pightle, 6 closes, 27 a. arable and 3 a. pasture. The contents of the house of Matthew Woodward of Barton[29] in 1591 were (in his hall or livingroom) a trestle table, chair, form, wainscot cupboard, painted cloths, and 5 cushions; his household equipment included a dozen trenchers and other "treen", a quantity of pewter and brass, kettles, posnet, skimmer, fryingpan, spit, gridiron, pothooks, bellows, tubs, pails, kimnels and firkins; there were spinning-wheels for wool and linen; in the chamber or sleeping-room, which also was hung with painted cloths, were 2 bedsteads and bedding; and he had 4 coffers, and candlesticks of pewter and latten. George Reeve of Toddington

22 C.R.O., PM 288, 290, 293, 402. An exhaustive study of the eventual owners of ex-monastic land in Devon has been made by Dr J. Youings, *Devon & Cornwall Rec. Soc.*, new ser. i, and fuller investigation might be attempted for Bedfordshire.
23 *B.H.R.S.* xxxii, 107.

24 C.R.O., ABP/W 1581/21.
25 C.R.O., ABP/W 1581/37.
26 C.R.O. ABP/R 20, f.51.
27 C.R.O., ABP/W 1561/64.
28 C.R.O., L 26/1442.
29 *B.H.R.S.* xxxii, 107.

had a painted bedstead.[30]

For the widow of yeoman or husbandman provision was often made, and sometimes even for himself in his last years. Richard Perkins, a husbandman of Tempsford, in 1597 wanted his wife Agnes to have the best milch cow, a hive of bees, half the poultry, a bed and bedding, the brass, linen and pewter she brought with her at their marriage, and the use for life of the room over the milk-house or dairy.[31] Elsewhere an incoming tenant's lease stipulated that the previous tenant, John Rowland, was to occupy half the house while he lived; and when he died, the new tenant must support Rowland's widow Agnes in sickness and in health, and supply her with wholesome meat, drink and cloth, and with all manner of other things meet and convenient for a woman of her age and calling.[32] Thomas Allbright of Kensworth, husbandman, in 1532 stipulated further that his widow Isabel was to have yearly 2 a. wheat and 2 a. barley ready carried and brought into her barn.[33]

What of the smaller agriculturalists who formed the majority? They are hard to trace. So far as the evidence goes, they seem more prominent in the north, where the heavy clay was hard to work, and where even in the present century before mechanisation 4 horses and 2 men were needed for ploughing, while for the lighter soil in the east 2 horses and 1 man would suffice. At Thurleigh the holdings on the Earl of Kent's estate seem to be anything from 6 to 30 a.[34] Elsewhere sometimes pressure of population reduced the size of holdings; at Blunham some half-yardlands had shrunk, apparently by sub-division, from 16 a. to 6 a., though each holder still claimed common for 6 cattle.[35] Often, probably, the husbandman with too small a holding for adequate subsistence merged into the craftsman (see above), and even thought of himself as primarily such. If this was not practicable, then he was barely distinguishable from the better-off cottager.

Yet it is perhaps worth mentioning here that (though evidence from tax returns is of limited value – see below) in this period nearly half the parishes in the county show a rise in the number of taxpayers: 35 of them by 50% or more; 22 of them by 100% or more.

COTTAGERS

There is another large class of dwellers in the countryside for whom unfortunately little information is forthcoming: the cottagers. This term is used in preference to the contemporary term, labourers, since, though in general they did some work for others, probably seasonally, the extent to which they depended for subsistence on their labour varied.

A cottager was not necessarily very poor; the most flourishing were probably little worse off than the poorest husbandmen. A cottager might pay tax, as did

---

30 C.R.O., ABP/W 1581/21.
31 C.R.O., BS 1288.
32 C.R.O., L 15/3.

33 C.R.O., X 125/1.
34 C.R.O., L 15.
35 C.R.O., L 24/643.

John Hall of Stotfold in 1581–2.[36] He might own his cottage; or he might lease it with a little land, as Thomas Norris leased 9 a. in 1604.[37] He might make a will, like Robert Allen of Barton, who in 1584 left each of his two sons £16 13s. 4d.[38] In Bedfordshire it is impossible to estimate the average cottager's livestock. It has been calculated that generally in the Midland common field areas many cottagers had one cow, perhaps more, a few sheep, and perhaps a pig; but that few had a horse.[39] Perhaps his house was like that of William Ward, an old lame shepherd of Thurleigh, in 1604; this was 40 x 15 ft., and had a hall or living-room, a chamber, and a parlour lofted over.[40] There were quite a number of these well-off cottagers; the ratio of their wills to those of other village dwellers is as follows: 1 cottager: 3 craftsmen: 3 yeomen: 7 husbandmen.

How many poorer cottagers there were is more difficult to determine. At Henlow between 1590 and 1599 the parish register mentions 22 cottagers or labourers, 7 yeomen or husbandmen, and 13 men following other occupations (weavers, tailors, smiths, millers, tanner, shearman, bowstring-maker, shepherd, servant); this would make half the population of the village cottagers.[41] At Eaton Socon in 1591 67 were paying rates and 25 (the majority women, mainly widows) were receiving relief;[42] with an estimated population of 879 and 207 houses, again quite half the population seem to be cottagers. These figures seem rather high (though for the 1524 subsidy, when wage-earners also paid tax, they were about half the taxpayers in 6 parishes in Willey Hundred[43] and they would not be likely to decline during the century). The national average has been suggested as from one-quarter to one-third, rising to 47% by 1700.[44] In extreme cases the poor labourer probably tried to seek work elsewhere, like the man noted in Campton register in 1586 "a poor fellow which came to the town for food, lately a shepherd at Southill"; and if unsuccessful died and was buried in a strange parish, as at Shillington in 1592 "a stranger died here and was buried", or at Campton again in 1598 "a boy of some 10 years old unknown, found dead upon Chicksands warren"; or Henlow in 1590 "a poor walking man whose name we could not learn, which then died in Ravens his barn".[45] (For poor relief see ch. 21).

GENERAL SURVEY

It is insufficient to consider rural society by classes. As always throughout Bedfordshire history, there is great diversity between one parish and another. An attempt has therefore been made to assess parishes in groups.

The grouping has been made primarily by considering the number of wills in

---

[36] P.R.O., E 179/72/183.
[37] C.R.O., L 15/15.
[38] C.R.O., ABP/W 1584/249.
[39] *Agrarian Hist.* iv, 415.
[40] C.R.O., L 26/1442.
[41] B.P.R. xxv.
[42] C.R.O., P 5/12/1.
[43] P.R.O., E 179/71/112: Bromham, Chellington,

Podington, Souldrop, Turvey, Wymington; also elsewhere at Clophill, Gravenhurst, Sundon and Tilsworth (the returns are defective, so the proportion for the whole county cannot be given).
[44] *Agrarian Hist.* iv, 398–9.
[45] B.P.R. xxv & xxxvi; and transcript of Campton in C.R.O.

relation to area, the range being from Over Stondon with under 500 a., to Eaton Socon with over 7,000 a. This has been compared with population (calculated from the registers and checked by reference to published population estimates for 1671 nearly a century later). Also taken into consideration is the number of taxpayers and amount of tax paid, but because of the unreality of late 16th cent. tax assessments (ch. 21), little reliance must be placed on the tax figures alone.[46]

In the first group, where there seem to be the largest number of yeomen in relation to area, the most striking is the medium-sized parish of Lidlington; then the much larger ones of Houghton Regis, Marston and Sandy; and those of Toddington and Shillington which are larger still; followed again by some medium parishes, Barton, Chalgrave, Potton, Roxton and Tempsford; and then Eaton Socon, the largest of all, but having in proportion to its area fewer wills and fewer taxpayers. In this group too are to be found three small parishes, Biddenham, Elstow and Pulloxhill. Thus these parishes vary in size, and are pretty well distributed over the county, except in the extreme north and northwest. There seem to be various reasons for the apparent prosperity of yeomen in them. Sometimes the cause may lie in their past development; freeholders were noted at Eaton Socon earlier (ch. 8). Perhaps following on from this is the absence of a large resident landowner in several of the above, though there was Gery at Eaton Socon, Conquest in Houghton Conquest, Snagge in Marston, and Cheney in Toddington; and at both Biddenham and Elstow William Boteler and Edward Radcliffe respectively paid half the total tax. Another factor may be the nature of the land; Biddenham, Eaton Socon, Roxton, Sandy and Tempsford are riparian parishes, four of them in what was about to become the market-gardening area. At Potton and Toddington some of their apparent prosperity may be due to markets.

The next group comprises most of the county. These parishes seem to have a number of yeomen, though not as many in proportion to their area as those in the first group. Here are some large parishes like Southill, Northill and Turvey; many medium-sized parishes, such as Bletsoe, Harrold, Sharnbrook, Streatley, Sundon and Sutton; and small parishes such as Milton Bryan, Milton Ernest and Tingrith. Perhaps the fact that their prosperity seems merely average is partly due in the north to the heavy clay land; thus Thurleigh's tax in 1597 is £8, but Houghton Conquest – almost exactly the same area – pays £11. At Bletsoe the St. John estate was building up; the St. Johns paid half the tax.

[46] Dr E. A. Wrigley has kindly contributed the following note on subsidies. In the early 16th cent. the subsidy assessments do not give an accurate indication of overall wealth, partly because the wealth that was assessable to the subsidies was restricted, and partly because there was some under-assessment; but for a time the subsidy returns can still be used to give a good indication of the relative wealth of individuals, and of the relative wealth of parishes. From about 1550 the accuracy of the sub-sidy assessments declines drastically, and they bear little relationship to the wealth of individuals; nor do they adequately reflect the changes in the relative position of wealth between parishes. They will pick up certain types of change; if a parish declines, the assessments of the declining parish will go down; but the reverse is not always true. Changes in relative wealth over time would have to be fairly drastic to upset the relative position of parishes arranged in groups.

In the last group are a few parishes with a very small population. Most are upwards of 1,000 a.; a few under that figure. There are scarcely any surviving wills, and the population in all but one is under 100 persons; a century later it is roughly the same, except that Battlesden has declined below 100 and Steppingley risen above. Others in this group are Edworth, Eyeworth, Higham, Potsgrove, Stondon and Whipsnade, the last being on the downs. Higham and Steppingley in 1597 each had only one taxpayer. Higham's population about 1600 is reckoned at 9; in 1671 as 17. It was the most notable case of 15th cent. enclosure (ch. 12). At Battlesden in 1597 William Duncombe paid £4 out of the parish tax assessment of £5 17s. 4d.

Some examples from each group are given below. The population has been calculated by taking a 10-year average of baptisms and multiplying by 30.

parish	area	wills 16th cent.	taxpayers (1581/2 or 1597)	tax £	population c. 1600
GROUP I					
Eaton Socon	7,602	60	46	27	879
Toddington	5,535	72	28	16	600
Marston	4,290	84	18	10	582
Roxton	2,941	49	24	13	369
Lidlington	2,544	72	19	8	468
Elstow	1,617	57	12	8	492
GROUP II					
Southill	5,734	42	33	7	720
Turvey	4,011	36	17	9	504
Thurleigh	3,418	20	15	8	351
Bletsoe	2,250	19	10	8	336
Tingrith	946	10	3	1	159
GROUP III					
Higham	1,298	3	1	4	9
Edworth	1,122	9	6	2	63
Whipsnade	1,088	5	3	2	36
Stondon	428	1	2	8s.	21

21 – ADMINISTRATION, 1530–1607

THE SHERIFF
The sheriff still performed the same duties as at the beginning of the century: he was responsible for writs and returns for the central courts, for arrangements for the assize judges, for the empanelling of juries, for the prison, for the county court which had declined, and for the return of M.Ps. The little prison in Gaol Lane was probably a wretched place. Kind-hearted people remembered the prisoners as objects of charity; John Norris of Luton[1] in 1537 left 5d. to 15 poor prisoners to be given to a man or woman bearing irons, and 3s. 4d. in beef. Till 1574 the county still shared a sheriff with Bucks., but thenceforward the two were separated, and George Rotherham of Luton was the first sheriff for this county only. The sheriffs were moderate gentry; Sir Thomas Rotherham held the office as well as George; so did Sir Humphrey and Sir Edward Radcliffe of Elstow; Sir Lewis and Sir John Dyve of Bromham; Sir Henry Cheney of Toddington; several held it more than once, such as Ralph Astry of Harlington, William Boteler of Biddenham, Nicholas Luke, Sir Richard Conquest, Richard Chernock of Hulcote. Perhaps Sir John and Sir Oliver St. John were the men of chief substance to hold it.

The sheriff held office for only a year at a time. Before the century was over, the government was to feel the need of an additional officer of higher status and longer tenure who could in emergency act as the king's lieutenant (see below). However, Bedfordshire rose neither for the monasteries in 1536, nor against enclosure in 1547; and there was no candidate of commanding position. The Marquess of Northampton seems to have been named in 1551 and Lord St. John in 1569, but for the moment the matter did not press.

JUSTICES OF THE PEACE
More important in county matters generally were the justices of the peace. Though a justice did not act in that capacity while he was sheriff, the justices were drawn from the same class, and included most of the above names with others more. Sessions rolls for this period have not survived. If later ones are any guide, it is probable that only a minority attended sessions regularly. At Easter Sessions 1585 those present were the Earl of Kent, Lord (formerly Sir Henry) Cheney, Thomas Snagge of Marston, and Lewis Dyve.[2] Scattered contemporary evidence seems to show that some justices were doubtful characters, and that animosity between them could still breed trouble even if not to the extent that it did so in the 15th cent.; while there seems to have been something haphazard

---

[1] C.R.O., ABP/R 4, f.90d. [2] Brit.Mus., KTC 115a 4, f.17.

217

about the conduct of business.

In the 1580's Robert Newdigate of Haynes was said by some of his colleagues not to co-operate with other justices, but to support evil and disordered persons; to have connived at the escape from Bedford gaol of a notable thief; and to have taken no action when his servant, Ellis Ap Rhys, beat up Thomas Percival in Haynes, Percival only being saved from death by the appearance of two poor women.[3] Newdigate's own account was that the Earl of Kent had conceived displeasure against him without cause; had, with 30 of his servants on horseback riotously assaulted him on the queen's highway, using terrible threats and outrageous oaths, saying that he would make Haynes "to whotte" [too hot] for him; and had persuaded Lord St. John of Bletsoe to bid certain simple justices to his house and set their names to a writing that he, Newdigate, was not meet to be on the commission of the peace.[4] Newdigate seems to have been a difficult character; but what perhaps gave edge to the clash of personalities was that he, though of an old Bucks. family, was a newcomer to this county (having married a Conquest); while the Earl was a member of an old Bedfordshire family reasserting its position, and hence perhaps touchy.

Another fierce dispute between justices was that between William Boteler of Biddenham (a comparatively new family which had thriven as the result of business in London) and Lewis Dyve of Bromham. Their lands adjoined and their purchase policy conflicted. Boteler alleged that in 1589, when he refused to fight a duel, Dyve with 9 named men armed with swords, daggers and staves, ambushed him on his way home from church on Sunday; he himself was stricken to the ground and bled; and of his servants, Peter Sampson was thrust through the gullet, Andrew Wright lost two fingers of the left hand, and Robert Sampson was wounded in the right arm, after which the attackers departed "in jollity, rejoicing greatly of that which they had done".[5]

A sidelight on proceedings at quarter sessions comes from an enclosure dispute at Podington in 1578.[6] Bredyman had set up a fence and Tyringham's men pulled it down; the former's agent wrote "I have arrested three of them . . . Mr. Tyringham came in this last quarter sessions, we being unprovided and not knowing of it before, until Mr. Conquest called me to him and asked me if you had any business there today, and bade me look well to it, for Mr. Tyringham had two counsellors there against us." He added that the clerk of the peace "hath stand you in great stead . . . and hath not as yet anything for his pains."

One action of the justices is known – their setting up in 1585 of a house of correction in Bedford, somewhat later than the act of 1576 directing this.[7] Here a justice could send rogues and vagabonds to be kept from their wicked and

---

3 C.R.O., L 24/647.
4 C.R.O., L 24/654.
5 C.R.O., TW 1016.

6 C.R.O., OR 1079.
7 See n.2.

ungodly course, corrected of their disorders, and forced to labour for their own living; and a parish constable who on warrant from a justice delivered such a rogue at the house of correction was allowed 1d. a mile travelling expenses.

SUBSIDY COMMISSIONERS

One of the accusations made against Newdigate was that, when made a commissioner for the subsidy or tax, he undervalued his own parish of Haynes, and increased the assessment of other parishes.[8] The assessment and collection of subsidies illustrates the role of the part-time amateur, on whom administration was to depend for centuries yet. A subsidy was in theory so much in the £ of a man's land or goods above a certain level; but in practice, owing to the inherent human reluctance to be taxed, it meant that there was no new assessment, but that approximately the same sum as was yielded by the previous subsidy was apportioned out in the county, thus ignoring any increase in wealth. The government appointed commissioners for the county (for the borough of Bedford the mayor and bailiffs acted). The county commissioners divided the hundreds among themselves, and nominated a collector for the county. Thus in 1550 William Boteler of Biddenham was collector; and among the commissioners for Barford, Stodden and Willey hundreds were Sir John St. John and Sir Lewis Dyve.[9] They sent for the constables of the hundreds and the previous lists, and made such alterations as they saw fit. Without detailed returns, such as are made to-day, it was impossible to produce a perfectly equitable list, and it must have been a tricky thing to put up a neighbour's assessment even when perfect integrity and goodwill prevailed. In the next reign an anguished taxpayer complained bitterly that "my Lord St. John with his own hand" had increased his assessment; "I cannot conceive, unless by some underhand misinformation, why he should deal so with me."[10] Thus subsidy lists are uncertain guides to the wealth of county or individual; but as they could not be completely divorced from economic reality, they are a rough basis for comparison of parishes (ch. 20).

THE CIVIL PARISH

It was in the 16th cent. that the parish, in origin ecclesiastical (ch. 1), became a civil and administrative unit. Since manors had first proliferated, and then much of their machinery had broken down, some such development had to take place. It came about by degrees. The first move was to give those parish officers of long standing, the churchwardens, a civil duty; thus in 1532–3 they were made responsible for reducing vermin; and though Tudor examples of this have not survived, churchwardens' accounts in the next century show entries such as "an otter's head, 2d."; "6 hedgehogs' heads, 1s."; "4 foxes' heads and one badger's head set up in the churchyard, 5s."; "widow Saffron for 4 polecats, 8d."[11]

Other duties became necessary. Clearly too much could not be put upon the

[8] See n.3.
[9] C.R.O., TW 875.
[10] C.R.O., OR 1749.
[11] J. S. Elliott, *Bedfordshire vermin payments*, 58–9.

churchwarden, but at the Easter vestry meeting other officers might be chosen; and though the archdeacon could not be expected to supervise them, there were the local justices of the peace to carry out this duty. The next officers to be appointed were the surveyors of the highways. For some time the state of the roads had been such that public-spirited people left money for the repair of particularly bad stretches, as John How of Houghton Regis did in 1503[12] (see also ch. 16). In 1555 each parish was made responsible for the upkeep of roads within its boundaries. Two surveyors were to be chosen; and under their direction each householder was to work on the roads 4 days a year, while the better-off were to send horse and cart. This parochial duty has produced fewer records than any other; obscure parishes probably neglected it as long as they could; bigger ones through which a main road ran could less easily avoid it; and later some accounts began to be kept when money had to be spent on materials or labour, or when the surveyor had some beer while he was "a-viewing the highways" to see what work ought to be done. The roads were infested with highwaymen, like the famous Gamaliel Ratsey, whose last exploit was taking £174 from a horseman near Bedford, after a fierce duel in which he was wounded. Through an accomplice turning king's evidence, Ratsey was traced to a hide-out in London, after which he was publicly hanged at Bedford in 1605, when he made use of the condemned man's privilege of making a speech long enough for a gathering storm to burst, so that "he might see them all [the spectators] well washed before he died".[13]

The pressing problem which no parish could avoid was that of poverty. The reasons why poverty was so acute in the 16th cent. are various, but their relative importance is not easily assessed. How far monastic alms[14] had helped to alleviate distress is uncertain; but certainly it was usual for a religious house to have an almoner, and a specific income was appropriated to him; thus of Newnham Priory's Bedford property rents totalling 28s. 10d. were earmarked for the almoner;[15] and therefore whatever was the whole extent of monastic relief in the county, after the dissolution there was none at all from this source. It is probable also that some charities for the poor were casualties when chantries were closed down; more than one later enquiry revealed mistakes that were made at this time.[16] While the abler yeomen and husbandmen were thriving and extending their holdings, the less efficient man's holding was shrinking, and he was becoming to a certain extent dependent upon his labour (ch. 20). More emphasis on the keeping of livestock, at first on sheep, later on cattle, meant less demand for labour than when grain was the first requirement. Population growth meant that the supply of labour exceeded the demand. Bedfordshire also, especially along Watling Street, received some wanderers from counties where these problems

---

[12] *B.H.R.S.* xxxvii, 12.
[13] *Shakespeare Ass. fac.* 10 (Life and death of Gamaliel Ratsey); *John Rylands fac.* 5 (Ratseis ghost).
[14] D. Knowles, *Religious orders*, iii, 264–6.
[15] *B.H.R.S.* xxv, 26–30, 36, 48, 68.
[16] C.R.O., L 24/418; cf. *B.H.R.S.* xlv, introduction.

were still more acute.

Almost every parish register shows such burial entries as "a beggar of unknown abode" (Wrestlingworth, 1597); "a wayfaring man" (Shillington, 1575); "a poor strange woman" (Milton Bryan, 1592).[17] Epidemics were another adverse factor; it is not unusual to find burials suddenly shoot up by anything from twice to ten times the normal average; the most striking case is Barton, where in 1559 57 people were buried instead of the usual average of 7.[18] These may have been due to smallpox or plague. Plague was spoken of as a visitation of God and was always a hazard when going to London, and liable to be brought back thence. Baldwin Payne of Podington wrote to his brother in 1543 recommending him to put up at the Pewter Pot in the parish of St. Andrew Undershaft, as so many inns were "visited"; "they die now in manner as fast as they did any time this year".[19]

Fumblingly through the century the public conscience (stimulated by the government) tried to cope with those in need by putting a few pence in the poor men's box at church; or arranging for a funeral distribution of loaves of bread; or (as Ann Spencer of Edworth did in 1560)[20] leaving a couple of cows to be let to two poor folks at 3s. a cow; or (as William Curtes of Elstow did in 1547)[21] leaving a flock of sheep to be hired out and the proceeds given to the poor – the constables were to see that the flock was properly maintained so that it might never die. A number of people left more substantial bequests for charity; thus in 1557 John Maynard of Broom in Southill, husbandman, left all his property to the parish, half to be used for the upkeep of the highways and half to the poor.[22] Only gradually was it realised that the responsibility must be borne by the community as a whole.

The government policy was at first, as in 1536, to try to stimulate almsgiving by Sunday collections, and to discourage beggars by whipping; till in 1563 it recognised the need for a levy. "The count of our gathering for the poor" appears in Northill accounts for 1563[23], and from then onwards sums are paid out varying from 1s. 6d. for the quarter ending midsummer, 1564, to 29s. 6d. at the previous Christmas. An average of 13 people were receiving relief; Playnemor had 8d. "for his children"; and widow Green in her sickness had 4d.

In 1572 the appointment of overseers (at first called collectors) was required;

---

[17] B.Par.Reg.

[18] B.Par.Reg. iv. Epidemics have been traced in B.Par.Reg. as follows. The normal average of burials is given, followed by that of the epidemic and the year in which it occurs.

Barton	7	57	1559
Bedford St. Mary	9	53	1557
Caddington	6	33	1558
Carlton	2	12	1560
Chalgrave	6½	38	1559
Dunstable	12	51	1559
Houghton Conquest	7	26	1557
Maulden	7	40	1558
Milton Ernest	7	23	1558
Sandy	10	71	1559
Shillington	15	50	1559
Southill	10	50	1557
Toddington	13	75	1558

[19] C.R.O., OR 1004; and cf. ABP/R 28, f.109d: "because of the hand of God by his visitation upon our town of Elstow", 1608.

[20] C.R.O., ABP/W 1561/64.

[21] C.R.O., ABP/R 11, f.240.

[22] C.R.O., P 69/25/1.

[23] Econ.Hist.Rev. iii, 102–8.

and in 1597 the law was consolidated, making the parish responsible for the sick and aged poor, for children, and for the able-bodied who should either be set to work or sent to a house of correction (see above). By this time more parish accounts are available. Those for Eaton Socon in 1591 show that Thomas Kippest and Robert Wright were overseers; they collected monthly sums varying from 1d. to 8d. from over 50 people and smaller sums from 1d. to 6d. from others. One man paid his 1d. in three instalments. The 25 recipients of relief got anything from 1d. a week, like Widow Ratford, to 4d.; the only one who received this large sum was James Proctor, who presumably was both sick and had a family. At the same time the overseers organised the making of pillow-lace by poor children for their own support (ch. 20).[24] The accounts were signed by the Earl of Kent and Oliver St. John. Something of the developing poor law during the century can also be traced at Shillington; here 25 people were receiving relief in 1596; and in 1597 10s. was spent on firewood for them.[25] The last years of the 16th cent. were years of bad harvests and rising prices so that, although the poor law machinery should have been functioning everywhere, distress was acute.

THE LORD LIEUTENANT

With Spanish invasion threatening, and with the restlessness caused by distress, it became urgent to appoint a nobleman of standing to act as the queen's lieutenant and arrange for musters, or periodical military training (unfortunately few details of Bedfordshire musters have survived). In 1586, two years before the Armada, Henry Grey, 6th Earl of Kent was commissioned as lord lieutenant. Henceforth, except for a confused period in the Civil War (ch. 23) the succession of lieutenants was unbroken.

In May 1607 there was a rising in Northants., which spread to Warwicks. and Leics. The Earl of Kent warned Bedfordshire constables to be on the alert; captains of musters, both horse and foot, to be ready at an hour's warning; and he had 4 post-horses in waiting at Bedford. On 6 June he wrote to the Privy Council that he hoped to keep the county in peace and good order. Some disturbance however did spread to this county; and on 20 June he had to confess that some discontented obstinate people had tumultuously disturbed public tranquility. He hoped his prompt action had settled the matter, and that offenders would presume no more hereafter. "That our Bedfordshire people should offend in this sort, I am very sorry for it."[26] The government, which all through the century had been uneasy about problems of the countryside, and thought enclosure might be the cause, ordered a commission of enquiry into seven Midland counties (ch. 17); the Bedfordshire commissioners included the Earl of Kent, Sir Edward Radcliffe and Sir Richard Conquest. No action was taken when the commission reported.

[24] *Op.cit.*, 108-16.
[25] *B.H.R.S.* xxxiii.
[26] *R. Hist. Soc. Trans.*, n.s., xviii. For the office of lieutenant in general, see G. Scott Thomson, *Lords lieutenant.*

With these darker strands of sickness and poverty and sometimes hunger running through the fabric of life in Elizabethan Bedfordshire must also be associated that of superstitious cruelty. Alleged witchcraft at Bedford has already been noted (ch. 19). It was found also in the countryside. Alice Smallwood of Blunham was accused in 1538 of being a witch; and Elizabeth Ocle of Pulloxhill was hanged at Bedford for witchcraft in 1596.[27]

LITERATURE AND ADVENTURE

Yet there were also some strands of colour and light not yet mentioned. Among young gentlemen who went to the university or studied law or went to court were some who had ideas beyond the old round of building up the family estate. In the secular drama which was now developing two Bedfordshire men led the way. Thomas Norton's career has already been given (ch. 18); in his youth he was joint author of the earliest tragedy in English blank verse, *Gorboduc*, which was performed in 1561 on twelfth night at the Inner Temple before the queen herself.[28] The second, *Jocasta*, was written by George Gascoigne in 1575. Poet, soldier, and at one time M.P. for Bedford, he contributed to a masque performed before the queen at Kenilworth; and when he published his *Posies* or poems, his preface "to all young gentlemen" describes himself as "a man of middle years, who hath to his cost experimented the vanities of youth and to his peril passed them; who hath bought repentance dear, and yet gone through with the bargain; who seeth before his face the time past lost and the rest passing away in post."[29]

Incidentally, London also exerted an attraction for more frivolous reasons. In 1543 Goodwife Keylsar of Podington sent a message to Baldwin Payne, asking him to bring her back a new hat. Somewhat embarrassed, he wrote back to his brother: "I pray you write me what manner hat she would, and I will buy one for her according to her desire."[30]

At a humbler social level, the invention of printing had brought books within reach of a far greater range of people than before; ordinary people might have a book, or (like Edward Welles of Luton in 1533) leave money to the church to buy a book.[31] There begin now to be references to teaching in several places. The Biggleswade school has already been mentioned (ch. 19). Woburn was lucky enough to have a schoolhouse actually built by the Earl of Bedford in 1582 (Joan Ball left 13s. 4d. to buy a lexicon for it);[32] but though in general village schools endowed by charitable bequest were yet to come, yet at Colmworth, Eaton Bray, Shillington, Streatley and Thurleigh references to teaching are known. Thus at Shillington in 1578 there was "Creke the schoolmaster", and in 1596 the church-wardens paid 6d. to Thomas Haire for "mending the school".[33]

[27] C.R.O., ABC 2, f.45; *B.Par.Reg.* xxii.
[28] *D.N.B.*; *B. Mag.* v, 113-8.
[29] G. Gascoigne, *The posies* (ed. J. W. Cunliffe), 9.
[30] C.R.O., OR 1004.
[31] C.R.O., ABP/R 3, f.81.

[32] C.R.O., ABP/W 1587/116.
[33] *B.H.R.S.* xxxiii. For Colmworth and Eaton Bray see ch. 18; for Thurleigh, C.R.O., ABP/R 15, f.142d; for Streatley ABP/R 15, f.54.

Then, even for this inland county a wider horizon was dawning. War had always been one means of seeing the world; thus Thomas Evans of Leighton was "at the wars" in 1585; he was probably serving in the Low Countries with the Earl of Leicester's expedition against the Duke of Parma; if he returned safely, he was to have a legacy of £5 from his father, and "a bedstead that standeth over the stairs".[34] In the past the other way had been pilgrimage; now trade beckoned to the adventurous man. Nicholas Laurence of Bedford, who became a merchant tailor in London, went to Morocco, whence he wrote in 1590 that he had travelled over 100 miles on foot. One item in which he was trading was sugar. While he was away, he was worried about his children; he asked his cousin "I pray you in any wise keep them to school; let them be lovingly used, cleanly kept and trained up." He adds "I am no good skoller to Red and nevr wayr." A statement of 1600 says that he "lately died in Barbary".[35]

[34] C.R.O., ABP/R 22, f.4d.   [35] C.R.O., TW 397.

Puritans and Parliamentarians

22 - THE CHURCH, 1603-89

THE ROMAN CATHOLIC CHURCH

The Roman Catholic church[1] in Bedfordshire had very few adherents. Its strongest foothold was at Turvey where, after the 4th Lord Mordaunt died in 1609, his widow lived. The government took away her eldest son so that he should be brought up an Anglican; but from 1625 to 1631 she even had resident in her house the Vicar Apostolic, "when he travelleth in his coach with 4 horses accompanied with 9 or 10 priests"; his jurisdiction extended over Roman Catholics in the whole of England and also in the American plantations. But England was dangerous, and from 1631 to 1685 (when a new order was set up) neither he nor his successors were resident in this country.

Two other Roman Catholic families are known. One was that of Hunt of Chawston by 1628. The other was the Watson family of Beckerings Park. With the Watsons, either in London or at Beckerings Park, lived for the last few years of his life, 1638–41, Father Augustine Baker, who helped to negotiate the re-erection of the English Benedictine congregation. He was also a writer, and in his *Secretum* he writes of "mystic contemplation . . . by which a soul, without discoursings and curious speculations, without any perceptible use of the internal senses or sensible images, by a pure, simple and resposeful operation of the mind, in the obscurity of faith, simply regards God as infinite and incomprehensible Verity."[2]

THE ANGLICAN CHURCH AND THE PURITANS

The Anglican church in 1603 had the loyalty of many clergy and laymen, not only because it was established by law, but from genuine belief, as a peculiarly English blessing, and a factor in national security. It also held those whose simple faith enabled them to accept what authority directed. This did not satisfy all. Even in Elizabeth's reign there had been some stirring of ideas in this county, as elsewhere (ch. 18). In the early part of the century two puritan trends in national thought[3] were to emerge clearly in Bedfordshire. Both were influenced in doctrine by Calvin, and in worship both desired more simplicity.

One was perhaps the more intellectual approach, and was found among incumbents and gentry; it got the name of Presbyterianism, though it never wan-

---

[1] *Northampton diocese centenary souvenir*, 1950.
[2] D. Knowles, *English Mystical Tradition*, 162–3.

[3] A helpful booklet is Studies in the puritan tradition (a joint supplement issued by the *Congregational and*

S

ted to take over completely the Scottish system with its synods. It accepted the parochial framework, but wished to institute ruling elders. In so far as it was frowned on by bishops, it became increasingly critical of episcopacy. This outlook (with its emphasis on order) was less strong in Bedfordshire than in some other parts of England.

The other trend was among men and women of more modest standing, who were beginning to read the Bible; it was called at first Brownist (after Robert Browne), later Independent. Instead of the parish as a basis, it insisted that those who met for worship should be guided by the Christian spirit; thus it was selective. It did not include the careless, ignorant and irreverent (like those who practised cockfighting in Knotting church in 1637);[4] and it too was opposed by authority, which had to think of the good of the whole flock. This outlook (with its emphasis on freedom) was to achieve a far greater hold on the county.

A national conference at Hampton Court in 1604 considered whether some changes could be made in the established church. The conference was unable to agree; and at it James I upheld the existing system. But authority cannot impose unity or prevent thought; repression hardens opinion and engenders counter-repression when opportunity comes. So pressure built up for nearly 40 years.[5]

This generation was concerned not with buildings but with ideas. The days of continued enlargement and enrichment of churches were over; church-wardens' accounts (where there was vigilance) show the need to keep the fabric in repair. A development which is in a way curious is the tendency of those gentry who could afford it to put in the church handsome sculptured tombs (sometimes with live-sized effigies of themselves), like those of the Mordaunts of Turvey, the Chernocks of Hulcote, or the Thompsons of Husborne Crawley. Perhaps the oddest is that of Sir Humphrey Radcliffe at Elstow, which is over the altar; while the most appealing inscription is that set up in 1641 by Lady Dyer at Colmworth for her husband, Sir William:

> "My dearest dust, could not thy hasty day
> Afford thy drowsy patience leave to stay
> One hour longer, so that we might either
> Have sat up or gone to bed together?
> But since thy finished labour hath possessed
> Thy weary limbs with early rest,
> Enjoy it sweetly, and thy widow bride
> Shall soon repose her by thy slumbering side,
> Whose business now is only to prepare

Presbyterian Historical Societies, 1964.)

[4] *V.C.H.* iii, 139.

[5] Gunpowder plot in 1605, when a few misguided Roman Catholics made an attempt on the govern-ment, briefly touched Bedfordshire when the fleeing conspirators changed horses at Hockliffe (*B.N.Q.* i, 156). The number of Roman Catholics in the county was negligible.

My nightly dress and call to prayer.
Mine eyes wax heavy, and the day grows old,
The dew falls thick, my blood grows cold.
Draw, draw the closed curtains and make room,
My dear, my dearest dust, I come, I come."

In the ferment of ideas, the book desired above all was the Bible. There had been more than one translation in the 16th cent., none completely satisfactory. As one positive result of the 1604 conference, James I appointed 54 divines, among whom were Francis Dillingham, rector of Wilden, and Andrew Byng, vicar of Everton, to make a new translation. The authorised version appeared in 1611 and displaced all others. The impact of the Bible, the vivid stories of the Old Testament, the teaching of the New Testament, translated into the language of their own day (a language used with mastery) was overwhelming. For many it was the only book they had, and kept in a special Bible box. Some had also simple devotional works, like the *The practice of piety*, or *The plain man's pathway to Heaven*.

Teaching brought it within the range of many. A teacher must be licensed by the bishop as a suitable man for his calling: at Bolnhurst in 1617 William Reeve was licensed; at Colmworth John Phipps; at Wilstead Thomas Wood; at Little Barford John Pittam; at Langford John Hemmyng.[6] But the demand was great, and some taught without licence, as did Thomas More at Riseley in 1610;[7] and in 1617 there were many others; at Cople Mr. Stringer; at Wootton Mr. Smythe; at Stevington John Gittens; at Melchbourne Paul Dodd; at Meppershall Mr. Noke; at Lidlington Bethuel Chapman; at Pulloxhill and Lidlington Mr. Millward; at Ridgmont Mr. Bower; at Clophill Hugh Hunt.[8] These were probably only part-time teachers, and the children they taught only a small proportion – those whose parents (yeomen, husbandmen or craftsmen, like Thomas Bunyan the brasier) could scrape together a few pence to pay for them; but reading was now to be found not only among the educated gentry but among those of more modest status.

In many parishes no doubt relations were smooth between incumbent and congregation. Of the best intellectual level among the clergy, John Donne, dean of St. Paul's, is an example. The Earl of Kent presented him to the rectory of Blunham (the Greys were discerning patrons – later they presented another poet, Thomas Traherne, to Credenhill on their west-country estate). Donne kept a curate at Blunham, but usually came down in the summer, and also presented the parish with plate. Just as he exercised the minds of his congregation at St. Paul's with teaching which still stimulates us, in beautiful prose which still delights us, he could also preach in simple terms to a country congregation. Thus on the text

[6] C.R.O., ABC 5, p.303 et seq.

[7] C.R.O., ABC 4, p.2.

[8] C.R.O., ABC 5, p.74 et seq.

"Father, forgive them for they know not what they do", given only by St. Luke, he explains why the gospels vary. "As an honest man, ever of the same thoughts, differs not from himself, though he do not ever say the same things . . . so the four evangelists observe the uniformity and sameness of their guide . . . And as, when my soul, which enables all my limbs to their functions, disposes my legs to go, my whole body is truly said to go, because none stays behind, so when the holy Spirit . . . directed one of them to say anything, all are well understood to have said it." Matthew's gospel was to supply a want in the eastern church; Mark's, out of Peter's dictates and by his approbation, in the western; Luke's because he was so individual a companion of the most learned St. Paul; John more diligently than the rest handleth his divinity. "So therefore all writ one thing, yet all have some things particular."[9] Afterwards, no doubt, his patron enjoyed Donne's conversation at dinner. Another writer has left a poem on the hospitality of Wrest; the house, he says, was not grand or ornate (probably it was that built by the 1st Earl); but it was a "house for hospitality", cheerful fires, a merry hall thronged with living men, piled-up dishes of choicest relish, while those whom "wealth, parts, office or the herald's coat" have severed from the common, sat with the lord.[10]

On the other hand there were parishes where a minister who tried to maintain a decorous Anglicanism found himself at odds with his parishioners, a situation where frustration on both sides led to undesirable incidents. Such was Dunstable, which had a puritan tradition going back to Lollardy and more recently to "an irregular and unconformable minister". The new incumbent, Edward Alport, was, he said about 1616, "much maligned by insolent and refractory persons" and was the subject of coarse practical jokes and rough treatment. Thus three young men pretended to baptise a sheep at the font (no doubt because they disapproved of making the sign of the cross). Others were said, after being late at the alehouse one night, to have gone into the rector's corn with staves, pitchforks and pistols, hoping to provoke him to "come out and be harmed". About 30 men were named in his petition, noticeable among them the Medgate family.[11] In the same year at the archdeacon's court Amy, wife of Edward Chauncellor of Studham, was presented as a Brownist; and in the following year so were several at Cranfield: Thomas Chambers, Richard Barrett, and the wife of John Wheeler.[12] When some years later in 1633 Archbishop Laud carried out a metropolitan visitation of the diocese, his visitors found Bedfordshire "the most tainted of any part of the diocese", and particularly given to "the sort of people that run from their own parishes after affected preachers".[13]

There were also parishes where a puritan incumbent found squire or

---

[9] *Sermons of John Donne*, ed. G. R. Potter & E. M. Simpson, v, 231–44.
[10] *Poems of Thomas Carew*, ed. R. Dunlap, 86.
[11] *B.H.R.S.* xi, 109–27.
[12] C.R.O., ABC 5, p.9, 18, 45.
[13] J. Brown, *John Bunyan*, 8–9.

parishioners of other views. At Podington Thomas Whitbie often did not wear a surplice, nor make the sign of the cross in baptism. All sorts of recriminations were exchanged which, whether or not they were true, show bad relations. Whitbie accused the lord of the manor, William Payne, of making a passage for carts across the churchyard and littering hogs there; of leaving church during sermon time in a scornful and tumultuous manner; and of encouraging young people to stay away and to swear; while Payne's version ranged over many points, such as that in a sermon Whitbie called St. Peter a malapert and saucy fellow; that he did not catechise the children, and when asked to do so "made a tush and scorn thereat"; also that he lived very poorly and kept a school, that his wife was a scold, and that his son robbed orchards.[14] Ministers with genuine puritan convictions were increasingly frustrated, and some began to think of a new world overseas where their views could prevail. Peter Bulkley, rector of Odell, accounting the surplice and the use of the cross in baptism "ceremonies, superstitions and dissentaneous to the holy word of God" in 1635 went to America and founded Concord; his *Gospel Covenant opened* was one of the first books printed there.[15]

In the archdeacon's court cases were brought of attending to business on a Sunday. At Sandy in 1617 two men were drunk in service time, and at Bedford some butchers killed beef on the sabbath.[16] High-spirited young men played games in time of divine service. Football quite often tempted young men; thus Gt. Barford, Roxton and Wilden were keen players in 1610, while Eaton Socon men looked on,[17] Pavenham, Stevington and Riseley also played at football;[18] Milton Bryan played at nineholes.[19] Provided the games were played after service, James I in 1617 declared them lawful, and in 1618 tried to encourage them by declaration from the pulpit. These cases serve as a reminder of the many ordinary people who were little concerned with controversy.

Young gentry travelling abroad imbibed the Calvinist atmosphere of Geneva. Sir Rowland St. John wrote to his son Oliver to avoid Paris, where there was too much expense and diversion; and in general not to see too much of Englishmen; "it hath ever been one of my principles that no traveller in a foreign country shall . . . improve himself by consorting with many of his own nation". But at Geneva "I would have you make the most of your residential abode."[20]

THE CRISIS, 1642

When in 1642 political and religious tensions came to open war between king and parliament, the Bedfordshire petition to parliament presented on 16 March by Sir John Burgoyne from the sheriff, knights, esquires, gentlemen, ministers, freeholders and others (i.e., the politically active) put religion first. "Your peti-

[14] *V.C.H.* i, 336–7; C.R.O., OR 1901–6.
[15] *V.C.H.* iii, 69; it has been said (Brown, *op.cit*, 10) that Zachary Symmes of Dunstable went with him, but this does not seem to be established.
[16] C.R.O., ABC 5, p.108, 205.
[17] C.R.O., ABC 4, p.1 et seq.
[18] C.R.O., ABC 4, p.55, 61, 64.
[19] C.R.O., ABC 5, p.199.
[20] *Elstow Moot Hall Leaflet* ii, 11.

tioners are truly sensible of your pious care in the reformation of religion from those scandalous and superstitious innovations which were introduced into the church", as also of their incessant labours for the commonwealth.[21] In the long parliament there were representatives from other counties who were ready to go still further. Those who inclined to a Presbyterian form of church government had the chance to try to impose it – they were even in danger of being pushed by the Scots (whose help they needed) rather farther than they wished to go. The Earl of Bolingbroke (Lord St. John) and Oliver Bowles, rector of Sutton, were members of the Westminster assembly[22] which conferred with the Scots on the "reform of religion in England", and agreed on a covenant by which this was to be promoted. In 1643 bishops were abolished (the bishop of Lincoln died in 1654 and no new bishop was consecrated till 1660) and congregations were ordered to elect elders; in 1644 committees were set up with power to eject "scandalous" ministers; and the prayerbook was forbidden, though the use of the directory, now introduced, was optional.

In Bedfordshire in 1642 the position was that there was a strong element of loyal Anglicanism; and even those (like Sir Oliver Luke and his son Sir Samuel) who had been increasingly hostile to the Laudian church, were not necessarily opposed to bishops as such or desirous of synods. There was also among yeomen and craftsmen and in the towns a widespread background of Bible study and a tendency to desire a freer form of worship, but this had not yet produced much overt action. What then actually happened during the struggle of the civil war and the uneasy changes of government in the commonwealth?

Though not all in the county were agreed, the parliamentarians gained control; thus clergy who were strong Laudians or who actively threw their weight into the struggle on the royalist side would be targets. About 30 were deprived of their livings or even imprisoned.[23] The rector of Yielden, John Pocklington, who had written in favour of ceremonialism a book called *Altare Christianum*, was deprived of all preferments. John Gwin, vicar of Cople, who said in church that "The scripture bid him obey the king, but there was no scripture commanding him to obey the parliament", was fined £100 and committed to Newgate for his "debauched, lewd and contentious disposition"; later he went to Virginia. Giles Thorne, rector of St. Mary's, Bedford, and Timothy Archer of Meppershall, were confined for years in the Fleet prison. Some, like Thomas Cookson, rector of Marston and of Millbrook, and Nathaniel Hill, vicar of Renhold, went to join the royalist army. The wives and families of those who were ejected were sometimes in distress – they were often allowed one-fifth of the income from the benefice. There were some incumbents who were deprived for reasons of conduct, like John Aylmer, vicar of Melchbourne, and William Pargiter, rector of Carlton,

---

[21] C.R.O., X 48/1.
[22] A. F. Mitchell, *Westminster Assembly*, pp.xii–xiii.

[23] J. Walker, *Sufferings of the clergy* (rev. A. G. Matthews).

for alleged drunkenness.

It was not always easy to get rid of an unpopular incumbent. The parishioners of Ampthill complained in January 1641 of the popish practices of their rector, Hugh Reeve, but over a year later he was still there, "converses with papists more than ever, and refused to give up the vicarage house".[24] Tingrith parish register has a note after 1641 "Four years omitted by reason of the civil war in the nation, which also occasioned civil war in this parish."[25]

New incumbents were normally favourable to parliament, but in the absence of episcopal ordination they were not always easily accepted by their congregation. They were appointed by an assembly of divines, who issued certificates to the commissioners of the great seal (one of whom was Henry Grey, 10th Earl of Kent), usually stating that the bearer was "painful [painstaking] in the ministry, well-affected to parliament"; thus in 1646 Nathaniel Hogan was certified as "fit to officiate in the cure of Whipsnade".[26] But it was possible to get ordination; Edward Rolt, rector of Tempsford in 1647, was ordained.[27] Civil marriage was instituted in 1653.[28]

How far church services were altered it is difficult to say. About a dozen parishioners of Tilbrook complained in 1645 that their rector, Savage, used part of the prayerbook, bowed at the name of Jesus, and preached against his parishioners who "went to hear other men preach, and said they were like daws that did fly from steeple to steeple"; but it is noticeable that he had used opprobious words against parliament.[29] The young John Bunyan, if his autobiography is chronological, on returning about 1647 from his military service attended church in Elstow, and venerated "high-place, priest, clerk, vestments, service and what else".[30] Of the two parishes for which churchwardens' accounts survive for the period, neither has an entry for purchase of the Presbyterian directory. One of them, Shillington, has an entry for 4s. spent at Potton when the churchwardens took the covenant; the parish also pulled down some crosses and other work about the church and got rid of their organs; they bought a new prayerbook in 1659,[31] when the end of the commonwealth was near. The incumbent of Luton, Thomas Jessop, in 1658 complained that, because he was not episcopally ordained, he had been struggling for years against a malignant and prelatical party, and that people withdrew from his communion and worshipped in prelatical form. The immediate cause of his complaint was Lady Crawley's burial, when the family broke open the church door and her son Thomas read the burial service.[32]

Thus, unlike London and Lancashire, Bedfordshire had apparently done little

[24] B.N.Q., i, 124–6.
[25] B.P.R., xvii, B. 4.
[26] C.R.O., L 29/66.
[27] A. G. Matthews, Calamy revised, 416. See also W. A. Shaw, History of the English church 1640–60, ii, 282.
[28] For Bedfordshire instances, see B.P.R. xvii; and for a marriage certificate, C.R.O. Guide, Pl. VIII.
[29] C.R.O., TW 926.
[30] Grace Abounding (ed. Sharrock), 9.
[31] C.R.O., P. 44/5/2.
[32] E.M.H. Leaflet vi, 10.

to approach even the standards of English Presbyterianism, except in a few cases. Of these Leighton Buzzard is the chief; here the parishioners in 1642 objected to their vicar, Christopher Slater, as a "promoter of superstition and of scandalous life", and said that they were obliged to maintain a lecturer, Samuel Fisher, for their better instruction in godliness.[33] Their next vicar, William Rathband, in 1644 wrote against the Brownists or Independents.[34]

Far otherwise was it with those men and women who had been reaching out for a simpler form of worship in a gathered church, and who now began to be known as Independents, and formally to set up congregations. Their chance had come. Those in Bedford were probably encouraged in 1644 and 1645 when detachments of Cromwell's troops (among whom the Independents were strong) were quartered in the town, and they seem to have met from 1645 onwards. In the county they were probably meeting too; Sir William Boteler in 1647 at Epiphany sessions denounced those who went "to hear some new-erected rabbi of their own choosing to poison them with principles of disobedience".[35] In 1650 those in Bedford definitely formed a congregation: "twelve of the holy brethren and sisters began this holy work . . . all ancient and grave Christians well known one to another".[36] The principles on which they entered into fellowship were "faith in Christ and holiness of life". The pastor chosen to minister to them was John Gifford, and in 1653 the town council invited them to take over St. John's church. The same year young John Bunyan, now practising his trade as tinker or brasier, was in Bedford and came upon three or four poor women sitting at a door in the sun; "methought they spake as if joy did make them speak: they spake with such pleasantness of Scripture language, and with such appearance of grace in all they said, that they were to me as if they had found a new world."[37] They mentioned him to Gifford, who invited Bunyan to his house, and the young man joined the Independent congregation. Soon "when some of them did go into the country to teach, they would also that I should go with them",[38] and before long he was "more particularly called forth". "I at first could not believe that God should speak by me to the heart of any man, still counting myself unworthy," but as his hearers so earnestly pressed after knowledge, "rejoicing that ever God did send me where they were, then I began to conclude it might be so".[39]

Thus Bedford became an Independent centre, with which many large or small groups were in touch, larger ones being more formally organised. For instance already in 1652 there was an organised congregation at Keysoe Brook End: "We this day give up ourselves to the Lord and to the word of his grace, to be guided, governed and directed by him in all his ways."[40] At Stevington the earliest

[33] R. Richmond, *Leighton Buzzard*, 73–4.
[34] *A most grave and modest confutation of all the errors of the Brownists*, 1644.
[35] C.R.O., OR 1882, f.78.
[36] Brown, *op.cit*, 80.
[37] *Grace Abounding*, 14–15.
[38] *Op.cit.*, 83.
[39] *Op.cit.*, 84–5.
[40] H. G. Tibbutt, *Keysoe Brook End and Keysoe Row Baptist churches*.

record is lost; that of 1673 states that "about 18 years ago some of the faithful in Christ did gather together to walk in the commandments and ordinances of the Lord with their beloved brother and teacher, Stephen Hawthorne".[41] In time some Independent congregations were to take up the further position, derived (as they believed) from the New Testament, that baptism should be an adult matter, and thus to be called Baptists; a group at Eversholt had done this by 1653;[42] but as yet this matter does not seem to have been prominent in the thoughts of most Bedfordshire congregations.

A new separate group appeared, that of the Quakers (Society of Friends) derived from George Fox, son of a Leicestershire weaver. These took the "priesthood of all believers" a stage further, in that they had no minister at all, and held that all life is sacramental. Quakerism was brought to the county by William Dewsbury, the "apostle of Bedfordshire", in 1654. The most notable convert was John Crook, who was a justice of the peace and who had recently bought Beckerings Park where Fox visited him in 1655.[43] There were soon many followers, in spite of hostility; Quakers were prosecuted under the commonwealth as they were to be later at the restoration. Isabel Parlour was whipped for exhorting people in Ampthill market in 1656; John Stevens of Wootton imprisoned for refusing to take an oath in 1657; and in 1658 several Riseley Quakers who "reproved the incumbent in a scriptural manner for his misconduct" were (not surprisingly) put by him in the stocks.[44] Among other places, Quakers are known at Barton, Cranfield, Pulloxhill and Woburn. In 1657 and 1658 3-day meetings were held at Beckerings Park to which Quakers came from all over England – the numbers were too many to get in the house, and they had to adjourn to the orchard.[45] From this developed what is known to Quakers as London yearly meeting.

Thus in 1659 there was a confused situation in Bedfordshire. There was a beleaguered Anglicanism of latent strength; a very slender Presbyterianism; flourishing Independency; fairly numerous Quakers; and scarcely any Roman Catholics. There were finally, no doubt, a large mass of "floating voters" or "don't knows", who would without great difficulty accept an imposed settlement. Cromwell was dead, and many men were thinking of a restoration of the monarchy. Once again the gentlemen, freeholders and inhabitants (and the accent is on gentlemen) issued a declaration. "We . . . having all our civil and religious rights and liberties daily invaded, cannot in this common day of calamity be silent . . . and having met and considered thereof do propose the assembling of a full and free parliament."[46] A new parliament met in April, 1660, and Charles II returned in May. Before the end of the year a new bishop of Lincoln was

41 Tibbutt, *Stevington Baptist Meeting.*
42 *Bapt. Hist. Soc. Trans.*, ii, 242.
43 *B.H.R.S.* xxv, 110–28. Sometime after 1661 Crook moved to Luton: *B.H.R.S.* xxv, 120, n. 40; and

cf. Austin, *Luton*, ii, 32.
44 J. Besse, *Sufferings of the Quakers*, i, 3–4.
45 *B.H.R.S.* xxv, 110–28; *B. Mag.*, iv, 163–6, 267–71.
46 C.R.O., X 48/2.

consecrated.

THE CHURCH RESTORED

That there would be a new attempt to reach or rather to impose unity, and that a parliamentary act of uniformity would be passed was clear. At Michaelmas sessions no doubt the new joint-Lieutenant was present; Robert Bruce, Earl of Ailesbury, had been associated with the old Earl of Cleveland (Lord Wentworth), who had been imprisoned for some years in the Tower; perhaps there was some discussion of the situation.

In November Bunyan was to preach at Samshill, near Harlington. Visiting a neighbouring justice, Francis Wingate, at Harlington, was Wingate's brother-in-law, William Foster, an able lawyer. It was probably Foster who suggested (pending the new legislation) using an old Elizabethan act against conventicles. The two hoped that a little firmness with a well-meaning but misguided man would restrain Independents and save trouble later – for already Independents were sometimes spoken of as "Bunyan his society".

Foster tried to reason with Bunyan "How (said he) can you understand the Scriptures when you know not the original Greek?" Bunyan made people "neglect their calling"; they should work six days and serve God on the seventh. These were only "poor simple ignorant people" that came to hear him. To this last Bunyan replied that "the foolish and the ignorant had most need of teaching and information". "If you will promise to call the people no more together, you shall have your liberty to go home, for my brother is very loath to send you to prison, if you will be but ruled." Bunyan refused. At Epiphany sessions (the justices were Kelyng, Chester, Blundell, Becher and Snagg) it was the same. Kelyng said "We might pray with the spirit and with understanding, and with the common prayerbook also"; Bunyan maintained that men might have many excellent words and yet not pray at all, but a man should pour out his heart.[47] He refused to conform and remained in prison.

Quakers were soon a target because of their objections to taking an oath to show their allegiance (affirmation was not allowed till 1833). Over 50 Bedfordshire Quakers were imprisoned after the assizes of March, 1661, though they issued a statement saying "We have been men of a quiet, sober, peaceable and upright conversation . . . We do believe and declare that the immediate hand of the Lord hath brought in Charles Stuart according to the laws of the nation . . . and we will not conspire nor plot against him."[48] They also resisted tithe. In 1662 John Crook was tried in London and was imprisoned; he survived several imprisonments, from one of which he wrote "to Friends in Bedfordshire and there-aways . . . as one that hath travelled with you and amongst you, I beseech you, stand fast".[49] John Rush of Kempston died in Bedford gaol in 1662 (earlier in the year he had

[47] A relation of my imprisonment, printed in *Grace Abounding* (ed. Sharrock), 105–31.

[48] Besse, *loc.cit.*

[49] From his *Collected Works* (copy in Bedford Meeting).

assigned his property to his son), and John Samm of Houghton Conquest in Northampton gaol (twelve steps underground) in 1664.[50]

Meanwhile the Anglican church was returning to normal with less disruption than might have been expected. By two acts the position was regularised. One of 1660 provided that ejected ministers should be restored to their livings. The next year was held the Savoy conference in 1661 on the prayerbook, at which the Presbyterians had hoped to gain concessions which would enable them to remain members of the established church – the Independents could hope only for toleration – but only minor changes were made. The act of uniformity in 1662 provided that no incumbent could remain or become beneficed without episcopal ordination and acceptance of the prayerbook.

Thus Timothy Archer returned to Meppershall; Theodore Crowley to Bedford St. John; and Giles Thorne to Bedford St. Mary. Thorne's will some years later was a confession of faith: "I, having lived, by the grace of God will die in the true religion established by law, and in the true, ancient, catholic and apostolic faith professed in the Church of England."[51] The number of clergy who either lost or gave up their livings under these two acts was surprisingly small.[52] Among them were Samuel Fairclough of Houghton Conquest, John Donne of Pertenhall (not the poet who died in 1631), Edward Rolt of Tempsford, William Dell of Yielden, and James Mabbison of Roxton; the precise number is uncertain, but it was not more than a dozen. William Wheeler's congregation at Cranfield apparently used the church, but he does not seem to have been rector.

Unfortunately no letters or diaries give illuminating details of how the parishes adjusted themselves. It is perhaps worth noting that at Bedford St. Paul through all the changes the office of parish clerk was held 1628–88 by three generations of one family, that of Marks.[53] No archdeacon's court-books survive till 1662 – the courts were probably not held until the coming of a new archdeacon in that year, Frederick Wilford. Where there was an active "prelatical party", as at Luton, they no doubt gladly regained possession of the church with their new vicar, in this case Thomas Pomfret. At Sandy the rector, Francis Walsall, gave a chalice "to his beloved flock 23rd May in the year of our salvation 1661 and in the second of the restoration of liberty".[54] But a new incumbent too much out of sympathy with his parishioners met with defiance, as at Flitton; "Thomas Daniel of Newbury was buried, with great contention against me, being the minister of the parish church, by William Wheeler of Silsoe, John Webb, Richard Wheeler of Flitton, and John Green junior, who did cast me out of the church by force and would not suffer me to bury him" (this William Wheeler was the Countess of Kent's bailiff).[55]

[50] B.H.R.S. xxv, 116–7. For Rush's assignment of property, see C.R.O., SX 107.
[51] V.C.H. i, 343.
[52] A. G. Matthews, Calamy revised. For Wheeler, see

Tibbutt, Cranfield Baptist Church.
[53] B. Mag. xi, 140–2.
[54] C.R.O., ABE 2.
[55] B.P.R. xviii, p.B 67; and see 3 Oct. 1668.

In many parishes there may not have been much change in the services – those clergy who had discontinued the use of the prayerbook resuming it. Curiously enough, even a new incumbent might be slow to use the prayerbook; Thomas Poynter, a new vicar of Goldington presented by the bishop in 1660, had to be reminded in October 1662 to use the prayerbook and to certify within a month that he was doing so.[56] Liturgy may have been approached with caution. So also were some other requirements. Some clergy who had come in during the civil war or commonwealth, like Hogan at Whipsnade, Baker at Battlesden and Chatterton at Chellington, were still not catechising in 1668.[57]

INDEPENDENTS, QUAKERS AND BAPTISTS

The archdeacon's court-books from 1662 record many cases of non-baptism of children, not coming to church, and non-payment of tithe. The civil authorities, who still believed that unity depended on religious uniformity, also carried on a campaign against those who would not return to the Anglican fold, the Independents and the Quakers. For the next few years regularly at the assizes many people were presented for not attending church.

These were not gentry (except for the occasional Roman Catholic or Crook the Quaker). Some of the gentlemen who had been active in 1641–2 were dead, like the Earl of Kent and the Earl of Bolingbroke; others, like Sir Samuel Luke, had long since withdrawn from public affairs; they were 20 years older, and perhaps they were tired; things had not gone quite as they expected. What they did was to retain their sympathy with Calvin's doctrine, but to relinquish their (never very strong) adherence to the form of church government devised by him. After all, a lord could have his chaplain to his liking; thus the Earl of Bedford went to the parish church on Sunday but had a Presbyterian chaplain.[58] Years later Geneva retained the hold it had earlier in the century; in 1690 the 11th Earl of Kent (under age at the restoration) wrote to his son "Spend all this next winter at Geneva, which is both a pleasant and as I am informed a wholesome place"; and in his next letter "You must not by any means go so far as Rome."[59]

Humbler folk, who had not this resource, showed tenacity. Though in south Bedfordshire the Independents seem to have been at this time largely leaderless, scattered as they were in small groups in the parishes, yet they kept in touch with each other, as later events showed. The Quakers, who needed no minister, were strongest in mid-Bedfordshire; over a dozen groups are known by 1667, meeting weekly, and once a month assembling in larger groups, or monthly meetings, at centres such as Cranfield, Kempston, Pulloxhill and Stotfold.[60]

[56] C.R.O., ABC 6, f.45.
[57] C.R.O., ABC 7, f.44d, 62d, 65d.
[58] T. Bruce, *Memoirs*, p. 181. Sir Robert Napier is said to have built or more probably enlarged the chapel at Luton Hoo because of his dislike of Jessop's services at Luton church (Austin, *Luton*, ii, 45); but he is unlikely to have afforded this during the commonwealth; and the dedication printed in H. Shaw, *History and antiquities of the chapel at Luton park*, 10–13, is 1674.
[59] C.R.O., L 30/8/32/3–4.
[60] B. *Mag.*, iv, 269.

At the winter assizes in 1663 over 80 persons were presented for not attending church. In 1664 an act imposed a fine on those who attended conventicles. From 1664 to 1668 an average of over 100 men and women from 67 parishes were presented each year at the assizes.[61] Nearly always they were described as yeomen, though other sources indicate that several were craftsmen. Among those who attended a conventicle in the house of George Farr, a grocer, at Blunham, were collarmaker, shearman and labourer. The leader at Oakley in 1669 was a lacemaker, John Read; while at Keysoe miller, dairyman and husbandman were prominent among those who met at the house of George Fowler, woodward; and at Cranfield one leader was a weaver.[62]

The Bedford Independent congregation, ejected from St. John's church, met in each other's houses. In 1670 nearly 30 of them were arrested in a body at the house of John Fenn, haberdasher, where they were being addressed by Nehemiah Cox, cordwainer. The subsequent distraint to obtain the fines imposed led to uproarious scenes in Bedford. A brass kettle was taken from Edward Covington, grocer; the officer paid a boy 6d. to carry it to an innyard, "but when the youth had carried the kettle to the inn gate (being hooted at all the way by the common spectators), the innkeeper would not suffer the kettle to be brought into his yard, and so his man set it out in the middle of the street".[63] In Bedford sympathy was with the accused; the crude horseplay at Sawbridgeworth in 1659 and Flamstead in 1682 shows that this was not always so elsewhere.[64]

Thus fines were sometimes difficult to exact. Imprisonment was not necessarily strictly enforced; Richard Laundy of Bolnhurst in 1669 "is commonly at home, although the king's writ *de excommunicato capiendo* was served upon him and he thereupon delivered into the common gaol";[65] and John Donne, the ejected minister of Pertenhall, though entered on gaol lists as "to be transported to the Barbadoes", was described in 1669 as usually preaching at his house in Keysoe and was still in the county in 1672.

At last in 1672 Charles II tried to bypass parliament by issuing a declaration of indulgence; congregations could apply for a licence to worship. For Bedfordshire[66] about 30 Independent congregations applied (more in proportion to area than anywhere else in the country); 6 Presbyterian congregations, now forced into an independent position (including Leighton Buzzard); and one Baptist (Shefford). Neither Luton nor Dunstable applied; at this time they seem to have been still leaderless; but that position was soon to change. Bunyan was released, and the Bedford Independents bought an orchard in Mill Lane, where a barn became their place of meeting and Bunyan their regular pastor. Quakers did not apply for permission, not recognising the competence of civil government to grant or

[61] C.R.O., HSA *passim*.
[62] *B.H.R.S.* xx, 177.
[63] Brown, *op.cit.*, 205.
[64] Besse, *op.cit.*, i, 241, 251-2.
[65] C.R.O., ABC 7, f.115.
[66] *Cal. State Papers Dom.* 1671-2, 1672, 1672-3.

withhold it.

The declaration of indulgence was not permanent; the king was obliged to withdraw it in March 1673; but a good deal of the zeal for authority felt by members of parliament and justices of the peace had waned, and they were uneasy about further prosecutions.

But William Foster, who in 1674 became commissary in the archdeaconry, made one more attempt against Bunyan. John Bunyan, tinker, was excommunicated for refusing to come to his parish church in Bedford and take the sacrament. Foster then got a writ from the civil authority for the imprisonment of an obdurate excommunicate. This seems to have been in 1676. Once more Bunyan was in prison.[67]

It was during his first imprisonment, besides making many hundred gross of long tagged laces to support his family, that Bunyan seriously began to write. Between 1656 and 1665 he had produced several short works. He then essayed a larger work of autobiography, *Grace Abounding*, published in 1666, which was at once widely read. It is somewhat wordy and confused, but he continued to write and to become more practised. He reflected on the chapbooks which had amused his boyhood, and gradually man's life in this world began to take shape in his mind in one of the greatest allegories of all time. Probably before his release in 1672 he had written the words "As I walked through the wilderness of this world I lighted upon a certain place where was a den, and I laid me down in that place to sleep; and as I slept I dreamed a dream." Friends, by going surety for him, brought about his release from prison in 1677. *The Pilgrim's Progress* was published in 1678. It was reprinted over and over again, reaching a far wider audience than he could have reached orally, and it soon began to be translated into European languages. Bunyan continued to preach and teach over an area extending beyond Bedfordshire. He died in 1688.

Meanwhile south Bedfordshire and north Hertfordshire had become organised in a large Baptist congregation based on Kensworth.[68] Their leader, Thomas Hayward of Kensworth, had begun to make an impact on Bedfordshire by 1669 when he was teaching at Houghton Regis. By 1675 his influence had spread so far that Luton, Dunstable, St. Albans and Leighton adhered to the group taught by this "laborious servant of Christ", besides an increasing number of villages. Within a few years these included Studham, Chalgrave, Sundon, Caddington, Totternhoe, Toddington, Eaton Bray and Tilsworth, besides others in Hertfordshire. No doubt they did not all assemble at Kensworth every Sunday, sometimes meeting at other places in the district; but probably many, as was the later practice, set out on Sunday taking with them their meal, which they ate

---

[67] *Cong. Hist. Soc. Trans.*, xvi, 23–32.
[68] St. Albans Library 3831; cited also Brown, *op.cit.*, 233; *B.H.R.S.* xxv, 138–9. The Kensworth church was already Baptist in 1653 under an intruded minister, Edward Harrison, who however left in 1656 (*Bapt. Hist. Soc. Trans.* ii, 242). For Thomas Hayward, see also *B.H.R.S.* xx, 177.

between morning and afternoon service. After six days of toil, Sunday was given up to fellowship and spiritual quest.

An ecclesiastical enquiry of 1676[69] gives the number of nonconformists in each parish at this time as estimated by the incumbent; this shows them in 99 parishes out of 131; but assize records and other sources reveal them from 1660 to 1689 in a further 14 parishes.[70] The 1676 return also gives Roman Catholics – a total of 40 persons for the whole archdeaconry, chiefly at Turvey and Carlton. The percentage of nonconformity is 8%.

An uneasy situation continued in the 1680's. Quarter Sessions declared in 1684 their belief that religion was the great instrument of political happiness, and unanimity in religion the most certain promoter of peace, and resolved that all dissenters should be reduced to a thorough conformity; and at their request the bishop of Lincoln issued a statement in their support.[71] Was this new initiative due to Thomas Bruce, who next year was to succeed his father as Earl of Ailesbury and as Lieutenant?

THE REIGN OF JAMES II

In the short reign of James II, his known Roman Catholic sympathies roused in the country as a whole greater, and probably irrational, fear on that side of the religious question. Such fear seems particularly irrational in Bedfordshire, where a contemporary said that there was not one Roman Catholic gentleman in the county "but Mr. Conquest that lived obscurely";[72] but in the background was always the fear of foreign domination, not now from Spain but from France. When in 1687 James II put out feelers to try to get members of parliament who would support a policy of toleration, this was a factor in the minds of those who replied. Several, like Sir Anthony Chester of Tilsworth, replied that they were "willing to live peaceably with all mankind", or "to live friendly with all persons of what persuasion soever, as becomes a good Christian", but "he cannot give his consent to take away such laws as do support the Church of England". Only a few gave limited approval, while several hedged: "he never designs to stand" or "he shall not be chose".[73]

After the revolution of 1688 had replaced James II by William III, the Toleration Act of 1689 was passed. Protestant congregations, except non-Trinitarians, could worship freely on registering with the archdeacon or with sessions; but nonconformists were still debarred from office and from the universities.

Why was not religious unity achieved in 1604, 1642-4, 1661 or 1689, though it was looked back to in memory as "the most certain promoter of peace"?

[69] B.H.R.S. xx, 159.
[70] W. M. Wigfield in an unpublished thesis on nonconformity in this period has compiled a nominal roll which provides a useful comparison with the 1676 figures (called the Compton return).

In general his nominal roll shows a similar picture.
[71] C.R.O., X 48/3.
[72] Bruce, Memoirs, 174.
[73] B.H.R.S. xx, 187-98; B. Mag., ii, 123-7.

National security was a complicating factor; the religious issue was not considered purely on its merits; but that was not all. Before the Reformation unity had been imposed from above by an authority accepted in western Christendom. Once authority had been challenged, there could be no resting-place on the slippery slope, and division would follow division, till complete freedom was achieved. Only then could all begin to see things in proportion, and to realise that what united them was more important than what divided; that the truth was sought by all; and that in the hurly-burly a fundamental good had been lost.

Meanwhile it was right that the Anglican church (left in the field in 1661) should not be allowed to exert that authority it would not concede to the Roman Catholic church. The men who gained a limited and grudging recognition were humble in status; and thus arose in English life, not an iron curtain, but perhaps a rubber curtain, dividing by religious persuasion and to some extent by social level; but their moral courage made a lasting contribution to our national life. In this Bedfordshire played no small part.

▲ *33a Room in Harlington House, traditionally where Bunyan was interrogated.*

▼ *33b Stairs in Harrold House (now demolished).*

T

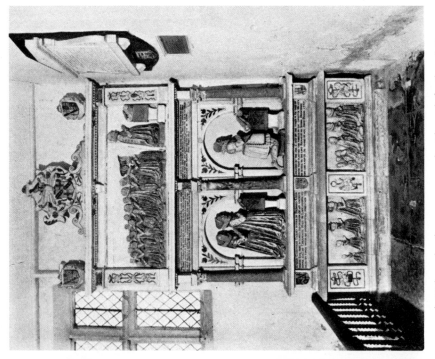

34b *Hulcote church: monument to the Chernock family, 1616.*

34a *Colmworth church: monument to the Dyer family, 1641.*

35b Countess of Kent, 1580–1651.

35a Earl of Kent, 1583–1639.

36b Dorothy Osborne, 1627–95.

36a Lord St. John, 1st Earl Bolingbroke, 1584–1646.

37b John Bunyan, 1628–88.

The Right Honourable
Thomas Earl of Ailesbury
& Elgin.
Aetat. 83 Anno 1738.

37a Earl of Ailesbury, 1656–1741.

▲ *38a Cottages at Turvey.*

▼ *38b Cottages at Battlesden.*

▲ *39a Parish chest in Husborne Crawley church.*

To do good
And to Distribute
Forget not: For with such
Sacrifices God is Well
Pleased

The Gift of M^rs. SUSANNA ROLT, late of
this Parish, & Tho: ROLT, in Twelve Two-Penny
Loaves Weekly to the Poor of the Said Parish
For Ever.

► *39b Charity shelves in Milton Ernest church.*

▲ *40a Almshouses at Houghton Conquest.*

▼ *40b Almshouses at Milton Ernest.*

▲ *41a Holme school, Biggleswade.*

▼ *41b Chew's school, Dunstable.*

42 Point-ground lace (in Luton Museum).

43 Straw-plait (in Luton Museum).

44a *Fire-hooks in Eaton Bray Church.*
44b *Fire-engine (in London Museum), made for Dunstable in 1678.*

▲ *45a Clay-mill, tile kiln and corn-mill at Husborne Crawley.*

▼ *45b Stone quarry at Totternhoe.*

▲ *46a Wrest Park: the old house before demolition.*

▼ *46b Wrest pavilion.*

▲ 47a *Southill park, print engraved 1782.*

▼ 47b *Luton Hoo, print engraved 1785.*

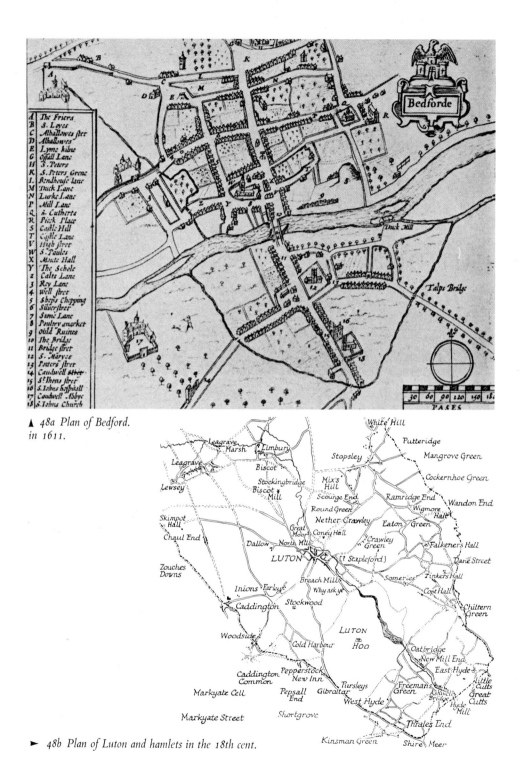

Bedforde

PASES

▲ 48a Plan of Bedford.
in 1611.

► 48b Plan of Luton and hamlets in the 18th cent.

23 – LORDS AND SQUIRES, 1603–88

THE LORDS

In 1603 in Bedfordshire the lords were comparatively modest. Henry Grey, Earl of Kent, was lord lieutenant; after its 16th cent. setback the family had begun to recover its former position of leadership, but the estate was still of moderate size. He died in 1615; after him there were four Earls in quick succession, followed by a minority; so till the end of the century the family was seldom prominent. In the north there was Lord Mordaunt at Turvey (created Earl of Peterborough in 1628), whose interest was divided with Northamptonshire. In the south the Toddington estates of Lord Cheney were to pass in 1614 to his widow's nephew, Lord Wentworth (created Earl of Cleveland in 1626, but this title died with him).

There were soon two accessions to the aristocracy. One of these was connected with the royal estate of Ampthill. At first in 1606 James I thought of restoring and remodelling Ampthill castle, and John Thorpe got out plans for this;[1] but probably decay had gone too far, and the project was dropped. In 1624 the king granted Houghton Conquest park to a fellow Scot who had come south with him, Thomas Bruce (created Earl of Elgin, 1633). There was already an attractive house recently built in the park by the previous grantee, the Countess of Pembroke, and the Bruce family began to build up an estate in the neighbourhood. They also acted as stewards for the Honour of Ampthill; it had dwindled, but included the manors of Ampthill and Millbrook, and lands or manors in Campton, Dunstable, Goldington and Steppingley.

The second was in 1625. Francis Russell asked permission from his cousin, the 3rd Earl of Bedford (whose heir he was) to borrow Woburn Abbey; the plague was raging in the neighbourhood of London, and he wanted to get his children to safety. They found the dilapidated remains of the old abbey, which had been neglected since Queen Elizabeth's visit about 50 years previously. Perhaps its forlorn state provoked the 4th Earl of Bedford, when he succeeded in 1626, to make Woburn his residence. The old building was past saving. The new one was built round a square courtyard, with gabled wings, high-pitched roofs, stone finials and grouped chimneys; a great hall occupied most of the west wing, while the family lived in the north wing; there were library and portrait gallery – about 90 rooms in all.[2] It was the most imposing house in the county, but the park was small and there was little estate. (Incidentally it was this Earl who was largely

[1] *Walpole Soc.*, xl, 30, 108 & pls. 120–1. See also B.H.R.S. xxxv, 74. For other buildings in Ampthill

park, see *Brit. Arch. Ass. J.*, 3rd ser., xiii, 14–23.
[2] G. Scott Thomson, *Life in a noble household*, 1–25.

responsible for initiating the drainage of the Bedford Level in 1634.)

Greater weight was carried by the family of St. John, who were widely connected with the squirearchy (Cheney of Sundon, Thompson of Husborne Crawley, Chernock of Hulcote, Becher of Renhold, Wingate of Harlington). They were active as well as numerous; the most able was one of the younger line, an Oliver St. John who in 1648 became chief justice.[3] Alexander and Beauchamp St. John, sons of the 3rd Lord, were successively members of parliament for Bedford, where by about 1600 it had become customary to have a St. John as titular recorder (the deputy recorder, who did the actual work, had the borough's other seat in parliament).

The 4th Lord St. John who succeeded in 1618 was then a vigorous man in middle life. When young he had been rapped over the knuckles by the king for hunting a stag just before one of the royal visits to Bletsoe. James I wrote to the 3rd Lord that this was "strange, as he could not but know that we are careful of the same, and found the number of deer less than we expected, not that we should have misliked your hunting in your own wood had you acquainted us therewith".[4] Another royal rebuke was occasioned by opposition to James I's irregular methods of raising money; the Privy Council regretted Lord St. John's cold dealings in the meeting held in Bedfordshire for promoting the benevolence, and also the absence of his name from the list of free givers; they advised a different course if he wished to preserve the king's good opinion.[5] However, the new Lord St. John entertained the king sumptuously, and in 1624 was created Earl of Bolingbroke (hereafter he will be referred to as Lord Bolingbroke).

They were an affectionate and serious family. A letter from Lord Bolingbroke as a young man to his brother Rowland abroad assures him that he will always pray for him, and signs himself "your most assured loving brother".[6] Rowland later, when arranging his daughter's marriage, comments on the couple's "youthful bashfulness, whereunto they are both subject, and which I for my part shall not endeavour much to extinguish, being in this age one of the rarest virtues".[7] One member of the family was different, Lord Bolingbroke's eldest son, Oliver (who bore by courtesy his father's second title of Lord St. John); he was one of the county members before Charles I's personal rule began; he had a ready charm and courtesy, and no money sense. Just before the civil war Lord Bolingbroke arranged a meeting with his son's creditors, and earnestly desired Rowland to be there: "I have always found you so faithful to me, as it emboldeneth me to desire your trouble."[8]

---

[3] There were several Oliver St. Johns alive at the same time, the chief being Lord Bolingbroke, his eldest son killed at Edgehill, and the chief justice. The title of Bolingbroke died out with the 3rd Earl; it was later recreated in another branch, only remotely connected with this.

[4] *V.C.H.* iii, 42.
[5] *Cal. State P. Dom.*, 1611–18, p.255.
[6] C.R.O., J 1443.
[7] C.R.O., J 1447–55.
[8] C.R.O., J 1463.

No estate was as yet very large, but Lord Bolingbroke's was one of the larger ones. It is described in detail in a survey made in the 1620's,[9] which shows a fair amount of property in Glamorgan and some in Huntingdonshire, besides that in this county. In Bedfordshire the main property was in Bletsoe and Melchbourne, in both of which he owned the greater part; and in Keysoe, of which he owned more than half; while there were smaller areas in several neighbouring parishes. At Bletsoe the park and woods occupied over 400 a., and the manorhouse was moated, with an inner court. At Melchbourne his father in 1608 had acquired from the Earl of Bedford the old preceptory; this, which Leland knew as "a right fair place of square stone", was already in great decay in 1587, and the St. Johns built a new house; the survey mentions both the ancient site and a mansion-house with great garden and bowling-ground; the park was 250 a., and there were over 300 a. of wood. Lord Bolingbroke enclosed Bletsoe in 1624, so that the survey shows the result "upon the new enclosure"; thus after each tenant's name his land is given in closes obviously recently derived from common fields; thus John Giles occupied two closes called Coplow, Coplow pightle, and New Coplow close.

Of the aristocracy's manner of living, some indication is given by an inventory of the Earl of Cleveland's furniture at Toddington in 1644. There were hangings of Arras and tapestry and gilded leather; Turkey carpets; leather and Turkey-work chairs; an ebony table; billiard table and shovel-board; and bed-furnishings of taffeta in red, yellow and blue.[10] Lady Mordaunt's house at Turvey at the same date had three parlours (one of them wainscoted), drawing-room (where were chairs of Turkey-work), red room and gallery, and 14 bed-chambers – her own contained a white wrought bed; among miscellaneous items were 5 bellows and 6 chamber pots.[11]

THE GENTRY

It was however the gentry who in this century in the country as a whole constituted what was largely a new source of power. The other county member in the early years of the century was Sir Oliver Luke; his mother was a St. John; he had studied at Cambridge; and his forebears in the previous century had been in public service and had made fortunate marriages (ch. 17). The other borough member, the deputy recorder, was Richard Taylor of Clapham; the Taylors were of more recent origin – Richard Taylor's father was a yeoman – but he had studied at Lincoln's Inn and he married a Boteler.[12]

The gentry's memories of 15th cent. insecurity had faded. The 16th cent. upheaval in the land market had subsided, and they were settled on their lands. They were reinforced by new blood, not only from rising yeomen. The county's nearness to London was convenient for merchants who wished to become gentry,

[9] C.R.O., GY 10.
[10] B.H.R.S. xi, 129–36.
[11] *Beds. A. & A. S.* xxxix, pt. 1, 184–5.
[12] B.H.R.S. xxv, 104.

like Anthony Chester, who in 1606 bought Tilsworth manor; he was the son of a citizen and draper of London and the grandson of a lord mayor; in 1619 he was created a baronet, and in 1628 was high sheriff. Similar cases are Becher of Renhold and Brandreth of Houghton Regis. Judges did likewise; the Andersons of Eyeworth derived from Sir Edmund Anderson, who bought the manor in 1594.[13] Similar examples followed in the 17th cent.; Samuel Browne (whose mother was a St. John) bought Arlesey manor in 1646,[14] and John Kelyng bought Gastlyns manor, Southill, in 1667.[15] From time to time there might be several Bedfordshire gentlemen in parliament, since some sat for other constituencies. It was an active, thinking, assured generation; and there were intellectuals too: Edmund Wingate of Harlington, the mathematician (d. 1656);[16] Edmund Castell of Higham Gobion, the orientalist (d. 1685);[17] and Edmund Wyld of Houghton Conquest, a would-be scientist.[18]

The political position gave the gentry their chance. The royal estate had declined, and it was only with great parsimony that Queen Elizabeth had managed with the minimum of taxation. Taxes for years had been granted by parliament, especially by the house of commons; and since boroughs had given up sending burgesses to parliament, the house of commons consisted of gentry. Thus in this century the ball would be at the gentry's feet, as it had never been before and would never be again. But at first opportunity delayed while the Stuart kings, finding difficulty with parliament, tried to avoid calling it, and to devise other ways of raising money.

Meanwhile some gentry, like some lords, were enclosing. Hockliffe seems now definitely to be enclosed; an early 17th cent. statement says that when the fields were open they used to get spoiled and trodden because of the nearness of Watling Street.[19] Some gentry were proceeding piecemeal, as at Aspley, when Thomas Sadler, lord of the manor, paid £5 to 5 husbandmen on enclosing 10 a. in 1633;[20] while at Chalgrave in 1629 Nicholas Potts, gentleman, had lately enclosed a close of 3 a.[21] At Sutton in 1638 John Burgoyne enclosed 54 a. by agreement; and at Potton in 1639 he made an agreement with 69 freeholders, copyholders and cottagers about tillage of the warren.[22] The practice was now beginning of forestalling trouble by making an agreement and getting it enrolled in Chancery, after a fictitious suit; this was done by Sir Thomas Leigh in 1630 with 100 a. at Leighton, where over 80 people were concerned.[23]

Some gentry too were building new houses. That at Haynes[24] (now replaced) was probably built in the late 16th cent. by Robert Newdigate, and about the

---

[13] V.C.H. ii, 231.
[14] V.C.H. ii, 262; B.H.R.S. ii, 137.
[15] V.C.H. iii, 258.
[16] D.N.B.
[17] D.N.B.; B. Mag. ii, 189.
[18] B. Mag. iii, 104–8.

[19] C.R.O., CRT 130/1.
[20] C.R.O., HO 45.
[21] C.R.O., CH 266.
[22] C.R.O., ABE 2; AD 961.
[23] C.R.O., BO 1335; KK 29.
[24] Shown on Gordon's printed county map of 1736.

same time Thomas Snagge seems the likeliest builder of Marston manorhouse, which still survives; while Stratton Park, recently pulled down, was of the same period, E-shaped, of brick with mullioned windows. Hillersdon House at Elstow was built by Thomas Hillersdon, who bought the manor from Radcliffe in 1616; over its renaissance porch were his arms. William Farrar or Farrer and his son-in-law Thomas Boteler built in 1608-10 Harrold Hall, only recently demolished; building accounts[25] show that some stone was dug locally and some came from over the Buckinghamshire border – one of the masons was old Grumbold; while the timber was brought from Colworth, Odell and Bletsoe. Later in the century the Caters built the old Kempston Bury; and later still Heath manor cost about £2,000 to build in the classical style.[26]

Of the gentry's style of living, an example is given by an inventory of the Francklin household at Mavorn, Bolnhurst, in 1633.[27] A century previously the family had been yeomen. The house was fairly fully furnished, but most of the things were plain and serviceable, some of them old, and there were few frills. In the armoury were 7 muskets and rests, 12 halberds, some pistols, and body armour for horsemen and pikemen. In the main rooms were a Turkey carpet and a tapestry carpet; one embroidered chair is mentioned; the curtains and bed-hangings were mostly of green and yellow say. In the beer cellar were 23 hogsheads of beer. Linen included 2 damask cloths and 8 dozen flaxen napkins; there were 7 pr. of flaxen sheets and many coarse harden ones; the silver included some tankards with covers to them, and a number of spoons.

The Bechers, who bought Howbury, Renhold, in 1624, lived in more elaborate style. Henry Becher of the previous generation had been a London alderman, and his furniture included court cupboards, cushions of crimson velvet embroidered with gold, or of green velvet, or of white taffeta; a painted cloth 33 yards long of the story of the prodigal son; a picture of Queen Elizabeth; coverlets, curtains and chairs of silk, velvet, satin or embroidery, or of dornix (Tournai) work.[28] Later in this century chests of drawers appeared; in 1644 Sir William Palmer of Old Warden had two.[29]

A tailor's bill for William Becher in 1606 came to £37 for a variety of doublets and cloaks, one trimmed with silver lace, and a hat with a pearled band.[30] We may compare an order in 1631 for material for dresses for two Boteler girls;[31] it was decided by "an artimask of tailors, a mournival of ladies and a gleek of gentlewomen" that 21 yards would be needed, allowing 6 breadths in each skirt. A little later Sir Samuel Luke set store by his coat lined with four or five black or sad wolves' skins; and in 1645 it took 6 yds. of scarlet cloth at 42s. a yard to

---

[25] C.R.O., TW. 818.
[26] C.R.O., AD 3346.
[27] C.R.O., FN 1097.
[28] C.R.O., PO 57.
[29] See *Beds. A. & A. S. loc.cit.* 169-71, which gives

some other inventories 1642-8 for papists and delinquents, but probably when the appraisers came round the best things were hidden away.
[30] C.R.O., PO 59.
[31] *E.M.H. Leaflet* ii, 9.

make him a cloak, with 8½ doz. buttons and loops.[32] Gold and silver buttons were obtainable from Ralph Smith, draper, who was mayor of Bedford in 1676.[33]

POLITICAL OPINION HARDENS

By 1626 political opinion was beginning to take shape. Charles I had dismissed his second parliament without obtaining a grant of taxes, and was driven to try to obtain money without parliamentary sanction. On 17 August a meeting of justices and constables of the six northern hundreds were held at Bedford. The justices present were Lord Bolingbroke, Sir Beauchamp St. John, Sir Oliver Luke, Sir John Osborne of Chicksands, Dr. Pocklington, rector of Yielden, and Richard Taylor. The justices were strictly correct; they could hardly have behaved otherwise, for they were almost certainly politically divided. The king's letter was read, and the high constables of the hundreds were left to confer with the parish constables. "And they found the opinion and vote of every hundred to be not to give to his majesty in this way, but in a parliamentary way." "We did divers of us speak with particular men, but we found them resolutely in the same opinion." Another appeal was made, when a Mr. Church from Essex, appearing for his nephew, said "he would give to supply his majesty's wants". Then the justices directed that all that would give should go to the right hand, all that would not to the left; "whereupon all the whole company went to the left hand, Mr Church only standing on the right". Finally two men spoke up: "they made some question whether this course now holden were not against law . . . and they feared future danger by such a precedent; they much insisted that the parliamentary way of raising money was most equal".[34] No record has survived of a similar meeting probably held by the three southern hundreds; here Crawley and Napier may have got a rather different result.

Yet the eleven years of Charles I's personal rule proceeded quietly for the most part, and when in 1635 he began to levy ship money on inland counties there was at first compliance. Bedfordshire was required to provide £3,000 for a ship of 300 tons, and the sheriff was responsible for collecting the money. Humphrey Monoux (the Monouxes derived from a merchant family from London who had settled at Wootton), sheriff in 1635 collected nearly this sum, and so did Sir Richard Gery of Bushmead in 1636. In 1637 Sir William Boteler was less successful; his list of defaulters shows a fair number in Houghton Regis, Husborne Crawley, Henlow, Stotfold and Dean, besides the towns; and often he had to distrain.[35] The legality of ship money was disputed at a higher level. Sir Francis Crawley of Luton, then a justice of common pleas, gave his opinion for it. Oliver St. John (the future chief justice) was Hampden's counsel in 1637, and made his reputation by his speech for the defence. In 1638 the receipts fell markedly, being less in Bedfordshire than almost anywhere in England, while in 1639 little or

[32] *B.H.R.S.* xlii, 126, 438.
[33] C.R.O., HSA 1678 W.
[34] *B.H.R.S.* xxv, 107–8.
[35] *B.H.R.S.* xviii, 43–88.

nothing was paid.

CIVIL WAR

In 1640 with the long parliament (while the Scottish army was invading) the head-on clash came. Parliament had nine Bedfordshire gentry in the commons, seven of whom were active parliamentarians. The county members were the elderly Sir Oliver Luke, returning to his former position, and Sir Roger Burgoyne of Sutton; the town members were Sir Beauchamp St. John and (instead of Richard Taylor) Sir Samuel Luke, who was Sir Oliver's son. Of those who represented constituencies elsewhere, one was Samuel Browne, another was William Russell (the Earl's eldest son till he succeeded), and a third was Oliver St. John the future chief justice, who in 1641 became solicitor-general. It was said that he was seldom seen to smile, but that at this time he was cheerful. It was he who promoted the bill for the attainder of the king's adviser, Strafford; "he that would not have had others to have law, why should he have any himself? . . . It was never accounted either cruelty or foul play to knock foxes and wolves on the head."[36] In the lords were Lord Bolingbroke; the 10th Earl of Kent; the 4th Earl of Bedford (he was convinced of Strafford's responsibility in contributing to the impasse, but reluctant to go to extremes; however he died of smallpox in 1641); and Lord Mordaunt, now Earl of Peterborough.

But there were also those who felt their loyalty to the king paramount; in the lords was the Earl of Cleveland, lieutenant of the county; and in the commons Sir Robert Napier of Luton and Edmund Wingate of Harlington. Petition and counter-petition went up to parliament from Bedfordshire. In 1642 came the outbreak of war, and by a parliamentary ordinance the county was associated with seven others in the Midland Association. The royalists (Cleveland, Napier and Wingate) left parliament, with others who took the same line. Sometimes there was division in a single family, like that between Sir William Boteler and his younger brother, who was a royalist officer.

In the confused struggle 1642–6[37] there were those in London, like the solicitor-general, Oliver St. John, and the old parliamentarians, Sir Oliver Luke and Sir Beauchamp St. John; those fighting on either side; and those directing affairs in the county – the Bedfordshire committee. By and large London and eastern England were for parliament; western England for the king.

The leading royalists were almost at once obliged to leave the county. The Earl of Cleveland and his son, Thomas Wentworth, both commanded brigades of horse. A party went to arrest Sir Lewis Dyve of Bromham; Lady Dyve said he was not at home; while reinforcements were coming up, Sir Lewis "made

---

[36] *D.N.B.* There are some MSS. relating to him in Peterborough Museum.

[37] For the general background of civil war and protectorate in this county, see *E.M.H. Leaflets* iii and vi; the following account is taken from them

unless otherwise stated. For individuals, see: Dyve, *B.H.R.S.* xxvii and xxxviii, 49–86; Luke xlii; Okey, xxxv. There are also in Dorset R.O. some unpublished Dyve letters.

escape by issuing out of his house with some men armed with pistols and muskets and calivers", crying "that he was commanded by the king and whosoever stayed him he would kill him" – in the scuffle three men were wounded. Sir Lewis also commanded a royalist regiment. In the panelling of Campton manor there are still bullets, where Sir Charles Ventris was shot at in his own house.[38] Sir Peter Osborne of Chicksands, governor of Guernsey castle, declared for the king. Among other active royalists were the Taylors of Clapham, the Gerys of Bushmead, Sir Lewis Dyer of Colmworth, and Richard Conquest. There were also some new adherents. Henry Mordaunt, 2nd Earl of Peterborough, who succeeded his father in 1643, was royalist; and the 5th Earl of Bedford, who was at first parliamentary general of horse and fought for parliament at Edgehill, when in 1643 his efforts at mediation failed, transferred to the king's side. When the king's headquarters were at Oxford, it seems that some students got involved; Thomas Cookson of Marston Moretaine "went to Oxford with an intent to study physic",[39] but said "he never did bear arms against the parliament"; none the less his sympathies seem to have been royalist.

Meanwhile the Bedfordshire committee tried to raise forces. Lord Bolingbroke was declared lieutenant in place of the royalist Earl of Cleveland; he died however in 1646. Prominent on the committee were Sir William Boteler of Biddenham, chairman, Sir Thomas Alston of Odell, Sir John Burgoyne of Sutton, James Beverley of Eaton Socon, and Edward Cater of Kempston; others were William Duncombe of Battlesden and John Vaux of Whipsnade. The initial contribution by Bedfordshire was 500 trained bands (i.e., from those mustered annually by the lieutenant for training); 500 volunteers; and a regiment of dragoons. Infantry were either pikemen carrying 15 ft. pikes; or musketeers, who supported their muskets on rests while firing; dragoons were mounted on inferior horses, and in battle they dismounted and fought on foot with sword or musket – the Bedfordshire dragoons suffered badly at Chinnor in 1643 when they lost 50 killed and 120 taken prisoner. Cavalry were the main deficiency. More demands were made on the county each year: 425 in 1643; 600 in 1644; 680 in 1645; and it was difficult to meet them by conscription.

Money was hard to raise. The Committee of both Kingdoms (i.e., England and Scotland) wrote to the Bedfordshire committee in 1644 that if it would not pay its proportion "why should not others forbear?" The estates of over 20 royalists in the county were sequestered.[40] Usually a fifth was allowed for the family; thus an order was made for the Conquest children, "it being certified unto us that they are in great necessity and that the six younger children are very young"; in fact, in desperation Richard Conquest returned home and tried to collect his own rent, and "swore he would destroy man, woman and child if he

---

[38] *V.C.H.* ii, 266.
[39] C.R.O., TW 895, f.18d.

[40] For particulars, see *Beds. A. & A.S.*, *loc.cit.* 169–71.

had it not".[41]

Those actually fighting on the parliamentary side were, like the royalists, normally outside the county, since the main fighting was elsewhere. Oliver (by courtesy) Lord St. John, the charming spendthrift, died of wounds received at Edgehill in 1642. But occasional flurries of war spilled into Bedfordshire. In October 1643 Sir Lewis Dyve with 400 horse surprised the Bedfordshire committee actually meeting at Ampthill, and went on to Bedford where the local parliamentary commander was in an alehouse and had to escape by the back door, and there was a skirmish on the bridge. The royalists then held a commission of array at Shefford. In the next June, 1644, royalists raided the southwest, shot the landlord of the Red Lion at Dunstable because he refused to supply them with horses, and fired at the minister in the church; then they plundered Leighton Buzzard. Again in August 1645 the king passed through the county; 300 royalist horse mustered on the meadows at Gt. Barford; moved on to Bedford where again there was fighting on the bridge; and plundered Luton. In November 1645 a large body of royalist horse was at Woburn, and "maliciously set fire to the town in many places at once, burnt down 17 or 18 dwellinghouses . . . whereby many families are left harbourless and utterly ruinated".

Bedfordshire's main concern with the war was with the garrison of Newport Pagnell. Because the king's supporters were mainly in the west of England, it was from the west that danger threatened. The royalists were driven out of Newport Pagnell in October 1643, and it was made a garrison town, under "great-spirited little Sir Samuel Luke". He had raised a regiment of dragoons in the county, had distinguished himself at Chalgrove Field, and become scoutmaster-general to the Earl of Essex. For nearly two years he held Newport Pagnell, maintaining its fortifications with often insufficient supplies and troops. His mustermaster was Captain Henry Whitbread.[42] In June 1644 he fought off an attack by the Earl of Cleveland – fortunately he had just received some artillery (culverin, drawn by 8 horses, firing a ball of 16–20 lbs.; and demi-culverin, somewhat smaller). His father, Sir Oliver, kept him informed of news from London.[43] He had continually to urge the Bedfordshire committee to send him supplies; thus in August 1644: "None shall be more desirous to spare his country [i.e., county] than myself, but now other countries have done their proportions to this garrison and far beyond you"; or again in February 1645: "I am sorry I should be a messenger of such a letter to my own country; therefore I hope you will pardon me if I am bold to tell you that if it be not now hearkened unto and more cheerfully obeyed than former letters have been, you must not expect any good account of this place from me." A month later (March 1645) Sir Beauchamp St. John wrote from London to the Bedfordshire committee: "You know how apt many are to accuse

41 C.R.O., TW 895, f.13d. 14d.
42 B.H.R.S. xlii, 94.
43 B.H.R.S. xlii, passim.

our county of sloth in these affairs . . . use all diligence . . . as also to take off all prejudice from yourselves of being backward."[44]

The situation seems to be that there were the active few, who took one side or the other and who would try to see the fight through to the end; the middle group who followed a lead, but soon became apathetic or obstructive when things became difficult; and the great majority who simply wanted to lead quiet lives. Of these we find an echo in a letter from Dorothy Osborne of Chicksands a few years later in 1653 when she described the husband she did not want: there was the gentleman who "understands nothing but hawks and dogs and [is] fonder of either than of his wife"; the one "whose aim reaches no further than to be justice of peace and once in his life high sheriff, who reads no books but statutes"; there was "a thing that began the world in a free school, was sent from thence to the university, and is at his furthest when he reaches the Inns of Court, has no acquaintance but those"; and there were tavern-frequenting gallants, and fops with the superficial polish of foreign travel; the ideologist is not even mentioned.[45] The sportsman, the justice, the lawyer and the gallant might all object to illegal taxes (even legal taxes are not popular); but when the struggle dragged on, with more and more financial levies, normal life disrupted, parliamentary troops quartered, and hostile troops raiding, things were different. Humphrey Monoux of Wootton was fortunate enough to get a warrant to excuse him from the quartering of soldiers, and even Sir Samuel Browne suffered from it till 1644.[46]

THE COMMONWEALTH

Thus there was already weariness when Cromwell's New Model Army succeeded in winning the war, but not in carrying to a successful conclusion the interminable negotiations with parliament and king, – negotiations, incidentally, in which Sir Lewis Dyve, prisoner in the Tower, shared.[47] They dragged on till renewed war broke out in 1648 in the north of England, from which defeated royalists retreated south, being routed at St. Neots; after this some royalist foot were "found about Luton dispersed under every hedge, and the most of them without either sword, pike or musket". At last Cromwell and the army believed that bloodshed would never cease while parliament haggled and Charles intrigued; they purged parliament of many members (mainly presbyterian); and the remnant of parliament passed an ordinance putting the king on trial. The king was beheaded in 1649. The crown lands were sold, often to army officers, one of whom was the regicide, John Okey,[48] who got Brogborough Park, Ampthill and Millbrook; and so were the lands of some royalists declared traitors, such as the Earl of Cleveland (who was captured at the battle of Worcester in 1651, where by making a cavalry charge he enabled the future Charles II to escape; and thus he himself

[44] B.H.R.S. xviii, 16.
[45] Letters (Everyman ed.), pp.152–3.
[46] E.M.H. iii, 14.
[47] B.H.R.S. xxxviii, 49–96.

[48] As a leading army officer, he was one of 53 commissioners named in the act of parliament setting up a court to try the king; B.H.R.S. xxxv, 33.

spent the years 1651–8 in the Tower).[49]

But the position in Bedfordshire, like that in the rest of the country, shows that the execution solved nothing. Among those who now either withdrew or were secluded from parliament were Oliver St. John, the chief justice, who was related to Cromwell by marriage, but had refused to act in connection with the king's trial; Samuel Browne of Arlesey; and the Lukes, father and son. Most of those who had hitherto made up the Bedfordshire committee dropped out of affairs, like Sir William Boteler (he died in 1656) and Humphrey Monoux; only a few like Sir Thomas Alston of Odell and Sir William Briers of Pulloxhill remained; and new men were brought in. At each stage the dilemma grew worse. The gentry's attempt to run the country had no more success than those of medieval barons.

Family life had suffered from war. George Nodes of Hertfordshire in 1642 was glad to see his Boteler grandchildren; "I am old and crazy [ill] and I doubt whether I shall see them again. We think the times more dangerous now than ever they were – I pray God amend them";[50] and this was a parliamentarian family. For the royalists it was worse. While Sir Peter Osborne was holding Castle Cornet in Guernsey, Lady Osborne with her children (Dorothy was 14) first took refuge with her brother at Chelsea, then went abroad to St. Malo. She sold her plate and jewels to provide supply-ships for her husband's men at Guernsey. Two sons were killed in the war; a third escaped arrest because Dorothy pleaded guilty in his stead. Lady Osborne fell ill and died before the Guernsey garrison surrendered in 1651; and Sir Peter, old and shaken, died in 1653. Thus it was from a girlhood spent in exile in poverty and anxiety that Dorothy returned to live with a surviving brother in a home straitened by debt, a home from which she wrote delightful letters to William Temple, whom she afterwards married.[51]

Yet some wounds healed and social relations began to be restored. By 1653 the Osbornes and the Lukes were exchanging courtesies, after a chance meeting on the road near Cople. Dorothy wrote "Sir Sam has grown so kind as to send to me for some things he desired out of this garden, and withal made the offer of what was in his, which I had reason to take for a high favour, for he is a nice florist".[52]

There were some years of uneasy peace and short-lived experiments in government. At quarter sessions in 1653 there were charges of speaking malicious words against the commonwealth. One man who still supported Cromwell was Edward Cater of Kempston, a member of the brief "Barebones" parliament in 1653, and brother-in-law of a regicide.[53] Cromwell became Protector; he unsuccessfully tried another parliament in 1654. In 1655, after an abortive royalist rising elsewhere, 4 Bedfordshire men were sent by the Bedfordshire committee

[49] E.M.H. vi, 5.
[50] C.R.O., TW 1107.
[51] B. Mag. x, 139–44.

[52] Letters, p.73.
[53] Kempston history, pp.27–8.

to London, including George Gery of Bushmead and George Parsons of Roxton; while other suspects in the county were watched. Then Cromwell tried to rule by major-generals, combining Bedfordshire under a Northamptonshire officer with that county, Hunts., and Rutland. England was a police state, and suspected people, like Richard Taylor of Clapham, had to give notice of their movements. Special taxes were levied on royalists; the Bedfordshire ones included Richard Taylor of Clapham; Francis Crawley, Luton; William Gery, Bushmead; and Richard Farmer, Westoning – there were sixteen in all.

Plotting continued during Cromwell's last months and under his son Richard. Among Bedfordshire plotters were John Mordaunt (brother of the Earl of Peterborough) and John Russell (brother of the Earl of Bedford). Some royalists from elsewhere, passing through the county, were arrested at a Turvey alehouse in May 1659. That spring Charles II in exile issued a commission to six men to act for him: they included Mordaunt and Russell. Their first moves were unsuccessful, and Robert Bruce from Houghton House was arrested and sent to London under suspicion. Then General Monk marched south from Scotland and declared for a free parliament.

THE KING RETURNS

By this time men of moderate views were ready to rally round a restored monarchy. Among the county militia commissioners now named were not only known royalists, like the Earls of Bedford and Elgin, but men who for several years had taken no part in affairs, such as Sir Samuel Luke and Sir Beauchamp St. John, and who were perhaps now sadder and wiser men. Charles II returned to England in May 1660, and the Earl of Cleveland was a member of his escort in London. The regicide John Okey fled abroad, but was captured, hanged and quartered, and his Ampthill estate was resumed by the king. Oliver St. John, the chief justice, was pardoned, but spent his remaining years in exile.

LIFE AT HOUGHTON HOUSE

As life returned to normal, we may pause to see how lords and squires lived in the reign of Charles II. This was the heyday of Houghton House, home of Robert Bruce, who in 1663 succeeded his father (who had taken no overt action in the civil war) as Earl of Elgin; and who for his own support of the king was almost at once made Earl of Ailesbury. Already in 1660 joint-lieutenant with the old Earl of Cleveland, he became sole lieutenant in 1664, and before long recorder of Bedford. In 1678 he was made a privy councillor. Thus a new family came to the fore in town and shire. But it was not easy for him. His son wrote later " 'Twas ever difficult for my father to gain their good will"; the Earl of Bolingbroke still "led the north part; and the gentlemen of the latter party rarely came near my father, notwithstanding at public meetings of assizes etc. outward civilities passed".[54] Before long he was also to be aware of opposition from the southwest,

[54] T. Bruce, *Memoirs*, p.441. See also the Earl of Cardigan, *Life and loyalties of Thomas Bruce*.

led by Russell.

At Houghton House there was on the ground floor a panelled hall, with shovelboard table, halberds, pikes and muskets: a smoking-room with table and leather chairs; and a parlour with 15 yellow velvet chairs; while in the cedar closet were about 150 books.[55] There were also great diningroom, withdrawing-room, red damask room and blue room. In the gallery were 39 pictures. The bedchambers were colourful; my lady's had flowered silk chairs and looking-glasses; and my lord's a crimson velvet bed lined with silk, while in his dressing-room was an escritoire. The house was lit by wax and tallow candles; over 9 months they cost £72 10s. By 1682 there was an icehouse where in winter ice was stored for summer use (that at Wrest was somewhat earlier – 1673[56]). Coal came from merchants on the river at Eaton Socon.

Most provisions came from the home farm. Livestock for it was bought from dealers and at markets as far away as Potton, where on one occasion 48 fat sheep cost £10; sometimes meat was bought from local butchers, like one at Silsoe who sold beef at 2s. 4d. a stone; a Flitton woman sold 10 geese for 28s., and Mr. Conquest's warrener was paid £7 10s. for 125 couple of rabbits. Duck came from the decoy on the estate; and pigeons, larks, quail and swan were also served. Some fresh-water fish were kept in the park; and bream and tench came from Bedford; salmon, no doubt from a distance, was also obtainable at Bedford; and the freight of 2 barrels of [salt?] fish from Yorkshire was 11s. Butter was sometimes bought, as much as 82 lb. appearing on one bill; vegetables included asparagus, artichokes and cucumber; and sometimes oranges and lemons came direct from Spain, while myrtle and oleander trees were imported from France. Home-brewed ale was the common drink; Lord Ailesbury also had claret, sherry, Rhenish, Canary, Malaga and Frontignac. Chocolate as a drink was a new fashion; 52 lb. were bought in the summer of 1684, and Lord Ailesbury had his own chocolate pot. Tea was rarely drunk, though tea cups were bought in 1684.

Round the house were gardens and bowling-green, and a well-stocked orchard which included medlars, peaches and nectarines, while melon-glasses were bought for the melons. Many horses were kept in the stables – riding horses for family and servants, coach-horses, pack-horses and cart horses. Coaches were now suspended on leather braces (springs not being yet invented); a new coach was bought for Lady Ailesbury in 1677; when Charles II died in 1685 both coaches were painted black. Once or twice a year the household went to London (to Elgin House in Clerkenwell), and occasionally they made a trip abroad – that to Holland in 1678 cost over £1,000.

Another royalist family which obtained a peerage from Charles II was that of

---

55 *B.H.R.S.* xxxii, 108–42; xxxviii, 97–104; *E.M.H.* v. For comparable life at Woburn Abbey, see Scott Thomson, *op.cit.*; for Wrest Park inventories of 1667 and 1691 see C.R.O., L 31/170–80. 56 C.R.O., L 31/194.

Carteret, defenders of Jersey. After the restoration, Sir George bought the manor of Haynes, and his grandson in 1681 became Lord Carteret of Haynes.[57]

LIFE WITH THE GENTRY

For the gentry families we may look again at the examples taken earlier in the century, Becher and Francklin. Sir William Becher of Renhold[58] was knighted at the restoration, and was one of Bedford's members of parliament in 1667. He and his second wife with 8 children and various relatives lived at Howbury Hall. In this household a year's supply of beef cost £62, with £37 for other meat. Sugar, spice, soap and "other small things" sent for to London came to £40 a year; bread, cakes and flour from a local baker cost £30. There were fires in most rooms, for twice a year 17 chimneys were swept at a cost of 17s. A good deal of spinning was done in the house ($\frac{1}{2}$ cwt. of flax cost 30s.), and a man was called in to full the cloth. Most clothes came from London, though gloves were bought at Northampton. In 1665 the garden was reorganised and 200 rose-trees put in. Sir William paid Mr. Zouch £10 for his wife's portrait in 1665, and gave her presents, such as a pair of pendants.

It was usually the husband who kept the accounts; but Lady Anne Burgoyne of Sutton, left a widow, kept hers neatly and carefully, with such items as "4 herrings 6d.", and "3 little patty pans and a pair of scissors, 8d."[59] It was also the husband who (since there were as yet no banks) kept the money locked up in the house; in 1688 Sir William Boteler wrote to his wife that she would find the key to the trunk of money in the lowest drawer but one in the study; in the same letter he asked for his horses, riding-boots and coat to be sent to the George at Luton to meet him when he alighted from the coach.[60] Lady Boteler's dress bills about this period include materials such as silk, satin, muslin, brocade, lutestring and persian, with gold and silver lace.[61]

Sir William Francklin of Bolnhurst too was knighted, and represented Bedford in 1679 and 1681. He had extravagant tastes, married the dowager Countess of Donegal, and died in debt.[62] Among the many bills left for his executor to settle were those to coachmaker, wine merchant, goldsmith, gold-lace maker, tailor and bookseller; this last bill included Dugdale's *Book of honours*, *The complete soldier*, *Synopsis of heraldry*, and acts of parliament. Either Sir William or his brother Sir John went to Winchester to school, for a school-list survived among their MSS. showing Francklin in the fourth form. Sir John was a master in chancery; he managed to get the estate on an even keel again, and bequeathed it to a distant cousin.

Love letters were not written only by Dorothy Osborne; one written by Dick Doughtie in 1630 "to her I love best" was enclosed in another to the lady's

[57] *V.C.H.* ii, 341.
[58] *B. Mag.* iii. 201–3; C.R.O., PO 3–5.
[59] C.R.O., X 143.
[60] C.R.O., TW 1121.
[61] C.R.O., TW 827.
[62] C.R.O., FN 1127–1226.

uncle, ending "The bells ring, the birds sing, the carrier stays, and I am almost starved for want of my morning draught."[63] But as a rule marriage was a matter for negotiation. A young Duncombe of Battlesden in 1644 held back from his courtship unless a dowry of £2,200 promised was made good, when "he will be very well contented to proceed therein again"; meanwhile he began to pay attentions elsewhere – "the gentlewoman is much distressed about it".[64] When Henry Brandreth of Houghton Regis in 1668 was treating with Ann Massingberd of Potsgrove for the marriage of his daughter Alice, Mistress Massingberd wrote: "Sir, I received yours. Since you have been informed of my son's estate in land, I shall tell you that for his wife's portion I shall expect £4,000 at least." The reply was: "Madam: in answer of yours, whoever gives £4,000 with his daughter will expect £1,200 p.a. at least, unless there is some defect of nature or morals."[65]

ENCLOSURE CONTINUES

On the gentry's estates enclosure was once more proceeding. Some, as before, was on a small scale, as at Felmersham in 1659, where Townsend close was "lately separated, ditched, fenced, and taken out of East Field";[66] or Pulloxhill, where in 1674 43 a. were lately enclosed.[67] But some was more extensive, as at Melchbourne in 1679 where Lord Bolingbroke enclosed about 900 a.[68] Again sometimes there were Chancery enrolments; at Hulcote enclosure seems to have taken place in 1648, the main parties being St. John Chernock and William Fallett, but probably because of the unsettled times the enrolment was not made till 1664;[69] and at Clapham in 1667 a Chancery decree dealt with exchanges made by Richard Taylor with 11 others, by which Taylor was to have Windmill Field and leave Peartree Field to them; a deed of the same year mentions common-field lands recited in a marriage settlement, and says that they "cannot now well be found without much difficulty and disturbance".[70] Pulloxhill seems to have been enclosed late in the 17th cent., probably by Sir William Briers.[71]

Charles II ruled for 25 years. His approaching end was awaited with foreboding by lords and squires, who feared the prospect of a Catholic king in James II, and whose dislike of Roman Catholicism was increased by fear of France. Some began to think of William, Prince of Orange, husband of James' daughter, Mary.

TORY ASCENDANCY

The Earl of Ailesbury would have liked his son, Thomas Bruce, to be one of the county members of parliament, but his influence did not stretch so far. The opposition came not so much from the Earl of Bedford; a hostile critic said of him that he was "a graceful old nobleman, and his outside was all";[72] and as yet only a

63 E.M.H. ii, 8.
64 B.H.R.S. xlii, 87.
65 B. Mag. ix, 201-4.
66 C.R.O., GA 1348.
67 C.R.O., WE 1630.

68 C.R.O., CRT 130 and B.P.R. vii.
69 C.R.O., AD 1651.
70 C.R.O., S/AM 74-5.
71 C.R.O., ABE 2.
72 Bruce, Memoirs, p.181.

beginning had been made in expanding the Woburn estate. It came from his eldest son, William, Lord Russell, who showed promise as a Whig leader (the names Whig and Tory had just come in), and was returned in 1679, when "the Russell faction was like a spring tide at full moon".[73] Wild rumours flew, and in 1683 some Whigs were accused of plotting to murder the king and his brother. On the flimsiest evidence Lord William Russell was executed. To the Whigs he became a martyr. Lord Ailesbury looked anxiously to the future: his last words to his son were "Dear son, you will see melancholy days; God be thanked, I shall not."[74]

Charles' illegitimate son, the Duke of Monmouth, had already been under suspicion, during which time he sought refuge at Toddington with his love, Henrietta Wentworth (granddaughter of the late Earl of Cleveland). It was said that "he regarded her as his wife before God, and she was as visionary on her side".[75] When James II succeeded in 1685 he made a bid for the crown; was defeated at Sedgmoor, captured and executed.

James II's reign was uneasy and autocratic. Thomas Bruce succeeded his father as lieutenant and as Earl of Ailesbury. He was obliged to make new deputy lieutenants of men he thought unworthy; he did not accept them socially, and sent their commissions with a note explaining that he did so at the king's command "notwithstanding I desire we may live for the future together as we have done formerly, for no one of the new ones had ever set foot in my house".[76] He had the difficult task of sounding out for the king prospective members of parliament who might support him (ch. 22). He asked those concerned on this occasion to Houghton House; "I pretended not to persuade, so on the other not to dissuade . . . I left each to go according to the dictates of honour and conscience and as good subjects withal";[77] and asked each to write his views "by reason I might mistake what each answered, by failure of memory".

When a son was born to James II, fear for the future alienated his remaining support, and he fled. Ailesbury, who was a gentleman of the bedchamber, was with him at the time, and begged him to stay. "I fell on my knees with tears, humbly beseeching him not to think of going," he wrote afterwards.[78] It was thought that Ailesbury's loyalty to the new regime was doubtful, and for a time he was imprisoned in the Tower. When he was released, church bells rang from Luton to Ampthill at his return, for he was personally popular; but he was removed from the lieutenancy; and after an uneasy period he went into exile, and died many years later in Brussels at a great age; while Houghton House, "that beautiful habitation that I doted on"[79] was shut up. The Earl of Bedford, as some recompense for the execution of Lord William Russell, "the ornament of his age", was given a dukedom. So ended the short-lived Tory ascendancy in Bedfordshire.

[73] *Ibid.*, p.53.
[74] Cardigan, *op.cit.*, p.105.
[75] Bruce, *op.cit.*, p.76. A popular account is given by
A. Fea in *The loyal Wentworths*.
[76] Bruce, *op.cit.*, p.166.
[77] *Ibid.*, p.163.
[78] *Ibid.*, p.194.
[79] *Ibid.*, p.443.

TRAFFIC BY ROAD

Increased trade promoted by a century of peace moved along the roads in 1603, either by chapmen, or with the help of packhorses, or in slow-moving carriers' waggons drawn by several horses. Several Bedfordshire carriers are known:[1] from Harrold and Wilden in the north, Arlesey in the east, Bedford itself, Cranfield in the west, Marston, Ampthill and Lidlington. In 1637 a handbook gives their usual port of call in London as the Three Horseshoes in Aldersgate; they went to London on Monday and returned on Thursday.[2] They prospered, especially as time went on. William Curfie of Lidlington was in a position to lend money on mortgage and to buy a few acres between 1663 and 1678.[3] Though about 1630 William King of Wilden seems embarrassed, Thomas King bought land in 1688 and a cottage a few years later.[4]

As well as goods, letters were often sent by carriers. Dorothy Osborne's letters to William Temple went by the Campton and Shefford carriers, Collins or Harrold, and Temple always had his letter by 9 a.m. If they were sent by the official postal service,[5] which was really for government business but by which private letters could also be sent, they were left at the post offices at St. Albans, Little Brickhill or Huntingdon. A commonwealth committee, on which John Okey of Ampthill served, was set up in 1653 to report on the postal service. However it was not till 1678 that there was a post office in the county; it was set up at the Swan Inn, Bedford, while Ampthill letters were left at the White Hart. Letters for the south were no doubt still left at St. Albans or Little Brickhill.

For the supply of meat, one method was for cattle and sheep from the north to be driven into Bedfordshire, where local graziers bought them to fatten for the London market. A drover near Doncaster in 1671 met with a Leeds boy going to London to look for work, and offered the lad 2d. a day to help him drive his sheep to Dunstable fair.[6] Similarly lords with estates elsewhere had cattle driven from other estates to their home farm for their own supply; driving beasts from his fen estate to Houghton House in 1681 cost Lord Ailesbury £2 16s. 8d., and from his Yorkshire property £7 7s. 0d.[7]

For goods like grain the roads served. At the end of this period Lord

[1] C.R.O. subject index.
[2] E.M.H. Leaflet ii.
[3] C.R.O., CH 443, 452; X 347/5; L 5/187–8.
[4] C.R.O., BD 1067; CH 497, 501, 504.
[5] E.M.H. Leaflet ii.

[6] C.R.O., HSA 1671 W 101. For drovers passing through Clapham in 1812, i.e., much later, see S/AM 271.
[7] C.R.O., X 289, f.237.

V

Ailesbury, setting out in his coach through the snow, was 3 hours going 3 miles, "the snow was so vastly deep", but "when I came into a great road leading to Luton, and it being market day there, the carts of corn made the way very good".[8] But the roads, maintained by parish surveyors, were often miry and rutted. They were of limited use for heavy freight like coal, now increasingly needed as fuel, since the supply of wood was declining. Hence the 17th cent. interest in water transport.

WATERWAYS

For the south, the nearest main river was the Lea. Here the lower reaches near London were cared for by commissioners of sewers, whose main object was to prevent floods. As a result, the Lea was navigable in this century up to Ware, only 18m. from Luton.

The north of the county was less well off. Here the nearest point for water transport was St. Ives, about 26 miles from Bedford. Coal was brought by sea from Newcastle to King's Lynn, and thence in lighters up the Ouse to St. Ives, whence it had to be carted.

There were problems involved in making the Ouse navigable to Bedford.[9] Technically these related to shallows and fords, mills and weirs; the main device required was a sluice for holding up the water in a shallow stretch; when the sluice was opened it produced a rush of water down which boats could ride, or up which they could be hauled with line and winch. In a dry summer boats could not get over the fords "unless a head of water was bought for them of the millers of Bedford or Newnham or Willington"; Tempsford ford (there was no bridge at Tempsford) was particularly difficult, and even later a waterman said that in summer he had sometimes had to go 8 m. to Bromham to get the millers to let down water to bring his boats over the ford. A cargo could be unloaded and "backed" as at Eaton Socon mill dams, but with coal this must have been slow dirty work.

Legally the river belonged to the owners of adjoining lands. A Middlesex man in 1617 got from the king a patent giving him general powers in such matters, and he assigned his rights in the Ouse to Arnold Spencer of Cople. Spencer by 1625 built sluices between St. Ives and St. Neots; then the work paused. Bedford corporation hoped to speed matters, and in 1628 the mayor and a number of supporters signed an undertaking that "knowing that great profit will thereby redound to the said town" they would be willing to pay for an act of parliament to promote the navigation. But the eleven years of Charles I's personal rule were about to begin, and the act was not passed. However Spencer resumed work. He obtained from the king his own patent to run for a term of years, and built a sluice at Eaton Socon, and scoured the river with "a strange kind of an iron instrument", "a sort of plough", drawn by horses, as far as Gt. Barford. The vill-

[8] T. Bruce, *Memoirs*, p.449. [9] *B.H.R.S.* xxiv, *passim*.

agers stared at the work in progress; John Gill, collar-maker, watched as he gathered rushes from the river for his collars; and Anne Waldocke years afterwards, when she was nearly 90, recalled how on her wedding day she saw men at work in Stone Holme ditch. Sometimes there was opposition; the men of Blunham threw the newly-dug earth back into the ditch that was being made. At Barford were built "shops, conveniences and yards near the bridge to lay coals and salt", iron and grindstones. But here the work halted again. Spencer had spent more than he could afford; existing sluices had to be kept up; and the tolls to which he looked for profit would not be extensive till the navigation could reach Bedford itself. Then "the troublesome times coming on spoiled the trade"; with the civil war trade itself slackened.

Even during the commonwealth Bedford burgesses did not lose sight of the project.[10] In the country too river navigation was a general concern, and in 1665 an act was passed to facilitate it. Arnold Spencer was dead, and his claims came to the hands of his granddaughters who had married Jemmatt brothers. The Jemmatts in 1674 leased their rights to an Eynesbury man, Henry Ashley, who also, under the act of 1665, got the backing of the justices of the peace in quarter sessions. He set to work energetically, built five sluices between Bedford and Gt. Barford, and repaired those between Barford and St. Ives. At Bedford wharves were built to receive goods. At last in the summer of 1689 lighters got through to Bedford. One of the first watermen to make the trip was Francis Browne of St. Neots.

The rates of toll were fixed at 5s. for 32 bushels of coal, with similar rates for timber, grain, malt, iron, salt and wine. A towing-path or haling-way along the river allowed horses or men to pass – it was not altogether popular with riparian owners. Sometimes there was difficulty with the millers, whose requirements for water might conflict with those of the lightermen, but Ashley's son managed to secure some of the mills. Bedford became a centre for coal distribution, and could also send agricultural cargoes down river in the returning lighters. In coming years coal merchants were to be among the leading burgesses. Trade increased; the earliest tollbooks have not survived, but one for 1710 has about 200 entries for April and May.

BEDFORD

A late 17th cent. traveller visiting Bedford noted the streets, small and old except for High Street which was pretty broad; the bowling-green on the castle mound with seats and summer-houses for the town and country gentry; the river, a source of fresh fish, with "gardens on its brink", "little boats chained to the sides", and "notches of ground set full of willows"; and the bridge "which has a gate on it and some houses".[11] In this century bridge repairs were the responsibility of the chamberlains, who each summer, when the water was low, went out in a

---

[10] B.H.R.S. xxvi, 73.   [11] Celia Fiennes, *Journeys*, p.340.

boat to see what work was required, and were allowed for their dinners 12d. apiece, besides the workman's labour and boat hire.[12] In the great storm of 1672 a tanner's man crossing it "was taken up from the ground and hardly escaped blowing over the bridge", while inn gates were blown off at the Swan, the Ram and the Maidenhead, two houses in Offal Lane were blown down, and a tree was "carried over Paul's steeple as if it had been a bundle of feathers".[13]

It had under 2,000 inhabitants.[14] Besides all the normal trades associated with food supply, with clothing, and with carpentry and building (these last included brickmakers), and the occasional yeoman, gardener, shepherd or blacksmith, there were miscellaneous trades such as bookbinder, combmaker, pipemaker, fletcher, roper, heelmaker, basketmaket, pewterer; one or two apothecaries or physicians; and the occasional notary and schoolmaster; and there was even a horse-courser; there were of course many labourers.

Town government tended to look to the neighbouring gentry, and they were not averse to this. The recorder and deputy recorder were respectively Lord Bolingbroke and Richard Taylor of Clapham (ch. 23). Later in the century an alderman left the 2nd Lord Bolingbroke "a gold ring in thankful remembrance of his goodness to me and mine".[15] The old town clerk, William Payne of Podington, died in 1624. Apart from his age, it must have been inconvenient to have a town clerk living 15 miles away; and in 1612 it was decided that after his death the town clerk should be resident.[16] On the other hand a nearby gentleman legally qualified had independent status with townsmen when friction arose, whereas a Bedford attorney depended for his living mainly on his local practice and so was to some extent involved. (The town clerk merely charged fees; it was to be centuries before there was enough work for a full-time officer.) So before long another country gentleman was appointed, John Cobbe of Sharnbrook. Parliamentary representation in the early part of the century went to the recorder's nominee (a St. John) and the deputy recorder, Richard Taylor.

There are two main points of interest in Bedford. This century saw the establishment of a semi-elective council; in the struggle between burgesses and freemen it was several times altered, but in the form in which it was established in 1660 and 1663 it lasted till 1835. The other is external: twice, in 1656 and in 1688, Bedford was subject to direct interference from the central government.

The burgesses were the prosperous men. They served the offices of mayor, bailiffs and chamberlains; and they attended, not only the court leet, but also a council when the mayor summoned one. Their sons inherited their rights. One who served as mayor was Robert Hawes, owner of Duck Mill (d. 1628).[17] He lived in a mansion house and his daughters were married to gentry (Boteler

12 *Lock Gate* i, 3.
13 *V.C.H.* iii, 4.
14 *B.H.R.S.* xvi, 144–9.

15 C.R.O., ABP/W 1675–6/69.
16 *B.H.R.S.* xxvi, p.xviii.
17 C.R.O., ABP/W 1627–8/225.

260

and Barnardiston). He left £10 to the poor of Bedford, with a further annual sum of 20s. to those of his own parish to be distributed at Christmas. To his brother (also more than once mayor) and to friends he left mourning rings, a form of bequest now customary among the well-do-to. Another burgess family was Beckett; several bore the name Simon, which occurs six times among mayors 1606–77; one who died in 1651 was a brewer, and left his son Simon his brewing vessels, coppers, furnaces, vats, coolers, cisterns and tubs.[18] Six times between 1624 and 1685 the name of William Faldo is found on the mayoral list; one of these was the son of a glover and inherited £100 from his father.[19] John Eston (d. 1663) was mayor four times and left to his son his old aldermanic gown.[20]

The freemen were usually of moderate means or poor; they were not at the beginning of this period represented on the council, and attended only the court leet, where however a "constitution" affecting town government could be made. For them there were only the inferior offices of constable, flesh-searcher and bucket-keeper. Most of them found the struggle to make a living enough to occupy them. One of them was Thomas Gibbs, a cooper (d. 1602); he left his working tools to his journeyman – probably his son Thomas was set up in trade; his daughter Faith was to have "the bed which I lie in at this present", and his other children 20s. each; he also left 10s. to the poor.[21] Another was Michael Smith, of whose furniture a list survives; in his hall or living-room, hung with painted cloths, were table, form, 3 chairs, 2 joined stools, a cupboard, 3 spinning-wheels (2 for linen, 1 for wool), 2 candlesticks, 14 pewter dishes, a brass pot, mortar, kettles, frying-pan, posnet, skimmer, hatchet and bellows; in the bed-chamber were 2 beds, 3 coffers in which probably his 12 pr. of sheets were kept, and no less than 5 books; he had some apples stored, and in the yard was a pile of wood.[22] Edward Glover was below the poverty line; he had a table, chest, cup-board, kettle, fryingpan, pewter dish and mattress; in all they were worth 22s.[23] There must have been many like him. In 1671 one householder in four was too poor to pay tax.[24]

But some among the freemen were reflective and energetic, and determined to make themselves felt. In 1610, by agitating at the court leet, they secured the right to be represented on the council by 13 men of quality.[25] It was not clear that the 13 representatives would necessarily be freemen; nor was the method and frequency of election laid down; in practice a new representative was chosen only when a vacancy arose. But it was a first step, and this system lasted till the civil war.

In 1640, when a parliament was summoned for the first time for eleven years, the town had a contested parliamentary election.[26] The royalist Richard Taylor

[18] C.R.O., ABP/W 1651/36.
[19] C.R.O., ABP/W 1625/162.
[20] C.R.O., ABP/W 1663/44.
[21] C.R.O., ABP/W 1602/16.
[22] B.H.R.S. xx, 68.

[23] Op.cit., 59.
[24] B.H.R.S. xvi, 144–9.
[25] Corporation MS.
[26] C.R.O., TW 891.

was no longer acceptable. Sir Beauchamp St. John was returned as before, but the other place was disputed between Sir Samuel Luke and Sir William Boteler, both country gentlemen. Canvassing lists were made out of "good voices", a vote at that date being an actual voice to shout. Among those who supported the successful Luke were John Eston and Robert Hawes, but the families of Beckett and Faldo were for the more moderate Boteler.

War broke out. Some Bedford men were drafted into the parliamentary army or the Newport Pagnell garrison or volunteered. This interruption of apprenticeship afterwards made difficulties for some; Samuel Gibbs, who had apparently served at least part of his apprenticeship in London and then was in the parliamentary army, and was "only the younger son of a freeman", was "molested and interrupted" by William Faldo when he later tried to set up in trade in Bedford.[27]

On the old castle mound a fort was set up, and walls with loopholes for shooting.[28] The commander, Captain Benjamin Hudson, conscripted labour for it from the nearby villages. Its garrison was about 100. Once in August 1643 Bedford was a rendezvous for 1,100 horse: and in June 1645 Cromwell passed through with 600 horse and dragoons. St. John's church was used by the troops, and the churchwardens' accounts show payments "for making clean the church when the camp was here".[29] Sometimes there were skirmishes when hit-or-miss royalist raiders appeared. Some burgesses were uneasy about the fort; they thought it made Bedford a target; others, including John Eston, called these the "ill-affected" and petitioned parliament for it to remain. Eventually in the autumn of 1645 the committee of both kingdoms decided to sleight the fort, and Captain Hudson removed to Leicester. The town was thus open when in the following summer, near the end of the war, the king marched through.

War was unsettling. At the court leet in 1647 when William Lavender was chosen to fill a vacancy on the council, the freemen demanded annual elections.[30] There was a hot dispute, which was referred to three representatives from either side; the three burgesses included William Faldo, grocer; and the three freemen included Thomas Gibbs, cooper. But the burgesses would not give way.

Then the freemen petitioned parliament, or what was left of parliament, demanding also a larger council.[31] The burgesses counter-petitioned; one objection they made was that if every year new freemen were on the council, and allowed to serve as chamberlain, bailiff and even mayor, there would not be enough responsible men left to be constables, flesh-searchers and bucket-keepers; in short, if everyone is somebody, then no one's anybody. But a parliamentary committee in January 1650 approved annual elections and a larger council.[32]

[27] B.H.R.S. xxvi, 10–11.
[28] E.M.H. Leaflet iii, 16–18.
[29] Op.cit, 19.
[30] Corporation MS: see court leet for 23 August 1648.

See also R.Hist.S.Trans., 4th ser., xxix, 151–65.
[31] Corporation MS.: petition of the freemen; and answer of the counter-party.
[32] B.H.R.S. xxvi, 28–32.

In April the new council took the revolutionary step of abolishing the distinction between burgess and freeman.[33] This was the highest point the freemen attained in their struggle.

In this same year the Bedford Independent congregation (ch. 22) was established. Among its early members were burgesses of old standing like John Eston, and freemen like Anthony Harrington. In 1653 the corporation invited the congregation to take over St. John's church, in their gift. Two years later, when the first minister died, there was some difference of opinion as to the next incumbent, but Cromwell decided in favour of the congregation's choice.

It is from this period that the first surviving minute-book of the corporation dates, from 1647 when William Scott became town clerk. Incidentally it illustrates the council's limited responsibility for public services. Street repair was a council concern only for the bridge and for a limited extent of High Street.[34] The remainder were "repaired by the occupiers of the houses, grounds, shops, stalls and tenements next adjoining thereto". The first ordinance for street-lighting was in 1649:[35] from October to February the inhabitants of High Street and St. Mary's were to hang out lights, "and the town bedell for the time being shall every evening at candle tinding go along and give public warning." For keeping the streets clean also the onus was on the townsman.

It was during the protectorate, when Cromwell was ruling through major-generals, that there came in 1656 the first arbitrary interference from the central government. The immediate cause is not clear, but no doubt Simon Beckett, who was mayor, was not in sympathy with the protectorate. The major-general removed him from office and also four members of the council, and substituted his own nominees.[36]

A few uneasy years followed, and then in 1660 came the restoration of the monarchy. The tide of the freemen's success ebbed. The council repealed the changes of the interregnum and renewed the distinction between burgess and freeman.[37] What remained however as a permanent gain for the freeman was annual election for the council. They may not have been altogether pleased with the method; nomination was to rest with mayor and burgesses; and by an amendment of 1663 nominees were to be burgesses only; but at least the final choice would be with the freemen and this choice would be exercised once a year.[38] Moreover, though no resolution was passed about it, at this time the general right of any burgess to attend the council seems to have lapsed; so that the 13 elected men with mayor, bailiffs and aldermen were in fact the council.

In spite of the royalist atmosphere of the time, the council remained loyal to the St. John family "under whose shadow and protection for 40 years together

[33] B.H.R.S. xxvi, 35.
[34] Op.cit., 11–14.
[35] Op.cit., 24.

[36] Op.cit., 95.
[37] Op.cit., 138, 149.
[38] Op.cit., 174.

our corporation once rested and flourished"; and when Sir Samuel Browne resigned in 1661 they appointed the 2nd Earl of Bolingbroke recorder.[39] Their members of parliament at this time included Paulet St. John, Sir William Becher and Sir William Francklin.

One disability was forced on the council: the test and corporation acts made obligatory taking the sacrament according to the church of England, and thus excluded dissenters. The names of John Eston, Anthony Harrington and their like disappear from the council minutes, while those of Beckett and Faldo remain.

For 20 years the position was stable. Then, in the uneasy 1680's when doubts about the succession to the monarchy made politics uncertain, came the second attack by the government on Bedford as on other old boroughs. Curiously enough, Bunyan's *Holy War*, an account of the siege of the town of Mansoul, was written just previously in 1682. Provoked by London, the government obliged boroughs to obtain new charters. Bedford's new charter in 1684 substituted Lord Ailesbury for Lord Bolingbroke as recorder. In 1688 James II, hoping to get nonconformist support for toleration for Roman Catholics, removed from office the mayor, Thomas Underwood, and 6 council members, including William Faldo and Robert Beckett; and substituted others who all seem to have been connected with the Independent congregation.[40] There was a storm throughout the country; James II revoked his action, but too late to save himself, and lost his throne in the revolution of 1688. So ended the second attempt at governmental intervention in Bedford.

These constitutional struggles were no doubt the concern only of the few. Most people in Bedford probably knew or cared little about king and parliament, burgesses and freemen, or governmental interference. One of these was probably Samuel Lane, a tanner, who one winter evening in 1668 went to an inn, having already had rather too much to drink.[41] The innkeeper's wife did not want to serve him, but he insisted, and sat down by the fire with a pot of beer, where also Richard Flint, apprentice, was sitting. A few minutes later she heard a great noise, found the candle out, and Lane lying on the floor, bleeding, and calling out "Rogue!" Or there were the would-be highwaymen who in 1679 "lay under a hedge at Putnoe gate all night to light of a prize, but could get none"; so they tried to persuade Thomas Branklin to break open William Faldo's stables and take out two of his best horses, which they would be waiting to receive.[42] A little gang of people in 1680 were clipping and coining money; when coins were of silver it was worth while to clip them.[43] William Smith seems to have been an arrant rogue; he stole material from a St. Neots draper; when he tried to sell it and suspicion was aroused, he said he had it "in swop for a horse"; then he told a hard-

[39] *Op.cit.*, 156.
[40] Corporation minute-book 1664–88, f.290–1.
[41] C.R.O., HSA 1668 S.
[42] C.R.O., HSA 1680 W.
[43] *Loc.cit.*

luck story about his wife, "a hard austere woman who would not afford him money to supply his necessary station"; finally he accused his son; and when the constable Josias Ruffhead searched his house, Ruffhead found there stolen shoes of his own making.[44]

During this period the free school continued, though it suffered from changes of staff; the salaries of £20 and £10 a year for master and usher were already too low to attract and retain good men.[45] One usher, Giles James, was often late at school; his corrections were "cruel, sudden, enormous", so that the whole street resounded with yells and sudden outcries. In the civil war period William Verney was master; and his usher was neglectful, so that the school was said to be quite desolate, and the inhabitants were forced at great charge to send their children elsewhere. Verney was ejected in 1656 when the town council was purged, and the council wrote to New College for a godly and fitting person to replace him; but at the restoration he was reinstated. The next master went off to be a naval chaplain. The warden of New College remonstrated: "what man of parts will come among you" for so small a return? The salaries were then raised to £30 and £20, but another master went to America in 1677. It was not till 1683 with Nicholas Aspinall that a master was appointed who was to remain for over 30 years.

The school's endowment, the Holborn estate, was not yet bringing in much income, and in 1629 its rent was £50. Perhaps salaries could only have been raised earlier by raising the 2d. per quarter paid by each child at the school. But already London was approaching the property. When in 1668 the land was let on long lease for £99 a fine of £100 was also secured. Later the lease was extended to 1760 at £149 p.a. When this lease fell in, there would be a harvest probably far greater than even the shrewd Harpur foresaw.

THE MARKET TOWNS

The market towns fall into two groups.[46] The chief were Leighton and Luton townships (i.e., excluding the agricultural hamlets). Each had a population of about a thousand, and so was approximately half the size of Bedford. The others – Ampthill, Biggleswade (excluding Stratton and Holme), Dunstable, Potton, Toddington and Woburn ranged in 1671 from 875 (Potton) to 599 (Ampthill); and this seems to have been the time of Toddington's greatest prosperity.[47] Harrold and Shefford were not yet important, in fact Shefford market seems to have lapsed.

All but Dunstable had a lord or squire resident or close at hand. The nearness of the Earls of Ailesbury, Cleveland and Bedford no doubt contributed to the prosperity of Ampthill, Toddington and Woburn. At Leighton was the Leigh

---

[44] C.R.O., HSA 1676 W.
[45] V.C.H. ii, 162–7; C.F. Farrar, *Harper's Bedford Charity*, 4–14.
[46] For population estimates, see *B.H.R.S.* xvi.
[47] V.C.H.. iii, 441.

family; this property was leasehold from St. George's chapel, Windsor; and Sir Thomas Leigh married the lessee's heiress, and was created Baron Leigh in 1643. Till 1671 the Leighs lived at Leighton, when the younger son succeeded as lessee (the elder line going to Stoneleigh). At Luton the Rotherhams gave place to the Napiers and the Crawleys. Sir Robert Napier, who had been a London grocer and a merchant trading with Turkey, bought the Hoo in 1601 and Luton manor in 1611. James I came to stay at the Hoo, and later made him a baronet. The Crawleys (chs. 17, 23) were adding to their estate, and in the mid-century bought Stockwood from another Rotherham. To Stratton Park near Biggleswade came early in this century Sir John Cotton, who was grandson of the famous collector of MSS. and who married an Anderson heiress. The Cottons almost entirely rebuilt the house, adding to it a richly carved staircase. Near Potton were the Burgoynes of Sutton Park, who owned the four Potton manors.

In all the manorial machinery was still in being. The court rolls for this period, where they survive, are almost full of entries of changes in copyhold tenancies; sometimes, as at Bigggleswade, held by prosperous men like Thomas Bromsall or by humbler men like Roger Foster and Edmund Rudd who each had only one hearth.[48] Only rarely are there entries of another kind, as when at Leighton George Wells, butcher, was fined 10s. because he "did blow his flesh".[49]

Their administrative machinery was parochial.[50] Their overseers, surveyors and constables were nominated at the Easter vestry meeting, and their appointment was confirmed by local justices of the peace to whom they were responsible. For the two latter offices early records are very rare; but for overseers beautifully kept books survive for Potton from 1638.[51] For 1638–9 the overseers were Thomas Waller and Francis Austen. In May they levied a rate on 93 persons, who paid amounts from 1d. to 8s. 4d., and this brought in over £4. They paid out relief to 20 people (7 of them widows) in sums varying from 4d. to 1s. Some other payments were "to Walter Langhorn for ridding the town of himself, his wife and children, 30s.", and "to the widow Knott to send her quite away" (this policy was reversed after the act of 1662 made a pauper chargeable on his birthplace). At Easter 1639 John Ward and Thomas Langhorn were nominated as new overseers, and on 9 May three justices, Sir Oliver Luke, Sir William Palmer of Old Warden, and Humphrey Fisher noted the balance in hand, passed the accounts, ordered the latter to be read out in church after morning prayer the next sabbath day, and formally appointed the new overseers for the ensuing year.

Gradually the accounts become more detailed. Hemp was bought to provide work for the unemployed. Henry Hall's boy was apprenticed to Robert Beamont. Goodwife Waters was paid "for looking to George Burgis". A bed

48 C.R.O., X 338.
49 C.R.O., KK 798.
50 Each of the Bedford parishes also had overseers, but they and the constables were appointed at the court leet. For road repair in Bedford see above.
51 C.R.O., P 64/12.

was made for Richard Barker; 6 boards, nails, straw and work cost 2s. 11d.; a flock bed, bolster, sheet and blanket came to 10s. Sometimes there are payments for shoes, stockings, an apron, a shift, shirts; and for firing and washing; Giles Darling, one of the overseers in 1670, occasionally went so far as to pay for milk and butter.

The overseers always worked closely with the churchwardens, and sometimes payments relating to the poor appear in churchwardens' accounts. Thus at Woburn in 1618 children were being taught to make pillow lace, and others were apprenticed.[52] The petty sessions when the justices approved the accounts seem for this hundred to have been held at Toddington or Dunstable; "paid for our dinners at Toddington when we went about the poor's account"; they also "paid for going with two rogues to be whipped at Dunstable".

This machinery was in kind exactly like that of the rural parishes, but simply tends to be better recorded at an earlier date because the market towns were on the whole bigger, more prosperous and more specialised. Wills proved and apprenticeship indentures during the period record the more prosperous town-dwellers, and the hearth tax of 1671 reveals the size of house occupied. Thus at Luton there were many yeomen and husbandmen; Philip Marshall (d. 1681) had 73 a. in closes and 28 a. in the common fields; his house had 4 hearths.[53] The next largest group at Luton was that of the maltmen; some were well-to-do, like Jn. Gutteridge (d. 1685) who also had a house with 4 hearths;[54] some operated only on a small scale, like Richard Reynolds with 1 hearth (d. 1688).[55] There were several in the clothing trades, weavers, glovers and tailors; and there were tanners, carpenters, blacksmiths, glaziers and brickmakers; there was also at least one barber chirurgeon, Cornelius Bigland.[56] Leighton had other occupations, such as shearmen, bodice-makers, ropemakers, collarmakers. At Dunstable, much smaller than either, there were several more innholders, a scrivener and two barber-surgeons. Before the end of this period the plaiting of straw for hats was established in Dunstable and Luton as well as in the surrounding villages (ch. 25). At Potton there were also basket-makers, hatter, locksmith, fellmonger, metalman, fuller, saddler, silk weaver and a notary. At Toddington there were no less than four tailors.

The market towns, with their shops, inns, markets and fairs, offered special temptations for theft. At Leighton Robert Perrott's shop probably had an open front and was shuttered at night; 20 yards of material stolen from him in 1684 were found with a Woburn upholsterer, Richard Gaseley, who was making it up for widow Cawkett.[57] At Luton in 1681 Peter Clark and John Collett stole quantities of goods (bracelet, rings, coats, breeches, buttons, penknife) before they were

---

[52] C.R.O., P 118/5.
[53] C.R.O., ABP/W 1681/20.
[54] C.R.O., ABP/W 1685/24.

caught.[58] Inns offered thieves a field of activity; it might be the occasional shirt from a passing traveller, as at Biggleswade in 1680;[59] from Ampthill inns Mary Williamson stole pewter flagons, erased the innkeepers' marks, and offered them for sale at Woburn.[60]

Markets were infested by pickpockets. It was a London man who in 1684 at Leighton stole from Robert Simons' breeches pocket.[61] Fairs were tempting; a Surrey woman stole bone lace at Woburn fair, which she concealed in the crown of her hat;[62] at Dunstable fair in 1684 an Ampthill tailor, Peter Sutton, had breeches stolen from his stall.[63] Fairs also gave a chance of disposing of stolen goods. Two Chalgrave men in 1678 stole sheep from Tebworth, sold them at Dunstable fair, and afterwards divided the money over drinks in an alehouse.[64] At the same fair John Taylor, who had stolen at Smithfield a dun mare with a star and a shorn mane, sold her for £2, and only when the fair was over did the Derbyshire owner of the mare arrive and find the sale entered in the fair tollbook.[65]

After fairs, footpads like Henry Benson at Leighton lurked in the dusk.[66] At Leighton in 1685 highwaymen stole two parcels of bone lace from a purchaser.[67] From carriers' waggons goods could be pilfered, as were hats (probably straw hats) from William Eames' waggon at Dunstable in 1682.[68] Coaches on Watling Street were apt to be held up by highwaymen; two men, one on a chestnut mare and one on a brown gelding, stopped John King's coach near Dunstable in 1678, shot a man passenger, and took 40s. from a woman.[69]

At the same time the market towns had their share of normal human problems. There were those of young women with illegitimate children; Margaret Rogers of Luton, servant to Elizabeth Wells, concealed her child under the straw in the malthouse;[70] while Alice White of Potton put hers out in Church close.[71] There were disputes over wages and conditions; in Luton John Winch called out to a fellow worker in widow Chapman's blacksmith's shop "Here's the rogue that works for 8d. a day when others have 12d.", and in the resulting quarrel ran a red-hot iron in his eye.[72]

Because the towns were congested, fire risk was greater than in the villages. Biggleswade had a bad fire in 1604.[73] Leighton had 12 fire-buckets hanging in church under the bell-loft; they were bequeathed by an innholder, Thomas Merieden, who wanted them hung near his seat in church.[74] Dunstable, alarmed apparently by the disaster of the great fire of London, acquired from John Keeling of London a fire-engine of a new type introduced from the continent; it was

[58] C.R.O., HSA 1682 W.
[59] C.R.O., HSA 1680 W.
[60] C.R.O., HSA 1671 W.
[61] C.R.O., HSA 1684 W.
[62] C.R.O., HSA 1671 W.
[63] C.R.O., HSA 1684 W.
[64] C.R.O., HSA 1678 S.
[65] C.R.O., HSA 1678 S.
[66] C.R.O., HSA 1664 W.
[67] C.R.O., HSA 1685 W.
[68] C.R.O., HSA 1682 S.
[69] C.R.O., HSA 1671 W.
[70] C.R.O., HSA 1677 S.
[71] C.R.O., HSA 1680 S.
[72] C.R.O., HSA 1680 W.
[73] B.Par.Reg. ii, p. C 65.
[74] C.R.O., ABP/W 1683/97.

worked by a pair of plunger pumps, filled by a bucket chain, and threw out jets.[75] Incidentally, Luton parish register notes that £3 was collected in the town for rebuilding St. Paul's cathedral; the vicar gave 5s. and two widows gave 1d. each.

On the whole the market towns were better off for teaching than most villages. Biggleswade or Holme school, set up in 1557, had a bequest from Benjamin Pigott in 1606.[76] Though at Dunstable the former schoolhouse seems to have been lost, there was teaching in the church, for John Riseley in 1663 wished to be buried "in the place where I taught school".[77] Leighton seems to have lagged behind till a Linslade curate, Edward Hargrave, taught there from the mid-century for 52 years.[78] At Luton Cornelius Bigland, the barber surgeon, in 1673 left money to clothe and educate 6 poor children.[79] At Toddington there was a school in 1652.[80] At Woburn the school founded in the previous century by the Earl of Bedford continued.

As they were on main roads, market towns tended to be vulnerable to the plague. Woburn lost 50 people from the plague in 1625–6; and 40 in 1665.[81]

How far their inhabitants were politically conscious it is hard to say. Probably most tradesmen thought of politics as an affair of the gentry. Many were copyholders and the electoral qualification was a 40s. freehold. Few would attend the county court where the candidates selected beforehand by leading gentry would be acclaimed; and those who did would think of themselves as supporters of a neighbouring lord or squire. Yet some feeling at least seems to have been stirred by James I and Charles I in their attempts to raise taxes without parliamentary authority. At Leighton, although Sir Thomas Leigh was a royalist, no less than 60 people were in arrears with ship money; two hats were distrained from George Shurruge for his, and from Henry Turney a silver cup.[82] At Luton there were 40 men in arrears, and cloth was distrained from Robert Wells and Tobias Seare, apparently drapers.[83] At Dunstable the number of 51 men in arrears, including William Metcalfe and Roger Finch, was larger in proportion to population than in either of the foregoing.[84] At Biggleswade and Potton the figures were 2 and 3 respectively.[85]

The civil war brought raids on some of the market towns. Watling Street was subject to attack, and more than once parliamentary supplies were sent by a roundabout route rather than trust to it.[86] At Dunstable the parliamentarian landlord of the Red Lion paid for his views with his life. (ch. 23). Woburn too suffered; wanton royalist destruction, it was said, burned down 18 houses "to the value of £3,869 7s. as appeareth by the estimation of 4 sufficient carpenters and 4

[75] This is still in the London Museum.
[76] C.R.O., ABP/W 1606/77.
[77] C.R.O., ABP/W 1663/42.
[78] Richmond, *Leighton Buzzard*, p.51.
[79] C.R.O., ABP/W 1679/32.
[80] C.R.O., Fac. 34, p.37; B.H.R.S. xvi, 115.

[81] *B.Par.Reg.* iii.
[82] *B.H.R.S.* xviii, 65.
[83] *Op.cit.*, 70.
[84] *Op.cit.*, 67.
[85] *Op.cit.*, 84.
[86] *B.H.R.S.* xlii, 345.

masons".[87] Luton suffered a plundering raid in 1645.[88] Sometimes there were sympathisers in the town, as at Ampthill in 1643 when Humphrey Iremonger welcomed the royalist raiders, and threatened to hang "traitors" at their own doors.[89]

In most towns economic life must have been disrupted, especially by the sequestration of the estates of Cleveland, Napier and Crawley. At Leighton Sir Samuel Luke seems to have made use of the Leigh house when in the neighbourhood.[90] Leighton, where the manor was owned by St. George's chapel, Windsor, was further affected in 1649 when deans and chapters were abolished: and Ampthill and Biggleswade were also drawn in when crown estates were confiscated in the same year. Ampthill was bought by a parliamentary officer, John Okey the regicide; Biggleswade by a Bedford burgess, Thomas Margetts, a supporter of Cromwell; while Leighton went to a group of purchasers. Toddington was sold when the Earl of Cleveland was declared a traitor.

During the protectorate, when support for the return of the monarchy began to build up, there were suspects who were obliged by the major-general to give notice of their intended movements. Among them were Humphrey Iremonger of Ampthill and John Marsh of Leighton. In 1656 Reuben Browne of Luton gave notice that "he now lodgeth at the sign of the Cock, the house of James Browne, innkeeper, in the parish of Botolph's, Aldersgate"; and four days later he notified his return to Luton.[91]

At the restoration the changes of ownership in Ampthill, Biggleswade and Leighton Buzzard were reversed. Former conditions were gradually restored. A sidelight on the feelings of some comes from the will of Frances Dobson, friend of the Napiers. Among her possessions was a gold locket with a picture of Charles I on it. She left to Sir John Napier her great silver pot, and to Lady Napier a silver candlestick.[92] Soon after this the Napiers enlarged and enriched the chapel at Luton Hoo, which was dedicated in 1674.[93]

All coins were still of gold or silver, and the only method of giving change was to break them up. Traders hit on the expedient of issuing tokens, each one with his own name and design, which he would honour.[94] These tokens were also issued in Bedford, e.g. by William Faldo in 1659 and by William Isaac (later intruded mayor) in 1666. The number known for each market town varies; there are most for Dunstable, in spite of the town's small size; that of Thomas Barret, carrier, shows a packhorse pannier. Next comes Potton, including Henry Rugeley, 1666 (a name we shall meet later), and Leighton. For Luton only a few are known; Luton was rather an agricultural than a mercantile centre. When in 1672 a copper coinage was for the first time issued, trading tokens were suppressed.

---

[87] *E.M.H. Leaflet* iii, 13.
[88] *Loc.cit.*
[89] *E.M.H. Leaflet*, vi, 7.
[90] *B.H.R.S.* xlii, 441.

[91] *E.M.H. Leaflet* vi, 8.
[92] *B.N.Q.* ii, 234.
[93] Shaw, *Luton chapel*, 10, 12–13.
[94] J. H. Blundell, *Beds. 17th cent. tokens.*

The market towns were not lacking in colourful personalities. Bedford is not the only local town to produce a Lord Mayor of London. Samuel Starling came from the Luton hamlet of Stopsley; he became a wealthy London brewer, and was master of the Brewers' Company in 1661.[95] Perhaps his early years were a struggle, for Pepys thought him ungenerous. After the great fire, when his house was saved, he "did give 2s. 6d. among 30 of them, and did quarrel with some that would remove the rubbish out of the way of the fire, saying that they came to steal". In 1669 he became Lord Mayor, but in the gloomy conditions of the time there was little pageantry for his show. Another Lutonian was John Pomfret (1667–1702), the poet; his father was vicar of Luton, and was the "nephew Pomfret" to whom Frances Dobson left all her books; he made his name after 1700 when he published *The Choice*.[96] From Dunstable came the restoration dramatist, Elkanah Settle (1648–1724), who wrote a series of bombastic plays, beginning with *Cambyses, King of Persia*.[97] Incidentally the Settles were alleged victims in a notorious case of witchcraft; but since fear of witchcraft was a general phenomenon this is discussed elsewhere (ch. 26). Another Dunstablian, Richard Finch (d. 1641) was a citizen and merchant-tailor of London.

The hearth tax of 1671 makes it possible to compare the market towns towards the end of this period.[98] There were few large houses with 10 or more hearths; none at Potton; 2 at Luton; most (7) at Ampthill. At Ampthill also the proportion of medium houses (2–9 hearths) was high, as also at Luton. Everywhere else houses with only one hearth formed the majority. A varying number of inhabitants were not listed because they received relief or alms; at Ampthill 12%; at Luton 15%.

[95] *B. Mag.* x, 265–6.
[96] *D.N.B.*
[97] *D.N.B.*
[98] *B.H.R.S.* xvi.

25 – YEOMEN, CRAFTSMEN AND COTTAGERS, 1603–89

IN THE first part of the 17th cent. the yeomen, craftsmen and cottagers were in much the same position as at the end of the previous century. But whereas the range of crafts and the number of craftsmen were growing, the yeomen by the end of the period were threatened with a disadvantageous trend.

CRAFTSMEN AND OTHERS

As before, almost all craftsmen cultivated some land as well as plying their craft. Except for a decline in bowstring-makers and fletchers, the same occupations (ch. 20) occur.[1] Butchers, bakers, grocers and millers were of course everywhere. So were those connected with clothing: even Chellington had a weaver, and some villages had two or three; at Haynes in the 1620's there were William Lynford and William and Edward Hickman;[2] while at Dean four members of the Fairy family were weavers between 1601 and 1666.[3] Thomas Albon of Southill in 1639 mentions his looms "to work linen, woollen and sacken".[4] Dyer, fuller, cloth-worker, shearman were also found. The majority of villages had a tailor, and some-times (as at Flitwick) a bodice-maker; Houghton Regis had a draper and Bletsoe a mercer; and at least ten parishes had a glover.

Leather trades were still important, and there were fellmongers, as at Aspley; tanners, as at Clophill; and saddlers as at Shefford.

Of the building trades, a Biddenham carpenter who apparently died while in process of building a house describes it in 1617 as standing on 6 posts and 6 pattens, with loose rafters and boards over; the chimney was already in position, and "it shall not be stirred but stand still".[5] All over the stone areas there were masons. Brickmakers occur not only at Wootton, but at Clophill, Campton, Stondon and Whipsnade; and bricklayers were widespread, showing the new trend to brick for large houses. Lidlington had a painter; there was a plasterer at Shillington, a plumber at Goldington, and a glazier at Pavenham. These trades often descended in families, as with the Castell family, who were thatchers at Stotfold.

There were several joiners, as at Pulloxhill; and a turner at little Astwick. There were more wheelwrights; the gentry's coaches came from London, but it might be necessary, as Sir Samuel Luke found,[6] to get a local replacement for a broken wheel; and carts and waggons were needed.

There were chandlers, as at Barton; coopers, as at Ridgmont; locksmiths,

---

[1] C.R.O. occupations index.
[2] C.R.O., SA 12, 712–3.
[3] C.R.O., PA 45, 60–2, 94.

[4] C.R.O., ABP/R 35, f.160.
[5] C.R.O., ABP/R 33, f.103d.
[6] B.H.R.S. xlii, 93.

as at Podington; collarmakers, as at Totternhoe; chapmen, as at Caddington; a badger at Meppershall; a salter at Sandy; a gelder at Northill; a gunsmith at Lidlington; a hopdresser at Eaton Socon; a ropemaker at Maulden; a musician at Wilstead; and hempdressers at Cardington and Houghton Regis. Plough-wrights were found everywhere from Odell to Houghton Regis and from Eversholt to Southill. The Ouse navigation is reflected in the occupations of coal-merchant and waterman at Tempsford.

Blacksmiths were in every village. William Goodale of Shillington in 1602 had blacksmith's shops also at Meppershall and Holwell, and mentions his anvil, bellows and coals.[7] Besides shoeing horses, they made and mended iron instru-ments, such as a jack to regulate the roasting of meat; and it was not a great step from such items to the simple clocks of those days. One of the earliest references to clocks is to that in the possession of a Toddington yeoman in 1623.[8] A little later James Ford (d.1697) made clocks at Goldington.[9] The son of an Ickwell blacksmith, Thomas Tompion,[10] went to London, met the scientist Robert Hooke, and became a member of the clockmakers' company in 1671. In 1675 he made for the king one of the first English watches with a balance spring; and he made clocks for the Royal Observatory in 1676. His skill was such that he was called the father of English watch and clockmaking. He still kept in touch with his home county; on a bell in Willington church is the inscription "Thomas Tompion fecit 1671".

All these occupations were found in other counties, but there also developed some particularly associated with this area. Pillow lace,[11] first heard of in the northeast at Eaton Socon, was now most strongly established in the west and spreading into Buckinghamshire. In the countryside and also in the towns poor children were taught so that they could earn money. Sometimes there was an actual lace "school", run by the overseers, as at Woburn in 1618 (ch. 24), where the children made lace under supervision. Sometimes a child made lace at home, and the overseer provided thread and bobbins; the Kempston[12] overseers note "given to Saunders his daughter to buy her thread and bobbins, 6d." in 1677; and at Podington[13] there were payments "for lace thread and learning", "learning the wench", and receipts for "the wench's lace", 1685. Probably in the country also non-pauper children made lace at home, for in the town we know that Ann

---

[7] C.R.O., ABP/W 1602/60.
[8] C.R.O., ABP/W 1623/189.
[9] C.R.O., ABP/W 1697/24; a clock by him is in Elstow Moot Hall.
[10] R. W. Symonds, *Thomas Tompion*; a clock by him is in Cecil Higgins Museum, Bedford. The first reference so far found to a watch owned (but not necessarily made) in Bedfordshire is in 1606 to one in the possession of Benjamin Pigott of Graven-hurst; ABP/W 1606/77. That the Willington bell is by Tompion appears from the fact that no

other Thomas Tompion of the right age is known at this time (his father d. 1665; and his nephew was too young). It is uncertain who made Northill church clock in 1706 (the famous Thomas Tompion d. 1708), but a connection of the Tompions, George Cooper, was churchwarden in this year.
[11] See *Pillow lace in the East Midlands* (Luton Museum publication).
[12] C.R.O., P 60/12.
[13] C.R.O., OR 975.

W

Smithson[14] of Ampthill in 1615 was "brought up at her book and needle" for 3 years, and for a further 3 years was "taught to make bone lace and to knit"; and so did women of good standing, like the wife of Henry Whitaker, master of the free school in Bedford (d. 1601).[15] Lacemaking was also practised by men, such as Richard King of Eversholt in 1621;[16] perhaps by those whose physique was too slight for heavy work but who had the needed dexterity.

The pillow used at this time was bolster-shaped; it was balanced on the knee; and bobbins had no beads. Whether there was yet devised the method of focussing light from one candle on several pillows, by means of inverted bottles of water round it, is not clear; but there must have been need for it in the lace "school" in winter. In summer work was done outside.

As time went on, the trade was organised by lacemen, who distributed thread and patterns (still called parchments because originally pricked on parchment); and collected and disposed of the finished lace. Lacemen are known in this century at Stevington, Harrold, Turvey, Marston and Cranfield; and sometimes Bedfordshire documents refer to lacemen over the Buckinghamshire border at Olney and Newport Pagnell. The lace which Richard Newman of Marston, laceman, had in his possession in 1641 was valued at £10.[17] At this date when lace was a feature of the gentry's dress, there was a ready sale for it at fairs, where it was sometimes stolen (ch. 24).

Matmaking was another craft which now came to the fore. How soon the early custom of strewing rushes on the floor gave place to weaving the rushes into mats is uncertain, but the first matmaker identified is Godfrey Basse of Elstow (d. 1628);[18] his name seems to have an occupational derivation, so the craft may be much older. Other matmakers are known in 1634 and 1639, and they increase as time goes on. In this century the trade was mainly along the river, as at Kempston, Oakley, Pavenham, Sharnbrook and Carlton; and also farther afield, presumably where there was a brook big enough to provide rushes, as at Cranfield or Wilstead. Probably at this time the matmakers catered for local demand; later they were to supply London.[19]

In the south of the county, as in north Hertfordshire, straw was already being used to make strawplait for hats.[20] In general this was a simpler process and a simpler occupation than pillow-lace, and the material was easy to come by. There appears to be no counterpart to the laceman as organiser. The method of disposal was to take the finished plait to the local plait-market at Dunstable or

[14] C.R.O., ABP/W 1615/47.
[15] C.R.O., ABP/W 1601/121.
[16] C.R.O., T 42/471.
[17] C.R.O., ABP/W 1640-1/93.
[18] C.R.O., occupations index.
[19] See V.C.H. ii, 124-5. The story there given of the industry deriving from a child Hipwell being sent from London in 1665 to escape the plague cannot

be true as it stands; but it may be that the first known matmaker in this family, Daniel Hipwell in the 18th cent., was the first to organise the trade on a larger scale.
[20] The story attributing strawplait to Mary Queen of Scots and the Napiers is on a par with that attributing pillow lace to Catherine of Aragon.

Luton (or Hitchin). In the next century, and possibly in this, plaiting straws were bought to set the poor to work.

One of the first local references to straw hats is in 1657 when Frances Fox of Wilstead left her straw hat in her will,[21] but this may have been a Leghorn hat. Hats were stolen from a Dunstable waggon in 1682 (ch. 24). The extent of the trade is known only from a petition in 1689 in which several villages joined with Dunstable and Luton to protest against an act to encourage the wearing of woollen hats. These villages were Caddington, Eaton Bray, Kensworth, Studham, Sundon, Totternhoe, Whipsnade and Wingfield, together with some in Herts. and Bucks. The petition said that more than a thousand families depended on the trade.[22]

The importance of the villages as trading centres in general is indicated by the survival of trading tokens from one village in four in the years preceding the introduction of copper coinage in 1672.[23] For instance, in Barton William Hopkins issued a token; at Clifton, John Samm's is dated 1664; at Wilden, Thomas Spring, grocer, 1667; at Husborne Crawley, Edmund Green, 1668; at Shillington, Jonathan Carter, 1667; and for Shefford there are five.

YEOMEN AND HUSBANDMEN

Though it was a basically arable economy with a mixture of stock and cereal, there now seems more specialisation. A scattering of dairymen occurs over the county from Pertenhall to Salford. A smaller number, mainly in the south, as at Potsgrove, Hockliffe and Eaton Bray, are called graziers; apparently they fattened for the London market animals driven down from the north of England or from Wales (a Welsh drover boy died at Hockliffe in 1669). The most striking concentration from 1610 onward is that of gardeners, who occur along the green-sand ridge and especially at Sandy, again probably producing for the London market. They operated intensively on a small scale, like John Palmer of Sandy, who when he died in 1661 left each of his 5 younger children small plots; thus his son David was to have "4 a. lying to one piece in Kenwick Field", 1 a. in Long Swarden furlong, and ½ a. adjoining "that I bought of ould John Wale".[24] The crops they grew are indicated by the will of Walter Caton of Old Warden in 1673, who left his two sons 2 lb. of carrot seed, 200 cabbage plants and a peck of peas; also 1s. each.[25] Woad was grown for dyeing; there was at Toddington a millhouse for woad.[26]

Of yeomen farming on more general lines, there is great variety. Some were still on the up-grade, adding to their holdings a few acres at a time. Some launched their sons into other walks of life. Some supplemented their holdings by renting additional land. Others seem to be only tenants, and on a small scale

[21] C.R.O., ABP/W 1660/44.
[22] J. Dony, *The straw hat industry*, 19.
[23] J. H. Blundell, *Bedfordshire 17th cent. tokens*.

[24] C.R.O., PM 414.
[25] C.R.O., ABP/W, 1673/89.
[26] C.R.O., Fac. 34 (original in Dorset R.O.).

at that.

The Beaumont family[27] of Flitton may serve as an example of the first. When Henry Beaumont of Greenfield, yeoman, in 1635 married a neighbouring yeoman's daughter, their marriage settlement dealt with only about 15 a. Many small purchases swelled the Beaumont holding: 2½ a. in 1651; 1 a. in 1655; 2 a. in 1662; 2 a. in 1663; 9 a. in 1667; 41 a. in 1668; 5 a. in 1677; and when in 1700 Thomas Beaumont married a gentleman's daughter, over 100 a. are mentioned. The Gambles of Pulloxhill were also rising. Richard Gamble, yeoman, died in 1581; one of his descendants was the lawyer George who became under-sheriff about 1637; and another, Henry, is called gentleman in the Flitton court rolls. They became Quakers; and when a Quaker meeting was held at the house of Thomas Gamble he was fined £20 in 1670; he would not pay the fine, and 5 cows were taken in distraint.[28]

Trade was another possibility. Thomas Johnson,[29] a successful merchant tailor of London who in 1624 founded a school at Lidlington, may well have been of yeoman origin. The Silsoe yeoman family of Sparkes took to trade; John went to Peterborough, and prospered as a grocer; he sold his 48 a. in Silsoe in 1682, by which time he was described as gentleman.[30]

Of a yeoman who was a tenant, but who was able to purchase land of his own, Henry Richards of Keysoe is an example.[31] He gives the impression of being a good man of business. He bought 4 closes from John Sharpe in Keysoe, and another from Walter Bennett, besides 2 closes in Huntingdonshire; and he also lent money on mortgage. The land he occupied as tenant on the St. John estate consisted of 46 a. in Keysoe Brook End, for which he paid £12 10s. p.a. rent. In 1654 he settled the greater part of his land on his eldest son Walter; and when he died in 1657 his younger son Henry had the purchases listed above and the money due on mortgage. He was still able to leave £3 to the poor. A more modest example is John Giles of Bletsoe,[32] yeoman (d. 1672), who rented 36½ a. and had been able to buy a close of 8 a. He left his best coat to his son John, his next best coat to his son-in-law, and 10s. each to two grandchildren.

Some men describe themselves in their wills as yeomen, though they seem to have no land of their own, and even the land they occupied as tenants appears (from a St. John estate survey) to be modest. The majority of farms on this estate contained less than 100 a. (an exceptionally large one of 279 a. was let to Robert Sampson, gentleman).[33] Some of these tenants had sizeable cash reserves; Silvester Addington of Melchbourne, yeoman, (d. 1651), who left each married daughter for her children an ewe and a lamb, had £100;[34] and Simon Latham

27 C.R.O., L 5/141–281.
28 J. Besse, *Sufferings*, ii Cf. C.R.O., L. 12/15–16/9.
29 C.R.O., X 196; see also *Charity Commission Reports*.
30 C.R.O., L 5/44–8.

31 C.R.O., GY 10, f.219; ABP/W 1657/36.
32 C.R.O., GY 10, f.131; ABP/W 1671–2/22.
33 C.R.O., GY 10. f.216d.
34 C.R.O., GY 10, f.280; ABP/W 1651/27.

of Bletsoe, yeoman, had deposited £50 for safe-keeping in his landlord's hands.[35]
Even John Marshall of Bletsoe, who rented only 18 a., was able to leave his four
younger children £5 each; while the five elder ones, apparently already launched
in life, had 12d.[36] But there were a number of small tenants who apparently
were not prosperous enough to make wills at all; perhaps three out of every four.

So far mention has been made only of freehold. In some areas copyhold
tenure was to continue for a long while to come. It was now purely a matter of
tenure and not of status; a yeoman, a gentleman, even a lord, would think nothing
of becoming a copyhold tenant for a piece of land that he needed to round off
what he already had; and some yeomen were simply copyholders. One copyholder
could buy from another, so long as the transaction went through the manor
court. But as quit rents stabilised and prices rose, it was less and less worth while
for the lord to pay for the collection of dues and the holding of the court unless
the manor was large. Throughout the 17th cent. manor courts were held at
longer and longer intervals. Copyhold tenure was strong, for instance, on the
old Ramsey manors of Barton, Cranfield and Shillington; also at Caddington,
Houghton Regis, on the Kempston manors, and at Stevington. With such of the
Wrest Park estate as had remained together it continued, as at Blunham, Clophill
and Gravenhurst. It had the best chance of survival where the ownership was
fairly stable, but even then the meetings of the court were often interrupted in the
uncertain period of the interregnum. Many courts of small manors had completely
disappeared long before then; in 1634 it was said of the manor of Budna in Northill
"this manor is long since extinct and fallen to the ground; there remains not
extant at this day any rental or court roll of it, nor any sign of such a manor;
but only some certain deeds and conveyances that mention that there was such a
manor once."[37]

The list of a Keysoe yeoman's farm equipment comprises all his ploughs
and carts, plough timber and cart timber unframed, 4 ladders, 2 iron harrows and
5 wooden harrows, an iron drag, rolls, 6 pitchforks, 3 muck forks, all his shovels,
a riddle, a ring sieve, 4 sacks and a gig.[38]

COTTAGERS

"The commonalty hate the yeomen", said Lord Ailesbury.[39] The St. John
estate survey in the 1620's gives information about cottagers; this estate being
one of the comparatively rare ones where in one or two cases practically the whole
of the parish belonged to one lord. In the small parish of Melchbourne there were
in the 1620's 11 small farms; there were also craftsmen – Thomas Hodgkin,
blacksmith, held 15 a.; Gilbert Bromwell, carpenter, had 3 a.; Peter Bromwell
was tenant of the windmill; and Hugh Woodfall kept the inn. Finally there were

[35] C.R.O., GY 10, f.133; ABP/W 1649/43.
[36] C.R.O., GY 10, f.134; ABP/W 1632/54.
[37] B.H.R.S. i, 251.

[38] C.R.O., ABP/R 33, f.68d.
[39] T. Bruce, Memoirs, p.441.

14 cottagers, of whom the largest, William Edmundes, held 5 a.; while John Mole and Widow Geery lived in two adjoining cottages on the waste with no land at all.[40] Nearly 50 years later the hearth tax return of 1671 shows much the same position; there were 35 householders (apart from Lord Bolingbroke); of these, 15 – no doubt mainly yeomen – had more than one hearth; and of the 20 with one hearth, 4 were receiving poor relief.[41]

Where the land in one parish was held by several owners, an estate survey is of limited use. Some parish books survive for this century. In the large parish of Shillington in 1610 175 householders were assessed for church rates.[42] Of these, 63 were paying only 1d. (the highest rate paid was 4s. 6d.). At Shillington the hearth tax return of 1671 seems to show a slight decline with 146 householders; of these, 73 had more than one hearth; of the remainder, 28 were receiving alms or were too poor to be assessed for tax.[43]

At Flitwick there is information only for the end of the period, and here only expenditure accounts survive (neither poor nor church rates). In 1671 there were 62 householders; of these only 17 had more than one hearth; of the remainder, 10 were too poor to be assessed for tax, and 8 of these (including several widows) apparently had no hearth at all.[44] The overseers' accounts bear out this picture; in 1677 they were paying relief to Goody Fountain, Goody Woodard, Goody Fipp, Widows Pracket and Sirkett, and Ben Crouch being sick.[45]

Thus in 1671 in these three parishes the numbers receiving alms or relief or too poor to be assessed for tax were respectively 11%, 16% and 19%; but there is no certainty that the standard applied was uniform. Even above this line there were probably several whose life was a struggle. In the county as a whole more than half the total number of householders (56%) lived in houses with one hearth; John Bunyan was of this number; however, such a house could have a modicum of comfort (ch. 26).

The proportion of cottagers with common right had declined with growing population. Only old cottages had common right. At Carlton in 1668 out of 47 dwellings, 27 were "new erected cottages that have no commons"; while several of the remainder have against them a second name in brackets, apparently indicating that ownership of the cottage and common right had passed from cottager to landlord; thus against "Grunden's" is "(Mrs. Godard)" – Mrs. Godard was a gentlewoman who died in 1670.[46]

The more prosperous cottagers made wills. A Stopsley cottager or labourer in 1619 left his youngest daughter Mary his cow, "the cow to remain in my wife's government so long as she thinketh good".[47] An Arlesey labourer in the same

---

[40] C.R.O., GY 10, f.278–97.
[41] B.H.R.S. xvi, 133.
[42] C.R.O., P 44/5/2.
[43] B.H.R.S. xvi, 81, 98.

[44] B.H.R.S. xvi, 119–20.
[45] C.R.O., P 59/12.
[46] C.R.O., GA 1122/6; B.H.R.S. xvi, 150.
[47] C.R.O., ABP/R 33, f.11d.

year mentioned in his will his copyhold of 2 a., and left two money bequests of £5 each.[48]

DOMESTIC SURROUNDINGS

The 17th cent. had much more of a money-based economy than any previous period; and as the century progressed bequests were stated in terms of money instead of objects. Yet enough evidence remains, either in wills early in the period or in inventories, to show an increasingly wide range and higher standard of domestic possessions: coffers may be painted or red; chairs turned; stools joined; there are cupboards; sometimes cushions; sheets may be double-stitched or plain-hemmed; some towels are coarse, but others are wrought with blue, and so are napkins; warming pans occur; exceptionally a pillow-bere may be laced. A Marston husbandman mentions a trunk marked "M.T. 1674".[49]

It is also clear that in all classes of country-dwellers there was a wide range of variation in their positions. As in the 16th cent., the label attached to a man tells nothing certain; his individual circumstances must be traced. Bearing this caveat in mind, three brief examples of the contents of a country home and homestead are given here.[50] They are in fact those of yeoman, miller and labourer (or cottager), but it would be better to think of them as first, second and third villager.

Edward Freeman of Stotfold (d. 1617) was fairly well-to-do.[51] His furniture included 5 chairs, 15 stools, 4 standing (4-poster) beds with curtains and 4 other beds, 2 cupboards, and a "fair press", and 40 pr. sheets; his extensive domestic utensils included 7 spits and 4 silver spoons; and his livestock ran to 9 horses, 60 sheep, 10 cattle, an unspecified number of pigs, 20 hens, 20 ducks, and 3 turkeys; while among his farm equipment were 5 carts, harrows and ploughs.

The house of Oliver Asplam was more modest (d. 1619).[52] He had no chairs, 6 stools, 2 beds with "furniture" and 2 other beds; and 2 chests.

Thomas Sexton of Eaton Socon (d. 1610) had a little money put by him; but the only one of his possessions, besides his clothes and a little barley, which was thought worth valuing was a chest worth 2s.[53]

The style of clothes worn by country folk changed little; they were for use and meant to last. A Stopsley cottager left his son his best doublet, sword and dagger.[54] Armour, incidentally, was owned by several; among the possessions of a Milton Ernest yeoman are noted his sword and fowlingpiece; a Blunham man had a pistol; and probably country neighbours of the Potton baker had, like himself, musket, bandolier and rest.[55] A Fenlake carpenter left to friends his best breeches, doublet and a pair of hose; and to his daughter his cloak.[56]

---

[48] *Ibid.*, f.8.
[49] C.R.O., ABP/W 1696–7/143.
[50] For many fuller instances, see *B.H.R.S.* xx.
[51] C.R.O., ABP 4/188.
[52] C.R.O., ABP 4/190.
[53] C.R.O., ABP 4/181
[54] C.R.O., ABP/R 33, f.11d.
[55] *B.H.R.S.* xx, 76, 89, 101.
[56] C.R.O., ABP/R 33, f.113.

Their grandmother's best and secondbest gowns were bequeathed to a husbandman's two granddaughters; and the elder also had her grandmother's best hat, a black stuff apron and a holland apron.[57] Sometimes there were colours; Cicely Woodward of Dunton had petticoats of red and russet;[58] and Mary Morton of Arlesey a green apron;[59] but "a silk girdle of a brown mingled colour" does not sound exciting; and velvet and chamlet such as Elizabeth Pendred of Dunstable had were not common in the countryside.[60] To judge by bequests, gloves were increasingly worn; and so were cross-cloths (head-squares) and kerchieves, whether "neckerchers" or "hankerchers"; a Roxton woman had one of needlework and another wrought with black silk.[61] There were also "safe-guards," or outer petticoats worn to protect the dress when riding pillion.

THE PARISH

Of the running of a parish, Pulloxhill gives an example.[62] In 1636 there were 58 householders; the chief landowner was Sir William Briers with 405 a.; and 8 men owned or occupied areas from 39 to 110 a.; but these were not the ones who ran the parish; neither, of course, did the 8 who had no land at all, some of whom may have had common right. It was the group of 42 men who held anything from 1 to 29 a. who alternated in the various offices. Some, like John Randall the blacksmith, served only once or twice. One who held office frequently was Edward Pennyfather, whose holding was 16 a.; in 1625 and 1629 he was churchwarden; in 1628 and 1634 overseer; and in 1627 surveyor. John Balls, who held 5 a., was surveyor in 1626, churchwarden in 1628, and surveyor in 1634; it is possible that he had land outside Pulloxhill, but he was a Pulloxhill resident, and he seems to have been too poor to make a will. Sir William Briers sometimes attended the vestry meeting; and occasionally better-off residents like the Gambles held office.

The work of the overseers of the poor was similar to that described for Potton (ch. 24) but on a smaller scale.[63] Of that of surveyors there is at this period little evidence for any parish, but probably at least a minimum was done on the main roads, otherwise pressure would be brought to bear. The constable had not only police duties, but was also responsible for collecting for the high constable of the hundred county rates when levied (they were kept at a minimum); and he had to make a general report on the parish to the judge at assizes. Usually he limited this to "all well"; but for Cople in 1667 one is unusually full. Slightly abbreviated, it reads as follows: "For popish recusants we have not any; we have not any persons that does absent themselves from worship on the Lord's day; our poor are provided for; we have not any that doth sell beer without license; our highways are in good repair; we have no engrossers of corn; we have no

57 *Ibid.*, f.53.
58 *Ibid.*, f.76.
59 *Ibid.*, f.98d.
60 *Ibid.*, f.62.
61 *Ibid.*, f.108d.
62 C.R.O., P 13/5.
63 Cf. also *Kempston history*, 48–52.

unlawful weights or measures to the best of our knowledge; we have not had any riots since the last assizes."

The public conscience now held that legally a poor neighbour could not be allowed to starve and a child must be cared for. There were also vague memories of old charities which had somehow lapsed, and official enquiries were held as at Northill in 1610 and Gravenhurst in 1613. Some were concerned to improve on the minimum. Some clergy set the example, such as Francis Dillingham at Wilden and Thomas Archer at Houghton Conquest. Joseph Bentham founded his charity at Wymington in 1665 in remembrance of the restoration of the monarchy. John Bryan in 1655 made provision for gowns and shoes for poor widows, and for penny loaves on Sunday at the church door after sermon in Ampthill, Marston and Maulden. Some benefactors, like Richard Grange at Cranfield in 1683, left money to provide for apprenticeships for poor children. But all this was haphazard: a few parishes had more than one benefaction; many at the end of this period still had none.

CIVIL WAR AND COMMONWEALTH

With the yeomen, as with the men in the market towns, it is hard to say how far they were politically conscious. Many of the constables who at the meeting in 1626 (ch. 23) opposed James I's demand for a benevolence must have been yeomen and craftsmen. Later there were parishes where many were in arrears with the payment of ship money;[64] at Husborne Crawley, Houghton Regis and Dean there were over 40 persons; and nearly as many at Kempston, Wootton, Henlow and Stotfold. But although a contemporary observer said that yeomen "care but little for their gentlemen",[65] even yeomen who had a 40s. freehold and who thought about public matters could at parliamentary elections do little more than acquiesce in what the gentry had arranged. Cottagers were still less concerned or even aware.

When war began, such interest as there may have been (and Henry Lowens at Bromham did try to obstruct parliamentary soldiers by putting a chain across the bridge) soon evaporated. Military service was not popular in any case;[66] response to summons was poor; and desertion soon began. In December 1644 it was given out in churches that soldiers who did not return in 8 days would be hanged without mercy. But in 1645 some recruits made off after they were equipped; and in 1646 80 out of 140 impressed men "ran away after they were delivered, before they were clothed and armed".

The conditions were not such as to encourage them.[67] Newport Pagnell had not adequate quarters for its garrison; some men had to sleep three in a bed. Clothing was often short; in May 1645 Sir Samuel Luke was demanding coats and breeches for a hundred; and there were two in his company that "had but

[64] B.H.R.S. xviii.
[65] T. Bruce, Memoirs, p.441.
[66] E.M.H. Leaflet iii, 5–7, 9.
[67] B.H.R.S. xlii, 48, 290, etc.

one pair of breeches between them, so that when one was up the other must upon necessity be in his bed". Pay was perpetually in arrears. There was a smallpox epidemic. It is not surprising that the garrison continually dwindled, and that parish constables were from time to time urged to apprehend straggling soldiers, and the constable was told that he would "answer the contrary at his peril".

Those who remained at home suffered from requisitions. In 1644 Manshead hundred said they could not send carts and labourers to strengthen the Newport fortifications; so much had been taken from them that "now, being seed-time, they have not horses to plough and sow their land".[68] Tools like picks and mattocks were also taken for Newport. Demands continued from parliamentary and Scottish troops quartered locally, who, being short of supplies, helped themselves. A troop in the Eversholt area in the spring of 1645 caused the inhabitants of Eversholt, Westoning and Ridgmont to make "divers complaints daily";[69] and even Lord Bolingbroke remonstrated with the committee of both kingdoms that the quartering of soldiers and the taking of horses had cost Bedfordshire £50,000 in two years; and that already some of the best farmers had given up their farms.[70] William Brasier of Pulloxhill, a small man with only 7 a., was probably lucky in that the parish allowed him 30s. when the soldiers took what was apparently his only horse.[71] Once at Elstow fair in 1645 local feeling erupted in "disturbances and violences" and the local people gave as good as they got; afterwards the soldiers "gave forth menacing words that they will be revenged", and the Bedfordshire committee wrote to Luke to appease them.[72]

When the actual fighting was over, times were still uneasy, even for parish affairs. At Pulloxhill in 1651 "three several meetings were appointed for neighbours to come together about the town businesses" without success.[73] In 1653 Margaret Pennyfather of Millbrook was indicted at Quarter sessions for speaking false and opprobrious words against the government.[74] During the protectorate such opinion as can be traced seems to be turning towards the monarchy. In 1659 a little group at Houghton Conquest and Millbrook planned to join a royalist rising and provided themselves with pistols;[75] these were Matthew Denton and his son, George Lawson, and two brothers Batt "whom I fetched out of a haymow, where they had lodged and in the woods near a fortnight, several other persons having been seen in the woods with them". Some of these were probably high-spirited young men, but George Lawson was rector of Millbrook.

As opposed to these, there must be remembered the many yeomen, craftsmen and cottagers who were now worshipping in Independent congrega-

[68] Ibid., 354.
[69] Ibid., 194.
[70] E.M.H. Leaflet iii, 14.
[71] C.R.O., P 13/5, p.39.

[72] B.H.R.S. xlii, 544.
[73] C.R.O., P 13/5, p.24.
[74] E.M.H. Leaflet iii, 5.
[75] Ibid., 12–13.

tions. Perhaps some of them were ex-soldiers who had served under Cromwell. After the restoration of the monarchy, they were to hold firm in their faith against the difficulties of years (ch. 22). Parliament was remote, even to the yeomen; but to thinking yeomen and craftsmen religion was immediate and personal. The ordinary man, in so far as he was perceptive, might feel himself to be politically of small account, but he knew that to God he was an individual of supreme importance. Perhaps this aspect of the spirit of the time is most vividly expressed in the will of Edward Snagge of Marston (albeit a gentleman): "My soul . . . I assuredly do hope shall fly with a merry note into heaven . . . as the bird doth into the air that hath escaped the fowler's net."[76]

SERVANTS AND WAGES

It is difficult to assess how far servants were recruited from country dwellers. A lord employed a great many; Lord Ailesbury's payroll for house and stables covered about 40 persons, from Mr. Tufton (for whom were bought periwig, silk stockings, and a silver-hilted sword) down to the woman who looked after the duck decoy for 6d. a week.[77] Often these are not given surnames; the accounts describe them as Susan laundrymaid, Betty dairymaid, Christopher postillion, or John foothuntsman. Laurence slaughterman killed the livestock on the home farm required for domestic consumption. Probably the men cooks, the butler, the ten footmen in livery, Lord Ailesbury's valet, and Lady Ailesbury's French maid were recruited in London; but some names like Joan and Mary Crouch and John Bartram have a local ring. Such service was well cared for; John coachman was tended when he was sick; and payment was made for "curing the kitchen boy's leg of a scald".

Even a gentleman, like Sir William Becher at Howbury, kept a good-sized domestic staff; his man cook had £8 p.a. and Lady Becher's maid £4, while Nan the washmaid had £2 10s.[78] Servants were employed on a humbler basis by yeomen and craftsmen; Peter Aucock of Keysoe, tailor, who died in 1681, left his maidservant his cottage "in consideration that she hath lived with me (and my wife when she was living) for 19 years and more, and hath done me very true and faithful service and never had any wages".[79]

Maximum wage rates were still laid down at quarter sessions, and one of these for 1684 has survived.[80] From this it seems that service in a gentleman's household might well exceed the legal rate, for the official annual rate for a washmaid was £2 (at Houghton Susan laundrymaid had £4).

Thus the other rates given may have equally little validity. In summer, when the working-day was longer, a master freemason should receive 1s. 4d. a day if food was supplied; a joiner the same; a bricklayer 1s.; a thatcher 11d.;

---

[76] C.R.O., ABP/W 1600/43; and cf. psalm 124, verse 7.
[77] B.H.R.S. xxxii, 122, 129.
[78] B.H.R.S. xxv, 133.
[79] C.R.O., C 1391.
[80] B.H.R.S. xxv, 129–37.

a carpenter 10d.; a tailor 6d. In winter the amount was less. Farmwork ranged from 1s. 2d. a day for reaping to 6d. for making hay (for a woman 3d.). A ploughman should have £5 p.a.

SIGNS OF CHANGE

By the end of this period there were signs of a trend which was to escalate in the next century – the growth of large estates. When in 1679 John Pearles of Flitton sold 14 a. to the Countess of Kent of Wrest Park, he agreed that if he ever sold other land adjoining hers, he would sell it to her at the same price.[81] A few fortunate landed families for various reasons (ch. 27) found themselves in a position where they could steadily expand. Why, however, did the small man sell, and why did the yeomen become, what some had always been at least in part, tenant-farmers? For this there seem to be various reasons.

Perhaps one is the continuing trend of able and active yeomen to turn to other walks of life, including trade. Again, the descendants of those who had become gentry did not always succeed in maintaining this position. In every walk of life there are ups and downs, failure of heirs and family mishaps (one testator referred to "money Abraham Dearmer that married my daughter against my will had and spent"; and another reduced a nephew's bequest because of "the great gains which his father and mother got clearly by me").[82] Another factor is that a yeoman did not necessarily aim at founding an estate, but at his death divided his holding among his various children, as did an earlier John Pearles (d. 1644).[83] Perhaps there were not now more sales of small amounts of land than there had been for centuries past, but among the yeomen such sales had evened themselves out; where one was unsuccessful, another bought from him. What was new was a determined purchase policy on the part of a few lords able to carry it out, with two centuries of peace in which to do so.

[81] C.R.O. L 5/25.
[82] C.R.O., ABP/W 1628/61 and 1685/80.
[83] C.R.O., ABP/W 1644/52.

THE HOME

Houses varied greatly. Of the more modest ones we get some idea from the parsonages of 1607.[1] Most clergy were vicars (the great tithes, at one time transferred to monasteries, now being in lay hands) and their stipends were low; so their style of living was like that of their neighbours. At Carlton the parsonage was of stone with a slate roof, and contained hall or livingroom, buttery and pantry, all "chambered over", that is to say, there were bedrooms above; the stone outbuildings were thatched and included kitchen, stable, dovehouse and barn. At Ravensden the vicarage was half-timbered and thatched. Further south, Husborne Crawley parsonage was half-timbered with a tiled roof, and it ran to a parlour. At Willington there was "a poor little vicarage house, unchambered" (i.e., with no upper rooms). Even when there were bedrooms upstairs they were often unceiled. Floors were sometimes earthen, as in part in Cardington parsonage, and probably all cottages had earthen floors. On the other hand, there were a few quite extensive parsonages, as at Barton, Blunham and Sandy (usually rectories), and these correspond with gentry's houses; they had from 20 to 30 rooms, boarded and ceiled; parlours; and many outbuildings, such as milkhouse, brewhouse, bakehouse, kilnhouse, dovehouse, cowhouse, stables, granary and barn.

A kind of slide-rule for gauging houses in the county is provided by the hearth tax imposed 1662–88 (the 1671 return is printed).[2] A fire of wood, peat or coal was then the only method of heating. For lighting a fire with flint and tinder, bracken or fern was used where available; at Haynes the rules were that no one should cut fern on the common warren before sunrise on Holy Cross day, that there should be only one scytheman for each house, and that he must carry only one load.[3] A Flitwick yeoman in 1634 left his wife 2 loads of fern and 3,000 turves.[4] The majority of houses had one hearth or fireplace for all purposes. Some houses no doubt had only two rooms, either one up and one down, and some like this survived into this century, or both on the ground floor. Others were more elaborate: round a central hearth, or rather built on at either end, there could be a number of rooms, Sometimes a new hearth was added; a Thorncote yeoman in 1621 directed his son to make his mother's room "fitting

[1] C.R.O., ABE 1.
[2] B.H.R.S. xvi.
[3] C.R.O., CRT 110/35.
[4] C.R.O., LL 17/80.

for her to make fire in it", and he left her half his firewood.[5] A Beeston yeoman who left his wife in 1611 the little parlour said that her sons were to bring her 3 loads of wood a year (and to see that her linen was washed as often as necessary).[6]

The hearth tax returns give the name of every householder, except the very poorest, with the number of hearths or fireplaces in his house, so that the rich man, having several hearths, paid more, and the man with one hearth less. Tracing parsonages in the 1671 returns, we find that the Ravensden vicarage had only one hearth, but the Carlton parsonage, perhaps extended since 1607, had 4, and that at Toddington had as many as 10. Investigating some of the actual yeoman families mentioned in the last chapter, we find Thomas Gamble at Pulloxhill had 4 hearths; and members of the Richards family at Keysoe had 3 or 2 hearths; but John Giles of Bletsoe had only 1. Of the tradesmen, Thomas Spring the Wilden grocer had 2 hearths; John Bassett of Cranfield, matmaker, had 1; two members of the Wooding family in Turvey, probably relatives of the 1687 laceman John, had respectively 3 and 1; and the Tompions, blacksmiths of Northill, had 1 hearth and 2 forges.[7] Some of these houses therefore could have been quite extensive.

Another way of describing a house is by the number of bays of building (a bay is the space between two main beams). At Thurleigh in 1604 on the Earl of Kent's estate the houses varied from 2 to 5 bays.[8] The 2-bay houses had two rooms on the ground floor and either a bedchamber or loft, and were less than 30 ft. long. The 5-bay house had hall, 2 chambers, kitchen and stable; it was 65 x 15 ft.

With the help of the hearth tax returns we can compare also the size of gentry's houses; and here the number of hearths is a better indication, for such houses had hearths or fireplaces with constant fires in all the main rooms, including bedrooms used by family and guests and upper servants. Here the number of hearths probably indicates the majority of rooms in the house (apart from attics for lower servants and larders and cellers for storage). The largest was Woburn Abbey as rebuilt by the 4th Earl of Bedford, with 82 hearths. Next was Luton Hoo (60), as reconstructed by Sir Robert Napier, but including part of the old Hoo house.[9] Much the same size was Lord Ailesbury's house on the boundary of Ampthill and Houghton Conquest (55). Wrest Park had 52; but in 1676 the young 11th Earl of Kent made a modest concession to fashion by building on to the old house a new north front in classical style.[10] The Earl of Cleveland's house at Toddington, inherited by Lady Henrietta Wentworth, had 45 hearths. Compared with these the St. John residences at Bletsoe and Melchbourne were comparatively modest (38 and 33). Of the gentry's houses, some were nearly

---

[5] C.R.O., CD 14.
[6] C.R.O., CD 10.
[7] Wrongly given as Thomkins. The cases cited are all from *B.H.R.S.* xvi.
[8] C.R.O., L 26/1442.
[9] Lysons, 109.
[10] C.R.O., L 31/228–43.

as large; Sir Oliver Luke's house at Cople had 27 hearths; that of Sir Francis Crawley at Someries had 23; but Sir William Boteler and Sir Lewis Dyve were more representative with 15 hearths.

The gardens of cottages were probably mainly devoted to herbs and vegetables, with perhaps one or two fruit trees. Yeomen had orchards; a Houghton Conquest yeoman in 1624, assigning some land to his son, stipulated that he was to have half the apples and other fruit from the orchard.[11] At Medbury, Elstow, 7 great walnut trees are specified.[12] Vegetables mentioned by the gentry include artichokes, asparagus, beans, carrots, cucumbers, cauliflowers, cabbage, mushrooms, onions, parsley, parsnips, spinach, sprouts and turnips; besides the ordinary soft fruits elderberries were used; and orchard fruits include prunes, damsons and apricots, besides warden pears.[13] Named varieties were obtainable from nurserymen in the neighbourhood of London; over 50 varieties of pear, nectarine, plum and cherry were bought by the Earl of Kent in 1693 from nurserymen at Knightsbridge and Twickenham; he even got his warden peartree from the latter.[14] Dr. William Foster, the opponent of Bunyan, was partial to an apple.[15]

For the gentry, gardening as an art was an increasing interest, as at Chicksands, Cople and Howbury (ch. 23). Helen Chernock, apparently recovering from smallpox, wrote to her mother that she was well enough to walk in the garden.[16] When Sir William Boteler let Harrold House, he stipulated that the tenant should preserve the garden and walks therein with pruning, weeding, new gravelling and rolling, in such sort as the beauty might be preserved.[17]

Educational opportunity varied. Children, even in gentle families, were taught to read by means of a horn-book. This consisted of a small sheet of paper on which was printed the Lord's prayer and the alphabet, mounted on a piece of wood to be held in the hand, and protected by horn. Sir Lewis Dyve's little son John in 1647 "tore the horn off his book with a pretence that it hindered him in coming to his letters".[18] Later the sons of lords and gentry might, like Lord Ailesbury, be taught at home by a tutor, or be sent away to school as a Francklin went to Winchester. For the rest, education in Latin grammar was obtainable for a few at the free school in Bedford or at that in Houghton Conquest. Here Sir Francis Clerke founded a school in 1632; the schoolmaster was a graduate and appointed by Sidney Sussex College, Cambridge; but whereas Harpur endowed his school with land in an expanding area, Clerke arranged a fixed charge of £24 on property in the parish; so that the two schools, starting from comparable origins, were to have a widely different future.

[11] C.R.O., HW 32.
[12] C.R.O., AD 1022. Leases mention preserving fruit trees; cf. KK 159.
[13] C.R.O., L 31/194, 291.
[14] C.R.O., L. 31/296.
[15] C.R.O., FN 270.
[16] E.M.H. ii, 10.
[17] C.R.O., TW 685.
[18] Dorset R.O., D 124 (Ilchester MSS.).

Others began to make permanent provision for country schools which would at least teach reading, writing and arithmetic.[19] The number of children to be taught free was always few, though the master could take other children who paid small fees; at Streatley in 1686 Richard Norton provided for 8 children. The premises were usually an ordinary cottage, the children being taught in at least one case in the upper room or loft. If the schoolmaster should "live disorderly or be contentious" he must be dismissed – so Thomas Peate laid down at Wilden in 1625. The largest school was that at Houghton Regis, where Thomas Whitehead, himself a schoolmaster at Repton, generously devoted his inheritance of a farm to provide for an "honest painful schoolmaster" to teach 20 children "in the place of my birth to which I give great respect". A uniform was provided at Lidlington in 1624, due to the special interest of the founder, Thomas Johnson, merchant tailor; it consisted of jerkins and breeches of grey frieze, stockings of blue yarn, and hats with watchet (blue) bands. With Thurleigh, Wilstead, and possibly Clophill, besides those previously mentioned (ch. 21), there were several of these village schools by 1689, besides those in the towns (ch. 24). In many other villages a schoolmaster or dame taught a few children for small fees (ch. 22); such schools were attended only by the children of those parents who could and did make the effort to afford it. The great majority of children received no teaching.

HEALTH

Many diseases were at this time unidentified. Occasional outbreaks of plague in the towns have been noted (ch. 24); and sometimes, as at Henlow in 1603 and Edworth in 1625 village cases occurred; or plague may be suspected from the large number of burials.[20] By the late 17th cent. plague died out. Smallpox replaced it as the main scourge, as at Flitton in 1685.[21] Typhus was known as gaol-fever. Gout, the stone, and ague were common.

Surgery was rarely attempted (it was only in this century that the circulation of the blood was first understood). One use of it was for the stone; Thomas Middleton of Lidlington went to Oxford to be cut for the stone, but died there.[22] Edward Cater of Kempston went to London in 1652 to be operated on for an abscess in the armpit, and he survived.[23] At the university of Cambridge students learnt anatomy by seeing the professor perform one dissection a year, and anaesthetics and antisepsis were of course unknown.

Medical training was little better, as it was based on the writings of Hippocrates. Dr. John Symcotts of Sutton, who was Cromwell's physician, had

[19] *Charity Commission Reports;* often the relevant documents have been deposited in C.R.O. by the parish concerned.
[20] *B.Par.Reg.* xxvi and ii. See in the same series Roxton, 1620 and 1625; Cardington, 1604, 1616–7; Felmersham, 1618; Cople, 1653–4; Odell, 1610; Swineshead, 1625; Stondon, 1631; Bromham, 1604–5; Tingrith, 1665; Cranfield, 1657–8; Thurleigh, 1657; Wootton, 1604.
[21] *B.Par.Reg.* xviii.
[22] C.R.O., ABP/W 1607–8/162.
[23] *Kempston history,* p.27.

a pragmatic approach. He kept a medical notebook in which he recorded cases in his practice and the treatment he tried out on them.[24] Thus in 1636 in what was apparently an epidemic of scarlet fever, he notes that the children were very sick, desired nothing but cold beer, and "fell presently into a general redness of the skin all over" and were very feverish. The cure was keeping them in bed or very warm and giving posset drink. Like his colleagues, he was very ready to resort to blood-letting (by venesection, scarification or leeches), emesis or vomiting, and purgatives and clysters (enemas). He used venesection for 14-year old Elizabeth Burgoyne's illness, which a recent medical writer has identified as pneumonia.[25]

There were few doctors. One or two eminent doctors had a local connection, Dr. Laurence Wright (another of Cromwell's physicians)[26] with Knotting, and Sir Charles Scarburgh, physician to Charles II, with Flitton; but they were called in only by a few of the gentry. There were also some lesser known ones, such as Francis Bannister of Bedford (d. 1666), who left his grandson his silver instruments pertaining to physic and chirurgery.[27] A doctor of Bedfordshire origin (he was born at Carlton) who practised at Stratford-on-Avon and died in 1635 was John Hall, who married Shakespeare's elder daughter.[28]

In general the lady of the house or the goodwife prescribed her own remedies, whether herbal or traditional. Those of the Countess of Kent had a great reputation and were printed.[29] A remedy for consumption handed down in the Gery household at Bushmead was: take 100 snails, bruise them and pick them from the shells, put them in 2 quarts of new milk scalding hot, and distil with mint and red fennel.[30] That for palsy recommended to Goodwife Viccar of Sutton by a neighbour was to lie for 24 hours together close covered with 2 large sheepskins new taken off the slaughtered sheep; "she endured 17 hours of her task, sweating exceedingly all that time, and so was recovered."[31]

The handicapped were at a great disadvantage. A father in 1634 hoped to cure his son's weak sight by means of a silk collar containing herbs.[32] William Goldsmith of Shefford, who had two deaf and dumb sons, urged their brother to provide them with all things necessary, "meat, drink, linen, woollen, hose, shoes"; and urged his kinsman in 1639 "to see that my deaf and dumb children be not wronged".[33] "Blind Hugh" (b. 1626) was a charge on Kempston parish all his life.[34]

Mental illness was still less understood and was treated with ignorant cruelty.

24 B.H.R.S. xxxi.
25 C. Newman, Diagnostic investigation (Medical History, iv, 322–9).
26 B.Par.Reg. xviii; and V.C.H. iii, 286.
27 C.R.O., ABP/W 1655-6/8.
28 Beds . Bib. supplt., 72. For other early local doctors, see J. H. Raach, English country physicians 1603–43, p.96.

29 A choice manual, or Rare and select secrets in physick and chirurgery, 2nd ed. 1653.
30 C.R.O., GY 7/3.
31 B.H.R.S. xxxi, 71–2.
32 C.R.O., X 125/59.
33 C.R.O., ABP/R 35, f.127.
34 Kempston history, p.49.

X

Among poorer folk the mentally sick man became the traditional village idiot. William Hanscombe of Shillington, yeoman, was detained in a madhouse and his friends not suffered to see him.[35] In the case of a man of property, some steps had to be taken; the court of wards could declare him unable to manage his affairs and appoint a committee for the purpose. This happened to Edmund Francklin of Bolnhurst about 1630. At sermon time in church he used these words "that his brother George was God the Father"; he also broke windows, threw things into the fire, threw a great stone at his brother and threatened to shoot him.[36] The visit paid him by Helkiah Crook, keeper of Bethlehem Hospital, is believed to be the earliest recorded domiciliary visit by a psychiatrist. Dr. Crook "came down from London in his coach and 4 horses, attended with 3 men, and carried him to London to the doctor's own house where he was fairly entreated and well used".

LEISURE AND PLEASURE

Indoors, cards were a source of amusement, though not for puritans.[37] The games played are not always recognisable, for instance "all fours" at Biggleswade in 1679.[38] So too were shovelboard, for which Edward VI shillings were preferred; dice and backgammon or "playing at tables".[39] Books were mainly religious; for the poor, the Bible and one or two simple devotional works; for the rich, perhaps a Bible with silver clasps, like Thomas Boteler's in 1654; he had also a commentary by the Dutch theologian, Grotius, works of religious controversy by George Abbot, Cornelius Burgess and Joseph Hall, histories, and a translation of Tacitus.[40] Drama also was read during the commonwealth. For ladies, embroidery was still a main activity; they embroidered bookcovers, caskets, and pictures in stumpwork showing figures in semi-relief; and Grace Dyve in 1647 was learning cutwork.[41] For men, "taking of a pipe of tobacco" was a common indulgence, as with the thief John Jones, found in the Crown at Ampthill in 1668.[42]

Of contemporary musicmaking an incident that occurred in Okey's regiment in the Civil War, though not in this county, gives an idea. An accusation of singing bawdy songs was brought against a captain, and he explained what happened. A soldier found himself billeted in a musical home, and asked his captain round. The householder produced from a press-cupboard fife, recorder and cithern, and the family played very well in consort, the captain meanwhile taking a pipe of tobacco. Apparently the family did not sing, but a soldier came in who had a good voice. The captain then sang over to the company once or twice "New oysters", and after twice or thrice, as he "struck time" with his hand, they sang their parts

[35] C.R.O., H/WS 789–97.
[36] C.R.O., FN 1060–84; and see R. Hunter and I. Macalpine, *Three hundred years of psychiatry*, 103–6.
[37] *Church book of Bunyan meeting* (ed. Harrison), f.54.
[38] C.R.O., HSA 1679 W 57.
[39] C.R.O., ABC 5, p.64.
[40] C.R.O., TW 1137.
[41] Dorset R.O., D.124 (Ilchester MSS.)
[42] C.R.O., HSA 1668 S 52–5.

very well. He then sang by himself "I met with Joan of Kent", and "There dwells a pretty maid". "I sang but merely for the music sake, not thinking any hurt at all."[43]

Most ordinary folk must have performed and sung by ear. The gentry had printed books of music, like *The lute's apology for her excellence*. They also had MS. music; an MS. book preserved by the Botelers has a tune called "Lady St. John's delight".[44] Two contemporary songs, one "In praise of tobacco", and one on the revolution of 1688, have been preserved in an ecclesiastical formulary.[45] It was in this century that the traditional tunes for country dances were first collected and printed.

Besides the lute there were virginals, an early form of keyboard instrument. Virginals were owned by an Eaton Socon yeoman in 1620; by William Bowstred at Toddington in 1623; and by the Wilden schoolmaster in 1628; and in 1668 a watch lying on a pair of virginals was stolen from the house of William Whitbread at Cardington.[46] The fiddle was played by Bunyan. There were also travelling fiddlers, and players on pipe and tabor, like William Norton of Wollaston who in 1671 inveigled away from a Shefford inn a maid (with some of her landlady's linen), telling her that he would carry her into a brave country and buy her new clothes.[47]

Outdoor games were growing in popularity, and gradually ousting archery, though there are references to the common butts as late as 1661.[48] Bowls were especially popular in town and village. Dunstable's bowling alley was in 1624 leased for 6s. 6d. p.a. to William Metcalfe of the White Horse[49] (who later was in arrears with his ship money). Gentlemen like Lord Bolingbroke had their own bowling-greens.[50] Ordinary villagers bowled too, as at Podington in 1616;[51] bowls are mentioned also at Clophill, Harrold, Renhold, Toddington and Wrestlingworth.[52] Football, originally a game for the open street, was now usually played in a close, as at Colmworth, Eaton Socon or Felmersham.[53] An early version of cricket was stoolball.[54] Tipcat was popular at Elstow. Nineholes (a kind of bowling game) was common.[55]

Seasonal festivities continued to be observed. The accounts of the Becher family of Howbury on several occasions show payments for Valentines, as in 1670.[56] Though puritan opinion might be hostile, May celebrations frequently continued.[57] The maypole is mentioned at Woburn in 1618, on which occasion there was a riot (whether caused by difference of opinion or by too much beer

43 *B.H.R.S.* xxxv, 54–5.
44 C.R.O., TW 1172–5.
45 C.R.O., ABC 20, f.87d. 151a.
46 *B.H.R.S.* xx, 54; C.R.O., ABP/W 1623/189 and 1628/40; *E.M.H.* iv, 15.
47 *E.M.H.* iv, 13.
48 At Gt. Barford; C.R.O. WW 141.
49 Cambridge University Library, Ee.3.34, f.32.
50 C.R.O., GY 10.
51 C.R.O., OR 1903.
52 C.R.O., AD 1057; L 4/299; PO 1; WW 94; X 222/5.
53 C.R.O., ABE 1; X 202/193; GA 1341; see also ch. 22.
54 C.R.O., OR 1901.
55 C.R.O., ABC 4 *passim*.
56 C.R.O., PO 3; also in 1684 and 1685.
57 C.R.O., P. 118/5.

is not clear). In 1672 incidental evidence in a case at the assizes shows that on May morning maybushes were stuck at the doors of divers people, again at Woburn.[58] Milkmaids had presents on Mayday, at least in Houghton Conquest.[59] At Christmas at Kempston the churchwardens from 1680 onwards usually paid about a shilling for holly to dress the church;[60] the gentry exchanged presents, tipped their servants, had music such as drummers or a fiddler, sometimes killed a Christmas bullock, and gave to the poor.[61]

Less commendable was cockfighting. It was practised for 3 years 1634–6 on Shrove Tuesday in Knotting church with the connivance of the churchwardens, until protest was made, not at the "sport" but at the place used.[62] At Ampthill it took place on Boxing Day; and John Newland, who in 1680 wanted money to bet at the "great cocking" took the opportunity of the Christmas Day service to break into a house while the family were at church and steal £6 from a trunk.[63] There was bear-baiting in Woburn church in 1612.[64]

For killing game, hawks were mainly used, – probably guns were not yet sufficiently accurate and precise. Bulstrode Whitelocke came hawking in Bedfordshire.[65] Sir Oliver Luke, while in London, sent his falconer to his son at Newport Pagnell, and Sir Samuel kept him supplied with game, including on one occasion in 1644 3 brace of pheasants, 2 couple of teal, 6 cocks, 2 brace of partridges and 2 dozen snipe; and once a heron is mentioned.[66] When in 1645 Luke captured Prince Rupert's falcon "one of the highest fliers that ever was seen", the general commanded that it should be returned, so a trumpeter took falconer and hawk to Oxford.[67] Dogs do not seem to have been well disciplined, for they often managed to demolish one or more birds. Larks were netted and sold for the table in quantities; thus "12 dozen larks" (1689).[68] Ducks were decoyed; a map shows the decoy near Houghton House.

Rabbits were sent weekly by Sir Samuel Luke to his father in London during 1644.[69] Besides being a delicacy, they were of use for their fur. When James Beverley let Clophill warren to a Silsoe poulterer in 1641, he stipulated that at the end of the lease there should be at least 560 rabbits in the warren, of which 300 must be black.[70] How this was ensured is not clear.

Gentlemen hunted deer in parks; and sometimes venison was killed by the keeper as required. In wartime it was an acceptable present for the officers or the general.[71] In peacetime lords and gentry distributed it to friends, and it made a festive occasion. William Symcotts of Clifton in 1684 sent some to his cousin Robert: "your excellent haunch of venison came sweet and good to me on

[58] C.R.O., HSA 1672 S 50.
[59] C.R.O., X 289, f.284.
[60] C.R.O., P 60/5/3.
[61] C.R.O., PO 3, pp.9, 15, 24, 53.
[62] V.C.H. iii, 139.
[63] E.M.H. iv, 14.
[64] C.R.O., R (bdle A.25).

[65] B. Mag. i, 317 & cf. 241–7.
[66] B.H.R.S. xlii, 74, 115.
[67] Op.cit., 181, 186, 199.
[68] C.R.O., L 31/195, p.253.
[69] B.H.R.S. xlii, 73.
[70] C.R.O., L 4/297.
[71] B.H.R.S. xlii, 267, 415.

Saturday morning; on Sunday we ate it. I had my brother Gregory, his son, and a neighbour or two; and if it had not been Sunday we should have been heartily merry."[72] Sometimes it was sent ready made into a pasty or pie.

Humbler country folk coveted game, and when the keepers came upon poachers there were bitter fights.[73] Two poachers in Ampthill warren in 1666, Ambrose Whittamore and William Evans, found the keepers at 4 a.m. removing the nets they had set to catch rabbits. In the fight that followed, Evans escaped, but Whittamore was fatally wounded. His body was taken to the Bell at Ampthill, with the net and a staff as evidence. George Sole of Flitwick and his friends, who had a greyhound, in 1679 stole horses to make an attempt on Woburn Park for deer. The Earl's servants, coming home at midnight, found the horses, took them to a stable, and went back and waited for the poachers till 3 a.m.

As yet, foxes were mainly thought of as vermin, and churchwardens were still paying out 1s. for a fox or 3s. 4d. for a vixen, as at Bolnhurst, Melchbourne and Milton Bryan.[74] But foxhunting was beginning. Towards the end of the period Lord Ailesbury hunted both deer and fox.[75]

Fairs flourished. Traders, and buyers and sellers of horses still came to them from a distance. The right to hold a fair on Ickwell green in March was obtained in 1676 by George Barnardiston, though he parted with this right a few years later to John Harvey of Ickwell Bury.[76] Even gentry shopped at fairs; in 1663 the Bechers got "several things for the house" at Elstow fair.[77] Extra supplies of beer were obtainable at local houses. In general fairs were a time of temptation. In 1674 Elizabeth Bizby of the Bedford Independent congregation was disciplined for "immodest company keeping with carnal and light young fellows at Elstow fair";[78] and Grace Andrew, lacemaker, leaving her furniture to her brother, stipulated "he must not meddle with it till the fair is past".[79] Much money changed hands; and as there were no banks, a trader stored his takings in a chest and hired a man to look after it; but even so on one occasion at Elstow £117 was stolen from such a chest.[80]

CRIME AND MISADVENTURE[81]

Theft was a common offence, even theft from poor folk. John Stokes of Hockliffe, labourer or cottager, found in 1670 that 20s. and handkerchieves were missing from his house. His neighbours told him that a youth in a brown periwig and blue stockings had gone by. He pursued the thief and found him on the road to Markyate with the handkerchieves in his pocket, but the money already gone.

[72] C.R.O., X 125/61.
[73] E.M.H. iv, 18–19.
[74] Bedfordshire vermin payments (Luton Mus. pub.), 31, 52, 55.
[75] B.H.R.S. xxxii, 131.
[76] C.R.O., HY 199.
[77] C.R.O., PO 3, p.5.

[78] Church book of Bunyan meeting, f.55.
[79] C.R.O., ABP/W 1665/73.
[80] E.M.H. iv, 20.
[81] Unless otherwise stated, all the following is based on assize records HSA in C.R.O., and much of it is published in E.M.H. iv.

Sheepstealing was common. Thomas Hensman took as many as 23 sheep and 4 lambs from a field at Keysoe, drove them to Oundle and sold them in the market; but his neighbours at Keysoe were suspicious when he returned and laid out "much money in household stuff". At Marston 6 men took a sheep and asked the landlady of an alehouse to cook it for them, but when she heard them whispering as to what they should do with the skin: "put stones in it and sink it in the brook?" she suspected the theft. The need to get rid of the skin was from fear of the theft being traced by the brand-mark.

Highway robbery was sometimes accompanied by violence. In 1670 John Poole, fellmonger, was attacked by 3 men near Woburn. They seized his wife and swore that if she spoke a word they would stab her; and dragged Poole up and down by the hair of his head and took from him £4; then they "did beat him and swear they would kick his guts out at his mouth", and one drew out a pistol and threatened to pistol him if he revealed what had happened. In 1683 John Jenkins beat John Wildes into the ditch crying "God damn you, deliver your money or else I will pistol you"; Wildes, an old man, gave up his purse, in which was only 14s. In 1678 a gang of highwaymen who used to work up and down Watling Street – going as far as Watford Gap to the north – regularly used the Swan at Flitwick as a hide-out; this came to light when Richard Rolph, a yeoman, and George Sole, called a tanner, but apparently the bad character mentioned above, refused to help their comrades in Newgate.

Too much ale sometimes produced a fatal quarrel. Two Ravensden neighbours returning from Bedford market fell to blows, and one killed the other with his knife. "Ah, Ned, what hast thou done!" cried the victim as he died, and the murderer ran home crying bitterly.[82] Violence could also arise from a dispute at work. At Northill in 1671 some men carrying dung out of Thomas Carter's yard played about, and in jest Oliver Brownall threw dirt at Henry Hannaway. Carter threw his pitchfork at him; Brownall happened to stoop at that moment, and it hit his head and killed him. At Honeydon in 1676 Arthur Ketch accidentally cut off Oliver Young's leg with a scythe; poor Young called out "Arthur, thou has undone me!" and Ketch cried "No, I hope", and helped to lead him while he died (tourniquets were unknown).

Sometimes children were involved in accidents. In 1672 8-year old Sylvanus Simpson of Maulden picked up his father's gun which was in the yard. No doubt he had heard his elders talk of the civil war, and he pretended to shoot his playmate, John Taylor, but the gun went off in earnest. His mother ran out, and poor Sylvanus cried "Indeed mother, and I did not know the gun was charged." Theophilus East of Ampthill, surgeon, came almost at once, and little John Taylor said before he died "I am sure Sylvanus did not think to shoot me."

Of another child who was a parish apprentice, some sad details survive.

[82] B. Mag. x, 211.

No doubt pauper children placed out in the parish varied, perhaps even from the intelligent and amenable to the unemployable; no doubt also the homes to which they went were good, bad and indifferent. Parish officers were sometimes in a quandary, but probably they would not knowingly send a child to a home that was flagrantly unsuitable. In 1669 at Houghton Conquest they appear to have done so. Ten-year old Sarah Mosse, technically apprenticed to Thomas and Elizabeth Willimott, seems to have been in fact their drudge, and her mistress actively disliked her. She drove the cows barefoot, but was said to have with her "good wheaten bread and cheese to eat"; but to John Riseley she confessed that she was hungry, and he wondered whether he ought to get a warrant to bring her before a justice of the peace. Her main bugbear seems to have been her fear of Elizabeth Willimott; "when her dame was abroad" she might be heard "merry and singing". At the Easter vestry meeting the parish considered making other arrangements for her, but for some reason this was not done. On Whit-monday she was found at the brook, crying; her shoulder was black and blue and her arm bloody; her mistress had flung her downstairs because, when she was called that morning, she fell asleep again. One evening about candlelight she slipped away through the orchard door and was later found drowned in the pond.

Witchcraft was alleged more than once in this period, as in the case of Emma Saunders of Little Staughton in 1653, and Mary Chamberlain of Stevington in 1693.[83] The best-known case is that of the Dunstable witch, Elizabeth Pratt, in 1667, probably a poor old crone. Perhaps she inadvertently smiled or muttered at Thomas Heywood's child, who later became sick. Then, unfortunately for herself, when she begged for "ale and toast" at the house of Josias Settle, barber-surgeon, she patted the heads of his two sons, one of whom soon afterwards died. This was enough to incriminate her. Probably crazed, the poor old woman under examination confessed to all kinds of malpractice. She had met the devil on Dunstable downs, and he had made a contract with her, and promised she should live as well as the best woman in Dunstable – but she found him a liar! She claimed that "George Heywood his back was her panel to ride on and she had ridden him up hill and down hill". She also said that she had three accomplices. The devil ordered her to curse William Metcalfe's livestock, which she did; and his pigs and a large number of his horses died (probably posting horses, as he kept an inn). So-called corroborative evidence was that, when the sick child was made to prick her with a pin, she did not bleed, and that when she was examined, witchmarks were found on her body. She was confined in Bedford gaol, but died before coming to trial.

The county gaol was still the old building at the corner of Gaol Lane, and prisoners who could not pay fines might be kept there. Escape was often attempted, as in 1684 when a Bedford man conveyed to prisoners a file, hammer and chisel.

83 *Beds. County Records* ii, 24; C.R.O., X 239/1.

The town lockup on the bridge was also defective, but was repaired in the 1670's. There were probably cages in the market towns, for in *The Pilgrim's Progress* Christian and Faithful were "put into the cage that they might be made a spectacle" and "remanded to the cage again", but references to village cages are not found till later.

Punishment for small offences was still largely by the stocks and by whipping. Arlesey had new stocks in 1647.[84] At Shefford when the constable, Oliver Spicer, in 1682 was putting two pickpockets in the stocks, "believing them to be dangerous rogues and full of beer", they resisted; the shoe of one came off, and out of it dropped a good deal of money. Whipping was in public; at Bedford the pillory stood in High Street; or if the offender was to be whipped somewhere where there was no pillory, he could be whipped at the cart-tail. Michael Merill, a poor boy, again of Shefford, was whipped in 1669 for stealing 12 brass farthings (probably tokens) from a grocer's moneybox.

For theft of articles worth more than 12d., the death penalty could be given; this level had been fixed much earlier when money was worth more. But there was an archaic survival of the privileges of clergy, by which anyone who could read might, instead of being executed, be branded; this lasted till 1822.

Another alternative to capital punishment was transportation to the American plantations or the West Indies. Transportation was not at this date so well organised as subsequently, and could be long postponed and eventually fail of being carried out.

THE NEW WORLD

Some Bedfordshire men were aware of the New World beckoning overseas. Of the humble emigrants we know little, whether transported or voluntary. It was possible to obtain a passage by going as an indentured servant to work in the plantations. On lists of arrears for ship money, Richard Lettin of Salford is marked "gone to New England"; so were two men from Kempston, Thomas Halsey and Richard Odell.[85] Communications were slow and uncertain; when in 1657 Martin Kitchener of Shillington died, he left £10 to his son Henry "if he should come to demand it, supposing that he is dead, being gone out of the country and not heard of of late years."[86]

Men of higher status leave some trace. The earliest reputed Bedfordshire emigrant was Edmund Helder, physician, whose tombstone, alleged to be dated 1618, has been found in Virginia.[87] Sir Saunders Duncombe of Battlesden is said to have introduced the sedan chair into England in 1634.[88] To Virginia went John Gwinn, vicar of Cople (ch. 22). New Jersey was founded by Sir George

[84] C.R.O., IN 81.
[85] B.H.R.S. xviii, 66.
[86] C.R.O., ABP/W 1655/7.

[87] B.N.Q. iii, 383–4.
[88] Lysons, *Bedfordshire*, p.42.

Carteret of Jersey, from lands granted to him by Charles II, some years before he obtained an estate at Haynes. Richard Nicolls of Ampthill (d. 1672) was one of three commissioners sent to North America to administer lands taken from the Dutch; he received the surrender of Nieu Amsterdam, which then became New York, and he was the first governor of Long Island.[89]

Some sense of the adventure and achievement of those early years comes out in the life of Peter Bulkeley, puritan rector of Odell, who went to Massachusetts in 1635. After spending some time at Cambridge there, he "carried a good number of planters with him up further into the woods, where they gathered the 12th church then formed in the colony, and called the town by the name of Concord". "He had many and godly servants whom, after they had lived with him a fit number of years, he still dismissed with bestowing farms upon them and so took others." As to his characteristics, he "avoided all novelties of apparel and cut his hair close". "By a sort of winning and yet prudent familiarity, he drew persons of all ages in his congregation." "He was a most excellent scholar and endowed the library of Harvard College." In his book *The Gospel covenant opened* he almost prophetically urged New England to rise to its destiny: "The more thou hast committed unto thee, the more thou must account for. No people's account will be heavier than thine, if thou do not walk worthy."[90]

[89] D.N.B.

[90] C. Mather, *Magnalia Christi Americana.*

Aristocratic Ascendancy

27 – LORDS AND SQUIRES, 1689–1771

IN THIS period the focus of interest shifts again. The aristocracy and some of the gentry began to go on a grand tour of Europe, collecting paintings and sculpture; and they planned great houses and gardens. A few great estates began to grow, a process which gathered momentum. Landowners used their economic position politically to influence tenants and boroughs. By the end of the period the slow age-long rationalisation of agriculture came to a head with a movement to enclose the remaining open fields by act of parliament.

LORDS

The three noble families who were active in the earlier part of the century were living quietly in 1689. The Earl of Ailesbury was in exile. The Earl of Bolingbroke was a childless elderly man, and when he died in 1711 the Bolingbroke title passed to a distant branch of the family, though a descendant of the 1st Earl's brother Rowland inherited the Bedfordshire estate and the barony of St. John. The 1st Duke of Bedford was an old man, and when he died in 1700 he was succeeded by a young grandson. But some new noble families emerged, and an old one which had latterly been in the background, that of Grey, came forward again.

The family of Grey in the earlier period and that of Russell in the later are the two leading Bedfordshire instances of the increasing importance of the aristocracy in the 18th cent. Three factors might help the rise of a noble family to power: successful marriage; small families (thus conserving resources); and ability. In both cases all are present to some degree. When Henry Grey died in 1651 he left a young son and daughter and an able countess who survived till 1698. She husbanded the family resources and began to build up the estate in nearby Clophill. Her son, the 11th Earl, married an heiress, who became in her own right Baroness Lucas of Crudwell in Wiltshire; he likewise had only a son and daughter, and lived quietly, except that he built a house in St. James' Square; he further enlarged the estate in Flitton and Silsoe. Henry Grey, 12th Earl, also married an heiress, the daughter of Baron Crewe of Stene; he continued to extend in Flitton, Silsoe, Gravenhurst, Pulloxhill and further afield at Harrold. He was Lord Chamberlain in 1704, Duke of Kent in 1710, Lord Lieutenant of the county in 1711. The list of Queen Anne's household staff survives among his MSS.;[1] it includes master of the revels, organ-maker, herb-strewer, rat-killer, and

[1] C.R.O., L 29/110.

operator for teeth.

In the career of Henry Grey, 1st (and only Bedfordshire) Duke of Kent, the new and wider interests of the aristocracy can be seen against this background of rising prosperity. In 1690–1 he went on the grand tour. To him his elders' preoccupation with particular forms of religion seemed stuffy and old-fashioned. At Geneva he found nothing to see but snow on the mountains all winter. Not only did he go to Rome, but privately to his sister he poked fun at parental phobias: "I shall have a sight of Anti-Christ [the Pope], but because his gown is so long I shall not see his cloven foot."[2] His letters home had more references to the carnival than to art and architecture. However he sent his own two sons abroad in 1716–17 with carefully selected tutors; they were to order from Chiari two paintings on the story of Aeneas and Dido, and were also to get the opinion of Juvarra (a famous architect) on the new plans for Wrest House. The elder son was delighted to buy books, prints and medals; the younger struggled against ill health and came home to die.

The plan for a new house at Wrest included a great oval hall with wings, a dome which was to rise in a handsome way above the roof, pilasters of the Corinthian order, and statues and vases. It had to be abandoned because the Duke lost money in the speculation craze called the South Sea bubble. However the gardens and park remained his lifelong interest.

His father had improved the small park north of the house and had made a formal garden to the south. The Duke created, beyond this garden, a new and larger south park with formal rides and water; by skilful use of the old moat and of a nearby stream, he made a "great canal", and erected beyond it a baroque pavilion designed by Thomas Archer; while smaller stretches of water led off on either side. Many trees were planted – oak, ash, elm, hornbeam, alder and fir, and walks were laid out in dignified regularity. Statues were placed at appropriate points. On Cain Hill, Hill House was built, also to Archer's plan, with views radiating in all directions. By the bowling-green rose somewhat later another building with gracious columned portico, designed by Batty Langley.[3]

Some other noble families built or enlarged houses. It was not always done: the Trevors (Thomas Trevor, chief justice, who had bought Bromham from the Dyves, was created Baron Trevor in 1712) did not rebuild Bromham Hall. But the Ashburnhams built a house in Ampthill park, where the old castle was no longer habitable. Service to the king brought to John Ashburnham the grant of the park. His grandson, to whom he had left "my watch with an enamelled case of imagery which was given me by my late dear master, King Charles I",[4] and who became the 1st Lord Ashburnham, built in the park in 1704–7 a great house with a fine classical facade, designed by John Lumley.[5] This house had a

---

[2] C.R.O., L 30/2/8.
[3] *E.M.H.* vii summarises the Duke's work.

[4] C.R.O., H/DE 2.
[5] E.Sussex R.O. (original correspondence).

sad beginning to its chequered history; the 3rd Lord Ashburnham's young wife, who was a daughter of the Duke of Kent, died; and after his own death a few years later the family withdrew to their ancestral Sussex. The 10th Lord St. John enlarged Melchbourne house in 1741.

Marriage greatly enhanced the fortunes of the Carterets, for the wife of the 1st Lord Carteret inherited much property elsewhere from the Earl of Bath; she was created Countess Granville, long survived her husband, and was said to be an old dragon. She probably extended the old Newdigate house at Haynes Park, where she lived,[6] but earlier work disappeared when it was refronted in 1790. The 2nd Lord Carteret (later Earl Granville), handsome, engaging and a scholar, with a driving capacity for work and a grasp of foreign affairs, but too aristocratic to manoeuvre or compromise, was once said to be "the ablest head in England".[7] His obvious sphere was not the local but the national stage; but Walpole and he were unable to work together; so after an early beginning as ambassador to Sweden, he came to power only in his latter years on Walpole's fall.

Naval prowess was the foundation for the Byng family's position. Sir George Byng was only 30 when he bought the Kelyng house at Southill in 1693. At that date in troubled times prize money swelled the fortune of a successful commander. After a long and distinguished naval career, in the course of which he shared in the taking of Gibraltar in 1704 and destroyed the Spanish fleet at Cape Passaro in 1718, he was made Viscount Torrington in 1721. It was probably he who enlarged or rebuilt the Kelyng house. Visitors in 1745 describe it as "worth seeing; long pleasant rooms, and several agreeable pictures – views of Messina, Naples, Gibraltar, where the late lord had command of the fleet".[8] The Torringtons too built up an estate round Southill. The second Admiral Byng was given, in the relief of Minorca, an apparently impossible task and a badly provided expedition; as a scapegoat, he was disgraced and executed.

Thus stately houses were rising in Bedfordshire, and it is not surprising that John Russell, 4th Duke of Bedford, who succeeded in 1732, was not content with Woburn Abbey as rebuilt by his ancestor a century ago. He was in a position to rebuild. The Russells are a classic example of the way in which family fortunes could soar. Ability in the 16th cent. had been rewarded by royal grants for services rendered. The marriage of William Russell in 1669 to Rachel Wriothesley brought them what was then country property at Bloomsbury, but was to increase tremendously in value with the accelerating growth of London. The 2nd Duke, Wriothesley, in 1695 married Elizabeth Howland, heiress of wealthy city merchants. Although he contracted debts while in Italy on the grand

[6] A. Ballantyne, *Lord Carteret*, 367–8.
[7] *Complete peerage*; see also B. Williams, *The Whig supremacy*, *passim*.

[8] *B.H.R.S.* xlvii, 28; see this volume for much information on aristocratic life in the period.

tour, and although his son, the 3rd Duke, was reckless in money matters, both died young; and so the able and ambitious 4th Duke, John, at the age of 21 could look forward to outclassing any Bedfordshire rival. As soon as he could afford it, he rebuilt the abbey with a stately west front, taking Henry Flitcroft in 1747 as his architect. Only the north wing of the former house and the quadrangular plan were preserved.

Neither was the 4th Duke content merely to have a foothold in the county, as the long-lived 5th Earl and 1st Duke had been. A few comparatively small purchases, for instance at Eversholt, Husborne Crawley and Potsgrove, had been made by the 2nd Duke and in the minority of the 3rd Duke. But it was with the 4th Duke that the great expansion began.[9] Where he could he bought whole estates. The chief (and he must have felt it also as a political triumph) was the purchase of the Ailesbury estate in 1738. The aged Lord Ailesbury in Brussels was near the end of his very long life; and it was already clear that his heir, brought up on the family's Wiltshire property, was never likely to return to Bedfordshire. So a large area of central Bedfordshire, and also a crown lease of the Honour of Ampthill came into the Duke's hands; and Houghton House in due course became the residence of his son, the Marquess of Tavistock. Already in 1736 he had been able to secure the Steppingley estate of the Abbots, who had contracted debts; and in 1737 for similar reasons the Oakley and Riseley property of the Levinz family, descended from the eminent judge, Sir Creswell Levinz. He did not neglect to buy farms and small areas when opportunity offered; where in the 17th cent. the Russells had made two small purchases, in the 18th cent. they made about 200. One local family of gentry – the Williamsons, comparatively recently established at Husborne Crawley – began to speak of him as "Ahab". Small landowners in this area might well be nervous, for it was the 4th Duke who created the great park, extending into Potsgrove, Milton Bryan, Eversholt and Husborne Crawley. It impressed by sheer size; whereas at Wrest Park the chief interest of the Greys was in design and embellishment.

This interest in Wrest Park was still maintained by its owners. The Duke of Kent died in 1740, predeceased by most of his children; the old title died out; but he had been able to secure for his granddaughter the Marquessate of Grey, in the hope that under this form the family would continue. The Marchioness, after a brief period of retrenchment, continued the steady expansion of the estate.

With the passionate interest of the time in houses and gardens, the young Marchioness Grey and her husband (Philip Yorke, heir of the Lord Chancellor, Lord Hardwicke) toured the country, seeing what was being done at Euston and Shugborough, at Stow and Normanton, at Holkham and Warwick.[10] Finally in 1758 they discovered the eminent landscape gardener of the day, Lancelot Brown, and with his help they re-planned Wrest Park, altered the course of the stretches

---

[9] See C.R.O. *Guide to the Russell estate collections*   [10] B.H.R.S. xlvii, 41–6.

of water, cleared some trees and planted others, giving the whole layout of water, rides and paths a subtler natural tendency instead of its former geometric regularity. They also added a romantic "root-house", and a building in the Chinese style (which has not survived); eastern art too now had its votaries.

Before this the great house in Ampthill park had come into the possession of John Fitzpatrick, Earl of Upper Ossory. He was brother-in-law of the 4th Duke of Bedford, for they had married respectively Evelyn and Gertrude Leveson-Gower. The Ossorys too began to build up a Bedfordshire estate; they bought manors in Marston, Wootton, Flitwick and Lidlington; they bought the Houghton Conquest estate from the Conquest family who had lived there 500 years; also where possible they bought farms, houses or cottages, and rounded off their Millbrook property with copyhold cottages and closes.[11]

Finally there came to the county in 1762 Lord Bute. John Stuart, 3rd Earl of Bute, had been friend and adviser to George III when the latter was a young prince; and when in 1761 the Countess (Mary Wortley-Montagu) became an heiress, he bought Luton Hoo (the last male Napier had died in 1742). The Butes had the Hoo rebuilt by Robert Adam; the rebuilding took some years, and a visitor in 1780 observed that "the mixture of an unfinished palace and ruinous offices is odd", though there was an immense collection of books and pictures, including a Velasquez, some Italian paintings, and many Flemish ones.[12] Lord Bute also much enlarged the Hoo park, which again was laid out by Lancelot Brown. He was a botanist and published botanical tables; and is considered to be the first director of Kew gardens, not in name but in fact.[13]

Save for brief scares over the Jacobite risings of 1715 and 1745, life was secure, and even the important wars of the mid-century (Austrian Succession and Seven Years) did little to disrupt it, apart from a riot in 1757 (ch. 31). Architecture, landscape-gardening, art, antiquity, books, foreign travel, all were of absorbing interest to those of the aristocracy who appreciated them, and they had the means to gratify their tastes.[14] The Marchioness Grey's husband was chairman of the committee which set up the British Museum; the famous Cottonian collection of MSS. made by that family had already been acquired for the nation. In London, where the aristocracy spent the winter season, there were plays ("Garrick is more the real character in whatever he personates that I ever saw before"), and the music of Handel ("prodigiously fine"). The summer was spent in the country with a succession of guests; here each noble family was the centre of its own little constellation of local gentry and clergy, for clumsy coaches and rough roads made journeys of more than a few miles unpleasant. Sometimes a house party put on private theatricals, as at Woburn in 1744, when the 4th Duke himself gave a very

11 C.R.O., *Guide* as above.
12 C.R.O., L 30/12/34/13.
13 Kew official *Guide*, p.2. See also J. Dony, *Beds. Flora*, p.18. Kew gardens were begun privately in 1759 by Princess Augusta, and Lord Bute helped both her and her son George III. The gardens were transferred to the State in 1841.
14 See *B.H.R.S.* xlvii.

good performance as Subtle in *The Alchemist*. Letters kept distant relatives and friends in constant touch. It was a good life for those few who were prosperous; and if they were few, at least they used their opportunities to add to the world's beauty, and created a heritage for us of the present day.

With this good life also went, for some at least, political power, and influence on economic development; but before approaching these aspects it is necessary to retrace our steps and look at the squires. They, like the nobility, were of varied origin.

SQUIRES

Some families of squires were by now of old standing, like Gery in the north, Becher near Bedford, Burgoyne and Osborn in the east, Crawley in the south, Leigh in the southwest, and several more. The Crawleys completed the rebuilding of Stockwood House by 1740, and probably enlarged Stockwood park then. But sometimes the main line faltered, or the family sold out and left the county. The last male Boteler of Biddenham died in 1703. The Dyves sold Bromham in 1708. The Lukes had already sold out. The Francklins renewed themselves in a distant younger branch, which came to live at Gt. Barford. The elder line of Brandreth of Houghton Regis came to an end in this period, but a younger line continued. The Cotton family, who in the previous century had obtained Stratton manor by marriage with an Anderson heiress, sold it in 1764. The estates of departing families sometimes swelled those of the rising nobility, as did those of Boteler and Dyve for Lord Trevor; Luke that of Carteret; Brandreth that of the Duke of Bedford; and Conquest (one of the oldest remaining families) that of Lord Ossory.

Like the nobility, a rising squire sometimes profited by marriage. The Orlebar fortunes had already benefited in this way when in the previous century George Orlebar (d. 1666) married the heiress Margaret Child (the one-time Payne estate at Podington having already passed by marriage to the Childs). His descendant, Richard Orlebar, rose further by marrying the heiress, Diana Astry, and in 1710 they built Hinwick House, with the goddess Diana on its pediment.

Another way to a landed estate could be through the legal profession. This was the case, not only with the judge, Lord Trevor, but with the Harveys of Ickwell Bury; they also inherited money from another lawyer, Hugh Audley, apparently through a connection by marriage.

Trade was a further source from which new blood came for the gentry. Samuel Ongley was a linen-draper in Cornhill and a director of the East India Company. He bought the former Palmer property at Old Warden about 1696. Advising a young man in 1717 on going to India, he wrote "the country is hot, and requires great sobriety and temperance, for the climate will admit of no drunkenness or excess of diet; in either case they fall into the bloody flux and die". His life of frugality and hard work had room for few pleasures, and the youthful insouciance of the nephew whom he educated as his heir often irritated him.[15] Another director of the East India Company was Sir Gregory Page, who bought Battlesden in 1724.

Marriage and trade combined to help Pym. William Pym in 1741 married the Sandy heiress, Elizabeth Kingsley, daughter of Heylock Kingsley, whose estate was partly derived from Heylock yeomen ancestors. The Pyms were merchants trading with Holland and also with India, and their account-books show in detail a career such as Ongley outlined;[16] receipt of salary at first as factor and then as junior merchant; expenses such as sepoy's wages and coolie hire; and trading accounts with Indian merchants, such as Dunjee Sorabjee; while items dealt with included pearls, silk, cloves, and elephants' teeth or tusks (cracked teeth fetched a lower price).

Sometimes a younger son continued in trade; Mark Antonie, who bought Colworth in 1715, apprenticed his younger son Richard to a London linendraper, but as the elder son died, Richard succeeded. One newly established family, that of Sambrooke (founded on the fortunes of city merchants called Vanacker), having created 1706–40 an estate at Yielden, Keysoe and Thurleigh, left only heiresses; and the property went by marriage to swell the fortunes of the south Beds. family of Crawley. John Dilly of Southill had two brothers who were London booksellers, who published Bunyan's *Books for boys and girls* in 1757, and who were friends of Samuel Johnson; in fact Johnson found at Southill "abundance of excellent fare and hearty welcome".[17]

The classic case of a young Bedfordshire man going to London to make his fortune in trade is Samuel Whitbread. The name Whitbread occurs as far back as 1254, and in the Elizabethan period the family were yeomen. By 1615 William Whitbread of Gravenhurst is described as gentleman. Thereafter the family moved to Cardington. In 1734 Samuel Whitbread, a younger son of the Cardington line, was apprenticed to a London brewer, and afterwards set up in trade himself.[18] At night he sat by the brewhouse copper, refreshing himself by washing in cold water; when the boiling permitted he read the Bible; and he never suffered the sabbath to be broken into. By 1742 he was in partnership with the Shewell brothers; and in 1761, when he bought them out, and the dissolution deed valued their assets – beer, casks, malt, hops, yeast, coal and utensils – the firm's net capital was £83,000. Another deed assigned to Whitbread the 13 London inns leased by the firm.

When a successful city merchant wanted to create an estate, it often happened that he chose another county than that of his origin; Ongley had come from Kent. But just as the Nortons had previously returned to Sharpenhoe, so Samuel

15 C.R.O., X 248; see also *B. Mag.* vi, 291–4.
16 C.R.O., PM 2745–62.
17 *V.C.H.* iii, 257.

18 *Whitbread's brewery*, p.8, citing C.R.O., W 1/924–5; see also W 3264–70.

Whitbread in 1766 bought 24 a. at Cardington and in 1769 the manor. As yet it was early in the firm's history and in that of the estate; the real build-up was to come later.

While it was in this period that the Whitbreads' fortune was being created, their time as patrons of art and architecture was still in the future; and it is at the established families that we must look. The outlook of the gentry, like that of the aristocracy, was widening. Some of them went on the grand tour. John Harvey who kept a travel journal, noted when he set out in 1688 that his fellow-passengers, in the coach from London included a Jesuit and "a north-country man that was popish likewise", but "we were agreeable enough in our conversation".[19] Of Geneva he said "though it hath made a great noise in the world, it is but a little town". He especially enjoyed Florence, which occupied about a quarter of his journal, and he saw there "many rare pictures of Andrea del Sarto's, Raphael's, Leonardo da Vinci".

Their houses and parks were a source of pride and pleasure to the gentry also. Sir John Osborn, when in 1705 he wrote directions to his son, sketched the history of Chicksands Priory; " 'tis a place I ever loved; and for the house, let no inducement whatsoever draw you to pull down one stone of the old building, being so antique as above 600 years, so strong and firm, so august and venerable . . . nothing of these new modern buildings are like it".[20] But he recommended planting in the park, perhaps walks and avenues of ash and chestnut – plant wide enough "or it will look pitiful and mean," water the young trees constantly for the first two years, and strongly fence them from cattle; a row of elms might also shield the house from strong west winds.

Some built new houses.[21] Aspley House was built about 1690, probably by the Chernocks. Eggington House was erected a few years later, perhaps by John Gardner, who by 1710 acquired the manor from the Man family who had been there centuries. The Orlebar house at Hinwick was built in 1710; and a little later Mark Antonie built Colworth House. Hasells Hall at Sandy seems to have been enlarged by Heylock Kingsley, but before the end of the century it was further extended by the Pyms. Sandye Place was built by a member of the younger branch of the Monoux family of Wootton, Humphrey Monoux (d. 1752).[22] At this date the profession of architect was emerging only slowly. The gentleman took a personal part in the building of his house, chose the general style, and discussed details with a local builder. The Hinwick accounts still survive among the Orlebar MSS.

A London season was not normal for the gentry. Some had occasion to spend time in London; Talbot Williamson (d. 1765) was gentleman usher to Princess

[19] B.H.R.S. xl, 6–34.
[20] C.R.O., O 168.
[21] See Beds. Heritage.
[22] C.R.O., F 635.

Amelia; and Richard Orlebar was clerk to the Privy Council, 1764-87;[23] but the play and the opera do not seem to have been in their line. The cultured gentry valued their libraries. Sir John Osborn reminded his son that the Chicksands library contained books of great value and antiquity of the best editions, now not to be had, and he must keep it up with care. Talbot Williamson was well versed in the classics, and also read Locke, religious commentaries, and of course the Bible and *The Pilgrim's Progress*.[24] He was fond of music; on one occasion on returning to London he found that he had left part of his flute behind; and on another he sent for fiddles left at Husborne Crawley.[25]

POLITICS

Politics, both for nobility and gentry, were now going through a new phase. Broadly speaking there was agreement on fundamentals, that is to say, on a protestant monarchy which would co-operate with parliament. After 1714 this monarchy was Hanoverian; incidentally at George I's coronation it cost Lord St. John £6 to have his coronation robes altered and new ermine added where necessary.[26] For the Stuarts there was still some sentimental attachment; the chief supporter of this way of thinking seems to have been Sir Humphrey Monoux of Wootton (d. 1757), who was said regularly to drink the health of the pretender, the exiled son and later grandson of James II; but even he took no step to join the Scottish risings of 1715 and 1745.[27] Men expected that the king would co-operate with parliament, as on the whole he did. Probably no one wanted another trial of strength between contending parties.

But all strove to get what advantage they could.[28] The king, especially George III, still felt that he had the right as far as possible to have ministers personally acceptable to himself. (The blustering John Wilkes, who attacked him, and who stood both for freedom of speech and for its abuse, did not belong to the Bedford-shire family of his name, but he was the husband of a Totternhoe heiress.) The more important nobility, in addition to the influence they derived from their position, had followings in the house of commons, these followers being actuated partly by hope of rewards. Though a gentleman's own ability and the esteem of his neighbours might get him returned to parliament, a lord's support would help him to get there, and a lord's favour might bring him place and profit when there.

These personal factors were the more important because there was as yet no proper party organisation, and party lines were not drawn hard and fast. In fact, there was a good deal of county spirit; and before an election there would be to-and-fro-ing and corresponding, to try to get the maximum agreement on candidates, and if possible avoid an actual poll. In the county in the 18th cent.

[23] C.R.O., OR 959.
[24] B.H.R.S. xxxiv, *passim*; for *The Pilgrim's Progress*, see p.53.
[25] *Op.cit.*, 115, 119.

[26] C.R.O., J 442.
[27] B.H.R.S. xxxiv, 25.
[28] See *History of parliament, The Commons, 1754-90* (ed. L. Namier & J. Brooke).

there were about 2,000 voters in a population of about 50,000.[29] Should there be a poll, the elector no longer had the comfortable anonymity of a "voice" to shout; his vote was recorded in a pollbook, which was afterwards printed for all to see; the first county pollbook to survive is 1685. In 1715 a Shillington voter sent a message to Sir Pynsent Chernock, one of the candidates, that he was in prison for a debt in which he had been bound for another, the sheriff having sworn that he would take him alive or dead before the election.[30] Much later, in 1780, a Wilden voter wrote to Lord St. John, to whose brother he had promised his vote, "I've had Lord Ongley's agent at Wilden, and Thursday I had esquire Harvey from Ickwell, and if I would grant 'em my vote they would do anything for me that lay in their power".[31] Bribery or intimidation might be used; and a doubtful claim to a vote would be challenged.

The use of bribery is exemplified in the career of Sir William Gostwick of Willington, who was one of the county members 1698–1713. It was a two-edged weapon. He was not particularly able, but he wanted to cut a political figure, and he fought seven elections. The first of these was challenged by a petition; for though bribery was general, if it was particularly open it gave opponents an opportunity to challenge the return. Some electors at the Bell Inn, Bedford, were heard to say that "honest Whigs ought not to be out of pocket", and got their money refunded; others were entertained at the White Horse by one of Sir William's tradesmen.[32] But there was not enough clear evidence to unseat him. At the end of his parliamentary career he was in debt to the extent of £26,700; and a few years later in 1731 his heir and grandson was obliged to sell the estate and leave the county.

There are clearer details of bribery for the election of 1713 in the accounts of the successful candidates, Sir Pynsent Chernock and John Harvey.[33] It must be remembered that there was no party organisation, and the candidate paid his own election expenses, unless he got rich friends to help. The total cost to the two men was £783. Some of this was for messengers all over the county. Then there were payments to the bell-ringers of all five Bedford churches, to fiddlers, and to five drummers (one came from St. Neots). A tactful contribution of £10 was given to the vicar of St. Paul's for his church organ. The largest item (over £250) was paid for free refreshment for hungry and thirsty country voters at Bedford inns. After all, they had given up a day's work on their farms, and it took time to ride in to Bedford and back; in the contemporary view, free refreshment seemed only common courtesy; but of course it did not stop there. Conviviality set in, as was natural on the occasion; and abuse followed. The Bell appears again to have been the Whig headquarters; for £80 was spent there. In 1715 however John Harvey

---

[29] The estimated county population in 1671 was 39,874; the census population in 1801 63,393.
[30] C.R.O., J 1494.
[31] C.R.O., J 1522.
[32] B.H.R.S. xxxvi, 109–14.
[33] C.R.O., WG 2653; cf. also J 466.

was unseated on a petition.

The manoeuvring before elections comes out most clearly in the 1730's, not because this time was particularly critical – though Walpole's ascendancy was then temporarily challenged – but because several letters have chanced to survive.[34] One of the existing members was Sir Rowland Alston, who seems to have been personally unpopular, but he had been returned since 1722 apparently in default of a better candidate; he has come down in north Bedfordshire tradition as "the wicked Sir Rowland". It was a second candidate that was required, and Walpole was anxious to have a suitable man.

The Duke of Kent, Lord Lieutenant but now elderly, replied to Walpole's request for help that he had "never lost an election here these 30 years", but latterly lived out of the world and thought it best not to do too much. The 4th Duke of Bedford had only just succeeded, but he wanted to secure the return of his brother-in-law (his first wife was Diana Spencer), John Spencer, and he wrote to Whig gentry to that effect. Lord Torrington told Richard Orlebar "The two Dukes are making what interest they can for Spencer . . . I do not see what hopes there can be of opposing him with success." A few days later he added "Lord Bruce is in a rage that his recommendation is not taken", but Lord Bruce, the heir to the Earldom of Ailesbury, was not likely to be able to effect much from Wiltshire. Spencer and Alston were returned.

Then a by-election was needed almost at once, for after all Spencer elected to sit for Woodstock. The next complication was that Sir Roger Burgoyne of Sutton was determined to get in; "Sir Roger is not to be prevailed on to desist; he says the Tories have all promised him." There was discussion at Epiphany sessions, 1735, where some urged that Burgoyne "was before pitched on by a great many gentlemen", so Denis Farrer reported; another correspondent wrote "the little baronet has been with Sir Humphrey Monoux, who promises all the Tory interest for him . . . so with them, his own, Sir Rowland and Mr. Cater's interest he thinks himself sure". Even the Duke of Kent wrote "Nothing can make him desist". Sir Roger Burgoyne carried the day.

By making an exhaustive analysis of all pollbooks, it might be possible to give some indication of the effect of property on votes. In default of this, however, one or two examples follow. In the 1734 election every Odell voter voted for Alston and Spencer, and so did most Flitton and Woburn voters. In the 1774 election, 33 out of 37 voters at Ampthill, and at Woburn all 18 voters voted for the 2nd Lord Ossory, the Duke's nephew.

The position that might be held by a powerful lord comes out most clearly in that held by the 4th Duke of Bedford (d. 1771). In Bedford borough his influence was felt (ch. 29). In the county he soon became predominant. Soon after the Duke of Kent died, the Duke of Bedford became Lord Lieutenant. The

---

[34] Orlebar documents, Pt. iii (at Hinwick); see also C.R.O., L 30/8.

Marchioness Grey, as a woman, could not take a leading role; and her husband, who would in due course succeed his father at Wimpole as Earl of Hardwicke, looked to Cambridgeshire as his sphere of influence, though political courtesies were exchanged between Woburn and Wrest. For years a relative of the Duke was one of the county members; first his brother-in-law, the 1st Lord Ossory; then his son the Marquess of Tavistock; then his nephew, the 2nd Lord Ossory. The other member from 1761 was R. H. Ongley of Old Warden; he has been described as "a mild Tory", but he frequently acted with the Bedford group, and he deferred to the Duke, so that when in 1766 Sir George Osborn asked for the Duke's support, the latter was reluctant to transfer it. Incidentally, Osborn's anxious grandmother commented "I am sure his fortune cannot support opposition to Ongley".[35]

As a political figure of his time, the 4th Duke must be seen in a wider context than that of Bedfordshire. One reason was the wealth he derived from his Bloomsbury estate; his followers were called "the Bloomsbury gang". Another was his estate in the southwest, a part of England which, because of its many small boroughs, had representation in parliament out of proportion to its size and population; here his chief power was that he controlled the representation of Tavistock and to some extent that of Okehampton also. Lastly his own personality, high-spirited, often wrongheaded and ungovernable, but loyal to his supporters, made him a force to be reckoned with, though neither temperament not ability were such as to give him the chief importance. His group in the commons was largely organised by one of his hangers-on, Richard Rigby. The highlights of his political career were his time at the Admiralty, where he carried out some re-organisation some years before the Seven Years War; his lead in 1745 when he raised a regiment against the Stuart rising; his period as secretary of state, 1748–51; his service as Lord Lieutenant of Ireland ending in 1761; his part in negotiating in Paris the peace treaty of 1763; and as Lord President of the Council, 1763–5.

He was personally brave, and more than once (not in this county) faced a riotous mob. A small incident is typical. In 1767 his coachman accidentally parked his carriage at the House of Lords in the place reserved for the Lord Chancellor and objected to moving it. When the Duke heard of his servants' behaviour, he ordered an instant enquiry; if guilty, they should either make submission or be dismissed at once.[36]

His last years were sad. In 1767 his only son, the Marquess of Tavistock, was killed in a riding accident. Crippled with gout and nearly blind from cataract, he died in 1771.

The Duke of Bedford was not the only Bedfordshire resident to have political power elsewhere. The Earl of Bute at Luton Hoo controlled a seat at Bossiney, Cornwall (where there were less than 30 freemen) in right of his Countess; he also

[35] E. F. D. Osborn, *Political letters of a lady*, p.147.   [36] C.R.O., R 369.

had extensive influence in Scotland in Buteshire, in some Ayrshire boroughs, and in Edinburgh itself. He was trusted by the king, and made prime minister 1762–3.

ENCLOSURE

After centuries of piecemeal adjustments in the open fields, both by squires and yeomen, in some parishes more extensive ones, in others less, and after similar piecemeal fencing-in of part of the common, there began a widespread movement to put agriculture on a new footing. Improvements in agricultural implements, more attention to crops and to cattle-breeding, all combined to give it special impetus, and would do so still more in the period to follow.[37] A simpler process for effecting enclosure was found by an act of parliament for each village, which provided for the appointment of commissioners to carry it out. The movement reached its climax in the next period, when the working of the process can be studied in detail in many parishes (ch. 34). In the period 1742–71 there were only seven parliamentary enclosures, and there is little information about its working at this time, apart from the final award in each case. But before discussing these, it is necessary to see what had been happening before enclosure, which is sometimes more important: that is, the concentration of land in estates, large and small.

Elstow is an example.[38] A map of 1767 shows the open fields with their strips. Practically the whole of the land belonged to the Hillersdon family, and was let to 13 tenant-farmers and some cottagers. Denis Farrer Hillersdon had it surveyed; and then he largely rearranged his tenants' land in the open fields, though not so completely as to bring each farmer's land entirely together: Robert Musgrove had a compact farm in the east adjoining Harrowden; Richard Willis' farm lay in six blocks; and James Cox's in even more. A second map of Elstow later in the same year shows the greater part of the parish in large blocks, though there were a number of strips which did not belong to Hillersdon, and which he could not control. In 1792 Samuel Whitbread bought the Hillersdon estate, and in 1800 put through a parliamentary enclosure, which allowed him to put fences round his tenants' fields. The independent land amounted to less than 50 acres. Enclosure was the last step in the transformation of Elstow; the main fact was the concentration of nearly all ownership by 1767.

In this period a like concentration of ownership is seen in some of the parishes where parliamentary enclosures took place (Aspley Guise, Felmersham, Pavenham, Podington, Souldrop, Sundon, Sutton and Tilsworth). The amount of open field land and common in the parish remaining to be enclosed varied from about half the area (as at Souldrop) to nearly the whole (as at Sutton). In four cases one landowner was predominant. This is most noticeable at Tilsworth, where out of 911 a. to be enclosed, over 900 belonged to Chester; and at Sundon, where out of 1,749 a. to be enclosed, nearly 1,500 went to Archibald Buchanan (including his allotment of 302 a. for rectorial tithes).

[37] R. E. Prothero, *English farming past and present*.   [38] C.R.O., X 1/6; and cf. W. 2864.

28 – ROADS AND WATERWAYS, 1689–1771

WAGGONS AND CARTS

Much freight went by road in waggons, and there was increasing preoccupation with the width of waggon wheels in relation to road surface. It was thought that broad wheels acted as a kind of roller, while narrow wheels made deep ruts. There were special rules for Puddle Hill on the Watling Street at Hockliffe:[1] heavily loaded waggons, provided their wheels were 9 inches broad, could be drawn up the hill by up to 10 horses; waggons with narrower wheels must not have more than 6 horses, and hence could take only light loads.

Among long-distance carriers[2] known in the towns were William Lake and William Bailey from Bedford; from Ampthill, John Child and William Poulton; from Harrold, Ebden; from Dunstable, William Edmunds and also the Cripps family; from Leighton Buzzard, Bull and Vaughan; and several at Toddington. The most northerly one, Ebden, left Harrold on Thursday; called at the Green Dragon in Bedford; and then proceeded to London, where his port of call was the Windmill in St. John Street;[3] thus his journey was about 60 m. each way. Some carriers distributed coal from Bedford and Tempsford, but it seems that some coal-merchants undertook the distribution themselves.

Carriers are also known for many villages, even for small ones like Tingrith (Robert Foulkes, 1721); and though it seems unlikely that every village had a carrier, probably no village was far removed from one. At Silsoe, conveniently placed on the Bedford–Luton road, there was a succession: William White in 1717; Hezekiah Penwright, 1729; John Best, 1742; Thomas Lilburne, 1763; and then Henry Sharp, who also had a footing in Bedford. Village carriers probably went only to Bedford or to the nearest market town.

On the road there might be regimental baggage being transported by reluctant local drivers. At Dunstable in 1727,[4] on one of many occasions, a justice ordered the constable to impress a waggon and a cart to be ready next day at 3 a.m. to transport army baggage to Ware (the cost would later be recovered from the county).

Almost every other day on the Watling Street there were carts conveying vagrants back to their places of origin. In 1749 Thomas Bigge, justice, ordered the Luton constable to convey Alexander Macleod with wife and children to Little

---

[1] QSR 1768/5.
[2] C.R.O. occupations index; B.P.R. indexes; B.H.R.S. xl, 57, 77.
[3] C.R.O., BS 2143.
[4] QSR 1727 passim.

Brickhill in a cart with two horses; the driver was allowed a guide (1s.), and when he arrived he took a receipt from the Brickhill constable for his passengers.[5] From Studham in 1727 there was an almost daily service sending back to Ireland and Scotland men like Michael Connor, Patrick Lamb and John Macdonald, besides English from the north to their places of settlement.[6] As the cost rose, the justices suspected that Studham men were lining their own pockets, and in 1740 drew up a scale of expenses allowed per mile, with an official mileage list for carriage of vagrants; this, at least in the Bedford area, was hardly fair, for the distance from Bedford to St. Albans was given as 20 m. and to Northampton as 15 m.[7] Still the cost rose, so in 1749 the justices reduced the mileage rate to 6d. a mile for a cart, or 3d. for a horse; and the claimant had to state on oath that the cart for which he claimed had actually been used and that the vagrants could not have walked, (on one occasion the cart is referred to as "the cripple cart".)[8] For Watling Street the justices in that same year hit on another expedient; they hired contractors, William Blow and Jonathan Munn, both of Markyate, for £100 p.a. Blow and Munn constantly found that their expenses outran the stipulated sum. The next busiest road was of course the great north road, where Wyboston constables' accounts show a similar picture; over 500 "passengers" were despatched in what appear to be the accounts for 1721–2, while earlier there are references to gipsies ("a parcel of gipsies"), and soldiers ("3 soldiers that came to look up some that had run from their collars").[9]

HORSEBACK

Gentlemen usually rode on horseback. Buying a new horse was an important matter; it was as well to be sure of his disposition. Captain John Salusbury of Leighton Buzzard in 1758 "rode a horse of young Mr. Sawell's this morning on trial, but did not like him"; till he could find the right horse, he had to borrow. The borrowed horse "ran away with me and I got a hearty fall"; next day he was very sore. After a few weeks he found one at Chesham that suited him, for which he paid 11 guineas.[10]

Convicts for transportation to the American plantations were taken manacled to London by the county gaoler with an escort. If there were only one or two, they rode pillion; but if there were several convicts a waggon was used.[11] The round trip took 5 days; the gaoler spent a night on the way, either at St. Albans or at Hatfield, and two nights in London, because it took him a day to transact his business there, hiring a coach to the waterside and then a boat to get to the ship. At night he paid a man 1s. 6d. or 2s. to watch the prisoners while he and his men slept. In the 1720's the cost to the county of conveying a convict to the convict-ship was £4 each; exactly the annual wages of William Gilbert, odd-job

[5] QSR 1749/77.
[6] QSR 1727.
[7] QSR 1740/128.
[8] QSR 1749/73.

[9] C.R.O. P 5/9.
[10] B.H.R.S. xl, 62–3, 67.
[11] QSR passim; for instance for one convict QSR 1724/83; for a waggon QSR 1727/194.

man at Leighton Buzzard a little later.[12]

Dangerous riding caused accidents. Two Bedford children in the 1770's suffered fractured thighs; little Mary Hull, when a butcher's apprentice rode "violently, and his horse running at full speed"; and 6-year old John Speechley, when another Bedford butcher rode full speed in the common street, so that he was "throwed down under his horse's feet."[13]

COACH AND CHAISE

When they could afford it, women or elderly men had their own vehicle, a coach or chaise. Even the coach, a substantial vehicle, could be overturned by the ruts and holes in minor roads. When in 1744 the Marchioness Grey made a trip to her Harrold estate (20 m.), the roads were so bad that she expected the coach to be stuck, broke or overset, and several times she got out and walked – it was 10 p.m. before she got back to Wrest.[14] The following year, when she drove with a friend to Southill, her husband accompanying them on horseback, "we were talking on, when we found the coach very gently laid down on one side . . . poor P. galloped up, who was riding far behind, and more alarmed at our fall than we who knew the worst of it".[15] At first cumbersome, coaches became more comfortable after the introduction of springs. The elderly were inclined to look on these adjuncts as a new-fangled fad. When old Lord Hardwicke, the Lord Chancellor, who visited his daughter-in-law at Wrest each summer, had a new coach, the family hoped he would have springs, for "his old travelling coach is an absolute cart".[16]

The chaise or chair was lighter and much used for short distances. Often on Sunday after morning or evening service, John Salusbury of Leighton Buzzard would go back in their chair with friends to Heath for dinner or supper, and afterwards walk home (2 m.); if dark, he took a lantern.[17] Floods made chaise-driving difficult: in December 1735 Mrs. Rogers drove from Carlton to Odell "with difficulty, the water running into her chaise".[18] Mud was another hazard; in 1772 Elizabeth Orlebar stuck fast in her chaise, with the horses plunging and the grooms tumbling about most sadly, till cart-horses were fetched from a nearby field to draw the chaise out of the bad road.[19] Nor had a chaise much chance when in collision with a waggon drawn by 8 horses, as William and John Addington found at Hockliffe in 1763.[20] The chaise could develop a defect; when Salusbury was driving Mrs. Hutton to Aspley Guise in 1759, "we had not got far before the chaise broke down; however we tied it up so effectively that it brought her home safe".[21] On another occasion "the horse being refractory we soon turned back."[22]

---

[12] B.H.R.S. xl, 70 (1758).
[13] QSR 1773/28; 1777/66.
[14] B.H.R.S. xlvii, 26.
[15] Op.cit., 28/9.
[16] C.R.O., L 30/9/56/51.
[17] B.H.R.S. xl, 64.

[18] B.H.R.S. xxx, 65.
[19] Orlebar documents at Hinwick, Pt. iv, 287.
[20] C.R.O., QSR 1763/89.
[21] B.H.R.S. xl, 78.
[22] Loc.cit.

For a longer journey people could use their own vehicle by hiring post-horses at inns en route; or hire both chaise and horses; or use the public coach, for there was an increasing public coach service. Wrest servants went to London by the Luton coach; and Woburn Abbey servants by the Woburn coach. The coach might be already full; "our Bedford coach was full last Thursday", wrote Thomas Bedford in 1702, "which prevented my cousin coming to town, but he thinks of going to Luton in order to get up in the Luton coach."[23] When in 1735 Sarah Rogers of Carlton came back from London, she took the coach to Bedford, and her mother met her there in the chaise – "God send them a good journey!" wrote parson Rogers in his diary.[24]

Accidents on main roads might be caused by a difficult horse, an unskilful coachman, or even by darkness. In 1665 an outside passenger travelling to Houghton Conquest fell from the coach as it was descending Barton hill, and the back wheel went over him.[25] Dorothy Kins, who was living at Stagsden about 1707, "was a cripple in her limbs by the overthrow of the coach going to London", so that she lost her post as housekeeper to Sir Anthony Chester.[26] A London coachman was buried at Streatley in 1732.[27] In case of accident, help was not easily had; sometimes the nearest parish did not want the trouble and expense of succouring the injured. One night in 1777 the Nottingham coach was overturned about a mile from Markyate, and the coachman was thrown from the box and his hip dislocated. A passenger walked to the inn at Markyate to fetch help. The innkeeper, Thomas Goosey (who happened to be overseer) came and drove the coach, but instead of stopping at Markyate he drove straight to Dunstable, where he left the coachman, who was in pain, at 2 a.m. "to be taken care of by anyone whose humanity might prompt them to it".[28]

Coaches especially risked meeting highwaymen. At Silsoe in 1751 a gang of four highwaymen fell out, and one was killed by the others.[29] But highwaymen were not always desperate characters. Talbot Williamson and his wife, returning to London in 1761 in their own coach, were stopped by a lad who had stolen a horse and had roughly hewed a piece of wood to look in the dusk like a pistol.[30] "I must desire you to give me some money." "You shall have what is in my pocket", replied Williamson, taking out some odd shillings and half a guinea. Meanwhile the Irish footman sprang at the lad and dragged him from his horse. He got off lightly, being handed over to the pressgang for naval service. A convicted highwayman would be hanged, and his body left hanging in chains on the gibbet.

Fatigue was inevitable on a long journey. One to Cornwall in 1760 took

23 C.R.O., FN 1255, p.427.
24 B.H.R.S. xxx, 63; see also 48.
25 C.R.O., HSA S 5.
26 C.R.O., FN 1255, p.449.
27 B.P.R. iv.
28 QSR 1778/70.
29 B.H.R.S. xlvii, 46.
30 B.H.R.S. xxxiv, 76–7.

Christian Russell (Williamson's sister) six days.[31] There were four passengers inside the coach, and at night they let the outside passenger, a young man, come inside because it was so cold, "though it crowded us much". After Plymouth, where they made a short stay, they travelled at first by post-chaise, and then (after waiting 3 hours for the Saltash ferry) on horseback at walking pace. She wrote "We have been one week here without one dry day." The Marchioness Grey too was unlucky with the weather when she went to Scotland in 1755, of course in her own coach; she took with her a supply of tea and plenty of books, and her journey to Perthshire took 3 weeks.[32]

WALKING

For ordinary people walking was the mode of travel. When Alice, Salusbury's housemaid at Leighton Buzzard, in 1757 had a rare holiday, a few days later she "came home wet and heartily fatigued, having walked all the way from St. Albans" (21 m.).[33] John Metcalf (the famous Blind Jack of Knaresborough) in 1741 walked from Biggleswade home in two days' less time than the coach journey of a man who had offered him a lift.[34] Most country people walked to their market town; oral tradition in the present century reports that it was quicker to walk back to Dean from Bedford (12 m.) than to ride in the carrier's waggon which stopped at every inn. Snow meant dangerous walking; in 1755 Joseph Samson of Barton was "smothered in the snow", and Thomas George of Luton was found on the moors – he had "expired from the severity of the weather".[35]

The vast army of vagrants also tramped. Sometimes we know their life stories. Christian Brown, aged about 91, who was taken at Chalgrave in 1725, had been born in Belfast and married a Londoner; Robert Turner, found at Eaton Socon in 1724, was born in Dorset; Elizabeth Amerson, found at Eaton Bray the same year, came from Durham.[36] One of the most picturesque was Richard Taylor, who was 43 in 1730; he did not know where he was born, but he went to sea at the age of 8. He had served on various ships to Guinea and to Jamaica with a cargo of negro slaves; on returning from this last trip, his ship was taken by pirates at the Azores, and he with others of her crew were put into boats; but they had the good luck to be picked up by another ship and were brought back to England. There he met his wife Alice, and they took to vagrancy; he begged; and she "got her livelihood by fiddling". They were apprehended at Potton.[37]

MAIN ROADS

Primitive road maps of main roads only were published in 1675. During the 18th cent. there became available atlases with county maps, at first sketchy, but gradually improving; sometimes they had also a rudimentary gazetteer. The

---

31 Op.cit., 61–2.
32 B.H.R.S. xlvii, 55.
33 B.H.R.S. xl, 52–3.
34 B. Mag., v, 237.

35 QSR 1755/88.
36 QSR 1725/70; 1724/54, 61.
37 QSR 1730/73.

essential matter however was the actual state of the road. By about 1700 it had become clear that parochial responsibility was not effective for main roads; for instance, Battlesden and Hockliffe combined had not the resources to keep their 2-mile stretch of Watling Street in repair. Gradually there came in a system by which an act of parliament set up for a term of years a turnpike trust for a particularly bad stretch of road.[38] As early as 1622 there was an abortive bill to establish one for the road from Biggleswade to Baldock.[39] In 1706 one was set up for the stretch of Watling Street from Hockliffe to Stony Stratford, and in 1710 one for that from Hockliffe to Dunstable. The great north road was similarly dealt with later; a trust for the stretch from Biggleswade to Stevenage dated from 1730 and one from Biggleswade to Alconbury Hill in 1725. More important for internal traffic, a trust for the Luton-Bedford–Rushden road was created in 1725, and one for the Bedford–Hitchin road in 1757; and there were a few others. At first it was supposed that the trusts were a temporary measure. Soon it was clear that they would have to remain; and nearly always, as the original term of years drew to a close, a new act was passed extending the trust for a further term.

There were two reasons for the success of the turnpike trusts. One was that the trustees were not, like the parish surveyors, villagers preoccupied with their own concerns, but the county gentry interested in keeping the roads open. Only a few of the many trustees named in the act attended meetings, but usually enough men did so to make an effective trust. For the stretch of the great north road north of Biggleswade, about eight usually attended; the Bedfordshire ones included William Becher of Howbury, Humphrey Monoux of Sandy, John Harvey of Ickwell, and William Astell of Everton.[40] They met at inns, usually alternately in Beds. and Hunts.; the Beds. inns included the Cock at Eaton Socon, the George at Tempsford, and the Sun in Biggleswade. For the Hockliffe–Woburn trust, active gentry included Francis Wingate of Harlington, John Chester of Chicheley (but with Tilsworth property), Francis Duncombe of Battlesden, and Sir Pynsent Chernock of Hulcote; they met at the George inn, Woburn.[41]

The other reason was a difference in financial method. The trusts raised money to carry out improvements. Because at first expenditure preceded income, they usually obtained ready money by mortgaging their future income from tolls; thus in 1728 the Hockliffe–Woburn trust mortgaged their tolls for £800.[42] This money of course they had later to repay. Tolls in the early days at the various gates along Watling Street were as follows: for a coach with 4 horses, 1s. 6d.; for a waggon from 8d. to 1s. 6d. according to the number of horses and the width of the wheels; for a horse, 1d.; for a score of oxen, 1s.; for a score of sheep, 5d. Exemption from toll was allowed for going to church on Sunday or for voting at

---

[38] B.H.R.S. Survey iii.
[39] I.H.R. Bull., xii, 108.
[40] C.R.O., X 261.

[41] C.R.O., X 21/4.
[42] C.R.O., CH 16/5.

parliamentary elections.

The frequency of toll-gates along a main road varied. At the first meeting of the Biggleswade–Alconbury Hill trust in 1725, gates were ordered on the great north road at Biggleswade, Tempsford and Eaton Socon,[43] i.e. about 3 m. apart On the Beds. stretch of the Watling Street there were five, i.e. about 2 m. apart. On lesser roads there might be a greater distance between them, but the traveller had constantly to stop and pay. It is not always possible to say exactly where the gates were; the Bedford–Hitchin trustees ordered gates at "the Dirthouse", at Deadman's Cross, and at Hammer Hill; and sometimes fenced the road on either side because travellers evaded toll by driving over the common fields.[44]

The initial setting-up of gates was unpopular. After what is now the A6 was turnpiked, the Bedford coal merchants in 1729 complained that the gates on the outskirts of the town were of great detriment to them, for their waggons made 5,000 journeys annually; and the aldermen, bailiffs and common council of Bedford petitioned both county and borough members of parliament, saying that Bedford trade suffered, because corn merchants were evading toll by arranging delivery at nearby villages, "nor can we, without stopping our ears, avoid hearing the daily exclamations of the people against the present situation of the turnpikes."[45]

The income from the tolls also went to pay for a salaried surveyor, for repairs and improvements to the road, for the erection of the gates, for the gatekeeper's salary, and later for a cottage built for him "in the most frugal and substantial manner". At the outset each gatekeeper on the great north road was allowed £30 p.a.; on the Hockliffe–Woburn road rather less – 9s. weekly or £23 8s. p.a.[46] It was difficult to keep a check on the gatekeeper; in 1766 Edmund Abbis, a gate-keeper for the Bedford–Hitchin trust, "having been deficient in his accounts, is discharged".[47] Eventually the trusts often met this problem by auctioning the tolls to the highest bidder; in 1779 the Bedford–Hitchin tolls were let to John French of Biggleswade for £624 p.a.[48]

The efficiency of committees varies, and all trusts did not always function effectively. Once in 1775 when the Bedford–Luton trustees were to meet at Luton, no Luton trustee attended, the minimum of business was done, and another meeting was fixed for the following month at Silsoe; "to this we suppose the Luton people will come in great anger, saying they were jockeyed in the first . . . The part Lord Bute's agents have acted is incomprehensible."[49] In fact the Marchioness Grey's son-in-law found the meetings stupid, and the trustees "all such buzzards"; and he himself was not the most businesslike of men.[50] None the less the increase in personal travel and in commercial traffic in the 18th cent. could not have taken place without a great improvement in the main roads.

43 C.R.O., X 261.
44 C.R.O., X 46/1, pp.99, 104.
45 C.R.O., OR 1883–6.
46 C.R.O., X 261; X 21/4, p.23.
47 C.R.O., X 46/1.
48 Loc.cit.
49 C.R.O., L 30/11/122/79.
50 C.R.O., L 30/11/151/19.

MINOR ROADS

Though by degrees the parish surveyors shed the chief responsibility for main roads, the parishes through which such a road passed still had to provide a team to work on it under the turnpike trust surveyor. They also had full responsibility for their minor roads. As the Bedford–Ampthill road was not turnpiked till 1777, in this period Houghton Conquest was responsible for all its roads.[51] For 1720-1 the surveyors were John Clarke and Thomas Impey. They spent 3s. 6d. on an account-book, and during the year they laid out just over £9, raised by a parish rate, which was authorised by the justices of the peace. A substantial item of expense was beer for the men at work, who were of course unpaid; another was their own expenses when periodically they went to petty sessions to report to the justices. They bought faggots, presumably to fill up some of the worst holes, and they spent a few shillings on some extra paid labour.

To keep the parish roads in a reasonable state of repair required a succession of responsible men to act as parish surveyors. Too often the surveyors for the year were content with half-measures, and the roads deteriorated to a condition where a major effort was needed to restore them. An unusual step taken by the justices at Manshead petty sessions in 1739 was to nominate an additional surveyor for Chalgrave, Edward Botsworth. Botsworth annoyed the parish by spending "several sums on the road over Wingfield heath", and 20 men bound themselves by agreement to share the costs of disputing at quarter sessions the legality of his appointment.[52] The more usual way to bring the parish to book was for a justice of the peace to indict it at quarter sessions. When alarmed by the prospect of having to pay a heavy fine for dereliction of duty, the parish would eventually go into action again. Thus at Michaelmas sessions, 1752, Melchbourne was indicted because Clayfurlong lane was in much decay; at Easter sessions, 1753, the lane was reported very ruinous so that people could not pass without danger to their lives; however representatives of Melchbourne appeared and confessed their fault, and the fine was postponed till they should have time to get the repairs done.[53] When eventually two justices were able to issue a certificate that they had seen the road and that it was repaired, the fine was waived; thus Marston, which had been in trouble, was cleared at Michaelmas sessions, 1759.[54] In 1760 Marshe Dickinson, a Dunstable justice, campaigned against the parishes through which the Icknield Way runs – Eaton Bray, Totternhoe and Houghton Regis.[55] A few years later Eaton Socon was constantly under attack.[56]

More remote parishes, especially if there was no persistent justice in the area, were often left unmolested, and probably their roads were as bad as, or worse than those of parishes which were brought to book. On the other hand, with a

---

[51] C.R.O., P 11/21.
[52] C.R.O., X 52/90.
[53] QSM xi, 156, 212.

[54] QSM xiv, 36.
[55] QSM xiii, 191.
[56] QSM xv passim.

well-drilled parish a word in the right quarter was sufficient. When the Wrest Park family found the Clophill road bad, it was enough to say a word to parson Rouse to get the parish machinery going.[57]

BRIDGES

Bridges are vital. Arrangements for their upkeep were complex, because the bridges themselves had arisen in various ways. Some were public, some not. Bromham bridge had been accepted by the county at an early date (it consisted of the three arches next Bromham which could take wheeled traffic, and of a causeway over the flood area for foot and horse passengers); Gt. Barford by 1651.[58] Since there was no county surveyor, the method of repairing a county bridge was to appoint one or two justices to supervise the work of a local builder. For several years from about 1753 to 1769 Luke Francklin supervised the upkeep of Gt. Barford bridge, where Uriah Clayson, stone mason of Harrold, put in a new arch in 1753 for £63, after advertisement had been cried in three market towns.

Two bridges, St. Neots and Turvey, were shared respectively with Hunts. and Bucks.[59] St. Neots was a timber bridge, and had a major rebuilding about 1617, when Beds. contributed a large sum towards its share of the cost; probably some stone from the old priory was used for foundations. The case of Turvey was more complicated, and here the county did not contribute. Villages on the Bucks. bank were responsible for a long causeway over the flood area on their side. In the main bridge, one arch was (according to a statement of 1630) the responsibility of Lord Mordaunt, and the other three of the inhabitants of Turvey.

At Harrold the position was still more involved.[60] One stone arch was repaired by the lord of Odell manor; two more by Lord Mordaunt; and one, which was only of wood, by the Earls (or Duke) of Kent; while the long causeway was the responsibility of the county. In 1757 it was suggested that the wooden arch ought to be replaced by a stone one, but the Marchioness Grey's steward insisted that the wooden one could be repaired at much less cost than would be involved in putting in a new stone arch. At Stafford bridge between Oakley and Pavenham the county repaired the causeway, but the bridge itself was kept up by local landowners, who sometimes, as in 1759, had to be prodded by quarter sessions.[61]

A demand for additional bridges was prompted by the increased traffic. The ford at Tempsford had long been a problem.[62] In January 1710 a carrier who attempted to cross in time of flood was drowned.[63] The interests of road and river traffic clashed, the lightermen requiring a flow of water, while road travellers desired to keep it at a minimum. The trustees of this section of the great north road had long wanted to build a bridge. In 1736, when they obtained a new act of parliament, they inserted a clause which forbade the stanch at Tempsford to be

---

[57] *B.H.R.S.* xlvii, 92.
[58] *Lock gate*, i, 128.
[59] *Op.cit.*, i, 237, 272.

[60] *Op.cit.*, ii, 37.
[61] *Op.cit.*, ii, 156.
[62] *Op.cit.*, i, 160.

put down between 4 a.m. and 8 p.m. until the new bridge was built (during this period the lighters had to pass at night). There were several tenders for making the new bridge, varying from £430 to £1,200; that for £430 for a wooden bridge of four arches was accepted. But the new bridge did not solve all problems; the road was often under water; the haling-way was too narrow and horses went on the road; so both travellers and lightermen remained dissatisfied.

Another new bridge was built at Radwell in 1766.[64] Here private subscriptions seem once more to have footed the bill.

No Ivel bridge was as yet a county bridge; and the main bridges over this river (Biggleswade and Girtford) were still of timber.

WATERWAYS

Meanwhile a steady trade was proceeding up the Ouse to Bedford in lighters. The responsibility for keeping the Ouse open was and remained in private hands (ch. 24). These rights were at first disputed between the Jemmatts, descendants of the original promoter, and Henry Ashley, the undertaker appointed by quarter sessions. At one point Ashley challenged the Jemmatts' agent to a duel, bringing two swords to the Bull inn at Gt. Barford for the purpose. After a protracted lawsuit 1688–97, the rights in the upper river remained with Ashley's descendants, while rights lower down the river were shared between them and the Francklins (through a Jemmatt marriage connection).[65] These private persons received the tolls and kept the navigation works in repair. The upkeep was heavy, and it seems that sometimes this cost could, as in 1732, amount to half the income; however Luke Francklin's accounts indicate that one month's tolls at the Gt. Barford stanch rose from just over £40 in June 1741 to just over £80 in June 1771.[66]

Tollbooks indicate that the main cargoes up river were coal, salt, fish (sent in trunks), and reed sheaves or sedge for thatching.[67] Coal was sometimes stolen from the wharves.[68] Down river the cargoes were agricultural products: corn, oats, barley, rye, malt, beans, pease, flour (60 sacks on one occasion), flax seed, hempseed, and cole-seed (which produces colza oil). Other cargoes noted are pipe-clay, fuller's earth, turves, iron, pitch, tar, oil, pots, wool, osiers, pigeon dung, and building materials such as stone, brick, tile, timber, deals, and laths. Some merchants, such as the Bedford fishmonger, John Thompson, and the coal merchants, Battison and Faldo, seem to have always used the same lighters and lightermen, possibly their own; other lightermen were free lances, taking whatever cargo offered.

So successful was the Ouse navigation that it was decided to extend it by making the Ivel navigable from its junction with the Ouse at Tempsford up to Biggleswade.[69] But for this river the system of management used was like that of

[63] B.P.R. xix.
[64] Lock gate, ii, 133.
[65] C.R.O., FN 1356–1473; see also B.H.R.S. xxiv, passim, and for the duel, p.13.
[66] C.R.O., FN 1492.
[67] C.R.O., FN 1490–1.
[68] QSR 1771/52.
[69] Lock gate, i, 30.

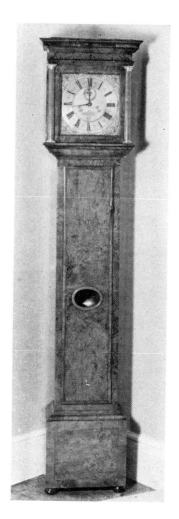

◄ *49a Clock (in Cecil Higgins Museum) made by
Thomas Tompion, 1639–1713.*

▼ *49b Chair (in Cecil Higgins Museum) embroidered by
Eleanor Welby, 1722.*

Z

▲ *50a The Alston house at Odell, now demolished.*

▼ *50b The Smythe house at Sharpenhoe, now demolished.*

▲ 51a Melchbourne Park.
▼ 51b Oakley House.

▲ *52a Battlesden House, now demolished.*

▼ *52b Sundon House, now demolished.*

▲ 53a Battlesden church exterior.
▼ 53b Battlesden church interior.

54b Duke of Bedford, 1710–71.

54a Duke of Kent, 1671–1740.

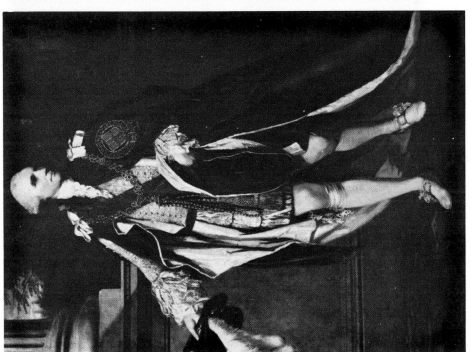

▲ 55b Talbot Williamson, 1711–65.

▲ 55a Earl of Bute, 1713–92.

56a A gardener at Wrest, (John Duell)
early 18th cent.

56b A woodcutter at Wrest (William Millward)
early 18th cent.

57 Rush-cutting and matmaking at Pavenham.

▲ *58a Bedford: Old (Bunyan) meeting-house, demolished 1849.*
▼ *58b Stevington Baptist church interior.*

▲ *59a Leighton Buzzard Quaker meeting-house interior.*

▼ *59b Bedford Moravian church with dwellinghouses adjoining.*

▲ 60a *General view from Lidlington hill.*

▼ 60b *General view from Sharpenhoe clappers.*

▲ *61a The village of Biscot, Luton.*

▼ *61b View from Chalton cross near Luton.*

▲ 62a Willington water-mill.

▼ 62b Turvey water-mill interior.

▲ *63a Sundon windmill.*
▼ *63b Leighton Buzzard windmill.*

64 The future Earl de Grey and his brothers.

the turnpike trusts; local gentry became trustees. In 1756 it was estimated that the cost of clearing the Ivel, making 4 locks and a haling-way, and obtaining an act of parliament to authorise the work, would be £4,000. In fact 5 locks were built, and they were actual locks 110 ft. x 12 ft. with double gates, not stanches which were a single barrier only. The work was complete by 1758. At first there was a deficit; soon the tolls began to bring in about £350 p.a.; and by 1780 the debts had been paid off.

The lightermen worked in gangs, that is, several lighters proceeded together up or down stream. Boys were apprenticed to them at 11 or earlier; these led or rode on the horses which hauled the lighters. When a halt was made, the boys fed and watered the horses; and in summer they slept near them. Thomas Watts, who began at 8 years old, remembered horses being impounded by the Roxton hayward for straying into Roxton meadow.[70]

[70] *Op.cit.*, i, 199.

AA

BEDFORD: TRADE AND NEW BUILDINGS

Between 1671 and 1801 the population of Bedford, like that of most of the market towns, nearly doubled, and it would probably not be far wrong to estimate the growth between 1689 and 1771 as over 40% to about 3,500. This was not due to natural increase only; trade was building up.

The Ouse navigation improved Bedford's prospects. For miles around the coal trade centred on Bedford. The number of coal waggons sent out daily by the coal merchants in 1729 (ch. 28) implies an average of 16 each weekday. Parson Cole at Bletchley complained in 1766 of the cost of coal which he had to get from Bedford; to eke out his fuel he used dried cow dung.[1] Thomas Battison, mayor 1691, 1701 and 1715 was a coal merchant, and so was his son Robert, mayor 1735 and 1741. William Theed, coal merchant, was county treasurer for 43 years from 1750 (it was customary to entrust this office to a Bedford merchant). The malt brought up the river helped Bedford brewers, not only the Becketts, but others such as Thomas Woodward, who was a member of the Independent congregation.

The build-up of trade snowballed. An increase in brewing meant a demand for more coopering. There were more tanners in Bedford than anywhere else, and so fellmongers, leather-dressers, glovers and harness-makers also multiplied. Rarities such as cabinets, brandy and pipes would naturally be sought in the biggest local town – there were a number of pipemakers in the parish of Bedford St. Cuthbert. The elaborate hair-styles of the period demanded skilled barbers and peruke-makers. The small craftsman increasingly found the town a better place than the village from which to ply his craft. Bunyan's father, Thomas, had operated as a brasier from Elstow, but Bunyan moved into Bedford about 1655, and no village brasier has been traced after 1674. As time went on, the improvement in main roads also helped.

The old rules for setting-up in trade were falling into disuse. In 1717 it was reported that Samuel Barker, a foreigner and not a freeman, had set up as a woollen-draper, and George Henesman, barber and periwig-maker, was to be sued for a like reason.[2] In 1738 the grocer, William Parker, was prosecuted for adding butchery to his grocery business;[3] he was later mayor and friend of Wesley (ch. 30). But these were among the last of such cases.

---

[1] W. Cole, *Blecheley diary*, p.81, 116 etc.
[2] The corporation minute-books at the Town Hall are not numbered, and some of them are not paged, but this reference and others which follow can be quickly traced by the date.
[3] C.R.O., QSR 1738/62.

The general appearance of Bedford altered little. There were two new public buildings (for the new chapels see ch. 30). One was a markethouse in the middle of High Street, near the crossing from Gaol Lane to Mill Lane, built in the late 17th cent. Later, in 1705, its upper room was converted for use at assizes at a cost of £60 (£20 from the council, the remainder being raised by subscription). When assizes were not in session, a schoolmaster, Benjamin Chesterton, was allowed in 1708 to use the upper room for 5s. p.a., provided he made good any damage done by the boys and did not let them go out on the leads. This markethouse lasted only till 1780, by which time its obstruction of High Street was found too vexatious, while another place had already been found for assizes, and it was pulled down. Meanwhile the old chapel of St. Mary in the Herne, used for assizes in the previous century, had become a storehouse.

The other new public building was a sessions house to serve town and county for official purposes, and built by public subscriptions from both town and county. The number of subscribers was 169, and the amounts varied from the Duke's 500 guineas, and £100 each from Lord Ossory, from Yorke, Alston and Osborn, down to 10s. from some of the more modest donors in the borough. Latterly, county quarter sessions, when held in Bedford, had been held at the Swan inn, since they had outgrown the little old guildhall near St. Paul's church. The first plan was to pull down the guildhall and rebuild there; but this site among the butchers' shops would not give sufficient room without clearance round it, and clearance would provoke opposition and involve expense. It was decided to purchase property for sale on the south side of the square – a house and brewhouse which had been the Castle inn in the time of Simon Beckett. While public subscriptions were coming in, the 4th Duke of Bedford advanced the necessary £500; and later he conveyed the site to 18 county and 4 borough justices, in trust to be used for assizes, for town and county quarter sessions, and for Bedford petty sessions. It was laid down that among the trustees there was always to be the Duke's heir in possession of Woburn Abbey.[4]

Other buildings mentioned in this period are the pesthouse off Bromham road; an engine-house in 1732 for two new engines (presumably these engines replaced the "two small water-engines for quenching fire" given by Thomas Christie in the previous century); and the taking down and sale by auction of the old lock-up on the bridge in 1765 – shortly afterwards a new one was built on the site of the pesthouse.

BEDFORD: TOWN GOVERNMENT

Town clerks were now townsmen instead of county gentry. Matthew Priaulx, town clerk 1734-9, was master of the free school in a rather turbulent period (see below); when he died his widow refused to part with the town books till his arrears of salary were paid.

[4] C.R.O., QSH 1/1.

The position of nonconformists was still restricted: they could not hold office without taking the sacrament according to Anglican rites. This was increasingly felt to be unjust. Parliament, instead of repealing it, from 1727 onwards passed an annual act of indulgence for those who had not complied. Thus it was possible for a nonconformist to act, but the law was an obstacle to a strict or conscientious man; and a corporation with a nonconformist mayor took a legal risk. The Independent church seems to have held aloof from town government; John Fenn, a deacon, was elected mayor in 1705 but died soon afterwards. The Moravians (ch. 30) came to Bedford in this period, but John Heaven, mayor 1768–9, was no longer a Moravian at the time of his mayoralty. However, the Methodists were not yet affected, as their break-away from the Anglican church came later.

The machinery for town government settled down in the 18th cent. into a pattern of limited nomination but free election, and struggles between burgesses and freemen gave place to struggles between Whig and Tory.

For the offices of mayor and bailiffs, each September the aldermen nominated 3 candidates; and the 13 men on the existing common council also nominated 3 candidates; the six candidates were then voted on at a meeting of all freemen.

For the common council itself, only aldermen could nominate, and they supplied a list of 26 candidates. A further meeting of all freemen then elected 13 common council men from this list. Michaelmas day was the date when the new officers and the new common council took over; and in 1734 a new pew in St. Paul's church was erected for them, the old one being too small.

The main power lay with the aldermen, and a freeman could not get far without some aldermanic approval. As long as there were 13 aldermen, the mayor was chosen from them. Should an alderman die or leave the town, the next mayor would be chosen from outside the existing ranks, thus creating a new alderman, to make the required number. The opposition's chance came when two or three aldermen died.

A further factor was the recorder, an aristocratic patron. He still considered himself entitled to dispose of one of the borough seats in parliament; William Farrer, deputy recorder, was one of the borough M.P.s from 1705 to 1710. As the office of recorder was held for life, there could be a clash between him and the council. Charles Bruce, later 3rd Earl of Ailesbury, a Tory, was recorder 1711–47. Under the early Hanoverian monarchy, the council was Whig. For George I's coronation the mayor was authorised to arrange a treat costing £15; and for its anniversary a year later the council met at the Swan to celebrate, "each member not to exceed his bottle". Relations with the recorder during this reign became strained; as a restive Whig in 1728 put it, "we have long laboured under a recorder perfectly disagreeable to us".[5] In February, 1747, Lord Ailesbury died, and the

[5] C.R.O., OR 1779.

corporation hastily appointed as successor Lord St. John, representative of the family which had formerly provided their patrons; and when he died he was succeeded by his son, the 11th Lord St. John.

BEDFORD: POLITICS

For the present-day student, the interest is less in the party politics of the time than in the infinitely slow process by which men learnt to allow each man his own opinion.

In Bedford the position was complicated by its connections with the county. For a century the borough had returned county gentry as members of parliament; and the recorder, a local nobleman, in return for his patronage, exercised influence. The Duke of Bedford did not attain this position till 1767. He was, however, of national standing, mainly because of his possessions elsewhere (ch. 27); and Whig townsmen of similar views were glad to have his help against Tories, or Whigs of a different group. In the main, Bedford was Whig; but there were varieties of Whigs, and there was also quite a strong Tory group.

The methods used in borough politics were four: outright bribery, as in the county; pressure from landlord to tenant, less applicable in the town than in the county; the bringing back of distant freemen; and the creation of additional burgesses or freemen.

Bribery was the chief. The 3rd Duke of Bedford was an anti-Walpole Whig. He declared that he knew the election of 1727 was to be bought and that he would buy it whatever the cost, even if it was 4 guineas a vote.[6] The names are recorded of several men who "confessed that they received money for votes". Afterwards on petition the seats were assigned to one of the Duke's candidates, James Metcalf, and to one from the other side, John Orlebar. Then Metcalf died and there was a by-election in 1731. By the Duke's orders, oxen were killed and beef distributed to the poor. The candidates were a newcomer to the county, Sir Jeremy Vanacker Sambrooke, and Dr Thomas Browne of Arlesey, the latter backed by the Duke. Sambrooke got in.

The pressure a landlord can put on his tenants was not a strong weapon in Bedford. It was only from 1749 that the 4th Duke began to buy property in the town, and he had not enough to make much difference. His help with the sessions house in 1752 was probably intended to show how useful he could be.

In the bringing back to vote of freemen who had left Bedford and were living elsewhere, the element of surprise was important; if both sides did it, the effect might be cancelled out. It was used with success by the Tories at the municipal elections in the autumn of 1731, when the death of 3 Whig aldermen improved their chances. Benjamin Rogers, rector of Carlton and son of a Bedford vintner and brother-in-law of a mayor, writes: "It was wonderful to see so many Tories come to town upon the election morning from all quarters, even Lincolnshire,

---

[6] C.R.O., OR 1788–9; for the distribution of beef, OR 1806.

Essex etc."[7] Tory mayor and bailiffs were chosen, and the Tories captured all the places on the common council. The Whigs used these tactics in 1768 but less successfully; a desperate search was made to round up Bedford freemen living on the Duke's Bloomsbury estate, but several would not comply: "will not engage"; "will not promise".[8]

The creation of additional burgesses or freemen of the desired political colour was the weapon of the party predominant in the borough at the time. At the parliamentary by-election of 1731 a townsman wrote to John Orlebar "whatever we lose by it [by the Duke's bribery], we are determined shall be supplied by burgesses or new freemen".[9] In 1741 before the municipal elections Rogers notes that "they made several burgesses and freemen to secure themselves against the Duke, who, they knew, was like to bribe high".[10] The most famous instance was in 1769 when over 500 new freemen were created. To explain the circumstances it is necessary to look back a little.

The 4th Duke had been making some headway. The borough M.P.s for 1754, R. H. Ongley of Old Warden and Francis Herne of Luton, were agreed on between Duke and borough. In 1761 he won his most notable victory; Richard Vernon, a gamester who achieved little in politics but voted as required and acquired places of profit, but whom the Duke backed because he was his brother-in-law, was accepted, and continued to be one of the borough M.P.s for the rest of the Duke's life.[11] When in 1767 the recorder, the 11th Lord St. John died, the 4th Duke at last succeeded in becoming recorder.

But he overreached himself. In 1768 he wanted to introduce as the other borough candidate Sir Thomas Hatton of Cambridgeshire. "Many here are averse to this", wrote James Belsham; "I cannot think it will be for the peace of the town".[12] Hatton was "an utter stranger", objected Samuel Whitbread. "Things are in such confusion at Bedford, and such a head seems to be making against His Grace's interest, that he thinks it will be necessary for you to come down", wrote one of the Duke's staff to another. In the end Samuel Whitbread, who was courteous to the Duke but was not overawed by him, and took his own (mainly Tory) line in politics, was returned; he was probably right in thinking that "all the dissenters would be with him". He sat as the other borough M.P. till 1790.

The corporation seem to have had a shock; they did not wish to become too deeply involved with the Duke, who, moreover, had had a lot to say about the free school and the Harpur Trust, the wealthy trust which had been set up in 1764 to manage the now important Holborn estate (see below). The corporation looked round for another patron, who should still be a Whig, but not too power-

[7] B.H.R.S. xxx, 30.
[8] C.R.O., R 503.
[9] C.R.O., OR 1806.
[10] B.H.R.S. xxx, 95.

[11] *History of Parliament*; 1754–90 (L. Namier – J. Brooks).
[12] C.R.O., R 201, 393, 404.

ful. They saw a possible one in Huntingdonshire in Sir Robert Barnard, a founder of the Bill of Rights Society, a warm supporter of equal representation, and a connection of the St. John family.

The mayor 1768-9 was John Heaven, a Holborn turner, who had become connected with Bedford as a young man, when he joined the Moravians, though he afterwards left them. He became a freeman in 1759, and a common council man and burgess in 1767. As the municipal elections approached, the Moravian church diary notes that "some persons cast bitter reflections on the brethren" because Heaven had formerly belonged to them; others "vindicated our innocency"; it notes that there were many strangers in town "full of a party spirit", and "no agreeable feeling attended it".[13] Over 500 freemen were admitted, several of them from Huntingdonshire. The opposition called it "such an arbitrary exertion of power as was without precedent or example", but their objection was rather to the scale of the operation than to the principle at stake. The 4th Duke died in 1771, and Sir Robert Barnard became recorder.

BEDFORD: SCHOOLS

For most of this period the free school endowed by Sir William Harpur was in an unsatisfactory state.[14] Nicholas Aspinall, the master, had 26 children when he resigned in 1717; the usher at that time was Benjamin Rogers; and their salaries still remained at the unrealistic figures of £30 and £20 p.a., plus a few pence paid by the children, though representatives from New College had tried to get the salaries raised.

When New College appointed Matthew Priaulx as successor to Aspinall, the corporation – apparently piqued at the unsought advice they had received – had the school locked against him, though Rogers let him in at the back. The corporation then withheld Priaulx's salary, till a Chancery suit resulted in 1725 in a decree against them. Priaulx eked out his living with other work, and eventually made good his footing with the common council sufficiently to become town clerk in 1734, but the number of boys sank. Of his usher, Gamble, Priaulx said "I could never determine whether impudence or ignorance was his superior quality." Priaulx was followed by George Bridle. In 1747 another Chancery suit for maladministration was brought by some Bedford inhabitants, as a result of which the Lord Chancellor, Lord Hardwicke, ruled that the master had been pocketing the usher's salary and must refund it.

The turning-point came in 1761. The falling-in of the long lease of the Holborn estate meant that some drastic step was needed. At this time a shilling rate in St. Paul's parish brought in £119; whereas the prospective income from new leases in Holborn, an actively developing area, was put at £3,000. As an interim measure, a Chancery decree of 1761 appointed a committee to deal with

---

13 C.R.O., MO.   *Charity*, 15-23.
14 *V.C.H.* ii, 167-72; C. F. Farrar, *Harper's Bedford*

the new leases: this committee consisted of the 4th Duke, his son, the Marquess of Tavistock, his agent, Robert Butcher, and also R. H. Ongley and John Orlebar.

A new permanent scheme came in 1764 when an act of parliament set up the Harpur Trust. The trustees were to be the mayor and other officers of the corporation and the common council; and also the ministers and representative inhabitants of the five Bedford parishes. The salaries of master and usher were raised to £200 and £100 and there was also to be a writing-master; sums were set aside for charity – for the marriage of poor maids and for apprenticing; and precise rules were laid down for administration, such as that trustees' expenses must not exceed a guinea for coach-hire in London and 10s. 6d. per day subsistence. (When in 1773 Goldsmith poked fun at the burgesses of Bedford for eating large suppers in London, he was already out of date.) The school building in St. Paul's square was restored and faced with stone.

There was other provision for education made in this period. Alexander Leith, vicar of St. Paul's (d. 1732), endowed a school for 20 poor children; and Gabriel Newton in 1760 provided for the education of 25 boys.[15]

MARKET TOWNS

Like Bedford, the market towns grew considerably during this period. They were gaining from the rural parishes a greater concentration of craftsmen than in the previous century, and a near-monopoly of the auxiliary trades that were attracted to centres of population: barbers, drapers and gloves, apothecaries and surgeons, glaziers and plumbers, ironmongers, scriveners, even saddlers. Their relative sizes remained much the same. If we may make deductions from the first census a generation after the end of this period, the largest, Leighton and Luton townships were in 1771 probably about 1,500 (not counting their spreading agricultural hamlets); Biggleswade and Woburn, which had grown more than the rest, rather more than 1,000; Dunstable, always a compact built-up area, barely 1,000; Potton and Toddington, which were growing more slowly, less than 1,000; while Harrold and Shefford were the smallest, with about 700 and 400 respectively. Some rural parishes were of course much more populous than these last; Eaton Socon, on the great north road, had over 1,000 inhabitants even in 1671; but as always the distinction between market town and village was not in size but in the degree of specialisation, and this specialisation was now more marked in the former than ever before.

Another feature which distinguished the market towns from most rural parishes was that occasionally quarter sessions met in the more important ones, as well as in Bedford. At Ampthill they met at the White Hart; at Biggleswade at the Sun; at Dunstable at the Black Bull; at Luton at the Bell, George, or Rose and Crown. Again, when an offender was sentenced at quarter sessions to be punished by public whipping, the county gaoler often went to the appropriate market

[15] C.R.O., ABP/W 1732/4; and Charity Commission *Reports*.

town to carry out the sentence; thus in 1716 Ann Low, for house-stealing, was sentenced to be whipped at Harrold at the cart's tail, stripped naked to the waist; and in 1751 Henry Potter was whipped at Ampthill at the cart's tail, from the market-house to Mr. Keling's and back again.[16] Market towns offered more temptations than the rural parishes. At Biggleswade in 1753 Thomas Hughes succeeded in extracting a hog from a pen in the marketplace and even in driving it home.[17] Tolls on the sale of livestock at Dunstable in 1743 were 4d. for a horse or bull, 2d. for a cow, 1d. for a pig, 8d. for a score of sheep.[18] At Leighton when horses were sold the inhabitants let their front rails or fence for the horses to be tied to them.[19]

The organisation of the market towns was parochial, like that of the rural parishes. They too every year chose their overseers and surveyors, who were responsible to the local justices in petty sessions; and also their constables who attended quarter sessions, like Thomas Hooton, a constable and bellman of Leighton in 1753. In the case of a large parish with many hamlets, like Leighton and Luton, the hamlets had a subsidiary organisation; thus Luton had no less than 7 constables, 2 for Luton itself, and one each for Limbury-cum-Biscot, Leagrave, Stopsley, East Hyde and West Hyde. Dunstable, on the other hand, required only two constables. (Rural parishes with many hamlets also had extra constables, as at Eaton Socon.)

The market towns fall into three groups. Dunstable and Biggleswade were the towns to benefit most from turnpike roads; and from 1758 Biggleswade also benefited from the Ivel navigation. Ampthill, Luton and Woburn had noble families living near, and Leighton with the Leigh family may be grouped with them; improved roads helped Luton and Woburn also. Of the other four, Potton, Shefford, Harrold and Toddington, none had a resident noble family, and the two latter were not on turnpike roads.

DUNSTABLE AND BIGGLESWADE

At these two towns were many inns. It is probable that only a few of them were first-class inns where gentry stayed on their journeys, and that several innkeepers, while they served drinks to inhabitants, cultivated a little land or had some other occupation as a side-line. It is not always possible to distinguish. At Biggleswade the known inns include the Angel, Bell, Crown, Golden Pheasant, Plough, Queens' Head, White Hart, White Lion, and Wrestlers. Much the most important was the Sun. When in 1770 George Fletcher, the proprietor, died, there were in his stables 44 horses, 6 post-chaises and 2 carriages. His two kitchens had massive equipment, including a range, stewpans, fish-kettles, cullenders, spice chest, coffee and chocolate pots, teapots, ladles, plate-warmers and bellows. Some cooking was also done on the open hearth, for he had a Dutch oven, lark spits, gridirons, pothooks and jack. There were about 100 pieces of pewter

[16] C.R.O., QSM ii, 215; ix, 133.
[17] C.R.O., QSM xii, 2.
[18] C.R.O., P 72/28/12.
[19] B.H.R.S. xl, 58.

and 60 of tinware, besides 7 punch ladles and a quantity of cups and saucers (some cracked). The beer and wine cellars were stocked with port, madeira, claret, hock, and brandy (also cherry and raspberry brandy). There were 85 pairs of sheets, some of them being holland or homespun; and about 90 tablecloths, some damask, some huckaback. The great and little diningrooms were each equipped with two mahogany dining-tables and chairs with leather seats. The bedrooms were named after the different coaches; the York bedroom had a 4-poster bed with needlework curtains, 6 mahogany chairs, a close-stool, mirror, and walnut toilet-table; while in the Durham bedroom the bedstead had crimson furniture (or curtains).[20]

More than twice as many inns are known at Dunstable, and the number was growing; thus in 1759 the Duke of Bedford's Arms is described as lately built by John Swindall.[21] Nearly all of them were on the Watling Street, the George, Bell, and Saracen's Head standing cheek by jowl; one or two, such as the Shoulder of Mutton, were in the Middle Row which formerly stood in the middle of the street; and the Goat was in Church End or Church Street. George Briggs (d. 1707) owned 7 inns: the Raven, White Lion, Goat, Woolpack, Star, Peacock and Sugar Loaf.[22] Goods were left at inns to be collected by rural customers, as nails were left at the Saracen's Head in 1685.[23]

Competition seems to have been acute, and we hear occasionally of an innkeeper in difficulties. The Black Bull, formerly the senior inn and used by quarter sessions, was apparently threatened by its newer competitors. The innkeeper William Ketteridge borrowed from a London coachman, Henry Earle, and was not able to pay back, so the inn became the coachman's property, or rather that of his son, for he soon afterwards died. The younger Henry Earle let the Black Bull to John Wright, who married his daughter, Sarah, in 1713; unfortunately this combination of business and romance failed, and a few years afterwards the inn had to be sold.[24] Some years later the Williamsons regularly used the Sugar Loaf; and quarter sessions held a recruitment meeting there in 1745.[25] One man in 1764 left directions for the relatives who attended his funeral to be put up at the Sugar Loaf.[26]

Dunstable, besides its inns, had now another speciality – straw hats. The coach traffic through the town made it a good place for selling, and possibly not all hats sold in Dunstable were made there; but we know that Widow Laurence in 1703 had a hat block, and that Mary Phelps in 1734 was apprenticed to William Willis to learn strawplait.[27] An early difficulty in this trade was competition

[20] C.R.O., P BwP/W 1770/53.
[21] C.R.O., ABP/W 1759/52.
[22] C.R.O., BS 153.
[23] C.R.O., X 119/32.
[24] C.R.O., GA 702-21.
[25] B.H.R.S. xxxiv, 20, 104.
[26] C.R.O., HW 87/279.

[27] C.R.O., P 72/18/1; 72/14/60. Sir R. Phillips, *Personal tour*, in 1828 said that the "chief seat" of straw-hat making had been transferred to Luton about 30 years since, "and it now extends about 16 miles round that place"; this seems to imply that there was modest production at Luton previously.

from imported Leghorn hats and plait, and in 1719 the straw-plait district of
Beds., Bucks. and Herts. petitioned parliament on this account;[28] but none the
less in 1725 Defoe noted that the manufacture of straw work was "wonderfully
increased" within a few years.[29] When in 1764 Samuel Whitbread, in memory
of his wife, founded in London a charity school for girls, he stipulated that there
should be bought yearly for the girls straw hats, green and white, made at
Dunstable, tied with green silk ribbon.[30]

In both towns the manorial machinery was still working,[31] and both were
still royal manors, though from 1674 Biggleswade was leased to the Carterets, and
from 1771 Dunstable to the Dukes of Bedford. The business before both manorial
courts consisted mainly of changes in copyhold tenancies; there were also elections
of officers such as constables, and fines such as for selling unwholesome meat.
At Dunstable many innkeepers were fined 1s. annually for "encroaching" with
their signposts; it looks as if the fine was the equivalent of an annual rent.

AMPTHILL, LEIGHTON, LUTON, WOBURN

To a lesser extent, and in some cases rather later, improved roads also
benefited Luton (linked with Bedford and St. Albans) and Woburn (linked with
Newport Pagnell and with Watling Street); but for Luton few inns are known,
and it was probably much more usual to stay at St. Albans; at Luton the George inn
seems the chief. At Woburn apparently the George and the Red Lion held the
palm, till a good deal later the Bedford Arms was built. On the other hand
Leighton, though not on an important road, continued to be a thriving local
centre; 30 inns are known here. Undoubtedly the White Swan was the most
important; here in the mid-18th cent. the Civil Society of about 20 local men
usually met, though sometimes they chose the Unicorn, or the Bull, or the Eagle
and Child; usually they drank beer, but if the attendance was lower than usual,
the drink was punch or wine in order to make up the difference to the innkeeper.[32]
At the Swan there was sometimes dancing.[33] At Ampthill the chief inn was the
White Hart, though there were also a number of others.

These towns benefited from their aristocratic residents, at Woburn the Duke
of Bedford, at Leighton at the Prebendal House the Leighs, at Luton Hoo the
Butes who followed the Napiers, and at Ampthill the Ossorys who eventually
took over the house built by Lord Ashburnham (ch. 27). At Woburn the Duke
of Bedford was only beginning to buy up the town; about a dozen small purchases
were made in this period – the beginning of a long process that was to go on till
the 20th cent. On the whole these towns seem merely to be developing normally.
Sometimes disputes arising out of apprenticeship were brought to quarter
sessions from them; thus in 1724 a Woburn mercer, Edmund Green, wanted to

[28] J. Dony, *Straw hat industry*, 26.
[29] *Ibid.*, 21.
[30] C.R.O., W 3271.
[31] Biggleswade: C.R.O., X 338. The Dunstable

court books are with Dunstable corporation.
[32] *B.H.R.S.* xl, 47.
[33] *B.H.R.S.* xl, 70.

cancel an apprenticeship because the lad was "idle, disorderly, embezzled his goods and laid out some nights";[34] and from Luton the father of George Taylor, apprenticed to a local surgeon, complained that his son was taught no Latin, but made to pound drugs and clean the shop.[35] Sometimes there were complaints relating to public health; at Leighton in 1740 Edward Walker was said to have put "muck and filth" into the highway; and at Woburn in 1789 a saddler threw lime used for dressing skins into the stream used by the inhabitants of Birchmore.[36] Strawplaiting was practised in Luton as well as Dunstable; it was taught in the workhouse, and straw hats were left in wills, as by Elizabeth Hillersdon in 1723;[37] (since this craft was also practised in a number of villages, see also ch. 31).

In all cases their manorial machinery was still in being, and the court books of Luton manor throw some further light on Luton.[38] Many encroachments on the waste were reported; "waste" meant any unoccupied land; thus when in 1732 Thomas Gurney enclosed a little patch by the new turnpike-gate, probably for a garden, it was an encroachment. Other encroachments were making wood-piles, dung-heaps, hog-sties, horse-blocks; offenders were fined 1s. 6d. or 2s. 6d., but next year the offence came up again, till the old list was quietly dropped in 1751. Sometimes dangerous chalk-pits were dug beside footpath or road (e.g., from Luton to Stockwood), "Necessary-houses" or privies were sometimes emptied into the town ditch; and John Watkins kept hogs next to Edward Ewer's pantry "so that the filth daily runs into the said pantry". There was great difficulty in getting the river Lea cleared out, and in 1762 the riverside-dwellers responsible were named for the whole stretch from Limbury common to Lot meadow.

For Leighton a picture of life 1757–9 is given in the diary of John Salusbury.[39] He had a house of moderate size, for he paid window-tax on 37 lights; and he was fond of his garden, with summerhouse, a few flowers, and a good supply of vegetables, and fruit-trees. He had a maid and a boy; also a bitch, Flora. Sometimes he gave little parties, and fed his guests on boiled chickens and roast duck, tarts and custard. He rode round to call on many friends, or drink tea with them; and though he himself was described as gentleman, his friends included grocer, tailor, draper and carpenters, besides attorneys. Sometimes he went shooting or fishing, and a favourite diversion was playing cards for small stakes. He was of course regular at church. Sometimes the Duke sent him venison. He did public work as charity trustee, turnpike trustee, militia officer, tax commissioner, and justice of the peace.

POTTON, TODDINGTON, HARROLD AND SHEFFORD

Potton still belonged to the Burgoynes of Sutton. Among the trades to which Potton lads were apprenticed at the end of the 17th cent. were weaver,

---

34 C.R.O., QSR 1724/51.
35 C.R.O., QSR 1777/14, 110, 152.
36 C.R.O., QSR 1740/154: 1789/166, 280.
37 Dony, *History of the straw hat industry*, 21; and
C.R.O., ABP/W 1723/78.
38 B. Mag. ix, 135–8.
39 B.H.R.S. xl, 46–8.

fuller, tailor, cordwainer, carpenter, turner, basketmaker, cooper, fellmonger, currier, saddler, metalman and dishman. The road running north–south (Biggleswade–St. Ives) was turnpiked in 1755. The overseers' accounts continued to be beautifully kept. Potton suffered from smallpox, and in 1721 several pounds were spent on the repair of the pesthouse, £1 being for "thacker, sarver and yelmer".[40] Somewhat later Potton made an agreement for medical attendance on the poor at £12 p.a., which however was not to include smallpox; and midwifery also was extra at a guinea a case. In 1783 they agreed with their workhouse-master for 2s. per head per week; for this, the poor were to have small beer, bread and cheese; and meat three times a week; the overseers would provide materials for shoemaking except new leather, and the workhouse-keeper was entitled to the profit of any work done.[41]

Toddington, after the death of Henrietta Wentworth in 1686, went to a distant branch of the family, and it was not on a turnpike road. Although strawplait was now carried on – bundles of hatting straws were bought for the poor in 1715, and Widow Fensham in 1734 had a hat-block[42] – Toddington had passed its peak. An apprenticeship was quashed at quarter sessions in 1743 because the master, John Webb, was poor and not of ability to take apprentices.[43] There were often cases of smallpox, a bad epidemic being in 1740.[44] The workhouse was frequently full; in 1757 an agreement was made with the workhouse-keeper for £15 per month for 6 months; "at the end thereof to receive £2 overplus if times prove bad and the parish thinks he deserves it"; times did prove bad, and the next agreement was for £20 per month.[45] In the following year, roundsmen were introduced;[46] this system, later to become widespread, meant that the unemployed were sent by the overseers "on the rounds" to any who would employ them (see ch. 35). In spite of its bad times, Toddington still had nearly as many inhabitants as Dunstable. It had to take fire precautions; in 1737 2 dozen buckets were bought from London, and pins to hang them upon (probably in the church).[47] However agriculture now seems to be its main stand-by, and the manor court rolls have many purely agricultural orders, such as not putting infected horses on the common.[48]

Though the road through Harrold was not yet turnpiked, Harrold was looking up in this period, for its present market-house was built early in the 18th cent. Shefford, though very small, and in fact a hamlet of Campton, had its market renewed in 1713,[49] and a little later it profited from the improved Bedford–Hitchin road. It had a strong concentration of fellmongers and tanners.

[40] C.R.O., P 64/12/2.
[41] C.R.O., P 64/18/6.
[42] J. H. Blundell, *Toddington*, 168.
[43] C.R.O., QSM vii, 116.
[44] Blundell, *op.cit.*, 169.

[45] *Ibid.*, 171.
[46] *Loc.cit.*
[47] *Ibid.*, 161.
[48] C.R.O., P 8/28.
[49] C.R.O., QSM ii, 57–8; PE 441.

SCHOOLS

The three existing endowed schools continued. That at Biggleswade was helped by a bequest from Sir John Cotton (d. 1731). That at Luton had two benefactions: one from Roger Gillingham of the Inner Temple in 1695; and one from Thomas Long, a successful merchant-tailor in London, in 1736.[50] One schoolmaster here, Thomas Gurney, invented a system of shorthand, and was later the first official shorthand-writer at the Old Bailey.[51] The school at Woburn also continued. (Incidentally Gurney was born at Woburn but married a Marsom of Luton.)

There were also new endowed schools. At Dunstable in 1705 the schoolmaster was in trouble because he had not provided himself with the necessary license from the bishop.[52] He was of course an occasional schoolmaster. However when Thomas Chew, a London distiller, died, his heirs at his wish built Chew's School in 1715 for 40 boys (Anglican).[53] At Ampthill in 1692 Elizabeth Emery provided a small endowment for teaching poor children. At Potton Dame Constance Burgoyne in 1710 endowed a school, which later also received bequests from Alexander Adkinson and from Henry Ward, a fellmonger.[54] At Leighton Joshua Pulford (d. 1710) had hoped to improve education, but his bequest for teaching was residuary, and seems to have had little effect in this period. Schoolmasters are known in Leighton, James Hill in 1724 and Thomas Wardle in 1746, but it was not till 1790 that Mrs. Leigh built Pulford School.[55]

There was teaching at Shefford, for 18th cent. schoolmasters are known, but no endowment; at Toddington no evidence of teaching has come to light in this period, nor has there at Harrold, though there may well have been dame schools at both.

[50] W. Austin, *Luton*, ii, 55, 65.
[51] *D.N.B.;* see also *B. Mag.* iv, 307.
[52] C.R.O., ABCP 90/2.

[53] C.R.O., X 277.
[54] C.R.O., CD 401, LS 48, 103.
[55] R. Richmond, *Leighton Buzzard*, 51.

THE CHURCH was now completely divided. It had of course been divided at the reformation, but this was less obvious because Bedfordshire had so few Roman Catholics. They, though not officially tolerated, continued, and in this period first began to show signs of revival. The various dissenting churches, who were tolerated after the act of 1689, ran in a series of parallel lines in a kind of co-existence with the Anglican church. It was not a tolerance of the heart, which is content to accept diversity of practice because it is conscious of fundamental accord; but one of the head; and so it was accompanied by soreness on both sides. So far as possible they ignored each other. Benjamin Rogers, rector of Carlton, scarcely mentioned nonconformists in his diary, though the Carlton congregation was large. If one church referred to another, it was grudgingly; the vicar of Stagsden complained that his parishioners gave "a freewill offering to their weaver that holds forth";[1] and in 1695 the Independent congregation in Bedford would not at first admit widow Bull until she could give satisfaction about her dissenting from the Church of England.[2]

Sunday was strictly observed. In 1748 a Swedish traveller noted that music, dancing or card-playing would put a man "in great danger and risk", though to be drunk at the beer-shop was another matter.[3]

ROMAN CATHOLICS

From 1685 England was divided into four districts, and Bedfordshire came under the Bishop of the London district.[4] Roman Catholics are known in a few places in the county at this time. At Houghton Conquest about 1725 Mrs. Conquest gave a gold and a silver pyx to the Benedictine order; but the Conquests were shortly to leave the county for Lincolnshire. At Turvey the 2nd Earl of Peterborough (d. 1697) was converted in 1687; and the 3rd Earl in 1722 married a Roman Catholic who maintained a chapel in the house at Turvey Park. After he died in 1735 a group still continued for some time, for Bishop Challoner in 1742 found 25 persons to confirm and a congregation of 35. At this time the main supporters were the Brand family, who lived at what is now Turvey Abbey, and later an old man remembered how mass was "constantly performed in a chapel which is now a garret in the middle of the house";[5] but the last Brand died in 1745. At Chawston in Roxton, Edward Hunt (d. 1726) founded a fund for

[1] C.R.O., FN 1255, pp.433–66.
[2] Bunyan Meeting church book, 86–9.
[3] Kalm's account of his visit to England (J. Lucas trans.), p.325.
[4] H. E. King, An ancient Catholic mission; Northampton diocese centenary souvenir, 1950.
[5] Scrapbook in possession of the Longuet-Higgins family.

"the priest assisting at Chawston", but the Hunt family died out. At the end of this period there can hardly have been more than thirty Roman Catholics in the whole county, apart from itinerant Irish. But there were the first signs of a revival. At Shefford, William Noddings, a butcher and innkeeper – that is to say, neither gentry nor dependant of gentry – was apparently a Roman Catholic; he died in 1743. Mary Noddings (d. 1783) left all her property to the Shefford mission; from this, more was to grow.

THE ANGLICAN CHURCH

The Anglican church claimed to be and largely was the national church. It had massive organisation, and the best (at first the only) buildings. It had the best educated clergy, having a monopoly of university education. It touched life at many points other than the purely ecclesiastical. Its members included the widest range, from the highest to the lowest social status, and the most scholarly to the most ignorant. Some in all ranks of society were true adherents; but just because it was the church from which some opted out, it had a residue of those who were Anglican in little but name; but as time went on, nonconformist churches were to have their proportion of members from inheritance or inertia.

The diocese of Lincoln in this period had some hard-working bishops. An episcopal visitation of the huge area in uncomfortable coaches on bad roads must have been an ordeal. The bishop did not go to every parish, but appointed centres where parish representatives and also candidates for confirmation waited on him. One incumbent in 1719 writes of having "more than 230" confirmation candidates, and says that the bishop confirmed 1,061 in one day.[6] A description of assembling for a visitation elsewhere would probably be true of Bedford archdeaconry: "Sometimes we passed a reverend divine upon a sober pad, sometimes two stuffed into a one-horse chair; then 4 or 5 tidy lads, some in clean white [smock] frocks, others in fustian suits; perhaps as many lasses in straw; hats and clean linen gowns, all trudging on foot; till we came nearer the town then we drove before us girls in waggons, on foot, on horseback, every way; surrounded with boys, old women, men, clergy, churchwardens and parish clerks without end; the bishop himself bringing up the rear; thus we entered the town in the midst of dust, noise and bustle."[7] At a Buckinghamshire visitation in 1766 it was noticed that not one of the 44 clergy who dined with the archdeacon "smoked tobacco", but the Bedfordshire practice is not recorded.[8]

Bishop William Wake, later Archbishop of Canterbury, kept a diary of his first visitation of his diocese in 1706.[9] In pouring rain he drove on 27 Aug. from Hatfield to Ampthill, for Ampthill was the centre at which parish representatives of the southern rural deaneries, those of Dunstable and Fleet, were to meet him on the following day. There was a service, and it fell to the rector of Milton

[6] C.R.O., X 326.
[7] C.R.O., L 30/9/111/49.
[8] Cole, *Blecheley diary*, 59.
[9] *Jnal. Eccles. Hist.*, ii, 203–4.

Bryan to preach – "an excellent sermon", noted the bishop. There was also a confirmation. In the evening he drove to Bedford. Next day the representatives of the four other deaneries attended (Bedford, Eaton, Shefford and Clapham), and the sermon was preached by the rector of Blunham. "Our confirmation was large, and everything done in great order." The bishop was amused to meet Dr. William Foster, former opponent of Bunyan, now very old, and "the greatest piece of antiquity in my diocese". The archdeacon, Thomas Frank, who was also rector of Cranfield, and Alexander Leith, vicar of St. Paul's, dined with him; after which he went on to stay a night with the archdeacon at Cranfield. He preached and held another confirmation there on 1 Sept., and the next day he went on to visit Buckingham archdeaconry.

Bishop Wake found time to compile with his own hand a kind of diocesan yearbook, noting for every parish not only the obvious facts such as incumbent, value of living, patron, and population, but also services, school, almshouses or other charity, and resident gentry (if any), besides numbers of Easter communicants and of nonconformists.[10] His successor, Edmund Gibson, Bishop of Lincoln 1716–23, continued this practice.[11] For Rogers' parish of Carlton with Chellington, Bishop Gibson noted that there were 110 families; services in Carlton and Chellington alternately, attended by both populations; catechising in winter, especially in Lent (the bishop apparently did not think this enough, for he added "he promises frequently"); holy communion three times a year and also at festivals.[12]

Also efficient was the archdeacon at this time, Thomas Frank. The best series of glebe terriers, c. 1707, dates from his term of office; and he had them transcribed into two beautiful volumes.

The archdeacon's court was still functioning. To some extent it still attempted to discharge its historic function of paternal care for the general well-being of the flock, but its sanctions were now more difficult to apply and of decreasing effect. The last cases of excommunication traced are in 1768 at Riseley and Caddington. For most of the 18th cent. it imposed penances for wrong-doing; and the printed forms notifying minister and churchwardens of the sentence were later returned to the archdeacon endorsed with their signed certificate of performance, as for instance in 1728, when William Thomas, who had called Mary Woodward a whore, made public acknowledgement in Potton marketplace from 9 a.m. to noon on market day;[13] or when two adulterers at Eaton Socon in 1735 stood in white sheets during divine service, and afterwards acknowledged their offence, and prayed for forgiveness, and for the congregation to have "grace to avoid the like".[14] The penance was originally designed not so much to humiliate the offender

---

[10] Notitia in Christ Church Library.
[11] Speculum in Linc. R.O.
[12] B.H.R.S. xxx, 106–7.

[13] C.R.O., ABCP 149–50.
[14] C.R.O., ABCP 243–4.

BB

as (in a simple visual age) to impress the congregation with the fact that such conduct was an offence. Such a penance was ordered at Turvey as late as 1772,[15] but it was less and less in accord with the outlook of the time.

The other function of the archdeacon's court was to ensure the smooth running of church machinery generally. Sometimes a pew was in dispute, as at Dunstable in 1769, when Eleanor Lee sold her house to William Hale, and with it the right to her pew, but her nephew F. Hill continued to sit in the pew.[16] There were also testamentary cases, for probate of wills was still a church responsibility: in 1737 Grace Ashton, widow, of Shillington was cited to produce the will of her husband Thomas.[17] Church rates and tithes, cases of which came before the court, were a legally enforceable obligation.

The system of church finances had scarcely been modified to meet changing times. Tithe had been appropriate for the early church in an agricultural society. Now in many parishes the great tithes were in the hands of lay rectors, or colleges and other corporations. The vicar still had small tithes but it was often difficult to collect them; at Pavenham for 1768–9 the vicar claimed that he ought to have had over £10 from William Newall's 240-acre farm from its stock of 39 cows, 200 sheep, pigs, 120 head of poultry, 10 hives of bees, and fruit and vegetables.[18] Hence in this period it was often the practice to accept an agreed money payment or modus. An agreed sum tended to fall in real value; at Wymington a modus fixed in 1617 was still in force in 1706.[19]

The incumbent usually had a small area of land (glebe) given to the church in early times, which he could farm or let; but this might vary widely from parish to parish.

Rogers was rector of Carlton 1720–69, and Bishop Gibson notes the "real value" of this as £80 p.a.; he had previously been vicar of Stagsden, 1712–20, when he also had a meagre salary as usher of the free school at Bedford; the bishop notes for Stagsden "real value £8". A poor vicar was in a difficult position; and as the great majority of parishes were vicarages, it is not surprising that there was some plurality,[20] though this could only be with the bishop's license.

Unfortunately it could easily happen that the parsonage house of a vicarage held in plurality deteriorated, so that it had still less chance of a resident incumbent. At Husborne Crawley in 1709 permission was given to sell the materials of the ruinous vicarage house, which was very much decayed, and much had already been taken by the poor for firewood; it was said that it was not possible to rebuild, as the living was only £15 or £16.[21]

[15] C.R.O., P 27/1.
[16] C.R.O., ABCP 319.
[17] C.R.O., ABCP 269.
[18] C.R.O., ABCP 318.
[19] C.R.O., ABE 2.
[20] A rough check of plurality in the Bedford archdeaconry 1700–50 indicates that the great majority of clergy held only one living, and that the combinations were usually obvious ones such as Arlesey and Astwick; Studham and Whipsnade; Hulcote and Salford; Bedford St. Paul and St. Cuthbert; Eaton Bray and Totternhoe; Flitwick (then small) and Sundon.
[21] C.R.O., ABF 3/115.

One modest step was taken to raise the stipends of the lowest-paid vicars. Queen Anne in 1704 relinquished a payment made to the crown since the time of Henry VIII of the first year's income of a benefice; this fund was used by degrees to make capital grants to the poorest benefices to augment their incomes. Thus during the 18th cent. there was some improvement in the clergy's status. The parson began to rank with the squire. When Rogers was ill, Lady Joliffe sent him many good things, and afterwards he waited upon her to thank her; when she died a little later in 1732 he wrote "in her I lost a very good friend".[22] At Wrest the local clergy were received, and a guest notes that the Marchioness and her husband were "properly civil" to them; and when the Wrest family were in London, the vicar of Flitton (at first Philip Birt, later Hadley Cox) and the rector of Clophill (Ezekiel Rouse) vied with each other as local correspondents in being first with the news. Philip Birt was one of the most active justices of his day (chs. 31-2); incidentally he was not poor, for he was also rector of Blunham, where he no doubt kept a curate. But though there was some improvement, it will usually be found that prominent or distinguished clergy were rectors and not vicars, and poor vicars remained.

Among notable rectors was Zachary Grey of Houghton Conquest (d. 1766). He published various works, was an antiquary of note, and built a delightful rectory. A Buckinghamshire colleague who had known him from a child called him "my ever-honoured and esteemed friend . . . Dr. Grey was the most humane, obliging, benevolent, good-tempered man I ever met with".[23] Another scholar was John Gay, vicar of Wilstead 1729–45, a philosophical writer.[24] The gracious 18th cent. rectory (now pulled down) at Sandy was built by a Monoux rector, brother of the Monoux at Sandye Place. At Pertenhall three generations of the King family held the rectory; the sister of one married John Martyn, 1699–1768, F.R.S., Professor of Botany at Cambridge and friend of Linnaeus, and in due course her son and grandson came to hold the living.

Most incumbents in this period of whom we have detailed knowledge engage our affection and respect. The personality of Edmund Williamson, rector of Millbrook, is mirrored in the way in which his serious and scholarly brother Talbot wrote to him.[25] In any other period John Berridge, vicar of Everton, would stand out; "to his church does the county flock for instruction and consolation . . . and his face is abundant of honesty, zeal and good works";[26] but he is dwarfed by his friend John Wesley (see below). Less well-known than these is John Lord, rector of Dunstable 1683–1728; his papers have survived, and he may stand as an endearing example of the best contemporary incumbent.[27]

The churchwardens and 30 inhabitants of Dunstable petitioned for John

[22] B.H.R.S., xxx, 25, 34.
[23] Cole, op.cit., 159/60.
[24] D.N.B.
[25] B.H.R.S. xxxiv.
[26] J. Byng, Torrington diaries, iv, 105.
[27] C.R.O., X 326.

Lord as their rector, because of his pious life.[28] His MS. sermons are extant; in one on Matt. xviii, 35 he paraphrases St. Peter's query as to how often one should forgive one's brother: "A man should forgive his brother again and again, 'tis reason, 'tis charity, God forbid but I should; but it were stupidity to let him trample me under his feet"; but he goes on to explain that "trespasses are alternate – we do and suffer them by turn". It is in his letters that he most reveals himself. He took pains to write to a deaf parishioner; thus in 1722 "I must by no means look upon you as one out of the world, although by the loss of that sense you may perhaps esteem yourself so, nor dare I be unconcerned for your salvation because you can reap no benefit from that part of my ministration in the church of Christ – I mean my preaching – because you cannot hear". To an adulterer he wrote: "Neighbour Shaw: I have sometimes determined to speak to you face to face, and sometimes to write, which would be most effectual. The matter of my letter is of great concern, no less than the eternal interest of your soul . . . [The woman concerned had died] But you are here, you my neighbour, whom I heartily wish well, and therefore do tell you that, as you was in a great measure the cause of her sin, so are you a partaker with her therein, and consequently will be a sharer with her in punishment. For you, my friend, I daily pray, and will do, that God will give you the grace of repentance . . . Consider what injury you have done the departed wretch, what wrong to your own wife, and what great injustice to all your family."

In any large body of men there are inevitably one or two unsatisfactory characters. John Draper, vicar of Stagsden early in the century, was accused of incest and died in prison.[29] John Bolton, who a few years later held the livings of Harrold and Sharnbrook, clearly had no vocation; he was sometimes seen "merry" at the Bell in Felmersham, where he went to read the news; he helped a friend, Brace of Astwood, with his brewing; he reduced the number of services and once forgot a funeral; while if parishioners died of smallpox he read the burial service from a distance, so anxious was he not to contract the disease. Yet when a case for neglect of duties was brought against him, a Sharnbrook labourer deposed that Bolton was "as honest a gentleman as lives, and very kind to the poor, and has given him money when in distress".[30] Antelmenelli Keeling, rector of Campton, like everyone else subscribed to lotteries and in 1726 bequeathed to his wife 22 tickets in the public lottery.[31] Vere John Alston, who was rector of Odell 1714–62 simply because he was a younger son for whom the family had to provide, liked his glass; in 1729, when "disordered with drinking", after dining with a friend, he fell from his horse and narrowly escaped.[32] William Dodd, rector of Hockliffe 1772–7, was executed for forgery, and was consoled, when in prison,

[28] C.R.O., X 171/188.
[29] C.R.O., FN 1255.
[30] C.R.O., ABCP 110.

[31] C.R.O., ABP/W 1726/27.
[32] B.H.R.S. xxx, 12.

by no less a man than Dr. Johnson.[33]

Patrons were usually concerned to get an active, able and worthy incumbent; none more so than the Turnors of Milton Ernest.[34] Their requirements in 1694 were: the incumbent should forbear resorting to a tavern otherwise than for the reproving of vice; he should promote peace, unity and love among his neighbours; he should read morning and evening prayer on weekdays as well as Sundays, a duty which he "shall not omit upon pretence of his parishioners' non-attendance"; he must preach, catechise, and administer the sacrament at stated times; he must visit and pray with the sick; and teach the children of those who cannot pay for schooling – this last after they had learnt to read in a dame school and until they were apprenticed.

The regular upkeep of church buildings had suffered during the 17th cent. In the 18th cent. therefore more than one church was in bad trouble, especially as regards its tower; and when the tower fell, the bells fell too. An expedient to which several parishes had recourse (with episcopal permission) was to sell these last to swell the repair fund, and there is associated with more than one church the rhyme:

> – – , wicked people,
> Sold the bells to build the steeple.

Pulloxhill steeple seems to have crashed in the 17th cent., "4 bells lying cracked and useless"; the money obtained by sale of the bells was not sufficient for repair; and in 1740 it was declared that the whole church was "so ruinous and decayed that the parishioners cannot assemble for divine service without danger of their lives, and the church must be entirely rebuilt" at a cost of £1,083; so quarter sessions approved application to the Lord Chancellor for a brief to enable them to collect donations outside the parish.[35] At Wilstead "the tower fell down Sunday night 11 April 1742 at 9.30"; the estimate to rebuild it was £474, which Wilstead felt unable to raise: and the bishop, "having considered the extent of the disaster and the inability of the parishioners to repair the steeple according to its ancient dimensions" allowed the parish to be content with making good the breach in the church and hanging one bell at a cost of £40.[36] At Dunton in 1710 it was said that the steeple fell down about 50 years since.[37] A more modest repair bill which survives among the papers of Leighton churchwardens is one for the weathercock; the mason undertook (1671) to keep in repair the top 6 ft. of the spire for 21 years; but in 1691 the blacksmith who repaired the clapper of the biggest bell would only covenant to keep it in repair for 7 years provided the bell's baldric did not break while ringing.[38]

Several churches added galleries. Some of these were for private pews

[33] D.N.B.; see also Boswell's Life, ch. xxxiii.
[34] C.R.O., X 266/11.
[35] C.R.O., QSM vii, 55.
[36] Par. reg.
[37] C.R.O., ABF 3/98.
[38] C.R.O., P 91/5/4–5.

(and this indicates the extent of congregations at the time). At Potton in 1723 and 1727 galleries were added respectively at the west end of each aisle, in each case to provide pews for three families.[39] At Ampthill in the beginning of the period there was almost a private war between the Earl of Ailesbury and the newcomer Lord Ashburnham.[40] The latter told the bishop "I cannot carry my family to church as I ought to do, for I have not due and proper accommodation", and he therefore wanted to build a gallery 16 x 9 ft. The bishop tried to smoothe matters over by getting the opinion of Sir Christopher Wren, who saw no objection to the gallery; however Lord Ailesbury's retreat into exile in 1696 left the way clear for Lord Ashburnham's gallery, designed by Hawksmoor, with green silk fringe with a sprinkling of gold, two easy chairs cased in green Persian taffeta, and green velvet cushions.

As to equipment in this period, some churches who had not previously possessed handsome plate for the sacrament now acquired it. That at Willington was given by the last of the Gostwicks between 1685 and 1697, and is in massive 17th cent. style. Plate made in the 18th cent. is on more graceful lines. Lady Wolstenholme gave plate to Harrold and to Odell in 1728; the Bechers to Renhold in 1734; and Thomas Gilpin to Hockliffe in 1752.

Bells need periodic recasting, and it was in this period that two successive families of bell-founders worked at Wootton.[41] In 1715 Thomas Russell, who also made clocks, cast a bell for Aspley Guise and another for Harlington. Helped later by his sons, he continued at intervals to cast bells for local churches till he died in 1745. Some years later, William Emerton reopened the foundry in 1768. He cast a ring of 5 for Tilsworth in 1776 and another of 6 for Biddenham in 1787, and continued to work at this trade till 1789. However, some parishes in this period had bells recast in Bucks., Northants., or London. At some places, such as Maulden, it was the custom for the ringers on Easter Monday to be entertained to breakfast by the rector. At Barton this breakfast consisted of tansies, roast pork and ale.[42]

Books were still collected by some parishes, and even libraries established, as at Cranfield.[43] An extensive library for Bedford was set up in St. John's church, and Bishop Wake inspected it on his visitation in 1706. Bromham's library, to which Lord Trevor contributed, has survived to the present day. Some parishes had only one or two books; Dean had Matthew Poole's *Synopsis of bible commentaries* in 5 vols.; and Toddington had Noel's *Institution of a Christian*.[44] The shortage of books among the laity is reflected in the importance attached to sermons; Caddington in 1770 complained that their incumbent removed the parish library from the church and that he did not preach two sermons each Sunday.[45] Leighton had no less than six endowments for additional sermons

[39] C.R.O., ABF 155, 159. Kempston had a gallery for musicians as early as 1618; *B. Mag.* iii, 100.
[40] *B. Mag.* ii, 277.
[41] T. North, *Church bells*, 37–40.

[42] C.R.O., ABE 2.
[43] *Loc.cit.*
[44] C.R.O., ABE 2.
[45] C.R.O., ABCP 323.

during the year.

The upkeep of the churchyard fence or wall was usually shared among parishioners. At Souldrop it was divided up among lengths varying from 2 yds. to 9½ yds.; at Shillington the list had been mislaid, and responsibility for some parts was in doubt.[46]

Services in this period began once more to be accompanied with music.[47] This had long been lacking; a metrical version of the psalms was used, but there were no hymns in the prayerbook, and organs had been discarded.

It was for the psalms that music first returned; and though there was no accompaniment, a simple pitch-pipe gave the singers the first note. In 1724 Robert Green, vicar of Everton, out of his own pocket paid the clerk 2s. weekly to teach the boys and girls to sing psalms. Dunstable was probably already singing psalms, for in 1726 they came to Ampthill to give a demonstration, and were paid a guinea. Ampthill's beginning was modest, the churchwardens paying 1s. 6d. for two boys to learn to sing; soon afterwards a musical parishioner left £1 every third year for teaching people to sing psalms; and by 1740 there was a regular choir. Perhaps Luton began to sing about the same time, for in 1779 Luton psalm-singers gave a demonstration at Caddington.

By degrees small orchestras came into use, originally of oboe, clarinet and bassoon. Often a gallery was appropriated to orchestra and singers. Where there were no local performers, another possibility was to instal a barrel-organ, as Ampthill did in 1760, paying Thomas Gale 5s. p.a. to turn the handle. These had a limited repertory; one which still survives at Sutton played only 5 tunes. Only Bedford St. Paul rose to the heights of a handsome pipe organ; the salary of the organist, William Weale, £20 p.a., was defrayed by the corporation (he wrote the tune Bedford).

Hymns came into favour only slowly, and were for long associated with evangelism. The first collection issued by John and Charles Wesley appeared as early as 1739; those of William Cowper and John Newton (*Olney Hymns*) were collected in 1779. Some parishes printed their own psalters or hymnbooks; Everton's *Sion's songs* had various editions; and Cardington printed a metrical psalter with music in 1786.

Amid all this evidence of group organisation, one wonders as to the views of the individual church-goer, whether aristocrat, gentry, or of humbler degree. Some examples are known. The Marchioness Grey looked on the wise and good Archbishop Secker almost as a second father.[48] At Wrest Park prayers were read twice daily; on Sunday all went to Flitton church, with another service in the afternoon in the private chapel. The Marchioness once wrote: "I thank God daily for a quiet mind. I think it is the foundation of all other blessings." Talbot

---

[46] C.R.O., ABE 2.
[47] B. *Mag.*, i, 257; iii, 99; A. Underwood, *Music in*

Ampthill church.
[48] B.H.R.S. xlvii.

Williamson, of Husborne Crawley, whose brother Edmund was rector of Millbrook, discussed Biblical commentaries with his brother.[49] When Edmund married, Talbot's wedding-present to his young sister-in-law consisted of a firestone necklace; he added "There is another set of ornaments which I doubt not but Miss has by her, those which St. Paul mentions, and seems to prefer to any that Ludgate Hill or Cheapside can afford." Thomas Pierson, a Bedford grocer, born in 1712, tells how his grandfather taught him to pray morning and evening, and how, when he was confirmed at the age of 13, "I was deeply concerned how I might give myself to God and serve and please him."[50]

Evidence from monumental inscriptions, which in this period reached their peak, is perhaps biased, but in the following for John and Sarah Bullock of Sharnbrook (d. 1763 and 1764) much seems to ring true.[51]

"A filial love, mixed with reverential awe, made him regard his parents next to his Maker. His conjugal affection shared every happiness with his consort and concealed from her every pain. As a parent, he tempered his authority so happily with his tenderness that the duty of the children was lost in their love for their benefactor. His friendships were few but permanent. His word was inviolate."

"Her inclinations were bounded by his will, not from his constraint but her choice. If she ever dissembled, it was to avoid giving uneasiness. Her regulation of her children was an intercourse of love, the freedom of a friend meliorated the authority of a mother. If she professed, she meant a friendship."

Obviously these standards were not attained by all, and John Pedley, the Great Barford farmer, probably had many counterparts. Extracts from his diary read: 1774 "Good Friday – was not at church. Easter Sunday – was chilled whilst I was in the church like an ague, did not receive the sacrament, did intend it before I went"; and again in 1774 "Christmas Day – was not at church"; 1775 "Easter Day – not at church"; 1776 14 April "sacrament at church – to my shame have not received the sacrament since 30 October 1774"; 1779 6 March "headache from drinking too much. Saw many lately inoculated for smallpox – the Lord my God protect me from it."[52]

Again, it is in the Anglican church with its wide-ranging membership that we must expect to find those oddities and eccentricities that go to make up the kaleidoscope of human nature. Of these Daniel Knight (d. 1756) of Luton is an example. He prepared his tombstone before he died:

> "Here lieth the body of Daniel Knight
> Who all my lifetime lived in spite.
> Base flatterers sought me to undo

[49] B.H.R.S. xxxiv, 57, 60.
[50] C.R.O., MO 607.
[51] An extra-illustrated Lysons in possession of the late Mrs. Shuttleworth (C.R.O. slide collection).
[52] B.H.R.S. xl, 95–109.

And made me sign what was not true.
Reader, take care whene'er you venture
To trust a canting false dissenter."

The dissenter in question was Samuel Marsom (see below), to whom he had had to apologise. He left directions as follows. "As soon as I am dead . . . let the brick-work stand till the middle of the night; then your men and you carry the stone down to the church and lay it down by Copt Hall seat, and then come back again and fetch the coffin and me . . . The bricks is to make a brick grave for the stone to lie on, with coigns to keep it from falling in. Make as small a funeral as you can. John Gillam to solder me up – he made the coffin." There was to be at his funeral a distribution of bread to the poor, but "no dissenters to have any".[53]

From centuries of past development, the 18th cent. church touched life at many points not purely ecclesiastical.[54] In many parishes, such as Clifton and Steppingley, the rector still kept a bull and boar for parish use; for the ownership of such animals had to be determined, otherwise there would have been fighting on the common. At Wilden when the parish was perambulated there were two recognised places for refreshment; at one the townsfolk made dinner; at the other the vicar provided ale and plum cake; perhaps the cake was made from some of his tithe eggs (3 for a cock, 2 for a hen) which were traditionally collected on Good Friday. At Souldrop the rector provided a stone of new cheese and bread and beer for a Christmas feast. Some clergy acted for their parishioners as amateur attorneys or physicians, not always with success; thus William Allen of Carlton in 1729 was blooded 3 times for pleurisy by the rector's directions, after which he died.[55]

The parish clerk was entitled to a small money allowance from each farm and cottage, and in many parishes once or twice a year he went round with his basket "to receive the kindness of his neighbours in victuals", though at Cranfield this had been discontinued by 1715 – John Odell did not care to exercise his right; and at Shillington, though it was formerly the custom that the clerk collected bacon and eggs all over the parish, the clerk had discontinued gathering for 20 years "by reason of the people's backwardness to part with their bacon". If there was a church clock, as at Eaton Socon, the parish clerk looked after it; and if there were none, in those days of shortage of clocks, it was often his duty to ring a bell at 4 a.m. and 8 p.m. At christenings, weddings and funerals he collected a modest fee; burial without a coffin cost less than with it; and briaring the grave (lining it with sweetbriar) was 8d. extra, as at Gt. Barford.

Those ancient parish officers, the churchwardens, still dealt with the control of vermin.[56] At Westoning in 1743-4 they paid for no less than 138 dozen

[53] C.R.O., ABP/W 1756/30; the inscription is printed in Luton *Yearbook*, 1906.
[54] C.R.O., ABE 2.
[55] *B.H.R.S.* xxx, 7.
[56] *Bedfordshire vermin payments.*

sparrows; at Houghton Regis and Harlington in this period they paid for hedgehogs and polecats; at Clifton for weasels; at Blunham for moles and otters; at Husborne Crawley for badgers, foxes and stoats. Sometimes, as at Odell, they provided a town plough.[57] Sometimes, as at Cranfield, they kept in the church leather buckets for fire, and hooks to pull off burning thatch. At Riseley on Good Friday they distributed cakes made from wheat grown in Cakebread-close. The newer, though also important, overseers always worked closely with the churchwardens. When on Easter Monday the new parish officers were chosen for the ensuing year, it was the custom at Haynes for the vicar to provide ale.

If the religious history of Bedfordshire may be compared to a tapestry, it is the Anglican church which provides most of the richly-coloured and varied design. But an essential part of the pattern, giving added depth and strength, comes from the quieter shades and the restrained but strong lines of the dissenting churches.

THE SOCIETY OF FRIENDS (QUAKERS)

Though the smallest denomination, the Quakers had had a national organis-ation almost from the first.[58] Local meetings, which met weekly, were grouped in areas, and once a month held a combined meeting; thus Barton, Clophill, Pulloxhill and later Ampthill formed such a monthly meeting area; so did Biggleswade, Clifton, Langford and Stotfold; and so also did Cranfield and Turvey. Once a quarter, representatives of all these met in Bedfordshire quarterly meeting. Once a year they went up to London yearly meeting to confer with representatives for the rest of the country. This system was flexible; it could be continually adapted to changing needs. Thus when Barton and Clophill meetings were discontinued, Pulloxhill joined forces with the meetings in the east of the county. On the other hand, by 1713 a meeting developed at Dunstable out of one which formerly met at Markyate; and by 1742 one at Luton; these, for their monthly meeting area, looked south to Hertfordshire. There was also a strong meeting at Hogsty End in Aspley Guise.

The silent worship, waiting on the spirit, practised by Quakers did not change, and they had no ministry, save that some "public Friends" from time to time travelled to other meetings. Of their outlook the diary of gentle Elizabeth Brown of Ampthill, 1778–91, tells.[59] When occupied in the house, she notes that she is "favoured with a sufficiency to procure everything needful to accommodate this body; but there requires a circumspect care not to indulge in things unneces-sary". When she visits one of an unhappy disposition, she notes "how necessary to keep the passions in subjection, observing to what a height that repining temper will grow if indulged". She loves "the beauty and variety of the creation"

[57] C.R.O., X 29/8.
[58] Full details at Friends' House, London.
[59] B.H.R.S. xl, 110–29.

and the privilege of reading serious books.

Less attractive are the Hows of Aspley Guise. Quakers, more than other nonconformists, were resistant to the payment of tithes and church rates, and the Hows must have been thorns in the flesh of several churchwardens. In 1735 Thomas How alleged that the balance of £3 brought forward had not been fully accounted for, that charges for churchwardens' horse hire were unreasonable, and that there should have been no item for repair of the church clock, as there was a contract with a clockmaker for 2s. 6d. p.a.[60]

The only Friends' meetinghouse which survives from this period is that at Ampthill.

PRESBYTERIANS

By this time Presbyterianism, even in the limited form in which it had occurred in England, seems to have almost completely disappeared from Bedfordshire. No more is known of the six congregations which had called themselves Presbyterian in 1672 (ch. 22), but there is a probably short-lived congregation in Sharnbrook. All that is known of it is that in 1763 ten men of Sharnbrook and Souldrop – such men as baker, grocer, carpenter, weaver – leased for 21 years a barn to be used for worship "by the people called Presbyterians".[61] Elsewhere in England most erstwhile Presbyterians had become Unitarian.

INDEPENDENTS AND BAPTISTS

At the passing of the Toleration Act Independents and Baptists consisted of many small minority groups in the various parishes. Few of these were well off, with the possible exception of some tradesmen in the towns. Some groups had friendly relations with others, but they were not formally united in a local, still less a national organisation. They lacked clearly formulated conditions of membership. They met in barns or members' houses. Few groups could afford the stipends of full-time ministers; and the universities were closed to those who wished to enter the ministry. Many therefore depended on local lay pastors, whose education depended on their own Bible reading and other study. In the circumstances, it is remarkable that these churches survived.[62]

As in their earlier days, Independent congregations formed themselves with a covenant. In 1693 a new group, at first based on Bedford but later to develop into a Southill congregation, wrote to five churches in Hunts., Herts. and North-

60 C.R.O., ABCP 216–29.
61 C.R.O., GA 871.
62 Information in this section is drawn from the following. Mr. H. G. Tibbutt has written a series of short histories of local churches; the relevant ones here are: Bunyan Meeting, Bedford; Blunham; Cranfield; Cotton End; Keysoe Brook End and Keysoe Row; Leighton Buzzard; Howard Congregational Church, Bedford; Little Staughton; Stevington. He has also written the history of Southill in *Trans. Cong. Hist. Soc.*, xx. The history of Ampthill has been written by A. H. Peer. For Luton see *B.H.R.S.* xxv, 138–65. The late G. E. Page covered several others in *Some Baptist churches in the Bedford area*. See also *B.H.R.S.* xx, 207, for a list of churches, 1715. The reference to Bolnhurst psalmody comes from Dr. Williams' Library MS 39 B Jones 13 and was supplied by Mr. H. G. Tibbutt.

ants.: "Grace be to you! We, a small remnant, do joyntly consent in purpose of heart to cleave to the Lord, and having appointed a day, even the 23 of June next, to enter into covenant by giving up our sellves up to the Lord, we have this day, after fasting and prayer, agreed to request you to come to advise and direct us"; this letter had 13 signatures or marks. At Carlton in 1688 there were 21 founding members, some of whom had formerly attended at Stevington. The covenant of a Blunham group in 1724 began "We do in the presence of God and of his holy angels give up ourselves unto the Lord"; here also the number was 21. Some small groups either ran into difficulties or have left no evidence for part of their history; from 1726 to 1768 nothing is known of that at Maulden, which had got as far as building a small chapel or barn; nor of Cranfield 1720–70; and there was an early Baptist church at Leighton Buzzard which disappeared.

Most congregations drew their members from a wider area than a single village. It was similarity of views which drew them together, but such combination also made a wider fellowship and concentrated resources. In such churches members from a distance brought their own food to eat between services, and at least at Luton beer for them to drink was a charge on church funds. Stevington drew members from seven parishes round and also from Northants.; but their equipment in early days was very modest: a pewter cup, an earthen platter, and a hassock or bass for the speaker; in 1674 this congregation met at Stevington, Oakley and Pavenham in rotation; in 1681 in Simon Peacock's barn. Kimbolton church had members from Bolnhurst, Pertenhall and Swineshead.

The two biggest congregations centred on Bedford in the north and on Kensworth in the south. If members came from a great distance, this had its own drawbacks; in time they began to feel the strain of the journey in all weathers. Inhabitants of villages close at hand had no difficulty in coming to Bedford, but Gamlingay members were amicably "dismissed" in 1710 to form their own new church; and 10 Blunham members in 1724 withdrew from Bedford to join the newly set-up group in their own village. When an individual moved he had a letter of recommendation to his nearest church elsewhere.

Separation of congregations might come on a note of discord, especially at the choice of a new minister. That the Kensworth church, comprising Dunstable, Luton, St. Albans and villages in the area, held together for more than ten years, is a tribute to the personality of the pastor, Thomas Hayward. When he died in 1688, divergences in views emerged which made it difficult to agree on a successor. First Brother Russell came on trial from London, but was not approved. Then Brother Marsom of Luton "provided one Mr. Tidmarsh to com upone tryall; one part of the church did like, the other did nott aproove of hym"; so he was paid for his time and went away. But Brother Marsom "did declere agaynst the said bretheren that did not aprove of Mr. Tidmarsh, and soe tooke an occation to draw awaie a certin number of members, and meade a rentt in the church". The split was largely, though not entirely, on territorial lines. The Luton group had over 70 members from Luton itself, and more than 100 from 15 places in Beds. and some in Herts. The remaining members again divided, one group centring on Dunstable and a third on St. Albans.

This question of a minister was one of the main problems. In general only a large church could afford to pay a full-time minister. At first there were no places of training from which a trained man could come when the money was forthcoming. Ebenezer Chandler (Bedford, 1690–1747) came from a London congregation. By degrees nonconformist colleges began to emerge. Chandler's successor, Samuel Sanderson, 1747–66, had been trained both at Jolly's Congregational Academy at Attercliffe in Yorks., and at Newington Green in London. Keysoe Brook End had as minister 1749–63 Richard Denny, who had studied at the Northampton Academy. But even the comparatively large church at Luton for long depended on local preachers, such as Nathan and Thomas Marsom and Samuel Chase, until in 1762 they appointed Christopher Hall at a stipend of £40 p.a. The first pastor at Little Staughton meeting at the end of this period was a Ravensden farmer.

The Bedford congregation seems to have been comparatively well off; it received bequests from quite early days; though Bunyan's granddaughter Hannah died in the workhouse in 1770.[63] In the villages, where the yeoman was giving place to the tenant-farmer, and the continuing transfer of crafts to the towns left the cottager with few resources besides his labour, church funds must have been raised at some sacrifice. Moreover there was still a legal obligation to pay both church rates for the upkeep of the parish church, and also tithe. Some village nonconformist churches managed to subscribe what for those days was a good income. At Carlton, which in 1724 had nearly a hundred members drawn also from Pavenham, Harrold, Oakley and Turvey, the contributions ranged from 2s. to £10 p.a. each, though on an earlier list is the note against Richard Green "never giveth now", and against Ellen Reynolds "giveth nothing", while Sister Margaret "promised sumthing". One of these contributors, Lewis Tysoe of Turvey, whose subscription was £1, was cited in 1731 before the archdeacon's court for non-payment of his tithes; unfortunately the amount is not given.

A live church nearly always had active members within its own ranks. If a man showed promise, a day would be appointed "to make trial of his gift". Sometimes opinion was divided, as at Luton in 1753 about Brother John Chamberlain; the vote was "privatly taken"; 38 thought that he "had a ministeral gift", but 7 "was not satisfied". The next year John Coles was luckier; "it was unanimously judged by all the members then present that the same was a ministoral one given for public usefulness".

The main responsibility for church management rested either on deacons, as

---

[63] C.R.O., P 1/12/1. For bequests to Bunyan Meeting, see ABP/W 1660/189; 1673/41; 1683/17; 1701/8

at Bedford, or on elders and deacons, as at Luton. In both cases these officers were appointed at a church meeting. At Luton in 1730 the elders were Nathan Marsom, Thomas Hickson and James Large; the deacons were John Bunker, Edward Hickson and Samuel Marsom. When Samuel Marsom was "called to the publick work of the ministry" another deacon was appointed.

All churches had the problem of providing premises, since before the Toleration Act no permanent building could be erected. For some years the Bedford meeting continued to worship in a barn, till in 1707 a meetinghouse with 700 seats was built. The minute-book of Dunstable meeting records: "In the year 1708 built then an house at Dunstable for the public worship of God; the ground cost £10, the writings £2; the charge for stufe and workmanship £81 and two pence."[64] Luton's meetinghouse must have been in existence by then, for in 1709 a gallery was added. Stevington was built 1720–1; Ridgmont by 1722; Blunham 1751; Carlton in 1760 with about 600 seats; Little Staughton probably in the 1760's. A new style of building was evolved, with plain oak columns instead of stone pillars.

At first music was not used in the services, and it made its way only gradually. In 1690 the Bedford meeting agreed that psalms could be sung, although none should perform it but such as could sing with grace in their hearts, and those who could not could be silent or not be present during the singing. This seems to have been on weekdays. In 1697 singing was allowed in the morning of the Lord's Day. At Carlton in 1703 "it is agreed upon to sing at the Lord's table". Much later, the Little Staughton meeting pronounced "singing of psalms, hymns and spiritual songs vocally is an ordinance of the gospel to be performed by believers, but as to time, place and manner, everyone ought to be left to their liberty in using it". In 1751 Bolnhurst agreed to practise psalmody once a week.

Regular attendance, especially at the Lord's supper, was expected, and enquiries were made if members were absent. Discipline was taken seriously. Offenders were first admonished, then suspended, and if obdurate excluded from membership. At the Bedford meeting in 1674 Oliver Thody was reproved for dancing; in 1702 Brother Butcher for unbecoming actions about the maypole; in 1718 there was a quarrel between Elizabeth Hern and her husband, "there being a great uproar, neighbours were obliged to go into their house to part them"; and in 1724 Brother Hurst played at quoits and ninepins and went cock-fighting. At Carlton in the 1690's Hannah Pye "was soon cut off again for her flying from the church and running into the world again as bad as ever". The Luton meeting in 1739 was embarrassed to find a minister, Brother Joshua Mead, drinking too much; he was suspended from partaking at the Lord's supper "and also from preaching, on account of his sad falls and sin, in over-charging and disordering himselfe with liquors to the great dishonour of God, reproach of religion, griefe

64 Minute-book in the church's possession.

and sorrow of the church"; and in 1744 Joseph Chandler "was cut off and separated from the church on account of his defrauding his creditors".

Congregations distrusted any association with the Anglican church. Marrying an Anglican might be cause for suspension; and at Blunham Ann Harris in 1750 was excluded after she had stood as a godmother and then refused to come to answer for her offence.

In general every church settled its own affairs, though there might be close relations between the mother church and small village churches which had hived off. When a pastor or leading church member died, the funeral sermon would be preached by a minister from a leading church elsewhere; thus the funeral sermon for Brother Killingworth at Southill in 1722 was preached by Ebenezer Chandler from Bedford; that at Bedford in 1766 for Chandler's successor, Samuel Sanderson, was preached by Samuel Palmer, who was of Bedford origin and then a minister at Hackney; and that at Luton for Marsom by a pastor from Hitchin. In case of schism in a church, as happened at Carlton in 1693 (see below), representatives of other churches were called in to advise or arbitrate.

Thus by the latter part of the 18th cent. the various practical problems which had faced the small groups in villages in the early years of their freedom had been surmounted. But the great question which vexed them was that of baptism. In a gathered church, whose members have come together, not on a topographical basis but spontaneously, or as they believe from a divine call, it is perhaps a logical deduction that a member cannot be admitted as an infant, but only when adult; if baptism marks entry into membership, baptism should be adult also. Independent churches came increasingly to take this view. Some, like the original meeting at Bedford, and for long that at Biggleswade, were tolerant on the point, leaving a member to follow his conscience; these came to be called Union churches. Others, such as the Kensworth church from which Dunstable and Luton derived, insisted on adult baptism; so also did Eversholt; these were known as Baptist (or later General Baptists). Some went still further, believing only in a particular baptism confined to the elect, and so became Particular Baptists; among these were Stevington, which sent representatives to a Baptist meeting in London in 1689; Ridgmont (1701); and Sharnbrook (1719). Churches might change their view from time to time, and Southill, originally Independent, went through the whole range. When members of the same church could not agree, dissension arose; this happened at Carlton at the beginning of this period, and at Bedford at the end.

Trouble at Carlton meeting began in 1693.[65] Their pastor, John Greenwood, had come to them in 1688 from Stevington, perhaps hoping that he was joining a more congenial congregation, for it was soon apparent that he believed in infant baptism. An increasingly vocal group at Carlton, led by William Bithrey,

[65] Transcript of minute-book in C.R.O.

one of the deacons, had come to be in favour of adult baptism. Church meetings were kept "with little comfort"; attempts were made to renew the covenant, "but after a proud and unorderly sort", and the dissidents began to meet separately. Greenwood probably would have done best to resign at once, but according to his own account he "mildly and gently admonished the dissidents", at which, so he says, Bithrey "fell into wicked passion". In 1695 representatives of eight churches in Beds., Hunts, and Northants. came to Carlton to advise, and they urged the groups to reunite and to invite a new pastor. For two months "things in the church went on broakenly and confusedly", during which time the church "conclouded not to dismember their pastor". Finally Greenwood acknowledged that the schism was partly due to himself, but it "could not be helped without sinning against his own light". In 1696 he "departed from us to North Crawley".

At the Bedford meeting much later there was a similar situation in reverse. The Bedford church had always avoided a hard-and-fast line on baptism; "we do not design to make baptism, whether of believers or infants, any bar to communion". When Samuel Sanderson (1747–66) died, he advised the church to appoint a successor of similar views, and not to be too hasty in making the appointment. Unfortunately the new minister, Joshua Symonds, in 1772 informed his congregation that his views on baptism had changed. He himself was then baptised at Hitchin by immersion. A compromise was reached, by which he was allowed to remain provided he did not mention baptism from the pulpit nor conduct any immersions. Even so, some members (one of whom was John Howard) were unhappy at his being allowed to stay; these seceded, and built a new church a few yards distant in the same street, Mill Lane, so that there were henceforward New Meeting, which practised infant baptism, and the original or Old Meeting, a Union church, where both views continued to be (and are still) allowed.

Generosity and broad-mindedness are not the qualities to seek in the non-conformist churches of this period; their characteristics were independence, courage and determination. Sometimes there came to them, as at Bedford in 1755, a feeling that they had missed the heights of their founding fathers; it was not that the church had suffered defection or scandalous conduct, but there was "too much lukewarmness"; they prayed for a revival of God's work; and it was resolved that all members should converse more frequently together and "more constantly attend meetings for prayer". Men, whether as individuals or in groups, cannot live always on the heights. Perhaps in spiritual life as in the natural world there has to be a rhythm, a rise and fall. Inspiration is not to be obtained by painstaking endeavour, and when it comes it is likely to appear in an unexpected quarter.

MORAVIANS[66]

To Bedford in the mid-18th cent. there came teaching from the continent,

[66] Short histories have been issued by the Bedford Moravian church; the records are in C.R.O.

stressing the need for life in the spirit of Christ. Ultimately this is the basis of every Christian church and of all Christian movements, yet few if any have yet succeeded in leading the Christian life, and so it has to be continually restated. This time the new impulse came from the Unitas Fratrum, known to us as Moravians. It went back to John Hus in the 15th cent., was currently active in Germany, and had spread thence to London. It taught an aloof attitude to the world; a complete submission to Christ; and a life as nearly as possible on the lines of the early church.

It arrived in Bedford unobtrusively. When in 1738 the town was gloomily recovering from a smallpox epidemic which had been worse than usual, young Francis Oakley, then at Cambridge, and son of a High Street milliner, helped his friend Jacob Rogers, curate of St. Paul's; and these young men invited down from London two Anglican clergy who had met with Moravian teaching there. Bedford was receptive. Rogers was won over, gave up his curacy and began to preach from a wagon on St. Peter's green, or a windmill on the road to Kimbolton. Once when he was allowed to preach in the gaol, many gathered outside in High Street and Gaol Lane to listen. On another occasion a preacher from London addressed a congregation in the house of Negus Eston, carpenter; the speaker stood in the passage, from which opened off two rooms occupied by the audience; and one of the audience, Thomas Pierson, has told how next day as he walked to Ampthill his heart was filled with peace. Soon members were meeting in a barn behind Mrs. Oakley's premises, but on their way to worship they encountered hostility from a crowd which lined High Street to "revile" them. New members had to go to London to be received, until in 1745 the Bedford Moravian church was officially constituted.

Mrs. Oakley backed her son. Her early life had been hard; her husband, a barber and peruke-maker, though mayor in 1719, was not a good man of business, and he died in 1734 in prison for debt. She brought up five children by working day and night, at first at dressmaking and later at millinery, till she had a prosperous business. The practice of charging fixed prices instead of bargaining, which else-where was usually initiated by Quakers, in Bedford is ascribed to Mrs. Oakley. But her premises in the heart of the town were not suitable for a permanent centre for an other-worldly movement, so in 1752 a Moravian settlement with church was built on the edge of the town. Some Moravian teaching also spread to the villages round, especially to Riseley.

In the new settlement the members lived a simple communal life, with daily worship. There were houses for single brethren and single sisters. The brothers worked at wool-combing, shoemaking, tailoring or tilling the soil; the sisters were occupied in spinning and lacemaking. The children were taught; James Gillray the cartoonist was at one time at school in Bedford. All decisions were church decisions, many important ones being taken by lot, because Moravians believed this to be a New Testament practice, and because it helped to subdue the individual will. The object was to have a complete and uncomplicated dependence on the will of God, and to recognise his intervention in the most ordinary of day-to-day happenings. Such an object made it unlikely that the church would ever become really widespread; thus it was not the Moravians but the Methodists who were to reach large numbers.

METHODISTS

The puritan movement of the previous century had come from individual Bible reading. John Wesley was an Anglican clergyman who had been impressed by the Moravians, and his unique contribution was that he reached those who could respond only to a direct personal challenge, many of whom probably could not read.[67] During the period of this chapter he was a galvanising force within the Anglican church. Among clergy, his helpers in Bedfordshire were John Berridge, vicar of Everton, and Samuel Hicks, vicar of Wrestlingworth; while the Luton curate, Coriolanus Copleston, was sympathetic.

It has been calculated that this amazing man in 53 years travelled 224,000 miles and preached over 40,000 sermons. Simply as a physical feat it is impressive. Most of his journeys were on horseback. In February 1747 on his first visit to Bedfordshire (apart from a hasty cup of tea at Dunstable in 1741 on his way north), the north wind blew exceeding hard and keen, and the snow drove full in his face. He preached at Potton at 6 p.m.; was off in the morning before it was well light; the frost would not well bear or break, the wind rose higher, a storm of rain and hail drove through his coat, boots and everything, and froze as it fell on his eyebrows, so that he had scarce strength or motion left when he got to the inn at Stilton; but he persevered through the snowdrifts, leading his horse, and reached Grantham next day. In January 1772 the snow was so deep that it was with much difficulty and some danger that he reached Luton. Even in spring or summer, heavy rain could make the minor roads almost impassable, as in March 1758 when on the way to Sundon he exchanged the road for the fields, and they, having just been ploughed, were deep enough. Finding the way was confusing on minor roads: sometimes guides came to meet him, but the weather or other delays might cause them to miss.

The place where he preached was sometimes the church, especially at Everton; sometimes out of doors, as at St. Peter's green, Bedford; sometimes in an unsuitable room, as at both Bedford (over a pigsty) and at Luton ("a miserable preaching-house").

The effect of his forceful preaching on the ignorant poor was such that sometimes they wept and cried out hysterically. These manifestations made him uneasy, for he realised their dangers, especially at Everton; but by 1761 in this

---

[67] All references taken from Wesley's *Journal*; a history of the Bedford Methodist church was also written by J. M. Anderson.

parish he was able to note "the greater part have found peace with God". He was even more acutely aware than most speakers of the effect of his words, and he certainly did not like it when once in 1764 the people of Sundon seemed very quiet and very stupid, or on one occasion at Bedford in 1768: "a more sleepy audience I have not often seen". What he preferred, and usually secured, was "a very numerous and serious congregation", as at Potton in 1762; or "a serious congregation" at Cranfield in 1769; or "a deeply serious congregation" at Gt. Barford in 1761. At Millbrook in 1766 he found "plain serious people"; at Lidlington "plain country people"; and at Wootton several had already found "the power of God unto salvation". Cople in 1766 was "at present the most lively of all the little societies in Bedfordshire". It was from these societies that twenty years later Methodism was to develop as a separate church (ch. 39).

To Bedford his first visit was in 1753. He came at the invitation of William Parker, a grocer who had at first joined the Moravians, but who was not able to go quite all the way with them in their other-worldly approach. A few like-minded friends began to meet at Parker's house. Wesley in 1753 stayed three days and preached twice on St. Peter's green; and in 1754 he came again. At his third visit in 1757 Parker was mayor, and he noted in his diary "Mr. Parker, now mayor, received us gladly".

Meanwhile he had also made contact with the south of the county. In 1757 he went to Sundon, where lived William Cole; Mrs. Cole had just received a large legacy, and Wesley expressed in the quaint language of the day his uneasiness at its possible effect on her: "it is a miracle if it does not drown her soul in everlasting perdition". But he need not have feared, for the Coles remained his staunch supporters. William Cole was high sheriff 1757–8 and invited Wesley to preach the assize sermon. Wesley's text was "We shall all stand before the judgement seat of Christ." The judge invited him to dine, but he had an assignment to preach elsewhere on the next day, so between 1 and 2 o'clock he was off again through snow, sleet, and a piercing northeast wind. (However once in June he took an hour off to visit Wrest gardens, and preferred them to Stow.)

These two men, Parker and Cole, were Wesley's chief lay friends in the county and he returned again and again to Bedford, Sundon and Luton, as he did to Everton and Wrestlingworth, where were his chief clerical supporters.

The singing of hymns was from the first a feature of Wesley's services, and his gifted brother Charles wrote over 5,000 hymns. It was from the evangelical movement that hymn-singing gradually spread once more to all the church.

The attitude towards Moravians and Methodists held by some may seem harsh. Talbot Williamson called them "pharisaical saintlings". Is not this like some attitudes towards modern missions: "In so far as the new message it true, it is what we have always held – why cannot others get it from the church in the ordinary way as we do?" But a new presentation startles others into awareness.

31 – FARMERS AND COTTAGERS, 1689–1773

TENANT-FARMERS

In the 16-17th cents. a number of yeomen had become gentry, or had gone into other walks of life, for instance as attorneys or merchants. Now those who were left were rapidly becoming tenant-farmers (holding farms on lease), as the big estates grew. The word "farmer" in place of the previous yeoman or husbandman began to come into use in the late 17th cent., for instance at Barton, though it was a long time before the term "yeoman" disappeared altogether.

The Woburn estate is the chief example of this growth of estates.[1] The 4th Duke of Bedford's major purchase of property in mid-Bedfordshire from the Earl of Ailesbury in 1738 has been noted, and his smaller purchases at Oakley and Steppingley from Levinz and Abbot (ch. 27). The family bought manors at Eversholt, 1702, Ridgmont, 1703, Eaton Socon, 1708, Husborne Crawley, 1721, Cranfield, 1729, Birchmore, 1747, and Houghton Regis, 1740, from Hillersdon, Stone, Ashley, Lowe, Monoux, Pickering and Brandreth. In these areas, especially at Eversholt, Husborne Crawley and Oakley, they also bought whatever smaller properties they could secure. Thus at Eversholt on several occasions 1702-61 they bought from smaller people houses with accompanying land; they bought cottages; and they bought a number of small areas of land varying in size from 1-11 a. At Husborne Crawley 1721-67 they made still more purchases of a similar nature; five purchases were sizeable houses with land; seven were only a cottage, or cottage and pightle; other purchases were of land only; and two were simply common rights. Oakley shows much the same picture. At Aspley Guise, Eaton Socon, Marston, Maulden, Milton Bryan, Potsgrove, Steppingley and Woburn purchases were made.

Who were these smaller people who were selling out to the big landowners? At this period the Wrest Park family were concentrating on purchases in Silsoe,[2] which gives an example. In three cases the vendors were women. Mary Wheeler, who in 1689 sold a cottage and 19 a., was a yeoman's widow. Elizabeth Lock, who in 1693 sold 30 a., was a spinster, formerly of Silsoe, who had gone to live in London. John Sellers, yeoman, had two daughters Elizabeth and Sarah, who married respectively into Caddington and into Hertfordshire, and from them a house and about 8 a. passed to the Wrest estate in 1718.

The Wrest family's major purchase in Flitton and Silsoe in this period was in 1755 from the Beaumont family. These yeomen (ch. 25) had steadily built up a

---

[1] Muniment books (photo-copies in C.R.O.).   [2] C.R.O., L 5.

position in the 17th cent., and had absorbed the lands of another yeoman family. that of Pearles. But in 1705 when Thomas Beaumont died, he owed £200 on his purchases. The family continued to mortgage. When at last the property was sold, the male members of the family were respectively Thomas, a salesman in London, John, a Silsoe maltster, and William, a Shefford apothecary. How far their departure was due to the attraction of other walks of life, and whether their inability to pay off mortgages was due to living beyond their means, it is hard to say.

Sometimes an existing older estate sold part to a newer one, as when the St. Johns sold Keysoe to Sir Jeremy Sambrooke. Sambrooke's agent met the principal tenants one Saturday at Bedford market in 1717, and found them inclinable to give the best satisfaction. Sir Jeremy meant to come to Keysoe himself, but the agent warned him that there was no suitable place in Keysoe fit to receive him, much less to lodge him, and it would be better to stay in Bedford. Later he reported that the tenants were "extraordinarily pleased with your kind entertainment", and were happy about the transfer, "having assurance of quiet continuance".[3]

It might happen that the lord of a small manor was obliged to sell and himself become a tenant. It must have seemed strange to John Man, whose ancestors had held Eggington manor for centuries, to write in 1721: "Landlord, I have sent you your rent, £40 . . . Landlord, mine with my wife's kind service presented to you."[4]

Tenancy did not solve all problems, and tenants were sometimes in difficulties. Heylock Kingsley of Sandy in 1724 wrote to his father-in-law about an impoverished tenant; he thought the man should be shown mercy coupled with strict oversight – "the fellow and family can't starve".[5] A Clophill tenant on the Wrest estate in 1712 was in arrears for his rent to the extent of £451, and his stock was listed as security; he had wheat, rye and barley growing on 62 a.; 56 a. of pasture and hay; 179 sheep; 35 cattle; 10 horses; 20 pigs; a waggon and 5 carts; besides some grain, beans and hay in store.[6] Incidentally, he was described as yeoman, though he was clearly a tenant-farmer.

Two other inventories indicate the stock carried respectively by a smaller and a larger man. The whole of the live and dead stock of Joseph Tearle of Stanbridge, including his household goods, in 1732 amounted to £100; he had 29 sheep, 3 cows and a calf, 2 horses, 3 pigs, poultry, and 9 a. under cultivation.[7] Those of Edward Edgley of Stratton in 1770 amounted to £1,080; he had 289 sheep, 8 cows, 5 horses, 37 pigs, and poultry; he had 65 a. under cultivation; and his grain, beans and peas, and hay in store accounted for £400 of the total.[8]

[3] C.R.O., C 2063–4.
[4] C.R.O., RY 56.
[5] C.R.O., PM 32.

[6] C.R.O., L 4/376.
[7] C.R.O., GA 507.
[8] C.R.O., PBW/P 1770/54.

Those leases which survive for this period (in the main for Clophill, Harrold, Houghton Regis, Husborne Crawley, Podington and Yielden) relate to farms varying in size from about 100 to 300 a.[9] They usually provide that the landlord will supply materials for repair (great rough timber, brick, tiles and lime), and the tenant carry out the work. Growing timber – young spires of oak, ash or elm – must be preserved. Sometimes the tenant is prohibited from sowing hemp, flax or woad; and almost always there is a penalty against his trying to get a short-term gain by ploughing up pasture. Sometimes in addition to his money rent, he must provide fowls at Christmas, or cart coal from Tempsford. The amount of rent varies surprisingly. Often the tenant covenants to consume on the farm the dung and straw produced; and to leave at the end of his term similar quantities to those found on entering.

On the bigger estates there begins now to be more evidence of the agent. Until the estate reached a certain size, such work did not occupy a man's full time, and Joseph Cole of Shefford had several other activities besides supervision of the Wrest Park estate. He was a schoolmaster. He made beautiful maps – an art which perhaps reached its peak in this century – coloured, with the title and other details framed in elaborate cartouches, and sometimes with coats of arms; one of Potton in 1754 was for Admiral Byng, for such maps were now in vogue among the gentry. The Marchioness Grey's husband spoke of him as "friend Cole", and though her son-in-law was on one occasion annoyed with him and called him a scoundrel, he had soon made it up, and "stopped at Shefford and had a jaw with old Cole". Where the manor was still functioning, a local attorney was usually employed to hold the court for copyhold tenants; the Duke of Bedford employed Samuel Davis.

For the farmer's political position as regards his landlord, see ch. 27.

From 1770, market prices of the chief cereals had to be recorded. The earliest surviving returns for this county show that Bedford was always the dearest market; Luton was the cheapest for wheat, Leighton for barley and oats, and Potton for beans; rye was sold only at Leighton and Potton, Leighton being the cheaper market.[10]

MARKET-GARDENERS

The specialists had a better chance of remaining independent than those who practised mixed farming. There were still many dairymen in southern and central Beds.; a Swedish traveller, Kalm in 1748, was surprised to see men and not maids going out with pails to milk the cows morning and evening.[11] To a much less extent there were also still graziers; horse-dealers too are known. Woad was still grown: the Ampthill family of Fox were woadmen c. 1740.[12]

[9] C.R.O., e.g., Clophill, L 4/383; Harrold, L 7/88–100; Podington, OR 174, 1329; Yielden, C 2167–9; Houghton Regis and Husborne Crawley, see R.
[10] C.R.O., QSM xv, 82; QSR 1775/167–82.
[11] *Kalm's account of his visit to England* (J. Lucas trans.), p.327.
[12] *B.P.R.*, xvii, burials for 1740 and 1744.

The small man who was best placed was the market-gardener, because he cultivated a small area intensively, and his London market was growing. The distribution of market gardening is reflected in the tithe arrangements prevailing about 1708.[13] At Sandy small tithes were paid by the acre on turnips, carrots, peas, beans, onions and parsnips. At Sutton "turnips have not been known in the field, till of late years a great part of our sand land has been sown with them; the parishioners will not pay tithe for them". At Maulden "turnips, onions, carrots, beans, peas and all garden stuff pay the tenth part". At Flitton-cum-Silsoe turnips were tithed by the acre. At Chalgrave, also on the greensand ridge, "turnips are only sowed by Mr. Atterbury". By contrast at Wymington in the north "turnips have never been known"; neither were they grown at Totternhoe and Eaton Bray in the south. Turnip-hoers in east Beds. are particularly mentioned in the anti-militia riots of 1757.[14] It may be that the use of turnips and clover as a substitute for fallow was spreading, but records of crop rotation at this date have not been traced.[15] The stability of market gardeners was especially marked at Sandy, even though here the estates of Pym and Monoux were building up.

OWNER-FARMERS

There were still some owner-farmers. John Blundell of Meppershall, who kept a notebook of miscellaneous jottings,[16] has an illuminating background. He may have been distantly connected with the better-known Blundell family,[17] but his grandfather was a labourer.[18] His father William seems to have got a little land with his wife Mary, who was hard-working, and got together money "by her extraordinary care and industry";[19] so that he was able to buy more, and he inherited a further 6 a. from a Hanscomb cousin. John's elder brothers either died young or had only daughters, so the whole modest farm may have eventually come to him; and he himself died, apparently a bachelor, in 1774.

Some of his jottings for 1763 follow. In January he made a little rick, carried 14 qtrs. of barley to Shefford, had his saddle mended, and paid the blacksmith a year's bill £1 13s. 10d. In February he sold 11 qtrs. of new malt at Shefford for 30s. a qtr. In March the local tailor turned his coat for 5s.; Mr. Pepper, the Biggleswade clockmaker, cleaned his clock for 2s. 6d., and he took physic, and also bought a pint mug for 2½d. He finished sowing barley, stacked ash faggots, paid land tax and poor's rate, and had some extra labour from Bland's boy for 2s. 6d. a week. In May he bought 6 white-hafted knives and forks. (Was his diet limited, as Kalm says, to "roast beef and pudding"?)[20] In June his housekeeper

[13] C.R.O., ABE 2.
[14] C.R.O., FN 1253, p.146.
[15] Twenty years after Turvey was enclosed, fallow was in occasional use there; Richard Pool of Grove Farm had no settled system, but in 1809–13 three of his fields were cultivated as follows (C.R.O., HG 104):
Fallow; wheat; beans; fallow; wheat.
Oats; fallow and turnips; barley; wheat; beans.
Vetches; wheat; oats; clover, sown wheat; wheat.
[16] I am indebted to Mr. T. W. Bagshawe for this reference. B.H.R.S. hope to publish the text in due course.
[17] Beds. Bib., 234.
[18] B.P.R., xxxviii.
[19] C.R.O., ABP/W 1726-7/81.
[20] Kalm's account, p.326.

caught the smallpox, and he was obliged to remove, taking with him 8 shirts, 5 pairs of hose, 8 "neckins", 3 wigs and 3 hats. In this month he sold his wheat, some at Hitchin for 19s. a load, some at an unspecified market, probably Biggleswade, for 18s. 6d. or 18s. 9d. When harvest began he took stock of his ale, for ale must be supplied to the harvesters: he had 4 kilderkins of ale and as many of small beer. On 10 Sept. he made harvest home (he does not say whether, as at Carlton, someone played the violin) and paid the harvest men. He sold a load of the second crop of clover for 15s. With winter coming on, he bought candles.

John Pedley of Gt. Barford was better off. His diary, 1773–95,[21] is mainly concerned with his own health. He attended a wide range of local fairs – Ampthill, Bedford, Biggleswade, Dunstable, Elstow, Ickwell, Potton and Woburn, besides some outside the county; and also "statute" or hiring fairs at local villages, probably to recruit workers. He sent his sheep (after branding them) to Elstow or Potton fair; cattle to Bedford; and horses to Woburn. He mentions harvest supper, and in 1777 he made the finest harvest he ever knew. Usually he travelled on horseback, but sometimes in a four-wheeled chaise. Pedley was a married man, and sent his sons to boarding-school at Aspley Guise (ch. 33).

THE CATTLE-PLAGUE

One factor which affected owner and tenant-farmer alike was the cattle plague (rinderpest) which raged intermittently from 1745 to 1754. So serious was this that an act of parliament ordered the slaughter of infected animals within 24 hours, after which they must be buried 4 ft. deep, the hides having been slashed to make them useless (lest thieves be tempted to dig them up). Compensation was at the rate of £2 for an adult animal, 5s. for a calf, this being about half value. Only a few months after the first outbreak, one justice of the peace (Philip Birt, vicar of Flitton) wrote that he had certified for about 60 sufferers. He felt that the legalistic severity practised towards Wrest Park tenants was less wise than the attitude of the Duke of Bedford; "his Grace chooses to allure rather than terrify", and promised a guinea for each beast killed.[22]

Quarter sessions appointed "inspectors"; in practice that meant an added duty imposed on an unpaid constable, though for this he was able to claim expenses. At first cattle fairs were still held, and cattle could be sold under certificate. There was evasion, and in October 1751 justices attended Leighton fair to make sure the rules were observed.[23] In January 1752 they at last prohibited the sale of cattle at fairs.[24] Leighton was impatient, and urged that Aylesbury was developing a trade in ox hair "where no such kind of market had ever been before", whereas that at Leighton "used to be very considerable" and was "in danger of being entirely lost".[25] As late as Michaelmas sessions 1754 the justices

[21] B.H.R.S. xl, 95–109.
[22] B.M., Add. MS. 35, 693.
[23] C.R.O., QSM ix, 135.
[24] C.R.O., QSM xi, 93.
[25] C.R.O., QSR 1752/51.

65 *Dunstable tournament armorial roll, later copy.*

66 *Foxhunting at Colworth*

67　*Carrier's waggon unloading at Toddington.*

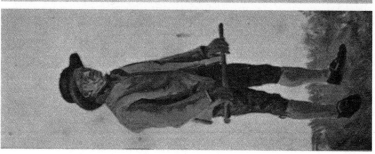

68 Preliminary studies for picture of the Woburn sheepshearing:
bull-feeder; R. Salmon, steward; Runciman, tenant; Holland, shepherd

were urging Bucks. and Herts. to cooperate.

While the epidemic was at its height, the clerk of the peace, William Goldsmith, sent out up to 1,000 notices and 580 letters annually. By the time normal life was resumed, he was dead, and in 1756 his widow sent in to quarter sessions a claim for over £500 for extra work done; it need hardly be said that she received only about a third of it, for the justices were of opinion that it was a dangerous tendency that an officer should receive more money every time parliament increased his duties; besides it would mean heavy rates for the farmers to pay.[26]

CRAFTSMEN AND OTHERS

In general the craftsmen now found in the villages were the essential ones of miller, blacksmith and carpenter. There might also be butcher and baker; weaver, shoemaker and rough tailor; mason and bricklayer. Most other occupations had gone to the market towns (ch. 29).

Exceptions to this are found in a village very near a town. Such was Elstow, which had joiner, matmaker, cooper, basketmaker and staymaker. A large village also offered better prospects; Henlow had millwright, woolcomber, carrier and ropemaker. Here and there a skilled man survived; Gt. Barford had a dish-turner; Caddington a bodice-maker; Westoning a chair-mender; and at Langford in 1759 there was a papermaker, Henry Dane. Other exceptional cases noted are: a gingerbread-baker at Clophill; a gunsmith at Lidlington; a pump-maker at Southill; a wickmaker at Kempston; and a woadman at Bromham. Clockmakers are known at Bolnhurst, Carlton, Cranfield, Goldington, Kempston and Wootton, as well as in the towns.

Along the western border of Beds. from Harrold and Odell to Leighton was a succession of lacemen or lace-merchants, who distributed patterns and thread to workers and collected the finished lace. They were also found inland as far as Bedford and Ampthill. Lacemen sometimes had difficulty in maintaining their rights to particular patterns. " 'Tis a common practice amongst them [the lacemakers] to get patterns, thread, money or goods from one and then sell their lace to another; and if prosecuted in Ampthill court [petty sessions] to make over their effects to a relation, so that there is nothing left to seize, and the creditor is only laughed at"; this was said in 1761.[27]

In the strawplait industry there was still no figure comparable to the laceman, though the industry had spread slightly by 1719.[28] The Bedfordshire poet Nicholas Rowe (d. 1718) wrote that "thousands get their living by the head". In 1748 Kalm described the process; the straws were cut to 9-inch lengths, made into bundles, and bleached with sulphur smoke. For the actual plaiting they were moistened to make them pliable. The finished plait was flattened in a

[26] C.R.O., QSM xiii, 119.
[27] C.R.O., HW 88/47.
[28] J. Dony, *History of the straw hat industry*, 20–5.

plait-mill – a simple wooden roller fixed to the wall; that in Caddington work-house had to be mended in 1771.[29] Kalm thought women looked pretty enough when "going out to pay compliments" dressed in straw hats which they had made, red cloaks, and with pattens to keep their shoes clean.[30] Boxes and baskets were also made, according to Arthur Young in 1768, the work being "carried to a great perfection of neatness".

Matmaking from rushes was now largely concentrated at Pavenham, though known also at Elstow and Cranfield.

Stone-quarrying at Totternhoe, though centuries old, is described for the first time by Kalm.[31] He says the freestone was dug deep under the hills. The entrance to the quarry was walled round for about 12 ft., and access was through an uneven passage 6 ft. broad by 7 ft. high, with water trickling everywhere in winter, but dry in summer. Light must be carried, "for after one had come 6–7 fathoms into the mine, there was no more daylight, but it was coal-black darkness as of night". On either side cross-galleries opened out; "this would have been to one unacquainted with them the worst labyrinth and maze there could possibly be", but they were mostly filled with stone fragments. The workers "hew with their picks" and then "knock wedges of iron into it, by which they spring it loose horizontally". The loosened pieces were then carried out on a low oak truck which, instead of wheels, had two rollers of ash; and which was hauled to the entrance by the workers; then wound along the road with a windlass to the place where the stone was to be hewn.

COTTAGERS

A cottager might own or rent his cottage, and (if fortunate) a small area of land; even so, the land would scarcely be enough to support a family. When those who owned their cottages got into difficulties and were obliged to sell them, they found ready purchasers. The 4th Duke of Bedford bought seven at Husborne Crawley between 1749 and 1760, besides several at Oakley; and others at Eversholt, Marston and Maulden over a slightly longer period.[32] Other landowners did likewise, as did John Harvey at Ickwell or Sir Jeremy Sambrooke at Keysoe.[33] Again, the cottager might be obliged to sell his land, even if he retained his cottage.

Common right appertained to ancient cottages. With pressure on the common it became more closely regulated, and it varied from place to place. When William Pain of Silsoe died in 1743 he left to his sister Mary his cottage and 3 cow commons.[34] At Yielden in 1704 a cottage is mentioned as having with it the right to common for 1 horse, 2 cows and a breeder, and 6 sheep.[35] Land on which a cottage had once stood could carry a common right, as a toft at Sundon

---

[29] C.R.O., P 35/12.
[30] *Kalm's account, loc.cit.*
[31] *Op.cit.,* 290–9.
[32] Muniment books (photo-copies in C.R.O.).

[33] For instance, C.R.O., HY 306–8; C 1378, 1392.
[34] C.R.O., WE 214.
[35] C.R.O., C 1344.

in 1771 which had common of pasture for 2 cows and a heifer.[36] Details like these are found among the muniments of gentry as old cottages came into their possession.

Common right was sometimes restricted by agreement, and gentry appear among the parties to these. At Clophill in 1714 the Duke of Kent agreed with 19 owners of common right to substitute 10 a. meadow and a money payment of £3 p.a. for Clophill warren, where formerly there had been a right to cut fern.[37] At Flitwick in 1752 Dr. Dell agreed with 74 persons owning common right that Church mead could be discharged of common in return for a money payment of £5 p.a.[38] Sometimes common right was threatened by encroachment, as at Kempston by Edward Edwards in 1717, when 27 persons bound themselves to share the cost of defending common right on both sides of Hardwick brook; here again, gentry are among the signatories.[39]

The cattle plague of 1745–54 must have borne heavily on those cottagers who still had a cow or cows. Unfortunately there is no way of ascertaining their losses exactly. As at least some farmers had closes in which it was possible to graze cattle, while a cottager would be lucky if he had a pightle and would normally graze his cow on the common where infection easily spread, it seems likely that the cottagers lost proportionately more than the farmers, and found replacement more difficult. Philip Birt, one of the clerical justices, sympathised with those "whose whole substance consists perhaps in a few cattle". "It is now", he said, "a very melancholy as well as troublesome office I have the honour to execute; it is foreign to my calling as a clergyman".[40] Probably in a number of cases common rights lapsed or were sold; the 4th Duke of Bedford bought two at Husborne Crawley in 1759 and 1767.[41]

Where there were still a number of cottagers owning common right and desirous of exercising it, there was sometimes difficulty in enforcing effective use over land which was in individual occupation for most of the year. This was the case with a field at Harrold on the Wrest Park estate, where there was common right from "old Lammas day". By the time the cottagers' cattle entered it, it was usually as bare or barer than the common, for the tenant, Knight, grazed it with 400 sheep. However, in 1770 he ploughed it up and sowed corn (for this he would probably have to pay his landlord a fine). According to his account, the field was of so little use to the cottagers that they would have accepted a small money payment in lieu of the grazing, but he feared to compromise his landlord's position. However, when the wheat was coming into ear, and the cottagers realised that they were losing the land for good and all, feeling flared up; they broke the fence, turned in a by-herd, and beat off the ears of wheat with whips

---

[36] C.R.O., T 42/418.
[37] C.R.O., P 45/28/1.
[38] C.R.O., LL 1/115.

[39] C.R.O., X 122/14.
[40] See n.22.
[41] Muniment book I, 176 (photo-copy in C.R.O.).

and sticks. They got little sympathy from the agent, Joseph Cole, who appeared to think common right an anachronism. "What advantage can it be to the cottagers to turn the herd to feed where nothing is to be had? It was downright malice."[42]

Besides those cases where common right had lapsed through lack of use or had been sold, there were newer cottages which had never been entitled to it, in particular any newly built on the waste, perhaps by a squatter.

The cottager's labour was still left to him, but it was a potential of which he could not always make full use. If the married man obtained paid work locally, it might be merely seasonal when there was particular demand. Hiring by the year was usually done at a statute fair; this was the obvious course for a single man, who might well be hired by a distant farmer, and go to live in. Occasionally married men attempted to do this also, leaving their families chargeable on the rates; in 1769 one man was indicted at quarter sessions for leaving his family for the third time.[43] Sometimes it happened, after a dispute with the master, that wages were withheld, as happened in 1743 to Joshua Knight, whom John Man of Potsgrove had hired at Luton fair.[44]

Whole families quite often wandered, in spite of the settlement act of 1662 which tried to restrict movement from one parish to another. The Branklins, who seem to have originated in Bedford or Ravensden, had moved about so much that in 1741 they had six children aged 2–14 who had been born in five different places in Hertfordshire.[45] Nathaniel Norris, apprehended the same year, was born at Shefford, had worked as a groom at Westminster, next spent some time at Maulden and Toddington, had another spell outside the county, and then arrived at Ampthill, having been twice married and lost both his wives.[46] Margaret Millard in 1773 was ordered to be sent back to Northill from as far away as Devon.[47]

With little scope for by-occupations, and with an uncertain demand for his labour, it is not surprising that the cottager was tempted to spend what money he had, when he had it, at the alehouse. In 1748 Kalm noted some men sitting all day in the alehouse killing time.[48] Inn doors, he says, were usually left open; hence the use of high-backed settles to keep out the draughts.

Any help the cottager's wife and children could give to the family budget mattered. In the west they made pillow lace. No laceman is known east of Bedford or Ampthill, so in the east it was more difficult to get thread and to dispose of the finished lace. In the south it was said that straw to the value of 6d. would make plait to the value of 8s. or 9s.; or alternatively that a 4d. bundle of

[42] C.R.O., L 24/231–7; Lammas Day was 1 August; as the calendar had been changed, at this date old Lammas Day would be 21 July.
[43] C.R.O., QSR 1769/28.
[44] C.R.O., QSR 1743/51, 64, 99.

[45] C.R.O., QSR 1741/21–8.
[46] C.R.O., P 30/13/4.
[47] C.R.O., P 10/13/3.
[48] *Kalm's account*, p.333.

straw would make three hats; thus women and children might earn £10–£30 p.a.[49] This is probably a maximum figure, and it seems likely that many earned much less. Moreover the area of strawplait had spread only slightly; probably it was limited to walking distance from the plait markets at Luton and Dunstable.

The cottagers' main diet was bread and cheese, supplemented with bacon. Many must have been able to have some meat, for in 1762 in Woburn workhouse there was meat (beef, mutton, pork, veal or lamb) three days a week,[50] as also at Potton. Sometimes their landlord gave them a joint of beef at Christmas; over 400 families were supplied from Wrest Park in this way.[51]

Distress did not make the countryman think of the army as a means of livelihood. (An exceptionally tall Gt. Barford man, William Willis, was kidnapped in 1736 for the Prussian king's famous regiment, but refused to take the oath and was eventually released; he however was a farmer's son.)[52] In 1757 rumour spread that by a new act of parliament men would be chosen by lot to fight in the American plantations. To Bedfordshire men it seemed obvious that, if the French must be fought, the place to fight them was in France; they were not prepared to be sent halfway across the world, whence they might never return, even if not killed. On 28 August 1,500 men from the hundreds of Biggleswade, Clifton and Wixamtree assembled round the Sun inn at Biggleswade, from which the deputy lieutenants, headed by Sir Roger Burgoyne, hastily withdrew. They followed him to Sutton Park, on which he surrendered the lists; then they told him "Now we will drink with you", and beer was brought in pails and tubs. They dispersed only on being paid 5s. per parish for their loss of time. A week later Stodden and Willey hundreds rose and converged on Mr. Bullock's house at Sharnbrook, and got him to discharge their warrants.[53] It was of course a mistaken rumour; the object of the militia act of 1757 was to provide for a home guard while the regular army fought the Seven Years War in America and India; but it was sometime before the Lord Lieutenant was able to get the new militia system functioning effectively.

Towards the end of this period, bad harvests made the price of corn exceptionally high. Just as in earlier centuries private courts of law functioned until public ones were sufficiently well established for the purpose, so on the big estates there appears an embryo welfare service. The Duke of Bedford sold corn to the poor at reduced prices, sometimes buying it for this purpose. His agent, Samuel Miller, at Woburn in December 1764 reported that on the previous Monday he had supplied 42 poor people with wheat at 4s. 8d. a bushel, and on the preceding day 103 poor people. In the winter of 1766–7 wheat was so short that it was necessary to mix barley and rye with it; Miller reported that people were prepared to take a

[49] Dony, op.cit. p.24.
[50] C.R.O., X 250/3; P 64/18/6.
[51] C.R.O., L 30/9/73/27.

[52] C.R.O., QSR 1737/38; see also Carleton Greene
   Roxton & Gt. Barford (1903 ed.), 11–12.
[53] C.R.O., FN 1253, 152.

proportion of from one-third to two-thirds barley; and some very large families took barley only at 2s. 5d. a bushel. The 4th Duke dovetailed together the interests of his estates, and used Devon cloth to make clothes for the Bedfordshire poor; the snow was deep, wrote Miller in January, 1767; he had fitted out Eversholt, and had enough left for men and boys at Steppingley, but would need about 110 yards more for the women's gowns.[54]

Cottagers did not write letters or keep diaries, and few of them made wills. Yet from parish records it is possible to attempt a few case histories, occasionally of men, more often of widows, children, and the handicapped.

At Eaton Socon at the beginning of the 18th cent., the Cooper family were paying rates, though only very low ones.[55] By 1733 John Cooper was receiving relief. When he died in 1739, the list of his furniture indicates what had been modest comfort; there was an elbow chair, 5 other chairs, some stools, table, dresser and cupboard; some pewter ware; 2 bedsteads, one of which had curtains, 3 coffers, 2 pr. sheets and 3 blankets. This compares well with the furniture of Widow Peak; when her goods came to be taken over by the parish, they consisted of 6 chairs, 2 tables, a cupboard, a bedstead, 1 pr. sheets, a blanket and small coffer.

In the same parish Widow Bleat seems to have put up a brave struggle to keep going. She was left with a young son, and owned her cottage, but could not afford to repair it, so several times between 1709 and 1715 the overseers repaired it for her; in the latter year it had extensive rethatching, for they paid for 2 loads of straw, 450 spits, and for the thatcher and his man. From 1712–14 there was a bad epidemic of smallpox, in the course of which Jane Bluck was brought back to Eaton Socon from Grafham, and Widow Bleat obtained work at 10s. a week nursing her, the overseers providing bed, firing, bread, cheese and candles. During the last fortnight, when Jane Bluck convalesced at Widow Bleat's cottage, Widow Bleat was paid 3s. for houseroom. Meanwhile her boy had been boarded out with Samuel Gray for 12d. a month, who "is to return the said boy up in as good a condition of habit as he receives him", that is to say, with new coat, hat, breeches and stockings, and with his shoes soled. But she was not able to carry on for long; "Widow Bleat in need, 1s."

Something similar was the case of the Lovells or Lovitts of Roxton.[56] William Lovell was probably glad of the weekly payment of 2s. for a parish boy whom he boarded out, and Goodwife or Goody Lovell earned a few pence for mending the boy's clothes and sewing on buttons. After William died in 1697 Widow Lovell was occasionally able to board a younger child at 1s. 6d. a week. Then she had to ask for occasional help and for wood. In 1712 she was allowed regular weekly payments of 2s. 6d. She died in 1714.

Whether Widow Spring of Roxton was more feckless or incapacitated by

[54] C.R.O., R 342–55.
[55] B.H.R.S., xv, 81.
[56] C.R.O., P 28/12.

poor health is not clear. Her husband, a labourer, died in 1733, leaving her ill and with a 6-year old son William. The overseers paid Widow Bishop to nurse her, and provided a loaf, 1 lb. butter, some cheese and firing; then regular payments of 1s. 6d. weekly, while William received breeches and stockings in August, shoes in October, and a shirt in December. Widow Spring was unable to cope. In 1736 when the boy was 9, there is an entry "for the warrant and whipping Widow Spring", [sic], and "for cleaning William Spring". William Spring was then "put out" apprentice, and 10d. was spent on ale when the indenture was signed. After this he disappears from view, for he had probably been apprenticed in another parish.

The mentally defective or mentally sick of course could not stand on their own feet. Such was "Pool's boy" at Roxton. In the 17th cent. the family had left wills, though John Pool was only a labourer, and Thomas, who died in 1674 and kept an alehouse, was able to leave his son only 12d., and an unspecified residue of goods to his two daughters; one daughter was out at service, and he feared she might become sick; if so, he asked his married daughter to give her lodging till she was better.[57] "Pool's boy" was probably the grandson of this Thomas Pool. He was boarded out, and was a continual expense for clothes and shoes; his breeches, at least in 1711, were made of sacking. On one occasion there is a charge for "stof to keel the boy's varment" (stuff to kill the boy's vermin). The last entry is in 1729: "paid 1s. 10d. for a bell and grave for Pool's boy". About the same date are also several payments for "the mad wench".

A workhouse was set up at Eaton Socon in 1719, and by degrees other large parishes followed suit. At first at Eaton Socon the management of the workhouse was rather erratic; the overseers bought supplies, and a caretaker supervised. Between those inmates who had made a brave effort to be self-supporting, but were now old and weak, those who were ill, and those who were incompetent, things must have been uneasy. An attempt was made to employ the children; Jane Harris taught the girls to make lace, which in 1721 brought in £14 p.a. (perhaps the overseers were able to arrange with a Bedford laceman); while some of the boys earned a little by small tasks such as keeping sheep or gleaning.

The cost of the workhouse in this very large parish rose from £227 p.a. in 1718–19 to £323 in 1727–8. The parish attributed this to the pampering of the poor, and resolved to "put off" the workhouse, and to follow a recent act of parliament in making those on relief wear "P" badges in red or blue. These badges must have been hated. But rates continued to rise, so the workhouse was resumed, and the sick were covered by a £5 contract with a local apothecary.

Gradually the bigger parishes made contracts with a workhouse manager. In 1769 Silsoe agreed with Wright Titmus to pay him £95 p.a. for 3 years; he was to provide the poor inmates with wholesome diet and good small beer and

57 C.R.O., ABP/W 1674/95.

decent apparel and bedding, and provide materials for them to work on; but no sufferer from smallpox, venereal disease, scabbed head or the itch should be introduced until recovered.[58] About the same date Potton and Woburn overseers were generous enough to stipulate that the poor should have meat three days a week.[59] The manager's solvency or profit depended on his keeping expenses below the contract price, so the plight of the inmates was likely to deteriorate as their number rose.

By the end of this period parish costs for poor relief were much higher than at the beginning.[60] Examples may be given from different parts of the county. In the north, Pavenham spent £15 in 1706; £83 in 1762. In the east, Roxton spent £13 in 1691; in the 1760's about £50. In the southwest, Chalgrave spent about £20 in 1708; £76 in 1755. Not one of these instances is taken from an enclosed parish. The plight of the cottagers relatively to that of other classes was at its lowest ebb since the 16th cent.; it was to go lower yet, but of this enclosure would not be the main cause.

ENCLOSURE

At the end of this period there began a widespread movement to rationalise agriculture through enclosure of individual parishes by act of parliament. It was in the next period that this movement escalated (ch. 34; see also ch. 27); so in this chapter it will be indicated only briefly. Apart from Sutton, 1742, which was not normal, there were seven parliamentary enclosures in this period, all between 1761 and 1771: Aspley Guise, Felmersham and Pavenham showing less concentration of ownership; Podington, Souldrop, Sundon and Tilsworth, showing greater concentration. Sundon also was slightly unusual, for here 92 a. of common were left unenclosed; but it is noticeable that only one cottager, Thomas Spiggins, had land, and he had only ½ a. Aspley Guise and Podington will be taken as examples.

At Podington the area to be enclosed was estimated at 2,426 a. Of this, nearly 2,000 a. went to Richard Orlebar in his own right and as impropriator of the great tithes. Neighbouring gentry owned 100 a. The Wagstaffes, yeomen, had about 200 a. The vicar was allotted 151 a. for small tithes, glebe and common right. The only other allottees were William Richardson and Thomas Clark with 2½ a. and 2 a. respectively.

At Aspley Guise there were 37 proprietors in all, only 17 of these being Aspley men, of whom 7 were gentry.[61] Of the remainder, there were 3 yeomen; Hutton who was awarded nearly 35 a. and who had also a close of 9 a.; William Brown was awarded 6½ a. and had a close of 3½ a.; and John Walduck, who was Richard How's bailiff and had only 3¼ a. There were 7 cottagers who owned

---

58 C.R.O., L 28/29.
59 In 1762. C.R.O., X 250/3.
60 C.R.O., Pavenham P 68/12; Roxton P 28/12;

Chalgrave P 114/12.
61 B.H.R.S. Quarto ser. ii, 32–3.

cottage and garden but had no common right, having presumably sold it. There were two men who owned common right but no land: Thomas Butcher, who was in fact a butcher, and John Byworth; and these two each received £6 5s. in compensation.

Thus the impact of these enclosures on lesser men was small. There were few yeomen left, and the cottagers had little to lose. The general standard of living was rising, but relatively that of the cottagers was declining.

To conclude with a picture of the 18th cent. village as a whole, we may summarise descriptions which have survived for 3 villages in different areas at varying dates.

In the north, Stevington in 1699 had 41 families, of whom about one-third (16) were labourers or widows or unspecified.[62] Two were described respectively as yeoman and farmer, and there were 2 shepherds. There were one or more of the following: miller; blacksmith; carpenter, mason (the village is in a stone area), and thatcher; tailor and shoemaker; baker and shopkeeper; laceman and matmaker. Their livestock is not stated.

Near Bedford, Renhold in 1773 had over 50 families.[63] The only crafts noted are blacksmiths, carpenter, thatcher and bricklayer. Most inhabitants are described as industrious, some "poor but industrious", one "middling", one "idle and thoughtless", and one "idle and his child in rags". Twelve of the cottagers had a cow or cows.

In the southwest Aspley Guise in 1782 had 82 families.[64] Of over 80 houses, 33 were not large enough to be rated for window tax and 21 were occupied by paupers. The poor were chiefly day labourers and farm servants; the women lacemakers; and the parish "greatly burthened with poor".

[62] B.P.R. ix, C. 48.
[63] C.R.O., PO 13, pp.68–71.
[64] C.R.O., HW 60–2.

THE ANCIENT office of sheriff continued, though with less responsibility. When held by an exceptional man like Johr. Howard it could be important; but as his year as sheriff was 1773, other county administration will be taken first.

LIEUTENANT

The Lieutenant was still the king's main representative, especially when disturbance threatened. During most of this period the office was held by Dukes of Bedford (though by the Duke of Kent 1711–40). The chief responsibility fell to the 4th Duke; he had to raise volunteers at the time of the Scottish rising in 1745; and later during the Seven Years War to implement the Militia Act of 1757 for organising defence at home – an act which at first caused much disturbance in the county (ch. 31).

JUSTICES OF THE PEACE: QUARTER SESSIONS

Justices of the peace carried the main weight of county administration and of the supervision of hundreds and parishes. For the first time this can be analysed, for after the Sessions House was built in 1752, quarter sessions minute-books from 1711 were stored in it, though some are only rough books, and there are gaps 1718–27 and 1762–7.

The number of local justices on the 1734 commission of the peace was 53. Had all attended quarter sessions, it would have been an unwieldy body, nor could they all have got in the Swan inn at Bedford, or inns elsewhere in the market towns and villages where quarter sessions occasionally met. In fact only a few turned up – those who were public-spirited, or had a talent for administration, or a love of self-importance.

From 1711 to 1717 the average attendance at any one session was barely four, the hard core being John Cater and William Hillersdon. From 1745 a justice had to appear once in order to qualify,[1] but a number only came once, like Heylock Kingsley of Sandy. About 1750 the most regular attender was John Nodes of Streatley, whose recorded attendance 1728–61 reached the record number of 187; another who came frequently was Humphrey Monoux of Sandy; while Harry Johnson of Milton Bryan came 74 times 1749–61. By 1770 the lay justices most active at quarter sessions were William Gery and R. H. Ongley; but still the average attendance was only marginally higher.

From the mid-18th cent. clergy begin to be noticeable. From 1739 to 1761 Philip Birt, vicar of Flitton, attended 99 times. About 1750 the impression given

---

[1] The justice took an oath that he had an estate worth £100 p.a.

is that, practically speaking, Birt, Nodes and Johnson administered the county, while a varying number of other justices came and went, without either lasting grasp of or much influence on county affairs; though some deference must have been paid to the 4th Duke of Bedford at his few appearances. A little later, clergy were represented by Hadley Cox, another vicar of Flitton, and by Peter Lepipre, rector of Aspley Guise.

At quarter sessions the justices' administrative responsibilities were very minor compared with county administration today. Not all bridges came within their sphere. Roads were not their direct province; but where a parish was negligent they could indict it, and by the threat of a fine stimulate it into action (ch. 28); and they also authorised parish highway rates. Footpaths could be diverted only with their sanction. County buildings came within their purview; at first these were the county gaol and the house of correction, of both of which more must be said below; and from 1752 there was also Sessions House, for which they bought candles, and added a hallkeeper to their staff roll. They licensed such wanderers as badgers, drovers, higglers and poulterers; and kept registers of gamekeepers. They had to cope with the cattle plague of 1745-54 (ch. 30). From 1770 they registered returns of cereal prices at the local markets.

Part of their work might be termed security. This was the enforcement on those holding office of oaths of allegiance to a new sovereign, and of registering for the same purpose certificates of those who had taken the sacrament according to the Church of England. The abortive risings of 1715 and 1745 help to explain why this was done.

Their chief paid officer was the clerk of the peace. The attorney who held this post was not necessarily a Bedford man. Ambrose Reddall (1721-31) came from the Woburn area; and William Goldsmith (1745-55) from Luton; he used to save postage by handing communications to those attending Luton market. When he held the office, he received a retaining fee of £10 p.a.; the annual value of fees he was able to charge the justices for other work was reckoned as about £140 p.a.[2] Though Jeremy Fish Palmer of Ickwell (1775-98) was after the period of this chapter, he may as well be noted here as the last clerk before the family of Pearse held the office for nearly a century; a visitor in his latter years in 1791 unkindly described him as "gouty, puddling, and knocked up; and looks only to the main chance".[3] The county treasurer was a Bedford merchant, who was considered sufficiently reimbursed for his trouble by the fact that he held the balance of county funds; for 43 years the office was held by William Theed, coal merchant. The justices themselves supervised local contractors for repairs to buildings or bridges. They paid the coroner for the inquests he held, and they also paid the hallkeeper and the keeper of the house of correction.

The justices usually ordered what they called a rate of ½d. in the £. For

[2] C.R.O., QSM xiii, 121. [3] *Torrington diaries*, ii, 313.

the whole recorded history of this period the same parish list was used,[4] so that Toddington, which though a large parish was on the downgrade, paid £5, while Dunstable, which though very small in area was growing in prosperity, paid £2. What in fact the justices meant when they ordered this rate was that they required a sum of nearly £300 to carry on with, and this was raised from the parishes in the same proportions as previously.

Much of their work arose out of the poor law. The law of settlement, though it did not succeed in confining parishioners to the parish of their birth, meant that when a man became a pauper he was compulsorily removed, under justice's order, to his supposed parish of origin; and that disputes as to liability arose between the parishes concerned. Some people when they left their birthplace had friends who stood surety for them; but none the less things might later go ill with them.[5] Often the original settlement was in doubt. In 1738 Maulden overseers disputed the removal to Maulden from Clophill of John Fowler with his wife and two children.[6] In 1742 Tetworth, Hunts., anxious to avoid the birth of another pauper in their parish, removed Ann Clark to Tempsford when very near the time of her delivery and unfit to travel.[7] Sometimes a parish entered a plea that a man's relatives in another parish should help him; Eyeworth in 1757 claimed that William Eyres' son John at Sutton was of sufficient ability to relieve his father.[8] Applications for affiliation orders for bastardy appeared at every sessions.

Quarter sessions were also a court of justice. A frequent offence was assault. In 1731 Mary Pearce of Maulden attacked Lydia Wells with an iron spit;[9] and in 1758 George Pearles of Barton, labourer, threw a hayfolk at John Read.[10] Theft was common. Sarah Scotchen of Battlesden in 1729 stole Agnes Verney's gleanings.[11] Articles stolen include livestock, such as poultry, sheep, horses; tools, such as a scythe; utensils such as a brass kettle; food or drink such as fish, sugar, malt and beer; and clothes such as cloak or stockings. Two unusual thefts were that of a prayerbook by William Peacock, a Silsoe labourer, in 1764; and of a book called *Preparation for death* by a Barton tailor in 1740.[12] Men were tempted to release their stray animals from the parish pound; at Langford Francis Stevens released 4 horses in 1729; and at Thurleigh in 1739 William Elsom let out 30

---

[4] C.R.O., QSM vii, 47; and cf. xxix, 415. Comparison with the subsidy roll of 1628 suggests a date of *c.* 1700 for the county rate list.

[5] In 1741, twenty years after he left Bedford for Shoreditch, Joseph Bletsoe died, leaving a widow and 6 children; the Shoreditch constable wrote to Bedford, saying that they were "almost in a starving condition", and recommending sending them a small allowance, as the widow could earn a trifle there (he did not mention that Bletsoe had owed him 28s., and when Bedford sent 40s., he deducted his debt). The widow wrote pathetic letters; "I am truly sorry to be so very burthen-

some"; "for God's sake do not forget me nor my poor children . . . or I must come down; pray for God's sake fail not, but consider my great want, and I will meet the carrier next Wednesday." C.R.O., P 1/16.

[6] C.R.O., QSM vii, 29.
[7] C.R.O., QSM vii, 97.
[8] C.R.O., QSM xiii, 141.
[9] C.R.O., QSR 1731/88.
[10] C.R.O., QSR 1758/31.
[11] C.R.O., QSR 1729/92.
[12] C.R.O., QSR 1764/89; 1740/48.

sheep.[13] From the market towns there were cases of using false weights, as Jeremy Barker of Luton did in 1728.[14] Other cases are breach of licensing laws (e.g. higgler); or occasionally poaching; or fraud, such as attempting to pass off a gilded shilling as a guinea.[15]

Sentences frequently included whipping. Early in the 18th cent. this was always done in public; in Bedford from the gaol to the bridge and back; or at the market cross on market-day; it was also carried out at Ampthill, Biggleswade, Dunstable, Luton and elsewhere. When in 1745 Henry Branklin stole 5 hens, a goose and a turkey from Sir Rowland Alston, he was ordered to be publicly whipped at the market cross next Saturday till his body was bloody.[16] Private whipping was beginning, for in the very same year Elizabeth Plevy of Woburn, who had stolen a pair of stockings, was ordered to be whipped at the house of correction;[17] but public whipping continued into the next century. The stocks continued in use; Wilstead had new stocks for 15s. 3d. in 1769.[18] For more serious offences, transportation to the American colonies (James Baker of Kempston was transported in 1770)[19] was a way of ridding the county of further liability. The county gaoler took convicts for transportation to London under escort (ch. 28); and from about 1731 the justices had a contract with a London merchant, at that time Jonathan Forward, for making the appropriate arrangements at that end.[20]

The most unpleasant thing must have been a sojourn in the little gaol in Silver Street for debt or awaiting trial. Normally food was not provided, but those who would otherwise have starved could petition for "the county bread", as did five poor debtors "in extreme want" in 1742, when they were allowed 6d. worth weekly till the next session.[21] The prisoners slept on straw.[22] Normally there was no heating, but in a very cold January in 1740 a chaldron of coals was bought.[23] The worst however was the risk of gaol fever (typhus). After this had broken out "several times" in 1754, "by means whereof several prisoners as well debtors as felons have lately died", the then sheriff, David James of Ampthill, suggested that a ventilator might extract the "foul and infectious air", so Harry Johnson arranged for a Northampton contractor to erect one at a cost of £50.[24] Escape was sometimes effected, but was not easy, as at least some prisoners wore irons: "ironing John Ray".[25] Once in the gaol (even if declared not guilty) there was no release till the gaoler's fees were paid, for he had no salary.

Oddly enough, the keeper of the house of correction in St. Mary's parish did have a small allowance, and was not entitled to fees; here short terms were

[13] C.R.O., QSR 1729/89; 1739/92.
[14] C.R.O., QSR 1728/100–1.
[15] C.R.O., QSM viii, 121.
[16] C.R.O., QSM ix, 2.
[17] C.R.O., QSM viii, 38.
[18] C.R.O., P 22/5/1.
[19] C.R.O., QSM xv, 80.

[20] C.R.O., QSR 1730/86.
[21] C.R.O., QSM vii, 104.
[22] C.R.O., QSM vii, 156.
[23] C.R.O., QSM vii, 54.
[24] C.R.O., QSM xii, 67, 100–1.
[25] C.R.O., QSR 1735/69.

served for small offences; the men beat hemp and the women span. These inmates could earn small sums by their work; thus the Kempston overseers in 1772 "paid Gadsby to buy him a loaf in Bridewell while he could earn one".[26]

SHERIFF

The incoming sheriff signed a receipt for prisoners and for outstanding writs received from his predecessor,[27] and appointed an attorney as under-sheriff to act in legal matters; William Pym of Sandy in 1764 appointed Jeremy Fish Palmer.[28] He also had to engage such bailiffs as were required; on at least one occasion they allowed an offender to escape (Francis Bishop of Luton in 1747).[29]

The armed escort provided for the judge, at one time a common-sense precaution, had now more or less become a piece of pageantry, when trumpets were blown, and young gentlemen bore halberds or "javelins". Richard Orlebar in 1721–2 reckoned that his expenses, including cleaning javelins, blacking the coach, trumpets, coats and hats, payments to ringers and for music, and largesse to the Bedford poor, besides a fee to the preacher of the assize sermon, came to £179.[30] John Francklin of Gt. Barford was less lucky; in 1739, after paying for 18 javelins and for 50 yards of broadcloth and 90 yards of shalloon for his escort, his whole expenses being £186, he was "extremely ill of a cold" and unable to attend.[31] William Cole of Sundon took the opportunity of being sheriff to invite John Wesley to preach the assize sermon (ch. 30).

John Howard, sheriff in 1773, viewed his position as rather more than a somewhat expensive status symbol with a few duties attached. His perception that the county gaoler ought to have a salary, in order that prisoners declared innocent might not be detained till they could pay fees, launched him on an investigation of prisons that extended ever wider. Little was known of him at first, as he was fairly new to the county; and even in 1775 the Marchioness Grey spoke of a visit from "little Mr. Howard". He is one of the few known cases in Bedfordshire of a dissenter holding office in spite of legal disability – he was a member of the New Meeting in Bedford (ch. 30).

Howard had served a short term in a French prison in the Seven Years War, and had a fellow-feeling for prisoners. When the justices agreed with the reasonableness of his suggestion as to paying the gaoler, but wanted to be reassured by precedent, "I rode into several neighbouring counties in search of one, but I soon learned that the same injustice was practised in them".[32] Thus he went on to a wider survey, and produced his *State of the Prisons* in 1777. At this time there were in Bedford gaol 8 debtors and 5 felons; it was kept clean, but there was no bath; and no fireplace in the felons' room; the fees due on release might amount to about £2. The public conscience was stirred by Howard's book. He was

[26] C.R.O., P 60/12/4.
[27] C.R.O., FN 1023–4.
[28] C.R.O., PM 2615.
[29] C.R.O., QSR 1747/17.

[30] C.R.O., OR 1768.
[31] C.R.O., FN 1027.
[32] *State of the prisons*, introduction.

indifferent to the fame which now attached to him, refused to sit for his portrait, and said that on his death he wanted only an inscription of the date added to his wife's tomb. But when, after visiting the prisons of Europe, he died in 1790 at Kherson, the tomb put up to him by the Russians was inscribed: "Whosoever thou art, thou standest at the grave of thy friend." A salary of £60 p.a. for the county gaoler was introduced in Bedfordshire in 1785.[33]

PETTY SESSIONS

Petty sessions were held for smaller areas by justices of the peace. It seems that the petty sessions for Flitt hundred met at Luton at the Bell inn; that for Manshead hundred at the Griffin, Toddington, since Toddington is more central for the hundred than Dunstable or Leighton; and that for Redbornstoke at Ampthill.[34] A combined petty sessions, probably meeting at Biggleswade, was held for the more sparsely populated hundreds of Biggleswade, Clifton and Wixamtree. Barford, Stodden and Willey hundreds also combined, and they may have met at Bletsoe, where the Falcon inn is known to have been a rendezvous for lieutenancy matters.

At such sessions parish poor accounts were passed. Justices' signatures in parish books show that a number who were rarely at quarter sessions did from time to time attend petty sessions. The St. John family in this century took little or no part in county affairs, and have no recorded attendance at quarter sessions; but Lord St. John's signature is occasionally found in overseers' books. Presumably also alehouses were licensed here, but registers for this date have not survived.

THE INDIVIDUAL JUSTICE

In his own parish, or in adjoining parishes, a justice was often effective. Without going near petty sessions or quarter sessions, he could stimulate parish officers by a word in the right quarter; this was the way of the Marchioness Grey's husband, the 2nd Earl of Hardwicke, who had responsibilities elsewhere as Lieutenant of Cambridgeshire, and whose interests in any case were academic. Equally, if easy-going or dull, the justice could sit back and let parish administration take what course it would; but he would probably have to deal with small offences.

An incident in 1735 illustrates this function of the justice. Two ducks were offered for sale in Carlton, and were said to have been shot from Harrold bridge by Hollis and another. It chanced that in the house was the rector's wife, helping one of her parishioners in childbirth. She recognised the ducks as stolen from her; confiscated them; and went in her chaise to William Aspin of Felmersham for a warrant. He had gone to London, so she turned back to Odell to appeal to Sir Rowland Alston; he agreed that the live and dead ducks were so much alike that they must have come from the same brood. He sent for the men, who came.

[33] C.R.O., QSM xviii, 27.   and 1735/49.
[34] C.R.O., HW 88/47; QSR 1740/24; QSR 1733/24

Sir Rowland said "Madam, they are guilty, or they would not have come without a warrant." On being questioned, Hollis insisted he had shot the ducks; but the ducks bore no sign of shot. "Sir Rowland said he thought he could punish him, having catched him in a lie. However he said Mr. Farrer was to be at his house the next day, and he would confer with him about it."[35] (William Farrer, though living at Cold Brayfield, was on the Bedfordshire commission of the peace because of his property at Harrold.) The end of the story is not recorded.

It would be a mistake to think of the justice as a petty dictator and of the villagers as quietly submissive. Thomas Walker of Leighton Buzzard in 1738 was foolhardy enough to defy a warrant signed by the 4th Duke of Bedford.[36] When the constable of Lidlington in 1727 got a warrant to fetch Mary Marshall before a justice of the peace, she shouted that "she did not care a turd for his warrant, and he might fetch another and wipe his arse of it."[37]

HIGH AND PETTY CONSTABLES

The high constable of the hundred was a key officer in county administration. He was of course unpaid, and if he omitted to attend quarter sessions he became liable to a fine of 6s. 8d.[38] For Flitt Hundred, Thomas White of Clophill, gentleman, held this office 1746–51.[39] For the long period of 1746–71 for Manshead hundred it was held by Abraham Baskerfield of Leighton Buzzard, gentleman.[40] He was a friend of the diarist, John Salusbury, a fellow member of the Civil Society, and land tax commissioner, and they had many social contacts as well as those on public matters.[41] High constables were responsible for bringing in the proceeds of county rates, and sometimes they were in arrears.[42] They produced lists of freeholders for elections, lists of jurors for sessions and assizes, authorised the passing of vagrants, and attended any whipping in the hundred ordered by quarter sessions. In all these matters the high constable acted through his subordinates, the petty constables in each parish.

To be a parish constable was a thankless task. It was not uncommon to be struck when trying to enforce the peace, as was Thomas Millard of Northill in 1748, when he attempted to quell a brawl between two men of his parish and a Mogerhanger carpenter, John Barr.[43] But to try to refuse service as constable, after being lawfully chosen by the vestry, as did Thomas Russell the Wootton clockmaker in 1738, only meant a summons to appear before quarter sessions and a fine.[44] To be negligent in duties had a like result, as John Partridge, yeoman, a Luton constable found, when he did not provide Richard Surkett, high constable of Flitt hundred, with a list of Luton men liable for jury service in 1745.[45]

[35] B.H.R.S. xxx, 65.
[36] C.R.O., QSR 1738/24.
[37] C.R.O., QSR 1727/51, 136, 167.
[38] C.R.O., QSM vi, 77.
[39] C.R.O., QSM viii, 205, ix, 128.
[40] C.R.O., QSM viii, 189; xv, 135.

[41] B.H.R.S. xl, 46–94.
[42] C.R.O., QSM xvi, 84.
[43] C.R.O., QSM ix, 56.
[44] C.R.O., QSM vii, 8.
[45] C.R.O., QSR 1745/52a.

33 – LIFE IN GENERAL, 1689–1771

COURTSHIP AND MARRIAGE

There were still negotiated marriages on grounds of suitability of rank and position,[1] but to a greater extent marriage was an individual choice. Love letters survive. "I beg leave to subscribe myself, dear Kitty, your most true and sincere lover and adorer till death", wrote a young naval officer in 1743. He anticipated shore leave, for he had been away 4 years; but his captain ordered him first to impress sufficient crew. The lady was Kitty Taylor of Aspley Guise. She was embarrassed to receive his letter, for in William's absence she had accepted another suitor. Soon came a further note: "Take pity on your dying and almost distracted lover."[2] Did William then come in person and find out the truth? Whether he did or no, Kitty never destroyed the letters.

A written proposal might be declined in a dignified manner. A Millbrook suitor in 1758 was told: "Sir, I have given your proposal the utmost consideration, but I cannot accept of your obliging offer."[3] A rejected Kempston suitor in 1772, setting out for Antigua, resolved "Miss J. I must try to forget, but I should like to know why she dislikes me so much".[4]

A trousseau might vary widely. Lord Ashburnham's bride in 1723 had nearly 200 yards of satin and sarsenet in white, cherry, pink and silver to make her dresses, and over 100 yards of lace, but only 18 handkerchieves.[5] Possibly the humbler woman's outfit was more like that of the Potton girl apprentice, Ann Castleman, in 1698: 2 shifts, a pair of stays, 2 petticoats, 2 gowns, 2 aprons, a straw hat, 2 headcloths, 2 handkerchieves, 2 pairs of stockings, and a pair of shoes.[6]

The wedding-day was kept quietly, even among the well-to-do, by bride and groom and their parents. The rest of the family were not invited, nor were friends. When, however, the Marchioness Grey's daughter and heiress was married in London in 1772, at Wrest Park an ox was roasted whole, and it was reckoned that over 2,000 joined in the celebrations there.[7]

For humbler folk their wedding was perhaps the one holiday they had in their lives, and they often made use of it by being married in another village; in 1750 William Addington of Roxton and Margaret Lowins of Tempsford were married at Little Barford.[8]

[1] *B.H.R.S.* xlvii, 105–7.
[2] C.R.O., M 10/3/1.
[3] C.R.O., M 10/2/28.
[4] C.R.O., M 10/4/18.
[5] C.R.O., L 31/133–42.
[6] C.R.O., P 64.
[7] *B.H.R.S.* xlvii, 87; cf. also p.54.
[8] *B.P.R.* vi.

Pauper marriages were enforced by the overseers. Ann Hudson of Northill was seduced by William Onions of Bolnhurst, who fled to Barnet. He was fetched back by overseer and constable, put in the house of correction at Bedford while the banns were read, and forcibly married to Ann at St. Paul's church, Bedford; then a removal order was obtained, and the couple were despatched to Bolnhurst. The total outlay, including coach fares, payment to the Barnet constable for his help, a "yellow ring" at 3d., eating and drinking at the wedding, was nearly £5, but Northill was rid of a bastard.[9]

FUNERALS

Funerals were another matter. For an important man the church was hung with black, and there was a large distribution of black scarves, hats and gloves, and mourning rings. The Duke of Kent's funeral in 1740 cost £3,000.[10] Pall-bearers formed a kind of guard of honour, and were sometimes stipulated in the will, as by O. T. Bromsall of Northill in 1731.[11] John Antonie of Colworth in 1760 was brought back from Bath (9 days) in a hearse drawn by six horses with black plumes and draped with black velvet; this funeral cost £138.[12]

Even John Rogers, an Ickwell carpenter, in 1733 left directions for a very good burying-suit and a coffin costing 18s., and that his neighbours were to be regaled with cake and good ale and given gloves.[13] The Roxton overseers, at least on one occasion in 1714, provided tobacco at a funeral,[14] and "brenches" (bread and cheese) was usual.

As early as 1742 there were signs of a change: John Kelyng of Ampthill, descendant of the judge, asked to be buried by daylight without pall-bearers.[15] At the end of the century the Marchioness Grey left directions that her funeral was to be private and that Flitton church should not be hung with black.[16]

There was a legal obligation to be buried in woollen material, though the well-to-do might pay a fine for exemption, and it was waived for paupers; Luton register has many instances of the latter. Poor folk also were sometimes buried without coffins (ch. 30).

HOUSEKEEPING[17]

For her housekeeping the young gentlewoman compiled her own cookery book from recipes supplied by her family and friends. A particularly full one is that of Diana Astry who married Richard Orlebar in 1708.[18] Her recipes are vague as to quantity ("as much butter as you think fit") and timing ("till it is done"), and rich in content. A good soup is made with a leg of beef, veal, mutton, a cock, lean bacon, a pigeon, cheese, ginger, mace, cloves, onions, carrot, turnip,

---

[9] C.R.O., P 10/12/3 (1810). This later instance is cited because of its unusual detail, but there are cases in the 18th cent.

[10] B.H.R.S. xlvii, 18.

[11] C.R.O., BS 11; and cf. B.H.R.S. xxx.

[12] C.R.O., BS 2060.

[13] C.R.O., ABP/W 1733/59.

[14] C.R.O., P 28/12/1.

[15] C.R.O., WE 1194.

[16] B.H.R.S. xlvii, 122.

[17] G. Scott Thomson, *The Russells in Bloomsbury*, 224–79.

[18] B.H.R.S. xxxvii.

horse-radish, anchovies and sweet herbs. For a good plum cake, take $3\frac{1}{2}$ lb. of flour, 6 lb. currants, 2 lb. butter, 20 yolks of eggs and the whites of 14, 3 pints of cream, and also nutmegs, cinnamon, almonds, sugar, sack and yeast. Mince-pies are made with good rump beef. Fresh fish are used; eels can be baked with butter, cloves and mace ("they do eat very well this way"), or made into a pie, or potted with onions and bay leaves; pike can be roasted (slashed with pickled herring), or boiled in white wine and vinegar. Warden pears should be first baked, then inserted in a high "coffin" of pastry and baked again. Various home-made wines can be made, as from cowslip and elder; and for bottling she recommended using corked bottles in a kettle of cold water; "let them be over the fire half an hour or more till there is a dew on the bottles, and then they are done enough". She kept a notebook for menus; one gives for the first course, calf's head, stewed carp, chine of mutton, and venison pasty; for the second course, roast turkey, roast venison, roast pigeon, and salmon; and for sweet, tarts, syllabubs, and "jocklett crames" (chocolate creams). Syllabubs were made from whipped cream flavoured with wine. The little use made of fruit and vegetables is noticeable.

No recipe book kept by a farmer's wife has survived, and probably few would have been handy enough with the pen to compile one. No doubt such women would be even more skilled than their gentle neighbours in fruit-preserving and in making home-made wine, but unless for a rare occasion their cooking would have been much simpler than that described above. That of the cottager's wife would be meagre. Hasty pudding was made with flour and hot water – not as a rule flavoured with arsenic, like that served in 1730 to Branklin by his wife – "she run away as soon as she had done it".[19]

An early form of cooking-range was introduced in gentry's households during the 18th cent.; there was one at the Hasells, Sandy, in 1761.[20] This made it possible to use lighter cooking utensils. When in 1759 a Millbrook housewife asked her sister-in-law in London to get her a new brass pot, a copper one arrived. "I hope you was not displeased at your copper pot, for a brass one is now quite out of date. They make none, for nobody asks for them."[21]

Wallpaper was coming into fashion. A French wallpaper of 1720 is still in position at Hinwick House, where it was discovered during recent restoration. The rector of Millbrook in 1751 proposed to prevent paper from rotting (owing to lack of a damp-course) by pasting it on canvas first, but he planned to wainscot the room chair-high.[22] Richard How senior of Aspley Guise in 1756 thought that wainscotting was in any case more practical.[23] The pavilion in Wrest Park was papered in 1754 "instead of the old gilt leather".[24]

[19] B.H.R.S. xxx, 20.
[20] C.R.O., PM 2578; and cf. L 30/9/17/118.
[21] B.H.R.S. xxxiv, 49.
[22] B.H.R.S. xxxiv, 8.
[23] C.R.O., HW 87/221.
[24] B.H.R.S. xlvii. 53.

SERVANTS

At Renhold in 1773, that is to say in the entire village, there were no less than 60 servants (the population in 1801 was 245).[25] Some of them were no doubt farm servants living in the farmhouses, but still a large number of domestic servants were required for the many tasks that have now been eliminated by modern methods, such as cleaning candlesticks and knives, pumping and heating water, making butter and cheese, curing bacon and hams, laundering, preserving and pickling, clearing grates and lighting fires. The squire, John Becher, had 10 servants. Many more were employed at big establishments like Wrest or Woburn. A common enquiry when writing for a testimonial for a butler or housekeeper was whether the applicant was of a peaceful disposition and sober.

Some servants remained for life with the same family, identifying themselves with its service. One wrote thus to tell the Marchioness Grey in 1769 of a sister-in-law's death: "Tryphosa Box presents hir Duty to Lady Gray & is sorry she has ocation to write thiss Maloncoly acount"[26]. The Marchioness took Tryphosa Box into her own service, and on retirement she was settled in a house at Silsoe. Such service must have varied, not so much according to the worldly wealth, as the kindness and good sense of the family concerned; and it is to be expected that at the other end of the scale there were cases of inhuman drudgery.

One use of all this labour was to maintain cleanliness in the home, and the Swedish traveller, Kalm, says that the standard was high. In the country such cleanliness might well be achieved. In London it was more difficult. When in 1759 the rector of Millbrook asked his London sister to put him up for a few nights, she replied "As to a bed with me you cannot, for having got some bugs, have pulled three beds down and sent two of them to be cleaned . . . But [a cousin's] house is free from bugs".[27] Personal hygiene too must have been more difficult when washing facilities were so much less than today.

FURNITURE

The range of household goods was now so wide, and standards might vary so greatly as between individuals in the same walk of life, that it is not possible to take any instances as typical. The following merely give some indication.

At Wrest Park in 1740 the Duke of Kent's bedroom was furnished in blue velvet, with a picture of Wrest house and gardens, and Gordon's county map, 1736; his dressingroom had walnut furniture, with portraits of his eldest son and daughter.[28]

As to gentry, Heylock Kingsley's widow at the Hasells, Sandy, in 1761 had a walnut dressing-table and glass, a mahogany pillar-and-claw table, a scalloped mahogany tea-board, a japanned tea-table, brass sconces and damask curtains.[29]

[25] C.R.O., PO 13, pp.68–71.
[26] B.H.R.S. xlvii, 82.
[27] B.H.R.S. xxxiv, 44.

[28] C.R.O., L 31/184
[29] C.R.O., PM 2578.

Francis Cooke of Milton Bryan in 1762 also had mahogany chairs; a bureau, a bookcase, a corner cupboard; and silver coffee-pot and tea-kettle; and china cups.[30]

James Ashwell, of a long-established farming family at Eaton Bray, had in 1753 a home with many comforts.[31] In the kitchen were dresser, 52 pieces of earthenware, pewter, knife-boxes, salt box and warming-pan; in the hall was a weather-glass; in his best room an 8-day clock and case, a turkey carpet, a worked dressing-box, and a dressing-glass in a worked frame. He possessed a chest of drawers, a number of small glazed prints, a clothes-horse for drying, a pewter bedpan, and a lark-spit, besides such conveniences as a yoke for pails and a mousetrap. Elizabeth Burrows, a Clophill widow who in 1735 married a Bedford husbandman, also had dresser, warming-pan, looking-glasses, and chest of drawers.[32]

Thomas How, wool-merchant, of Aspley Guise in 1722 had two corner cupboards, tea-table and set of china, and various silver items, including cups, mug, porringers, spoons, salt, and tobacco box. In his countinghouse, besides office furniture, was a Bible.[33]

A Milton Bryan blacksmith in 1707 (John Robinson) and a Biddenham carpenter in 1710 (Robert Leader) had simpler furniture: table, form, a few chairs, one or two cupboards, pewter.[34] Robinson had also a hanging-press; and Leader a dresser, a chest of drawers, and a warming-pan.

Richard Deane of Sandy, who in 1699 was a fairly well-to-do cottager, (owning a horse, 3 cows, pigs, and another cottage besides his own, besides a pightle of 1 a.) had tables, chairs, 2 chests, pewter, and 3 bedsteads.[35]

DRESS AND FASHION

At the beginning of this period, gentlemen's dress especially for social occasions or in town was still gay. The Duke of Kent, when a young man in town, bought laced cuffs and cravats, cherry and peach-coloured waistcoats, and a silver sword.[36] Handsome buttons and buckles were used; William Poulton, an Eversholt falconer, in 1754 left to his son John a gold-laced hat and a set of plate buttons, and to his son Robert silver knee-buckles and shoe-buckles.[37] As late as 1765 John Orlebar had an apple-blossom suit.[38] In the country gentlemen's dress was more informal, normally a cloth suit.

Wigs were worn; the Marchioness Grey's husband had two made in Paris in 1749;[39] and even the modest Meppershall farmer, John Blundell, thought it necessary to take three with him in 1763 on a short absence from home (ch. 31).

30 C.R.O., X 21/593.
31 C.R.O., BS 161.
32 C.R.O., SA 500.
33 B.H.R.S. xxiii, 96.
34 C.R.O., GA 400; WW 406.
35 C.R.O., PM 107.

36 E.M.H. Leaflet vii, 4.
37 C.R.O., X 52/103.
38 Shown at the Moot Hall for the County Record Office jubilee exhibition in 1963 (no. 121).
39 B.H.R.S. xlvii, 49.

By the 1770's when the young Edmund Williamson (grandson of his name-sake of Husborne Crawley) was at Cambridge, dark colours were in fashion; "I prefer one of the dark browns," he wrote to his mother, "likewise fustian breeches"; though when he had a new coat he did refer to the "yellowish colour worn in Cambridge".[40] By this time wigs had given place to powdered hair. Then in the next decade powdering began to go out. The young 5th Duke of Bedford excited comment from an older man when he appeared with his hair worn naturally: "Why this singularity?"

Though references are occasionally found to the clothes of humbler men, little detail is given, and such clothes would be plain and serviceable. Robert Harrison, an Odell mason, in 1705 left his son his best coat, waistcoat, breeches, hat, stockings and shoes, but did not describe them.[41]

Ladies of rank bought their silks in London. Sometimes the most pleasing patterns the mercer offered were still being woven, and then it was difficult to get the desired one in time to be made up for the King's birthday, when a new gown must be worn. In 1746 the Marchioness Grey was offered a choice of silks (all with white ground) as follows: one with silver diagonal and running gold stalk with lively coloured flowers; one of soft purple, yellows, green and silver; and one with yellows and silver only; the first much the most expensive.[42] Such country ladies as seldom or never went to London relied on friends or relatives there for sketches of styles or information as to fashionable colours.[43] In 1744 Elizabeth Hurst of Luton had gowns of blue damask, green, cherry derry, and speckled crape, and also one of new printed linen.[44] These must be contrasted with the humbler outfit of two gowns given to a girl apprentice (see above).

All ranks wore aprons to protect their clothes, for neither the gentry's elaborate silks nor other folks' heavy handwoven clothes were readily washable. When Fanny Cater of Kempston "greased her gown very much", she tried to clean it with French chalk.[45] A Luton woman in 1723 bequeathed her best white apron and her best blue apron.[46] A fine muslin worked apron, bordered with Mechlin lace, could be worn by a bride.[47] For everyday purposes a lady could wear one of black gauze.

Ladies' shoes for house-wear were of silk, and often embroidered by the wearer or by a friend. The material was left with the shoemaker to be made up. Fanny Cater in 1778 needed some new shoes in a hurry for Bedford races, and asked the shoemaker not to make them so round at the toe as the last, nor the roses so deep-coloured; also "as they are to dance in, be careful they keep up well behind".[48]

40 C.R.O., M 10/4/252, 265.
41 C.R.O., GA 1/1.
42 B.H.R.S. xlvii, 32.
43 B.H.R.S. xxxiv, frontispiece.
44 C.R.O., X 216/13.

45 C.R.O., M 10/4/55.
46 C.R.O., ABP/W 1723/78.
47 B.H.R.S. xlvii, 87.
48 C.R.O., M 10/4/53.

For mourning the intricate rules are a study in themselves. They varied with every degree of relationship down to a 4th cousin (and possibly beyond!) However, when a letter of advice on this subject refers to a "black silk night-gown", to which there could be added coloured ribbons after a certain time had elapsed, the reference is not to sleeping attire but to evening dress.[49]

Fashion reached perhaps its peak of elaboration in the 1770's under the influence of the French queen, Marie Antoinette, and especially was this true of hairdressing. In 1775 the Marchioness Grey wrote to her elder daughter that a lady's powdered and dressed head of hair should be 12 inches in diameter and no less in height; to be worn with a cap decorated with flowers, fruit, beads, gems, feathers or ribbons. It was even said that the French queen had used a Savoy cabbage. "I beg you will enquire of the gardener if he has any cabbages of this sort, and rehearse in the country the method of wearing them" (she had of course a twinkle in her eye when she wrote this).[50] Here, too, the revulsion soon came, and in a few years the Marchioness' younger daughter was sitting to Romney for her portrait with unpowdered hair.

Children's dress was like that of their elders. Little girls wore long dresses, and it was not appropriate that even a 7-year old should show the calves of her legs when learning the minuet.[51] Little Critty Williamson had morning gowns of purple and white, and a black bib and apron for every day, but this was after her mother had died.[52] Muslin came increasingly into use for girls.

Servants in noble households received liveries. Those at Woburn Abbey were orange in colour; lengths of orange cloth of 60 or 70 yards, with matching shalloon for lining, were bought for footmen and others; and the tailor's bill for liveries in any one year might come to £150.[53] Ladies' maids often received their mistresses' cast-off clothing. For outdoor workers, the linen smock (at first called a frock) was coming into use. The first local mention found of what may be a smock is at Roxton in 1714: "for a frock and making for Nicholes"; by 1796 at Totternhoe it is called a smock.[54]

CHILDREN

In every walk of life the advent of children was often a joy of short duration: death was a frequent visitor to most families. Edmund Williamson of Husborne Crawley rejoiced when his eldest son was born in 1709 – nine relatives and friends were present – but the child died a fortnight later. Of his eight children, five were stillborn or died within a year of birth (one of smallpox); and then their mother died.[55] John and Mary Croot of Croot's farm, Willington, lost seven of

---

[49] C.R.O., M 10/4/67.
[50] B.H.R.S. xlvii, 95.
[51] C.R.O., M 10/4/109.
[52] C.R.O., M 10/2/99–100. 104, 112.
[53] Scott Thomson, op.cit., 237, 263.
[54] C.R.O., P 28/12/1; P 58/12/1. See also A. Buck,

The countryman's smock, in Folk life, i. In the middle of the century the word "frock" is also used for a coat with turned-down collar, as worn in the country.
[55] B.H.R.S. xl, 35–7.

their thirteen children born between 1756 and 1770.[56]

Diet was not well understood. As late as 1783 the future Earl de Grey was given no protein till he was 18 months old, when he had chicken twice a week.[57]

After the dangers of infancy, childish diseases took their toll. In 1770 Edmund Williamson, grandson of the above, had measles while staying in London with his aunt, who fed him on whey, barley-water and sago; "nothing could be fuller than he was yesterday of spots from head to foot; today they are a little abated".[58] Accidents happened then as now. Rogers' 5-year old son John "fell backwards into the potage pot just as it was taken boiling off the fire for dinner, but was taken out immediately by the maid. The fleshy part of his backside was miserably scalded."[59] Ridge's house (probably in Bedford) was burnt down in 1728; "the fire was occasioned by his sister's looking under the bed with a candle for a halfpenny that one of the children had lost there".[60]

All kinds of children's letters survive. "Honoured Madam", wrote little John Harvey of Ickwell to his grandmother in 1739, "I am very well, tho' it is very cold."[61] One from Edmund Williamson in 1772 at the age of 11 to his mama reads more naturally (slightly abbreviated); "I am very well, and eat a hearty dinner upon salmon and strawberries. My aunt gave me half-a-crown, saying money was acceptable at school. Went to see Westminster Abbey, then went to supper on a small lobster and a cherry tart and a quart of porter. I beg you would excuse my writing, as I have a very bad pen and am in a hurry."[62] Seven-year old Mary Grey's first letter in 1763 was written from the Grey town house in London: "Dear Mama: we went to Richmond, which was very pleasant. The hyacinths begin to come out very prettily. We went to see the goldfish, who were very civil to us; the sun shone very bright, which made them extremely handsome and shining."[63]

SCHOOLS

Children such as these, if girls, were taught at home; or if boys, were sent to well-known boarding-schools. Some Bedfordshire boys of more moderate status went to Houghton Conquest school, though this never attained large size or much reputation. Much better known, and indeed known outside the county, was the boarding-school at Aspley Guise. The first reference found to the Aspley Guise school is unprepossessing; in 1724 the headmaster was asking for recommendations, as the smallpox had caused some vacancies; but by 1782 it had over 100 boys, and the headmaster, William Wright, had 9 assistants.[64] John Higgins (ch. 34), then of London, went to school here.

The village child was lucky if there were a charity school in the village.

[56] B.P.R. x.
[57] B.H.R.S. xlvii, 114.
[58] C.R.O., M 10/4/105.
[59] B.H.R.S. xxx, 49.
[60] B.H.R.S. xxx, 6.

[61] C.R.O., HY 925.
[62] C.R.O., M 10/4/204.
[63] B.H.R.S. xlvii, 72.
[64] C.R.O., HW 60-2, 68.

Some additional charity schools had been established, such as one set up by Joseph Neale at Dean to teach 20 poor boys from the neighbourhood; and others at Bolnhurst, Renhold, Maulden and Hockliffe. At Meppershall there survives for 1698 "an account of the scholars and their learning"; here the children were taught by dames. "Elizabeth Deer can read well and hath knit 3 pair of stockings"; 3 other girls were making similar progress, one of them beginning to read in her Testament; these were taught by Dame Gurny. Of those taught by Dame Soal, 5 children were learning their letters, and one boy, Thomas Ruff, could read pretty well; their handwork was spinning hemp tare, and of Ann Endersby Dame Soal reported that she could spin 2 lb. in a week and "she makes a good thread".[65] At Woburn the Duchess in 1721 provided the girls in the charity school with material for samplers.

The position of charity schoolmaster was not always easy, as William Sheepey found at Lidlington in 1727.[66] Mary Marshall struck him over the head with a long pole. The trustees certified that Sheepey had lived a very honest and civil life in Lidlington for 7 years, and that as to Mary Marshall "some of us which live near her can give no worthy commendations of her".

In villages not fortunate enough to have charity schools, there was often some teaching for a small fee. Thus in 1736 at Carlton "Mr. Bordley, schoolmaster, came to this town, and began to teach the Monday following, Jenny, Jack and Sam going that day to his school. I gave him 5s. for their entrance."[67] A number of schoolmasters are known in this period, for instance among others at Eaton Bray, Sundon, Steppingley and Northill, and there were probably more for whom evidence has not survived.

OUTDOOR ACTIVITIES

Outdoor activities still included some May celebrations, since at least one member of the Independent congregation at Bedford was once tempted to dance round the maypole (ch. 30); and "wood for the maypole", also garlands and flag, are noted at Wyboston in 1714;[68] while there was a maypole at Silsoe in 1741.[69] (Incidentally, in 1751 there was even an attempt to revive witch-hunts at Leighton and Luton, but fortunately it petered out.)[70]

Cricket was played. The 4th Duke of Bedford was fond of it, and there were matches in Woburn Park, as in 1757 between teams captained respectively by Lord Sandwich and Mr. St. John, "which was won hollow by the latter".[71]

The village feast was still kept. Originally this was the festival of the patron saint, but it had become an occasion for merrymaking. Parson Rogers attended the feasts of some villages near Carlton.[72] The Moravians discouraged their members from attendance; in 1746 "the people seeing Brother Negus and family

[65] C.R.O. Guide, Pl. X.
[66] C.R.O., QRS 1727/51, 136, 167.
[67] B.H.R.S. xxx, 67.
[68] C.R.O., P 5/5/1.
[69] C.R.O., L 30/10/5/7.
[70] B.N.Q. i, 43.
[71] B.H.R.S. xl, 49.
[72] B.H.R.S. xxx, 28-9, 73 (Melchbourne and Yielden).

EE

going to Stevington feast wondered much, and said 'Ah, I thought they were too good to go to such places'. It is not good that any of our people go to them."[73]

Bedford races were first held on Cow Meadow in 1730, "there not having been one at Bedford before in anyone's memory".[74] The promoters were the 3rd Duke of Bedford and Sir Humphrey Monoux; and the plate (won by a London owner) was worth £25. These races soon became a settled event, and later a spectator recalled how Mrs. Becher of Howbury used to come in her coach and six.[75]

With nobility and gentry foxhunting became increasingly popular. As early as 1708 Richard Orlebar had bred foxhounds at Hinwick.[76] In the mid-18th cent. the 4th Duke of Bedford's eldest son, the Marquess of Tavistock (who did not live to succeed) apparently founded the Dunstable hunt. Of this hunt's Bedfordshire activities, little or nothing is known, but they also used to hunt on the Duke's property at Lyndhurst.[77] The Dunstable hunt seems to have collapsed with Tavistock's death in 1767.

When the Marchioness Grey's son-in-law (Lord Polwarth who married the Wrest heiress in 1772) took up foxhunting, he negotiated with Lord Ludlow and Lord Fitzwilliam a partition of hunting "country".[78] Some people, like his father, thought it a frivolous pursuit, and his father-in-law Lord Hardwicke had difficulty in tolerating kennels at Clophill. Polwarth too died young, and the establishment of a permanent hunt was to wait for another generation and for the 5th Duke of Bedford.

INDOOR PURSUITS

Indoors cards were for men and sometimes also for women a standard leisure occupation: commerce, cribbage, ombre, picquet, quadrille, tredrille and whist. As a young man, the Duke of Kent betted for fairly high sums; so also did the 2nd Duke of Bedford in his short life. The Leighton Civil Society in the 1750's limited themselves to sixpences and shillings.[79]

When the young folks had a ball, cards were provided for the older generation. At the Bedford assembly in 1757 the ball was opened by Lord Russell and Lady Caroline Russell; there were but 14 dances, which included minuets.[80] At a ball at Bedford in 1777 there were 15 couple; first there was cake and coffee or tea; then Sophia Cater of Kempston began the dance with Captain Urquhart, while John Cater danced with Charlotte Jackson (that same Miss Jackson who in 1779 turned him down, so that he sailed from Portsmouth with a heart distracted by tortures);[81] at 10.30 there was a genteel cold collation, with great order and decorum; after which the young people danced again, and those that chose

[73] C.R.O., MO 2. pp.85, 454; 34, p.16.
[74] B.H.R.S. xxx, 21, 44.
[75] Torrington Diaries, ii, 315.
[76] B.H.R.S. xliv, 1.
[77] C.R.O., R 228.

[78] B.H.R.S. xlvii, 95.
[79] B.H.R.S. xl, 48.
[80] B.H.R.S. xl, 49.
[81] C.R.O., M 10/4/42.

played cards. Mrs. Cater, who had lost two rubbers of whist before supper, chose to sit in the dancing-room for the rest of the night. The ball ended by 3 a.m. At Leighton Buzzard there was sometimes dancing at the Swan; at Woburn there were assemblies at the George; and no doubt there were dances also at Luton and Dunstable, though references to them have not been found.

Strolling players gave occasional performances, and the bill of entertainment for the evening included more than one play. At Woburn in 1753 *The Beaux Stratagem* and *The Miller of Mansfield* were given in a stable; at Leighton town hall or moot hall in 1759 a company gave *The Miser* and *Damon and Phyllida;* and about the same time *Lionel and Clarissa* was acted in the George yard at Bedford.[82]

Embroidery still occupied the time of many ladies. When Eleanor Welby of Lincolnshire married William Gery early in the 18th cent., she brought with her a set of chairs (now in Cecil Higgins museum) for which she had embroidered the seats and backs.

HEALTH

There were now rather more doctors, such as Thomas Brown of Arlesey (who took his M.D. at Cambridge in 1724), John Godfrey of Sharnbrook, Humphrey Dell of Flitwick, and John Crawley of Dunstable. These were consulted by gentry from a distance. When in 1729 Mrs. Gibbons of Carlton "from the gout in her stomach was so ill that 'twas thought another fit would carry her off", a messenger who went on horseback to Arlesey found the doctor had gone to Bath.[83]

The aristocracy might prefer to get a doctor down from London, as the Wrest Park family did for little Bell in 1759; here again there was disappointment; Dr. Watson was not in town, and Dr. Taylor could not go till next morning. A famous doctor with local connections was Richard Mead (d. 1754), who had taken an M.D. at Padua. He was the son of Matthew Mead (an Independent minister born at Leighton Buzzard), and he married Ann Alston and often visited at Harrold.

The lady of the house or the housewife still produced her traditional remedies. A book of remedies compiled by Hester Benyon who married Charles Gery in 1701 has the following remedy for consumption: "take 100 snails, bruise them and pick them from the shells, then put them into 2 quarts of new milk and set them on the fire till it be almost scalding hot"; add mint and red fennel.[84] For cancer she suggests a compound of herbs, including dock roots, sow-thistle leaves and pimpernel. Colic may be prevented by taking spirits of nitre in cold

[82] C.R.O., HW 87/200; *B.H.R.S.* xl, 82; *B.Mag.* iii,
[83] *B.H.R.S.* xxx, 8.   [93.
[84] C.R.O., GY 7/3. These recipes are parodied by "a receipt how to make a right Presbyterian in 2 days" in the Hanscombe collection in C.R.O. (HE 425). "Take the herbs of hypocrisy and ambition, of each

2 handfuls; of the flowers of formality, 2 scruples; of the spirit of pride and malice, 2 drams each; of the seeds of contention and stubbornness, of each 4 oz.; of the cordial of reflections and lies, of each 50 oz.; of the root of moderation as small a quantity as you please."

ale morning and afternoon.

The humbler apothecary or surgeon, who had got his qualification by apprenticeship, was to be found in most of the market towns, and it was with him that the overseers of bigger parishes made medical contracts for care of the poor. One for Kempston in 1773 is noted in the overseers' account-book as follows: "Nathenl Taylor agreed with the Churchwardens and Oversears to take Care of pore as Potecarrey and Sugen and Bonesetr and to Say [see] all woomen in Cases of midwiferey and Fracurs of Broken bones and Smaulpox and all For the Sum of Five pounds and allwayes to have an oder From one of the oversears when wanted until Easter next."[85] Women surgeons were not unknown; the Bedford Moravian Brother Negus in 1746 applied to a woman surgeon, "but he says if it does not do well, he will employ a proper one".[86]

The great scourge of the time was smallpox. It was a recommendation when applying for a vacancy to have had it (i.e., to have got the danger over), and sometimes an employer stipulated that he would suspend a servant's wages during smallpox, as Captain Salusbury of Leighton Buzzard did in agreeing with William Gilbert in 1758.[87] Inoculation against smallpox was known early in the 18th cent., and soon became generally practised by the gentry, but it was a long while in making headway with other classes. Popular ignorance supposed it to be another way of contracting the disease; and in 1766 24 inhabitants of Dunstable bound themselves to prosecute a local apothecary, Thomas Warren, if he practised it in their town.[88] Within a few years a better understanding was growing, and the Bedford overseers apparently arranged for it in 1777, for it was thought necessary for 5 Bedford apothecaries to sign an agreement to inoculate only Bedford householders and inhabitants, and not (apparently) to allow nearby villagers to profit from the proposed arrangements.[89] The control of smallpox, now within sight, eliminated much suffering and grief; but – so complex are human affairs – the solution of this one problem magnified all others, for it helped to cause a population explosion for which no one was prepared.

Operations carried out by local surgeons without anaesthetics or knowledge of antisepsis must have been grim; and those in London little better. One in London in 1780 is described by the patient, Lord Polwarth, who was braver than the friend holding him. "Gough most valiantly shut both eyes, and if he had not held fast by my arm he would have dropped; he pretended to hold the water glass, but soon began to totter, so I helped myself; his phyz would have made a good picture. I neither bawled nor uttered, but I whispered 'Oh dear.'" The operation was an unsuccessful attempt to remove a loose piece of bone, probably the result of a hunting accident.[90]

[85] C.R.O., P 60/12/4.
[86] C.R.O., MO 2, p.7.
[87] B.H.R.S. xl, 70.

[88] C.R.O., P 72/18.
[89] C.R.O., P 1/18.
[90] B.H.R.S. xlvii, 102.

Dentistry was primitive, the only remedies for bad teeth being filing or extraction. Those who could afford it could obtain dentures made from teeth extracted from healthy persons (who sold them) and wired together.[91]

For poor eyesight it was possible to buy a pair of glasses which gave a little help by magnifying; the farmer Pedley bought himself such a pair in Bedford.[92]

One forward-looking development in Bedfordshire was the issue in 1701 of proposals for life insurance by Samuel Rhodes of Flitwick, Michael Arnald of Ampthill, William Barnwell of Millbrook, and Charles Dymoke of Cranfield.[93] These proposals do not seem to have come to anything, but life insurance was to develop in London during the century.

COMPASSION

More and more individuals were becoming moved by a sense of compassion, by the awareness that "no man is an island". To some who themselves were fortunately placed, the legal public provision by the overseers, guaranteeing existence on the minimum level, did not seem enough; and like subscribers to relieve world hunger today, they felt impelled to try to help, even though they could only touch the fringe of the problem.[94]

Some charitable provision began centuries before this; its origin was often forgotten, in which case it was known vaguely as "poor's land" or "town land". During the 17th cent., in spite of other preoccupations, it had increased. In the 18th cent. it grew still more. It took several forms.

A favourite one was the actual provision of bread, just as the relief poster today pictures a starving child. At Dunton in 1717 the Rev. Robert Bamford provided for bread to be available in church each Sunday throughout the winter. At Goldington in 1732 James Haselden preferred to arrange that 4 poor persons in the parish should receive bread each Tuesday. At Milton Ernest the Rolt charity provided twelve twopenny loaves each Sunday. At Studham the Rev. George Burghope in 1707 arranged for bread to be available on the anniversary of his death.

Clothes were sometimes given. Hockliffe and Chalgrave benefited from 1690 under Francis West's will by clothes for poor children. At Ampthill William Carter in 1703 arranged for coats for 3 poor men. John Bryan, whose extensive charity went back to 1655, provided that 4 poor widows both at Ampthill and at Maulden should receive each Christmas gowns of blue cloth and shoes, the same widows not to benefit two years running. At Bedford Gabriel Newton in 1760 provided clothes for 25 boys aged 7–14; each to receive a green cloth coat, waistcoat and breeches (not under 20d. per yard), a shirt of flaxen cloth (not under 13d. per yard), and such stockings, caps and other apparel as he had usually

[91] B.H.R.S. xlvii, 117.
[92] B.H.R.S. xl, 108.
[93] C.R.O., LL 15/5.

[94] For details of this section see Charity Commission's Reports, and parish documents in C.R.O. (P).

allowed for some time past.

Housing was not forgotten, In 1697 Sir Edmund Turnor of Milton Ernest provided 6 almshouses. Ann Joliffe in her will of 1723 feared she would not complete her arrangement at Harrold for 6 almshouses before she died: "I strictly order my executor to buy ground and build as many as will make those I leave six. I will have them tiled; one good room below, and a chamber over it; to every one of them a buttery, and a place to lay wood in, strongly built."

Some benefactors (as mentioned above) provided for education; some for apprenticing children, as Ursula Taylor did at Clapham; some provided for sermons, as at Little Barford; Blandina Marshe at Dunstable was concerned for gentlewomen; and a number simply left money which the minister and church-wardens could distribute as they thought fit.

The achievement of this growing tendency was necessarily uneven. The towns, with their larger population, had several charities; Dunstable, for instance, those of Ann Morton, Daniel Marsh, William Avery, Mary Lockington, and Jane Cart among others. Most large villages had them, especially where there were resident gentry; but a number of parishes, mainly small ones, had none; parishes lacking charities include Odell, Souldrop, Pavenham, Stagsden, Astwick, Edworth, Higham Gobion, and Lower Gravenhurst.

Some people were willing to enlarge their sense of the common human bond outside their own parish, and to devote energy to London foundlings. The Foundling Hospital, 1756, put out to nurse the younger children it received; as there were at first very many, arrangements were made over an area extending into Bedfordshire. Local inspectors were appointed, who organised transport and found foster-mothers. One of the Bedfordshire inspectors was Samuel Chase, a Luton Baptist. By 1764 he had dealt with 86 foundlings. The mortality rate was high – 19 died in the first six months. By 1769 the "bulge" was over, and only one girl was left under his supervision; Chase wrote " 'Twill be almost a heartbreaking [to the foster-mother] to part with her – she is an excellent house-wife, and the child is as fond of her as she is of the child".[95]

It took an exceptional man like John Howard to extend compassion to prisoners in Bedford gaol and gaols elsewhere, living in bad conditions, exposed to disease, and unable even when innocent to leave gaol without paying gaoler's fees (see ch. 32).

Still fewer were able to visualise the distant slave trade and to be concerned by the wrong involved in it and in the possession of slaves at all. When in 1772 Samuel Crawley bought a coffee plantation in Grenada, he bought with it 10 negroes, listed in the conveyance as Jacques, Francois, Philibert and so on.[96] Sir Gillies Payne of Tempsford had sugar plantations in the West Indies; when he

[95] From the records of the Thomas Coram Foundation (details kindly supplied by Greater London
Record Office).
[96] C.R.O., C 1523.

made his will in 1787, he requested his trustees to set free such of the negroes as through age or infirmity were incapable of labour and not likely to recover; and these were to be allowed houses, provisions and clothes as if they were able to labour.[97] One who was concerned was Richard How of Aspley Guise (he had no economic interest involved and was in some ways an unattractive character). When in 1788 the Society of Friends (Quakers) organised a petition to parliament, he wrote to several people to try to enlist their support. Among others he wrote to the 5th Duke of Bedford. "May I, without too great presumption, humbly recommend the cause to my Lord Duke's attention"? The Society had "long lamented the grievous oppression under which those most wretched of all human beings, the Africans, groan", and urged "the restoration of that inestimable blessing, liberty, a natural right, whereof (to the disgrace of humanity and the British name) the sordid avarice of free men has cruelly and unjustly deprived them".[98]

THE WIDER WORLD

The wider world drew Bedfordshire men from three causes: office, trade or war (not to mention those involuntary emigrants, the transported convicts; see chs. 27, 32).

Appointments to office overseas affected only gentry, and comparatively few of these. Before the period of this chapter there had been some examples, such as Richard Nicolls of Ampthill, governor of Long Island (ch. 26). An Earl of Peterborough was the first English governor of Tangier from 1661, and took with him as secretary John Luke, son of Sir Samuel; for part of his time there John Luke kept a diary, 1670-3.[99] Sir Danvers Osborn was governor of New York in 1753, and John Osborn was ambassador to the King of Saxony at Dresden in 1771.

Overseas trade has already been mentioned as founding the fortunes of some gentry, as Indian trade did for Sir Samuel Ongley and William Pym (ch. 27); and that of the West Indies for Sir Gillies Payne of Tempsford, while it contributed to that of Crawley of Luton. Africa was at this date mainly unknown, but Philip Francklin of the Gt. Barford family was stationed at Cape Coast castle 1727-8 for the Royal African Company. The company was not flourishing, and a letter from Francklin dated 17 Oct. 1727 acknowledges the news just brought by the company's ship that writers or clerks' pay was to be reduced to £60 p.a.[100] Robert Ramsay of Woburn, an unsuccessful tradesman, died at Gambia in 1761 or 1762.[101]

Trade also drew the more adventurous younger spirits from among tradesmen in the market towns. Such were the Rugeleys of Potton and St. Ives.[102] The shrewd old father, Rowland Rugeley (d. 1781) thought his sons flighty; he had meant to resign his shop to William, "but alas! you was above my instruction";

---

97 C.R.O., BS 684, 1443 (pr. 1801).
98 C.R.O., HW 87/396, 402. For his pernickety behaviour in the parish, see *B.H.R.S.* xxiii; and his love for a married woman, *B. Mag.* x, 50-4.
99 *The journal of John Luke* (ed. H. A. Kaufman).
100 C.R.O., FN 1055.
101 *B. Mag.*, x, 54.
102 C.R.O., X 311; especially, 75, 93, 96.

and again "Your temper will not long let you be easy yourself nor anybody with you. . . . You might have been worth many hundreds if you had followed my advice." Three of Rowland's four sons went to South Carolina from 1765 onwards, originally enticed by hope of the favour of the govenor, Lord Charles Montagu. Their letters throw light on settlers' lives. Rowland junior wrote from Charleston in 1766 that, if he had capital, cotton "planting [would be] much more eligible than to enter into business"; it would enable him "to live tolerably genteel"; not much knowledge was required – that could be left to the overseer. The heat was great; in the hottest weather clothes were "thrown aside". Bridges were shocking contrivances, and after a sudden storm they broke down, and man and horse had to swim.

Unsettled conditions came to a head with the war of American Independence. Henry served as colonel on the loyalist side and was taken prisoner. All three Rugeley brothers overseas got into difficulties; and only Matthew, who had stayed quietly at home and was sheriff of Bedfordshire in 1786, ended life as a prosperous man.

An army career appealed to some of the gentry. William Orlebar fought under Marlborough at Malplaquet in 1709. John Burgoyne (1739-85) of Sutton, who did not succeed his father as 7th baronet till 1780, had a distinguished career, served in India and became a major-general.[103] William Gibbard of Sharnbrook gives details of Indian service. Bengal had been pleasant for the last few months, but the hot weather was beginning to set in, and there was no stirring out without running the risk of fever. The men had been very unhealthy; and at Madras "most of the officers have been but poorly ever since they arrived"; but "the Colonel seems to think the whole of the regiment will be ordered round to join us here with the ships that come out next season, when we are to relieve the 73rd at Corrompore, where we shall be stationed for 2-3 years".[104]

For the ordinary man the army had less appeal, especially at the time of the war of American Independence. The recruiting sergeant, who in 1775 assembled village groups by beat of drum and began his speech "Ye heroes of Bedfordshire!", found the heroes unresponsive.[105] At Deadman's Cross, Haynes, in 1778 Francis Mee assaulted Sergeant Evan Jones "on his duty when beating up for soldiers for his Majesty's service"; and in the following year there was trouble in Bedford and at Cotton End when Thomas Ingram "pretending to shake hands with William Somerfield, flung a halfpenny into his hand and told him he was entered to serve King George".[106] In the early 18th cent. regiments had been known either by numbers or by the names of their commanding officers; now to improve recruitment they were associated with counties. In 1782 the 14th Foot was re-named the 14th or Bedfordshire Regiment of Foot, and Bedfordshire was

[103] D.N.B.
[104] C.R.O., GA 2488.
[105] B.H.R.S. xlvii, 97.
[106] C.R.O., QSR 1778/71 and 1779/81.

assigned to it as a recruiting-ground. Perhaps this produced better results. At all events young Cox, son of the Flitton vicar, was a casualty in the American war.[107] It was the Marchioness Grey's younger son-in-law, Lord Grantham, who as Foreign Secretary had the unpleasant task of negotiating the treaty which brought this war to an end.

[107] *B.H.R.S.* xlvii, 97.

War and Distress

34 – LORDS AND SQUIRES, 1771–1832

THE PERIOD was in some ways like our own. It was overshadowed by a war which affected life more than war had done for many years; agriculture advanced; social justice began to cause concern; administration was developing; traffic increased; the towns grew. Yet in one way it was far removed from us: the big estates, though the Woburn estate was not yet at its maximum, were greater than they had yet been; and the big landowners were the leaders of society.

LANDOWNERS

The new Lord Lieutenant in 1771, Lord Upper Ossory of Ampthill Park, was 26. A wry comment made at the time on such an honour going to a new family was that perhaps "being nephew to the Duchess of Bedford makes up other deficiencies".[1] But he had qualities which made him generally liked. Horace Walpole found him sensible, with an engaging manner, good-natured without being weak; he liked gaming in moderation; and could "be in fashion without folly".[2] He held the office till his death in 1818. In 1804 he secured by exchange from his cousin, the Duke, a lease of the Honour of Ampthill. He was interested in Ampthill's past, had a model made of the old castle, and put up in the park a cross to the memory of the "injured queen", Catherine of Aragon.[3]

Incidentally, a "Gothick" revival was gaining ground, and when in 1789 John Byng of Southill called on his neighbour, Sir George Osborn, at Chicksands, he remarked how the cloisters "afford a most pleasant and gloomy passage to the library" and how he himself had contributed some of the items on the cloister walls, including two brasses collected on his travels.[4] "I agree with Sir George in taste as to the invention of old chapelries . . . in a pleasant wood he has erected by a pond side a well-constructed heap of ruins." Later in 1813 Sir George had Chicksands altered and extended in this style by James Wyatt.[5]

At Woburn the redoubtable dowager Duchess of Bedford was the main force. It was probably she who in 1774 bought what had at one time been the Gostwick estate in Willington, Cople, Ravensden, Renhold and Goldington; and in 1776 Monoux property in the west. An amusing account has survived of a large reception she gave in London at breakfast on a cold blustery May morning. The meal consisted of cold beef, tongue, fruit and radishes; there were no fires,

---

[1] C.R.O., L 30/9 17/155.
[2] *Complete Peerage.*
[3] *V.C.H.* iii, 270.
[4] *Torrington Diaries*, ii, 34; iv, 116; the brasses came

from Bolsover and Wrotham.
[5] N. Pevsner, *Bedfordshire, Huntingdon and Peterborough*, 67.

the fireplaces being filled with greenery; the doors were left open and the wind was nearly enough to blow the guests away. At last the Marchioness Grey managed to find a cup of tea. The courtyard was crammed with cold, cross and impatient coachmen, and it was 4.30 before her coachman managed to bring her home.[6]

The Duchess' young grandson Francis came of age in 1786 and soon asserted himself. He began to make alterations at Woburn, where he commissioned Henry Holland to build a south wing to the abbey and to add a Chinese dairy; at Oakley to transform the hunting lodge on a ducal scale; and at Bedford to rebuild the Swan hotel. He was a keen foxhunter, kept his own hounds, and also subscribed to the Quorn. Nor did he neglect the expansion of the estate. In 1787 he bought Priestley manor, Flitwick, from Egerton; and in 1794 the Williamson property in Husborne Crawley. His lavishness scared his staff; "the vast expenditure here is beyond conception", wrote the steward, Jones, to the Bedford Office in London in 1790; and Jones' successor, Farey, in 1796 found "the call for money so great I have scarce known how to get on".[7]

At Bletsoe the young Lord St. John was a minor, who had succeeded in 1767 at the age of nine. At Wrest the old Marchioness Grey lived till 1797, and was followed by her daughter (created Countess de Grey in another attempt to preserve the family name). The Countess de Grey, widowed after a vain attempt to save her husband, Lord Polwarth, from consumption by wintering at Nice, lived quietly, but made some additions to the estate. At Luton Hoo a young Lord Bute succeeded, and was created Marquess in 1796; the second Marquess (his grandson) had Luton Hoo altered in 1829 by Sir Robert Smirke;[8] (incidentally, Smirke was educated at Aspley Guise). At Haynes the Granville title had died out, but the late Earl's nephew in 1784 was created Lord Carteret; and in 1790 he added to the mansion a south front with a Corinthian order of pilasters. At Bromham Lord Trevor, after a life of public service, was created Viscount Hampden in 1776. At Warden was still R. H. Ongley (created Lord Ongley – an Irish peerage – in the same year). At Southill there was George Byng, 4th Lord Torrington. His youngest brother, John Byng, kept from 1781 to 1794 amusing diaries of his tours, and sadly chronicled the dismantling of Houghton House in 1794; "Down go the floors! Crash fall the rafters!"[9] But Lord Torrington sold Southill, so when John succeeded in 1812 the family had severed connection with Bedfordshire.

It was Samuel Whitbread who bought Southill Park in 1795, and it was the younger Samuel Whitbread who, even before his father's death in 1796, was the young 5th Duke of Bedford's chief local ally. He succeeded to the brewery created by his father – one of the first examples of brewing on a really large

[6] B.H.R.S. xlvii, 96.
[7] C.R.O., R 1704, 1717.
[8] C.R.O., G/DDA, 149.
[9] Torrington Diaries, iv, 32.

scale. It had the most up-to-date equipment: in 1785 a steam-engine was intro-duced for grinding malt; "our wheel required 6 horses to turn it, but we ordered our engine the power of 10, and the work it does we think is equal to 14 horses".[10] In 1787 George III himself visited the brewery, while a great crowd gathered in the street and "repeatedly huzzaed".

The younger Whitbread also succeeded to an estate and a position of influ-ence in Bedfordshire. In Cardington at first the elder Whitbread and Howard had both been purchasers, and Byng wrote that they "strive which shall most benefit and adorn it; for what cannot the riches of the one and the charity of the other accomplish";[11] Subsequently the Howard property was united with that of Whitbread. At Elstow Whitbread's main purchase was from Hillersdon in 1792. Then in 1795 came that from Lord Torrington in Southill, Warden and Potton.

The younger Samuel Whitbread had been educated at Eton; he married the daughter of Lord Grey of Howick, and his sister married the young Lord St. John. He patronised men of talent, engaged Smeaton to build a bridge at Carding-ton and to design machinery for the mill there, encouraged the artist, George Garrard, and commissioned Holland to extend and remodel the house in Southill Park where he made his home. It has been called "a refined and reticent house, one of the most exquisite English understatements".[12]

Some of the older families of squires like Burgoyne, Crawley, Francklin and Osborn continued. So did Orlebar and Pym; the young Francis Pym, when he succeeded his father, had the grounds at the Hasells laid out by Humphrey Repton.[13]

Some others slightly changed their names. Hester Gery, heiress of Bushmead, married Hugh Wade, and the name became Wade-Gery. A letter which her mother, Mary Gery, wrote to her from Bushmead Priory in December 1792 is a reminder what an infliction coughs and colds were in those days of inadequate heating. "We have all colds and coughs, not a person in the house has been exempted from them, and we stand but little chance of getting rid of them at this season. Mr. Gery has increased his very much by going to Huntingdon last Saturday to a public meeting. The sessions house was much crowded, which made it very warm, and then coming out in the cold and riding home in a great wind must add to it considerably." Hester Wade-Gery kept a note of the christen-ing dinner for her little son and heir in 1794 – it included oysters, venison, turkey, celery, artichokes, and hot apple-pie.[14]

Similarly the Pages of Battlesden became Page-Turner when Sir Gregory Page-Turner succeeded his great-uncle in 1775. A charming poem to his little

[10] *Whitbread's Brewery*, 11.
[11] *Torrington Diaries*, iv, 109.
[12] Pevsner, *op.cit.*, 145.
[13] *Torrington Diaries*, ii, 289.
[14] C.R.O., GY 7/4; the letter quoted is in the family's possession (no. 12)

son Gregory on the latter's 12th birthday begins:

"Dear Gregory, thou graceful boy,
Thy father's pride, thy mother's joy"

but though it seems to have been this boy, who succeeded in 1805 as Sir Gregory Osborne Page-Turner, who assembled the family collection of local water-colours, his later life was clouded by mental illness.

The Antonie property of Colworth went to a Lee relation, who took the name of Lee Antonie; William Lee Antonie was a keen foxhunter, and was also for several years one of the members of parliament for Bedford borough.

Some new families also came. A London merchant, Charles Higgins, in 1786–7 bought Turvey from the Earl of Peterborough. Two branches of the Higgins family succeeded in Turvey. One in 1794 built Turvey House. The other settled at and improved the house called Turvey Abbey, where John Higgins delighted in everything to do with the village, sketching it in many watercolours, drawing its inhabitants, and keeping a notebook of its concerns. Another new arrival from London was that of the Polhills, who took over the Becher property at Howbury. To Milton Bryan came the East India merchant, Sir Hugh Inglis, on marriage with the heiress Catherine Johnson in 1784. In 1777 Mogerhanger passed to the Thorntons; Godfrey Thornton was a director of the Bank of England, and a graceful house in Grecian style in Mogerhanger Park was designed for him and his son by Soane. In 1806 John Cooper acquired the former Wentworth estate in Toddington. Earl Brownlow's Ashridge estate began to spread from Herts. and Bucks. to Studham and Totternhoe about 1808.

WAR

The shadow of war with France darkened most of this period, for the war lasted with brief intervals from 1793 to 1815. France, originally on the defensive against continental attempts to restore her monarchy by force after the revolution of 1789, passed to the offensive; and soon Napoleon's ambition and ability dominated Europe till Waterloo, with England at times almost alone against him. Taxation mounted. The militia was embodied for home defence (ch. 35), and among its officers were John Osborn, colonel from 1805, and St. Andrew St. John, who preserved papers relating to his service.[15] The Sessions House was used for a drill hall, and its furniture suffered – there are bills for mending forms and tables "when the soldiers went away". A depot for the militia was built in Bedford in Mill Street in 1804.[16] Patriotic subscriptions were raised – Caddington has a receipt dated 1798 for a voluntary contribution of £51 10s. 6d. for the defence of the country.[17]

Nationally there was established in 1796 a chain of signalling stations to report fleet movements or weather, or to give warning if invasion came, and one

[15] C.R.O., J 1078–1162.
[16] B. Mag. viii, 265.

[17] C.R.O., P 35/28/5.

of these was on the downs at Kensworth near Dunstable, on the line from Yarmouth. The station comprised posts on which were pivoted six pierced shutters, which gave a choice of 63 positions when signalling. It was dismantled in 1814.[18]

Most gentry were concerned rather with volunteer forces than with the statutory militia. In 1802–3 an uncertain peace revealed that Napoleon was planning to invade England. While the government organised formal preparations to meet this (ch. 35), it also legalised the formation of volunteer troops. Already in April 1798 cavalry had been raised; General Egerton reviewed those for the south in Wrest Park – 52 men on tolerable good horses; they had received arms in the previous week, so could only draw their swords and put them up again; he went on from there to review northern volunteer cavalry at Bedford; and in May an Ampthill troop was being raised – upwards of 20 were inclined to come forward.[19] For infantry the Lieutenant, Lord Ossory, on 1 August 1803 held a meeting at the Swan of deputy-lieutenants and justices to promote further efforts. This was followed everywhere; at the Potton meeting on 5 August, organised by Matthew Rugeley, 45 men signed a resolution offering their services, and offers came in from the villages, from Wrestlingworth 6 and from Eyeworth 4.[20] London firms with an eye to business offered to tender for uniforms – the gay uniforms of those days no doubt encouraged volunteers; there was a government grant of £1 per man, and the rest had to be raised by subscription. At the first muster in October, Mrs. Whitbread presented colours; Colonel Whitbread gave the word of command, and Major Lee Antonie (so wrote a spectator) made a conspicuous figure on his grey mare.[21] It was not only gentry who served as officers; Matthew Rugeley was a tradesman, and John Lesley of Houghton Regis a schoolmaster. In December Sir Montague Burgoyne inspected the force; and though only 100 out of a complement of 430 had arms, he complimented them "on their advanced state of discipline, which vastly exceeded his utmost expectations".[22] After this there was a dinner at the Swan for those who had provided their own uniforms, while the others were given tickets to present at public houses.

Had an invasion taken place, there would have been need for artillery, especially on the coast, but also inland if the enemy penetrated. John Harvey of Ickwell Bury, whose portrait in his scarlet coat with facings hangs in the Shire Hall, raised in his area a troop of volunteer horse artillery; its green embroidered banners still survive, and its muster roll, with rules providing for a fine of 2s. for wearing uniform off duty, and of 1s. for sergeants and 6d. for other ranks who did not appear punctually on parade, with arms, accoutrements and clothing

[18] C.R.O., CRT 140/3 (ex inf. C.W. Davis).
[19] C.R.O., L 30/11/215/55–7; Pawsey says that the cost of outfitting oneself was 16–20 gns.
[20] C.R.O., X 202.
[21] C.R.O., BS 583.
[22] C.R.O., BS 582.

in good order.[23]

With the navy Bedfordshire had less connection. At first, owing to neglect, conditions were so bad that in 1797 there were mutinies at Spithead and the Nore, arising out of genuine grievances. Mutiny in wartime had to be put down swiftly, and Sir Hugh Inglis of Milton Bryan was chairman of a committee of London shipowners, merchants, and insurers to help do so.[24] They passed resolutions saying that they beheld the mutiny with concern, indignation and abhorrence, and they raised a fund (as they put it) to bring lurking traitors to justice. The logbooks of Captain Henry Bayntun of H.M.S. Leviathan, covering the Trafalgar campaign, came to be preserved at Dean because his granddaughter married a Dalton; they show the entries for that memorable day, beginning: "Light airs and cloudy; at daybreak observed the enemy fleet to leeward."[25]

POLITICS TO 1815

A long period of Tory government began in 1783 when the younger William Pitt came to office. He gradually established a strong position; and when war broke out (little as he wished it) he became a great war premier. But Bedfordshire remained Whig. Those most active in the county were two young men, the Duke of Bedford and the younger Whitbread. They had fallen under the spell of Charles James Fox, the brilliant but individual Whig leader, who hailed the French revolution as the greatest event of the day. They felt the challenge of the problems of their time; the Duke especially in advancing agriculture; while Whitbread, who was a member for Bedford borough 1790–1815, had a burning concern for the poor, the sick and the ignorant, and a restless energy which found its outlet in work for the county (ch. 36), as well as for the oppressed and the ill-treated wherever they might be. Another Whig was St. Andrew St. John, one of the county members for about 20 years till he succeeded his brother as Lord St. John in 1805, and who in 1791 at the trial of Warren Hastings spoke against extravagance and corruption among servants of the East India Company in India.

The correspondence of Whitbread and Lee Antonie, for some years his fellow-member for Bedford borough, shows how even after Fox's death his memory held the Whigs together. Whitbread conjured Antonie "by the immortal memory of Fox and by all that is attached to his great name and character" to be in his place in the commons when "that most atrocious act", the 1808 bombardment of Copenhagen to break Denmark's adhesion to Napoleon's continental system, was to be debated. Political association, cemented by personal friendships, permeated many local activities; for instance, the militia; "in the present political situation of this country I feel that the command of the local militia may be made a means of political influence and I know that our adversaries are at work . . .

[23] C.R.O., HY 832, 967–8.   [25] C.R.O., X 170.
[24] C.R.O., X 52/86.

I have therefore secured the command . . . My good old companion and friend, don't desert me!"[26] It even extended to sport; by 1798 the growing strain of taxation was felt even by the Duke; private foxhunting had become too costly to sustain; and thus was formed the Oakley Hunt on a subscription basis, mainly by the instigation of the Duke and Whitbread, with Lee Antonie as first master. "I will continue my subscription of £500 so long as Mr. Pitt leaves me the money", wrote the Duke to Whitbread, and Whitbread said to Lee Antonie when he agreed to be master "I knew it would answer, and without you we could do nothing".[27]

The Tory side had its supporters. The Wrest Park family had now definitely moved to the political right; and the steward sourly described to the old Marchioness Grey a county meeting in 1795 when few gentry could gain access, and the Duke and Whitbread harangued at length "the lower order of mechanics and some labourers"; "this attempt to set up the people in a mass is highly censurable".[28] The Tory candidates at first were Lord Ongley and then John Osborn of the Chicksands family; John Osborn succeeded in being returned for the county five times.

Sometimes the struggle was a close one, as in 1784 when the first return showed that St. Andrew St. John had a majority of one vote over Lord Ongley. Ongley challenged the vote of William Lugsden of Little Staughton as being intended for himself. St. John then counter-petitioned, and every vote was scrutinised. Among those who had to go up to Westminster Hall to give evidence was John Pedley of Gt. Barford, the diarist; he went reluctantly, felt sure he would catch smallpox, and got very cold and much fatigued at Westminster Hall, where were many people from Bedfordshire; but as soon as he was dismissed with 6 guineas expenses, and had some tea, he felt better, and set out for home in a post-chaise next morning at 7 a.m.[29] The result of this enquiry shows how imperfect the electoral machinery still was. Out of 2,998 votes cast, 297 were disqualified for various reasons – some had freeholds of less value than 40s., some were copyholders or leaseholders, some were under 21, and some had polled twice.[30] The seat was adjudged to St. John.

Both sides spent freely at elections. In 1802 Whitbread's expenses at his headquarters, the Swan inn, Bedford, came to £240, and included over 500 bottles of port, 136 gallons of beer and porter, and a good deal of punch, while "glass broke the three days" was 95 glasses, 3 decanters and a window.[31]

The pressure on individual voters was heavy, especially as elections went on for days. John Chase, surgeon, of Luton, who attended Lord Bute professionally and was allowed to fish in the park, was in an agonising position, because he had

[26] B.H.R.S. xliv, 37.
[27] Op.cit., 17, 19.
[28] C.R.O., L 30/9/73/16, 18.

[29] B.H.R.S. xl, 104–5.
[30] C.R.O., HA 14/1, pp.117–81.
[31] C.R.O., X 27/20.

▲ *69a Chicksands Priory, interior.*
▼ *69b Woburn Abbey, the Chinese dairy.*

▲ *70a The Sessions House at Bedford, built 1753.*

▼ *70b The Shambles at Potton, rebuilt late 18th cent.*

▲ *71a Luton, Park Street.*

▼ *71b Leighton Buzzard, marketplace and town hall.*

▲ *72a Dunstable, the Watling Street.*

▼ *72b Ampthill, Church Street.*

▲ *73a Shefford, Ampthill Street.*

▼ *73b The market-house on Harrold green.*

▲ *74a The White Horse yard, Hockliffe.*

▼ *74b The Cock Inn, Eaton Socon.*

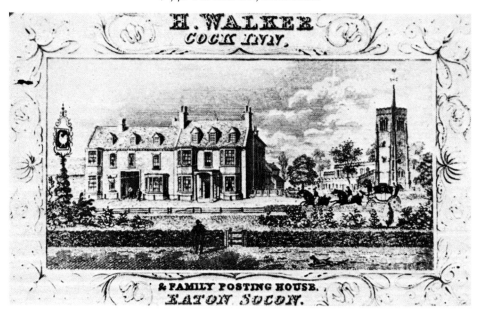

75a *Sutton toll-gate.*

75b *Gt. Barford lock, as repaired in 1841, with initials of Cullum and Francklin.*

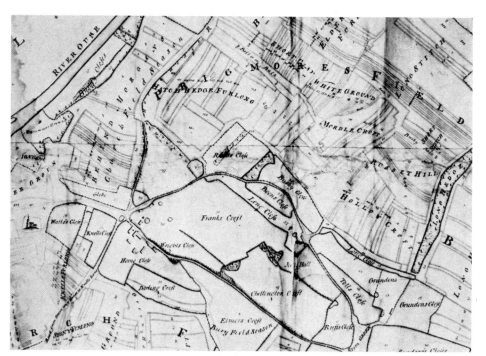

▲ *76a Strip map of Chellington, 1798 (detail).*
▼ *76b Strip map of Houghton Regis, 1762 (detail).*

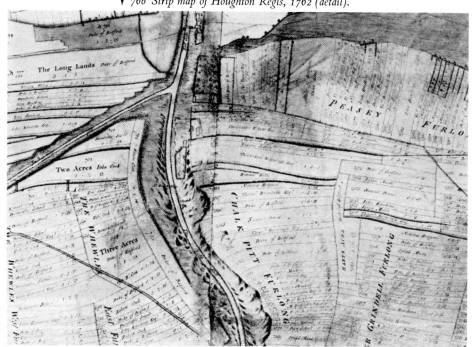

▲ 77a Enclosure surveyors at Henlow, c. 1798.

▼ 77b Open country.

78b Samuel Whitbread, 1764–1815.

78a John Howard, 1726–90.

79b Theed Pearse, Clerk of the Peace 1798–1843.

79a Lord Upper Ossory, 1745–1818.

▲ *80a Bedford infirmary and fever hospital.*

▼ *80b Bedford asylum.*

▲ *81a Bedford Gaol.*

▼ *81b Bedford house of industry.*

82a Parish
stocks and
workhouse
at Eversholt.

82b Parish cage at Wootton.

83a Parish clerk, schoolmaster and sexton:
Thomas Gregory of Toddington, 1742–1816.

83b Poacher: James Clare of Woburn, 1762–1834.

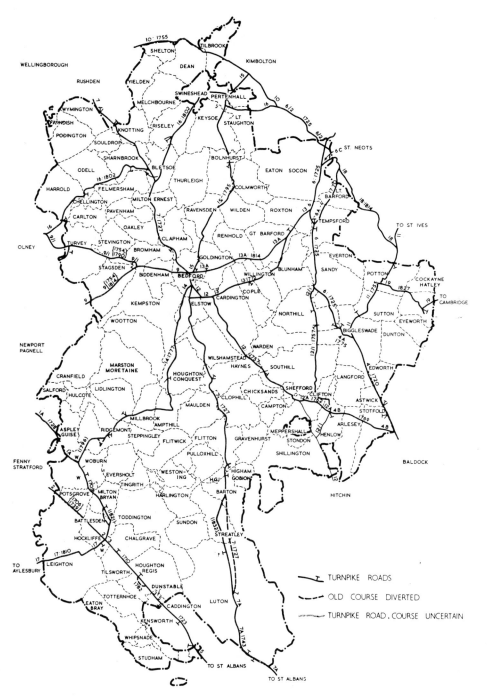

84 Map of turnpike roads.

long had friendly relations with the Osborn family (John Osborn was Tory candidate for the county), but Lord Bute's agent had claimed his vote for the other side. He tried to extricate himself by going on a journey, but had to return before the poll was closed. Osborn sent him expresses. "In point of honour I was obliged to go to Bedford." At Bedford Brown, Lord Bute's agent, came up and spoke to him very warmly. "I well know that Brown will thwart me in everything in his power in every little concern between me and your lordship." Yet Chase stuck to his guns; if it really was to be the case that his fishing and his professional attendance were to be forfeit, "I will relinquish them with greater satisfaction than I could honour and integrity".[32] The claim which a noble neighbour could make on a vote is instanced by a letter to Countess de Grey from the vicar of Flitton (and Flitton advowson did not belong to her) in which he said that he would not think of promising his vote without consulting her ladyship.[33]

Whitbread's own constituency was Bedford borough, but he worked indefatigably to secure the return of his party in the county also. He had, he wrote to Lord Bute,[34] "by agents in different parts of the county ascertained alterations in the freeholds, digested the information, and matured a plan of collecting it abroad and arranging it at home". His register[35] has comments such as "a respectable farmer", or "supposed friendly if he could be induced to vote", or of Samuel King of Langford "self appears to be this man's motto – no dependence whatever upon him". It also has details of qualification or change. A Colmworth entry reads "John Topham; freeholder; lives at Wyboston; a friend"; then is added "lately dead, Mr. James Topham succeeds him, interest friendly". A Luton entry is "Charles Fullwood; sold to William Gillham, a new freeholder". It was to keep the Luton section up to date that Whitbread sought help from the Marquess: "will you think me too bold if I solicit such instructions as may further my plans and relieve my anxiety?"

Whitbread was the greatest local figure in the politics of the time, and was of national importance in that he helped to keep alive the progressive spirit when everything was overshadowed by the war and when movements for reform were suspect. One target for reform was the disproportion in parliamentary representation through the country, which had been practically unchanged for centuries, and with every year that passed became more marked. In Bedfordshire it was not acute; there was, it is true, discrepancy between having two members for the county (population in 1801: 63,393) and two members for the borough (population in 1801 3,948); but nationally it was urgent, with new towns in the north unrepresented, and tiny rotten boroughs in the southwest having members.

---

[32] C.R.O., G/DDA 146/5. John Chase was the son of Samuel (ch. 33); see C.R.O. C 1039–41; and not apparently an attorney, as suggested by Austin, *Luton*, ii, 110; it was Frederick Chase in the next generation who was an attorney, and (fortunate to relate) was employed by Lord Bute.
[33] C.R.O., L 30/11/157/3.
[34] C.R.O., G/DDA 148/3-4.
[35] C.R.O., RV 11–12.

Whitbread saw that reform was needed, but though he would support it in parliament, he did not, like some, try to rouse outside opinion, for such agitation provoked further repression.[36] He opposed the slave trade (abolished 1807) and thereafter slavery itself. He led the impeachment of Melville for financial irregularity. He championed the cause of the ill-treated Princess of Wales. He found time to make great efforts in such a different field as the rebuilding of Drury Lane theatre after it had been burnt down. He never ceased to be member for Bedford borough, partnered for a time by Lee Antonie and then by Lord George Russell. His life was spent in opposition, but there are times when opposition is of prime importance.

AGRICULTURE

All over England in the late 18th cent. many were considering agricultural problems: improved stock-breeding; the use of machinery; and (in areas where common-field cultivation still prevailed) enclosure, which would make it easier to adopt new methods. But till now no one in a leading position in Bedfordshire had seriously taken up these matters. Lord Polwarth (Marchioness Grey's short-lived son-in-law) read Arthur Young and obtained from his mother-in-law in 1773 a farm at Clophill where he could experiment. Polwarth wrote lyrically about his farm, but he was not very practical. He died in 1781.[37] It was Francis, 5th Duke of Bedford, who led the way.

At Woburn Park farm all kinds of experiments were carried out. Livestock formed one subject. Thus in 1794 four equal sections of the park were hurdled off, and into each was put a different breed of sheep, who were weighed after being at grass, and later weighed after being fed with turnips. On the whole, the South Downs seemed to do best, though some favoured the new Leicester breed. Again in 1797 different breeds of cattle were given similar diets of oil-cake, turnips and hay, and the result checked.

By this time, oxen were less and less used as draught animals, and cattle were usually reared for meat and milk. Cheese-making, except for small cream-cheeses, was disappearing.[38] Transport facilities, both by road, and in this period by canal, made it easier to bring in cheese from more pastoral counties. At the end of this period Joseph Coleman, a Bedford grocer, used to buy 54 Leicester cheeses at a time, which were conveyed to him via the Union and Grand Junction canals to Linford wharf in Buckinghamshire, and thence by waggon; in 1830 36 of them were stolen from the waggon; some were found behind the hedge at Astwood before the thieves could get them away, and others had been buried in a garden.[39] A Clophill shop was selling Dutch cheese in 1824.[40]

---

[36] C.R.O., W 1/4430, 4436.
[37] B.H.R.S. xlvii, 93–5.
[38] T. Batchelor, Bedfordshire Agriculture, 528.
[39] C.R.O., QSR 1830/479, 521. Cf. Stilton cheese, which was apparently brought by road from Leicestershire to Stilton early in the 18th cent., after a Stilton innkeeper got his Leicestershire relatives to produce it because he could not get enough locally; V.C.H. Hunts. iii, 222.
[40] C.R.O., QSR 1824/410.

The annual shearing of sheep in June became an occasion for progressive agriculturalists to visit Woburn. Arthur Young was there in 1795; many were present in 1797; and each year it attracted increasing numbers from all over the country and even from Europe and America. The artist, George Garrard, made many sketches of personalities there, and finally painted a picture, of which a popular engraving was made in 1811. Arising from these gatherings there was formed in 1801 the Bedfordshire Agricultural Society, with the Duke as first President, and with over a hundred members drawn from gentry and substantial farmers. (Peterborough was a few years earlier in 1797.) In the following year the 5th Duke died suddenly of a neglected rupture, but his younger brother, John, 6th Duke, was as much of an agriculturalist as his brother, and was backed by his agent, Robert Salmon, who was ready to try out any new method.

One of the society's first activities was the organisation of an annual ploughing contest, where the width and depth of furrows made by different makes of plough were measured. Farm machinery was occupying much attention. There was still no large-scale production of such machines when Thomas Batchelor (a Lidlington tenant of the Woburn estate) wrote his survey of Bedfordshire agriculture in 1807. Thus as regards seed-drills, he mentions that a 1-row drill-plough was in use in the Ampthill area; Pedley had one with two rows; at Colmworth was one with four rows; while at Woburn Park farm was one called the Northumberland drill which could do seven rows at a time. Years afterwards it was said:

> "Batchelor, thy memory will
> Live in connection with the drill."[41]

Harrows usually had 5 beams or rows with 5 tines or spikes in each beam, but Mr. Brown at Dunton had one with only 2 rows of tines. Mr. Runciman of Woburn had a horse-hoe, but throughout the county much hoeing was still done by hand. The Duke had a cast-iron drill-roller, and Mr. John Foster (a progressive farmer at Brickhill, Bedford) had a fluted iron roller, "an implement of great service".

Till now threshing had been done by flails, and flails continued in use for many years, but on bigger farms there were sometimes threshing-machines. They were usually worked by 2 horses; Lord Ongley had one at Warden; Mr. Bricheno of Biggleswade had one which cost 50 guineas and threshed 10 loads of wheat in 9 hours; while Mr. Pickering of Harrold had a small one which in the same length of time threshed only 5 loads. Waterpower however could be used to drive the machine, if available; Mr. Cowley at Hulcote had one made by a common carpenter which was turned by an under-shot water-wheel about 12 ft. in diameter; and Mr. Grant of Leighton also had one worked by water. A chaffcutter was invented by Robert Salmon.

These early machines were not always fully effective. A farmer at Eaton Bray

[41] W. Franklin, *The Plough*, 1857; this was James Batchelor, brother of Thomas.

said that some threshing-machines left so much corn in the straw, which later sprouted, that he had seen ricks almost as green as a meadow. Nor was it easy to get them mended when they went wrong; at Mogerhanger Godfrey Thornton's threshing-machine was laid aside because the iron horse-wheel was broken.

The urge to introduce improved methods was strengthened by two other factors. One was the need to feed a growing population (ch. 35). (At the same time, there was the dilemma that there were more men requiring work than ever before; and even the marginal reduction in jobs made by primitive machines was unfortunate.) The other was the incentive of rising prices, increased by the pressure of war. The importation of corn was not allowed till the price of corn reached a certain level; this level was raised in 1804 to 66s. a quarter. The average price of corn 1804–12 (the peak period of Napoleon's economic war) was 88s. 11d., which shows both the scarcity and the growing need.[42]

ENCLOSURE

Thus in this period came a greatly increased drive to enclose the common fields, and it was especially promoted by progressive landowners. Where a landowner owned the entire parish, he could rearrange the tenants' farms as he chose. On the St. John estate much had already been done by this method (ch. 23). On the Woburn estate it seems to have been used at Cople and Willington after their purchase, for Batchelor refers to their enclosure as recent.

But the usual way was by an act of parliament for each parish. Before setting this procedure in motion, a big landowner sometimes found it worth while to buy up such smaller properties as he could secure. The prospect of enclosure enhanced the price he had to pay, but such purchases eliminated some of the other proprietors; the newly-acquired properties swelled his claim, and would be allocated conveniently with his other land. Elstow was enclosed in 1800, and between 1792 and 1798 Whitbread bought 17 dwellings, small amounts of land, and 4 common rights.[43] On the Woburn estate the Duke made 17 similar purchases in Husborne Crawley (enclosed 1799); 10 in Maulden (enclosed 1803); 6 in Oakley (enclosed 1804); and 11 in Eversholt (enclosed 1808).[44]

Parliamentary enclosures did not run on exactly identical lines, but with growing experience the procedure became more and more streamlined; and that of Carlton, Chellington and Stevington in 1807, at or just after the peak of the war-time enclosure boom, gives an example. There was no predominant proprietor; three neighbouring estates (those of Sir Thomas Alston, Lord Hampden, and the future Countess de Grey) ran into Carlton, and there were also the local squire, Thomas Battams of Carlton Hall, and the rector.

First a list of proprietors' names was taken from land tax returns, and individual approach made to each one, their names being marked off as they were

[42] J. S. Watson, *Reign of George III* 520.
[43] C.R.O., W 2804–987, 3414–54.

[44] Register of Russell purchases (photo-copy in C.R.O.).

persuaded to sign, or "consents but has not signed", or (only one) "dissents" (John Gurney of Stevington with 7 roods), or in one case "not found".[45] A formal meeting was then called at which application to parliament for an act was approved, and an attorney (whose identity was probably already determined) appointed to deal with the application; in this case, John Garrard of Olney.

The act named commissioners who were not as a rule connected with the parish; in this case Edward Platt of Lidlington, the Duke's agent, was one, while the other two came from Oxfordshire and Northants. (For Chalgrave one was Joseph Pawsey the Wrest Park steward, while the other two came from Bucks. and London.) The commissioners received claims and assessed them; reallotted lands; where necessary revised the course of roads; and meanwhile directed the course of husbandry for the few years which the work occupied. During this time a map of the reorganised parish was prepared. At a final meeting the map was produced and proprietors were put in possession of their new lands.

The land dealt with by the enclosure award was that which remained in open fields and common. In every parish there were some closes of old enclosure (chs. 17, 23, 27) sometimes few, sometimes many. At Husborne Crawley, 1,610 a., the area estimated to require enclosing was 1,400 a. At Cardington, which then included Eastcotts and was over 5,000 a., the estimate was 3,000 a. At Eversholt, area 2,146 a., it was only 130 a., but this was exceptional. Perhaps a fair average would be two-thirds of the parish.

In this period over 70 parishes were enclosed in this manner. Twelve of them were on the Woburn estate and were enclosed between 1796 and 1817. The Whitbread parishes were enclosed between 1800 and 1811. Crawley enclosed Keysoe and Thurleigh in 1806 and 1808. Pym was probably largely responsible for the enclosure of Sandy and Everton in 1804; and Willes for the enclosure of Barton in 1814.

On the Wrest estate things went more slowly. Though Blunham, Henlow and Harrold were enclosed in 1798 and 1799, the initiative probably came from local squires and not from the ageing Marchioness; and the steward, Pawsey, though he might occasionally act as commissioner elsewhere, does not seem to have pushed enclosure with his own employer. However, when he retired in 1807 the Marchioness was dead, and the Countess de Grey chose as his successor a man who urged that "spending a considerable sum of money in enclosure will not only produce double the interest it can make in the funds, but will mean a substantial improvement on the estate".[46] He proved unsatisfactory, and was replaced by Thomas Brown, who was to be active in several enclosures; and Flitton, Silsoe, Clophill and Pulloxhill were finally enclosed in 1826.

Similarly reluctant was Viscount Hampden. When the Carlton enclosure was proposed, he said that he was not desirous of gaining any advantage nor

<hr>

45 C.R.O., GA 1120/9.   46 C.R.O., L 30/11/132/29; 30/11/301/179.

inclined to promote the project, but he would not object "provided he is franked from all charge except in the proportion that he may reap of any contingent profit".[47] Biddenham and Stagsden, where he was the main owner, were not enclosed till 1828. In short, though the trend of the time was towards enclosure, there were always some who were indifferent and unwilling to change.

There were also the rights of the church. Glebe in the common fields could be reallotted near the parsonage. For tithes there must either be an allotment of land in lieu (and where the great tithes were owned by a layman or institution, this would go to him or it, and an allotment for small tithes to the vicar); or else an annual payment called a corn-rent would be charged on an allotment to one or more of the larger proprietors, who in consequence of bearing this liability would gain an increased area of land; thus at Toddington a corn-rent of £296 was charged on 638 acres allotted to Thomas Conolly, son of a Wentworth heiress. Sometimes the better-off clergy were not cooperative. William Hooper, rector of Carlton, wrote: "In the first place I expect to be allowed to appoint a commissioner; [secondly he wanted his allotment to adjoin the rectory]; thirdly and as a matter of course I expect to be put to no manner of expense."[48]

Moreover, though a long-term advantage was to be expected from improved farms and increased rents (at Cardington it was thought that arable rents could be raised from 11s. 6d. to 15s. and meadow from 22s. 6d. to 27s. 6d. per acre), this would take time to mature, and meanwhile the initial outlay was considerable. First there was the cost of the act, of fees for solicitor, commissioners and surveyor, and for making new roads, all shared out between proprietors. The final figure often exceeded the estimate. At Cardington an attempt was made to keep down the expense, and there was only one commissioner, Whitbread's efficient agent, James Lilburne (this was in fact illegal, but the commissioner named in the act refused); Whitbread's two-thirds share of the cost had been estimated at £1,250, but actually it was £1,841.[49] The individual proprietor then had to pay for fencing his own allotments. Where outlying farms were created, he had also to build a new house and buildings for the tenant; such outlying farms dating from enclosure are Harrold Lodge farm at Harrold and Hill farm at Willington. Whitbread found in 1804 that he had to give up hunting; "I am not justified in continuing the expense; and unless some new arrangement can be made I fear the Oakley establishment must be given up."[50] At Wrest, even with the earlier enclosures not instigated by the estate, part of the cost was met by melting down some of the leaden statues in the park – Queen Anne suffered by mistake: "I clearly understood your ladyship" wrote the steward "Queen Anne was of the number desired to have been taken down, and the Bacchus was much disfigured."[51]

[47] C.R.O., GA 1120/1.
[48] C.R.O., GA 1120/14.
[49] C.R.O., HA 16/3, 98.

[50] B.H.R.S. xliv, 29.
[51] C.R.O., L 30/11/132/40.

POLITICS 1815–32

From 1812 till 1831 the 6th Duke's eldest son, the Marquess of Tavistock, was one of the county members. John Osborn's last success was in 1818, in which year he succeeded his father at Chicksands; he was weighed down by accumulated election debts which he and his friends (such as Edmund Williamson and William Astell) struggled for years to pay off. In 1822 he wrote that he must make every practicable reduction, and this included the gratuity for his chaplain. His creditors suffered: Mary Blackshaw of the Red Lion, Bedford, wrote to the Countess de Grey in 1826 that there was £600 outstanding, and begged her to help an aged widow and fatherless children;[52] in 1829 there was still £305 due to William Dawson of the Bull, Bedford, and he feared imprisonment for debt. Legal proceedings threatened Osborn in 1830.[53]

The time after Waterloo was an uneasy one. The price of corn fell, and to protect agriculture the price at which corn could be imported was raised in 1815 to 80s. a quarter. In 1828 this was replaced by a sliding scale. But all was not well, even for big landowners and large farmers. Between 1801 and 1831 the county population increased by more than 50% (ch. 35), as much as it had done in the previous 130 years. There was a heavy burden of rates: Toddington in 1821 petitioned quarter sessions about "the heavy burthens with which we are loaded. The vessel is sinking; add a little more to her cargo and she must go down . . . We are encircled by a black chilling tempest of taxes, without one star to illuminate the horizon."[54] Unrest was common and arson appeared. For some time the village constable had been unable to cope with crime, and associations of local gentry were formed to offer rewards for the apprehension of felons. The Olney, Turvey and Harrold Association was formed in 1796; that of Hockliffe, Chalgrave, Battlesden and Tilsworth in 1800.[55] Often the offences were thefts of food: beef or mutton from butchers' shops, and vegetables or fruit from gardens and orchards.

In the country as a whole the demand for parliamentary reform grew, and the opposition to it became more entrenched. For any real attempt to grapple with the problems of the time, it was the first essential, and it was the great aim of Lord John Russell, a younger son of the Duke. He sat first for the Duke's pocket borough of Tavistock. In 1820 when still in his twenties he introduced in the commons a motion for this purpose; it was lost like others during the decade. In 1830 he unsuccessfully proposed the enfranchisement of Leeds, Manchester and Birmingham. Then Lord Grey of Howick (brother-in-law of the late Samuel Whitbread) became prime minister, and once more Lord John Russell introduced a bill for reform. After a long struggle it was passed in 1832. He was a short man, and when in Devonshire cheering crowds were disappointed with his stature,

[52] C.R.O., L 30/11/26.
[53] C.R.O., M 10/5/10, 85–95, 176–7, 622, 640, 667.
[54] C.R.O. QSR 1821/538.
[55] B. Mag. ii, 145; C.R.O., GT 3.

it was said that he had been bigger, but had been "reduced by excessive anxiety".

Of Bedfordshire celebrations the diary of Emily Shore of Potton gives some idea. "All the mob of Potton made a great riot to celebrate the passing of the reform bill, and paraded the town with the most hideous yells, accompanying a triumphal car in the shape of a waggon covered with fresh boughs and bearing flags . . . I do not suppose that any of them understood what they were so noisy about".[56] In fact, the direct effect on Bedfordshire was not great. The representation of two members each for town and county was unchanged, but the county franchise now enabled leaseholders, copyholders and tenants-at-will to vote, and the need to check these qualifications caused proper electoral registers to be compiled and printed annually henceforward. Bedfordshire and Bedford borough continued to be represented in parliament by members of county families for nearly 50 years.

Among the very small boroughs which had been disfranchised was Bossiney in Cornwall, so the Marquess of Bute lost his power there. Tavistock in Devon escaped for the time being, and was still controlled by the Duke of Bedford and often represented by a Russell. The reform of 1832 was rather a first step towards equal representation than a fundamental change.

[56] *B. Mag.* iii, 251.

35 – THE VILLAGERS, 1771–1834

The ordinary countryman's military service was usually done in the militia. The militia's function was to provide for home defence while regular troops were overseas; so during much of this period the militia was embodied, that is to say, it was doing full-time service.

The method of recruiting the militia was by lot. The high constable of the hundred summoned the petty constables from the parishes to bring to a sub-division meeting lists of the men in his parish liable to serve. From these lists the required number of names was drawn. If a man was chosen, he was not compelled to serve himself if he could pay for a substitute; but cottagers were not likely to be able to buy themselves off in this way.

The militia did not go abroad; it was usually guarding the coast of Norfolk, Sussex, Hants, or Devon. It also did two spells of duty in Ireland in 1799 and 1814. Thus, except while there was unrest in Ireland, it did not face danger; what it had to contend with was boredom. Small causes of irritation arose, such as in January 1798 when the men were reprimanded for wearing their best coats, and they objected that it was cold and the old ones were worn out. It was probably boredom that led to the court-martial in the same year of two young lieutenants, Stevenson and Carpenter. The charges were behaving irreverently in church at Lewes, being rude to the Colonel, and using improper language on being refused leave to go to Brighton. Stevenson was allowed to resign and Carpenter was dismissed.[1] Tedium led also to desertion; the Dunstable constable took three deserters in 1793.[2] Sometimes militia service gave opportunity for fraud; George Kirk of Luton, who was medically unfit, managed to get money from more than one of his co-parishioners by offering to substitute for them, when in fact he had been discharged for having a bad arm.[3] Towards the end of the war, in 1814, the Beds. militia spent some time guarding the depot of French prisoners in Hunts. at Norman Cross.

It was possible for militia men to volunteer to be transferred to the regular army for active service. Till 1809 such transfers were probably made to the 14th Foot, for which Beds. was the recruiting-ground. In May 1809, owing to the whim of a Bucks. officer, Beds. and Bucks. exchanged regiments, and the 16th Foot became the Beds. regiment. It was then doing a spell of several years in the

---

[1] J. M. Burgoyne, *Regimental records of the Beds. militia*, 30–37.　　[2] C.R.O., QSR 1793/68.
[3] C.R.O., QSR 1807/68.

West Indies, where it lost 27 officers and more than 500 men by disease, so it was not an attractive service. It also fought in the war of 1812–14 against the United States, and did not return to England till after Waterloo.

For the navy there were occasional volunteers, like the brothers Richard and Samuel Summerland of Harrold, who served on H.M.S. Polyphemus 1804–12, and each allotted 4d. a day from his pay to their mother Elizabeth.[4] On their record of service appears "that mamorable action of Cape Traffalgar".

When invasion threatened in 1803, the Beds. militia was in the southwest, so this like other counties had to take extra precautions. For some parishes the returns still survive as to how many waggons and carts could be produced in an emergency; what mills and bakehouses there were; and what extra stocks of flour and bread could be supplied. Thus at Colmworth were 3 waggons and 7 carts, but neither miller nor baker; at Stagsden 12 waggons and 5 carts, and Thomas Bass could supply an additional sack of flour per week. Some of the surviving returns reflect farmers' impatience at being asked to fill in forms in a busy summer. William Baker of Tilbrook wrote on 6 August 1803 "I cannot spare time, for our wheat is mildewing very fast at this time, but when we have got our harvest I and my men are at your searvast".[5]

ENCLOSURE

A definitive history of parliamentary enclosure in Bedfordshire has yet to be written; and for the present account it was not possible to make an exhaustive analysis; what follows is a series of trial soundings.[6]

To what extent did the owner-farmer exist? Some actual awards for different parts of the county have been searched, mainly those with schedules. They are Carlton, 1807; Wilden, 1817; Gt. Barford, 1824; Wilstead, 1811; Ridgmont, 1803; and Toddington, 1800. Three have a preponderant proprietor: Toddington (Thomas Conolly); Wilstead (Lord Carteret); Ridgmont (Delmé-Radcliffe). In the others the main ownership is distributed among three or four; thus at Gt. Barford beside the resident Francklin family are Polhill of Howbury, Metcalfe of Roxton, and Trinity College.

---

[4] C.R.O., X 50/3–5.
[5] C.R.O., HA 15.
[6] Many printed accounts of enclosure, such as the following passage from a reputable series, are misleading as far as Bedfordshire is concerned:
"The result [of enclosures] was more corn grown; it was also the dispossession of the smallholder and the independent yeomen farmers, the destruction of communal rights and consequent poverty for the cottar who had lived on the margin of subsistence."
The student who has read attentively chs. 17, 20, 23, 25, 27 and 31 will realise that early piecemeal enclosure could be practised by a yeoman as well as a squire or lord; that the point of prime importance is the ownership of land; and that in Bedford-shire the change in ownership (i.e., the build-up of the big estates) had largely taken place before the main enclosure period (parliamentary enclosure) began. To form his own opinion, the student is advised to choose a particular parish, to study the pattern of landholding and of other occupations there in the century before it was enclosed, then to study the enclosure award, and to find out from other sources as much as he can about every owner who received an allotment; at the same time he should study its population pattern and its poor law expenditure. For contrast he should take a parish of late enclosure, like Eaton Bray or Stotfold, and ask himself what differences there are, what similarities, and why.

In what follows the factor of old enclosures (ch. 34) must be borne in mind. A farm with open-field land and common right always had also some closes of old enclosures, sometimes quite extensive ones. Unless there is a schedule setting out both open-field land and old enclosures it is often difficult to ascertain the size of farms (not to mention that the farm may run into an adjoining parish).

At Gt. Barford Pedley is clearly the son of Pedley the diarist (ch. 31); he has 191 a. in old enclosures and an allotment of 189 a., in all 381 a. Benjamin Jefferies had only 14 a. of old enclosures and an allotment of 72 a., but he had a paid post as Francklin agent. At Wilden John Wagstaff has 83 a. of old enclosures and his total holding is 208 a.; he appears to be an owner-farmer.[7] But few others are recognizable. At Toddington Gilpin with 116 a. is the Hockliffe landowner. For Wilden, Robert Lloyd (141 a.) lives at Croydon; George Smith (277 a.) in London; and James Dyson (135 a.) belongs to local gentry; in all three cases this is their total holding in the parish. At Wilstead John Crooke (211 a.) is domiciled in Hants.; James Lucas (206 a.) in Herts.; and William Lowndes (112 a.) is described in the Whig electoral register,[8] where these personal details have been traced, as "esquire, Tax Office"; here too the figures are of the total holding. On this showing just a single farm in a parish, as well as one on a big estate, can belong to a distant owner and be let to a tenant.

With holdings of less than 100 a. similar results are found. Some small owners are farming their own land; at Wilden John Clare farms his 74 a., and John Smith his 69 a. But often these smaller areas too are let to tenants; and it is clear that the same man may rent land from more than one source, so that the extent he occupies is hard to deduce. At Carlton, Pinkerd, whose holding was 48 a., lives at Turvey and lets the land to Goodes; at Gt. Barford, Alders lives at Buckden and lets his 62 a. to Benjamin Jefferies above-named; while at Wilstead Mary Leroux's 52 a. and John Parkers' 53 a. are both let.

What of the smallest allotments of all, those of less than an acre, among which might be expected the poor cottager in so far as he was still an owner? First it may be as well to investigate the purchases sometimes made by a big landowner before enclosure: were cottagers bought out then? Elstow, where Whitbread made 20 purchases in the decade before enclosure, seems to show that there were few independent cottagers left.[9] Six of his purchases, though some were of a cottage only and one was as little as a rood, were from gentry, often living at a distance; four were from tradesmen, including a draper at Huntingdon; one was from a Biddenham yeoman; five involved a share-out of family property; and one was from Richard Kefford, a substantial tenant on the Whitbread estate. Three were from cottagers; two of these were in a better-than-average position: John Buckle owned another cottage in which he lived and on which he paid

[7] C.R.O.: cf. ABP/W 1848/19.

[8] C.R.O., RV 11–12.

[9] C.R.O., W 2804–987, 3414–54.

land tax; Philip Prigmore also owned another cottage, and when he died in 1828 he left his grandson a silver watch;[10] but of the third, William Knight, no more details have been found. It seems worth looking more closely at one of the cases of a family share-out mentioned above; William Malden, wheelwright, had died; all but one of his sons were living at Bedford and Biggleswade and practising the trades of baker, carpenter, cordwainer and tailor. The impression given by Whitbread purchases in Elstow 1790–1800 is of able men leaving the village where they could, and of only one or two exceptional cottagers maintaining their independence.

Both because ownership of his cottage (where he once had it) had in many cases passed from the cottager, and because new dwellings were not entitled to common right, few small allotments solely in lieu of a cottager's right to pasture cattle on the commons are to be expected in awards. As a very rough indication, the following are the figures for allotments of less than an acre (which is what one might expect such an allotment to be) in the parishes considered above, while at the same time the number of dwellings in the 1811 census is given: Carlton, 76 dwellings (1807: 6); Wilden, 54 dwellings (1817: 6); Gt. Barford, 107 dwellings (1824: 8); Ridgmont, 122 dwellings (1803: 15); Toddington, 258 dwellings (1800: about 30). Incidentally, Toddington now ranks as an agricultural parish; its market had already been discontinued for some years when the markethouse was pulled down in 1799.[11]

With Wilstead, which had 108 dwellings in 1811, and whose enclosure award in that year includes 13 allotments under an acre, we can be more precise.[12] The commissioners' minutes list claims for common right, both allowed and disallowed; and only two claims were from the cottager himself. That of Thomas Liles was allowed; that of William Tompkins disallowed. The other claims were all from landowners on the ground of their cottage or other property, and five of these were disallowed. It is unsafe to assume, without proof, that the claimant or recipient of a small allotment is a poor cottager. Confirmation of this comes from Carlton; Mary Lett was allotted ½ acre; when she died in 1809 her will was proved at under £450 (at this time a considerable sum).[13] In Toddington small allotments include one to Joseph Bright at the Queen's Head, another to George Osborn at the wheelwright's shop; and two to butchers.

Where the original claims survive, the question of the small cottager may be viewed from another angle. At Stevington, disregarding those recipients of small allotments who are known to be of higher status (like Peregrine Nash, the Bedford brewer), five successful original claims survive. Robert Bowyer, who was allotted 10 p., said that his father bought his cottage in 1752; "therefore I lay cleam to part

[10] C.R.O., ABP/W 1828/35.
[11] V.C.H. iii, 439, 441, 444.
[12] C.R.O., A 36/3, p.55. Thurleigh (WG 2642, p.35)

lists claimants for common right, but does not distinguish between owner and cottager.
[13] C.R.O., ABP/W 1809/40.

of the commons";[14] his father was probably the matmaker of that name who died in 1788. Mary Odell, an illiterate and somewhat confused claimant, who received 1 r. 15 p. and who could only make her mark, said she was "in possession of her own cottage, and Thomas Coles a tenement adjoining the same, with a pickle or cloase sittuate in Stevington Park End [and] has a rite and title to a full cottage rite in claim of hir estate exlcaimed in hir surendor and a writing or the same alowed from the coart of the manor"[15] (much of Stevington was still copyhold). All five of these small allottees are found paying land tax in small amounts both before and after the award; only Mary Odell's allotment passed (presumably by purchase) after her death to Daniel Nicholls, who had been allotted 130 a. and who apparently was a small owner-farmer.

Harrold was enclosed in 1799. The population in 1801 was 763. Here rather more claims for common-right were submitted, under 20 in all, and a digest of them has survived.[16] More than half of them seem to have been disallowed, as they do not appear in the award. Three were sold: those of Ann Allen, Thomas Bottle and John Ross.

Turvey was enclosed in 1785. A preparatory list of the "state of property"[17] made out a few years previously shows the common rights almost entirely concentrated in the hands of the Earl of Peterborough – this was before his sale to Higgins (horses: 83 out of 108; cows: 207 out of 259; sheep: 1,329 out of 1,681); only 10 others had common right, of whom none appear to be cottagers. Peterborough's common rights were shared out among his tenant-farmers.

Thus in investigating awards the big owners stare the investigator in the face; but surviving small owners and independent cottagers are harder to find. By the latter half of the 18th cent. the generality of occupiers of cottages had become day-labourers paying rent for their cottages; and the enclosure of the parish, at whatever date it took place, was of little relevance to this fundamental fact.

One qualifying observation must be made. A parish of which we should be glad to know more is Maulden, but very little relevant material has survived. Nearly two-thirds of it was already enclosed when it was the subject of parliamentary enclosure in 1803, and as the award has no schedule it is impossible to assess the total holding of each allottee. Yet among those to whom small allotments were made, when people like Morris the brewer, Gostelow the surveyor, and Bolding the surgeon have been discounted, there remain several who appear to be small men, for three of whom wills survive in which they describe themselves as yeomen. Maulden was not typical; on the greensand ridge, it was a market-gardening area, and so was favourable for the survival of the small man. It is the only parish for which an actual disturbance at the time of enclosure has so far been traced (see below). It is however a warning that a final statement

[14] C.R.O., GA 1125/6.
[15] C.R.O., GA 1125/18.
[16] C.R.O., A 12/3.
[17] C.R.O., X 21/628

on Bedfordshire enclosures can be made only when each parish has been investigated exhaustively.

POPULATION

Still more important however for the countryside in this period is the increase of population. This appears most clearly at Luton where, though the township was urban, the large area of hamlets was rural, and all were in one Anglican parish, so that the number dealt with was big enough to show trends.[18] Though, in quoting from Anglican registers, we must bear in mind that nonconformists are not included, and that this period saw the rise of Methodism, yet it is not probable that vital statistics differed as between one denomination and another. In 1755 69 children were baptised and 25 children were buried; in 1800 the numbers were 91 and 36; thus it might be said that in the 18th cent. out of 3 children born, 2 had a chance of growing up. Between 1800 and 1810, on a similar basis, out of 10 children born, 8 or 9 could expect to live.

In the 19th cent. the census gives more reliable figures. Between 1801 and 1831 the county population increased from 63,393 to 95,483, that is, by 50%. The increase was not perfectly even everywhere. Some parish populations nearly doubled; Clapham from 157 to 298; Lt. Barford from 80 to 176; Houghton Regis from 784 to 1,424. One or two show only small increases, like Cockayne Hatley from 102 to 125. The majority are in the region of 50%, like Barton from 448 to 720, and Marston from 709 to 1,007. Since many cottages consisted of only two rooms, one up and one down, and several shared an outside privy, the overcrowding must have been frightful. But worse still was the redundancy. For centuries each village community had grown very slowly.[19] There were now more men than could be employed, and the number was increasing all the time.

A main cause of population growth was probably the diminution of smallpox caused by the spread of inoculation. For instance in 1802 Southill overseers paid £26 5s. to have the inhabitants inoculated.[20] In 1804 there was smallpox at Clophill; a Silsoe girl caught it, "in the centre, next door to Woods at the shop – I fear we shall have to inoculate the whole parish" wrote Pawsey, the Wrest Park steward;[21] however she recovered, and there were no other cases. Improved hygiene helped. In the 1770's Howard had campaigned for cleanliness in the gaol, for an oven to destroy vermin, for a pump, and even for a bath "to wash prisoners that come in dirty, and to induce them afterwards to the frequent use of it. It should be filled in the morning and let off every evening."[22] This attitude may have had an effect outside the gaol also. There may have been other causes which we cannot fully assess, for the population grew in Ireland also, where conditions were not identical.

---

[18] B. Mag. ix, 135.
[19] Cf. ch. 8, n. 76.
[20] C.R.O., P 69/18/4.

[21] C.R.O., L 30/11/215/144–5.
[22] State of the Prisons, 3rd ed., p.23.

The extent of the population increase was only dimly realised at the time, in spite of the census; and the reasons for it still less. Batchelor was aware of it, and in 1807 investigated several parish registers to disprove its connection with enclosure. As late as 1834 the Duke's steward, Thomas Bennett, urged on the new poor law commissioners that there was a surplus population, which they were "not hitherto disposed to admit".[23]

Had the fact been clearly perceived, it is difficult to see what remedy could have been applied and how suffering could have been avoided. The towns were growing (ch. 38) and the day of many small crafts or by-occupations in the countryside was definitely past; only important men like blacksmith, carpenter and miller could hold their own. Emigration had not yet begun on a large scale; the American colonies became independent in 1783, and helped France against us, so that we were at war with them 1814–15; and Australia, though soon used for penal purposes, was at first slow in attracting settlers.

Charity was a palliative. The French wars raised the price of food. In January 1800 at Wrest, old does in the park were killed and given to the most distressed poor. The following winter even respectable farmers were eating barley bread, wrote Pawsey, the steward, and the potato crop failed. He got barrels of herrings down from London; the cost was $\frac{1}{2}$d. per herring, and he sold them at $\frac{1}{4}$d.; at first the cottagers would not eat them, but as they got used to them about two barrels a week were consumed in Silsoe; "they are almost the only meat the poor can get in these very dear times".[24] This was 26 years before Flitton and Silsoe were enclosed.

What became practically universal was the roundsman system, already in occasional use.[25] By this an unemployed man who applied to the overseer was sent by him "round" the parish, sometimes with a printed application for work; the farmer paid something and the overseer made up the payment, but to less (usually 2d. a day less) than the normal wage. This was demoralising in two ways. It discouraged good work; men left early, or tried to make the work spin out; and in any case, till retirement pensions were introduced in recent years, the workers included old and decrepit men and boys. It also tended to keep down wages, as farmers might be tempted to employ men on relief rather than on normal wages.

Under centuries-old legislation, justices had the power to fix maximum, though not minimum wages. In 1795 Whitbread was far-sighted enough to introduce a bill into the commons empowering justices to fix minimum wages, with penalties for employers who did not comply; but it was thrown out.[26] Had it been passed, however, there would still have been the problem of the

[23] C.R.O., R 3827.
[24] C.R.O., L 30/11/215/106–11. Herrings were sometimes distributed by the overseers also, as at Shefford in 1819 (P. 70/12/2).

[25] Cf. C.R.O., QSM 31, p.246, where Joseph Reynolds of Luton in 1834 forged signatures on his form of application.
[26] R. Fulford, *Samuel Whitbread*, p.51

unemployed.

Relief costs became swollen. Relief expenditure included roundsmen, the aged in their homes, and those who for whatever reason had been transferred to the parish workhouse. These increased costs can be illustrated from any parish in the county where the records survive, whether or not the parish was enclosed. At Lidlington in 1780–1 poor relief cost £134; in 1807–8 £719. At Eaton Bray poor relief in 1776–7 cost £142; and in 1812–13 £777. The former parish was enclosed in 1776; the latter not till 1860.

To show what this meant in terms of numbers of people is more difficult. Overseers' methods of accounting varied; besides, roundsmen usually appear as a collective entry; and there are seldom details of the inmates of the parish work-house. None the less, the accounts of Eaton Bray (an unenclosed parish) for January 1813, which occupy 5 pages, give a picture of distress. There are constantly accounts of children being ill; "Francis White, his children ill"; "Hannah Goodson, her girl ill"; and often there follow entries such as "2 coffins for William Osborn's children, 2 shrouds for them, bread and cheese when they laid them out, beer for ditto". There are many payments for faggots and coals, for shoes, shirts, flannel, cotton and calico. The workhouse was repaired. Every week comes a payment for the roundsmen. The total expenditure for the month was £79 14s. 7½d., a sum which not many years previously would have sufficed for a year.

Men no longer looked on relief as a disgrace. In 1816 the Duke's steward, Salmon, commented gloomily that 40 years ago able, willing and industrious men would shudder and lament at the idea of parish relief, but this was no longer the case.[27] He said he well knew that the price of necessaries of life was such that the wages of no labourer with a family was adequate to buy a sufficiency of the trash sold for bread; but yet he doubted if a better way than going the rounds could be devised; it was better than relieving them without employment. In 1819 the Duke proposed at quarter sessions a resolution that the roundsmen system was "destructive of the moral energies of the labourer and injurious to the interests of the farmer",[28] and it was carried unanimously and circulated to the press, but it seems to have had no effect, for once again it did not face the question of the unemployed.

The policy of the Duke and his steward was to try to set a lead in the matter of keeping wages up, without allowing too great a gap between wages paid by the Duke and those paid by neighbouring farmers; and also to employ as many men as possible and to encourage his tenants to do the same. A farm labourer's weekly budget in 1830 on wages of 10s. a week was calculated by Salmon's successor, Crocker, as follows:[29]

[27] C.R.O., R 2119.
[28] C.R.O., QSM 26, p.393.
[29] C.R.O., R 2855.

	s.	d.
rent	1	0
1½ quartern loaves at 10d.	1	3
3½ lb. bacon at 8d.	2	4
1 pint beer daily at 3d.	1	9
tobacco		6
tea, coffee, sugar		6
clothes and firing	2	8
	10	0

but farmers often paid 9s. or 8s.[30] Incidentally, in considering these figures it should be borne in mind that the man's wage was not the whole income of the household; the wife and children also earned what they could, whether at lace, strawplait, or other work.

Bread prices were noted in his diary by Edward Arpin, parish clerk of Felmersham.[31] "I do remember in the year of 1763 that bread was sold at 1s. 1d. the peck." He was a bit of an historian, and when he had anything unusual to record he would add "It never was known in the oldist age". The highest price that he notes for a peck loaf was 6s. 8d. in 1816.

When the farmers would not take on any more men, the overseers set them to work on the roads in gangs. Here they were paid even less, sometimes 3s. to 5s. a week[32] (but see above); even with the meagre sums earned by wife and children such families must have nearly starved. In these gangs they discussed their grievances and brooded over them, and so was "produced in their minds a general and settled feeling of hostility".[33] Inns (when they had money to buy beer) were also places of ferment. At Milton Ernest the constable, Thomas Hine, was fetched from his bed at midnight on Saturday, for fear that "murder would ensue". He turned out men from the Queen's Head, but some of them went down the street into the Swan. It was a moonlight night, so he saw them do so, followed them, and told them to go home, and when he threatened to arrest one, Solesbury, they rescued him and nearly threw Hine in the pond.[34]

By 1831–34, over much of the county, relief was costing in the neighbourhood of £1 per head annually. In some places it was even more. Marston, with a population of 1,007, spent on an average £2,082; and Hulcote, with a population of 49, averaged £195.[35]

UNREST

The first disturbance traced in this period was at Maulden in 1796 and arose

[30] C.R.O., R 3647.
[31] B.H.R.S. xl, 135-43.
[32] C.R.O., R 3571.
[33] Petition from Redbornstoke justices presented to the house of commons by Tavistock, 1829: PUBC 2/6, p.375.
[34] C.R.O., QSR 1821/348.
[35] First. Ann. Rep. of Poor Law com., p.394.

directly out of enclosure (see above). There was a right of cutting peat or turf from the moor for fuel, and it was planned to make an allotment of part of the moor to trustees, so that peat-cutting could continue when the rest of the moor was enclosed. In August a riotous assembly of about 200 prevented the commissioners from surveying the ground, and in response to a request from a local justice, the War Office stationed a troop of cavalry at Ampthill to protect the commissioners.[36] The eventual allotment made for fuel was 19 a. (whether increased in deference to the feeling roused cannot be traced). The justice who wrote to the War Office for help was the Rev. James Webster, no indifferent man, but a concerned justice who was Whitbread's ally in improving the conditions in parish workhouses. He wrote "part of it [the moor] is to be given up to the poor . . . but they are not contented with part of the common, and claim a right to the whole". It is possible that incompletely-informed rumour had aroused an emotional response, like that in Blunham in 1604 and Harrold in 1770.

The next trouble was an attempt to raise wages.[37] In 1819 4 Marston men were imprisoned for refusing to work for normal wages. Then 6 Keysoe men in 1822 combined to demand an increase, and went to neighbouring farmers, such as William Cunington, "with intent to alarm and terrify . . . and by threats and menaces" to get wages raised. A few years later there was a similar case at Roxton; and in 1831 at Flitwick. At Meppershall in 1834 8 men went to the farms of John and Charles Pestell, John Ivory, Samuel Jarvis, and John Kirkby and intimidated several workmen "to depart from their respective hirings"; in the end the riot was said to involve a hundred people.

Then feeling found vent in damage to parish property. Shillington men damaged parish wheelbarrows in 1827; and so did Lidlington in 1830. Millbrook did the like in 1829, and broke windows, after which about a hundred men imprisoned the constable for an hour. Constables became the target of attack, as at Riseley, Southill and Luton in 1832; at Ampthill, Kempston, Shefford and Wilstead in 1833; and at Toddington, Biggleswade and Cople in 1834 – again at Cople the crowd was said to number a hundred.

But perhaps the most sinister sign was recourse to arson. The damage inflicted could be great, the offender was hard to trace (though James Addington of Wilstead, aged 18, was hanged for this in 1832),[38] and feelings of alarm and insecurity became widespread among farmers and landlords. "Last night several corn-ricks at Hoare's new farm near Hulcote were burnt", wrote Crocker, the Duke's agent, in November 1830; "fortunately the wind shifted, but a clover rick, 2 bean

---

[36] W.O. 40/17 (I am indebted for this reference to Mr E. Thompson.) In point of fact, peat-cutting was abandoned when only about one-tenth of the area had been cut; see the small area marked as "waste" on land utilisation maps of 1930 in C.R.O. The allotment was therefore adequate. A.G.L. Shaw, in Convicts and the colonies, found in his investigations that in Bedfordshire villages crime had no connection whatever with the enclosures of various parishes.

[37] Details of these cases have been extracted from quarter sessions records and will be found in C.R.O., CRT 150/11–12.

[38] C.R.O., QSS 4.

ricks and 2 wheat ricks were burnt".[39] A few days later he wrote "Another fire – at Benson's farm at Wootton Pillinge; all the buildings and rickyard destroyed; nothing saved but the farmhouse and dovehouse."[40] Meanwhile he was visiting local vestries and persuading the farmers to employ more men; the Duke had a labour force of nearly 400 in parishes round Woburn, but "I think there are 20 at Ridgmont, 25 at Crawley, and more at Eversholt unemployed, on the roads, or digging sand. The farmers do anything but help; as fast as we take on, they discharge".[41] In December he wrote "fire between 12 and 1 a.m. at Robinson's farm, Wootton Keely".[42] The following October (1831): "I dread the approaching winter – I have had all engines put in order, and would like 4–5 dozen more buckets and two more lengths of hose-pipe",[43] and very soon he was again reporting fires: "at Lewsey farm all destroyed except the house and granary; 10 stacks of corn, 2 of hay, carts, waggons, upwards of 50 pigs, all poultry, a colt, calf and 5 cows; 2 others dreadfully scorched and must be killed".[44] Unpleasant too was the maiming of animals; of cattle at Houghton Conquest, and of an ass at Stotfold, both in 1834.

If the evidence of a Hertfordshire parson is to be accepted, the nearest approach to widespread violence came in December 1830 at Stotfold (a parish not enclosed till 1851).[45] The Rev. John Lafont of Hinxworth may have been officious, but he seems to have thought an actual rising was imminent. He rode over to Wrest hoping to see Earl de Grey (who had succeeded Ossory as Lord Lieutenant), but not finding him, left a note that unless men were taken that night consequences might be dreadful. He consulted a local justice, Edwards, and they assembled 120 special constables and took 10 of the ringleaders – one, James Sharpe, escaped to London. "If we had not put down Stotfold, a coalition of 2,000 men would have been effected in 24 hours." He found much popular sympathy with the rioters; there were some who said "We won't oppose the poor men in their rise for wages." Lafont seems to have been disappointed that he did not get more recognition for his action; a few months later he wrote to Earl de Grey that he had "saved all this side of Herts., Beds. and Cambs. from insurrection".

REMEDIES?

How were these problems to be solved? Farmers and parish officers seem to have been fatalistic. Their unenlightened outlook might depress a man trying to stand on his own feet; for instance, Ridgmont and Husborne Crawley would not allow relief to a man who had a pig, but when he was no longer able to make this effort he would get relief. Crocker notes a case in 1831 when a man, refused on this ground, replied "I have not got one [a pig] now, and when I had it never did you any harm."[46] It was a kind of means test.

[39] C.R.O., R 3566.
[40] C.R.O., R 3569.
[41] C.R.O., R 3567.
[42] C.R.O., R 3572.

[43] C.R.O., R 3591.
[44] C.R.O., R 3593.
[45] C.R.O., L 30/18/27.
[46] C.R.O., R 3574.

Some tried to give publicity to the poor men's case. T. P. Macqueen of Ridgmont, though he seems not to have been able to get cooperation from his own tenants as the Duke was at least always trying to do, wrote a booklet *Thoughts and suggestions on the present condition of the country* in 1830. He said that of 96 prisoners in Bedford gaol, 76 were of good character, driven to crime by sheer want. He instanced a poacher from Kempston, called Lilley, who had a pregnant wife and two small children; "I was allowed 7s. a week for all, for which I was expected to work on the roads from light to dark"[47]; he and his brother were hanged for wounding a keeper.

Some gentry introduced schemes for parish allotments for poor labourers, as at Sharnbrook, Toddington and Eversholt.[48] The Harlington rules stipulated that allotment-holders must be regular attenders at divine service; the advice given to them was to raise vegetables for the family, to keep a pig, and to make compost from vegetable refuse and dung.[49] The Bedfordshire Agricultural Society from the very beginning had offered prizes to labourers who brought up families without recourse to parish relief; thus in 1803 Thomas Lawrence of Shillington won 5 guineas for having brought up 9 children still alive without such help.[50]

Some parishes had schemes for setting the poor to work. Marston had a parish brick kiln; in 1830 they arranged with William Franklin to manage it, finding a horse to work the mill, and taking $7\frac{1}{2}\%$ on sales of bricks.[51] (This is comparable with Dunstable's chalk pit for the manufacture of whiting.)[52]

Friendly societies are also found, which helped members when sick or unemployed and were encouraged by the gentry. Sometimes these were associated with a church, as at Turvey (probably because of Higgins influence), but more normally they met at an inn. Podington must have had one for some years, for a Podington man won a prize for long membership in 1803.[53] Barton's club met at the Rose and Crown; Streatley's at the Chequers; Cople's at the Dog. The Westoning Amicable and Brotherly Society of 19 members under 41 years of age (13 of them could not write) met at the Chequers inn once a month; they had a strong-box with 3 locks in which their funds were kept; and a new member must put in 2s. 6d. and spend 6d. – no doubt on beer; but any member who came drunk or swore or offered to bet was fined 2d. If sick, a member would receive a small weekly sum and attendance from an apothecary; and if he died, £5 would be paid for his funeral.[54] By the end of this period at least one parish in four had such a club; and some, like that at Sharnbrook, embraced smaller parishes nearby.[55] These benefit clubs are a reminder that, whatever the difficulties of the times,

[47] Macqueen, p.13.
[48] C.R.O., AD 531, 1749; X 21/511-20.
[49] C.R.O., X 21/510.
[50] C.R.O., X 136/1, p.40.
[51] C.R.O., X 135/80-5.

[52] C.R.O., P. 72/8/3, in 1833.
[53] C.R.O., X 136/1.
[54] C.R.O., HA 33.
[55] C.R.O., CRT 150/29.

there were always some who, through character or ability, managed to keep their heads above water.

Some men, as others had been doing before them for many years, made their way to the local towns (ch. 38).

Some families went to the industrial north, where expanding industry needed labour. A little group from Cranfield went to Mellor, a small town with cotton factories, a few miles from Manchester. In Cranfield Philip Peddor had earned 7s. a week as a farm-worker, his wife and daughters 5s. 10d. by lace-making, and a son 2s. 6d. as ploughboy. At Mellor in 1834 he was working on the land, and his wife and children in a factory, and their total earnings had doubled to 30s. a week. The mill-owner, Mr. Clayton, found his new hands "very gentle". Peddor wrote to friends that if they would not join him, they deserved to be starved in Bedfordshire. He would rather cross the sea than go back to Cranfield.[56]

Some in fact did cross the sea. Emigration became more common. Macqueen had 10,000 a. in New South Wales which he called Segenho, and he introduced the first free settlers to Australia in 1824. Arpin notes in his diary for 1828 "John Turnor to North Amereca", and for 1829 "39 men women and children set off to go to Boston in Massachusetts in the united states of North of America".[57]

Finally in 1834 the reformed parliament passed a new poor law, which grouped parishes in unions with elected boards of guardians. For the troubles attending the initiation of this system, see ch. 41.

---

[56] *First Ann. Rep. of the Poor Law commissioners*, 324–5.   [57] *B.H.R.S.* xl, 142.

36 – GROWING RESPONSIBILITY, 1771–1834

ADMINISTRATION

With the advent of Theed Pearse, clerk of the peace 1798–1843, county administration became more assured. He is the first clerk whose appearance is known; pleasant, equable, competent, we can imagine him holding courteous but capable converse with the genial Lord Ossory, Lord Lieutenant; being suitably but not excessively deferential to the 6th Duke of Bedford; and able to hold discussions with the driving Whitbread without being too much deflated. He probably had a pretty good knowledge of the gentry who in increasing numbers regularly attended quarter sessions. At his house in Potter Street (Cardington road) he had a thriving legal practice. He saw that the county records were properly kept, and for over 40 years his familiar writing in a letter or a marginal note indicates that a matter is in good train. Only as to one point was he remiss; in presenting his annual bill to the treasurer for payment; and when he finally did so in 1822 the justices were staggered at the sum outstanding; £500 was paid down, and the rest was to be paid by instalments,[1] but higher authority forbade this, and Theed Pearse lost it.

The county treasurer continued to be a Bedford merchant; William Watkins, coal merchant, acted from 1793 to 1803, and was followed by Francis Green, 1803–36. During the Napoleonic wars the work in connection with militia men and their substitutes became burdensome, and he was paid an honorarium in recompense for his excessive trouble. It now became necessary occasionally to have recourse to a professional surveyor, both in connection with county bridges (ch. 37) and for the new county buildings which were required. John Millington of Hammersmith was appointed for this purpose in 1816, and followed in 1825 by Francis Giles, also of London.[2]

At quarter sessions 1800–10 there might be 12–20 justices attending; as time went on, 20–30. The Duke sometimes came, and so did the Marquess of Tavistock. Samuel Whitbread was regular, and after his death his sons attended. The Pyms of Sandy were frequent, and so was Hugh Wade-Gery of Bushmead. New gentry took the duty seriously, like the Higgins of Turvey, and Sir R. H. Inglis of Milton Bryan. Those from the south joined in, occasionally the Marquess of Bute, more often Samuel Crawley. From Wrest Park there was the Countess de Grey's nephew and heir, the future Earl de Grey, who succeeded Lord Ossory as Lord Lieutenant. Then came energetic clergy like the Rev. George Cardale of Millbrook

[1] C.R.O., QSR 1822/124.   [2] C.R.O., QSM 25, p.229; 28, p.248.

and the Rev. James Webster of Meppershall. In short, the climate of opinion had changed; it was the thing to go to quarter sessions; and there the active intelligent gentleman or cleric might expect to meet his fellows.

GAOL

Perhaps one reason for more participation was the increasing demand made by county affairs. There was for instance the new county gaol. It had long been realised that the old gaol did not come up to the standards set since Howard's day. Again, it was small, and when the American war held up the overseas transportation of convicts it became overcrowded; and since it stood in the middle of the town an epidemic at the gaol could easily spread. In 1783 the government was pressed about this, and in 1789 was requested to send convicts to Botany Bay. The gaol was also rat-ridden. At first in 1786 the plan was to secure additional land in High Street and rebuild on a larger scale, with cells above ground, separate accommodation for men and women, and a sick bay. But the land could not be obtained, and more time went by. There seems to have been a bad outbreak of typhus in 1799, when there are charges for sitters-up with sick prisoners (victuals, beer and rushlights) while the sufferers even had brandy and port, and, when convalescent, broth and sago; and the place was fumigated and the walls washed with oil and vinegar.

However in 1798 a committee resolved on a site outside the town in Dovehouse close. The building was to replace both the old gaol, and the old house of correction in Cauldwell Street. John Wing was the architect. It for the first time included a bath; there was a chapel; there were also facilities for executions – a movable machine could be erected on the roof of the turnkey's lodge (protected, when not in use, by a tarpaulin). On 18 June 1801 the move was made, and a few weeks later the execution took place of William Pepper of Millbrook for sheep-stealing and John Brown for burglary and horse-stealing. The old gallows on the road to Biddenham were taken down in 1802. The prisoners were employed on work of various kinds, such as beating hemp and making lace and strawplait. Typhus was not eliminated from the new gaol – it broke out in 1816 and 1825.

The gaoler at this time was a rather unusual man, and we shall hear more of his descendants. His name was John Howard, and he is *not* to be confused with the humanitarian (who was no relation, and whose only son died young). Howard the gaoler had some land, and employed the prisoners on it, but the justices were shocked, and dismissed him in 1814, and so ended this unofficial attempt to make Bedford an "open prison".[3]

The new building soon proved insufficient for both purposes, and in 1819 a new house of correction was built beside the gaol. It was to be used, the justices said, for "bastardy, lewdness and light offences". But they still found difficulty in preserving what they called "regularity of behaviour", and in 1821 they added a

[3] C.R.O., QSM 24, p.225.

treadmill for grinding corn; they found that this "subdued the mind and fatigued the body without affecting general health".

Physical conditions were much better for the prisoners than they had been. On Christmas day they had beef and plum pudding for dinner. Attempts were made to care for them; the chaplain taught them the Lord's prayer and the ten commandments, and justices inspected the gaol regularly. And yet all was not well. Indeed the justices themselves in 1828 feared that wages of 3s. a week (that is, 6d. a day on the roads) were in themselves enough to drive labourers to despair. Eliza Grant in 1829, who had "led a profligate life", sullenly tore to pieces everything the overseers had given her, using obscene language; and in 1831 the chaplain found that many Bibles had been lost or destroyed.[4]

CRIME

Though the gaol was the justices' responsibility, many prisoners there (especially those under sentence of death or awaiting conveyance to the hulks for transportation) had been sentenced by assize judges. What were the offences for which men were most commonly brought before justices at quarter sessions? Theft covered almost every possible object. All kinds of livestock were stolen; food – meat, grain, vegetables, fruit, eggs, cheese, honey; so were clothes, whether outer clothes such as cloak, waggoner's frock, jacket, breeches, shoes; or under-clothes such as shift or shirt; and one man stole two blankets from the workhouse to keep himself warm; while fuel was broken from hedge or fence. Surprisingly all kinds of tools were taken also, from ploughshare, dibbing irons, and grindstone, to pig-trough, spade and harness. Valuables, such as silver spoon, watch or gold ring occur more rarely. Lace and strawplait could be converted into a little extra cash. A grim case was the theft of bodies from the churchyard to be sold for medical purposes; in 1826 George Lester and William Smith were found attempting to convey one from Biggleswade to London in William Carrington's waggon, but his suspicions were roused, he fetched the constable, and inside the suspected box was found a corpse in a fresh and perfect state.[5]

Gleaning afforded a chance to pilfer. In 1785 at Blunham some poor women were following Matthew West's cart in Ham Field in Merfurlong, when a heavy shower put a stop to carting for that day; they all exclaimed at having to go home without their gleanings, when Mary Emery took "a couple of laps' full of loose barley in her apron" from adjoining land where the grain had not yet been carried, and put it in her sack.[6] Sometimes gleaning gave rise to a brawl. At Silsoe in 1816 Ann Stormer would not join with the other women in sending for beer on a hot day – they called her "a mean niggardly devil" and a fight ensued.[7]

There were cases of assault with hedging bill, waggoner's whip, dung-fork or scythe. John Pruddon of Bromham, blacksmith, in 1786 kicked his wife about

4 C.R.O., CRT 130/23.
5 C.R.O., QSR 1826/350.
6 C.R.O., QSR 1785/81.
7 C.R.O., QSR 1816/227.

the room.[8] John Cutler of Gt. Barford in 1823 cheeked his mistress, Mrs. Jeffries, when she told him he had not cleaned the knives properly, and then Edward Jeffries beat him till his shoulders were black and blue.[9] Elizabeth Page of Gravenhurst in 1818 threw a saucepan at her daughter-in-law which hit her on the temple.[10] William Soames, a Stevington farmer, in 1826 was set upon at night by three of his own men after his harvest home.[11] Sometimes the threats were worse than what actually took place: "I'll let your damnation guts out!" or "Damn my heart to hell if I do not shoot you!"

The ugliest scenes arose at poaching affrays. When John Cooper in 1792 was searching for poachers in Sandy warren, he was confronted by several men from Potton, who said "Damn you, if I get or have the first blow, them that I hit shall not have a second!"[12] (Incidentally, though Potton and Sandy rivalry was traditional, inter-village feeling was often strong elsewhere also; at a disturbance between Haynes and Wilstead in 1826, not caused by poaching, Wilstead people said "they would not go while [until] all Haynes people had left the field, they would not be drove".)[13] An armed gang of 7 men from Clophill and Maulden, poaching at Cainhoe in 1820, was met by the keeper and several assistants, and in the affray William Giddings, who was helping the keeper, was knocked down and his head beaten with the butt end of a gun.[14] In 1828 Smart, one of the Duke's men at Woburn, had his leg broken with a flail by a gang of poachers, and was wounded in the head while he lay on the ground, while another, Jeffs, was dangerously hurt.[15]

There are still several references to parish stocks. Thus at Old Warden in 1813 a prisoner broke the lock of the stocks and escaped; and at Dunstable in 1826 a travelling carpenter who beat his wife in Church Street was put into the stocks for a couple of hours; while stocks are shown on some early 19th cent. watercolours, as at Eaton Bray, Upper Gravenhurst, and Wootton.[16] But the provision of cages, either to supplement stocks or as an alternative, was extending to at least the larger parishes; thus while we get references to cages in the market towns, such as providing straw for the cage at Shefford in 1816, breaking open the cage at Potton, also in 1816, and the difficulty of getting a drunken man into the cage at Woburn in 1823, we also get references to the building of cages at Harrold in 1824 and Eaton Socon in 1826; while there was trouble at Houghton Conquest in 1825 about the taking of beer to a prisoner in the cage; and an early watercolour of Turvey shows a cage.[17]

[8] C.R.O., QSR 1786/66-7.
[9] C.R.O., QSR 1823/347-9.
[10] C.R.O., QSR 1818/258.
[11] C.R.O., QSR 1826/299.
[12] C.R.O., QSR 1792/51.
[13] C.R.O., QSR 1816/287, 630.

[14] C.R.O., QSR 1820/274.
[15] C.R.O., R 3517. For a similar affray on the Whitbread estate in 1815, see B. Mag. ix, 333-8.
[16] C.R.O., subject index to cages.
[17] C.R.O., subject index to stocks.

ASYLUM

Another county building which had to be provided by the justices was an asylum. Such entries in parish records as "the mad wench" show that there had long been cases of mental illness or sub-normalcy. Occasionally overseers managed to place these in Bethlehem hospital in London, as happened with Jane Stocks of Langford in 1799;[18] the matron was particularly fond of her, even having her to sleep in her own room when indisposed, and she usually conducted herself with propriety, but she was subject to occasional variations and could not be described as cured.

At last in 1808 an act of parliament enabled public provision to be made in a county asylum where patients would be maintained by their respective parishes. Whitbread was chairman of the justices' committee to put the act into effect, and again Wing was the architect. The Bedford asylum opened in the Ampthill road in 1812, and was the second in the country. (Northampton, 1811, was the first).

It had accommodation for about 60 patients. According to the ideas of the day, the windows had iron bars, and the equipment included strait-waistcoats and handcuffs, but these were only occasionally used. There was gruel for breakfast, meat at midday four times a week, and supper of bread and cheese; vegetables were grown in the garden, a brewhouse provided beer, and there were various workshops, so that where possible the patients' work could contribute towards their own support. John Harris, superintendent, was enlightened for his day, and even unsuccessfully suggested the construction of mounds, whence the inmates would be able to see, over the high walls, what was happening on the road below, and so keep alive their interest in the outside world.[19]

Because the parish had to bear the expense when the family could not, there was sometimes difficulty in getting the parish to make use of the asylum. Peter Warren, a Riseley plumber with 12 children, one of whom was an unmanageable lunatic boy, was required to pay half the cost, the parish paying the other half, but he was unable to keep up his payments.[20]

HOSPITAL OR INFIRMARY

This period saw too the building of the infirmary or hospital. At present care of the physically sick was regarded as a parochial liability; the provision of a hospital was a field for private charity. Here it was the elder Whitbread who took the initiative by leaving £8,000 for the building and upkeep, "which appears to me to be very much wanted", and the younger Whitbread who, with the help of a committee of landowners and others, carried the project into effect.[21] Here too Northants. was before us (1793), but Herts. did not have such provision till the 1820's and Bucks. not till 1833.

[18] C.R.O., W 1/150–1.
[19] C.R.O., CRT 130/34.
[20] C.R.O., QSR 1818/367.
[21] C.R.O., W 3306.

A site for the infirmary was chosen near the Ampthill road in Bedford, and once more the architect was John Wing. It was opened in 1803. The furniture included 50 iron bedsteads; the operating room had an operating table and 3 pairs of oilskin sleeves (this was of course before the discovery of anaesthetics).[22] There was accommodation for 4 nurses, a matron and a house-surgeon. No chairs are listed for the patients' waiting-room. About £50 a year was spent on leeches for blood-letting. An extensive medical library was built up by gifts.

Most county gentry and a number of townsmen subscribed towards the building, and continued to give annually towards its upkeep. An annual subscription of at least 2 guineas entitled the subscriber to recommend a patient for admission. They also organised fund-raising efforts. A letter from Ann Skevington of Bedford about 1829 says that a fancy-dress ball at Bedford raised £50; and £500 was produced by a bazaar where the Marchioness of Tavistock, elegantly attired, had a stall, and the writer purchased a handsome reticule.[23]

There were also collections in churches and chapels. Some parishes subscribed, but parish subscriptions were difficult to extract. A Flitton overseer, when told in 1812 that his parish was in arrears, wrote that this demand "much alarms our parishioners"; he also did not think that the parish had benefited much; "one man was sent and was soon sent back uncurable".[24]

One of the early reports in 1811 gives the average number of patients as 32; they were admitted on Saturdays only, 11 a.m. to 2 p.m., when the physician Dr. D. G. Yeats and the surgeons (of whom there were now two) were in attendance.[25] An application for the post of matron in 1814 has absolutely no reference to nursing experience,[26] and as late as 1835 Mr. Tomkins of Harrowden gave Nurse Watson 1s. to give his wife better attention.[27] Nurse Hipwell was reported in 1829, after 21 years' service, as incapable of attending to her duties, on account of age and infirmity, and in 1830 she was released with a pension of 6s. weekly – the governors congratulating themselves on their enlightened policy of generosity.[28]

WORKHOUSES

Whitbread's energy found time not only for county institutions but also for parish workhouses, and he brought accounts of their deficiencies to quarter sessions and got orders made for their improvement. By this time almost every parish had its workhouse – one or sometimes several cottages belonging to or hired by the parish to house those who could not manage to keep a roof over their own heads. With growing destitution, it is not surprising that some of these were in a very bad state, and that in 1808 72-year old Samuel Binyon of Cranfield,

[22] C.R.O., W 1/187. For the library, see HO/BM 5, pp.237–42.
[23] Undated letter of 1828 or 1829 in the possession of Mrs. Wade-Gery, (no. 194).
[24] C.R.O., W 1/210; for instance Dunton subscribed (P. 51/18/15).
[25] C.R.O., W 1/207.
[26] C.R.O., W 1/219.
[27] C.R.O., CRT 130/15.
[28] C.R.O., HO/BM 5, pp.212, 252.

who found that he was unable to maintain himself and his wife on the 3s. weekly allowed him by the overseers, petitioned quarter sessions to order the sum to be raised; "he has a real objection to be put into their workhouse, which is in a very filthy and uncomfortable state, as he has always been till lately in a clean and comfortable situation as a tradesman".[29]

The first brought to book by Whitbread was Shillington in 1790; 9 of the 12 beds had only one pair of sheets, "and the poor lie without while they are washed and dried".[30] Langford in 1802 had an epidemic, and was ordered to repair the poor houses, drain the ground to prevent damp floors, provide furniture and clothes, and "rescue themselves from the disgrace of a system of management so cruel and oppressive to the poor;" similar directions were given to Haynes; and Houghton Conquest was told to make the poor houses "fit for human habitation".[31]

Next year Stotfold poor houses were found to be in a worse state; Whitbread had found them without windows or floors (by this time the old earthen floors were usually covered with a layer of brick), with no proper separation between men and women, and the poor without bedding, furniture, clothes and cooking utensils. At Maulden 5 of the 10 houses were in a deplorable condition, and the poor therein "an offence to the common feeling of humanity". Arlesey's fault was limited to neglected thatching.[32]

Latterly he was helped by the Rev. James Webster, who in 1807 reported on Lidlington as follows. "The workhouse is not fit for the habitation of man . . . the poor are in want of food, clothing, bedding, fire . . . there are 21 inhabitants living in the most wretched condition, without any master, or care or attention from a parish officer. In one bed, consisting of little more than a few rags, are sleeping 5 persons, namely Ann Goodman and her children . . . Amelia Goodman, aged 19, sleeps on the ground with a few rags to cover her; she wanted a little straw, the parish officers would not give it to her, and she purchased 3d. worth."[33]

There may well have been workhouses in very bad condition in other parts of the county not reached by Whitbread or by some other energetic justice. Where the workhouse was efficiently managed, the complaint might well be that of severity. Thomas Peck of Stagsden, who absconded for two days, was refused supper on his return till certified by the overseer, and he struck the master's wife, Sarah Davis, with a tin vessel.[34]

In all this the main point to note is not that so many workhouses were badly run. There were more workhouses and they had more inmates, but the condition of a workhouse had probably always varied with the humanity and efficiency of the overseers for the time being. The main point is that individual consciences

29 C.R.O., QSR 1808/149.
30 C.R.O., QSR 1790/57.
31 C.R.O., QSR 18012/1-4.

32 C.R.O., QSR 1803/3, 4, 9.
33 C.R.O., QSR 1807/78.
34 C.R.O., QSR 1815/175.

were stirred by a growing sense of responsibility to get them improved. The phrase "the common feeling of humanity" is a new one at quarter sessions.

SCHOOLS

Schools, like hospitals, were still not thought of as a public obligation – Whitbread in 1807 introduced into the commons a bill to make them so but it was rejected. However the public-spirited were increasingly aware of the need for them. Except for the fortunate few in the comparatively small number of parishes with endowed schools, like Houghton Regis and Wilden, only those whose parents or benefactors paid for them were taught to read and write.

Cost was not the only obstacle; one was child labour. For many children the only day when they were not at work was Sunday. A growing movement for Sunday teaching appeared in Bedfordshire as elsewhere. At Turvey in 1792 Charles Higgins left £300 to be invested to pay a master to teach on Sundays, if others would add sufficient to make up his salary to £20 p.a.[35] At Elstow in 1802 Whitbread contributed £5 to each of two Sunday schools, one for 25–30 boys kept by Buckle and others for girls kept by Prigmore; and in 1812 a Sunday school for dissenting children was opened in the Moot Hall.[36] At Cardington he supported (as well as day schools) two Sunday schools kept respectively by Cox and Izzard. At Old Warden he gave £7 a year to one for 30–40 children kept by Bunting.[37] The Countess de Grey provided a dinner of meat, plum pudding and beer for the girls of her Sunday schools at Clophill and Pulloxhill.[38] Occasionally a Sunday school might be purpose-built; the Duke built one at Willington opposite the church in 1832 – the contract was for £132 and included two privies.[39]

Sometimes such a Sunday school arose through local effort or through a church. Riseley vestry resolved to set up one in 1805. At Harrold in 1809 there was one associated with the Independent congregation; its object was to instruct poor children in reading, writing and the principles of religion; the teachers were to be of good moral character and unpaid, but fined if late; the classes were to be held at 9 a.m. on Sunday and after afternoon service; the children must be clean, and must not be given corporal punishment, but the disobedient or truants were to be dismissed with every mark of disgrace.[40] At Ridgmont there seems to have been a Baptist Sunday school by 1830.[41]

Weekday teaching was rarer. Some weekday "schools" were in effect places for the production of lace or strawplait under supervision. Such was that in Ampthill where 7-year old Henrietta Timms was taught in 1833; after the morning's work she had to wait for her plait to be measured off, so one day she did not get home till 1.30, when her father, a breeches-maker, beat her black

---

[35] C.R.O., HI 47.
[36] C.R.O., W 1/2076. For a time the children attended church and meeting alternately.
[37] C.R.O., W 1/849.
[38] C.R.O., L 29/120.
[39] C.R.O., R 3732.
[40] C.R.O., X 242.
[41] C.R.O., X 347/2.

and blue.[42] At such schools some simple teaching was also given, and Henrietta learnt to read the Bible there. Boys sometimes went to them; James Jackson of Sundon, who left his plait-school in 1831, and later got into trouble, was said by his plait-teacher to have been a "a steady and careful lad".[43]

When there was provision for a regular weekday school, it was sometimes necessary to allow the children to do some work because the small amounts they could earn in this way were necessary for the family budget. At Clifton where in 1807 the rector, the Rev. D. S. Olivier, established a school at his own expense, taught by one William Morgan, the hours were 8–12 a.m., 2–5 and 6–8 p.m. (for some were glad to come in the evening), and most of the children did some strawplait; and strawplait was taught in Emery's charity school at Meppershall.[44]

Efforts were made by landowners and others to encourage weekday teaching. The elder Whitbread had for years paid for the teaching of children at Carding-ton,[45] and the younger Samuel Whitbread continued this by making grants to three people in Cardington who took pupils, to Evans, Waterfield and to Miss Morgan; and he provided clothes annually for some of the children who attended; while at Old Warden he made a grant of £8 p.a. to Bunting for his weekday pupils; but there fewer than 12 boys attended on weekdays, while on Sunday the number might be as many as 40.[46] At Stotfold H. O. Roe, son of a former vicar, provided school and site in 1808 – the children were to be of Anglican parents.[47] Edward Willes of Barton in 1807 left property for the teaching of 40 children, mainly from Barton, also from Higham Gobion and Pulloxhill.[48] The Countess de Grey provided a school site at Blunham in 1816.[49]

As yet there was little emphasis on the actual building; more often sums were paid to a man or woman who taught in his or her own house. At Southill in 1809 Whitbread negotiated an agreement to use the Baptist meetinghouse; this required serious consideration by church members, who eventually agreed, provided it was understood that they always had the prior claim. He also rented a house at Shefford for teaching. Willes altered a house at Barton to make it suitable for his school, and left money for desks. At Oakley in 1802 the Duke of Bedford converted the townhouse into a school. Roe actually erected a building at Stotfold; and at Kempston William Joyce of the Bedford Independent congrega-tion built a school by 1828. Even when the trustees of the old free schools at Sharpenhoe about 1820 built a new schoolhouse, the old one having fallen into ruin, the new one contained four rooms "one of which is a schoolroom" – that is to say, it was a master's house.[50]

Teachers' salaries, even at the low rates of those days, were a factor in the

[42] C.R.O., QSR 1833/707–12.
[43] C.R.O., QSR 1835/533.
[44] C.R.O., W 1/853; Charity Com. Rep., 187.
[45] C.R.O., P 38/28.
[46] C.R.O., W 1/849.

[47] C.R.O., P 83/25/21.
[48] Charity Com. Rep., 159.
[49] C.R.O., L 30/11/40/5; the site was not conveyed till 1842 when the school was enlarged, L 28/39–43.
[50] Charity Com. Rep., 41.

cost of schools, and in bigger places use was made of pupil-teachers by the monitorial system.[51] An example is Woburn, where the Duke repaired the old school, and it was reopened in 1808. There was a monitor to each of 8 classes. In the lowest class the monitor taught the alphabet by printing on a sand-desk. The next class had the use of slates; the monitor gave out words, syllable by syllable; and when the slates were full the master inspected them. For reading and spelling, 8 boys assembled round a card hung up by the monitor. The monitors also give Bible readings or read hymns while the boys were silent.[52] But the monitorial system was mainly used in towns (ch. 38).

Thus the curriculum was very limited, but it was more extensive than it had been. In the early days it was a great thing to be taught to read; to learn to write was one step further; and to learn arithmetic, or "to cast accounts" was advanced.[53]

Meanwhile some of the charity schools founded many years previously sometimes ran into difficulties of their own, mainly because the master's salary was no longer economic. At Lidlington in 1815 the salary was raised from £2 13s. 4d. to £3 13s. 4d. p.a., but even so Robert Batchelor found it necessary to keep shop as well. Incidentally the rules for this school in 1818 provided that each child on entering or leaving had to bow or curtsey. At Houghton Regis, John Lesley, schoolmaster 1773–1815, was also clerk to the justices. He had been there so long that when he died the family felt they had a hereditary right to the school, and when a new master was appointed, and it was clear they had to leave, they destroyed everything their father had added or planted in house or garden; as the new master wrote to a trustee: "I am concerned to state to you that yesterday during divine service the whole family of the Lesleys (not excepting the females) were employed in cutting down all the fruit-trees, shrubs etc., and pulling down one of the outbuildings . . . they have been committing still greater excesses destroying the inside of the house, untiling the schoolroom, and I know not where it will end."[54]

As has been seen, the drive for providing more teaching came partly from individuals and partly from churches. The main Anglican effort came in 1815 with the founding of the Bedfordshire Institution. It was inaugurated at a meeting at the Sessions House, with Sir George Osborn in the chair; the President was the Marquess of Bute, and John Gibbard of Sharnbrook became secretary. The Institution stood for training children in the principles of the established church, and the method to be used was again the monitorial system. It collected subscriptions to help set up new schools, and it was in touch with the already (1811)

[51] At the time this was sometimes called the Madras system, from its use in Madras by Andrew Bell, sometimes Lancasterian, from a Quaker pioneer in England, Joseph Lancaster. A Lancasterian Association was formed in 1810, and the term 'Lancaster-ian' can mean a school founded in connection with this Association, as at Leighton Buzzard (ch. 38).

[52] C.R.O., W 1/852.
[53] Cf. C.R.O., L 30/11/215/104.
[54] C.R.O., B 695.

formed National Society, which often made grants for this purpose of up to one-tenth of the cost. Some of the schools mentioned in the early papers of the Bedfordshire Institution are Blunham, Everton, Kempston, Thurleigh and Turvey.[55] For nonconformist schools, help could be obtained from the British and Foreign School Society (1814), which superseded the earlier Lancasterian Association (1810).

SOME INDIVIDUALS

In this period of unemployment on the one hand, and on the other of conscious efforts to improve matters, there is a temptation to think of people in groups. It is worth while perhaps to stand beside Whitbread's chair in the justice's room at Southill Park, and see some of the people who came to him as he saw them, as individuals.[56]

Every day that he was at home, from two to ten people came, some with justified complaints, some without, some merely to ask his advice. Sometimes there were wage disputes, as when a man hired at Michaelmas wanted to break his contract; Whitbread assessed the amount due, as with Abraham Woodard and his servant George Wheatley; Wheatley was to have 32s. Sometimes a young woman expecting an illegitimate child came for a warrant against the supposed father, as Anne Horth did. Sometimes a poor cottager's house was in a bad state; "rafters in Stephens' cottage to be mended, the wet stopped out and the stair mended. If Mr. Oliver will not do it, the overseers must, and that out of hand". Some came from a distance. John Lincoln of Clophill, whose boy was sick, complained that his allowance was too small; he earned 13s. a week, his wife 1s., the boy normally 1s. 6d.; "ordered the boy to be visited by the doctor, if necessary to be sent to the infirmary; 2s. a week to be continued whilst the boy is sick". There was a like complaint from Frances Thompson of Cardington, whose husband was ill, and who had 8s. from the club, but from the parish only 2s.; two of the six children were at work; "wrote to the overseer to allow nourishment, and to the doctor to instruct the overseer". John Adams came from Langford, "wants linen; wrote to overseer to give him some and have his shoes mended". On the other hand, if he thought fit, he could write firmly against a claimant's name "dismissed". A constable brought Robert Stevens, an army deserter; he issued a warrant to commit him to Bedford gaol. A farmer, William Saville, came to ask if the poor had a right to glean without leave; his answer was No. The time, thought and trouble that Whitbread gave to all the demands made upon him can hardly have been exceeded by any other justice. He had a clear conception of public service.

[55] C.R.O., X 25; GA 2568. [56] C.R.O., PSI 1/1.

37 – ROADS AND WATERWAYS, 1771–1832

Traffic increased greatly in this period. Whereas the Marchioness Grey in a long life only once (1755) journeyed to Scotland to see her father, Lord Breadalbane, her daughter, the future Countess de Grey, when she married in 1772 visited Scotland almost every year.[1]

Stage-coaches multiplied. Wheareas the 1785 directory gives only one coach leaving the Swan, Bedford, for London on alternate days (fare 12s. or 6s. 6d.), that for 1824 lists 5 coaches for London leaving the Swan or the Red Lion, and also coaches to Cambridge, Oxford, Kettering and Leeds; and that for 1830 notes a daily coach to Manchester. The coaches given in 1824 as picking up in Biggleswade for London, Leeds, Oundle and York number 15; and by 1830 there is one to Glasgow. As for the position at Dunstable, the directories do not attempt to list coaches stopping there, but merely note in 1824 that there were nearly 50 coaches for London, Birmingham, Chester, Liverpool, and elsewhere; and these had of course multiplied by 1830. Coaches had regular stopping-places also at Ampthill, Leighton, Luton, Potton and Woburn. Some had striking names, like the Lark, the Rocket, or Peveril of the Peak. From nearly all the above places at least two carriers' waggons plied weekly to London.

For one of the coach services, in which John Rawlins of Bedford was a partner, we have some detailed papers.[2] This service was from Kettering to London. Between Bedford and London, probably because there was more competition, a small coach plied; it carried 6 passengers, and the monthly tax on it was £12 10s. The Kettering coach was bigger and could carry 10 passengers with luggage or 12 without. Breakdowns were one problem; on one occasion Rawlins had to send out a new axle-tree to Sharnbrook, and a chaise to fetch the passengers. There were running repairs to harness, lamps and windows; sometimes new wheels or ironwork or a coat of paint; and some bills are vague, such as "doing a gobe to the kotch", or "expenses when the man was lost in the snow". (From the passenger's viewpoint, cold was not the only hazard; when Edmund Williamson went to London in July, 1772, he was "choked with dust".)[3]

It was necessary to have a reliable driver; "we cannot appoint a more proper man than David Lambert, a steady good coachman, well known and respected on the road" – but Lambert was not to be tempted. Some customers had to be

---

[1] *B.H.R.S.* xlvii, 91.
[2] C.R.O., X 37.
[3] C.R.O., M 10/4/204.

brought in by post-chaise: "Please to secure me two places in the coach for London on Monday next, and send a post-chaise over to Felmersham in the morning, time enough for us to be at Bedford." There was the question of customers' comfort at inns on the way; in 1815 there were "two passengers down per coach this day who dined at the Swan, who was not satisfied, having only cold beef and nothing hot, and was charged 2s. 6d. for the same"; this was the more annoying, since there had been previous trouble at the Swan, resulting in a move to the Red Lion; and when the coach returned to the Swan a promise had been made that inside passengers should have a room, and "likewise the outsides be equally attended to and made comfortable".

And there was the problem, in a time of inflation, of when to raise fares, which might mean pricing the coach out of the market, for there was no general agreement between proprietors. Rawlins and his partners in 1811 put up the fare to London by 1s., with some misgiving on his part. "Continual complaints are being made. Several people remain a day longer sooner than be so imposed on, they say. Mr. Brooks of Bedford, which was a constant customer every week before we raised that shilling, will not go with us now. I plainly seen what would be the consequences of it".

On the Bedford coach the annual profit in 1806 and 1807 seems to have been about £700. On the Kettering coach, where there were several partners, Rawlins received £94 for the March quarter in 1809, and £361 for the September quarter in 1813, as the share for his $16\frac{1}{2}$ mile stretch.

The length of time taken by a coach journey at any particular date is not easy to trace; directories give times of leaving, but no times of arrival. However it seems that in 1810 a journey from Fetter Lane in London to Eaton Socon took nearly 11 hours (including stops).[4]

ROADS

With increasing traffic, the main or turnpiked roads needed ever more attention. The Luton road was much improved.[5] This was after a well-attended meeting in 1775 of the turnpike trustees at Luton, where on this occasion the innkeeper provided a good dinner and good port and there was "but little squabbling". A traveller wrote in 1776 "the road down Barton hill is almost entirely new made, and when the work is finished and a little beat it will be perfectly good – just about Barton is the worst"; and again in 1777, "I think we never found the road over Luton downs in better condition." Barton was always a difficult spot, till in 1832 a cutting was made, and the winding stretches of the old road were sold off.

By the end of the period, main roads round Bedford were exceptionally

[4] The Rev. Hugh Wade-Gery wrote to his wife from London that he would catch the 7 a.m. coach to Eaton Socon, and walk to St. Neots (at most $1\frac{1}{2}$ miles), so that if she went in the carriage and drank tea there he would join her about 6 p.m. (letter in the possession of Mrs. Wade-Gery, no. 303).

[5] C.R.O., L 30/9/60/65, 75, 100.

good. In 1828 a traveller was prepared to recommend them "to the imitation of road-makers throughout the kingdom". Bailey, who was mayor that year, and was surveyor to more than one turnpike trust, "considered it an opprobrium if a rut were visible within 20 miles of Bedford".[6]

Expenditure continually outran income. There was some difficulty in letting the tolls; in 1808 John Walker of Shefford bid £1,251 for the Bedford–Hitchin tolls, but repented of his bargain, and the trustees had to hold him to it.[7] In 1812 these trustees found that they must spend £2,000 in the next few years, and that they would have to suspend payment of interest on loans; even so, they had to raise tolls in the following year.[8]

Still the cry was for more and better turnpike roads, and in this period more roads came under the management of turnpike trustees. Two of them were revivals of trusts which seem to have lapsed after a false start in 1754; Bedford–Newport Pagnell and Bromham–Lavendon; the latter was re-started in 1790 and the former in 1814. The Bedford–Woburn road was turnpiked in 1777; and the Bedford–Kimbolton road in 1795; while Bedford's eastward links with the great north road were also turnpiked. Further north in the county, an east-west route from near Kimbolton to Lavendon (through Riseley, Bletsoe, Sharnbrook and Harrold) came under turnpike trust in 1802; the Wrest Park steward, in reporting to his lady on the proposals, looked at it somewhat askance; it would be useful to Alston and to Lord St. John, and to the tenants on the Harrold estate, but he doubted its financial success; he suggested a subscription of £100, and that she should not expect to see interest or to see her principal again.[9]

A parliamentary enquiry in 1812 into the finances of turnpike trusts shows that the most viable was the great north road; from Biggleswade to Alconbury the tolls brought in £3,966 p.a., and from Biggleswade to Stevenage £3,128 p.a., but the outstanding debt on the two stretches combined amounted to £7,219. Apart from very recent additions, like the roads to Kimbolton and Newport Pagnell, the worst financial position was that of the Bedford–Hitchin trust; this had an income of £1,794 and a debt of £9,509.[10]

Minor roads in the care of the parish surveyors were still often unsatisfactory. In 1790 the road to Oakley was said to be so bad that a carriage could not pass with safety, and one of the Duke's staff called a parish meeting to try to stimulate action: "I hope to surprise the Duke."[11] Sometimes heavy traffic took to the side-roads to evade toll on the turnpike road; John Morris, the Ampthill brewer, whose waggons had made a detour through Wilstead with disastrous effects on that road, promised amendment in 1814.[12]

Cases at quarter sessions throw sidelights on travel, whether on main or minor

[6] Sir R. Phillips, *Personal tour.* p.14.
[7] C.R.O., CRT 160/3.
[8] C.R.O., W 1/170, 577.
[9] C.R.O., L 30/11/215/107/11.

[10] C.R.O., CRT 160/2.
[11] C.R.O., R 694.
[12] C.R.O., W 1/603-4. His house recently belonged to Sir Albert Richardson.

roads. Evasion of toll was practised by unloading before the waggon was weighed as Arthur Rock of Woburn did at Puddle hill in 1786.[13] Benjamin Knibbs, the tollkeeper at this gate in 1799, was beaten by a horseman with his horsewhip.[14] John Drage forced his way in 1781 through the Lidlington gate without paying toll.[15] There were opportunities for theft or other malpractice: goods to the value of £50 were stolen from the Manchester coach at Houghton Regis in 1787;[16] and James Giddings of Eaton Socon, a guard on the mail coach, bought hares and pheasants from Sandy poachers in 1820.[17]

There were also highway offences. Robert George of Bedford in 1800 drove a 6-horse waggon against the chaise of Sarah Hodson of Haynes.[18] Thomas Ward, an Olney laceman, in 1804 purposely drove his cart against William Munday on horseback, who was talking to a young woman at the roadside near the new gaol.[19] Samuel Foxley rode on his coal-waggon at Elstow in 1824, without having anyone on foot to lead the team.[20]

And there was trouble over the nearness of windmills to the road – they caused accidents by scaring the horses. One on the Kimbolton road had to be taken down in 1802;[21] and another on the Hockliffe road in 1814, though the owner, James Ball, prevaricated as long as possible – he had nowhere to move it to, and would have to sell it at a loss.[22]

Against these various troubles it is pleasant to record the more cheerful case of Thomas Barber on the Bedford–Hitchin road. His father had been tollkeeper; and when the father died in 1783, young Tom worked on the road for 8s. a week, while his mother kept the gate in the daytime and he did so at night, and he will "also maintain his said mother out of the said weekly payment". For a month at harvest time he was allowed to be absent to work as a harvester, during which time the turnpike trust would pay 5s. only, which 5s. he was to remit to his mother. A few months later, the trust surveyor reported that Tom "by his industry is of great service to the road, and it is thought he is not sufficiently paid for his services", so Tom was given a rise of 1s. a week.[23]

BRIDGES

In this period one more bridge over the Ouse was built by public subscription. This was Felmersham, where hitherto there had been only a ford. It was the enclosure of Sharnbrook which brought matters to a head. The commissioners in setting out roads did not allow for one to the ford, so 22 inhabitants of Felmersham and the neighbourhood, including Lee Antonie, petitioned for a road over Sharnbrook meadow to the ford by Felmersham church; if this could be done,

13 C.R.O., QSR 1786/105.
14 C.R.O., QSR 1799/132.
15 C.R.O., QSR 1781/63.
16 C.R.O., QSR 1787/39.
17 C.R.O., QSR 1820/76–8.
18 C.R.O., QSR 1799/52; 1800/165–6.

19 C.R.O., QSR 1804/46, 70.
20 C.R.O., QSR 1824/158.
21 C.R.O., QSR 1802/76, 156.
22 C.R.O., W 1/607, 613.
23 C.R.O., CRT 160/3.

they proposed to raise money for a bridge. Arpin's diary records the bridge's progress: "1818 Feb. 16 begin to cutt stone . . . begin to bild . . . turned the 1st arch . . . turnd the 2 arch . . . turnd 3th arch . . . turned the 4 arch . . . Thomas Eyels of Carlton went over the bridge with a cart . . . Oct. 8 turnd the 5 arch . . . Nov. 14 finished the bridge."[24] However the road on the Sharnbrook side, though marked out, was not made up until 1820, for Sharnbrook maintained that Felmersham had undertaken this too. At first the new bridge gave trouble; two arches fell in 1819; and in October 1823 "it was the greatest flood that ever was known, it drove the walls down from the bridge".

But the conception of a bridge as a necessity, to be borne from public funds, especially where the road was an important one, was gaining ground; and of this, Tempsford is an example. Incidentally, the position of the low-lying road here had continued to cause friction between the proprietors of the Ouse navigation and the trustees of the turnpike road (whose responsibility the bridge was). Erosion of the river bank meant that the lightermen sometimes used the road as a haling-way; in 1779 the turnpike trustees tried to prevent this by erecting oak posts and rails, but the proprietors pulled them down in 1781; at the assizes in 1783 the case went against the navigation. But the turnpike trustees were still in difficulty from the decay of their timber bridge, and for lack of funds to build a better one. In the end it was quarter sessions which in 1815, by a special act of parliament, obtained permission to build a new bridge and charge tolls to pay for it. The justices would probably have been wise to accept Wing's design, but they chose both designer and contractor from London. The foreman was dismissed for debt and the contractor had to be replaced, and it was not till 1820 that two justices, viewing the completed bridge made of Sandy stone, were able to certify that "His Majesty's subjects may safely pass and travel over the same."[25]

This principle of public responsibility was extended in some other cases. That for Radwell bridge was disputed in 1775 and 1805; but it was taken to assizes, and in 1806 the county was adjudged liable.[26] On the more important great north road, increasing traffic obliged the turnpike trust to rebuild in stone the timber bridge over the Ivel at Girtford in 1780 (by John Wing senior), and that at Biggleswade in 1797,[27] but both were a few years later acknowledged to be county bridges. Another Ivel bridge, that at Clifton, was reckoned a county bridge in 1807; when it was washed away in 1824, an iron one replaced it. Bromham bridge, long a county bridge, was extended; hitherto the carriage bridge, $11\frac{1}{2}$ ft. wide, had only been over the actual river, and approached by a wide southern sweep; while over the flood area was a 6 ft. causeway for horse and foot-passengers; but between 1813 and 1815 the causeway was widened to link up with

24 *Lock Gate*, ii, 78.
25 *Lock Gate*, i, 177, 190.

26 *Lock Gate*, ii, 134.
27 C.R.O., X 106/79–80; QBM i, 34.

the bridge, and so permit all traffic to take the direct route.[28]

But public responsibility still did not apply to all bridges. For Turvey bridge, though on the main road to Northampton, the Higgins family still accepted liability.[29] Private repairs continued to be made to the less-used bridges at Harrold and Oakley–Pavenham (Stafford). And about 1813 another bridge was privately built – the Duke of Bedford built a second bridge at Oakley on the site of the old mill.[30]

WATERWAYS

Along the Ouse and the Ivel lighters continued to ply. Winter always slowed down the traffic, February being a particularly slack month; and in December 1796 for three weeks the river was blocked with ice.[31]

A report on the navigation of the Ouse made in 1812 by B. Bevan notes that the haling-way was out of order in several places. He comments that the problems of navigation were not understood in the early days, for the width of 3 ft. then adopted was insufficient, especially where the bank had since been eroded; and there were also too many places where the haling-way changed from one side of the river to the other, which delayed the traffic. He noted where the early sluices or stanches had been made of timber and needed repair; brick or stone would be far more effective; that at Eaton Socon was extremely bad, and repairs were also needed at Roxton, Cardington and Bedford.

The tolls had declined in real value, owing to inflation,[32] as Bevan remarked. They also were sometimes evaded. In 1800 Francklin's agents were threatening Watkins of Bedford with proceedings; and the next year they taxed Barnard of Bedford with a similar offence, having brought to light a discrepancy between his loadings at King's Lynn and the amount on which he had paid toll. Barnard excused himself on the grounds that "having so much business in his bank, that the freight tolls he leaves entirely to be settled by his clerk".[33]

A suggestion was made by Lord St. John that the Ouse might be made navigable above Bedford[34] – he was thinking particularly of the stretch from Newport Pagnell to Bletsoe, which might be continued eastward by a canal in the Kimbolton direction (see below), but nothing came of it.

However, though the Ouse navigation was not extended, that of the Ivel was continued for 6 m. to Shefford. The number of waggons and carts bearing merchandise (especially coal) unloaded at Biggleswade wharves and destined for Shefford, Henlow and beyond, was checked for a 10-week period in 1806 and

[28] B. Mag. viii, 129.
[29] Lock Gate, i, 272.
[30] Lock Gate, in press.
[31] C.R.O., L 30/9/73/27.
[32] Two account-books of this period, though entitled "Navigation", are inadequate for assessing the financial position. They were kept by Jefferies, the Francklin's Gt. Barford agent, and they include other matters besides those relating to the river. However if, as appears probable, the Baker who makes regular payments is the Gt. Barford toll-collector, it seems that the tolls at this time averaged £400–£600 p.a.
[33] C.R.O., FN 1348/41, 43.
[34] C.R.O., L 30/11/253.

1807, and found to have increased in the interval from 342 to 472, i.e. by 38%.[35] It was estimated that 1s. 6d. toll on nearly 7,000 tons would bring in nearly £500 p.a., and amply repay the outlay. Perhaps the war caused delay, for it was not till 1822 that the extension was carried out, to plans prepared by Francis Giles. As far as Langford it was treated as a river navigation, and a Bristol firm was paid 5s. a yard to make the channel 5 ft. deep and 40 ft. wide. Above Langford, so many new cuts had to be made that it was treated as a canal at $3\frac{1}{2}$d. per cubic yard cut, with a £40 bonus for filling in the old stream. Five locks descending in all 26 ft. were made at Shefford, Clifton, Stanford, Holme and Biggleswade.[36]

The importance of the Ivel route was its value for north Hertfordshire. A deputation from Hitchin waited on the commissioners in 1825, advocating a further link with Hitchin and Baldock.[39] It was even hoped to link up with Hertford.[38]

Incidentally, the market-gardening area offered special temptations to lighter-men to jump ashore and collect some potatoes en route, but on one occasion at Clifton the theft was seen, and the constable met the boat at Stanford lock.[39]

The hopes for further extension for the Ivel were a reflection of the general belief in waterways as the best transport method of the day for goods traffic. Canal building to complement river navigation reached its peak. Between 1793 and 1805 the Grand Junction canal linked London with Warwickshire, passing within a short distance of Leighton Buzzard. Henceforward this was much used for traffic for the southwest of the county, e.g. for Woburn Abbey; the cost in 1830 for wharfing and cartage from Leighton or Fenny Stratford to Woburn was 10s. per ton for heavy goods such as Bath stone (less likely to be stolen) and 11s. 8d. for light goods.[40] On this waterway the temptation for lightermen was to take hay for their horses, as some did in 1823.[41]

It was next proposed to link the Grand Junction canal with Bedford, and the Mayor of Bedford called a public meeting in 1811, and a printed prospectus was issued.[42] The line proposed was through Wootton, Marston and Lidlington; the distance 14 m.; and the estimated cost over £100,000. If local subscriptions amounted to £50,000, it was hoped the Grand Junction Company would supply the remainder. But though notable names appeared on the prospectus, like Lord Ossory, the Duke of Bedford, and Samuel Whitbread, in private some of them were hesitant as to whether the amount of traffic forthcoming would justify the outlay, and many landowners on the route were actively hostile.[43] An opposition meeting was held at the White Hart, Ampthill, with H. H. Hoare in the chair, on 17 December 1812. At this time subscriptions amounted only to £20,000. A

[35] C.R.O., M 6/8.
[36] Lock Gate, i, 61–4, 80–3.
[37] C.R.O., M 10/5/405.
[38] C.R.O., X 67/846a.
[39] Lock Gate, i, 81–2.

[40] C.R.O., R 3548.
[41] C.R.O., QSR 1823/195, 344–5.
[42] C.R.O., X 37/39.
[43] C.R.O., W 1/639–735.

few weeks later, Theed Pearse wrote to Whitbread "I am afraid we must not flatter outselves with the hopes of proceeding." The canal never materialised. Still less chance had the 1817 proposal for a canal from Bletsoe through Riseley to Swineshead (see above).[44]

[44] C.R.O., QCW 7.

BEDFORD: BUILDINGS

Bedford, thought a local schoolmaster in 1831, J. H. Matthiason,[1] was "one of the most desirable places of abode that can probably be found;" it was not yet all that could be desired, but it was well placed "so as ere long probably to vie with some of the proudest cities in the world". It was a parochial view, but it showed the confidence bred by changes during this period, when Bedford's population increased by 76% from 3,948 in 1801 to 6,959 in 1831.

One of these changes was enclosure. In the late 18th cent. the open fields – Conduit, Windmill, Bury, Oak, Muswell and Mother Fields still came close up to the town. The parishes north of the river were enclosed in 1797, St. Mary's south of the river in 1799. The land thus enclosed remained largely agricultural; John Foster of Brickhill was a farmer of note (ch. 34); and even in 1831 the London road by St. Leonard's farm had an airy rural appearance, while to the north St. Peter's parish was neat and rural, and at the back of what was then called Harpur Street (now Dame Alice Street) there were spacious fields. "On the way to Goldington" (i.e., Goldington Road) was the mansion of a recent mayor, G. P. Livius, a place of dignified retirement with an extensive garden with dark and woody shrubberies, where rooks cawed and doves cooed. In Cauldwell Street was a mansion in "cottage" style, with open verandah and trellis-work covered with roses and jessamine; and in Potter Street were handsome modern residences. By 1831 a "New Town" was developing near the gaol, and the Crescent was a new street with large and genteel houses.

Commenting on public buildings, Matthiason noted appreciatively the Sessions House; the rebuilt Swan Hotel "plain but chaste", with its great room next the river used for assemblies, and its riverside gardens pleasingly arranged; the new bridge over the river; St. Paul's Square, consisting of no less than 10,000 sq. yds.; High Street with "neat and regular shops, many vying in taste and show even with those of the metropolis"; the other county buildings, gaol, infirmary and asylum (ch. 36); the new buildings put up by the Harpur Trust and the house of industry where Bedford's paupers met with "humane and liberal treatment" (see below). There was the markethouse on the north side of St. Paul's Square, with two sections of shops or covered stalls for meat and a third section, of cool and airy construction, for butter and poultry. He was less happy about St. Cuthbert's

---

[1] Matthiason lost money by the publication of his book on Bedford and was imprisoned for debt. The number of visitors who came to see him made trouble for the gaoler.

church, small, low and mean-looking; and "Bunyan's or the Old Meeting", old and rather mean-looking, plainly built with a triple-ridged roof, and densely furnished with pews. The New Meeting, on the other hand, was neat and regular.

What he could not approve was the area of Silver Street, Well Street, White Horse Street and Angel Street, thickly inhabited by the operative classes who, confined in close courts and low houses, and toiling at their lace pillows and other sedentary employments from morning till night, inhale an atmosphere unchanged by the salutary breezes of the streets, and entail sickness and disease on themselves; but he was glad to think that all one side of Angel Street and part of Well Street was shortly to come down.

Those new buildings which Bedford owed to the county (gaol and asylum), to the Duke (Swan Hotel) and to Whitbread (infirmary) have already been discussed. When came the house of industry, the clearing of St. Paul's Square, and the rebuilding of the bridge?

Though the poor law as a whole was not revised till 1834, it was possible before that for groups of parishes to combine by special act. Such an act was passed in 1794 for the five Bedford parishes, and the house of industry (or combined workhouse) was built in 1796. It was 4 stories high and could house 200 persons; it had a master's room; workrooms for trades; and schoolrooms for children; while other inmates were "occupied in garden and farm-work according to their abilities". It was managed by a committee of 12, chosen from inhabitants rated at £10 annually, which met weekly. It was, thought Matthiason, "one of the most complete parochial establishments in the kingdom".

The clearing of St. Paul's Square came through the Bedford improvement act of 1803. This recites that the gildhall was ruinous; that the streets were greatly obstructed on market-days, and by the slaughter of cattle and sheep, and that they were ill-paved and not sufficiently cleansed and lighted; and that the mayor and burgesses had no adequate funds. Commissioners were therefore appointed to "improve" the town; in effect they were for the most part prominent members of the council under another name. They included well-known men: William Belsham, the nonconformist radical writer; John Foster; Theed Pearse; the brewers, William Long and Peregrine Nash; the architect, John Wing; the physician G. D. Yeats; the banker Joseph Barnard; attorneys like Thomas Kidman; and a number of others who had already served as mayor or were shortly to do so. Incidentally Theed Pearse was town clerk 1810–15, but then he handed over that office to his son, Theed Pearse junior.

These commissioners were empowered to borrow up to £3,000; to raise rates (in practice rates had hitherto been parochial) up to 8d. in the £ in any one year; to take down the gildhall and other buildings, and to lay out streets; to arrange for slaughter-houses and take other measures for public health; and finally to build a new gildhall and a new bridge.

They did in fact take down the gildhall, and in 1806 the mayor and burgesses obtained permission to use the Sessions House till a new gildhall should be erected.[2] The commissioners also began to clear St. Paul's Square. The list of property for purchase and demolition scheduled in the act includes 82 houses in High Street, Stonehouse Lane, Butcher Row, Church Alley, the Fish Market, and Vines Corner. The numbers in this small area show how small the houses must have been, and how congested the network of alleys.

By 1810 however the commissioners had lost momentum. They found their funds inadequate to build a new gildhall, to pave and light the streets, and to rebuild the bridge. Another act of parliament was obtained, allowing them to raise up to 1s. by rates; while their borrowing ceiling was slightly raised to £5,000, though even this was much below the cost of a new bridge. On the bridge the main effort was now to be concentrated and it was hoped to recover the cost gradually by means of tolls.

In this project they could count on such support as their member, Whitbread, could whip up among the more well-to-do and public spirited county gentry. He himself lent £2,000, as did the Duke; and the Marquess of Bute lent £1,000; in all 27 county gentry subscribed. John Wing was given the task. Funds began to run out; a second appeal to gentry drew injured protests, though the Duke, Whitbread and Lord Bute converted their loans into gifts. The efforts and controversy dimmed enthusiasm. There were no invitations to the opening in 1815. As Theed Pearse put it, the intention "should be generally known in conversation"; there was no parade of music; just a quiet progress over the bridge by Whitbread, with the commissioners meeting him. Tolls were levied on traffic, till the debt was cleared off in 1835.[3]

The Bedford Rooms, or Assembly Rooms, were built in 1834 by a company formed for the purpose. To one of the rooms in this building was transferred in 1836 a library, made up of the old one at one time kept in St. John's vestry (ch. 30), and the newer general library formed in 1830[4] (they were amalgamated in 1831).

BEDFORD: HARPUR TRUST

In describing the Harpur Trust, Matthiason says that "Bedford shines forth with a lustre peculiarly its own". The original grammar school in St. Paul's Square had been refurbished in 1765, but educationally it was not of much consequence till in 1811 a notable headmaster was appointed, Dr. John Brereton. In all the schools which either then were or have since become recognised as public schools,[5] the quality of the individual master was at this time a vital factor, and for some time to come. Harrow grew under George Butler, appointed 1805.

[2] C.R.O., QSM 22, p.107.
[3] Lock Gate, i, 19–23; see also C.R.O., W 1/131.
[4] T. A. Blyth, History of Bedford, 164–5; D. G. C. Elwes, Bedford, 52–3; Bedford Museum Guide, p.3.

[5] Bedford is given in the first Public Schools Yearbook, 1889; see T. W. Bamford, Rise of the public schools, p.189.

Much later Uppingham grew considerably under E. Thring. When Brereton came to Bedford, there were 6 boys; his salary was to be £200, with an extra £3 per boy to 20 boys if the number grew so far. He therefore took boarders to give himself more scope. A new regulating act in 1826 raised his salary and also his capitation fee, giving him 5 guineas per day-boy without limit. Henceforward he had less financial inducement to take boarders, the more so as his reputation was attracting families to settle in Bedford. Hence the residential development in Bromham Road, Adelaide Square and the Crescent. "Took poor Willy to Dr. Brereton's", wrote Catherine Young, a clergyman's widow who had come to live in Bedford, in her diary in 1832.[6] Dr. Brereton was a stickler for attendance: "School opens on Monday, August 4th, and it is particularly requested that each boy should return *as soon as possible*; any boy absenting himself after Wednesday will subject himself to the loss of prizes." He had also a way with parents; of the Gibbard boys he wrote "Your good little boy has by application gained the honourable post of second senior in his class"; or, less favourably, "he discovers no want of ability when he chooses to exert himself".[7] The numbers in 1830 were 61 boarders and 60 day-boys, and the day-boys continued to increase.

Another school had grown up within the old building; this was for boys who did not require to learn Latin grammar. It had begun in 1765 with the appointment of a writing-master who taught boys from the ages of 8 to 14. It did so well that it was necessary to provide separate premises for it, and it was for this purpose that the west side of Angel Street was cleared in 1833, where it became known as the Commercial School. In the same range of buildings were new premises for the preparatory school, set up in 1815 on the monitorial system, where boys were admitted at the age of 5, and girls on afternoons when the boys had a holiday.

The Harpur Trust also erected purely charitable buildings. One was a "hospital" in the old sense of charitable premises, for poor boys and girls, who wore dark blue suit and cap, or dress and bonnet. And finally there were the almshouses. The regulating act of 1794 provided for almshouses for 20 poor men and women (these were in Bromham Road). But, so much had the Trust's income increased, that when a disastrous fire in 1802, which broke out in a black-smith's shop in St. Loyes, caused an acute housing shortage, the Trust built 46 houses on the north side of what was then called Harpur Street, to ease the situation (later, in 1816, they were converted to almshouses).

BEDFORD: BUSINESS AND PROFESSIONS

It was not only as a county and an educational centre that Bedford was advancing; there was business development too; and a marked sign of this is the establishment of Barnard's bank. By 1776 Joseph Barnard was established in Bedford as a coal merchant; and by 1793 he had already begun to have banking

[6] *B.H.R.S.* xl, 156.   [7] C.R.O., GA 47.

transactions with local gentry, when John Byng applied to him for "the sinews of war; 'Will you accommodate me with £50?' 'Oh Sir, what you choose – £150 or more.' "[8] The bank was formally established in 1799, with a total capital of £10,000. Like other small local banks, it acted virtually as a collecting agency for the London money and stock markets, and helped to provide the capital for England's industrial expansion. Unfortunately Barnard was misled by a clerk in the Bank of England, George Corner, who was caught in 1811 in a stock market collapse. Whitbread came to Barnard's help, but he lost £15,000. It taught him a lesson in sound banking. He preserved the papers for his descendants: "this packet contains the whole of the lying and villainous correspondence from George Corner . . . this will I trust be a warning to those who may succeed me".[9]

Savings banks emerged also in Bedford and other towns.

Brewing developed on a larger scale. In Bedford the chief representative of this is perhaps William (afterwards Sir William) Long, by origin the son of a Stondon farmer. From 1784 he was in partnership with the Whittingstall brothers, whom he subsequently bought out; and they busily acquired public houses in and around Bedford, as was now the practice. In 1800 Long purchased the brewery on the south side of St. Paul's Square, which at one time belonged to William Belsham. Long was mayor of Bedford in 1803, 1813, 1822 and 1829; and when he died in 1841, leaving three daughters, the extensive inventory of his business assets survived.[10] Another brewery worth mentioning is that in Horne Lane, built by Stephen Benson before 1836.[11]

As the centre of an agricultural district, it was appropriate that Bedford should provide the improved agricultural machinery of the day. This was done mainly by John Howard (son, not of the philanthropist, but of the gaoler), who had been apprenticed in 1805 by the Harpur Trust to an Olney ironmonger. He set up in business in Bedford in 1813 in a shop on the west side of High Street, and in 1817 he moved across the street and built a shop with an extensive foundry behind it, as his billheads show. Here he produced many iron goods, from hot-air stoves and kitchen ranges to palisading and "all sorts of agricultural improvements"; but his great success was in "Howard's patent plough", which was soon to be in great demand outside the county as well as in it.[12]

BEDFORD: POLITICS

Politically the borough remained Whig. All through this period one of the borough members was a Whitbread; Samuel Whitbread was succeeded by his son W. H. Whitbread. Lee Antonie, Samuel Whitbread's colleague for several years, stood last in 1807. By this time the recordership had once more, on Sir

[8] *Torrington diaries*, iii. 198.
[9] *Westminster Bank Review*, Feb. 1960, p.10.
[10] C.R.O., WL 626.
[11] C.R.O., WL 61–2.
[12] C.R.O., BR 1.

Robert Barnard's death, gone to the Duke of Bedford; and the Duke's son, Lord William (less able and less active than the third son, Lord John) took over the seat.[13] He would leave for the continent on the day of the mayor's feast, was slack in attending the house of commons, and took no notice of Lord John's warning "Where is our brother William that in this day of strife he wrestleth not with us? It shall be remembered to him in the synagogue." At the critical election of 1830 it was clear that Lord William would have no following, and although Lord John was in demand elsewhere, his name was put forward. But Bedford was having one of its periodical revolts against the Russells; "the houses of Russell and Whitbread have absorbed us all; the people of Bedford will now teach the house of Russell that they can and will be free".[14] By one vote Lord John lost the seat to Frederick Polhill, and Bedford lost the chance to return a leading figure on a great occasion.

Though Bedford's parliamentary representation was disproportionately greater than that of the county, it did not lose one of its two members by the reform of 1832; the reformers dared not attempt too much at first; only boroughs with a population of 4,000 or less had their representation curtailed or abolished, and Bedford was nearly 7,000. But the act put an end to the manipulation of elections by the creation of freemen; henceforward freemen would be entitled to vote only when they lived within 7 miles of the town – unless of course they had a property qualification also. The new uniform borough franchise for householders rated at £10 or over slightly increased the resident electorate.[15]

Bedford's institutions which had evolved over the centuries were, like those of other boroughs, revised by the municipal corporations act of 1835. Henceforward the mayor was elected annually by the council; councillors were elected for 3 years by ratepayers; and aldermen were appointed for 6 years by councillors. A borough police force was set up under the act.

MARKET TOWNS

The number of effective market towns was shrinking. Toddington has already been mentioned; at Harrold it was said in 1811 that the market-house was no longer either useful or ornamental;[16] Ampthill's population increased only 36% and Woburn's 16% between 1801 and 1831 when the general county increase was 50%. On the other hand, those market towns which were growing did so faster than the county. Dunstable and Biggleswade, both with heavy road traffic, increased respectively by 63% and 80%; in 1805 the old markethouse at Dunstable was removed and rebuilt on the site of the present town hall.[17] (Incidentally, Biggleswade manor, long held on crown lease, was sold by the

13 *B.H.R.S.* xlix, (to be published).
14 *V.C.H.* ii, 65.
15 In 1820 for the unreformed parliament 914 electors voted. This includes freemen. The first electoral register in 1832 printed after reform lists just under 1,000 householders and property owners entitled to vote. With it is printed a list of about 600 free-

men – the town clerk supplying the full list, whether entitled to vote or not; and it seems that a few non-resident freemen tried to vote at the next election, and one or two in fact got away with it (annotated copy at Town Hall).
16 C.R.O., L 30/11/132/96, 100.
17 W. Smith, *Dunstable*, 185.

crown in 1807.) The townships of Leighton and Luton (excluding hamlets) were in 1831 respectively 3,330 and 3,961; that is to say, they were approaching what had been Bedford's size in 1801; in 1831 they were half (Luton more than half) as big as Bedford, and were her nearest rivals. Potton suffered a disastrous fire in 1783, and Potton's increase 1801–31 was only 50%; however, the shambles in the marketplace were rebuilt in Georgian style about 1800 (the old shambles were out of repair, and the butchers complained at paying 1s. or 1s. 6d. and "having to sit in the wet").[18]

Because towns, especially developing ones, had so much more scope than the villages, increasing population with them was an asset rather than a liability. In 1831–34 the market towns spent only about 10s. a head on poor relief, compared with a more usual 20s. a head in the villages. The exception was Leighton, which spent 17s. a head.

Like Bedford, and like the rural parishes, the market towns normally required enclosure, except for Dunstable, whose area of less than 500 a. had never had much agricultural scope. But here there is a difference between those two ancient Saxon royal manors of Leighton and Luton, which had kept in step for so much of their history. At the end of this period, Leighton's agricultural land was still nearly all in strips in the common fields, and nearly all copyhold. This is probably because of the conservative policy of the lord of the manor, the dean and canons of St. George's chapel, Windsor, for the Leigh family of Prebendal House were their lessees. Leighton's enclosure was yet to come. On the other hand, much of Luton was already enclosed except for the Great Moor. Exactly how and when the greater part of Luton's enclosure took place is hard to determine; it was probably piecemeal down the centuries, as manors proliferated and disappeared, families came and went, and land constantly changed hands. The enlargement of the Hoo park by the Butes, and of Stockwood park by the Crawleys, no doubt contributed. There was still a manorial entity known as Luton manor, to which a certain amount of copyhold land was attached, and which belonged to Lord Bute. Luton enclosure award of 1810 deals only with 18 a. Apparently at this time Lord Bute enclosed some other land, and this latter was allotted for common for various small claims that would be too expensive to enclose separately.[19]

As for the smaller market towns, or those which had had this status, Ampthill, Harrold, Potton, Shefford and Toddington were all enclosed between 1775 and 1832; but neither Biggleswade nor Woburn was the subject of parliamentary enclosure. In the former case market-gardening probably contributed to piecemeal enclosure, but at the end of this period there were still 200 a. of cattle common. In the latter, early piecemeal enclosure was probably supplemented later by private enclosure by the Duke.

[18] C.R.O., HA 326–32; W 11/1–6.   [19] Cf. also C.R.O., BO 1325.

By 1830 directories show in the towns a wide range of callings: clothing trades (breeches-makers, drapers, dressmakers, glovers, hatters, milliners, tailors); attorneys, apothecaries and auctioneers; gardeners and seedsmen; ironmongers and saddlers; besides the usual food trades there were confectioners and dealers in wines and spirits; and there those who supplied more special requirements, such as booksellers, cabinet-makers, druggists and watchmakers. It was not only in Bedford that brewing was on a larger scale, and that brewers bought public-houses; an example is Thomas Burr of Dunstable.

Banking began to develop in the bigger market towns. As elsewhere, it arose where a man engaged in other business accumulated sufficient capital to begin banking transactions. At Leighton a bank was opened in 1812 by the Quaker, Peter Bassett, towards the end of his successful career as a draper. Early details of this bank have not survived, but when Peter Bassett retired in 1813, and his son John Dolin Bassett took over, his capital in the drapery business was £9,000 and a partner brought in another £3,000.[20] Bassett's bank, though smaller than Barnard's, remained steady, and by 1823 had a branch in Dunstable. At Biggleswade[21] Wells the brewer began banking in 1812, and Hogg "dealer in sea-coal, bar iron and timber" about the same time; they joined forces; and in 1830 this united bank, now called Wells, Hogg and Lindsell, opened in new premises. But Luton was not so lucky; here it was a solicitor, Leonard Hampson, who began banking with the help of a partner (at first J. Griffiths, later C. Austin); but when he died in 1824, Austin had not enough capital to continue alone.[22] Soon afterwards a Hitchin bank opened a branch in Luton; the partners were Exton (who derived from an Ampthill Quaker family) and Sharples.[23]

Why was Leighton less prosperous than Luton, Dunstable and Biggleswade? The answer seems to be twofold. One factor was the relative value of road and water communication. Though there were at Leighton in 1830 3 wharfingers, the canal, with its through traffic of lightermen and heavy cargoes, was not comparable in effect with a main road carrying traffic of all kinds, such as brought benefits to Biggleswade and Dunstable. Luton's road communications were less important than theirs, but probably the main road from Bedford to St. Albans helped.

The other factor was the strawplait and hat industry.[24] Here the war promoted development, The import of fine plait from Leghorn in Italy was interrupted; duties were imposed on imported plait in 1805 and increased in 1819. Meanwhile tools had been invented for splitting straws to get a finer plait. Straw-splitting tools were in use even in Bedford gaol in 1804,[25] and quarter sessions

[20] C.R.O., X 292.
[21] Information from the bank; but note C.R.O., L 30/11/132/80, which indicates a bank in 1810.
[22] Dyer–Stygall–Dony, *Luton*, 137–9; Austin, *Luton*, ii, 117, 140.
[23] Directory, 1830; cf. *B.H.R.S.* xl, 110–125 for the Extons at Ampthill, and the connection of Sharples with them.
[24] Dony, *Straw hat industry*, 31–52; Dyer–Stygall–Dony, 115–20.
[25] C.R.O., QSR 1804/142.

records show the purchase of as much as 100 lb. of straw for plaiting in the prison in 1820. The demand was such that Thomas Waller, a Luton strawplait merchant, got plait made by French prisoners of war; and after the war he visited Leghorn to get ideas there. At the plait markets of Luton and Dunstable there was such competition for plait that sales would begin before the market was opened, till this was forbidden in 1802 and 1814 respectively. The making of straw hats and bonnets developed. At first hat-makers worked in their own homes, but by degrees factories were opened also. In 1830 there were 15 straw-hat manufacturers in Dunstable and 17 in Luton, with others who called themselves "Leghorn merchants", besides plait-dealers and plait-bleachers; supplemented in the latter by a number of small domestic producers. At Dunstable in 1823 are also mentioned fancy straw manufacturers, who produced straw boxes and toys called Dunstable ware, such as were illustrated by Isaac Cruikshank as long ago as 1796.[26] Hats of low quality at 2d. each were made in the prison at Bedford.[27] Toddington reopened its plait-market,[28] and even little Shefford developed as a subordinate plait-centre, and this may account for the rates of Campton-cum-Shefford being phenomenally low. But though Leighton in 1830 had 4 straw-hat makers, it was in the main outside the area of this industry.

Now, perhaps because of prosperity, there appears at Luton a note of assertion, like that found centuries previously in medieval Dunstable. In 1820 Luton petitioned quarter sessions, saying that it was "excessively aggrieved by the enormous county rates".[29] Luton was not alone in this, but it was better off than the villages.

At Leighton there were mutterings of another kind. In 1821 the steward said that he was "surrounded by Quakers, dissenters and radicals of the worst kind . . . I am almost alone, with the exception of Mr. Wilson the curate and a few other friends, as church and king men".[30]

Education was progressing at all the market towns. At Leighton, Pulford's school was housed in a building in Church Square put up by Mrs. Leigh in 1790. There was also a monitorial school – in this case an actual Lancasterian school – opened in 1813, mainly by the efforts of Quakers; they wrote to Whitbread before the opening session to "ask the favour of thy attendance".[31] At Luton, besides the old church or free school, a monitorial school was opened in Park Square with the help of the Marquess of Bute, and in 1819 it took 135 boys – the master was paid £52 1s. for the first 60 boys, and 10s. for each additional boy thereafter; while his wife received £31 10s. for teaching girls in the evenings. A National school in Church Street on a site given by Lord Bute was opened

[26] Isaac's son George, the artist, married a Dunstable girl in 1827; C.R.O., ABM.
[27] C.R.O., QSR 1820/454.
[28] C.R.O., X 21/408.
[29] C.R.O., QSR 1820/457.
[30] C.R.O., KK 867.
[31] C.R.O., W1/856.

in 1835.[32] A monitorial school was running at Biggleswade in 1815.[33] The monitorial school at Woburn has already been mentioned (ch. 36).

At Dunstable Chew's School continued, and the many surviving documents for it give a picture of a good charity school of the time.[34] An inventory of 1791 includes master's desk, cupboard for books, 10 forms for the boys to sit on. 9 desks for them to write on, a long bench, a short bench for them to stand on when they were asked to read, 3 rows of pegs to hang their caps on, and the orders of the school in a black frame with glass. The annual cost of their uniforms rose by 1820 to £110; they had 2 cambric bands, a pair of stockings, a black cap with scarlet band and tassel, a coat, waistcoat, breeches, and 2 shirts of home bleached linen, a pair of low shoes, and one of "high shoes, well nailed". The political views of their parents are reflected in the names of some boys, such as Benjamin Reform Tofield and George Liberty Smith.

In these thriving towns there was also a demand for small "academies" where parents could pay fees for a more select education. At Biggleswade Nicholas Salmon had rather a struggle with his school, and Whitbread (helpful as always to a lame dog) for a time employed him as tutor to his own children. Salmon's school is known too because a bonfire in the schoolyard at the time of celebrations after the battle of Waterloo caused trouble.[35] In 1830 there were also in Biggleswade James Porter's academy for boys, and two day and boarding academies for "ladies". Similar establishments were to be found at the other market towns, and of course in Bedford also.

[32] Dyer–Stygall–Dony, op.cit., 129–32.
[33] C.R.O., L 30/11/20/8. Probably the school derived from Peake's foundation, now actually functioning in Biggleswade instead of Holme.
[34] C.R.O., X 277.
[35] C.R.O., W 1/2184–263; QSR 1815/391.

39 – THE CHURCHES, 1771–1836

"THE SPIRIT OF CHRISTIANITY" was a phrase used by Samuel Whitbread in 1812 in writing of fuller toleration, to which he looked forward with "great eagerness".[1] Parliament in 1829 allowed the Roman Catholics freedom to worship; in 1828 repealed the test and corporation acts which had made it difficult for dissenters to hold office; and in 1836 allowed marriage by other than Anglican rites. In 1828 a non-sectarian college was opened in London, which led in 1836 to the setting-up of London university, though Oxford and Cambridge remained Anglican preserves. Only compulsory church rates continued for another generation.

These advances were not achieved easily. Whitbread, in the letter quoted above, referred to those "who only consent to lessen the fetters of some that they may use their efforts to draw tighter the bonds by which others are bound". The old Countess de Grey, when over 60, wrote a long letter to her nephew and heir, urging him, if he could not conscientiously vote against Catholic toleration, at least to abstain from voting; it was not "the poor quiet English Catholics" she feared, but the Irish – "a people famous for revengeful violence".[2]

Nor did legislation mean that tolerant attitudes prevailed everywhere and in all relations of life. For every example of tolerant behaviour, it would be easy to cite several instances of stubborn suspicion and continuing estrangement. Although John Byng had said of Methodists in 1789 that if they "preach the word of God they appear to me as men most commendable",[3] to get a site for a Methodist chapel was often difficult, as at Clophill or Silsoe.[4] In considering an application for a farm tenancy, religious persuasion would be thought relevant; in 1835 the Duke's steward wrote of a farm at Lidlington that James Thomas was "the most likely applicant . . . he is a member of the Society of Friends, but I imagine not a rigid one", for he had "liberal and independent ideas".[5]

The period covered by this chapter does not, for church purposes, provide a satisfactory division. To some extent earlier trends continued. The Methodist movement reached its logical conclusion. More Independents tended to become Baptist. Some Anglican clergy, especially the more well-to-do, were active as justices (ch. 36), or as trustees for road and river (ch. 37), and hunted and shot with the gentry with whom they consorted (ch. 40). On the other hand there is the

[1] C.R.O., W 1/4320, 4344.
[2] C.R.O., L 30/18/24.
[3] *Torrington diaries*, iv, 105.

[4] C.R.O., L 30/11/132/108, 122, 124, 141.
[5] C.R.O., R 3840, 3844, 3847.

beginning of a new movement in the Anglican church, with an altered devotional approach, and an increased desire to serve, which was to flower in the Victorian era.

CONTINUATION OF EARLIER TRENDS

Methodism grew. Wesley, now an old man, continued to visit the county.[6] In 1784 he found at Bedford his old friend Parker "quivering on the verge of life"; and in 1785 at Luton Cole "was now gone to his long home. The room prepared for me was very large and very cold." He now had to travel in a chaise instead of on horseback, and in 1787 the roads were so bad that he went to Wrestlingworth in a farm cart. He died in 1791. Already the first step towards separation from Anglicanism had been taken – almost accidentally. In 1784, the first year in which the national Methodist Conference was held, Wesley ordained men for overseas work.[7] The actual separation virtually took place in 1795.

There had been ups and downs in membership. Joseph Pescod wrote regretfully in 1784: "When I designed to have made trial at some new places, the Lord afflicted me with a severe fever, by which I was hindered. I now leave upon the list 263."[8] By 1804, when a church was built in Angel Street (now Harpur), Bedford, the membership was over 300.[9] It was drawn, not only from Bedford and the towns, but from over a dozen villages in the county (one of the first village chapels was built at Lidlington in 1805). It also extended into Bucks., Herts., Hunts., and Northants., for at this time the Bedford circuit (or administrative unit) extended well outside the county. With a growing membership, such a big circuit became no longer practicable. The Luton circuit was formed in 1808; and as the little building put up there in 1778 was already too small, in 1814 a new one was opened in Hog Lane, which lane soon changed its name to Chapel Street.[10] At Bedford in 1830 it was said "such crowds flock to our prayer meetings as I never saw before", and the Bedford church had to be rebuilt in 1832.

At Shefford the Roman Catholics were increasing under the care of the Rev. Christopher Taylor, who began to hope for a chapel. "My flock is small, I allow," he wrote in 1791 to the Vicar-Apostolic of the London District, "but more numerous (thank God) than when I quitted Essex for Bedfordshire; in fact, it is too big for my bedchamber. The five or six found at my coming hither have been multiplied to above twenty. We hope for more, with heaven's blessing." The first small permanent church[11] was built in 1800, unobtrusively behind three shops given by the Noddings family. To Shefford came later the Rev. Jean Potier, one of many French refugee priests for whom a house had been opened at Thame. About 1812 he set up a private boarding-school, but it ceased with his death

---

[6] *Jnal.*, vii, 35, 123, 338.
[7] Wesley wanted to send two men to work in America, and the Bishop of London (in whose diocese the former American colonies had been) was unwilling to send out ordained preachers.

It was just after the American War of Independence.
[8] C.R.O., MB 1, p.65.
[9] J. M. Anderson, *Early Methodism in Bedford*, 18–22.
[10] Dyer–Stygall–Dony, *Luton*, 115, 136.
[11] H. E. King, *Ancient Catholic mission*, 6.

in 1823.

Quakerism gained strength in Leighton, where the meetinghouse dates from 1789, and in Luton, where a new and larger one was built in 1799, adjoining the old site, in Castle Street; but it had died out in north and east Beds.

Among Independents the belief that membership (and therefore baptism) must be an adult matter continued to gain ground. In Bedford the Old (or Bunyan) Meeting in 1793 suffered a second seccession, this time of 19 Baptists who formed Mill Street (now Brickhill) Baptist church.[12] More often an entire congregation became Baptist, as at Ridgmont in 1770; Keysoe Brook End and Southill a little later; and probably Toddington (1812). Some new churches were Baptist from the first: Leighton, Lake Street, 1775; Cotton End, 1776; Westoning, *c.* 1790; Keysoe Row, 1812; Barton, 1830; and Stotfold, 1832.

But Independent churches multiplied also. Bunyan Meeting developed daughter churches at Kempston (1813), Elstow (1817), Stagsden (1820), and Goldington (1825). Harrold and Roxton were founded by 1808: Hockliffe in 1809; and Shillington was developed from Hitchin before 1825.

The Rev. William Bull's academy at Newport Pagnell was a favourite training place at this time. Samuel Hillyard of Bunyan Meeting studied there; and Joseph James, originally a Keysoe miller, who became a minister at Leighton in 1776, used to walk from Leighton to Newport Pagnell academy.

It could happen that another denomination became established where the Anglican incumbent was not one of that church's best representatives. Of the Harrold incumbent, where the living was poor and its holder apparently did not command respect on other grounds, the Wrest Park steward wrote in 1802 that he was "in a deplorable state amounting to want; the family so totally without firing or money to procure it that they burned part of the stable rack and manger boards".[13] Similarly, in such circumstances an old-established dissenting church could gain access of strength; at Blunham from 1780 for nearly 30 years there was a particularly vigorous Baptist minister, the Rev. Martin Mayle; here the Wrest Park steward said that its congregation was swollen because the rector seldom resided, did not visit the sick, or give alms to the poor.[14] But the establishment or enlargement of a dissenting congregation does not necessarily reflect on the Anglican incumbent of the parish concerned. The increased population gave scope for more churches, and soon the Anglicans would have to create additional parishes in the towns and hamlets. Conversely, there could be, as at Sutton, an unsatisfactory Anglican incumbent without an alternative place of worship.

One factor in extending work in the villages was co-operation. It was hoped that Baptists, Independents, Methodists and Moravians could all work together for

[12] H. G. Tibbutt, *Bunyan Meeting*, 43. For what follows, see *op.cit.*, 110, 121, 125, 132; J. Brown, *Bedfordshire Union of Christians*, 51, 53, 55; and the respective church histories.
[13] C.R.O., L 30/11/215/123.
[14] C.R.O., L 30/9/73/19.

this purpose. The idea came from the Rev. Samuel Greatheed of the Woburn Independent congregation, who in 1797 convened a meeting of ministers at Ampthill. After a further meeting that autumn in Bedford, which had the ill fortune to take place in a devastating storm, the Bedfordshire Union of Christians was formed. Its membership went as far as Newport Pagnell, Kimbolton and Gamlingay geographically, but remained Baptist and Independent.[15]

It was not till some years later that national federations were formed for these two denominations. The Baptist General Union was formed in 1813, though some Bedfordshire congregations like Barton, Southill and Westoning ignored it.[16] The Congregational Union of England and Wales was formed in 1832, since when Independent churches have been known as Congregational; thus Bedford New Meeting became Howard Congregational church.

In the Anglican church the use of music continued to spread. More and more churches had orchestras of clarinet, flute, violin, oboe, bass viol or bassoon, or some of them; and others had barrel-organs.[17] Luton replaced its barrel-organ with a pipe organ in 1823; and Dunstable had a pipe organ at least by then.[18] Gentry paid for children or young people to be taught to sing psalms; it would not only enrich the service, but "keep the young men from the public house and conduce to sobriety and morality"; at Silsoe the cost was 2d. a head.[19]

A brief mention must be made of the Potton carpenter, Thomas Seamer, who at first sounds like a new Moses. He sent in to the churchwardens in 1824 a bill "for making new commandments and finding the stuff". He had of course lettered the ten commandments on a new board to hang in the church. Another intriguing bill is from Riseley in 1829: "for sweeping the chimney and lighting the fire in Mr. Pickering's pew".

A NEW ANGLICAN TREND

Anglican clergy in this period covered a wide range. Those acting in public office have been noted. There were the naturalists. Charles Abbot was usher at Bedford School from 1788 – this was in the pre-Brereton period when numbers went down to six. His teaching duties sat very lightly on him, as did his ecclesiastical ones as vicar of Oakley and later of Goldington, besides two Bedford livings; but he was an energetic botanist, and in 1798 published a county flora, *Flora Bedfordiensis;* his herbarium is preserved at Luton Museum.[20] Another botanist was Thomas Martyn; like his father he was professor of botany at Cambridge, and from 1804 rector of Pertenhall, where he built a dignified rectory. There were

[15] Brown, *op.cit.*, 15–28.
[16] There were some regional Baptist Associations, including an intermittent Bedfordshire one, 1815–38 and 1879–89; one for S. Beds. and Herts., 1835–78; and a Northants. one c. 1800 to which some Beds. churches belonged; but none of these ever included all the local Baptist churches.
[17] *Beds. Mag.*, iii, 99; A. Underwood, *Music in*

Ampthill church. Some other examples are known from churchwardens' accounts in the C.R.O., but where such accounts have not survived evidence is lacking.
[18] H. Cobbe, *Luton Church*, 635; C.R.O., P. 72/8/3.
[19] C.R.O., L 30/11/133/5–7.
[20] Conisbee, *Bibliography*, 225.

those indefatigable antiquaries, the cousins Oliver St. John Cooper, vicar of Podington, and Thomas Orlebar Marsh, vicar of Stevington, whose tomes of notes are in the British Museum,[21] and the former of whom published some of his work. There were those who went shooting, like Edmund Williamson, rector of Campton, and hunting, like J. W. Hawksley, rector of Souldrop,[22] not necessarily with adverse effects on their care for their parish. There were the absentees like G. Davies, who for many years combined the livings of Hull and Upper Gravenhurst, and kept a curate at the latter.[23] And there was one of the most unsatisfactory Anglican clergy at any time, Edward Drax Free, rector of Sutton, who in 1823 was accused by his own churchwardens of drunkenness, swindling, shop-lifting, selling the lead off the church roof, pasturing cattle and horses in the churchyard, and of having three illegitimate children.[24]

There was also the beginning of a new line in Anglican clergy. One of these was Robert Beachcroft, rector of Blunham 1806–30 (successor of that earlier rector who earned Pawsey's disapproval).[25] He was a gentleman, and was at school with the future Earl de Grey; it was probably this schoolboy friendship that introduced him to the Countess de Grey, who presented him to Blunham at the age of 25. We know him from many angles, from his relationships with his patroness, his mother, his parishioners, and from his private journal; and we see his views develop. Soon he began to write articles for the *Christian Observer* on such points as the use of music, the importance of residence, and the running of Sunday schools (it was said that in his own parish the older boys regarded him as a friend and father – he had no children of his own, and latterly his wife was an invalid). The Countess, who was by no means heedless in the standards she expected of her clergy, put sporting facilities at his disposal; and he enjoyed this, though he only shot late in the day when his parish work was done. However, he began to feel guilty about it; "I lamented the pangs of the dying animals . . . I judged my own conduct as a minister to be faulty", so at the age of 30 he gave it up. One day about this time he noted in his journal "Found a great truth, that unless I forgive, I cannot look for forgiveness from my heavenly Father." Another day he notes how muddy the road was when he was visiting at the workhouse. (Incidentally, Francis Hews, Baptist minister of Westoning and Dunstable, writes in 1798 of walking 20 miles to preach, "up to the middle of my leg in water and dirt, as I often have done, and must do, to carry the gospel to Edlesborough and Totternhoe. Many times have I been wet to the skin."[26]) The hamlets of Mogerhanger and Chalton were at some little distance from the parish church, and at Mogerhanger there were 4 or 5 cripples, so he began to hold prayer-meetings in the hamlets in different cottages, "and the poor take a pleasure in

21 B.M., Add. MSS. 21, 067; 34,364–85.
22 *B.H.R.S.* xliv, 19.
23 C.R.O., M 10/5/159–75.

24 C.R.O., ABCP 391.
25 T. A. Methuen, *Memoir.*
26 F. Windridge, *Nevertheless*, 11–12.

455

getting their chairs borrowed and the room ready and the Bible on the table", and these meetings were "admirably attended". He was on good terms with the Baptists, and when they asked him if he would be offended if they began a Sunday school, his reply was "It always gives me pleasure when good is done." Some of his more conservative parishioners called him "a saint and a methodist" (in this context neither meant as a compliment). He was also an active promoter of the Bedfordshire Bible Society.

In Legh Richmond, rector of Turvey 1805–27, we see the same outlook taken a little further.[27] It was said that every Sunday outside Turvey church there were rows of carriages and other conveyances which brought people from other parishes to hear him preach. He was a secretary of the Religious Tract Society, and his tract *The Dairyman's Daughter* sold by millions. It is the story of the good life of a woman who died young (in fact one of his parishioners in his previous parish in the Isle of Wight). Asked how she felt about the darkness of death, the young woman replied "It is not dark, my Lord is there and he is my light."

Incidentally a point of quite other significance is worth mentioning in connection with these two clergy. Beachcroft as a baby nearly died of smallpox, and his recovery was said to have begun from the moment when someone (against doctor's orders) opened the bedroom window. The dairyman's daughter died of consumption. Consumption, though not as devastating as smallpox, was now to replace it as the chief scourge to health.

A CAVEAT

Religious history must centre round the leaders and trend-setters, through whom light comes to many others, and if they are lacking the period goes dead. In another metaphor, they are the leaven that leaveneth the whole lump, spreading slowly and seldom completely. To keep a sense of proportion, it is necessary to remember the "lump", whether represented by heedless youth, by sullen prisoners in the county gaol, or any other form of non-receptivity. Such for instance were the boys at Beeston who in 1811 interrupted a Methodist service by talking, whistling and coughing;[28] the sleepy folk at Shefford who dozed off in sermons and had to be prodded awake by James Haddow, who in 1825 was paid 52s. p.a. for winding the church clock, keeping the building clean, and walking round once or twice during service to prod sleepers;[29] or the half-dozen labourers at Shillington who in 1828 made a disturbance in the belfry when the parish clerk came to ring the bell, and disturbed the teachers in the Sunday school;[30] or the condemned prisoners, Costin, Hewlett and Parsons, who, when in 1825 they were reprieved from execution to transportation, were far from exhibiting gratitude, but were "silent and apparently unaffected . . . Hewlett was smoking his

---

[27] G. F. W. Munby & T. Wright, *Turvey and Legh Richmond. The Dairyman's Daughter* has been reprinted recently.

[28] C.R.O., QSR 1828/375.
[29] C.R.O., P 70/8/1.
[30] C.R.O., PSI 1/1.

pipe at the time".[31]

EDUCATION AND OUTREACH

Outreach was to a greater or less extent a feature of all denominations. Partly this was expressed in promoting education, especially Sunday schools. Education had from the first been a preoccupation with the Moravians, as were Sunday Schools with the Methodists; and now the older denominations were making greater efforts in the cause of teaching. In Bedford for a time the nine Anglican and dissenting Sunday schools were under a common management, and once a year in June they assembled on St. Peter's green, processed by High Street, and a collection was taken in St. Paul's church for their expenses, but this system seems to have come to an end about 1810.[32] Mary Woodward, a Sunday school teacher at Bunyan Meeting, rewarded with ½d. any pupil who learnt by heart psalm 139, "O Lord, thou has searched me and known me". The Bedfordshire Institution, founded in 1815 and concerned more with weekday schools, has already been discussed (ch. 36).

The promotion of Bible reading was another object fostered by all denominations. After a public meeting in Bedford in 1811 the Bedfordshire Auxiliary Bible Society was formed, with the Duke as president, Sir George Osborn as vice-president, and the Rev. Samuel Hillyard as secretary.[33] Hillyard wrote to Whitbread that he had ordered a large consignment of Bibles, had paid £400 to London headquarters, and that there was still £200 in hand. The following year the wife of the Rev. Edmund Williamson wrote to her son "Father has a cold, but went to Bedford to the annual meeting of the Bible Society."[34]

Missions were a growing concern. The Moravians had from the first made efforts out of proportion to their numbers. Among their records is preserved the detailed diary of Brother George Carie's mission to Jamaica, 1754-6;[35] thus Dec. 1754: "there came in the morning a pretty company of negroes, about 70 . . . I spoke to them with a warm heart, and they heard attentively and eagerly. The dear negroes saluted me all very friendly after the meeting. In the afternoon visited some negroes in their houses, who testified their joy that they could hear preaching." Thomas Blundell, a Baptist minister at Luton, was one of the founders of the Baptist Missionary Society in 1792, and Samuel Greatheed of Woburn was a founder of the inter-denominational London Missionary Society in 1795.

A private mission venture was sent out in 1817 to the 400 slaves on his Jamaican plantation by Robert Hibbert (later founder of the Hibbert Trust), of West Hyde, Luton.[36] His emissary reported: "I preached to them as often as I could get them together, visited their huts, and buried their dead. Some came to my house and talked on religion. I formed the children into classes, and tried to

---

[31] C.R.O., QGR 4.
[32] Tibbutt, *Bunyan Meeting*, 44, 67-9.
[33] C.R.O., W 1/2058-66.

[34] C.R.O., M 10/7/17.
[35] C.R.O., MO 983.
[36] J. Murch, *Memoir*, 5, 15-17, 22-3.

teach them to read." Other slaves on nearby plantations became discontented, and other masters unpopular, and Hibbert believed he was not justified in undermining slavery so long as it was allowed by law. After 3 years he ended the venture. Slavery was abolished in 1833, the plantation market slumped, and Hibbert, in spite of government compensation on emancipation, lost heavily when he sold his estate.

40 – LIFE IN GENERAL, 1771–1839

THE COUNTRY

In the countryside there was a simple round. The statute or hiring fair in larger villages took place at Michaelmas, when men or women fortunate enough to be hired for a whole year were engaged. Shepherds and horsekeepers, dairymaids and laundrymaids, all stood with the symbols of their work, and prospective masters and mistresses made their bargains accordingly. But there was all the fun of the fair as well. For instance at Eaton Socon in 1827 inverted cups were disposed on a stool, and wagers laid as to which cup had a ball under it.[1]

Then there was the 5th of November, when there were usually fireworks and bonfires. Luton seems to have been unruly on Guy Fawkes nights, and in 1828 the justices forbade fireworks. This incensed Lutonians. "Let's go up to Dickey Jones", cried some – Jones was a straw-hat manufacturer, who for some reason was unpopular. Men blacked their faces (for anonymity), and a mob converged on Jones' house. Squibs, crackers and stones were thrown. When a blazing tar-barrel was rolled up to the fence, Jones fired into the crowd and wounded some. Charles Austin the solicitor, who lived nearby, said that the noise from the guns, and fireworks and the yelling of the mob was tremendous. However, after a struggle the tar-barrel was quenched and removed before too much damage was done.[2]

The sowing of wheat for next year's crop was celebrated with a dough-cake flavoured with carraway seeds and spice.[3] In 1821 two Renhold labourers, James Birch and Richard Hight, finding themselves with only 8d. each on which to celebrate "wheat-seeding cake-night", stole 6 geese from Mr. Polhill to set themselves up in funds.

In some parishes which kept a town [or parish] plough, a good deal of beer was consumed "at the town plough going out"; Riseley overseers spent 25s. on this in 1786, which must have been enough for more than a pint for every able-bodied man in Riseley.[4]

At Christmas churches were "stuck" with holly – at Oakley the parish clerk, James Agutter, was paid 2s. 6d. for doing this in 1821.[5] Some churches had holes for this purpose bored in the pews. At Kempston old Captain Newland, a Waterloo veteran and somewhat irascible, one Christmas morning plucked out the holly bough behind his head and hurled it with some force into the aisle.[6]

[1] C.R.O., QSR 1827/350-2.
[2] C.R.O., QSR 1828/1828/392–408.
[3] B. Mag., v, 281; C.R.O., QSR 1821/383–8.
[4] C.R.O., P 50/12/1.
[5] C.R.O., P 40/5.
[6] E. W. and E. C. Williams, Kempston, p.4 (typescript in C.R.O.).

On Valentine Day the children went the round of the village asking for gifts.[7] When May came there might be Morris dancers, as at Silsoe: "Mayers, alias Morris dancers, who go about with a fool, a man in woman's clothes (Maid Marian), and music."[8]

Then in the summer came harvest. Casual labourers engaged for the harvest would celebrate by getting drunk the first day they were hired. When gleaning was due to begin, notice was usually given by a church bell being rung at 6 or 7 a.m. Even an unpopular farmer like William Soames of Stevington celebrated harvest home with a supper for his men and plenty of beer (in his case in 1826 with unfortunate results to himself).[9]

At some time during the year there was still kept in most places the village feast, at the usual season, though the reason for it was forgotten. The alteration of the calendar in the mid-18th cent. had thrown out the reckoning, so that it was now celebrated some days after the festival of the patronal saint. Thus in 1825 Steppingley feast was kept on 30 August, though its church dedication is to St. Laurence whose day is 10 August; Daniel Mann records how, later in the evening, he stood in the Horseshoes public-house watching the dancing, "it being the feast".[10] At Radwell feast in 1824 they bowled for tea, sugar, bread, butter and snuff; on this occasion Dickins Prigmore and his wife fought, and the blows "was as if they was rending wood" – "she was in fault", noted Arpin judicially.[11]

Sometimes a small travelling amusement fair might visit the village; there was one such at Cardington in May 1789 "a little fair and a stall, and a turnabout to make the children sick after their gingerbread", noted Byng.[12] At this same fair a good many years later, a Bedford tinplate-worker had his pocket picked of 3s. 6d., an orange-and-yellow coloured handkerchief, and $\frac{1}{2}$ lb. of gingerbread nuts.[13]

If a local musician struck up his instrument, open-air dancing followed spontaneously, if there were enough people present. We can imagine the scene at Houghton Conquest in 1825. Outside the inn some boys gathered to see the blue-jacketed soldiers of the Yeomanry Cavalry, who had been exercising in Houghton meadow, and had come for a drink. A sharp-eyed 8-year old saw James Grummit take a prize pistol from a holster on one of the horses left in the yard. There was a scrimmage while Grummit and Redman (who had possessed himself of another pistol) were put in the cage, kicking violently, and bystanders gathered. Then the shepherd took out his flute, and dancing began.[14]

By now, belief in witchcraft had practically disappeared, but occasionally there is a trace of it. A Cardington labourer, whose watch was stolen in 1824,

---

[7] References occur in later school logbooks; but the reference in Cole's *Diary* in 1767 to children hallooing under his window before he was awake seems to indicate that it was probably an old practice in Bedfordshire as well as in Buckinghamshire.

[8] *Torrington diaries* iv, 100.

[9] C.R.O., QSR 1826/299.
[10] C.R.O., QSR 1825/324.
[11] *B.H.R.S.* xl, 139.
[12] *Torrington diaries*, iv, 109.
[13] C.R.O., QSR 1830/431
[14] C.R.O., QSR 1825/310.

said "I went to the wiseman at St. Neots, and could get no assistance from him", so then he tried the village constable.[15]

Special occasions called for special celebrations. In 1814, after Napoleon had been sent to Elba, Henlow bells were rung, houses decorated with oak boughs and flowers, and 500 people sat down in the street to a feast which had been provided by subscriptions from the farmers and gentry.[16] In 1821 when George IV was crowned, the subscription list at Clifton amounted to £28, and the provisions included 50 stone of meat, 50 lb. plums, 54 quartern loaves, 7 score eggs; each man was allowed a quart of ale, each woman a pint, and children half a pint.[17]

GENTRY AND TOWNSFOLK

Of the gentry and townsfolk we know more. Children had pets. "Tell sister to take care of the blackbirds in the garden hedge, and tell James to look after the larks' and thrushes' nests", wrote the schoolboy Edmund Williamson in 1773; perhaps sister forgot, for next year he appealed to his mother "Pray take care of all my live animals, and tell me how my rabbits are, and when she has young ones again."[18]

Bowls were still played, though they were less popular. There were cricket matches. At Biggleswade they took place on the common, and in 1829 Biggleswade juniors (under 20) defeated Potton by 111 runs to 77.[19] At matches at Luton a marquee was put up, where players changed their shoes, and in 1822 shoes which George Clark and Edward Taylor had left in the marquee were stolen.[20] In Bedford football was played on St. Peter's green, a practice not welcome to the Moravians in their nearby settlement, and they discountenanced it as much as possible.[21] Boxing matches were so far as possible suppressed by the justices, who were "convinced of their ill tendency" and "determined not to suffer them to take place".[22]

Hunting was enjoyed, not only by the gentry. The Silsoe carrier, John Edwards, was drowned hunting in 1823. An eye-witness says that the fox crossed the river at Turvey, although it was in a high state of flood; the hunt followed; Polhill's horse slipped off the causeway, and so did others, and soon there were "seven horses, men and hats all swimming in this tearing flood. I saw Edwards swimming and holding his chestnut horse by the bridle. The horse reared and came down with his forefoot upon Edwards' head." The body was later found at Turvey mill.[23]

The supporters of the Oakley Hunt were still apt to rely on the Russell and Whitbread families to make good all financial deficiencies. In 1829 when the Marquess of Tavistock, then master, gave up hunting, the hunt nearly fell through.

[15] C.R.O., QSR 1824/384.
[16] C.R.O., AD 3283.
[17] C.R.O., P 7/28/12.
[18] C.R.O., M 10/4/224, 242.
[19] C.R.O., X 356/1; and cf. QSR 1816/245-6.

[20] C.R.O., QSR 1822/354.
[21] C.R.O., MO 35/1792.
[22] C.R.O., QSR 1791/3.
[23] B.H.R.S. xliv, 76.

Then a stranger, G. F. Berkeley, offered himself and established his own kennels and pack at Harrold. He was touchy and individualist and was not liked. In 1832 he challenged S. C. Whitbread to a duel, and arrived at the Swan with pistols. Fortunately the wiser judgement of the seconds prevailed on him to apologise. Soon afterwards he retired, and then permanent kennels were built at Milton Ernest for the hunt.[24]

Bedford races continued. On Sir Philip Monoux's silver sauceboats (they had formerly belonged to Sir Humphrey) there was a racehorse engraved;[25] was it a former Bedford winner? There was comment when Mrs. Salmon, wife of a man who kept a private school at Biggleswade, was seen at Bedford races in 1812, though her husband said she only went because of the desire of some parents that their children should attend.[26] There were pickpockets there; that same year a pickpocket from Essex was found in a ditch with a purse and money belonging to John Bonnet of Peterborough.[27] People were apt to drink freely; in 1811, the day after the races, Robert Farnell wrote "A friend of mine informed me I abused you on the race-ground yesterday ... I was very much in liquor, and I humbly beg your pardon."[28] There seem also to have been races elsewhere; at least a sketch survives of Potton race-ground in 1813.[29]

Then there was coursing. John Trevor of Bromham (Lord Hampden's heir) wrote to a friend in 1811: "I should be glad any day to match our greyhounds in Biddenham fields, where I think I could show you and your young folks some sport, when the hares are got a little stronger."[30] Captain Moore, retired from the navy, in 1820 asked Countess de Grey's permission to course at Maulden.[31] Whitbread in 1814 had 11 dogs, mostly pointers and spaniels.[32]

Fishing-rights were jealously safeguarded, whether or not the owner wished to exercise them personally; and those at Carlton and Harrold were the subject of a lawsuit between Grey and Alston in 1791; the fish mentioned are trout, carp, tench, perch, bream, roach, dace, jacks, eels and even gudgeons.[33] If the owner did not himself fish, or was away, he allowed friends or dependents to fish by permission, as Lord Bute did in Luton Hoo park;[34] or else he had the steward send him fish as required – from Leighton fish was sent by canal to the Leighs at Stoneleigh.[35] John Gibbard of Sharnbrook bought two new rods in 1818 at 5s. and 7s. respectively, and 4 lines at 1s. 6d.; he got them from Kilpin in Bedford.[36] Villagers were tempted to poach; however when one parish constable found 3 men with a casting net one night, "having no person at hand to assist me, and being close to the river, I did not deem it prudent to attempt then to apprehend them".[37]

[24] B.H.R.S. xliv, introd., and p.57.
[25] C.R.O., F 639.
[26] C.R.O., W 1/2254.
[27] C.R.O., QSR 1812/160–3.
[28] C.R.O., W 1/6223.
[29] C.R.O., P 64/25/9.
[30] C.R.O., W 1/6224.
[31] C.R.O., L 30/11/191.
[32] C.R.O., W 1/6173.
[33] C.R.O., L 24/239–41.
[34] C.R.O., G/DDA 144/1, 13; 146/5.
[35] C.R.O., KK 874–9.
[36] C.R.O., GA 50.
[37] C.R.O., QSR 1830/487.

(A noted poacher of game in general was James Clare of Woburn. For over twenty years he appeared constantly before quarter sessions for poaching, but his last appearance in 1831 was for threatening the mistress of Woburn workhouse with a poker because she would not give him more meat pudding and potatoes.)

Gibbard bought his guns in London, preferably from Thomas Stevens in High Holborn; also copper caps, up to 600 at a time; and in 1825 Stevens cleaned his duelling pistols for him; gunpowder he got locally, 2 lb. at a time.[38] Among the gentry boys took to shooting at an early age; and a well-to-do clergyman with private means, like Edmund Williamson, rector of Campton, often went shooting; he wrote to his schoolboy son how he had taken William and Richard (aged 10 and 8) with him, and that he had shot 14 brace of partridges, 5 of hares, 4 couple of rabbits, a brace of pheasants and a snipe.[39]

For indoor amusements, there was occasionally a concert in Bedford. In 1812 the Messiah was given, or part of it; but fewer than 100 attended.[40] However, in 1825 a greater effort was made, again with the Messiah.[41] The performance took place in St. Paul's church, and was patronised by many from town and county. It was in aid of the infirmary and of new schools. Several musicians from London, Cambridge, Peterborough and elsewhere gave "gratuitous assistance in the most handsome manner"; the organist presided at the organ; and there were violins, violoncellos, double bass and drums. Tickets ranged from 2s. 6d. to 10s. 6d. A little later, when the new rooms were built, it was expected that concerts there would be very well attended.

From time to time in Bedford there was an assembly, with dancing for the young people and cards for their elders. Here the minuet was giving place to the waltz, or to "volsing", as one writer spelt it in 1785; "I took it by the first description to be some foreign phrase for plain English romping"; at a later ball at Bedford "the waltz appeared the rage of the night".[42]

Drama continued to be occasionally available in the towns. When John Byng was at Biggleswade in 1791, a rather inferior company was performing in a barn; he thought they seemed starving; "one fiddle and 13 candles composed our music and lights . . . more barnish misery exists not". However, he went again a few weeks later, and on the last night they had a full house, with poorer folk outside peering through holes in the walls.[43] At Bedford plays were sometimes given in the Sessions House, as in 1785 and 1786; or in the yard of the Old George inn.[44] In 1809 a travelling company gave The West Indian and The Agreeable Surprise in St. Loyes Street.[45] A barn in the yard of the Hop Pole inn in Cauldwell

38 C.R.O., GA 49.
39 C.R.O., M 10/7/8.
40 C.R.O., M 10/7/11.
41 C.R.O., X 37/35.
42 C.R.O., L/30/9/60/332; M 10/4/42, 109, 243, 279; also an undated letter (1828 or 1829) from Ann Skevington of Bedford to Ann Milnes, afterwards

Ann Wade-Gery, in the possession of Mrs. Wade-Gery (no. 194).
43 Torrington diaries, ii, 308–9, 411.
44 C.R.O., QSR 1785/129; 1786/120, 142; and Fac. 21.
45 C.R.O., X 254/66.

St. was also used for plays.[46] Charles Frewin of Shefford in 1822 paid nearly £200 for a portable theatre, but it landed him in gaol for debt.[47] At Dunstable in 1804 "the much admired comedy of *John Bull*" was given.[48]

There was in Bedford a small so-called museum of curiosities collected by James Read the painter. John Byng laughed at this "twopenny museum" and never tells what the exhibits were, but he usually called to see Read in the 1790's when in Bedford.[49]

In 1817 there was formed the Bedfordshire Horticultural Society, with over 50 members from town and county, including such names as Pym, Whitbread, Livius, Higgins, Dr. Brereton and Theed Pearse. They organised spring and autumn shows of "auriculas, polyanthuses, cucumbers, carnations, picotees, melons, gooseberries and currants", at which they had a common meal, of which the cost was not to exceed 4s., including ale. Cucumbers were not to receive a prize unless they were at least 10 inches long.[50]

Somewhat rarer was the study of astronomy. For several years James Pettit of Leighton Buzzard kept an astronomical journal.[51] Most of the entries are technical, but in 1820 he noted that his mother in her 78th year had such excellent sight that she could see the satellites of Jupiter through a small telescope. On one occasion when he had trouble with his calculations about Jupiter, he wrote "Now this difference, I have but little doubt, must have been caused by the uncertainty of our town clock", on which he had to depend at the time. In 1835 he entered many observations on Halley's comet. Another Leighton astronomer was Benjamin Bevan, the surveyor; Pettit wrote of him, when he died in 1833, that "though self-taught, he was a very good astronomer . . . he was perhaps better known on the continent than he was at Leighton Buzzard", where most people confused astronomy with astrology. In Bedford a retired naval captain (later Admiral) W. H. Smyth,[52] who came to live in the Crescent in 1828, built himself an observatory, with an outer meridian room 17 ft. long and a circular one adjoining, 15 ft. in diameter; Pettit thought it "one of the best observatories in England", and that it contained one of the best telescopes.

Among the county's more unusual characters was Dr. Rodomonte Dominicetti,[53] who published a *Dissertation on the artificial medicated baths*. When he went bankrupt in London, he came down to Ampthill whence his bride had come, and took East End House, Flitwick, on a long lease. Here he erected "neat and convenient apparatus for the preparation and application of his various artificial medicated water, vaporous and dry baths," and was prepared to board any lady or gentleman. The Flitwick venture seems to have been of doubtful success, and he left in 1806.

[46] B. Mag. iii, 92.
[47] C.R.O., QSR 1824/642.
[48] B. Mag. iv, 82.
[49] Torrington diaries, ii, 287, 313–4; iii, 191, 200.
[50] C.R.O., AD 1744; X 37/32.
[51] C.R.O., AD 1011.
[52] B. Mag. x, 25; and B.N.B.
[53] B. Mag. vii, 165.

The Victorians

41 – THE GREAT ESTATES, 1832–88

FROM ABOUT 1830 to 1870 was the golden age of the great estates. They were at their peak of size, power and beneficence. For their tenant-farmers things went well; and after a time and to a less extent things improved for their cottage-tenants. The political power of nobility and gentry was scarcely undermined; and though, under pressure from manufacturing interests, the corn laws were repealed, this repeal did not at first affect agricultural prosperity. Only in the 1870's and 1880's did sudden alarming cracks appear in the foundations of landlordism, and brought also disaster to the farmers and hardship to the cottagers.

THE ESTATES

The Woburn estate reached a new maximum in 1842, with the purchase of the Ampthill estate, which had once been Lord Ossory's, and had descended from him to his nephew, Lord Holland. (It was Lady Holland who planted the Alameda avenue at Ampthill.) A conscious Woburn policy was formulated with regard to purchases and/or sales. Curiously enough, it was enunciated by the steward, Thomas Bennett, who was more ducally minded than the Duke (Francis, 7th Duke, succeeded in 1839). The Duke asked him whether it would be advantageous to buy any part of the Ampthill estate. Such a query was routine practice when there was any sale nearby; the steward then reported on whether such-and-such a farm, close or cottage would or would not work in well with the existing estate. On this occasion, Bennett took time to consider, then replied: "I beg to suggest buying the whole; not so much for increasing our estate as consolidating; and sell Eaton Socon and Wilden. The estate from Woburn to Maulden would be connected, and it certainly would then form one of the grandest properties in the kingdom . . . Although the county estates altogether are large, yet so many being far apart, the domain at home does not quite correspond with the extent and magnificence of the Abbey. I suggest it with great deference."[1] The Duke was impressed; consolidation became the policy; the Ampthill estate was bought; and Eaton Socon and Wilden sold soon afterwards. This concentration on the area from Woburn to Ampthill (and also over the border in Bucks.) meant that purchases for in-filling were still to be made; and the actual peak of the Beds.–Bucks. estate was reached in 1877 with 37,186 a.[2] (The Page-Turner estate at Battlesden was bought in 1885, but it was offset by the sale of Houghton Regis in 1880 and Knotting and Souldrop in 1882.)

[1] C.R.O., R 4390.   [2] Duke of Bedford, *Great agricultural estate*, 224.

Consolidation was in the air. In the north, Lord St. John made purchases in Bletsoe and Riseley, selling off more distant property at Radwell and Tilbrook.[3] In mid-Bedfordshire, Earl de Grey pulled down the old house at Wrest, and rebuilt it in 1834 on a larger scale,[4] largely according to his own ideas (he was the first president of the R.I.B.A.), but helped by the architect James Clephane. He consolidated his estate, especially at Silsoe. Practically the only major changes in the general pattern of landholding were that after a disastrous fire at the Hoo in 1843 Lord Bute sold it and most of his Luton estate; and in 1871 Lord Ongley sold his Warden estate to Joseph Shuttleworth. When in 1873 the government compiled details of landownership, the main estates in Bedfordshire were given as:

the Duke of Bedford (Hastings, 9th Duke)	33,589 acres
S. C. Whitbread, Southill	13,257
Countess Cowper, Wrest (heiress of Earl de Grey)	8,888
J. S. Crawley, Stockwood	8,240
Lord St. John, Melchbourne	7,806
Miss Trevor, Bromham	
(Lord Hampden died in 1824, when the property passed to Rice Trevor)	6,229
Sir E. H. Page-Turner (sold to the Duke in 1885)	4,879
the Rev. John Thynne, Haynes	
(the Carteret title became extinct in 1849)	4,717
J. G. Leigh, Luton Hoo	4,265

In the 3,000 a. range were Cooper Cooper of Toddington and the Osborns of Chicksands; in the 2,000 a. range were about a dozen squires, including Alston, Burgoyne, Harvey, Orlebar and Polhill; and in the 1,000 a. range over twenty, including Francklin, Higgins, Pym, Stuart, Thornton and Wade-Gery. Half the county was owned by fewer than 50 persons.

This period saw the end of parliamentary enclosure:

Wootton	1838
Cranfield	1840
Westoning	1842
Leighton Buzzard	1848
Stotfold	1851
Goldington	1852
Streatley	1858
Eaton Bray	1860
Meppershall	1863
Totternhoe	1891

PROGRESSIVE FARMERS AND NEW METHODS

It may seem contradictory that the earlier part of this period was a good

---

[3] C.R.O., X 158/58.   [4] C.R.O., L 30/18; X 219.

one for farmers. The days of independent yeomen were far distant, and farmers even took some pride in the estate to which they belonged. When young Queen Victoria, one fine July day in 1841, visited Woburn, 150 mounted tenantry were drawn up on either side of the park entrance to receive her (the best mounted near the gate), and they escorted her to the Abbey, falling in rank two by two behind the carriage.[5] The rent audit was a pleasant occasion, on which there was a dinner for the tenants, sometimes of venison.[6]

Tenants' farmhouses or buildings were improved by good landlords. Piped drainage was also promoted by them, sometimes by contributing to the cost or by supplying materials; on the Woburn estate Bennett preferred to control the whole operation, so that the work was not skimped.[7]

Agricultural implements were gradually improved. In the early 19th cent. an individual farmer might have an idea for a better design, or even for a new implement altogether, and get the local blacksmith to carry it out. Such a happy knack was possessed by the Armstrong family of Wilstead. William Armstrong (d. 1845) had several sons, four of whom farmed at Wilstead, Haynes or Wootton (John, William, Joshua and Thomas).[8] One of the family got the local blacksmith to execute a design for an improved plough. Its possibilities were seen by the Bedford ironmonger and foundry-owner, John Howard (son of the former gaoler) who was able to produce and market it on a large scale, and who exhibited it at the first show of the Royal Agricultural Society in 1839: "a plough by Mr. John Howard of Bedford, of small size, with a mould-board or furrow-turner of excellent form, calculated to give the least resistance in turning over the furrow".[9] It became known as the "champion plough of England"; produced at the Britannia Ironworks (completed 1859) at Bedford, it was widely exported. Armstrong is also credited in a contemporary poem with an improved harrow and horse-rake:[10]

> "Now
> I'll speak of England's champion plough . . .
> Still the palm bedecks that plough
> Of Armstrong's made by Howard now,
> Remitting by one-third the toil;
> While other ploughs take horses three,
> Two draw the champion easily.
> And other honours yet belong
> Unto the genius of Armstrong:
> When you commit the seed to ground,

[5] C.R.O., R 4423, 4430–3.
[6] Loc.cit.
[7] C.R.O., R 4644; for Wrest, cf. X 159/3.
[8] C.R.O., ABP/W 1845/46; and Wilstead parish register.

[9] V.C.H. ii, 126.
[10] W. Franklin, The Plough, 1857. For Beds. ploughs, harrows and drills, see also Jnal. Roy. Ag. Soc., xviii, 21–3.

The zig-zag harrows best are found;
'Twas he conceived the happy knack,
No tine to trace another's track . . .
A third good honour, too, he won . . .
At harvest, when the crop of grain
Is carried off, some will remain,
This with the fork you cannot take,
But can by using Armstrong's rake."

The horse-drawn reaper, which superseded sickle and scythe, was invented in America and first shown in England at the Royal show in 1851; by the 1870's it was improved so as to bind sheaves as well as reap.

A new source of power was found in steam. Howard manufactured a plough for use with a steam-engine; the engine stood at the side of the field, and drew the plough over it by means of a windlass. Steam-power was also used for threshing, and the mid-19th cent. threshing drum was more effective than the crude threshing-mills of 50 years previously. Small farmers could not afford to own a steam-engine, and had to hire one. In 1869 such equipment could be hired from E. Spencer of Harrold, T. Dynes of Cardington, W. Stocker of Eaton Ford, G. Hawkes of Arlesey, or W. Cripps of Hockliffe. For threshing small quantities flails continued in use for some time. One in the Bedford Museum is said to have caused the death of a man who poked fun at it – the user hit out at him with more force than he realised.

Cropping in 1857 in Bedfordshire was said in general to follow a 4-course rotation (on the clay: fallow, barley, beans, wheat; on gravel and loam: fallow, barley, clover, wheat); while on the chalk, oats were often added before fallow, making a fifth course.[11] But now new fertilisers were coming into use, which emancipated farmers from the old rotation. In 1842 super-phosphate was patented just over the county border by J. B. Lawes at Rothamsted, and was soon in use in Bedfordshire. Phosphatic nodules (locally called coprolites) occur in a narrow area of land about 5 miles wide, stretching across the south of the county from Leighton Buzzard to Arlesey, but they require to be dug and ground for use. Lawes contracted to have them dug at Shillington in 1869,[12] and in the 1870's and 1880's they were systematically extracted and sent to a mill at Royston to be ground. Guano was imported. Scientific weed-killers and pesticides however were as yet unheard of, and boys were paid a few pence for pulling charlock by hand or scaring birds.

In the farming journal of Robert Long of Upper Stondon, a tenant on the Wrest Park estate, we see these improved methods in use.[13] He first had one

[11] Loc.cit.
[12] B.Mag. iii, 310. True coprolite is the fossilized dung of prehistoric saurians, but for trade purposes the term was used to denote any phosphatic nodules.

For Lawes' Shillington contracts, see C.R.O., HE 188–94.
[13] C.R.O., X 159/3.

steam-engine; a 7-horse single-cylinder one; then in 1863 he bought a 9-horse one in addition (unfortunately the under-horsekeeper, William Simkins, had an accident with it, and had to be taken to Hitchin infirmary to have his fingers amputated). For fertilisers he used horse-dung and soot from London, and also super-phosphate and guano. Improved drainage was put in on his farm; when the steward came over to see about it, "told him I would rather do it myself, even if I paid for materials as well as labour". He attended the Royal show to see whether there was anything new. The practice of selling livestock by auction at Hitchin market was instituted by him, and by 1865 this had become the practice at Bedford also (Hitchin was his market, and he presided over the market ordinary at the George, the third generation of his family to do so). Sometimes also his journal touches on other matters, such as sparing men and carts to help build Lower Stondon school, or the death of the Prince Consort.

The principles of stock-rearing were studied. At Woburn Park farm in the 1850's feeding experiments on cattle were carried on for Rothamsted by the permission of Francis, 7th Duke of Bedford – these were more intensive than the earlier Woburn experiments (ch. 34).[14] Comparison of weekly live weight with dry food consumed by oxen, sheep and pigs showed that pigs were the most economical food producers, cattle the most extravagant. A successful stock-farmer was Samuel Bennett of Beckerings Park farm on the Woburn estate. For several years from 1839 his sheep won prizes at the Royal show, and he was on the council of the Royal Agricultural Society from 1843 till his death in 1853.[15]

Disease gave some trouble; Long notes some foot and mouth disease in 1862, though this was not taken as seriously then as later: "milking cows are the worst; the milk is very bad, what little they give; and the pigs seem to have caught the same from drinking the bad milk; there is a deal of it about just now, I am told; they eat scarcely anything while they are at the worst, which is about 6 days".[16] A serious outbreak of rinderpest came to England from the continent in 1865. It reached Bedfordshire first at Beckerings Park. "At Little Bramingham early this week John Eve had one died with it, and all the rest he had killed, being 20",[17] – an act of 1866 ordered slaughter with compensation.

Though there are no precise figures to prove it, it seems certain that production greatly improved in the first half of the 19th cent. in this county. In 1857 an old Bedfordshire farmer estimated that there were in the county scores of farms producing 50% more corn than in 1794; and supplying the metropolitan market with a stone of meat for every pound supplied in 1794.[18] Incidentally, Bedfordshire was the subject of the first attempt of the government to get such figures in 1838 through the clergy; but so few figures were obtained that the project was

[14] E. J. Russell, *History of agricultural science*, 151–75.   [17] *Loc.cit.*
[15] *B. Mag.* in press.   [18] *Jnal. Roy. Ag. Soc.*, xviii, 28.
[16] C.R.O., X 159/3.

dropped.[19]

In 1876 Hastings, 9th Duke of Bedford, founded a permanent experimental station at Woburn, with Augustul Voelcker as director, under the Royal Agricultural Society.[20]

Local agricultural and horticultural societies were formed.[21] The Olney, Turvey and Harrold Agricultural Society was formed in 1848; and Sandy and District Floral and Horticultural Society in 1869; this latter ran a successful show until the middle of the 20th cent. The Bedfordshire Agricultural Society of course continued. There was always an annual dinner with a formidable toast-list; in 1852 there were 21 toasts, beginning with the Queen and Prince Albert. The show was not always held in Bedford; in 1854 it was at Biggleswade, 1856 Woburn, 1857 Leighton, 1861 Luton. But thereafter it was usually at Bedford, and in 1871, as the result of a request from Bedford town, the month was changed from October to July.

The Royal show was held at Bedford in 1874, and was attended by over 70,000 people.[22] Many prizes for stock went to Bedfordshire farmers, such as George Street of Maulden, Henry Purser of Willington, and George Hine of Oakley. The class for the best all-round farms was limited to Bedfordshire, and the 1st prize was won by Richard Checkley of Brogborough, the 2nd by Thomas Crouch of Lidlington.

POLITICS

Political power was still largely with the landowners. After the reform of 1832 there were only approximately 4,000 electors for the county (1 in 23 of the county population at the census of 1841); and the reform of 1867 made little change in rural districts (1 in 20 at the census of 1871). One, if not both, the county members was a Whig, and usually a Russell; and both were almost always from county families. It was one of the duties of the Duke's steward to act as election agent, at first for Lord Charles Russell (M.P. 1833–47), then for Hastings Russell (M.P. 1847–68), who was later 9th Duke. Printed pollbooks reflect fairly closely the interests of the landowners concerned; thus in 1857 on the Woburn estate the majority of the votes were cast for the Whig Hastings Russell (in Woburn itself all but one); while at Tempsford 18 out of 19 were cast for the resident Conservative, William Stuart, and at Hockliffe 13 out of 15 for the resident Conservative,

[19] The Board of Trade addressed queries to 126 Bedfordshire incumbents as a trial venture, but only 27 replied. Even those did not answer all questions; to most questions the Arlesey incumbent wrote "the farmers decline answering". So far as these returns go, they indicate that, on the average, 2½ bushels of wheat were sown to the acre, and the average return was 23 bushels. The largest number of sheep given was at Blunham (including Mogerhanger): 2,200; the largest number of cattle (other than milch cows) Turvey (200). The largest amount of butter given was at Keysoe (10,000 lb.). Scarcely any cheese was made. At Henlow 3,000 bushels of potatoes were produced. (*Agricultural Returns*, 90–6).

[20] See annual *Report on field and feeding experiments at Woburn*; and also E. J. Russell and J. A. Voelcker, *Fifty years of field experiments* (Rothamsted Monographs).

[21] C.R.O., GA 4; LS 408–47.

[22] See n.15 above.

R. T. Gilpin. Gilpin was one of the county M.P.s 1852–74.

It was during this period that England's policy with regard to agricultural imports changed. The growing industrial population needed cheap food, and townsfolk in the manufacturing north were increasingly opposed to the law which, by a sliding scale depending on the home price, restricted the import of corn. The Anti-Corn Law League was formed in 1839. Richard Cobden, its leader, even addressed a meeting in Bedford.[23] Sir Robert Peel repealed the corn law in 1846. During all this time Bedfordshire farmers were very uneasy, and feared to sign leases committing themselves to payment of rent for years ahead. Bennett, the Duke's agent, tried to convince them that their fears were exaggerated; to the tenants he said that, if there was a ruinous fall in prices, the Duke would feel bound to set aside contracts made on the faith of the present law; while to the head office in London he wrote "the way to meet . . . their objection as to terms, you say 'I do not mean to sacrifice my property, but . . . I offer you a proviso which will secure you from alternate loss, and your lease still be in full force in other respects' ";[24] that is to say that, should the farmers' position deteriorate, the Duke would reduce rents, but the tenant would still have security of tenure. However, William Bennett, tenant of Lewsey farm, a strong protectionist and incidentally a Methodist, protested to such an extent that the Duke was obliged in 1849 to release him from his lease and compensate him.*

Bennett's view of the outcome was right at that time. English farming was efficient enough to stand some competition, and there were not in Europe vast surpluses of corn waiting to enter the country; so the price of corn was little lower than it had been. Robert Long in the 1860's was still a prosperous man. Of the corn market in Bedford on 12 October 1867 David Stanton, a young Keysoe farmer, wrote "The corn exchange has been crowded, the wheat in large supply, and business firm", the prices for best quality being up to 72s. a quarter.[25]

Thus though the nobility and gentry had the main power, they could be convinced of the need of a change not in their tenants' interests. The Whig Duke of Bedford might still (like Trollope's Earl of Brentford) use his pocket borough of Tavistock till it was disfranchised in 1885, but the Whigs were the party most committed to extending the franchise, with all the consequences which must eventually follow. Nowhere is the change in outlook more evident than that between John, 4th Duke of Bedford in the 18th cent., and his greatgrandson, Lord John Russell. Lord John Russell was prime minister 1846–52 and 1865–6. When he spoke in the commons, though his voice was small and thin, the house was hushed; "you felt that you heard a man of mind, of thought, and of moral elevation". Under him the ten hours bill of 1847 was passed, limiting factory hours. He initiated the original grant for education in 1839, and in 1853 vainly

[23] J. Coombs, *Recollections*, 10.
[24] C.R.O., R 3792, 4673.

[25] C.R.O., CRT 160/54.
* I owe this point to Mr Brent Rogers.

proposed to allow a local rate for education. He was unsuccessful in coping with the Irish famine of 1846–8, but this was a disaster on a scale to challenge even the resources of today. His last words were "I have made mistakes, but in all I did my object was the public good."

MARKET GARDENING

Market-gardeners continued, especially at Sandy, where the names of Sutton, Jeeves and Braybrook recur; and also elsewhere along the greensand ridge. An exceptional market-gardener, like John Read of Maulden, did very well; he was said to have begun in a small way without a shilling, and by industry brought up a large family with great credit, and in 1834 was worth a considerable sum.[26] In general, however, in the early part of this period they were small men, with a cottage and a very few acres; and their wills were usually proved at under £100. They are sometimes found mortgaging an acre, perhaps after a bad season, or perhaps because they had just succeeded in buying it. The growth of towns enlarged their market. Then the great northern railway gave Sandy and Biggleswade quick access to London for their produce, and also brought them large supplies of horse manure (more important to them than to the farmers, because they had little of their own). In the 1864 directory (i.e., after the opening of the railway) over 200 market-gardeners are listed for the county, half of these being at Sandy and Biggleswade; and nearly all the remainder are in the surrounding villages. They were still small men, but gradually they began to operate on a bigger scale.

THE COTTAGERS

At the beginning of this period there was surplus population in the villages, with low morale, living in hardship, and breaking out in violence. At the end of it, living standards were still low, but the population trend was reversed. How had this come about?

There are many references in the early 1830's to the low morale which the poor law of 1834 was intended to eradicate. Many active and able-bodied men were going the "rounds" of the parish, or were put by the overseers to work on the roads, and were conscious that this was merely a way of trying to dispose of them. On the other hand, some in regular work were feeble and ineffective, and humane employers hesitated to discharge old men; thus in 1830 "Saunders is almost blind; when he comes to get his money, he can't see 2s. 6d. if placed a foot away from him, and a sixpence has to be put into his hand"; in 1831 "old Stopp carries a broom about the park to show what his work ought to be if he would do it"; the time came when his legs were swollen to enormous size and he was incapable of walking, but he still expected his money.[27] This lowering of standards was bad for boys, who "come at a very early age, do nothing, learn nothing, and become a burden"; "all consider themselves fixtures" (1829).[28] A conscientious

[26] C.R.O., R 3822.
[27] C.R.O., R 3556, 3586.
[28] C.R.O., R 3527.

attitude to work was hard to attain when wages were kept low by the availability of roundsmen. It was a vicious circle.

The poor law of 1834 attempted a radical change. Parishes were grouped in unions round Ampthill, Bedford, Biggleswade, Leighton, Luton and Woburn; while (since county boundaries were not respected) some Bedfordshire parishes found themselves attached respectively to St. Neots and Wellingborough. Boards of guardians were elected for these new areas. By transferring social responsibility to a larger unit than the parish, it was hoped to care more efficiently in a large, well-run workhouse, for those who really needed it, and to avoid the evils of the old parish workhouse (ch. 36). It was hoped to make the status of able-bodied paupers less desirable than the position of the worst-paid labourer, in the expectation that this would put pressure on every man who possibly could do so to get a job, and would put employment, especially in agriculture, on a more realistic basis.

The early stages were difficult. The newly-elected guardians had to learn their functions, to get the new workhouses built, and to engage appropriate staff. At the same time the parish overseers (who now were responsible to the guardians) had to cope with numbers of militant unemployed, and some made mistakes. At Marston in October 1834 the overseer thought that money might no longer be paid to roundsmen and roadmen, and so he distributed loaves. Nearly a hundred men (no doubt including some from other parishes) assembled at the house of a nearby justice, the Rev. G. Cardale of Millbrook, and threatened to pull the house down unless he came out. Cardale told them he had not ordered the distribution of loaves, and advised them to send a deputation to petty sessions at Ampthill on the following Thursday (though it was said that some justices were "so wedded to the old system . . . that they would probably direct something opposed to the act to be done").[29] At Ampthill on the day of petty sessions nearly 200 men assembled, but when the justices explained that work was still to be paid for in money, and that it was only relief of need that would be given in kind (food and clothes), they dispersed.[30] At Cople the overseers discharged surplus men and told them to find work for themselves, so the others struck.[31] At Eversholt the overseer said the men were "got beyond his management".[32]

Lidlington was a danger-spot. To help the overseer, the Duke's steward, Bennett, arranged some digging on a farm at the piece-rate of 3d. a pole, at which he reckoned they could earn 1s. a day. About 40–50 men marched in a body to Bennett's house and surrounded him with a menacing appearance; "I told them threats were no good; by this work they could earn bread but not beer."[33] This was in November 1834. When on 11 May 1835, a Monday, the newly-appointed relieving officer for the Ampthill union came to Lidlington, he was met by a mob

[29] C.R.O., R 3820.
[30] C.R.O., R 3648, 3817.
[31] C.R.O., R 3802.
[32] C.R.O., R 3819.
[33] C.R.O., R 3819–22.

demanding "blood or money". The following day, Tuesday, Millbrook followed suit.

The justices were alarmed. There were hasty consultations, and on Thursday 96 special constables from the various parishes of the union were sworn in. The Lidlington ringleaders were arrested. As they were being brought back through Millbrook to Ampthill, a threateningly large mob gathered and released them. Then a huge crowd assembled in Ampthill. The guardians, who had hastily met, tried to explain to the crowd the working of the act, but could not be heard. Stones were thrown, and almost every window in the workhouse broken; the reading of the riot act had no effect; the high constable was knocked down, and some of the guardians attacked. Others of the mob turned on the justices in petty sessions at the King's Arms. A message was hastily sent to ask help from the metropolitan professional police. At last, evening brought calm.

By 10 a.m. next day, Friday, 21 men of the metropolitan police had arrived and they proceeded to make arrests, while over a hundred more special constables were enrolled, some reluctantly. Thus the Ampthill riot was quickly quelled. Lest violence spread elsewhere, the yeomanry were called out and stationed at Luton. Some of the rioters were tried at quarter sessions, some at assizes; 5 were sentenced to death, but this sentence was commuted to imprisonment; in all, 22 men served terms of from 3 months to 2 years.[34]

Three years after the passing of the poor law, a select committee of the commons, including Lord John Russell, was appointed to examine into its working. The unions of Ampthill, Bedford and Woburn were selected for special attention. The committee found that some mistakes had been made, but that most complaints were unfounded, and that there had been a great improvement.[35]

MIGRATION AND EMIGRATION

The key to the whole situation, perceived only by a few, was surplus population. "Without some means devised to dispose of this redundancy, the workhouse system will fail", wrote Bennett in 1834.[36] What then happened to those who were redundant and who did not go into the workhouse? The personal and private details of many a weary struggle we shall never know; all that can be given is a broad outline. In brief, the answer is twofold: migration and emigration.

Many went to the towns. The main local towns were Bedford, Luton and Dunstable – the two latter both became municipal boroughs in this period

---

[34] C.R.O., CRT 150/11–12 (extracted from QS records).

[35] *Report of Select Cttee. on the Poor Law Amendment Act*, 1838. The detailed investigations were made by two men, James Turner and Mark Crabtree, who were not local, and seem not to have had rural experience; some of their information appears to have been inaccurate. However, the committee censured two cases: one where a man had been refused relief for his sick wife unless he came into the workhouse ("harsh and improper"); the other where relief to a widow was made conditional on her migrating to a manufacturing district. The committee also stressed that payment should be made at a room provided in each parish, not in the street, church porch, public-house or shop.

[36] C.R.O., R 3830.

(ch. 42). The census figures show a considerable rearrangement of population within the county:

	county population	increase or decrease	
		towns	villages
1801	63,393		
1831	95,483		
1861	135,387	154%	24 %
1891	160,621	90%	-4 %

One poor boy who is said to have come penniless to Luton from Stopsley, eating acorns on the way (more probably it was beech-nuts), was Asher Hucklesby, whom we shall meet later.[37] The Luton hat trade drew women even from Bedford; in 1851 a young widow, left with twins, carried one twin to Barton, hid the child in a hedge, went back for the other, spent the night in Barton, and next morning carried both twins to Luton.[38] Local towns did not necessarily draw only on the Bedfordshire population – Luton no doubt also attracted villagers from north Hertfordshire; and probably some Bedfordshire people went to towns in surrounding counties.

Others went, as some had done previously (ch. 35), to the industrial north. This migration was actively promoted by some guardians. The Rev. James Beard, rector of Cranfield, justice of the peace, and one of the guardians for Ampthill union, went in 1835 for a 3-month visit to Lancashire. Some Cranfield families already there had got on exceedingly well; "he is now sending away a lot more; altogether by the end of next week he will have got 16 families (about a hundred, old and young) from Cranfield, where they were destitute, into full and regular work at high wages".[39] On this, the Ampthill Board resolved to send an intelligent man to make a circuit among the manufacturers to ascertain likelihood of work; and, if the prospects were good, to arrange with someone on the spot to send information as to where people were wanted, as well as to meet the paupers when sent and help them to get work; and Woburn Board hoped to follow suit.

For the man who was prepared to live hard and to migrate in gangs (like the Irish) to wherever work offered, railway building offered better wages than farmwork (ch. 44). Already in 1838 an official report found that many men from the unions of Woburn, Ampthill and Bedford had gone to work on the railway,[40] which must have been the London to Birmingham, opened in that year.

Some went to London. Probably they did so in the early part of this period, though figures cannot be given, but certainly they did so in large numbers in the later part of it. In 1881 there were distributed over the various London boroughs 15,543 people born in Bedfordshire, the highest figure (2,379) being in Islington.[41]

37 Dyer–Stygall–Dony, *Luton*, 164.
38 Information from a grandson of one of the twins, now a respected Luton resident.
39 C.R.O., R 3889.
40 *Report of Select Cttee.* cited above.
41 *Life and labour*, statistical tables.

There was also emigration. Bennett had said "The owners of the soil can never look to any permanent relief until a considerable part of the population will leave the country altogether."[42] Transportation was one means. Richard Dillingham of Flitwick was transported to Tasmania in 1832 for stealing from a house at Steppingley. In 1836 he wrote "I am now ... in a large market garden ... and my imploy is to drive a horse and cart into Hobart town with the produce of the garden for sale. As to my living ... I want for nothing in that respect. As for tea and sugar, I almost could swim in it."[43] Charles Cartwright of Millbrook was transported to New South Wales in 1837 for stealing 15s. 6d. with violence. At first he was set to work building a new gaol near Sydney; then on a dock; and later on a farm. He wrote home in 1844 "i have plenty to eat, more than you do i ham Shore, and plenty Cloes to ware ... but i Cannot go ware i Like, not with out a pass."[44]

Emigration could be helped by the parish. Seven men were sent to Canada in 1834 by Riseley vestry, "with his Lordship's approval and assistance" [Lord St. John], and each was to receive two sovereigns on landing; the same parish cautiously provided Job Smart with shirt and a pair of shoes, but he was not to have them till the ship had actually sailed.[45] Emigration could be assisted by the poor law union: besides help with their passage, emigrants received each a knife, fork, spoon and plate for the voyage, and if they behaved well they were allowed to keep them. In the first decade of the new poor law, about 250 emigrated in this way, most to Australia, about one-third of them to Canada, and a few to South Africa.[46] They were mainly from north Bedfordshire, from the cold heavy land; 48 from Stevington, and a number from Riseley, Bolnhurst, Sharnbrook and Colmworth, but there were also some from further south – 34 from Wilstead. These were of course young people, who either took a few children with them, or would raise families overseas.

Probably some emigrated to Australia privately; the steamship companies regularly advertised their sailing dates in local papers such as the *Bedfordshire Mercury*, with a reminder that an immigrant could receive a free allotment of land. Some of the settlers' difficulties in their new homes are reflected in a letter of a later generation, written by Priscilla Dodson of Elstow, who went with her husband and father to Australia in 1863. Writing in 1886 she reported her father as saying that "the emigration lecturer's fair tone and full description of this land flowing with milk and honey, as it were, was a sad day for him and us".[47]

There was private emigration to the United States. How many could raise

[42] C.R.O., R 3830.
[43] B.H.R.S. xlix in press. For convicts in general see A. G. L. Shaw, *Convicts and the Colonies*.
[44] B.H.R.S. xl, 228–31.
[45] As regards clothes, a reasonable outfit was provided for the convict; see that for Lydia Sanders of Eversholt (transported in 1829 for helping to steal a lamb), QSR 1829/723, 751. Her age was 19.

An 1819 logbook of a ship transporting women convicts was found at Ampthill in 1956; the convicts were locked below at night, and those who gave trouble were made to wear a wooden collar and their hair was cut off; see C.R.O., X 240/19 and Mic. 83.
[46] *Annual reports* of the Poor Law Commissioners.
[47] B.H.R.S. xl, 237.

the money for this it is impossible to say, but occasional references in unlikely places, such as in the minute-books of Ridgmont Baptist church, show that it was done. One who went was William Baxter of Sharnbrook; when his mother died in 1838 she still remembered her dear and only son, but being but very poor and having but very little to leave, she felt bound to leave it to her daughter.[48] Rogers of Wilstead went in 1853, and the next year sent £20 towards a passage for his wife and 4 children; the parish explained that they could not help her officially, but because of her excellent character they sanctioned her making private application to such of the parishioners as she deemed fitting.[49]

Later, when gold was found, both in the United States and in Australia, it was an inducement to adventurous spirits, but one which probably led to success for only very few. Joel Croxford of Silsoe, who sent his niece "a smol nugit of gold", wrote in 1864 from "Iornbarks" gold fields in New South Wales to explain why a letter had been delayed in reaching him: "we gold diggirs are never satisfide for we hear of a new gold feilds braking out in some other country wher thay say people are makeing rapped fortune",[50] but there is no news of Croxford's making a fortune.

In the natural course of things, there was a time-lag before the exodus from the countryside began to show in the population figures and before the overall figure for each parish began to decline. The peak year varies from parish to parish. Some figures are given below:

	1881	1891
Lidlington (peak 1841: 926)	657	600
Melchbourne (peak 1851: 290)	219	165
Pulloxhill (peak 1861: 704)	529	492
Wrestlingworth (peak 1871: 725)	638	524

The cottager who stayed at home had fewer competitors as time went by, and the situation eased a little for him. His wages were still low – Robert Long in the 1860's was usually paying from 10s. to 12s. weekly; but he had his self-respect since he had a job, and the good worker shared with his employer the tie which binds all who serve the land faithfully. His place might be humble, but it was a definite place in the scheme of things; even if he were ill or unfortunate and had to go to the infirmary or workhouse, that was his place.

Towards the cottager some at least of the gentry and clergy had a new attitude. The hymn speaks of "the rich man in his castle, the poor man at his gate", but the poor man was a person to be considered. (Incidentally, we who treat the developing nations as the poor men at our gate have no right to be smug at the

---

[48] C.R.O., ABP/W 1838/34: "I beg of my dear son . . . not to think that I, Elizabeth Baxter, am wanting in proper maternal feelings . . . but he has already had from his mother prior to his leaving England for America and since then . . . . more than she in justice to her daughter Sarah Baxter perhaps ought to have given."
[49] C.R.O., P 22/8/1.
[50] B.H.R.S. xl, 235–6.

expense of the Victorians). When there was an epidemic of typhus in Silsoe, Earl de Grey's daughters distributed blankets and flannel, and saw that the infected cottages were whitewashed; when their great-aunt remonstrated, they replied "We are very careful not to put ourselves in the way of infection, and only go to the healthy cottages." When they returned to London, they wrote "We took the opportunity of its being so fine to go round the village to see if any of the poor want anything before we leave them."[51]

Some idea of what bad housing might be like can be gained in 1866 from a report on Biggleswade, where the housing standards were probably much like those of the villages. There were 45 houses with only one bedroom; and in one case 14 persons slept in the bedroom. In Mill Lane there was only one privy to 9 cottages in which 45 persons lived. "The pigsties are generally very close to the dwelling-houses, and the accumulation of manure is usually kept close to the sty." Of a house in Anchor End it was said: "No privy, no back door, rains in, and [inhabitants] obliged to get up or cover themselves over with sacks in bed; cesspool 6 ft. from door."[52]

For some cottagers housing was improved – this was on the best estates, which had standard designs. Old Warden in 1871 was described by an inspector as a model village (Lord Ongley). Good housing is especially noticeable on the Woburn estate, not only from that estate's size, but also because the Duke, with his London rents, was not as dependent on the income from his land in Bedfordshire as some other landlords were. To go through the county, looking out for the familiar style bearing the "B", coronet, and date of building, and note how the houses grew in size and the windows were enlarged, is to realise how much rural housing owed to the best landlords, before it became a public responsibility. But the Duke's estate at its maximum was only one-tenth of the county, and there were landowners who were less conscientious, less efficient, and who lacked other resources. An old farmer in 1857 said that in the same parish might be seen tastefully built cottages, with 3 bedrooms and 2 living rooms, a neat stone sink, and a good spacious garden, all at moderate rent; and miserably small, crowded cottages, devoid of all convenience, without a foot of garden ground, paying 2s. 6d. a week.[53]

In many villages there was more schooling available for the cottager's children, though if boys could earn a few pence by casual jobs about the farm, they would be kept away from school, while many children were sent by their parents to lace or plait schools to work under supervision, because the children's earnings were necessary to the family. However, there was more teaching than there had been. Most new schools were built by the churches (ch. 43) but a number were due to the landowners; thus the Duke built Aspley Heath, Husborne

[51] C.R.O., L 30/11/241.
[52] C.R.O., PUBWM 9, pp.310, 315, 318.
[53] Jnal. Roy. Ag. Soc., xviii, 26.

Crawley, Knotting, Millbrook, Oakley and Stevington between 1840 and 1868; Lord St. John built Melchbourne; Milton Bryan was built by the Inglis family; Tempsford by the Stuarts. So much did some landowners consider this a private matter that when an enquiry was made into schools in 1846, the return for Tingrith read "There is in this parish a Sunday and infant school, containing 65 children, of which the master and mistress are paid by the ladies of the manor [Trevor family], who wish no return to be made."

Though the cottager's job was more secure, and often his cottage and his children's chance of schooling improved, the traditional stand-bys of his wife – lace in the north, strawplait in the south, were being undermined. The competition of machine-made lace made it almost impossible to earn money by making the old fine (point-ground) lace. As early as 1821 a Bedford lace-dealer was insolvent, and in 1822 two Sharnbrook lace-dealers who were in difficulties dissolved their partnership.[54] Unexpected help came to the lace-makers as the result of the Great Exhibition of 1851 at the Crystal Palace, at which was shown pillow-lace from Malta, much cruder in design and requiring less time in the making. The old point-ground designs fell into disuse, and lacemakers concentraded on coarse Maltese patterns. Even these were not in great demand; the curate of Odell, in asking for help for the poor of his parish in 1860, mentioned the "dullness of lace".[55]

In south Bedfordshire the difficulties arose later, and in this case the competition came, not from machines, but from the importation of cheap plait in quantities from the Far East about 1870 (ch. 42), so that the demand for local plait rapidly declined.

As for the lace and plait "schools", where children worked under supervision in these two crafts in which it was increasingly difficult to get a living, conditions may be judged from a description of a plait school at Clifton in 1871: "I saw 51 children sitting in a room 10 ft. sq. by 7 ft. high; the window was shut, the door open . . . but it opened into a small kitchen, and this into a yard, with a filthy drain close to the door, and pigsty and privy close by. It was really impossible for anyone coming from outside to stay in the plaiting-room for a minute without a feeling of nausea."[56] Lace schools were less congested, as room had to be found for each child's pillow.

Wages for the ordinary worker in 1835 ranged from 8s. to 12s. a week (boys 1s. 6d. to 4s. 6d.); with higher rates at harvest time; piece-rates were sometimes used, by which more could be earned; and skilled men like horsekeepers and shepherds had more. In 1857 9s. to 12s. is quoted, with skilled men getting 14s. Free beer was provided at harvest, and small beer for the rest of the year.[57] Hours

[54] C.R.O., X 37/46; X 198.
[55] C.R.O., BS 600.
[56] C.R.O., PUBWM 10, p.256.

[57] Agricultural returns; and Jnal. Roy. Ag. Soc., xviii, 25.

were long. At Sharnbrook they were from 6 a.m. to 6 p.m. for labourers while horsekeepers began in winter at 5 a.m. and in summer at 4 a.m.[58]

Drunkenness seems either to have been more prevalent or to have been deprecated by more people. Though the cottager might be more secure, the monotony of long hours and no holidays except at church festivals (August Bank Holiday from 1871) encouraged a tendency sometimes to break out and go on a "blind". This last was more easily practicable because public houses then opened at 6 a.m. Hence arose in the late 19th cent. a temperance movement (ch. 43).

Mid-19th cent. prosperity emboldened farm-workers to demand higher wages, and Joseph Arch began to organise in the country as a whole an Agricultural Workers' Union, like those existing elsewhere for industry. One man near Luton was discharged for speaking at a meeting; others collected for him and he moved to Derbyshire. In March 1874 men in some villages near Bedford asked for a rise in their weekly wages from 13s. to 15s., and when this was refused, they struck (their strike pay was 9s.). From a van in St. Paul's square, lit by oil lamps, one evening Arch addressed a meeting estimated at 3,000; many wore the strikers' badge, a blue ribbon. Next day he spoke at Lidlington. At Cople a blackleg was assaulted. Two friends to the workers were the Rev. H. E. Havergal, vicar of Cople; and Henry Wright, who had a private school at Luton, and was one of the first members of Luton town council.[59] The Duke of Bedford refused to take sides. But the time for this movement was not propitious (see below), for already wheat prices were falling.

Other country-dwellers felt the effect of the machine age. The work of blacksmiths and saddlers diminished somewhat, as coaches gave way to railways (ch. 44), though the change was gradual; for the rest of this century harness and shoeing were still required for the gentry's carriage and riding horses, for the farmer's trap or gig, and for horses used in farm-work. The custom for rural inns on the main roads fell off, and some closed down, like the Cock at Eaton Socon. Steampower began to be used for milling; some mills were converted, or used steam as an auxiliary, as at Biggleswade and Shefford;[60] but in the middle of the century others, like Willington, were already going out of business.

THE DEPRESSION

For all dwellers in the countryside things worsened in the 1870's. This worsening began with the import of American corn. The prairie lands of America, virgin soil and ruthlessly exploited, had come into cultivation. Steamships had become larger and faster. Foreign competition was on a scale and in conditions unforeseen in 1846 a generation previously at the repeal of the corn law.

Some indication must be given of wheat prices. It should perhaps first be explained that *a quarter is 8 bushels*; the weight however depends on the type of

[58] C.R.O., X 25/39.
[59] *Beds. Mercury*, 14 March to 9 May 1874.

[60] *B.H.R.S. Survey* i; C.R.O., WJ 34, 317.

85 Map of administrative boundaries in 1834.

86 Turvey villagers: John Warren, mason, William Dalley, ploughwright, cooper and carpenter.

▲ *a Carlton thief in 1863.* ▲ *a Luton murderer aged 16 in 1868.*

87 Prisoners in Bedford gaol.

▼ *an Irish hawker – thieving at Bedford in 1863.* ▼ *a woman tramp – stealing at Bedford in 1872.*

88b James Pedley (grandson of diarist).

88a Catherine Maclear, 1842–1935 (daughter of diarist).

89b Justices at Quarter Sessions:
John Lee, John Trevor, Sir R. H. Inglis, John Foster, John Green.

89a T. C. Higgins, 1797–1865,
chairman of Quarter Sessions.

HOWARD'S NEW PATENT STEAM CULTIVATING APPARATUS
WITH COMBINED PORTABLE ENGINE AND WINDLASS.

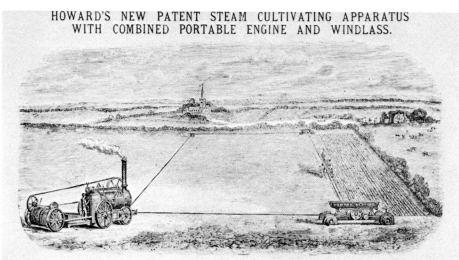

J. & F. HOWARD have introduced important improvements in Steam Cultivating Apparatus, which render the ordinary Portable Thrashing Engine more thoroughly fit for the difficult task of Steam Tillage. One of these improvements is, that the weight of the Engine is used as an anchorage both for the Windlass and the Pulleys which lead off the ropes, and the separate snatch blocks and anchors, hitherto necessary and troublesome to fix, are dispensed with.

The Engine and Windlass although detached for convenience of removing from field to field, are connected when at work by a single rod or bolt. The driver has therefore perfect control both of Engine and Windlass, and is in a favourable position for overlooking the ploughing as it proceeds.

▲ *90a Howard's patent steam plough, 1878.*

▼ *90b Straw hatmaking at Luton.*

▲ *91a Wheelwright's shop of William Kendall at Wilstead, c. 1910.*

▼ *91b Daniel Albone, 1860–1906.*

▲ *92a Railway engine from the Sandy – Potton line, opened 1857.*
▼ *92b Southill railway station.*

▲ *93a Vauxhall car made in Luton in 1905.*

▼ *93b The R 101 airship made at Cardington.*

▲ *94a Sunday school at Kempston Church End and Up End: the top two classes, c. 1870.*
▼ *94b Board school at Lidlington, c. 1896.*

▲ *95a Late Victorian cricket team, probably Tempsford.*
▼ *95b Late Victorian football team, Bedford Town.*

▲ *96a Victorian Biggleswade.*

▼ *96b Edwardian Bedford.*

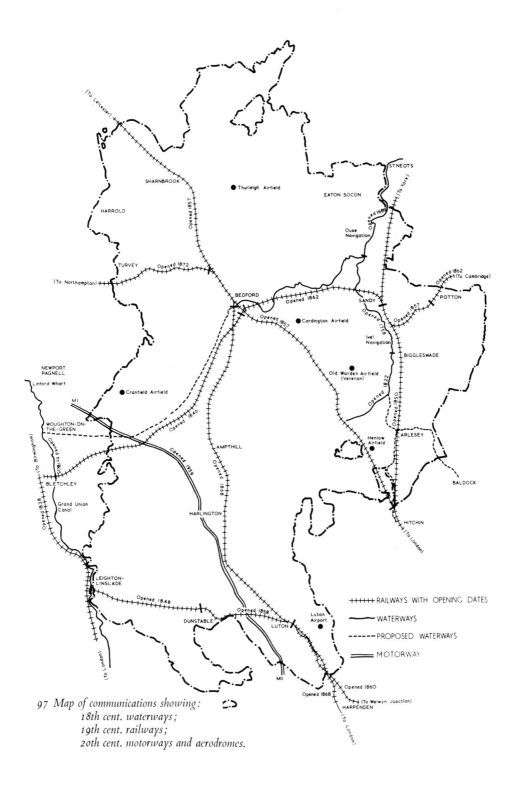

(To Leicester)

SHARNBROOK

● Thurleigh Airfield

ST.NEOTS

EATON SOCON

(To York)

HARROLD

Opened 1689

Ouse Navigation

Opened 1857

TURVEY

Opened 1872

Opened 1862 (To Cambridge)

(To Northampton)

BEDFORD

Opened 1862

SANDY

Opened 1857

POTTON

Opened 1857

● Cardington Airfield

Opened 1758

Ivel Navigation

BIGGLESWADE

NEWPORT PAGNELL

Linford Wharf

● Old Warden Airfield (Veteran)

MI

● Cranfield Airfield

Opened 1822

WOUGHTON-ON-THE-GREEN

Opened 1846

AMPTHILL

Opened by 1805

Henlow Airfield

ARLESEY

Opened 1850

BLETCHLEY

Opened 1838

Grand Union Canal

Opened 1859

Opened 1868

HARLINGTON

BALDOCK

HITCHIN

(To London)

LEIGHTON-LINSLADE

Opened 1848

╫╫╫╫╫ RAILWAYS WITH OPENING DATES

DUNSTABLE

Opened 1858

LUTON

Luton Airport

——— WATERWAYS

- - - - PROPOSED WATERWAYS

═══ MOTORWAY

(To Birmingham)

(To London)

MI

Opened 1860

Opened 1868

HARPENDEN

(To Welwyn Junction)

(To London)

97 Map of communications showing:
   18th cent. waterways;
   19th cent. railways;
   20th cent. motorways and aerodromes.

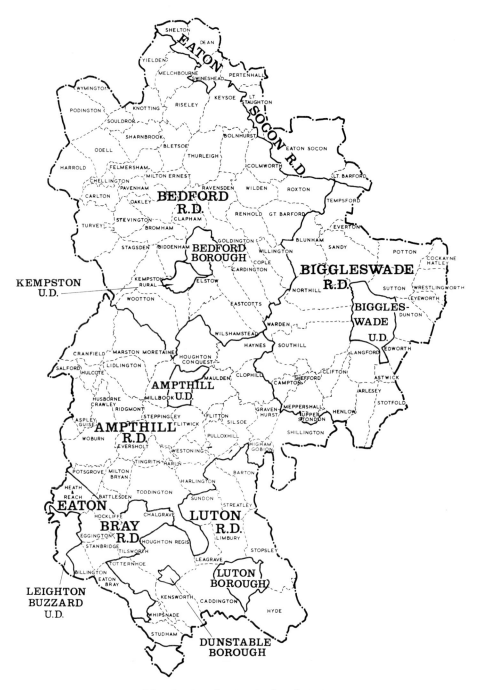

98 Map showing administrative boundaries in 1900.

99 Map showing administrative boundaries in 1968.

▲ *100a Leighton Buzzard Urban District Council, 1891.*

▼ *100b Bedfordshire County Council, 1889:*
Front row: C. S. Lindsell, R. Orlebar, H. H. Green, R. Barton, Marquess of Tavistock,
  C. Howard, C. Magniac (chairman), S. Whitbread, F. Howard, H. Blundell, J. I. Wright,
  C. D. Broughton, A. Pym;
Second row: R. Purser, T. W. Pearse (clerk), J. H. F. Peppercorn, J. Wilson, W. Inskip,
  J. King, C. Mees, R. Mossman, J. Carter, T. Smart, R. H. Lindsell, Lord St. John,
  J. Hawkins, E. T. Leeds Smith, A. Hucklesby, E. Crouch, J. Brown, T. Barnard (treasurer);
Third row: T. J. Jackson, G. M. Johnson, J. Pedley, B. Cole, C. Cook, J. Dover, J. Daniels,
  J. N. N. Shillito, H. Pettit, J. W. Green, J. H. Limbrey, H. Trethewy, J. Crouch;
Back row: A. Macnamara, B. Dimmock, J. F. Hatfield Carter, T. Fardon, G. Haynes,
  W. H. Jacksom, E. E. Dymond, W. P. Becket, J. Cumberland, H. C. G. Brandreth,
  W. H. Derbyshire, G. Horn C. J. Pope.

cereal, a quarter of wheat, the heaviest, being $4\frac{1}{2}$ cwt., barley 4 cwt., and oats 3 cwt. Nationally the average price of wheat was:[61]

1873	58s. 8d. a quarter
1886	31s.
1894	22s. 10d.

On the other hand, locally sometimes a different measure was used, namely *a load is 5 bushels*; a load of wheat therefore is just under 3 cwt. The best surviving local accounts are those of J. S. Peacock of Stanford farm, Southill, a tenant on the Whitbread estate, and he uses this latter measure in accounts 1855–82.[62] He sold his wheat crop in about ten instalments annually, partly to catch the best price so far as possible, partly to fit in threshing with other work, and partly according to cash requirements. After 1856 he never again got as much as 50s. a load; after 1872 he only once got 40s. a load; often the price was below 30s.

Another glimpse of Bedford corn market in February 1879 is given by David Stanton, now farming at Thurleigh (like Keysoe, part of the Crawley estate). "Took a sample of my barley, also a sample of Father's, and a sample of wheat for him too . . . I was bid 38s. a quarter for the wheat by one man; thought it was worth more . . . but found to my surprise that I could not get any more . . . Have been to the first five markets at Bedford this year. I don't remember going to such bad markets before."[63]

This year, 1879, was one of the wettest years on record. Stanton did not begin to reap wheat till 3 September, and then had to stop, as the crop was not ripe enough. He finished harvest on 7 October.

For the local millers too the new situation in corn meant disaster. Big new mills were built at the ports where the imported grain was unloaded, and gradually local millers were driven out of business. Several closed down in the late 19th cent.; and of all the mills that formerly existed in the county, less than twenty were still working after 1900.[64]

In the farmer's new circumstances, livestock became more important. The old saying "down corn, up horn" meant that his risk was distributed, so that if the yield of the one fell, he hoped to recoup on the other. But just as the weather made things worse for corn-growing, so towards the end of this period disease militated against the trade in livestock. Legislation tried to help by organising measures to control the disease. Between 1878 and 1882 over 1,000 pigs were slaughtered in Bedfordshire in an attempt to stamp out swine fever, mainly in the south (Luton, Chalgrave, Eaton Bray, Tingrith and Hockliffe).[65] Foot and mouth disease was widespread in 1883.[66]

And then came the importation of frozen meat. Long ago in 1842 Bennett had

[61] *Enc.Brit.* i, 388; Russell, *op.cit.*, 176.
[62] C.R.O., X 98/3.
[63] C.R.O., CRT 160/54.
[64] *B.H.R.S. Survey* i (windmills only).
[65] C.R.O., QAV 4/5.
[66] C.R.O., QAV 4/2.

said "I presume no live fat stock will be sent from America; notwithstanding the voyage is much shortened by steam, yet the expense, and the waste of flesh by confinement will prevent sending."[67] He had reckoned without the advent of refrigeration which made it possible to import chilled or frozen meat. The first cargoes of mutton and lamb arrived from New Zealand in 1882; the first beef from the Argentine in 1883.[68]

Landlords of course were obliged to reduce rents – their tenants were unable to pay them. Lord St. John's rental, which in 1872 was just over £10,000, had sunk by 1887 to £6,779.[69] At Turvey, W. F. Higgins' nominal rental of £2,549 was short in 1880 by £1,210.[70] The Duke of Bedford remitted 50% of his rents in 1879, 1885 and 1887, with smaller remissions for intervening years; and in 1895 he revalued the whole estate, reducing the rental by 55%.[71]

Not many people will feel excessive concern for the landlords. But for the farmers it was disastrous. An early farmer to go bankrupt was Joseph Topham of Wyboston in 1874,[72] and there began to be a number each year. Arable land went out of cultivation; buildings decayed; hedges and fences were neglected. Old people living today, who derive from farming ancestry, were brought up on long memories of hard times. Cottagers suffered; some lost their jobs; and wages could not rise though prices did. Octogenarians living in the 1930's and 1940's have told how breakfast consisted of a slice of bread on which boiling water had been poured; and how, if there was illness in the family, a jug of skimmed milk was an acceptable present.[73] The drift to the towns accelerated. Industrial England forgot the dwellers in the countryside. Indeed, it had its own problems, in growing competition overseas, and in the international financial crises of 1873 and 1882. Nationally the great era of economic expansion had come to an end.

LATER POLITICS

Before the worst trough of the depression was reached, political change had begun. Already there had been the ballot act of 1872. Farmers, unable to see their position as clearly as we see it today, were discontented on many grounds, such as the malt tax, and the rights of tenants on settled estates. There was projected, not only in Bedfordshire but elsewhere, a Farmers' Alliance. In 1880 James Howard, who had once previously represented Bedford borough, and who, as a maker of agricultural machinery, knew the problems of farmers, was prevailed on a week before the poll to stand as one of the county members and was returned, but the only other county to return a land reformer was Herefordshire. The malt tax was converted into a beer duty, and a settled land act was passed, but nothing

[67] C.R.O., R 4519.
[68] Enc.Brit. i.
[69] C.R.O., X 158/58, 60.
[70] C.R.O., HI 193.
[71] Great agricultural estate, 122–7. See also R. Prothero, Whippingham to Westminster, pp.200–2.

[72] C.R.O., X 67/826.
[73] The late Levi Webb and the late Annie Dawson, Willington. Cf. the statement of Elizabeth Denton of Harlington 1823: "I got up at 6 a.m. to make my husband a mess before he went to work;" QSR 1823/266–8.

vital was done to help agriculture. When in 1884 a wider franchise was introduced for rural areas, the end of the old political era had come. In 1885 the county was divided into two constituencies of north and south. (Incidentally in this year there was an election riot at Potton.)[74] The electorate in 1891 for these two constituencies was 25,919 out of a population of 132,598 (1 in 5).

[74] C.R.O., QSM 47, p.698.

THE TOWNS fall into two groups. Bedford no longer stands alone; Luton overtakes it; and Luton and Dunstable (though Dunstable was very small) become municipal boroughs. Between Bedford and Luton on the one hand, and the market towns on the other the gap widens. Some of the market towns eventually become urban districts. However, there are some features which most urban communities have in common in this period.

THE LIFE OF TOWNSMEN

Queen Victoria's coronation was celebrated at Ampthill in 1838 by a public dinner in Church St., where 20 tables were set out. The houses were decorated with evergreens. A subscription committee had collected £100 (Lord Holland gave £15), and there was beef, plum pudding, ale and tobacco. Afterwards there were sports, dancing and fireworks; and a balloon inscribed "Victoria" was released.[1] (Fifty years later, for the queen's jubilee, tables were similarly set in Bedford High Street).

For the man who was comfortably off, town life was pleasant. Mark Rutherford has preserved it inimitably.[2] The attorney did business from his house – Charles Austin lived in George St., Luton. The vicar of St. Paul's, Bedford, lived in St. Paul's square. The tradesman lived over and behind his shop; it was open for long hours, and he stood at a little desk at the end of the counter, with a pen behind his ear, but there was no rush and little competition, and he knew all his customers. At midday Bedford High St. was empty from end to end and the profoundest peace reigned. On Saturday he might keep open house for farmer friends who had come in to market. On Sunday no avoidable work was done; the meal was cold, except for potatoes; and the family attended two if not three church services. One postman sufficed to deliver Bedford's letters.[3] Town criers at Bedford and other towns gave notice of such events as the county show.

Bedford boys at the Grammar or Commercial schools on their half-holidays wandered into the country, fishing or bathing in summer, skating or playing football in winter. Among the private residents whom education had attracted to Bedford, ladies like Catherine Maclear[4] played the harp or piano, drank tea with each other, and went for walks (though the streets were dirty in wet weather) or for drives. An occasional concert, the visit of a travelling theatrical company,

[1] M. S. F. George in the *Ampthill News*.
[2] C. M. Maclean, *Life*; and his own books, e.g. *Autobiography*, and novels such as *Catherine Furze*.
[3] J. Coombs, *Recollections*, 9.
[4] *B.H.R.S.* xl, 144-62.

or the excitement of an election which might lead to a riot, was of interest to all.

The private residents with their new houses on the town's outskirts heralded a change. "You ought to go with the times", said Mrs. Furze to her husband;[5] she wanted him to turn the parlour into a counting-house, use the drawingroom on the first floor for storage, and live away from the town centre. At Bedford John Howard (ch. 41), who in 1837 lived over his shop in High St., which had a foundry behind it, before long built or rather enlarged Cauldwell House; and the attorney and town clerk, Theed Pearse the younger, moved out to Cauldwell St. to a pleasant house called Rye Close. At Luton, the Bedford road and Hart Hill became residential; and in 1864 Edmund Vyse, the straw hat manufacturer, lived at Holly Lodge, and Thomas Sworder, the brewer, at the Bury.

For poorer inhabitants conditions were worse. At the beginning of this period no town in Bedfordshire had a piped water supply; people still depended on wells, either their own or a public well. It was often the practice to throw slops out of the door. Sanitation was mainly by means of earth closets, too few in number. Graveyards were congested. Newcomers came from the overcrowded villages; speculative builders put up small streets of mean cottages, and these too became overcrowded. The connection between dirt and disease was only gradually becoming clear (the study of bacteriology was in its infancy). There was a constant threat of epidemics.

The worst danger was from cholera. There were some cases in Bedford in 1832, and the mayor issued health hints; cleanliness in the house, keeping bedroom windows closed at night, wearing flannel next the skin, and avoiding salads. In an outbreak in 1849 the monthly death-rate in Luton doubled, and that in the central parish of Bedford St. Paul (especially All Hallows and Gravel Lanes, and Newnham, Hawes and Thames Streets) quadrupled.[7] In 1854 there was a particularly bad outbreak at Luton,[8] in the centre of the town, where 33 houses (each containing only two rooms) stood back to back and had 4 privies, an open cesspool and a well); fire-engines were brought to swill out the accumulated filth, and the street was covered with lime. In 1868 cholera occurred in the Biggleswade area;[9] here, in a street called Cage Hole, water for household purposes was drawn from a well which was 4 ft. from a privy, and this privy was in an abominable condition; and in Cowfair Lands cowsheds and heaps of manure were close to cottages, and there were horrible sheds for privies, with faeces lying about on the floor.

Some of this disease spread to the villages roundabout. The trouble at Biggleswade in 1868 reached Stotfold, where people complained that they had to walk 6 miles in summer heat to Biggleswade for medicine, and were "almost tramped to death" – the union medical officer justified himself by saying that

[5] See n.2.
[6] Actually London; C.R.O., AD 1739.
[7] Parish registers. The Bedford streets are given in

C.R.O., AD 1755.
[8] *Bedford town and townsmen*, 83.
[9] C.R.O., PUBWM 10, p.249.

he had entrusted 450 doses for free distribution to Mrs. Green, the Stotfold publican.[10]

From smallpox the danger had much diminished; inoculation had been replaced by vaccination, and from 1840 this was obtainable free (eventually it was more or less compulsory). But there was an occasional outbreak, as at Ampthill in 1882; a nonagenarian[11] there can recall how afflicted families put a basket at the gate for neighbours to do their shopping, and tradesmen dropped all money in a basin of disinfectant; some victims were taken to the union workhouse, whence burials were made at night, deaths being posted up on the gate.

The need for improved practice and standards, if large numbers were to live safely in urban communities, was learnt by painful experience.

UTILITIES AND AMENITIES

It might be thought that townsfolk would demand an increasing range of services, but to think thus is to project back into the early Victorian age the outlook of our own. Some improvements were passionately opposed; in the local press the formal reports of town council or of public meetings give glimpses of battles as fierce as those in *Middlemarch*. Leading townsmen thought in terms of a small community; lesser townsfolk were poor and struggling; the expense (it was said) would be enormous; besides, to criticise the water of Bedford or Luton was to affront local pride. To support their case, opponents could point to many other towns without new-fangled schemes – Bedfordshire was by no means unique.

Today a main agency for town improvement is the town council. But the act of 1835 had given boroughs few powers. And in 1835 the only borough was Bedford; its rate income (a precept on the poor rate) was under £500, while another £500 came from rents and tolls; the town clerk was paid £50; and the only large item of expenditure was the cost of police. It was the improvement commissioners, with special statutory powers (ch. 38), who had carried out recent alterations in Bedford, and they were not merged with the town council till 1860. All other towns (except in so far as their poor authority was the union of which they formed part) were simply administered by the churchwardens, overseers, surveyors and constables appointed at the Easter vestry meeting. The machinery of Luton (3,961) was on a par with that of Astwick (97), though no doubt more activity would be found in the vestry minutes of the former, had they survived. The central government had no plan for local government to match the great expansion on the way (expansion which, with our hindsight, is so clear to us). When faced with a new need, it either passed a special act giving the town council a new power (as for libraries), or it set up a new body – a local board of health could be set up on application to the central board of health, and there could be a burial board to arrange for cemeteries. (For other special bodies, see chs. 44 and 46).

---

[10] C.R.O., *ibid.*, p.24.   [11] Mrs. Grimmer.

Some steps, in fact the earliest ones, were taken by companies in which better-off inhabitants took shares, from which they hoped eventually to get dividends. For a tradesman or professional man to help plan a venture, either because it was for the good of the town, or because he was shrewd enough to realise that in time it would prove a worth-while investment, and to see it eventually become secure, must have been in its own way as rewarding as to launch a great enterprise today. Bedford Gas Company was formed in 1832.[12] It began with a capital of £6,000 (200 shares of £30 each). Among the shareholders were John Howard, ironmonger and industrialist, Alexander Sharman, attorney, Joseph Trapp, banker, and Isaac Hurst, surgeon; and 5 directors were appointed. A site was bought in a close between Well St. and Bromham Road, in what is now Greyfriars. Gas-lighting for the streets was welcomed, but at first many thought it dangerous to introduce gas into the home. To set an example, the chairman of the company installed a "gas-cooking apparatus" in his own house. By 1841 private consumption amounted to nearly £1,000. In 1864 it was necessary to transfer the works to a larger site in Ford End Road.

Luton's Gas Company was formed in 1834.[13] It aimed at a capital of £2,500 in £10 shares, and the promoters hoped to provide 40 street lamps. This company had among its early shareholders Edmund Waller, a straw-hat merchant, Benjamin Harrison, draper, Frederick Burr, brewer, and R. M. Brown, miller. It was some years before they were able to pay a dividend; and often the lights went out, especially, it is said, on Sunday evening. In fact, not till W. Phillips, a chemist on Market Hill, in 1843 gave up his business and became manager and secretary, with a salary on a sliding scale according to the amount of gas consumed, did the company really go ahead.

The other gas companies were on a smaller scale. Leighton's was formed in 1835 (gas cost 15s. per 1,000 ft.);[14] Dunstable followed in 1837; Ampthill and Woburn in 1850; and by the end of the period there were gas companies in Biggleswade and even in Kempston, Potton, Sandy and Shefford.[15] Sandy gas-works[16] were built by a local gentleman (A. W. Peel, son of Sir Robert Peel; he enlarged Sandy Lodge in 1870 from an existing house).[17] He erected 23 lamps in Sandy in 1862. The works occupied 24 p., and consisted of retort house, meter-house, sheds for coal, coke and lime, gas-holder, tar tanks, and a cottage for the man in charge. There were 57 customers. Eventually, in 1890, the works were taken over by a Sandy Gas Company.

The method of the company was also tried in connection with water supply. The installation of a supply of clean piped water was perhaps the most vital measure for an expanding Victorian town, and here it was that the greatest battle

---

[12] C.R.O., X 133/12–13.
[13] Dyer–Stygall–Dony, Luton, 128; Austin, Luton, ii, 132–4.
[14] R. Richmond, Leighton, 41.
[15] And actually one at Turvey; see 1894 directory.
[16] B. Mag. ix, 1.
[17] C.R.O., X 344/33–51.

raged. In Bedford an attempt was made in 1859 to form a water company, and plans for waterworks were prepared; but a storm of opposition arose, and the project hung fire.[18] Then there was an outbreak of typhoid. The Privy Council called for a special report, which showed that there were in the town 3,000 cesspools and that the wells were usually near them.[19] The London *Times* commented: "It is the autumnal habit in this town to suffer from typhoid fever."[20] Then the town council took up the matter. The mayor was the industrialist, John Howard, now retired; and his son James proposed that a deputation be sent to investigate Leicester's methods. "Who is to pay?" angrily demanded the opposition.[21] But the reformers had their way; they took over the plans prepared for the abortive water company, and erected waterworks in the Clapham road in 1866; while in 1864 they put main drainage in hand.

At Luton, however, the water company succeeded, but not without difficulty. In 1860 a petition against the project was signed by 1,600 ratepayers. In 1861 a public meeting was held, with J. S. Crawley in the chair, and leading townsmen like James Waller, F. W. Vyse and T. E. Austin on the platform; Robert How, a straw hat manufacturer, supported the new proposals; but a resolution was passed that the waterworks were not needed.[22] Eventually in 1865 the water company was successfully formed; a reservoir was made on Hart Hill; mains were laid by 1870; and public baths were built in Waller St. in 1872.[23]

Some other services were produced by the method of the company, for instance cemeteries; Luton Cemetery Company, 1854, issued £2 shares. (Bedford cemetery, 1855, was provided by a burial board; and so was Dunstable's in 1863, and Leighton's in 1882.) A company was formed to build a corn exchange on St. Paul's square, Bedford, in 1849; its opening was celebrated with a dinner at the Swan, when a Lidlington farmer, J. Thomas, proposed "prosperity to the elegant, useful and ornamental building".[24] This building soon proved inadequate, and the present corn exchange took its place in 1874,[25] the year of the Royal show at Bedford, and unfortunately at a time when the agricultural depression was about to set in. The company method was also used for some town halls – meaning by town hall a place for public assembly: Luton town hall, built by a small company, was opened in 1847.

Another possible agency was the local board of health. The government,

[18] At a meeting of Bedford town council on 14 Dec. 1859 Col. Mellor's resolution that "a public water company for the town of Bedford appears to be of very doubtful advantage, and this council decline to give their assent" was carried unanimously; and at a meeting of the improvement commissioners the same day, Mr. Shelton believed that no sane man would enter into such a speculation – there would be so few to take water that it would never pay, and the company would soon become bankrupt, and "sarve 'em right"; *Beds.*

Mercury.

[19] *Letter from Privy Council to Town Council,* 1860 (printed).

[20] Cited *Beds. Mercury,* 24 June 1861.

[21] *Beds. Mercury,* 18 Feb. and 23 Sept.; Coombs, *op.cit.,* 18.

[22] *Beds. Mercury,* 9 Nov. 1861.

[23] Dyer–Stygall–Dony, *op.cit.,* 128; Austin, *op.cit.,* ii, 181, 184, 189.

[24] *Bedford town and townsmen,* 71, 73.

[25] *Op.cit.,* 129.

alarmed by cholera scares, set up a central board of health, which could create local boards on petition by the inhabitants. An existing town council could obtain the powers of a board of health, and this Bedford did in 1862. In Luton, which had as yet no town council, some forward-looking inhabitants sent up a petition in 1850, with the minimum of publicity. Nevertheless, since it was known that the matter was being discussed, a public meeting was held, with Frederick Chase in the chair, and a resolution was passed that such a board was unnecessary. However, the reformers had got in first; a board was set up; George Bailey became its clerk, and John Cumberland its surveyor. This board instituted a sewerage scheme for Luton, with sewage works off Windmill Road; in 1886 the works were removed to a new site and extended, and new pumping plant was installed.[26]

Luton's board of health did not stop at this. It created better market facilities. In 1868 the dilapidated old market-hall was pulled down; the Middle Row on Market Hill cleared; and a corn exchange built in 1869. Till this time straw-plait had been sold on boards and trestles in George St. in the open air; but in 1869 plait-halls were erected in Cheapside and Waller St.; they were opened by the Lord Lieutenant, Earl Cowper of Wrest, after which there was a banquet, and the manufacturers treated 1,200 women hat-workers to tea in the corn exchange. Unfortunately, like the Bedford corn exchange, they were built at the wrong time, for the plait trade was shortly to decline (see below). Live stock were still sold on the verges of Park St. till 1882, when a cattle market was opened off Castle St.

However, though local boards of health temporarily served a useful purpose, the long-term future in municipal government was to be with the town council. Incidentally it is worth noting here how salutary was the wider range of opinion now that nonconformists were free to take part in local affairs. James Howard, the protagonist of clean water and of drainage in Bedford, was a Methodist. He, by the way, was mayor 1863–4, when Garibaldi visited the Britannia Iron-works to see steam ploughing, and planted a tree there. There were also mayors who were members of Bunyan Meeting, like the physician James Coombs (1871, 1889, 1891) and the timber merchant, J. T. Hobson (1875–6, 1880). Bedford town council missed the chance to set up a public library, thinking existing facilities adequate; but it completed the clearance of St. Paul's square. It had an eye to gardens and parks[27] – it bought the land on which the park was laid out, which was opened in 1888; and began to open up the river embankment; in this it was led by Joshua Hawkins (mayor 5 times between 1883 and 1899), a newcomer who had developed the Lansdowne Road area and had urged the building of Prebend St. bridge. The town clerk all through this period was a Pearse: Theed Pearse the younger, 1816–54; and Theed William Pearse, 1854–90. The rates by

[26] Dyer–Stygall–Dony, 127; Austin, ii, 203.
[27] *Bedford town and townsmen*, 145; Coombs, 26.

See also *Beds. Times* for 30 Ap. 1892 (obituary of Joshua Hawkins).

1880 produced nearly £4,000, and salaries had risen to £700. Municipal offices were established in 1891 in St. Paul's square, in the former premises of the Grammar School (on the school's removal).

By this time Luton and Dunstable also had acquired town councils. A very odd point in Bedfordshire history is that Dunstable was incorporated in 1864 at a time when its development, which for centuries had been slow, was arrested. Because of the cessation of coaching traffic and the decline of its trade in high quality hats, it was at this time smaller than Leighton or Biggleswade, and about a quarter the size of Luton. Rules governing the formation of boroughs and county boroughs were not then as explicit as they are today; Dunstable applied for a charter of incorporation and obtained it.

It was not till 1876 that Luton got its charter. Agitation came to a head in 1874, when the company which owned the town hall wanted to sell it, and the board of health at first refused to buy it. Pressed by the ratepayers, the church-wardens and overseers called a public meeting to consider applying for a charter. Some deprecated the move; they said that, though Lutonians were "most industrious and worthy . . . from exuberance of spirits [they were] not so amenable to control as persons living at Bedford".[28] The majority were in favour, the charter was obtained, and George Bailey, clerk to the board of health, became first town clerk. There were 3 wards, each represented by 6 councillors, and there were 6 aldermen. The first mayor was William Bigg, who had been concerned both with water and gas schemes, and had now retired from being a bank manager. He was followed by John Cumberland, who had been surveyor to the board of health. Thereafter the mayors were mostly straw-hat manufacturers, except for Henry Wright, 1883, the proprietor of a private school, who had helped the agricultural workers with their union (ch. 41).

Before long Luton's hamlets were detached, and in 1894 they were formed into a civil parish as Luton rural; in the next year they became the parishes of Hyde, Leagrave, Limbury and Stopsley.[29]

There was still one more method by which services or amenities were provided in Victorian towns; and that was by voluntary effort, often with the assistance of a noble patron. Fire brigades were still voluntary, though fire damage could be severe – a fire at Dunstable in 1841 destroyed 19 houses.[30] Luton's fire brigade was formed in 1844, and later taken over by the board of health. The arrival of the fire engine at Houghton Conquest in 1849 was celebrated in verse:

The fire engine came with speed from Ampthill to their aid,

Which threw a watery stream in need, and soon the flames it laid.

Thus God did bless the means they used to quench the flaming fire,

And though their minds were much confused, they trembling did admire.[31]

[28] *Report on Luton*, p.21.
[29] All but Hyde have since been reabsorbed.
[30] Worthington Smith, *Dunstable*, 185.
[31] C.R.O., P 11/28/6.

The rules for Leighton brigade in 1857 cautioned members to avoid letting water from their hose-pipes fall on spectators; Leighton's brigade was partly paid.[32] The rules for the Biggleswade brigade about 1875 laid down charges for its services at the rate of 3 guineas per engine, and 1s. per hour for each member of the brigade; there was also a fine of 6d. for members who missed the monthly drill for testing the engines.[33] Bedford volunteer fire brigade, to cover all five parishes, was formed in 1869; their annual dinner in 1885 had a sumptuous menu, including salmon, oyster patties, truffles, turkeys and ptarmigan;[34] the Duke gave them a new steam fire-engine in 1887.[35]

Voluntary effort also provided funds for a hospital at Luton; there were concerts, fetes and garden parties; the first step was a cottage hospital in High Town road, converted from two houses in 1872. The Bute trustees gave a site in the Dunstable road. Then in Whitweek 1882 a bazaar in the plait-halls raised £1,400; and the hospital was built.[36] Statues of famous men were beginning to be thought civic additions, and the Duke of Bedford presented Bedford with a statue of John Bunyan in 1874.[37] Public subscriptions built Bedford suspension bridge in 1888 and helped with the park, which was opened in the same year.

At the same time, facilities for reading improved. At Bedford the General Library, which in 1836 had moved into part of the Bedford Rooms, was of limited membership; but a Working Men's Institute, which later had newspapers and a library of 2,000 volumes, was opened in 1856 by the Duchess of Bedford, with a brass band in attendance.[38] These Institutes were a feature of the time; Luton had one as early as 1845 – membership cost 2s. 6d. a quarter; Biggleswade by 1851; and Woburn about the same time. At Luton a free library was established in 1883, and ten years later the corporation adopted the public libraries act and took it over.

INDUSTRY

Thus by one method or another, by the end of this period many characteristics of town life as we know it today had come into being. How was it that, in spite of the gloomy forebodings of early Victorians, there were the resources to finance them? Though the forces of expansion were not so clear to contemporaries as to us looking back, the wealth of towns was rapidly growing.

A guide to this is the multiplication of banks. They are too many to note them all individually, for small banks proliferated, till experience showed that there could be safety only in larger units. Private banks continued. Barnard's bank at Bedford was housed in a new building at the foot of the bridge, and Thomas Barnard went to live at Cople House. At Leighton John Dollin Bassett

---

[32] *B. Mag.* x, 333.
[33] C.R.O., X 276.
[34] C.R.O., X 67/250.
[35] Coombs, *op.cit.*, 43. Some large villages also had fire engines. Eaton Socon in the days of its coaching prosperity in 1831 collected £191 for a new engine in light blue, picked out with vermilion, with

"Eaton Socon 1831" written on it in gold. There was an allowance of £10 for the old engine. C.R.O., P 5/28/9.
[36] Austin, *Luton*, ii, 197.
[37] *Bedford town and townsmen*, 129.
[38] *Op.cit.*, 85, 89.

built a private residence, the Cedars, in 1855, and a new building for his bank in 1866. There were a number of other banks, both local ones as at Biggleswade, and in the south that of Sharples & Co., mainly based on Hertfordshire. One of the growing national banks, the London and County, had 5 branches in the county in 1864.

Brewing was one of the first industries to increase its scale. Purchase or amalgamation resulted in fewer and larger units. At Bedford Sir William Long died in 1841; his brewery went in 1873 to Jarvis (and eventually in 1910 to Charles Wells); while Newland took over Nash; there were 9 maltsters in 1864. At Luton, where in 1864 there was only one maltster, the chief brewery early in the period was that of Thomas Sworder, but future development was to be with J. W. Green (1869). At Biggleswade Wells, Hogge and Lindsell (also bankers), were later to become Wells & Co and subsequently Wells and Winch. Breweries which for their day were on a fairly large scale, but which were eliminated in the growing concentration, included that of John Morris at Ampthill, and that of the Burr family at Dunstable.

The first steps towards engineering were naturally first taken in an agricultural area by small foundries producing agricultural implements. In the small towns some such undertakings continued through most of this period. In the 1860's there were T. B. Kitchener at Potton; Morton & Kinman at Biggleswade; W. Goss at Shefford; W. Whitehouse at Ampthill: George Brown at Leighton; and W. Hensman at Woburn. At Bedford the Victoria Ironworks in Mill Street was built by E. Page (later a builder's merchant). But the biggest venture was the Britannia Ironworks built in 1859 in Bedford by John Howard's sons, James and Frederick. In 1874 these works were described as vast, and occupying 15 a.; "thousands of tons of iron are here worked up in the course of the year . . . into implements and engines of many different patterns, suited to different soils, climates, and means and habits of working".[39]

At Luton engineering took a different line. Brown and Green's foundry, set up in 1840, concentrated on kitchen-ranges and stoves, and they also made gates, fences, pipes and castings of every description. Hayward-Tyler, an old firm, opened a new factory in 1871, and worked in brass as well as iron; they made soda-water machinery, and later hydraulic pumps. T. Balmforth made boilers.

In the smaller towns, however, no big firm developed, in this or other fields. An example of their small-scale undertakings is that of a herb farm for herbs like peppermint, lavender and henbane, from which oils were distilled in a drug mill; this was in Church St., Ampthill; it was begun by Charles May and later (1857) carried on by George Allen.[40] The enterprise which in the 1880's showed most promise was the Ivel Cycle Works established at Biggleswade by the racing cyclist, Dan Albone, who produced a tandem in 1886 and a woman's bicycle

---

[39] *Illustrated London News* for 11 July.   [40] *B. Mag.* i, 115.

in 1887;[41] but Albone aimed at quality rather than quantity.

This then was the main background of town development, but Bedford and Luton, the two main towns, had each a special feature.

THE HAT INDUSTRY

At Luton the hat industry was the most important.[42] London firms such as Vyse opened branches in Luton (and sometimes Dunstable also, which in the early part of this period still had a reputation for making better quality hats). An association of straw-hat manufacturers and plait-dealers was formed in 1852.[43] Hat-blocks were made by skilled wood-workers; the 1864 directory gives 8 block-making firms at Luton (and one at Dunstable). Most blocking was still done by hand in small firms, though by 1860 blocking machines were used by some bigger firms. The sewing was done by women, who could do this by hand better than the earliest machines could; but by 1874 it was possible to do the work by machine, and this technique was gradually improved. The colour range was extended; the old dyes from wood and vegetables were black, brown and blue; but Thomas Lye, who in 1857 set up in business in Luton, developed aniline dyes. About 1870 a new source of cheap plait was found in the Far East. The new machines and the cheap plait so much reduced production costs that Luton, with its inexpensive hats, could cater for the expanding Victorian home market and even develop an export trade (while Dunstable's small higher-quality production declined after the removal of tariffs in 1842). The working season was mainly from February to May, when all available workers were mustered, and work continued till late in the night and all night on Friday till 1 p.m. on Saturday. The export trade helped to relieve the dull period; and so did the making of felt hats, introduced by the Carruthers brothers from Scotland in 1877. Engineering and the hat industry between them occupied nearly all Luton's energies.

HARPUR TRUST SCHOOLS

It was the Harpur Trust Schools that constituted the special feature in Bedford's development – that is to say, the Grammar School in its cramped old premises, and the Commercial School, soon to be known as the Modern School, in new premises in Harpur St. In the early 19th cent. they had begun to attract a residential population.

Then for twenty years there was a setback. The Trust, whose other commitments had expanded, economised by restricting the Grammar School.[44] Bedford's development was checked at the very time when, both in and outside Bedford, the demand for grammar school education was growing. There was a new

---

[41] B. Mag. iv, 135.
[42] Dyer–Stygall–Dony, Luton, 120, 142–8; Dony, Straw hat industry, 53–84.
[43] Austin, Luton, ii, 158.
[44] Farrar, Harper's Bedford Charity, 45. By the 1853 scheme the master's salary was £250, with a

capitation grant up to 167 boys, and under Brereton's successor the salary was to be £300, with a capitation grant up to 140 boys. Boarders were limited to 70. Fees were nominal or none. The 1873 scheme imposed fees, but they were low.

conception of what it meant to be a gentleman; a gentleman needed education; if so, then someone who had such education was likely to be a gentleman, whether or not he was of long family descent. So to meet the thwarted Bedfordshire demand there was formed a middle-class public school company, which built at Elstow a county school.

Nationally the movement had wider consequences; a royal commission enquired into foundations like Bedford, and in 1869 the endowed schools act was passed. The Harpur Trust was obliged to adopt a new scheme in 1873; the schools were not to be restricted to Bedford children; there were to be low fees for all; and boarders were allowed. Local feeling was adverse; George Hurst, the draper, said that it was "plundering that which was intended for the necessities of the poor, and giving it to the more wealthy".[45] But the schools were set free to develop.

A notable headmaster, J. S. Phillpotts, came to the Grammar School in 1874; it moved to new premises on its present site in 1891; and when the *Public Schools Yearbook* appeared for the first time in 1889, listing 30 schools, Bedford was among them. From 1877 there was a notable headmaster at the Modern School (R. B. Poole). From 1882 there were opportunities for girls (Bedford High School and the Girls' Modern School at first were in a single building, till the latter moved to St. Paul's square in 1892). So again there was a residential influx from men returning to England from overseas service, with families to educate. A generation later, in 1913, one such wrote: "The society in Bedford is just what Anglo-Indians have been accustomed to . . . In many places . . . the retired officer [finds] no companionship to his taste during the greater part of the day, but this is not the case at Bedford."[46]

The residential population which came for Bedford's schools needed goods and services. It is perhaps partly on their account that we find in Bedford in 1864 16 cabinet-makers, while at Luton there were only 4; and 5 sellers of musical instruments, while at Luton there was one; this tendency was strengthened after 1873. Partly also this difference is due to the greater number of people who resorted to Bedford for various county purposes, and the large area served by its market and shops. Yet all these factors, added to its brewing and its ironworks, were not enough to enable its size to keep ahead of Luton.

POPULATION

Population figures reflect these developments, and reflect also the inrush from the over-populated villages. In every decade from 1831 to 1881 Bedford's population grew by about 20%; and between 1881 and 1891 it grew by 50% to 28,023. Far greater was Luton's development; between 1831 and 1861 it quadrupled (3,961 to 15,329); between 1881 and 1891 it doubled to 30,053. Thus it had overtaken Bedford. By comparison Ampthill and Leighton grew only slowly,

[45] *Bedford town and townsmen*, 120.   [46] C. J. Maltby, in *Bedford town and schools*.

though steadily. Dunstable between 1861 and 1891 remained practically stationary (4,465 to 4,513), having lost the coaching traffic and having little to replace it, while its hat production was dwindling (see above). Woburn declined with declining road traffic. On the other hand, the railway greatly helped east Bedfordshire; a new urban area emerged in Sandy, the market-gardening centre, which between 1831 and 1891 grew by 58% to 2,755; and Biggleswade, though it had lost the coaching traffic, held its own, and with a population of 4,943 in 1891 was bigger than Dunstable.

URBAN DISTRICTS

The market towns remained small. Leighton's long connection with St. George's chapel, Windsor, was severed when the manor was sold in 1863. Leighton had a few plait-dealers, a few basket-makers and watchmakers, and a few sand merchants; some sportsmen kept horses there and came down from London to hunt with the Whaddon Chase, as Trollope did in 1873;[47] but in the main it remained a market centre for the villages around. At Ampthill the great house was at first let by the Duke of Bedford to tenants. In 1884 Lady Ampthill came to live there; she was widow of Lord Odo Russell, who was ambassador to Berlin 1871–84, and was created Lord Ampthill in recognition of his important diplomatic work. (He was brother to the 9th Duke.) These towns continued with their parochial machinery, and the bigger ones began to need other powers. The government was still fumbling towards a new conception of local administration, which gradually emerged. Poor law unions were made rural sanitary authorities in 1875. A little later urban districts were separated from their surrounding villages; Ampthill, Biggleswade and Leighton became urban districts in 1891 and Kempston followed in 1895 (Sandy not till 1926).

POLITICS

Till 1885 Bedford returned two members to parliament, and usually one was liberal and one conservative. Representation still normally went to a member of a county family. For nearly all this period the liberal was a Whitbread, at first W. H. Whitbread, then Samuel Whitbread; the conservative was at first Frederick Polhill, then Henry and later William Stuart. Many more urban workers were enfranchised by Disraeli's reform of 1867. Bedford, like many places elsewhere, had formed a branch of the short-lived Reform League. In 1868, for the first time for many years a townsman (the industrialist, James Howard) was returned as co-member with Samuel Whitbread; and the Reform League celebrated electoral victory with a public banquet.[48]

As late as the 1880's the rival candidates concurred to fix a time to begin the campaign. "I well remember" wrote J. W. D. Harrison, "seeing Mr. Guy Pym on the east side of the High Street and Mr. Whitbread on the west, each

[47] A. Trollope, *Autobiography*, ch. 19; also *The way we live now*. [48] *Bedford town and townsmen*, 112–4.

attended by a little group of agents and prominent supporters, starting their personal canvass."[49] When polling-day arrived, the rival candidates marched in procession, each arm-in-arm with his proposer and seconder, and followed by his supporters with flags and banners, all wearing rosettes or streamers in his colours, from their respective headquarters at the Swan and the George, to the hustings on St. Peter's green.[50] At the poll there was often roughness or violence, and in 1851 George Hurst, a town councillor, was knocked down by Polhill's horse when Polhill was jostled by the crowd.[51] It was the introduction of the ballot in 1872 which did much to keep election tempers cool.

Whitbread was more than once offered office, but always refused. When pressed by Gladstone in 1882 to become a Privy Councillor, he replied that, though it was painful to refuse Gladstone, "it seems to me that an independent member, especially in times of political difficulty, has less chance of being useful if he is seen to be accepting for himself marks of distinction which fall quite naturally and properly to those who have borne the burthen of official life".[52] Individual Victorian members of parliament enjoyed a liberty of action much greater than that of their modern counterparts.

Both liberals and conservatives built substantial club premises in Bedford, in Midland Road and St. Peter's Street respectively; there was a Luton liberal club in Bute Street[53] "to provide for the social, moral and intellectual improvement of its members", and a South Beds. conservative club on Market Hill, Luton (this was opened with a dinner at the Plait Hall in 1883, J. S. Crawley being in the chair);[54] and there were other political clubs at Dunstable, Leighton and Sandy.

From 1884 Bedford had one member only. On a numerical basis it was still over-represented as opposed to the county, which had two members for a population four times as large. But in point of fact it continued to return the county figure Samuel Whitbread for the remainder of his parliamentary career.

VIOLENCE AND POVERTY

Though Bedford and Luton were growing in wealth as a whole, there was poverty among their inhabitants. In 1842 1,000 blankets were distributed to the poor in Luton to mark the birth of the Prince of Wales.[55] Things were worst in Luton each year during the dull season of the hat trade; in November 1890 at Hitchin Road school many children had such old boots that their stockings were wet to the ankle, and in December the mayor's wife provided hot dinners twice a week; sometimes the mayor gave schoolchildren free breakfasts.

There were also violence and coarseness. In Luton in 1854, in a time of

[49] *Echoes of old times*, 16. For Victorian elections in general, see Trollope's *Autobiography*, ch. 16; and his political novels, especially *Ralph the Heir*, ch. 29, *Phineas Redux*, ch. 4, and *The Duke's Children*, ch. 14. But in Bedford the candidates were almost always known county figures.

[50] Coombs, *op.cit.*, 11.
[51] *Bedford town and townsmen*, 77.
[52] C.R.O., W 1/6436.
[53] C.R.O., X 95/379.
[54] C.R.O., LL 17/319.
[55] F. Davis, *Luton*, 179.

unemployment owing to war, and again during the hat industry's dull season; there were riots for no apparent reason other than a mistake about a meeting; the mob smashed the windows of one firm of straw-hat manufacturers after another – Munt & Brown in George St.; Gregory, Cubitt & Co. in Bute St., Webster & Grundy in Wellington St.; and even of private houses, and of Mr. Everitt's conservatory in the Bedford road.[56] In 1868 on 5 November some people in high spirits set fire to a temporary wooden shanty which had been put up on Market Hill pending the erection of the corn exchange.

In Bedford in 1859 there was a free fight on St. Peter's green between the boys of the Grammar and Commercial schools over the use of a playground.[57] Executions still took place in public.[58] One in 1860 was of a Luton man, Joseph Castle, who had cut his wife's throat and thrown her body over a hedge. On the day of his execution, the streets began to fill from early morning – it is said there were 15,000 spectators; he was hanged at noon in heavy rain; and the body was not cut down till one. The last public execution in 1868 was again of a Luton man, William Worsley. Both Castle and Worsley were commemorated by lace bobbins, as was Sarah Dazeley of Wrestlingworth, hanged in 1843.[59]

At Luton the large number of inns had no good effect. In 1870 there were 226 inns, estimated at one to every 48 persons over the age of 13. When some licences were withdrawn, the number of commitments to gaol fell between 1869 and 1871 from 257 to 73.[60]

THREE TOWN HISTORIANS

Charles Farrar was born in 1860, the grandson of the Bedford industrialist, John Howard. He has described his childhood at Cauldwell House, where he played with his Noah's ark and with his brother George (who later went to South Africa), and did his Greek and Latin prose, and listened to family prayers (Monday for missions); and whence he accompanied his grandfather, a lay preacher, to Methodist services in the villages (on one occasion at Radwell on a very hot summer afternoon, a member of the congregation removed coat, waistcoat and shoes). When he grew up, the future of the County School at Elstow was in doubt, because the situation which brought it into being had changed; and friends and relations bought it for him as a wedding-present; he ran it as a private school till 1916, when it came to an end. His boys had a great loyalty to it; for long they kept up the Elstonian Association. *Old Bedford* was published in 1926. Farrar sensed the fact that history is about people; the documentary evidence we now have was not available to him; and so, when he felt restricted, he gave rein to his fancy. Today this method is not acceptable; but in his own day he gave a new awareness to history to many people. He could also write serious

[56] Austin, *Luton*, ii, 159.
[57] *B. Mag.* ix, 179, 245.
[58] *Bedford town and townsmen*, 91, 113.
[59] T. Wright, *Romance of the lace pillow*, ii, 167; Farrar, *Old Bedford*, 254.
[60] Austin, *Luton*, ii, 185.

history, as he did of the Harpur Trust.

William Austin of Luton, born in 1850, was the son of T. E. Austin, clerk to the guardians, and related to Charles Austin. He attended the school kept by Henry Wright (see earlier), and in due course succeeded his father, and also became clerk to the justices and steward of the manor. In a long life he knew from the inside much of Luton's development. Active and energetic, his practice as a solicitor prospered. In his house in Cromwell Hill was a hall for dances, and nearby were croquet and tennis lawns. Family prayers were said, and on Sunday morning immaculately dressed, he walked to Christ Church with his wife and daughters, and then in People's Park. A favourite maximum was "if a thing is worth doing at all, it is worth doing well". On summer evenings the family cycled in the country. In their household was a house-boy, taken as an orphan from the workhouse; the maids were considered, and the little girls were taught to help them. He took and developed photographs and played golf. He wrote the history of the Crawleys and of Luton freemasonry. When he got older, he at first hired a landau; then in 1913 bought a car and employed a chauffer-gardener. At the age of 70 he thought of learning to drive, but decided that he was a menace on the roads. At the age of 78 he was still working, but one June morning while taking a photograph on Blow Downs on the way to the court at Dunstable he had a heart attack. His history of Luton was published posthumously in 1928.[61]

Worthington Smith (1835–1917)[62] came to live in Dunstable in middle life. He was originally trained as an architect, but became known for his book illustrations on botanical subjects, and his *Outlines of British Fungi*, and *Man the primeval savage*. At his house, 121 High Street South, all interested in archaeology were welcomed, from the hungry schoolboy who was given a sumptuous tea, and the brickmakers from Caddington who came to show their finds, to scholars with a national reputation. His history of Dunstable was published in 1904.

---

[61] Information kindly supplied by Mrs. Milner.   [62] *B. Mag.* iii, 341; xi, 73.

FOR THE churches this was a time of expansion, both because of the growing population, and because all denominations had a sense of purpose and took a wide view of their responsibilities.

In the Anglican church one outward and visible sign was the creation of new parishes (by stages, after a period as "district"). In Bedford there emerged Holy Trinity, St. Leonard and St. Martin; in Luton, Christ Church, St. Matthew, St. Paul and St. Saviour. The hamlets of Leighton and some of the Luton hamlets became parishes. Mogerhanger (formerly hamlet of Blunham) had a church built; and at Silsoe (chapelry of Flitton) the future Earl de Grey and his daughters flattered themselves that their church, rebuilt in 1831, was a perfect model; their own pew was lined with blue cloth, the Grey colour, with blue Bibles and prayerbooks to match. (Incidentally they distributed Bibles and prayerbooks to the poor of the village also.)[1] Some older churches that were too small or in bad repair were rebuilt, such as St. Cuthbert in Bedford near the beginning of the period, and Cardington near the end; while at Woburn an impressive new one on a new site was designed by the architect Clutton. All churches were vigilantly inspected by Archdeacon H. K. Bonney, who kept careful notes of the directions he had given, so that at the next visit he could check that they had been carried out.[2] Thus at Sundon in 1823 he directed that the seats within the communion rails be removed, the communion table be placed against the wall, there be a new door to the chancel, the south porch be rebuilt, and the earth taken from the walls on all sides.

Among the Anglican clergy a new spirit gained ground, with a greater emphasis on the sacraments, and on colour and symbolism in the services. We can follow it closely at Souldrop,[3] where G. D. Newbolt was rector 1856-95, and it may be noted incidentally that a relative of his was a friend of Charlotte Yonge. In this small parish he usually prepared 6 young people annually for confirmation. He gradually increased the number of celebrations of Holy Communion, till by 1869 it was weekly. In 1870 he introduced the 3-hour service on Good Friday. Gifts to the church, often by his friends and relatives, included in 1861 an altar-cloth and alms-bags of crimson velvet, white and violet bookmarks, new plate and much new furniture; in 1865 there was a green silk frontal for the altar; in 1868, red, green and violet stoles; and in 1870 the choir acquired cassocks

---

[1] C.R.O., L 30/11/241.
[2] C.R.O., ABV 28.

[3] B.H.R.S. xl, 200-25.

and surplices, the men black, the boys violet. He introduced a parish guild, which was rather like a revival of the old medieval religious guild or fraternity; members undertook to pray and attend church regularly, and to try to do some work for God.

Most characteristic was his introduction of a religious harvest festival to counteract the drunkenness common at harvest time. He was not alone in this; a printed pamphlet at Eaton Socon in 1848 urged men to be thankful and not to make themselves "more stupid and senseless than the dumb animals". However, in 1859 his celebration was so striking that it was reported in the local press. Over the church gateway was an arch, with white lettering on red "Let us give thanks"! and in the church was a red and blue spiral scroll "Thou crownest the year". Round the windows were neat and elegant laurels; the nave was decorated with geraniums and asters; over the chancel arch were purple and white asters; and behind the altar a cross of dark red dahlias, surrounded by purple asters and yellow marigolds, the work of tasteful young ladies. At 1.30 the procession assembled, headed by a band from Bedford, a wheatsheaf on a pole, and a banner "Souldrop harvest home"; each farmer walked with his men, all wearing coloured favours with an ear or two of corn, while other villagers followed behind. The church was quite full. After service, the procession, again with band playing, walked to the rectory close, where, in a tent made with rickcloths, there was served cold meat, 20 plum puddings, and a limited quantity of beer. Later there were races, cricket and dancing; then, as dusk fell, fireworks; and finally God Save the Queen. (The Bedford Arms public-house by special arrangement closed at 8 p.m. that day.)

At the same time that Newbolt was trying to bring his parishioners to a new spiritual awareness, he tried to help with their material problems. He reorganised the clothing club, into which each subscriber put 1d. weekly, and himself doubled members' contributions at the end of the year. He also let part of his own land as allotments.

That something of a new spirit pervaded the diocese as a whole is shown by reports of diocesan conferences. Incidentally, it had now been found impossible, with increase of population, to work effectively the great area of the old Lincoln diocese, and in 1837 the archdeaconry of Bedford was transferred to the diocese of Ely. The Ely diocesan conference of 1867 has a curiously modern ring. It was the fourth of its kind. On the first day clergy met, mainly archdeacons and rural deans; and on the second day there was a lay representative from each deanery; the Bedfordshire ones included St. Andrew St. John, Charles Longuet Higgins of Turvey, Colonel Stuart of Tempsford, John Harvey of Ickwell, Joseph Tucker of Pavenham, Captain Pollhill Turner of Howbury, and Lionel Ames of Luton. One subject discussed was family prayer; it was thought there was need for a form of prayer and a lectionary for such churchmen "as might not have much leisure at their disposal"; members were to send suggestions to Archdeacon Rose at Houghton Conquest. It was thought also that cottagers might like framed prayers with illuminated borders. The conference was concerned about education (still not thought of as a government responsibility); there were a number of youths requiring better education than the National [i.e., Anglican] schools could provide, and some parents would be willing to pay modest fees for a boarding school; could there be a large central diocesan school? But since at this time in Bedfordshire plans were going ahead for a County School run by a company, a diocesan grammar school seemed impracticable. Other social matters considered included the religious needs of gangs, (such as those working on railway construction); and the need to improve rural housing; the conference felt that this last had important moral and religious bearings, but did not quite see how to act; members thought that the government ought to make loans, as for needful public works. There was discussion on the introduction of weekly offertories; most thought this desirable and practicable; the Bishop advised going cautiously, and getting goodwill first; it was important not so much for gain, as for teaching to give by way of privilege. With regard to metrical psalms and hymns, the deaneries were recommended to consider whether greater uniformity in practice could be introduced. This latter question soon solved itself, for *Hymns Ancient and Modern*, published in 1861, became almost universal. Incidentally, organs were ousting the old village orchestras; H. E. Havergal, vicar of Cople and member of a noted musical family, built his own organ.

There were both some gentle and vivid personalities in the Anglican church, clerical and lay. Archdeacon H. J. Rose, rector of Houghton Conquest 1837–73, found on his arrival that in his church part of the East window and the chancel arch were blocked up, and he restored the church largely at his own expense; his brother-in-law, Dean Burgon, said of him that in his rectory there was unfailing loving-kindness, unbroken peace and joy. Augustus Orlebar, for 54 years vicar of Willington, was at Rugby under Dr. Arnold, and it was his fight with a boy who was later another distinguished cleric which figures in *Tom Brown's Schooldays* as Brown's fight with Slogger Williams. The layman C. L. Higgins (d. 1885) of Turvey abbey, restored Turvey church, was an early visitor to Palestine, built a working-men's room for the railway navvies, and ran an annual choral festival.[4] John Linnell, vicar of Pavenham 1882–1919, preached in a Geneva gown, welcomed any denomination to the communion table, and carried the loads of all the marketing women he overtook; when attacked by thieves at night on Oakley hill he fought them to a standstill, and then made them kneel in the road and say the Lord's prayer.[5]

---

[4] *B. Mag.* v, 213. Another religious layman was J. H. Brooks of Flitwick; see his diaries in C.R.O., for instance LL 17/283, 1 Jan. 1856.

[5] J. Linnell, *Old Oak*, has as preface a memoir written by his son.

The other denominations expanded also. At Shefford the tiny Roman Catholic chapel had an access of Irish members, probably due to the Irish influx for railway construction. In 1850 Bedfordshire was included in the newly-formed diocese of Northampton. In the Shefford register appear such names as Peter McShane, who died in Bedford infirmary in 1857, and Patrick Walsh of Bedford in the same year. The main growth at Shefford dates from 1868 when Canon William Collis opened a diocesan orphanage for 67 boys; it was dedicated to St. Francis of Assisi; and a new church of St. Francis was opened in 1884. Gradually development began elsewhere. Bedford was the next place; mass was said in 1863 in a washhouse near the prison by Father Warmoll, who lived in a single room in Offa Street and had about 20 church members; then in 1865 a site was bought in Brereton Rd.; at first there was a small chapel; then the present church was built 1874–1912. At Luton a mission in 1845 was evanescent; then in 1884 there was a resident priest; and an iron church was built in Castle St.

New Methodist circuits were formed; at the beginning of this period there were already Bedford, Luton and Biggleswade; Dunstable circuit was formed 1843 and Ampthill circuit 1875. Gradually little groups in the villages which had formerly met in private houses built themselves small chapels, which they later improved or enlarged. Thus Wilstead's first chapel was built largely by the farmer, William Armstrong, in 1808; and in 1841, a few years before his death, he laid the foundation stone of a bigger building. The larger Methodist churches, like the Anglican, discarded their orchestras for organs; Biggleswade acquired an organ in 1856; smaller ones had harmoniums. The Methodist church in Chapel Street, Luton, was rebuilt in 1852. Kempston West opened its new chapel in High Street in 1860.

The Methodists' widespread use of "local preachers"[6] was at the same time a sign of their strength and a source of it. A promising young man would be sent out with recognized local preachers, and after being heard at least four times might be promoted to this office. Thomas Twitchell, a Willington farmer, became one at the age of 20 in 1841; and John Howard, the Bedford industrialist, continued in old age. Local preachers for each circuit met together quarterly with their professional ministers – the average attendance was about 20 – and were concerned to maintain the standard of their work. At Bedford in 1831 Brother Ward was rebuked for taking a service in a hurried and improper manner, while in 1841 Brother Knight was requested to preach shorter sermons.[7] (The Anglican office of lay reader, initiated in 1866, was long in coming into general use.)

With both Methodists and Baptists, the impulse to diversify (an impulse which had been running in the churches for 200 years) was still in spate. The Primitive Methodists, who at first concentrated on whole-day meetings in the open air, and, being discouraged by the main body, organised themselves separ-

<hr>

[6] C.R.O. MB 9, pp.19, 83.   [7] C.R.O., X 347/3.

ately from 1811, established a number of churches, as at High Town, Luton, in 1838; Lidlington 1863, Girtford 1868, and also at Bedford and Dunstable. With the Baptists, the emphasis was on the degree of strictness to be observed; hence Strict and Particular Baptists, and Gospel Standard Baptists. Usually it was a stricter group which broke away from a parent church. Long ago Keysoe Row (1808) had broken away from Keysoe Brook End; Blunham suffered more than one secession, one of them to Sandy; at Cranfield a group seceded to form a second church in 1849; at Leighton a group seceded from Lake St. in 1833 and met in Thomas Matthews' granary, till they built a chapel in Hockliffe St. in 1847. Luton Park St. Baptists suffered more than one secession; but one of them in 1865 was a Congregational group which built a place of worship in King St. Incidentally, a noted Baptist minister was William Cuff, afterwards President of the Baptist Union in 1900; he enrolled 51 new members at Ridgmont in one year (1867).

To understand the impulse behind all this, we need to get away from lists of places and dates to see how it seemed to one man at the time. An example is John Corbitt, a Baptist minister who wrote his own life.[8] His father was a tenant farmer just over the Cambs. border, and he himself was a light-hearted young man. Once when gleaners intruded into his harvest field before it was fully cleared, while he was at work on the stack, he rode out to the field on a desperate kicking mare at full speed, cracking a whip and hallooing, and all the gleaners ran tumbling over each other into the ditch. However, after losing his young wife and two children, he began to reflect, and to discuss serious matters with all and sundry – he recalls the surprise of a minister to whom he gave a lift when he was driving to Potton market in his horse and gig. He married again, and began to wish he had a Baptist place of worship in his own village. The minister of the chapel where he attended "told me I had better ask my landlord's leave first, or else he might be offended". However, he did ask people to his house, and when his landlord sent for him he feared he would be given notice; but in fact this summons was on business only. Gradually he began to preach at Potton, Blunham, Biggleswade and elsewhere, but especially the last. "In going constantly to Biggleswade once a fortnight, I formed such a sweet union with the people that I can say I loved them as my own soul." He began to neglect his farming, forgot to take a corn sample to market, or forgot the price offered, till at last he moved to Biggleswade as minister. He describes his first baptism in the Ivel in 1845. He had obtained the squire's permission beforehand, and the squire himself attended in a boat, while a large crowd of people who had come out of curiosity listened quietly while he spoke.

This spirit is also found in the most unconventional figure of the time, Timothy Matthews. Originally an Anglican curate at Colmworth and Bolnhurst, he was a law to himself. He made a name in Bedford, where he was chaplain to

[8] *The lion slain.*

the House of Industry till 1832, and finally his supporters built a special church for him, called Christ Church[9] (not the present Anglican church). He would summon his congregation with a bugle or trumpet, and he had such a stentorian voice that people outside the church would stand listening. One "ungodly man", who was angry because his wife attended, fetched her out and "beat her with a great stick, running her up first one street and then another . . . She took it with the patience that must have its perfect work."[10]

The Congregational churches expanded less, but they grew in public esteem. The original church of Bunyan Meeting was rebuilt in 1849. Later, in 1876, the Duke of Bedford presented it with fine bronze doors. John Bunyan was now seen in historical perspective for the great figure that he was; not only was his statue erected (ch. 42), but his life was written by the meeting's most notable minister, John Brown, 1864–1903. This *Life* is still indispensable. Brown said afterwards "I have pored for hours over old letters and journals in the handwriting of the men of the 16th and 17th centuries till I seemed as if I knew these men almost as well as my own contemporaries"; and so indeed he did. He also laid the foundations of the Bunyan museum adjoining the church, and collected copies of the ever-increasing foreign translations of *The Pilgrim's Progress*. He refused an invitation to leave Bedford for Oxford. He was chairman of the Congregational Union of England and Wales in 1891. In politics he was an admirer of Gladstone. The life of the Brown family in the old manse in Dame Alice St. has been described by his daughter;[11] it had a big garden in which croquet was played. John Brown lived in retirement for some years, and one who heard him in 1919 at the City Temple wrote "What a picturesque figure he was as he stood there, his lovely English in his silvery voice entrancing the vast audience, and that too in his 89th year!"

Perhaps because of the strength of Methodists and Baptists, more Quaker (Society of Friends) meetings closed; Cranfield in 1849; Aspley Guise in 1873; and Ampthill in 1880; but Quakerism continued to be strong at Luton and Leighton Buzzard. The Moravians celebrated their centenary in Bedford in 1845 and opened their new church in 1865. For a time from 1862 there was a Unitarian group meeting in Bedford. Intermittently there was also in Bedford a small Jewish group, the leading families being those of Joseph and Lyon (the question of whether Sheba Lyon was to be allowed to attend a Harpur Trust school was a noted case in 1818; the Harpur Trust had allowed it, but the Lord Chancellor ruled against); and about 1853 there was a small synagogue.[12] There were, too, in Bedford in 1894 a Catholic Apostolic church, a Huntingdonian one, and also

---

9 A building in Bromham Rd., subsequently converted to lay purposes.

10 T. Wright, *Life*, 60.

11 F. A. Keynes, *Gathering up the threads*. John Brown was grandfather of J. M. Keynes.

12 C. Roth, *Rise of provincial Jewry*. The Ecclesiastical Census of 1851 says that there was a synagogue from 1803 to 1827; and that the existing congregation dated from 1837; there were 5 members, and they met in Offa St. for New Year, The Day of Atonement, and the Tabernacle.

the Salvation Army (also found in Luton). And at Thorncote and Biggleswade in 1850 there were small groups of Mormons or Latter-Day Saints. Matthews at one time allowed Mormon missionaries in his church at Bedford,[13] for he was connected with the Mormons by his marriage to a Fielding. His sister-in-law, Mary Fielding of Honeydon, emigrated in 1834, married Hyrum Smith, and after her husband was murdered trekked with her two small children to Salt Lake Valley in 1847.[14] All members emigrated to Utah, and so the Bedfordshire Mormon churches existed only a few years.

Though in many ways denominational feeling was still strong, there was also cooperation. The Bedford Sunday School Union formed in 1860 comprised all the dissenting churches. In the towns there was almost a family or paternal spirit with some of the large firms. At Bedford the industrial family of Howard was the mainstay of the Cauldwell St. Methodist church, and it was whispered (though it may have been a calumny) at the Britannia Ironworks that a regular attender there had a better chance of becoming a foreman than had a non-chapelgoer. Hayward-Tyler's at Luton provided a chapel on their premises, where daily services were alternately Anglican and Nonconformist, but attendance was not compulsory.

Especially was there cooperation (mainly Nonconformists but to some extent Anglican also) in the campaign against drunkenness. A Band of Hope appeared in Bedford in the 1850's, and soon there were a number of denominational Bands. A Band of Hope Union was formed in 1872. By 1890 there were over 100 Bands in this Union, including 9 in Luton and 4 in Dunstable, besides many villages and hamlets. Each Band had its coloured banner, and members who took the pledge to abstain from alcohol wore an enamel brooch in the shape of a bow of white ribbon. The first president of the Union was Joseph Tucker of Pavenham Bury, an almost fanatical teetotaller, who instituted at Pavenham a reading-room where a cup of tea or cocoa could be got for a penny. His attempts to ensure abstinence had a dubious effect, for it was said that workers on the Home Farm took their beer to the fields in teapots. (Incidentally, the solid food taken into the fields by the farm-worker was traditionally the clanger, a suet roll with bacon at one end, jam at the other.) The late C. D. Linnell said afterwards that he signed the pledge at the age of 7 because he got a slice of cake. One Pavenham man was said to have signed the pledge 19 times. Temperance literature, depicting the effects of "the demon drink", had the vogue of the modern thriller.[15] But probably improvements in education, housing and pay did as much as the temperance campaign to promote responsible living.

All denominations were concerned to help education. In fact, when in 1833 the government first voted an annual grant towards education (in 1833 it was

[13] B. Mag. xi, 43.
[14] B. Mag. v, 146.
[15] The writer remembers as a child being highly edified by the maid's temperance tracts, till forbidden to read them.

£20,000 for the whole country), there was so little support for a national educational policy that the grant was at first administered by the National Society (Anglican) and the British and Foreign (Nonconformist). In 1839 on Lord John Russell's initiative a committee was set up for the purpose.

By this time the Bedfordshire Institution, a lay Anglican organisation formed in 1815 for promoting schools (ch. 36), which still had its original secretary, John Gibbard, had lost momentum. Other dioceses were forming archdeaconry boards of education, and the archdeaconry of Bedford followed suit. John Gibbard was somewhat chagrined, though Archdeacon Bonney wrote a tactful letter referring to his kind and beneficial work in the past. The new Board, like the old Institution, cooperated with the National Society, and the promotion of new schools went ahead more actively. The main initial effort to set up a school was always a local one; there was usually a grant from the relevant religious society; and a grant from the government. The running of the school depended partly on local voluntary contributions; partly on the few pence paid weekly by children as school fees; and partly on a small annual capitation grant from the government.

In 1846 the National Society made a survey of all schools then existing. Among places which had only Sunday schools were Aspley Guise, Caddington, Marston and Wootton; and also Gt. Barford, where "the people are miserably poor and there are no resident gentry". Sometimes the incumbent and his wife do all the teaching, as at Eggington Sunday school; "it is thought that a daily school would not answer, unless the children were allowed to plait half their time". In more than one case the incumbent is the main financial support of a weekday school, as at Odell, where 11 boys and 36 girls were taught; "a schoolhouse and a good master are sadly wanted". At Luton "a girls' day school has been tried, but has not answered, from the nature of the business of this place – straw bonnet-making". At Keysoe there was weekday teaching, but "great difficulty in keeping a school together – the children are all brought up to lacemaking". In several places plans for improvement were in hand. At Flitwick there was no school at all, but the incumbent was anxious to have one. Husborne Crawley was about to apply to the society. At Potton where 40 girls attended on weekdays and 50 boys on Sunday "These schools are maintained by the clergyman; a schoolroom is wanted, for which £100 has been collected." At Felmersham "the new schools are completed, and a master, and if possible a mistress will be appointed immediately". But at Shillington the need was very great – most people were unable to read and write their names. At Sundon a schoolroom would be very desirable, "as it would be in the centre of a district of parishes and hamlets containing a population of 4,000 inhabitants". Summing up its returns, the society notes that 13,530 children were receiving instruction, but more than half of them were being taught on Sunday only (the total population of Bedfordshire in 1841 was over 100,000). In 58 cases the premises used were parts of the church or rooms in dames' cottages.

Some idea of the part played by Anglican laity is given by the correspondence of Thomas Barnard, the banker, who, when he went to live at Cople, wrote to Caroline Fitzpatrick of Kempston Hoo for advice about schools. She told him that at Kempston the schoolmaster was paid £20 p.a.; and that the children paid 2d. a week on Monday morning, except for farmers' sons who paid 4d. and expected to receive more attention.[16]

Many of the early school plans survive,[17] showing an allowance of 6 sq. ft. per child; thus at Heath in 1845 a room 36 x 20 ft. was thought to have a capacity for 120 children. There were no refinements; the Tebworth plan in 1854 bears the note "town pump about 60 yds. to NW". At Eaton Socon in 1859 the appeal for extension said that the school was originally built for 120 children, but nearly 200 were attending; a subsequent report in 1861 shows that Eaton Socon had collected £417; the National Society had granted £30; and the government grant was £531; the contract was £995.[18] Help was given by the laity in kind as well as money. Robert Long, the Stondon farmer, noted in his diary in March 1861: "some of my labourers working at Lower Stondon where the new school is to be . . . excavating earth for a cellar under the part to be used for a dwellinghouse for the mistress; carted bricks to spot for building; Hull, too, has carted materials"; when the school was opened in October he wrote "a lot of company came, and at the church and school doors we collected about £20".[19]

An example of the running of the school is given by Tebworth National School, opened in 1855.[20] The managers consisted of vicar and churchwardens, plus 5 elected members, who must subscribe at least £1 p.a. and were elected by those who subscribed 10s. p.a. The teacher here was paid £35 p.a., and the meagre furniture provided in her parlour and bedroom is listed at the front of the account-book. In the first year of working, voluntary contributions and collections brought in £17, school-pence £22; while the capitation grant (6s. p.a. for a boy, 5s. for a girl) brought in £10. Cleaning the school cost 9d. weekly.

The teachers who opened some of the new schools, though they themselves were not highly qualified, had a daunting task. At Husborne Crawley, finally opened in 1867, the teacher admitted 54 children; "only 9 can write even small words or do a simple sum – the rest can hardly form a letter". The children themselves were probably like those described in *The Daisy Chain*: "they all came pushing in, without order or civility, rough heads, torn garments, staring vacant eyes, and mouths gaping in shy rudeness . . . they had no power of attention, even to a story, and the stillness was irksome to such wild colts". There was often difficulty in collecting fees; at Toddington in 1865 "lowered the school fees from 2d. to 1d. for labourers' children". Sometimes the teacher was obliged to have a cam-

---

16 C.R.O., BD 1259.
17 C.R.O., AD 3865.
18 C.R.O., X 67/688–9.

19 C.R.O., X 159/3.
20 C.R.O., P 114/25/4.

paign for cleanliness, which was done by washing some children in front of the others. Often children would be kept away to work; in 1865 at Cranfield many boys were "twitching" (pulling up twitch) in the fields; in 1863 at Dunton boys were pulling charlock; sometimes children would glean, or help with harvest by making bands for sheaves. Often there is an entry in the school logbook "left for the pillow" or "gone to the plaiting school for the winter". But sometimes absence was from lighter causes – picking cowslips, or a meet of the hounds, or a parish feast, or a Wesleyan tea-drinking.

In these schools most clergy continued to visit regularly, as for instance did the vicar of Luton, J. O'Neill, and often to help with the teaching as well. However at Shillington in 1868 the curate not only took scripture, but "preached a sermon against the master in church because he caned for bad conduct". Apparently the master had it out with the vicar, for a week or two later there is a logbook entry: "Rev. J. Freer visited the school. Punishment allowed."

Because the Anglican church was the largest and numbered among its adherents the most well-to-do, so also was its contribution to education the largest in Bedfordshire; it ultimately helped over 60 schools. But there were also Non-conformist schools, for instance at Ampthill, Dunstable, Eaton Bray and Todding-ton; and at Luton the Quakers opened an Adult School in 1862.

Details of the running of a Nonconformist school are provided by Eggington, where from 1848 one was held in the schoolroom at the back of the Congrega-tional church. A single child in a labouring family here paid 2d. a week, but each additional child 1d. Saturday afternoon was a half-holiday. Boys left at 10 years of age. Among the school records are bills for a dozen slates ($1\frac{3}{4}$d. each), a gross of pens and a pint of ink. One teacher, Emma Baker, died of cholera in London in 1854 while visiting an educational exhibition. Her successor, Leonora Taylor, had various troubles. The inspector said the school was too crowded, though on that particular afternoon there were only 50 instead of the usual 60. "He requested me on no account to admit any more children if I valued their health and my own. I trust I do both, nevertheless feel most unwilling to act according to his wishes in that point, especially as I expect some new ones on Monday whom I pressed to come." But when she could get no permanent lodging but a public house, she hastily returned to London. Her minister there defended her: "Had anything happened to her character she would have been reproached, as a single woman, for living in a place of temptation . . . I am at a loss to conceive how the committee could permit, much more suggest, such a home for their teacher."[21]

Some Nonconformist churches had libraries and mutual improvement societies. Hockliffe Congregational church had both; the library in 1855 had 59 books, and that at Eggington 58 books, including *British Birds* and *Female Excellence*.[22]

[21] H. G. Tibbutt, *Hockliffe & Eggington Congregational church*, pp.19–23.　　[22] Tibbutt, *op.cit.*, p.14.

Government involvement in education, though at first indirect and small, led first to inspection, and then to action to bring about improvement of standards and equality of provision (ch. 46).

All denominations also felt concerned to help missions to spread Christian teaching overseas in the wider world of Africa and Asia, of which they were becoming increasingly aware The Bedfordshire district societies for the S.P.C.K. and S.P.G. (Anglican) met annually in Bedford, usually under the chairmanship of a leading figure, such as the High Sheriff, Colonel Gilpin of Hockliffe, in 1850, or the Lord Lieutenant, Earl de Grey, in 1851; and this meeting was often accompanied by a service with a sermon from an overseas cleric, such as the Bishop of Guiana in 1850, or the Bishop of Labuan in 1861; and village meetings were also held – in 1863 the Rev. J. L. Kearns "of India" spoke in the schoolroom at Blunham.[23] One local supporter of missions was Mrs. Long, wife of the Stondon farmer, Robert Long. In 1863 she had to stay with her two girls from Sierra Leone who were being educated in England by the Church Missionary Society for teaching overseas. Their dark skins caused much interest in the little village.

All other denominations had of course their own missionary societies. During this period young men were trained for overseas work with the London Missionary Society (predominantly Congregational) at two Bedfordshire academies. The first was kept at Turvey by Richard Cecil from 1829 to 1838; on Sundays his students went by twos to the villages to preach; later one of them, John Frost, when a minister at Cotton End, himself trained others for the Home Missionary Society. Somewhat similar training was given in Bedford from 1840 by John Jukes, minister of Bunyan Meeting, who had previously run a similar academy elsewhere. He was helped by William Alliott, the minister of Howard Congregational church. The young men they trained went afterwards to such places as China, India, New Guinea, and the West Indies. Most of them came from elsewhere, but S. J. Whitmee was a Stagsden man and friend of William Hale White ("Mark Rutherford"). Whitmee was afterwards a missionary in the Pacific; he sent botanical specimens to Kew, one of which they called after him "oleandra Whitmee"; and he taught R. L. Stevenson the Samoan language: "we went down at 4 p.m. to my Samoan lesson from Whitmee. I think I shall learn from him; he does not fool me with cockshot rules."[24] Another student, J. S. Moffat, went to Matabeleland; he later said – thinking of Bunyan – "I have never lost the sense of that presence in my own life."[25]

[23] C.R.O., X 67/714–28.
[24] B. Mag. xi, 195–6.

[25] B. Mag. v, 321; vi, 8, 84.

RAILWAYS

The great fact in Victorian communications was the development of railways. They affected people in many ways: those who promoted them and invested in them; the landowners and farmers through whose land the new lines passed; the gangs of navvies (joined by some local men) who came to work on them, and whose rough living and not particularly law-abiding ways caused apprehension; those who used the railways and suddenly found their mobility much greater and swifter, whether for trade or for social reasons; and those who had painfully to readjust – the coachmen and innkeepers, the turnpike trustees whose receipts dropped wholesale, and the watermen who found trade slipping from their hands.

The promotion of railways was on two levels. The main lines were promoted nationally, and no Bedfordshire town was important enough to be a prime consideration. Those lines which affected Bedfordshire were: London–Birmingham, 1838; London–King's Lynn (Eastern Counties), 1845; London–York (Gt. Northern), 1850. A prospectus circulated in 1836 for a London–Boston line via Bedford,[1] but it did not materialise. So at first it seemed that Bedfordshire would benefit little by railways, and people from this county had to get to the main lines at the nearest accessible point. When the London–Birmingham line was opened, this was the station situated in Linslade parish but actually called Leighton. A coach ran daily to meet the trains here; and it is this station which is referred to on an occasion in 1841 when the visiting justices failed to find the governor at Bedford gaol, because he had unexpectedly been called to meet a person on business "at the railway station".[2] When the Eastern Counties line was opened seven years later, Cambridge provided an alternative for the east of the county; soon this line had a branch to Hertford; and by 1847 a coach from Eaton Socon was meeting trains at Hertford station. The first main line to run through Bedfordshire was that from London to York (Gt. Northern), and it ran through Sandy and Biggleswade.

Thus the need for branch lines was obvious, and hence came local action. For a long while there was only talk. Already in 1836 people were discussing the possibility of one from Cambridge via St. Neots, Bedford and Newport Pagnell to join the Birmingham line.[3] In 1844 George Stephenson came to Bedford

[1] C.R.O., R 3957.
[2] C.R.O., QGR 5. "The station" was even the place where Leighton Buzzard enclosure award was signed by one commissioner.
[3] C.R.O., R 3957.

to discuss a Bedford branch; and in 1845 a group of Bedford businessmen negotia-ted with the London to Birmingham company to the effect that, if they could get a line built from Bedford to Bletchley, the bigger company would take it over and run it; and so was formed the Bedford Railway Company.[4] The chairman was T. J. Green, mayor of Bedford 1843–4, and also county treasurer; as a coal merchant he hoped to use railways. Of the directors, Robert Newland, a brewer, again had an eye to business; and there was also T. A. Green; the others were probably investors – Thomas Barnard, Isaac Elger, Henry Littledale and George Witt; and one of the auditors was W. B. Higgins, a county figure. Shareholders' meetings were held in the Bedford Rooms. Their task was completed when the line was opened in 1846. As the directors pointed out, "a short branch could not be worked as an independent line without disproportionately great expense"; and it became a branch of the London–Birmingham line.

Meanwhile a branch from the same railway to Luton was canvassed unsuccess-fully. In 1844 George Stephenson met some men at the George to discuss it, but Luton did not want the line to run across the Gt. Moor.[5] A branch was therefore made to Dunstable instead of Luton, and opened in 1848. This caused reflection in Luton. Again time passed. In 1855, chiefly through the efforts of James Waller and Henry Tomson (the latter was a farmer) a company was formed to promote a branch line to join the Gt. Northern at Welwyn – it was to run from Dunstable via Luton. But once more there was trouble, this time about the site of the station; Waller and Tomson were outvoted, and Thomas Sworder the brewer and John Everitt a hat manufacturer took their places. The Dunstable–Luton section was opened in 1858; and the Luton–Welwyn section in 1860.

Another local line, opened in 1857, had beaten it by a short head This was the 4-mile railway from Sandy to Potton, built as a naval captain's hobby.[6] William Peel was a son of Sir Robert Peel. He had already explored Africa and written up his tour when he bought an estate at Sandy in 1852. Sandy could not contain him – in the Crimean War he won the V.C. by throwing back at the Russians a live shell with fuse burning – but he found time to plan the railway and engage a railway engineer. The engine (which still survives – it was called after his ship, the Shannon) cost £800. The opening of the railway found Peel away in India, commanding a naval brigade in the mutiny, and in 1858 he was injured at the relief of Lucknow and died at the age of 34. His stretch of line was taken over by a line from Bedford to Cambridge in 1862.

Finally the Bedford–Northampton railway was promoted by local supporters in Bedfordshire, Buckinghamshire and Northamptonshire, after a meeting at Olney in 1864.[7] The mayor of Northampton attended the initial meeting, and the

[4] C.R.O., AD 565.
[5] Dyer–Stygall–Dony, *Luton*, 140. Luton references are taken from here.
[6] *B. Mag.* v, 55. The estate later passed to his brother

Arthur, who became Viscount Peel, and rebuilt William's house, Swiss cottage, to become Sandy Lodge, and also built Sandy gasworks.
[7] *Bedford town and townsmen*, 103, 124.

chairman of the company was at first W. H. Whitbread, then W. B. Higgins. The line was opened in 1872.

Meanwhile also that main line which was to be of the most importance to the county, the Midland, had opened its first stretch. The line from Leicester via Bedford to Hitchin (on the Gt. Northern) was opened in 1857. The Hitchin-London stretch became increasingly congested, so eventually a Midland line was built from Bedford to St. Pancras via Luton, and opened for goods in 1867 and passengers in 1868. This time Lutonians made no protest about the Gt. Moor; the southern stretch of the Moor was taken by J. S. Crawley for building development; and in exchange he gave the open spaces known as Pope's Meadow, People's Park and Bell's Close.

Investment in railways was widespread among those who could afford it. In fact, there was in 1845 in the Bedford Rooms a special "railway news room", where were railway prospectuses and lists of prices of railway stock.[8] The investment book of Francis Wythes of Ravensden[9] shows that between 1846 and 1872 he bought shares in the East Anglian, Gt. Eastern, Norfolk Extension, N. Staffordshire, Gt. Northern, London & Southwestern, Royston & Hitchin, London & Northwestern, York, Newcastle & Berwick, Shropshire Union, Caledonian, and Somerset & Dorset railway companies. It seems likely that conversely many people at a distance invested in railways which were to pass through Bedfordshire. Such was the railway fever that nearly 20 railways to pass through the county were planned which were never built. To get a railway act passed would at least stake out a claim and warn off competitors, in case it was later needed. Plans had to be deposited with the clerk of the peace for public inspection, and sometimes there was a rush to get them finished in time; those for one abortive railway (an early proposal for Bedford–Leicester in 1845) were deposited at 11.46 p.m. on 30 Nov. 1845, and some of them are in manuscript because there was not time to lithograph them.[10] Among the abortive proposals were: Ely–Bedford; Biggleswade–Bedford; Wolverton–Bedford (or rather, Ridgmont); and Northampton–Cambridge, running through Eaton Socon.

Landowners and farmers no doubt viewed with mixed feelings the construction of railways over their land. There was one compensation for landowners with well-wooded estates; railway construction increased the demand for and so raised the price of timber. Bennett, the Duke's agent, noted in 1836 that prices at his recent wood sale were the highest he had ever known.[11] The income from woods on the Duke's Beds. and Bucks. estate in this year was nearly £9,000; it was to reach its record figure in 1846 with £26,446; then it dropped; from 1858 to 1860 it rose again to over £10,000. By the 1880's it had fallen to an average

---

8 *Op.cit.*, 7.
9 C.R.O., X 98/7.
10 C.R.O., PDR 18. After this a rule was made that

plans must be deposited by 8 p.m.
11 C.R.O., R 3912.

£4,500.[12]

Other people of Bedfordshire saw the situation in varying terms. In those villages – the majority – which were still overpopulated, the railways offered the adventurous man who could stand rough living a chance to get away. The wages of navvies from 1843 to 1869 were anything from 15s. to 22s. 6d. a week,[13] higher than those of farm workers. He could join a gang working on a local stretch of line. (Under the main contractor were sub-contractors, who took on a cutting here, an embankment there; the sub-contractors appointed gangers, and each ganger organised his own gang.) Once a member of a gang, he might migrate with it wherever railway work required; and sometimes even his name was obscured by the nickname his mates gave him.

Secure people feared lawless outbreaks, for the navvies lived practically without comforts in wooden shanties, and would occasionally break out and drink to excess. The Rev. George Maclear tried to help those working on the Bedford–Bletchley line, and would go out to read the Bible with them – what his reception was is not recorded.[14] Some at least of the men were Irish – Irish names appear at this time in the Roman Catholic register at Shefford (ch. 43).

Public nervousness is understandable, since the professional constabulary was not only small but inexperienced, for it was formed only in 1849 (ch. 46). At its formation several Luton residents, including Charles Austin and Thomas Waller, had petitioned quarter sessions; they feared that Luton would get less protection than under its old system, when the township had one day-constable and two night-watchmen; they urged at least that the area superintendent should have the means of speedy communication with his subordinates, "for which purpose they humbly suggest that he should be provided with a horse".[15] This was five years before any railway construction began in Bedfordshire; and at the time the total county force was 47, of whom six were area superintendents. Later, when the Midland railway from Leicester via Bedford to Hitchin (opened 1857) was in progress with many men at work, quarter sessions did enlist one extra constable.[16] The county force grew by degrees, and in 1865 the Luton contingent comprised 15 men; but because in that year work was about to begin on another Midland line to run from Bedford to London via Luton, in which work it was thought 3,000 men would be employed, 40 Luton inhabitants petitioned quarter sessions that their coverage be increased by five.[17]

Throughout the period the varying response continued. When the Bedford–Northampton railway was under construction (opened 1872), C. L. Higgins

[12] Duke of Bedford, *A great agricultural estate*, 220–4.
[13] T. Coleman, *Railway navvies*, 67. Further details of navvies are taken from this vivid account.
[14] *B.H.R.S.* xl, 152. On the other hand some canal navvies at Brickhill in 1800 gave rise to the Baptist church there – they had prayer meetings in a local house, and were "violently persecuted" as "the whole parish was strongly attached to the established church, being full of pharisaical pride"; see Tibbutt, *The Baptists of Leighton Buzzard*, p.23.
[15] C.R.O., QEV 3.
[16] C.R.O., QSM 38, p.227.
[17] C.R.O., QEV 3.

built a readingroom for the men at Turvey (ch. 43), while Charles Magniac of Colworth complained that the navvies, in gangs of 18 or 20, went poaching with guns and dogs, and broke hedges and fences.[18]

The navvies' work was hard. Because railway lines had to be as level as possible, great amounts of earth had to be removed, and it was the navvies who moved it. Labour was plentiful and cheap; and though a mechanical excavator was patented in America in 1843 its cost was high (£1,500). The quickest method of excavating earth was to undermine the lower part of a bank till the upper part gave way. This involved judging the right moment to withdraw and the navvies constantly took risks. When the Leicester–Bedford line was under construction, there were "several very severe accidents", and in 1855 the infirmary applied to the contractors for an annual subscription as recompense for the heavy expense. At Ampthill in 1867 Charles Bostin had undermined a large area, when 10 tons of earth fell on him without warning; he was not buried but his neck was broken; while his mate, who had to be dug out, survived.[20]

A normal day's work for each pair of navvies was 14 sets; that is, they 14 times filled a horse-drawn waggon by shovelling earth and rock over their heads, i.e., about 20 tons. The directors of the Bedford–Bletchley line reported that there had been difficulty at the Brogborough cutting. With a cutting, the waggons might be waiting above; planks were laid up the side of the cutting, up which barrows connected by rope with a horse-drawn pulley were wheeled; a slip on the muddy plank might cause the man to fall with his load on top of him. But this method was mainly used with longer cuttings to save time; here it was usual to have carts at the bottom of the cutting.

Most dangerous was tunnelling. The men worked with pickaxes in darkness lit only by candles, in foul air, and sometimes standing in water, for 12-hour shifts. As they cleared a stretch, centre supports were put up, and the bricklayers took over. Ampthill tunnel was completed in 1867.

For the general public the opening of a new railway was an occasion for rejoicing. When the Bedford–Bletchley line was opened on 17 November 1846, Bedford Brass Band played, church bells rang, and large crowds watched 600 people leave for Bletchley in 30 carriages drawn by two "powerful engines". The passengers inspected the works in progress to make Bletchley station, and then returned to Bedford to be received by the Duchess of Bedford. Then a "brilliant company" dined in the Bedford Rooms.[21]

Perhaps excitement was even more intense at the opening of the Sandy-Potton line in 1857.[22] The stations were decked with banners and evergreens; there was a triumphal arch, and slogans such as "The Queen – God bless her!"

[18] Coleman, op.cit., 106.
[19] C.R.O., HO/BM 8 (1 Jan.).
[20] Beds. Mercury, 11 Dec. 1867.

[21] Bedford town and townsmen, 61.
[22] B. Mag. v, 55.

and "Captain William Peel and progress!" At Potton the Bedfordshire Militia Band played, and conducted the company to the marketplace, where in a giant marquee 400 people had lunch (2s. 6d., including a pint of beer), while the Sun and the Swan inns were full, and the 44 navvies were not forgotten. London professionals sang glees and songs, and the toasts were many. In 1858 when the line from Luton to Dunstable was opened, there was again a brass band, and there were so many passengers (not all of whom had bought 6d. tickets) that they sat on the top of carriages or hung on to the sides. Perhaps this was why the train broke down.[23]

Travelling by railway was less comfortable than it is today. Charles Dickens, who left Leicester at 9.35 a.m. in January 1867 said that the "reckless fury of the driving and the violent rocking of the carriages" obliged him to leave the train at Bedford, although he was an experienced traveller. James Howard rose to the defence of the Midland line; it "runs as smoothly as any I have ever journeyed by", – and he had travelled, he said, in three-quarters of the globe; in fact it was "one of the best pieces of permanent way in the kingdom".[24]

Today we are accustomed to many accidents on the roads, but we expect the railways to be safe. Railway safety was only achieved after long struggle. The first accident on the Bedford–Hitchin line was in 1862, when an excursion train returning from Bedford regatta ran into some cattle trucks near the junction with the Gt. Northern, and several passengers were injured.[25] In 1867 at Arlesey on the Gt. Northern in the December dusk a truck loaded with 9 tons of coprolites became derailed, followed by two other trucks and the guard's van; lamps were lighted, and a repair gang got to work, but an express crashed into it, killing the driver, stoker and three others, while 30 were injured.[26] F. L. Pym of Sandy was killed in 1860; a man was killed at Luton in 1861; and the rector of Souldrop in his church diary notes on three occasions the death of a parishioner "killed by the railway".[27]

Railways had some levelling influence. Even royalty went by train, though a special train. When a lord like the Duke of Bedford or Earl de Grey went to London, he did so by train, as his humblest neighbour did, even though he went in a first-class compartment. His carriages were kept for short trips at home.

There was another result of railway travel which was less desirable. Then, as today, offenders were not slow to make use of modern methods. Luton, always anxious on police matters, and continually pressing for an enlarged force to cope with its growing population, pointed out in 1860 that "since the opening of the railway from Luton to Hatfield, thieves have much greater facility in disposing of their plunder, by taking an early morning train to London before the police

[23] Dyer–Stygall–Dony, op.cit., 141.
[24] B. Mag. viii, 32.
[25] Bedford town and townsmen, 96.
[26] Op.cit., 135.
[27] Beds. Mercury, 10 June. B.H.R.S. xl, 202.

are aware of the transaction".[28]

The impact of the railways on Bedfordshire trade and travel was both short-term and long-term. In the former, existing traffic was simply transferred from roads and waterways to railways. After the opening of the London–Birmingham line, the innkeeper at the George, Woburn, found by 1839 that there was so little demand for posting horses that it would not answer him to continue.[29] On the Saturday after the opening of the Bedford–Bletchley line in 1846, which gave access to London via Bletchley, the Bedford Times coach left the Swan inn, Bedford, for the last time.[30] Its speed was 10 miles an hour, but as the local press commented, the public now expected 20 miles an hour. So this coach, with its rose-pink upholstery, and its curtains – green in summer, scarlet in winter – the favourite among Bedfordians among the coaches which started from or passed through the town, and always watched by a crowd, is remembered only in a picture painted by the local artist, Bradford Rudge. And as people transferred to railways, so also did goods traffic leave the waggons and the waterways, especially coal.

But the railways' real importance was in the long-term effect which came in the next period. In mid-Victorian times Luton grew, although it had no railway till 1860 and was not on a direct line to London till 1868. Though Bedford by 1872 had an extensive railway system, no special immediate growth resulted. But in late Victorian and Edwardian times, when the whole of the infrastructure was in being, there was to come a massive development of industry in both Luton and Bedford. There was also to come large-scale brickmaking, which drove out of business the many small brickworks all over the county from Dean to Stopsley. The first sign of this was in 1852, when Robert Beart of Godmanchester opened brickworks at Arlesey on the Gt. Northern railway,[31] and by 1890 Beart's Patent Brick Co. was making large quantities of perforated white bricks here. Arlesey in 1890 showed another pointer for the future in its lime and cement works.

ROADS AND BRIDGES

As the railways developed, the roads declined. From the first, the turnpike trusts had borrowed money to improve the roads, and had never quite caught up with their initial expenditure. Now they were increasingly in the red. That stretch of Watling Street which was under the Puddlehill trust (Dunstable–Hockliffe) in 1835 brought in £2,770 in tolls; when the government made enquiries in 1840 after the opening of the London–Birmingham railway, this income had sunk to £1,030; tolls on the Hockliffe–Woburn road were halved; and even those on the Bedford–Luton road were already less than they had been.[32] As other railways were built, so for other trusts the income from tolls fell; on both the Hitchin road

[28] C.R.O., QEV 3.
[29] C.R.O., R 4098.
[30] *Bedford town and townsmen*, 61–4.
[31] *B. Mag.* ix, 20.
[32] C.R.O., QT 30.

and the Gt. North road it dropped steeply; only on the Kimbolton road, which had no competitor and in any case had little traffic, was it maintained.

Examination of minutes and accounts of the Dunstable–St. Albans trust provides a few pointers. The Wonder coach from London to Shrewsbury, itself in trouble, asked in vain for a reduction in tolls. The trustees constantly considered whether a reduction in tolls would produce an increase in traffic, but usually decided against. The salaries of clerk and surveyor were reduced, with the illusory suggestion that they would be restored when times improved; then in 1842 the surveyor resigned, and no successor was appointed, but one of the four labourers, Thomas Lee, was appointed overlooker at 12s. weekly. The trustees lost interest; attendance declined from 7 to 3, and once in 1856 no one turned up. Representations to parliament were made in vain. In 1847 a meeting of representatives of some trusts was held in London; they urged the government to nationalise or consolidate trusts and take over their responsibilities; while the Dunstable delegate, J. S. Story, had the ingenious idea of "putting their debts upon the different railroads, or imposing a small sum upon persons travelling by them according to the distance they go".[33]

At last in 1862 the government decided to set up machinery to deal with roads, and since the current fashion was to set up a new elective board every time a new need was realised, quarter sessions were empowered to set up highway boards. In Bedfordshire therefore quarter sessions established five highway boards, Bedford, Biggleswade, Bletsoe, Luton and Woburn; and one by one between 1868 and 1877 the old turnpike trusts were wound up. The system of highway boards was unpopular. In 1876 representatives of over 80 parishes, after a meeting at the Sessions House, petitioned quarter sessions that it had been an expensive failure, that the cost was greater and the roads sometimes worse, and that it would be better to return to the old system of parish surveyors. In the following year the highway boards of Bedford, Luton and Woburn sent in resolutions to the same effect.[34] The highway boards lasted only till a new pattern of local government emerged at the end of this period (ch. 46).

Meanwhile, the conception of a bridge as a public responsibility had now almost come to hold the field. Turvey bridge was repaired by the Higgins family until 1881, when it was at last declared a county bridge.[35] Harrold nearly became a county bridge in 1847;[36] at this time quarter sessions proposed a new iron bridge, which should become a county bridge, but on condition that the proprietors made one last contribution. These were Earl de Grey, the Alston family, and the Misses Trevor. But the Misses Trevor astonishingly held out; they were responsible for only one arch, they said, and it was proposed that they should pay for two. To them we owe the preservation of Harrold bridge; for as a result of their firm-

[33] C.R.O., Fac. 6/2.
[34] C.R.O., QSM 46, pp.518–20, 568.
[35] *Lock Gate*, ii, 2.
[36] *Lock Gate*, ii, 38.

ness, the old bridge was repaired, and did not become a county bridge till 1930.

Just as we are now finding that some, even comparatively recent, bridges cannot take modern traffic, so there was trouble in 1873 at Holme bridge, Biggleswade, when a 10-ton steam engine belonging to T. B. Kitchener of Potton caused it to collapse. It was an iron bridge, and not very old, but there was a known crack in one girder. (This may have been the result of the canal freezing in 1823 when it was in transit; the forwarding agents disclaimed responsibility; and as it was an outside girder, and normal traffic over the bridge was not at that time heavy, it was thought that it would not matter.)[37] But the steam engine was too much for it. At the assizes in 1873 an attempt was made to make Kitchener bear the repairs, but the conviction was quashed.[38]

WATERWAYS

Traffic left the waterways even more promptly than it left the roads. Coal, for so long their mainstay, was still better adapted for railway trucks than for lighters and barges. With the Ivel navigation trust, an act was passed in 1876 to bring it to an end. £14,350 was owing, which was to be paid as far as possible out of assets. The haling-way was sold off piecemeal.[39] A few years later there was a dispute about liability to maintain the banks at Tempsford; William Stuart complained that the miller kept an excessive head of water which damaged the banks.[40] One sidelight on the period during which the navigation was declining is provided by a letter from John Harvey of Ickwell, complaining in 1849 that the locksman made difficulty about eel-pots in the sluice gates; "I am deprived of a dish of which I am very fond."[41]

The Ouse navigation was private property. In this period part of it still belonged to the Francklins of Gt. Barford, and the other part (the original share of Henry Ashley) to a Suffolk family called Cullum. It became less and less worth while for the joint proprietors to collect tolls and repair sluices, so in 1864 and again in 1865 they advertised for sale the navigation rights of the 31 miles from Bedford to St. Ives, together with Eaton Socon mill, the haling-way, and collectors' cottages. They optimistically valued the tolls at £2,000 p.a. By 1867 they were glad to sell the whole for £1,500.[42] The purchaser sold the navigation rights in 1883 to L. T. Simpson, who tried to restore the works and bring the river again into use.[43] His efforts were the first of a series which continue to the present day.

SUNK WITHOUT TRACE

It is almost impossible to discover what happened to those whom the railways made redundant. There were no schemes for helping them, other than through poor relief; they were left to the law of supply and demand. Baker, innkeeper at

[37] C.R.O., QSR 1823/675, 686.
[38] C.R.O., QSM 46, p.148.
[39] For instance, C.R.O., X 147/20.
[40] C.R.O., WG 2743.

[41] C.R.O., HY 57.
[42] C.R.O., FN 1324–9.
[43] C. F. Farrar, *Ouse's silent tide*, 211–2.

the George, Woburn, was fortunate in 1839 in being offered the tenancy of a farm at Sundon on the Page-Turner estate.[44] H. D. Walker, proprietor of the Cock at Eaton Socon, was less lucky; his assignees sold it in 1845; its sale notice points out that it possessed carriage drive, shrubbery, and stabling for 60 horses; while the house had 7 bay windows, 5 dining and drawingrooms and 20 bedrooms. It had been "long justly appreciated by the nobility and gentry", and it would make a gentleman's residence, or with a small outlay it could be converted into business premises or a manufactory.[45] Actually it was bought by John Woods who kept the Angel inn at St. Neots,[46] and who had an omnibus running 3 days a week to meet trains at Bedford; and in 1847 he was still trying to run the Cock as an inn. The 1847 directory notes of Eaton Socon; "this parish had formerly the main north road, through which ran 36 coaches daily to and from London"; now, it says, "the Magnet passes through to and from Hertford station at 7 a.m. and 10 p.m." Dunstable on the Watling Street stagnated for 30 years.

There were not only the innkeepers, but the waiters, maids, ostlers and grooms. There were the long-distance carriers (the short-distance ones continued). There was reduced trade for saddlers, blacksmiths and coach-builders. There was less demand for horses. On the waterways, lightermen and lock-keepers were less and less needed. How did all these redeploy? A groom at Eaton Socon, for instance, could not get a job as porter, for there was no railway station within miles; he must have had to move elsewhere. A coach-builder at Bedford was not helped by possible vacancies many miles away where railway-carriages were being produced. What did a redundant lighterman do? Somehow, if still young enough to do so, they must have had to find other work, as the superfluous farm-workers did (ch. 41), perhaps by migration to London or the north, or by emigration overseas. Or, if they were elderly, there was always the workhouse.

[44] C.R.O., R 4098.
[45] C.R.O., WG 2373/2.

[46] C.R.O., X 67/622-3.

45 – LIFE IN GENERAL, c. 1830-90

A GENERAL account of homes in Victorian Bedfordshire is scarcely practicable, for the possibilities were now infinitely varied and the range of incomes very great. Perhaps it is also unnecessary, since Victorian fiction, photographs and survivals are familiar. Two items may help to evoke the Bedfordshire background of the time.

One is a middle-class sale notice of 1868 which lists the furniture of an Ampthill commercial traveller, William Bennett. He had a house with kitchen, scullery, living-room, and front and back parlours; while upstairs were 4 bedrooms. Among his ornaments were a pair of buffalo horns, two oil paintings, and a stuffed squirrel in a case; and he had about 120 books and a piano. Upstairs, the furniture in the best bedroom was mahogany, and there was a 4-post bed. In the outbuildings was a capital 4-wheeled dog-cart.

The other is a macabre incident of 1849, which recalls the squalor portrayed by Dickens. A Marston woman died in childbirth, and the husband was refused help in providing her coffin because he was at work (in Luton). It was feared that her death was accelerated by want of proper nourishment. The dispute with the Ampthill Union was still unsettled when the rector, the Rev. T. Tylecote, and Mr. Stimson gave a positive order to the overseer to do what was necessary, "in consequence of the decomposed state of the body and the alarming effluvia arising therefrom at a period when cholera was so near to them as Bedford."[1]

OUTDOOR PURSUITS

However, compared with those in previous centuries, living standards were higher, and recreational possibilities, both outdoors and indoors, were now diverse. Some were increasingly being organised by clubs or societies.

To take first those outdoors: there was the occasional prize-fight, though forbidden by quarter sessions. In 1845 one was organised on the Biddenham side of Bedford between Robert Goddard and Charles Johnson; the police intervened; but the promoters made what seems to have been a planned withdrawal to Fenlake on the other side of the river, where additional spectators brought the number present to about a thousand. The police at first did not realise what had happened, and they were on the wrong side of the river without a boat. The fight continued uninterrupted for 42 rounds; Goddard won; and the injured Johnson was removed to the infirmary.[2]

---

[1] C.R.O., PUAC 1/20, p.109.   [2] *Bedford town and townsmen*, 55.

Horses and dogs were as popular as ever. The Oakley Hunt continued,[3] and by the end of the period the financial difficulty of finding a master who could afford to provide hounds had been solved in 1876 by Hastings, 9th Duke of Bedford. He bought the pack and presented it to the hunt. From 1850 to 1885 there was a redoubtable master, Robert Arkwright. Bedford races were still held on Cow Meadow till about 1874. A race-stand company, of which Whitbread was the chief shareholder, had provided a race-stand, and there was also a refreshment room. Several race-cards survive, and show that some of the horses were entered by local owners, such as G. Ongley in 1844;[4] those which came from a distance were stabled at the Horse and Jockey inn for a fortnight's previous training.[5] There was also greyhound racing, as at Cardington in 1852 for four days in February, for dog puppies, bitch puppies, and all ages, the stewards on that occasion being George Inskip, William Vipan and John Purser.[6]

Aquatic sport was beginning. Though we know little of the earliest regattas, we know there was one at Bedford in 1848, for little Simon Lamb ran out of his father's hairdressing shop by the bridge to see the boats, and was knocked down by a horse. (He was unhurt, but the driver pulled up so sharply that the shafts broke, the horse bolted, tangled in the reins, pitched by St. John's church and broke its neck; hence a press report.)[7] By 1853 the regatta had become formal for sculls, fours, pairs and randans (a pair of oars and a pair of sculls), but it was still at a primitive stage, for many boats leaked, and the water had to be bailed out before or after a race. Proper precautions were not always taken with the starting gun. In 1869 the sergeant in charge allowed another man to fire it, and unfortunately a little girl chose this moment to run in front of it and was killed.[8] When in 1886 Bedford Rowing Club was formed (it kept its boats in Chetham's boathouse, which had formerly been Halfhead's coal wharf)[9] rowing was firmly established as a major Bedford sport, and the popularity of Bedford regatta was growing.

Natural history attracted more attention. The gentry listed plants they found, as the Squire ladies did at Basmead manor about 1860; or pressed wild flowers like the Stuarts of Tempsford about 1880; or sketched them, as Alston ladies did in Odell wood about 1830.[10] (The gentry sketched not only flowers but also landscapes and buildings, and the Higgins family of Turvey produced up to about 1842 watercolours of high standard.)[11] This interest in natural history began to reach a wider range of people. Not only was there the occasional naturalist, such as William Crouch of Clophill (d. 1846), but a Natural History Society was formed in Bedford in 1875. Perhaps a contributory cause was the velocipede or primitive bicycle, which was said in 1869 to have "an enormous number of devotees" in

---

[3] B.H.R.S. xliv.
[4] C.R.O., AD 1144.
[5] Bedford town and townsmen, 51.
[6] C.R.O., PM 2742.
[7] Bedford town and townsmen, 69.

[8] Op.cit., 115.
[9] Op.cit., 25.
[10] C.R.O., SQ 185, CC 433–4, X 48/5.
[11] Belonging to Dr. M. S. Longuet-Higgins.

Bedford. One of them rode to Hemel Hempstead and back in $3\frac{3}{4}$ hours.[12] By 1894 there was a Cycling Club at Biggleswade, where Dan Albone was making bicycles. Fishing ceased to be a preserve of the gentry; and in order to acquire fishing rights to practise it lawfully, the Ouse Angling Association (president, James Howard) was formed in 1872.[13]

Parks and gardens developed. Parks in Bedford (ch. 42) and Luton (ch. 44) have already been mentioned. Gardening, whether on a grand scale or a smaller scale, had long been an interest of the gentry; and it was their cultivation of fruit under glass (Earl de Grey's orangery at Wrest was built by Clephane in 1836) that gave Sir Joseph Paxton the idea for the Crystal Palace for the 1851 exhibition.[14] (Paxton came from Milton Bryan, where his father was the Page-Turner agent.) Now gardening developed a hold on an increasing public. The Bedfordshire Horticultural Society (ch. 40) centred on Bedford; Luton launched a Horticultural Society in 1842;[15] both Dunstable and Leighton had one; and even so small a place as Odell held a horticultural show in 1864.[16] Sandy show (ch. 41) drew entries from beyond the county borders. Smooth lawns became possible with the advent of the lawn-mower. The better type of farmhouse had a large walled kitchen-garden with trim box hedges, plenty of vegetables to feed the large household of children, servants, and the man living in, and a well-stocked orchard; while the front garden had circular flower-beds cut out of the lawns. The newer estate cottages were invariably supplied with gardens; and in some villages with old-style cottages lacking gardens, arrangements were made for allotments, as at Eversholt. Even in towns, houses in the newer residential areas had gardens of a fair size.

Garden games gained favour. The South Beds. Croquet Club was established in 1871 with nearly a hundred members drawn from all over the south of the county.[17] These were gentry, such as Major Cooper Cooper of Toddington, Major J. H. Brooks of Flitwick, Col. R. T. Gilpin of Hockliffe, Mrs. Crawley of Stockwood, and the Rev. G. G. Harter of Cranfield. Ladies and gentlemen competed separately. From 1878 tennis was added to this club's activities. For a time the Duke and Duchess of Bedford were members, and in 1883 one meeting was held by invitation of Earl Cowper at Wrest Park (Earl Cowper had married Earl de Grey's daughter and heiress). But it is noticeable too that Bunyan Meeting manse in Dame Alice Street, Bedford, had a lawn large enough for croquet.

In much of the above, the tacit assumption is that leisure was for the gentry, or at best for the middle classes, but this was decreasingly so as time went on.

For most young men, the old favourites of cricket and football kept their pride of place. Luton had two football Clubs (Wanderers and Excelsior), who in

[12] *Bedford town and townsmen*, 115.
[13] *Op.cit.*, 123.
[14] *B. Mag* ii, 299.

[15] C.R.O., G/DDA 151/6.
[16] C.R.O., AD 3238/6.
[17] C.R.O., LL 17/323.

1889 amalgamated to form Luton Town Football and Athletic Club, which had a ground off the Dunstable road.[18] At Bedford the new form of football developed at Rugby became popular, and the Rovers, founded 1876, and Swifts, founded 1882, amalgamated in 1886 to form Bedford Rugby Football Club.[19] Both Luton and Bedford had cricket clubs, as did also some villages, for instance Flitwick in 1889.[20] A Town and County Cricket Club was formed in 1870, and a score-book for 1879 has survived with details of its inter-county matches; J. W. D. Harrison recalls that in 1882 the captain was H. G. Tylecote, son of the rector of Marston mentioned above.[21] But by the end of the period, this club had lapsed, and county cricket was temporarily at a low ebb.

Amid this growing organisation, traditional county customs continued (ch. 40). The village feast was still kept, as at Houghton Conquest.[22] So was Plough Monday (ch. 16), at least in the north; a Thurleigh version of the song the plough-boys sang when they went round to collect money was:

> Think of the poor old ploughboys
> When the dirt sticks like glue.
> No one knows what the poor old ploughboy
> Has to go through.[23]

The Shillington and Clifton logbooks note that not many children attended on Valentine's day – they "stayed away to go round the village to obtain valentine gifts", "excuse – been round singing as usual"; at Shillington school in 1873 "Mrs. Frere kindly brought halfpence for those who attended as an encouragement." At Tilsworth on Mayday eve young men stuck a branch of may by every house for each girl who lived there, singing a song of which one verse ran:[24]

> A branch of may I have you brought
> And at your door it stands –
> It is but a sprout, but it's all budded out,
> It is the work of our Lord's hands.

In many parishes the gleaning bell still rang for gleaning – the vicar of Eaton Socon in 1851 cautioned his flock about scolding and scandal-mongering in the gleaning-field.[25]

Royal events were heartily celebrated. When Edward, Prince of Wales, was married in 1863, Sharnbrook provided dinner in the schoolyard for all men and boys over 15. In the afternoon there were sports, including sack race and wheel-barrow race. At 4 o'clock there was tea for the women and children; followed by climbing a greasy pole for a leg of mutton, and catching a pig by his tail. Finally

[18] Dyer–Stygall–Dony, *Luton*, 162.
[19] *Bedford 1166–1966*, p.54.
[20] C.R.O., LL 17/321. There were also occasional matches played by scratch elevens, such as the eleven from Sworder's brewery at Luton (*Beds. Mer.*, 30 Aug. 1858).
[21] C.R.O., X 188; *Echoes;* 85–8; *Bedford town and townsmen*, 117.
[22] C.R.O., P 11/28/2, p.143.
[23] Information from Mr. F. Hamer.
[24] *Beds. N. & Q.*, i, 143.
[25] C.R.O., CRT 150/22.

there were fireworks and a bonfire. The prizes were: for men, a spade or hoe; for women, tea; for boys, money; and for girls, scarlet stockings. Sharnbrook must have been rather proud of its effort, for the printed notice warns that intruders will not be allowed to participate.[26]

For Queen Victoria's diamond jubilee in 1897 Sandy festivities were still more striking. The bells rang; there was a service; then there was a public luncheon at 1s. 6d. a head. After singing God save the Queen, a procession proceeded to Sandy Place for sports, followed by tea for the children, dancing, and again fireworks and bonfire. The races included a thread-needle race for girls, and a treacle-bun-eating competition for boys. All prizes were in money.[27]

Royal visits were great occasions, for they gave the only chance to see royalty. When in 1867 the Grand National Hunt steeplechases were held in Bedfordshire, crowds with flags lined the approaches to the Midland station to greet the Prince of Wales.[28] When the Prince and Princess of Wales stayed at Luton Hoo, as they did for instance in 1886, the town was decorated, and two women were allowed to bring hats for the Princess to select.[29] Even when royalty passed through on a train, mayor and corporation sometimes attended in their robes to present an address.[30]

Travel abroad was still mainly for the gentry. In those leisured days they kept journals of their tours, as the Brooks did in France in 1880, or the Burgoynes of a yachting cruise in 1872.[31]

INDOOR ACTIVITIES

Of indoor leisure pursuits, music was the first to be the subject of organisation. (Perhaps music might also be called an outdoor activity. Bedford had a brass band as early as 1846 – ch. 44 – and bands were in demand for all ceremonial occasions, such as opening railways.) Bedford Harmonic Society appears to have been formed in 1836; the Rev. John Brereton was president; and it began to organise six concerts a year at the Bedford Rooms.[32] The Rev. E. Williamson, writing to his son in 1837, mentions a grand concert which was expected to be very well attended. Perhaps this society lapsed in time. But there was a revival in the 1860's, for in 1864 a concert was given by Mme. Grisi, who had sung in European capitals.[33] In 1866 a new society arose, the Bedford Musical Society, president Frederick Howard.[34] Luton Choral and Orchestral Society was formed in 1870.[35]

In the villages, various instruments such as the clarionet were still played, as at Eyeworth and Husborne Crawley,[36] especially in church orchestras, though gradually organs were coming into use in those churches which could afford them;

[26] C.R.O., X 25/42.
[27] C.R.O., PM 2737.
[28] Bedford town and townsmen, 109.
[29] Austin, Luton, ii, 204.
[30] Bedford town and townsmen, 112.
[31] C.R.O., X 143/23; LL 17/291.

[32] C.R.O., X 274/35–7.
[33] Bedford town and townsmen, 103.
[34] Coombs, Recollections, 19.
[35] Dyer–Stygall–Dony, op.cit., 163.
[36] C.R.O., P 19/5/1; P 49/5/2.

and likewise harmoniums were being acquired by chapels. The justices thought an organ too expensive for the prison chapel, and installed a seraphine (an early type of harmonium) in 1852.[37] There were now pianos; Mrs. Manning of Wrestlingworth in 1833 had one which cost £67 – it was a Broadwood; and Frances Ongley of Sandy mentions hers in her will in 1841.[38] Soon they were within the reach of the well-to-do farmer or business-man, and it became incumbent on young ladies to entertain the family with music.

Drama for most of this period continued on the same basis as previously, that is to say, travelling companies came round from time to time, and performed in the best temporary accommodation that could be arranged. At the Wheatsheaf inn, Woburn, in 1842 the play was *The Bridal Bed of a Murderer*, which sounds like a regular Victorian melodrama; and no doubt the whole affair was somewhat different from the amateur theatricals given at the Abbey in 1844 and 1850.[39] Then in Bedford there emerged Wells' Pavilion Theatre in Commercial St.; and sometimes the Corn Exchange was used, as when the D'Oyly Carte company came in 1890.[40] Theatres as we understand them today did not come till 1898 in Luton, when Lily Langtry opened the Grand Theatre, and 1899 in Bedford, when the Royal County Theatre was opened by Violet Vanbrugh.[41]

A great advance was the magic lantern. The Bedford Band of Hope Union had one which could be hired for 3s. 6d. a night; among the subjects in hand in 1893 were Little Joy's Mission, and Friendless Bob.

Astronomy was still the interest of a select few. Pettit at Leighton Buzzard (ch. 40) continued his observations till 1837; S. C. Whitbread had his own observatory at Cardington; and there was some public interest, for a lecture on astronomy was given at Eaton Bray National school in 1844.[42]

Archaeology and architecture had a greater following, though still among the gentry, clergy and middle classes. In 1847 the Bedfordshire Architectural and Archaeological Society was formed, with the Duke of Bedford and Earl de Grey as joint presidents; and until 1886 this was an active society, making expeditions and issuing annual papers in a combined publication with Leicestershire, Northamptonshire, Lincolnshire and Yorkshire. Among its members were the Rev. W. Airy of Keysoe, the Rev. H. J. Rose (later Archdeacon) of Houghton Conquest and the Rev. C. C. Beaty Pownall of Milton Ernest, a justice; also T. C. Higgins of Turvey, and James Wyatt of Bedford (proprietor of the *Bedford Times*). One achievement was that in 1850 they helped to save Willington stable and dovecote from demolition; the Duke's steward, Bennett, was then planning new farm buildings on the site; and, though a good estate-manager, he had no architectural appreciation whatever (a few years previously he had contemplated

[37] C.R.O., QSM 37, p.271.
[38] C.R.O., X 202/190; BS 1465.
[39] C.R.O., AD 3238/1; CRT 130/9.
[40] C.R.O., X 67/252–61.
[41] Dyer–Stygall–Dony, *op.cit.*, 180; C.R.O., X 279/1.
[42] C.R.O., AD 3467, 3805.

pulling down the great house in Ampthill Park). The society drew the Duke's attention to the matter, and the new farm buildings were erected nearby.[43]

Architecture, then, was arousing interest, mainly as regards the study of churches and their restoration – the latter was not always carried out sympathetically. But understanding of archaeology did not get very far. There was haphazard collection by two Bedford men, Charles Read (perhaps a relative of James – ch. 40), who looked out for fossils found in railway excavations;[44] and Dr. G. Witt; and a small group of antiquities, including some Roman pottery from Sandy, accumulated at the Bedford Rooms under the care of the Literary and Scientific Institute and the General Library.[45] When important Saxon finds were made at Kempston in 1864–5, these went to the British Museum. Scientific excavation awaited the arrival of Worthington Smith at Dunstable (ch. 42).

History began to be considered. At the inaugural meeting of the Architectural and Archaeological Society, Archdeacon Tattam expressed the hope that a county history might be compiled. Though Bucks. had one long since, Beds. lagged behind; in the previous period Oliver St. John Cooper published only parts, and Thomas Orlebar Marsh did not get beyond the note stage (ch. 39); while in 1817 Thomas Fisher, a non-Bedfordshire man, printed only drawings. A contributor to the *Gentleman's Magazine* in 1838 said that the county had been "lamentably neglected . . . yet it contains abundance of materials".[46] W. M. Harvey of Goldington Hall produced a *History of Willey Hundred* by 1878. The one who did most to lay foundations for later studies was F. A. Blaydes of Bedford (later mayor), who between 1886 and 1893 published much useful material, including *Beds. Notes and Queries*.[47] As for the county history, a writer in 1895 said "That is a task which still remains unaccomplished."[48]

As regards literature, the books of Mark Rutherford (W. H. White) were written away from this county, but never lost the impress of Bedford. A non-Bedfordshire author who loved the county was Edward FitzGerald, whether he was staying at Goldington with William Kenworthy Browne, or at the Falcon at Bletsoe. In 1839 he wrote "Here I am again in the land of old Bunyan . . . by a row of such poplars as only the Ouse knows how to rear – and pleasantly they rustle now."[49]

By now Bedfordshire was developing its own press, instead of depending on the *Northampton Mercury*. In fact, local newspapers proliferated. Communications were not yet good enough to make national newspapers generally available, even to those who could afford them – and many could not. Therefore local newspapers reported national news; and in order to give different political points of view

---

[43] C.R.O., X 69/16, pp.75–80.
[44] *Bedford town and townsmen*, 9.
[45] Bedford borough *Museum Guide*.
[46] C.R.O., AD 1717.
[47] Mayor 1892, 1895; he took the name Page-Turner

on succeeding to the family estates. See also B.H.R.S. xiv, 1–2.
[48] *Bedford town and townsmen*, 68.
[49] B. *Mag.* v, 253–5.

to an electorate extended by the reform act of 1832, they rapidly multiplied. Often they declined equally rapidly, or amalgamated, so only a few are mentioned here.[50]

The *Bedford* (later Bedfordshire) *Mercury* began in 1837 and lasted till 1912; then at Bedford came the *Times* (1845) and the *Standard* (1883), which amalgamated in the present century. At Luton in the 1850's and 1860's several papers appeared, including the *Luton Recorder* (1855) and the *Luton Times* (1855), which later amalgamated with the *Advertiser*; and it was not till 1891 that Luton's regular paper took its present form in the *Luton News*. The Dunstable *Chronicle* began in 1856; the Leighton *Observer* a little later; and the *Biggleswade Chronicle* in 1891.

SICKNESS, MISADVENTURE AND CRIME

Medicine, surgery (notably by anaesthetics and antisepsis) and public health made great advances nationally in this period, but it took some time for the effects to filter down to the local level (ch. 42).

The records of coroner's inquests make horrifying reading, from the number of infants or toddlers who were overlaid, burnt by accident, or died from convulsions. Others suffered from ignorant treatment; thus in the early 1850's babies died (among others) at Felmersham from an overdose of opium, at Potton from repeated doses of syrup of poppies, at Pertenhall from an overdose of laudanum, and at Luton from a pernicious concoction known as Godfrey's cordial.[51]

Cholera and typhus were the bane of growing towns, and have been mentioned with the growth of Bedford and Luton. Scarlet fever was often prevalent; in 1871 at Biggleswade a girl with scarlet fever was sent by her mother to one of the most crowded plait-schools up to the actual day of her death; and at Meppershall six children, of whom one died, had it in one house.[52] Venereal disease occurred in the gaol, and there was also a case of leprosy in 1841.[53] The main scourge of the time was consumption, fostered by under-nourishment and bad living conditions. (For understanding of the long-drawn out decline produced by consumption, the reader is referred to the novels of Charlotte Yonge.) As it was highly infectious, it was found in all classes. Joanna Fitzpatrick of Bedford, granddaughter of Sir William Long, had an incessant cough, and in 1840, when she was 18, her brother (later vicar of Holy Trinity) was summoned home from Cambridge to see her die.[54] It was probably consumption of which Earl de Grey's son and heir died in 1831 a few weeks before what would have been his 21st birthday; his sister wrote that he was "so very weak", and his symptoms had latterly changed much; a few

[50] For a complete list, see C.R.O., CRT 120/25.
[51] C.R.O., CO 11/1–2, nos. 1715, 1773, 2005, 2045. See Dr. May's denunciation of Godfrey's cordial in Charlotte Yonge, *The Daisy Chain*, when his grandchild died from it; her account seems to be strictly true.
[52] C.R.O., PUBWM 10, 253–4.
[53] C.R.O., QGR 1/7.
[54] N. R. Fitzpatrick, *Memoir of R. W. Fitzpatrick*, p.11.

weeks later she said "Papa and Mama bear the heavy blow better than I could have dared to hope."[55] Prisoners in the gaol or house of correction died of consumption, like Jabez Holland in 1841.

For some years the infirmary at Bedford remained the only hospital provision in the county, though in addition in 1848 a fever hospital was opened at Bedford. At the infirmary the patient's diet in 1841 still included beer, and suet pudding was discontinued only in that year; while bread apparently was baked from flour ground by the prisoners in the house of correction on their treadmill.[56] The infirmary depended entirely on funds raised voluntarily, and so economy was always in the governors' minds. In 1854 it was desired to buy a microscope for £30, an "essential instrument in the investigation of disease", "but the funds were not in a sufficiently good state".[57] A sick person who needed to enter the infirmary had to get a letter of recommendation from some subscriber; each subscriber of a guinea annually could recommend one in-patient; and a subscriber of two guineas was a governor; while various benefit clubs subscribed varying amounts. There were also collections and other fund-raising efforts. In 1883 there were 607 in-patients and 2,602 out-patients; and 114 operations took place. Meanwhile the provision of a hospital in expanding Luton (ch. 42), again by voluntary effort, had met the need of the south. By 1895 the old infirmary at Bedford was out of date, and a new hospital was built, towards which the Duke and Whitbread each subscribed £5,000.[58]

Meanwhile the profession of nurse had been transformed from that of inferior drudge to one of honourable and enlightened service. How low was the former estimation of nurses is indicated by the sneer of a wounded Bedfordshire officer (see below) in the Crimea when Florence Nightingale and her nurses arrived; he referred to them as "40 unprotected females" who were a regular object of ridicule.

By the end of the period attempts were beginning to be made to form local district nursing associations which raised funds to engage a nurse to serve the locality. One of the earliest was Ampthill in 1893; Bedford association was formed in 1896 and so was Dunstable; and the county association in 1897. These efforts never completely covered the county.

A medical oddity at this time was the chalybeate spring at Folly farm, Flitwick. At first the farmer, H. K. Stevens, sold its water at 2d. a bottle. After it was the subject of comment in the *British Medical Journal* in 1880 and the *Lancet* in 1891, it was marketed on a large scale for several years.[59]

There was a greater number of doctors available, and they of course charged fees. It was necessary to help the poor to pay the fees, or at least to pay something,

[55] C.R.O., L 30/11/241/9–10.
[56] C.R.O., HO/BM 22; HBO/BM 5, p.267.
[57] C.R.O., HO/BM 8 (6 Nov.).

[58] *Bedford town and townsmen*, 150.
[59] B. *Mag.* xi, 185.

and thus arose the Provident Dispensary. The dispensary enrolled the services of certain doctors, and perhaps also a dentist; and thrifty poor people (at Bedford their wages must be below 25s. weekly) enrolled as members, paying 1d. a week if single, or not more than 3d. for the whole family. If too ill to come to the dispensary, they would be visited at home by the surgeon if he received their card by 10 a.m.[60]

Self-help like this was widely practised. There was a Friendly Society in almost every parish to help in time of sickness or with burial expenses. In the larger parishes there was more than one, for the usual meetingplace was an inn, and each inn had its own clientele. At Leighton, the Union Society met at the Unicorn, the Amicable and Brotherly at the George, the United Brotherly at the Ewe, Lamb and Shepherd, and the Fraternal at the Golden Bell. On the other hand, there were a few religious or teetotal societies; in Luton the Total Abstinence Society met at the Temperance Hall; at Turvey the meeting place was the vestry; and one Bedford club met at Howard Congregational church. Sometimes, as at Renhold and Stagsden, the club met in the schoolroom. As time went on, these societies tended to be branches or lodges of national organisations such as the Oddfellows, the Foresters, or the Free Gardeners.

In many villages there were coal clubs, clothing clubs, or savings clubs pure and simple, often helped by landowner or incumbent. Thus with a clothing club members paid in a few pence throughout the year, and then were able to obtain clothes to the value of their contributions (plus their share of the charitable donations). In the towns arose building societies to help the active small man buy his house; Biggleswade had one as early as 1846, and so did Dunstable, while those at Bedford, Leighton and Luton followed soon after. The County Building Society dates from 1853.[61]

But there were many people who through age, ill health, or misfortune began or ended their lives in the workhouse. This was not the small, squalid, haphazard workhouse of a previous generation, but the large, central, efficiently-run establishment of the Union. Guardians made rules about the quantity of food per person, finding at Bedford in 1853 that it was too large; or directing in 1848 that there should be more suet pudding and pease pudding to make up for the potato shortage; or in 1846 cavilling at buns for the children. The local press account of Christmas in Bedford workhouse in 1859 has a somewhat hollow ring. The hall was tastefully decorated with evergreens, the mayor and leading towns-men were present, and there was dinner of roast beef and plum pudding, with home-brewed ale. After grace had been sung, the mayor (John Howard) made a speech of considerable length, followed by Alderman Hurst; and the greatest attention was paid – the speeches were listened to in perfect silence, except for the clapping. One inmate then made a short speech of thanks, and the inmates returned

60 C.R.O., X 275/18.   61 C.R.O., AD 1978.

to their own rooms, while the children had oranges and nuts.[62]

In spite of the efficiency of the Victorian workhouse, the general attitude towards it was probably reflected in a long doggerel poem written by John Bundy, aged 87, of Eaton Socon, of which the refrain is "They must go and die in the Union." (It was apparently prompted by a case at Kimbolton of an old man who was taken to the workhouse and died next day.) One verse runs:

> A poor old man when he reaches fourscore,
> And has done all he can, can do no more;
> To ask for relief it makes him afraid.
> Since they have took up with this body-snatching way
> He must go and die in the Union.[63]

Crime was the way taken by others. At the gaol in this period was a remarkable governor, R. E. Roberts, who compiled statistics 1801–78 analysing the incidence of crime in every possible light.[64] He found that the age of 21–25 was the most common for an offender, whether at quarter sessions or at assizes. Larceny was by far the chief offence at either court. At assizes the next was burglary, and then horse or cattle-stealing. At quarter sessions the next was assault; then poultry and rabbit-stealing. At petty sessions the order was: poaching; vagrancy; assault. Whipping ceased in 1850, and up to then there were 277 whippings in the century. Transportation ceased in 1857; here the figure is not easy to get; but from 1801 to 1857 there were 281 death sentences, of which only 15 were carried out; so that most of the remaining offenders were transported. The death sentence, still the legal penalty for many offences, was, as indicated above, not often carried out; and between 1823 and 1841 legislation abolished it as a penalty for almost everything but murder.

Murder came quite low in the list of crimes, with 45 cases from 1801 to 1878, but it bulked large in public interest. A feature of the time was the broadsheet, with lurid details of the crime and a crude illustration of the gallows. Such was one produced in 1833 for Thomas Crawley of Luton, who struck a poor old man Joseph Adams, with a stick cut from the hedge, in order to rob him, having previously sent away his own 13-year old son; and the blow was fatal. The boy shed tears in court, for his father's life depended "upon every word the poor boy uttered". Crawley "underwent the awful sentence of the law with great fortitude. The crowd of spectators was immense."[65]

The gaol register of this period has personal comments on some prisoners, such as: "a bad fellow (Irish)"; "a troublesome old man"; "this is a bad man, but for fear of punishment he kept himself in order"; "indifferent"; "very quiet and well-behaved".[66]

[62] C.R.O., PUBM 12 (2 Jan. 1860).
[63] C.R.O., X 67/704.
[64] C.R.O., QSS 4.

[65] C.R.O., CRT Luton 130/9.
[66] C.R.O., QGV 10.

The problem of the unmarried mother began to be recognised as one needing sympathy and help. By the end of the period the Ely Diocesan Association for rescue and preventive work was in action.[67] In 1885 there were 17 children in the Bedford home; two girls had lately been rescued; and during the previous year two girls had left for domestic service and one to learn dressmaking.

MILITARY

While those who were unable to maintain the pace of ordinary civilian life subsided into workhouse or gaol, those whose active spirits chafed at it might seek a military outlet.

In the earlier part of this period, such an outlet had to be in the regular army or in that of the East India company, for in the long years of peace after Waterloo volunteer effort died down. The militia was dormant, with a small depot, at first in Castle Lane (now part of Cecil Higgins Museum), later in Goldington Road; and a skeleton of officers.[68] Even of the regular army we have little information till the mid-century brought a sharp change in England's situation; and when we do it is not of the rank-and-file but of the gentry.

When the Crimean War broke out, Sir John Burgoyne of Sutton was a captain in the Grenadier Guards. His voyage out took 4 months – it was a "wretched morning, rainy and cold" when they called at Constantinople on the way; but in the Crimea in July 1854 it was very hot, and on march the waggons stuck in the deep sand of the road, while there was soon cholera among the men. In September the English, French and Turkish forces confronted the Russians at the river Alma, where they forced the ford. "Without any hustling the men formed on the edge of the bank under a tremendous fire . . . just then the smoke cleared . . . we received orders to advance, and before we had done six paces I felt a blow on my right shin, and, on putting my foot to the ground, fell. Young Hamilton took the colours from me, and the battalion went on." After some time stretcher-bearers collected him; "when the doctors came near me, and I saw their bloody hands and knives, I felt sure they would have my leg off", but he was lucky. He passed the night on hay under a wall, the moans of the wounded sounding in his ears. In his brief stay in hospital he had time to note that the commonest medical appliances were lacking and that men were dying by scores for want of them, but he did not see things at their worst, for in November he was invalided home.[69] After the war, Bedford was allotted a captured Russian gun, which was eventually placed on the Embankment.[70]

After the Crimean War came the Indian mutiny. J. H. Brooks of Flitwick was a Major in the East India company's service. He went out in 1843. The mutiny of 1857 broke out in March while he was on the march from Lucknow to Mhow, and it was not until July that trouble reached nearby Indore. With a small troop,

[67] C.R.O., X 67/243.
[68] B. Mag. viii, 265; see also C.R.O., QSM 46, p.698.
[69] B.H.R.S. xl, 163–83.
[70] Bedford town and townsmen, 138.

Brooks captured from the rebels two 9-pounder guns. "It was midday, and the heat of the sun teriffic. The shock of the charge up to the gun had dislodged my helmet, which fell to the ground; to pick it up was impossible", as the rebel infantry were surrounding them menacingly. "For the best part of an hour, which seemed an age, we remained parrying their spear thrusts, and parleying with them, till reinforcements arrived. I recovered my helmet, and without resistance the men were disarmed, the bullocks harnessed to the guns, and we marched back to cantonments." However, as the situation was uncertain, the commanding officer ordered all women and children into the fort, and directed the regiments to camp outside. That night in the moonlight the sepoys rose, yelling "Kill the infidel", but some of the officers managed to get clear and were hauled up the fort walls "in a somewhat exhausted state", while the rebels made off to Delhi. Brooks remained in the fort till reinforcements arrived from Europe.[71] (For Capt. William Peel, see ch. 44.)

The change for the worse in England's security brought an awareness of the need to be prepared. The militia was reanimated. Volunteer effort was encouraged again; a Bedfordshire Rifle Association was formed with a number of companies and regular competitions for accurate shooting were held. Thus in 1862 the 7th Coy. (Biggleswade) held squad drills each month at Biggleswade, Shefford, Eaton Socon and Potton; and company drills also monthly at Biggleswade, Henlow and Potton; and in 1865 at their annual prize meeting in Wrest Park the prizes offered included a silver watch, field-glasses, and the works of Shakespeare.[72] The county uniform was grey, trimmed with green braid; and for a parade a green shako with a plume of cock's feathers.[73] The Rifle Volunteer public house on the way to Whipsnade was where the Dunstable volunteers refreshed themselves on the way to and from shooting practice.

Horsemen, especially those of higher social standing, preferred a cavalry corps, and so those in north Beds. turned to the troop of light horse raised by the Duke of Manchester of Kimbolton castle in 1859; in fact, Capt. Polhill-Turner's troop even included a Hockliffe man, Sergt. H. Meux Smith. Its uniform was a scarlet tunic and white breeches. When in 1870 the Prince and Princess of Wales stayed at Kimbolton castle, the Duke of Manchester's Light Horse escorted the royal carriage at a sharp trot; and a few days later a Volunteer Ball was held at the castle (the Princess wore lavender satin). In 1877 the troop acquired a regimental song, of which the chorus ran:

> Then raise your sabres high, and as a battle cry
> Ring out aloud three hearty British cheers
> For our Duke so brave and true, and our noble Duchess too,
> And his Grace's gallant Light Horse volunteers.[74]

[71] B.H.R.S. xl, 187–99.
[72] C.R.O., X 67/546–7; see also X 95/215–6.
[73] Bedford town and townsmen, 91.
[74] C.R.O , X 25/38; see also CRT 140/6.

Fortunately the volunteers never needed to go into action.

It was still the regular army that attracted daring spirits like F. G. Burnaby, son of the rector of St. Peter's, Bedford. He made a balloon trip in 1866. His book, *Ride to Khiva*, describes his 1875 mid-winter ride 300 miles across the steppes en route for Kabul and India, but at Khiva he was recalled by the government for fear of trouble with the Russians. At the age of 43 he went without leave as a volunteer to help his friend Gordon in Egypt, and was killed at the battle of Abou Klea.[75]

The men of humbler station who enlisted in the Bedfordshire Regiment saw less exciting service. It was usual for a regiment to do 5 or 6 years of garrison duty at home, and then about 20 years overseas. The regiment was in Ceylon and India 1820–41; and was in the new world (West Indies and Canada) from about 1846 to 1869; so it missed both the Crimean War and the Indian Mutiny.[76] In the 1870's the government resolved to give each regiment a depot in its territorial area, and so Kempston barracks were opened in 1878, and the old militia depot in Goldington Road was given up. Henceforward one battalion was at the depot while one was on foreign service.

THE WIDER WORLD

However, it was not only through the army that Bedfordshire had contact with the wider world. Archdeacon Tattam visited Jerusalem, on which he gave a lecture in Bedford in 1847; and James Howard in 1868 lectured on his travels in Egypt; S. C. Whitbread went to the United States, then such an unusual trip that on his safe return in 1854 a dinner was given him at the Swan; foreign visitors came to Bedford, such as Garibaldi in 1864, and General Grant, ex-President of the United States, in 1877.[77]

From Australia there was news from local families who had emigrated. Some young people were sent by their families because they had been difficult at home. Such a one was John Feazey of Wilden at Melbourne; on the whole he was happy; and he acknowledged that "it is the best thing that fathers can do with troublesome sons to send them across the sea . . . that will bring them to their thoughts very soon"; he was working on a sheep farm, and thought he had good prospects, but could not help regretting his lost love, Miss Dean.[78] Dr. G. Witt was a professional man from Bedford who emigrated to Sydney. "I sometimes talk of taking a trip to England for the summer months," he wrote to Thomas Barnard in 1851, "but my wife vows that if she once gets back she will take her chance and remain." Mrs. Witt was bothered by the servant problem. "You can form no idea of the wretched servants here and their impertinence. Miserable Irish girls come to the door of the best houses without shoes or stockings, as ignorant and dirty as savages; they literally know nothing . . . I often think what

[75] *B. Mag.* i, 111–3.
[76] F. Maurice, *16th Foot*, 81–9.
[77] *Bedford town and townsmen*, 69, 81, 102, 111–2, 137.
[78] *B.H.R.S.* xl, 231–2.

would Mrs. Barnard say?" Dr. Witt himself was more worried about the mosquitoes; but on the other hand he enjoyed the fruit: "oranges by cartloads, grapes by the ton, the vineyards are attached to almost every house".[79]

From South Africa Thomas Maclear (brother of the Rev. George) wrote in 1839 that the mountains were rugged beyond conception, and stored with wolves, panthers, jackals and baboons.[80] Later George Farrar (grandson of John Howard) developed Benoni.

It was to Canada that Arthur Barnard, nephew of Thomas, went in June 1878, after being seen off at Liverpool by his uncle. He found the heat intense, 98° in the shade. Land was only 8s. an acre, and he asked his uncle to transfer £200 to Winnipeg, where he proposed to buy about 160 acres. By November he had built his house or shanty, and was planning to extend his farm and buy 100 head of stock.[81]

In the United States the loyalist Rugeley family's Carolina estate was not finally cleared up till 1848, for the sale of building plots in Charleston was involved; by this time over $14,000 had been remitted. The number of middle-class emigrants from Bedfordshire in this period is impossible to assess.

Some families like the Paynes still had West Indian estates. The Paynes' agent wrote in 1865 after negro slaves in the United States had been freed that sugar prospects would be "good for some time . . . the emancipated negro will hardly be induced to do as much work as in a state of slavery".[82]

Trade made other overseas contacts. In 1865 Edward Pettit of Leighton Buzzard was a merchant in Canton, China.[83]

Then there were the roving spirits. Such was Albert Culpin,[84] one of the large family of a Congregational minister at Shillington, and a grief to his father. He ran away from his apprenticeship in Birmingham; enlisted in the army and deserted; stowed away to America. In 1881 he returned to England, and his family tried hard to settle him in regular work. Soon he was off again, writing from San Francisco, Wyoming, Texas, New Orleans; then again from Liverpool, ashamed of himself for writing for money, but nevertheless doing so; then once more off to sea, and in 1892 writing from Sydney. Such men, whatever their class of origin, never settled anywhere.

To all these must be added the humbler emigrants, the convicts transported, the farm-workers helped to emigrate by the poor law authorities, those who managed to scrape up a fare to the United States by means of savings augmented by charitable donations, and the gold-diggers; for some of these managed to keep in touch with their families also (ch. 41).

By the end of the century there was a Bedford in South Africa, a Cape

[79] Op.cit., 233–5.
[80] C.R.O., M 10/5/535.
[81] C.R.O., BD 1345, 1392.
[82] C.R.O., D 7.
[83] C.R.O., X 233/22.
[84] C.R.O., X 345.

534

Bedford in Queensland, and several Bedfords in the United States (New Jersey, Massachusetts, Pennsylvania, Kentucky, Iowa, Indiana, Montana, Illinois); but oddly enough no Luton.

46 – ADMINISTRATION, 1834–94

SOME ASPECTS of administration have already been covered: the boroughs of Bedford, Luton and Dunstable; the fumbling piecemeal Victorian system of elective boards, especially for poor and later for roads; and the responsibility of quarter sessions for bridges. It remains to deal with county administration as a whole; with the last of the elective boards, the school board; and with the new administrative set-up which took shape at the end of the period.

The structure of county administration resembled a building which had been altered and enlarged during many centuries. It had, so-to-speak, Saxon foundations, but little of the Saxon structure remained except a main doorway (shrievalty) and traces in the walls (hundreds). It had a substantial medieval hall (quarter sessions). In the Tudor period a defensive porch had been added (lieutenancy). The building was venerable, but there was no plumbing (elections); so it was ill-adapted for modern living. The French or Russians would have pulled it down and started again. The Victorians, after years of procrastination, retained the main structure, but built on a modern wing (county council). Thus until nearly the end of this period, till 1888, quarter sessions were still responsible for county administration as well as for justice.

QUARTER AND PETTY SESSIONS

The chairmen of quarter sessions were Francis Pym of Sandy, 1832–48; T. C. Higgins of Turvey, 1848–65; John Harvey of Ickwell, 1865–79; and William Stuart of Tempsford, 1879–91.

The most notable of these was T. C. Higgins, who carried on the humanitarian tradition of Howard and Whitbread. In his time gaol and asylum were rebuilt, and the Carlton reformatory established, though he failed to carry the other justices with him in a plan to rebuild the inconvenient old Sessions House. But lest we think of him only as a dedicated county figure, it is as well to recall the charming letters which he wrote in 1838, as an eager young lover, to his future wife, Charlotte Price. "You have entirely occupied my thoughts since we parted yesterday" (in fact, in thinking of her he forgot to attend a county meeting). Humbly he admitted that he was sometimes called particular, strict, and even fussy; but these qualities would "perhaps take flight the moment that gold hoop shall be placed on your finger". And again from Turvey in June just before the wedding: "Everything seems to smile at the near prospect of enjoying the fostering care of a mistress."[1]

[1] In the possession of Mrs. Hanbury. Characteristically Higgins asked his bride-to-be what time her family had

At quarter sessions there was a strong feeling of responsibility. The proportion of justices who attended sessions increased, till at Michaelmas 1853 attendance reached 36. Though there were still clerical justices, such as the Rev. W. C. Chalk of Wilden, the Rev. C. C. B. Pownall of Milton Ernest, or the Rev. F. C. G. Passy of Wilstead, lay justices predominated, such as Lionel Ames of Luton, R. T. Gilpin of Hockliffe, J. Tucker of Pavenham, and the families of Higgins, Pym, Russell, Thornton, and Whitbread. Some were uneasy at the fact that they were not elected: in 1860 Lord Charles Russell proposed to sessions to petition parliament that "the time is come when the representative principle may be with advantage admitted into the management of the county", but he was out-voted.[2] By the end of the period the social range from which justices were drawn had been extended; there were solicitors like Henry Trethewy and E. T. Leeds Smith; and there was Asher Hucklesby, who owned the largest hat firm in Luton, and was on the county commission even when Luton had its own commission of the peace.

An embryo local government service was emerging. Towards this the Pearse family, who were clerks of the peace for the whole of this period, contributed. Theed Pearse senior, that amiable and able gentleman who might be called the father of our modern county administration, retired in 1843. Theed Pearse junior succeeded him. Theed William Pearse served from 1857 to 1890; and by his time there was a salary of £650 p.a. for the clerkship, though he himself still engaged and paid what staff he required.

The responsibilities of county surveyor increased, though these were not yet concerned with roads. Now that nearly all bridges were county bridges, there was more work in supervising them (ch. 44). County buildings were also more demanding; there was pressure on the Sessions House; the gaol was rebuilt and enlarged in 1848 (the house of correction being pulled down and converted into a garden); before long, police stations had to be built; and a new asylum was required (see below). From 1858 to 1874 the experiment was tried of having two surveyors, one for the north and one for the south; but in 1874, after the unfortunate affair of Holme bridge (ch. 44), William Watson became surveyor for the whole county with a salary of £200 p.a.

The office of county treasurer continued to be held by a Bedford business man, the coal merchants T. A. Green or T. J. Green, or the banker, T. Barnard. In 1845 the justices ordered a new rating valuation to be made by the churchwardens and overseers; Bedford was assessed at £37,232; Luton £33,000; Biggleswade £12,430; Leighton £11,370; and Dunstable £7,000;[3] the total for the county being £451,444; that is to say, the urban centres provided less than one quarter of the whole. Till now, county rates had been collected by the high constables of the hundreds; in fact this was one of the high constable's main

---

morning and evening prayers – "I shall think of you
most particularly then."

[2] C.R.O., QSM 40, p.494.
[3] C.R.O., QSM 35, p.293.

functions; but in 1847 county rates were first collected in the various unions by a precept on the poor rate.[4] The hundred was losing its significance, though the office of high constable was not formally abolished till 1870, and the land tax was collected by hundreds till the present century.[5]

Petty sessions no longer met by hundreds, but this alteration took place somewhat earlier than the alteration in rate-collecting. In 1828 an act required quarter sessions to define petty sessional districts. The new arrangement, which came into force in 1830, made six districts instead of the old five (there were nine hundreds: Flitt, Manshead and Redbornstoke had met individually, but the three northern and the three eastern hundreds had combined). The new districts were based on the urban centres of Ampthill, Bedford, Biggleswade, Luton and Woburn; with one for northern rural parishes at Bletsoe.[6] The reason for Woburn being one was probably the Duke's residence there, for it was not populous, and Leighton would have been the more logical choice. In fact, in 1854 an additional petty sessional district was made for the Leighton area. The northern rural petty sessional district was at first known as Bletsoe, because this had been the old meetingplace for the three northern hundreds; but before long it became known as Sharnbrook, where a courthouse was built.

POLICE

There was a new county officer, the chief constable of the new professional county police.

For long the old system by which parishioners each year nominated one or more of their number to serve as constable had been inadequate. Its defects were stated as early as 1821 by a Bedfordian, J. H. Warden. The inexperienced constable was, he said, new to his office every year, must first of all attend to his own business, and could not be aware of the manoeuvres of loose and desperate characters; besides, if the active constable was a shopkeeper, the lower classes would attack him with every opprobrious name and seek to injure him. If there were professional police, they would "become acquainted with the artful devices of experienced robbers, their modes of communication with each other, and the disposal of their booty . . . the old offender will find his old devices fail and the juvenile depredator will be deterred from crime by speedy exposure".[7] Professional help from London had had to be sought for the Ampthill riot in 1835 (ch. 41). When a police act was passed in 1839, quarter sessions endorsed all Warden's statements, and added that there was little or no cooperation between one rural parish and another, and that the high constable of the hundred concerned

[4] C.R.O., QSM 35, pp.545, 553.

[5] The land tax was imposed in 1692. In 1798 it was legally fixed at 4s. in the pound (which it had in fact been for some time), and redemption was encouraged. Many redeemed it. The unredeemed tax remained a fixed charge until the present century and was still collected by hundreds. For the abolition of the office of high constable, see QSM 45, p.127.

[6] C.R.O., QSM 30, p.74.

[7] C.R.O., QSR 1821/711.

himself very little with crime.[8] The ease with which offenders escaped had long ago led to private associations for the suppression of felons (ch. 34).

At first there were doubts about the cost of a force, and quarter sessions thought perhaps 15 men would suffice – three in Bedford, and one constable in each of a dozen larger places, of which Luton was one. In the end the initial force consisted of a chief constable, Edward Boultbee, who was to live at Ampthill, 6 superintendents, and 40 constables.[9] A constable was paid 19s. a week and had a clothing allowance and a lantern. A tradition of professional conduct was not easy to establish. It may be that only "toughs" were attracted to enrol, or perhaps it was thought these were what was required. Not all constables could shed their old habits easily.[10] Frederick Porter joined in March, 1840; was suspended in July for being drunk; and dismissed in October for general bad conduct. James Cooper who joined in April was in July allowed to resign, "there being doubts as to his honesty in money matters". Several were found drinking and smoking on duty; Charles Kitchener played skittles on duty; 3 constables played cricket at Potton fair; Charles Vear neglected his duty at Cranfield feast; and John Rayner did likewise at Biggleswade races. However, in time the steady type began to enrol; Edward Scott served for 26 years and retired in 1866 on a pension of 14s. weekly.

Both because of the early force's cost and its doubtful nature, it was slow in winning public confidence. In 1841 36 ratepayers of Houghton Regis represented to quarter sessions "our utter disappointment . . . the amount of crime being in our estimation in no respect diminished, and the enormous cost being totally dispro-portionate . . . We therefore respectfully entreat your worships [to relieve] us altogether from the rural police";[11] and one signatory added "I am that I am weary of the police." In 1843 Turvey petitioned that the police force should be discontinued except for the chief constable and superintendents.[12] But soon the attitude changed. It was even urged that the force should be extended (it was by one constable) to deal with railway navvies; and Luton with its increasing popu-lation more than once petitioned for extra constables; in 1860 72 Luton townsmen said that recently "two well-known and experienced thieves" were apprehended in the church vestry; "two constables were knocked down, and if there had not been two others within call their lives would probably have been sacrificed".[13]

By 1875, when the chief constable was A. J. Warner, a sergeant was paid 27s. a week and a constable 22s., with 9d. for boots. Warner admonished his force as follows: "It should be understood at the outset that the principal object to be obtained is the prevention of crime . . . There is no qualification more indispen-able to a constable than a perfect command of temper, never suffering himself to

---

[8] C.R.O., QSM 33, p.395.
[9] C.R.O., QSM 33, p.531. After 1842, petty con-stables were continued only where they were thought necessary; QSM 34, p.428.
[10] C.R.O., QES 8.
[11] C.R.O., QEV 3.
[12] *Loc.cit.*
[13] *Loc.cit.*

be moved in the slightest degree."[14]

One result of the new system was the gradual disappearance of parish cages.[15] An enquiry was made in 1840, when it was recommended that cages should be built at Riseley, Shillington and Turvey; and that some existing ones, like Gt. Barford and Cranfield, should be repaired; but there arose a doubt whether county rates could be used for this. It was not always clear to whom an existing cage belonged. Some cages became dilapidated; Cardington pulled down theirs in 1853; Dunton followed suit in 1875; but Wilstead in the same year restored their cage with an iron roof. That at Stotfold had a useful, if ignominious, end as a toilet for the Strict Baptist chapel.

A new development in the treatment of young offenders under 16 was the establishment of a reformatory school at Carlton. The government was not prepared to provide such schools, but by an act of 1844 would in effect take them over when built and after inspection. For a small county Bedfordshire was very quick in acting on this. (Two schools elsewhere preceded the act, and seven other counties were moving by 1857.) Its promptness was mainly due to T. C. Higgins – and it is not every landowner who would promote the establishment of a reformatory on his own doorstep. A public meeting was held in 1855. Subscriptions realised £1,679, and land was bought on which were erected house and workshops and farm buildings. The first superintendent was Joseph Roberts, and under him about 30 boys were variously occupied in lessons, farmwork, shoemaking and tailoring; while the gaol chaplain and the vicar of Harrold gave religious instruction once a week.[16] The reformatory was approved in 1857; and in 1861 the committee reported that the school had "fully answered the expectations of its most ardent promoters", and that, with government assistance, it was now self-supporting.

Under the prison act of 1877, the government also took over gaols. Justices retained only the right or duty of visiting; and so the long history of local control of the gaol came to an end.

THREE COUNTIES ASYLUM

For many years the energetic and enlightened John Harris continued as medical superintendent of the asylum which Bedfordshire had so early provided (ch. 36); and in 1837 he also set up a private asylum for 30 patients at Springfield house, Kempston, which was later carried on by Henry Harris, subsequently by David Bower, and continued until recent years.

Meanwhile other counties began to seek help from the Bedfordshire asylum. First Hertfordshire began to participate in 1837; Bedford borough in 1846; then Huntingdonshire in 1847. But the asylum began to be crowded, and the parish

---

[14] C.R.O., QEV 2/4.
[15] See C.R.O. subject index on cages. Houghton Regis cage door recently found its way to Luton Museum.

[16] C.R.O., QSM 41, p.93. Mrs. Hanbury of Turvey House, descendant of T. C. Higgins, is still on the Board of Managers, and one house is called Higgins House.

of Bedford St. Mary petitioned quarter sessions that deceased asylum inmates were filling up its small graveyard! A report of visiting justices in 1857 says that there were then 307 patients, of whom two-thirds were occupied in active work, the men outdoors or as artisans, and the women on needlework, strawplait, lace, or working in the laundry. The justices thought the amount of work done most creditable – they ventured to suggest as a possible addition knitted stockings; and they also recommended the provision of a better description of dress for Sunday. All patients were tranquil except one; this was a woman who had arrived the previous Sunday, lightly bound in a straitjacket, and covered with bruises, having also a large wound on her shin-bone, while her wrists and angles bore marks of ligatures which had ulcerated.[17]

It was decided to erect the new premises at Arlesey, as a more central place for the three counties, and the move took place in 1860. There were then 422 patients, of whom nearly half came from Herts., 156 from Beds., 9 from Bedford borough, and the remainder from Hunts. By 1880 the total number had nearly doubled.

SCHOOL BOARDS

By 1870 it had become clear that voluntary efforts to provide education (ch. 43) could not ensure equal provision, and were difficult to maintain. For 40 years the state had supervised voluntary efforts. It had sent inspectors to schools receiving grants. It had tried to secure better teachers by providing that a pupil-teacher who had served 5 years in a suitable school was eligible for a grant at a training college, and by giving a teacher with a training college certificate a government grant in addition to his ordinary salary. It had introduced a system of payment by results, by which the school grant was related to tests passed by the children in reading, writing and arithmetic; but unfortunately withholding or diminishing a grant to a bad school did not necessarily help the school to improve. In 1870 an act was passed which accepted state responsibility for seeing that education was generally available. Since this was the age of elected boards for any and every purpose, the machinery set up was an elected school board, wherever required, which could levy a rate for school purposes, though school fees were still collected from all parents who could afford it.

Sundon is an example of a school provided in this way in a place where hitherto there had been little or no provision. A school was built in 1873 and opened in the spring of 1874. The master had an uphill task. Parents were un-cooperative, for many of them had no education whatever and could not see the benefit of it; the children were very backward, several not knowing even their letters; the girls went to morning plait-school, the boys went weeding; and in the first month there was an outbreak of scarlatina; so that the average attendance was 51 out of a possible 80. The master wrote in his logbook: "I sometimes think that

[17] C.R.O., LT 5.

if I had known the true state of affairs I would never have undertaken the mastership."

Sometimes two or three small villages combined in one board, as with Stanbridge, Eggington and Tilsworth. The first meeting of the board was held at the Five Bells, Stanbridge, and the board resolved to build two schools, one at Stanbridge and one at Eggington, and discussed suitable sites. To their mortification, the owners were not cooperative; several were applied to; "all refused to sell a site"; and it was several months before the Eggington charity trustees agreed to sell part of the charity land. The two schools were not built and opened till 1880 and 1881 respectively.

When there was an existing school which had been built by a landowner the transfer was usually straightforward. Thus at Cople, where the school and teacher's house had been built by the Duke of Bedford, the Duke agreed to let these at the nominal rents of 10s. and £5 p.a. respectively, and gave the board the school furniture and books.

A minority of voluntary schools (usually National, i.e., Anglican) were taken over by boards. At Flitwick the managers and subscribers of the National school voted to transfer the school and teacher's house, provided the board would take over the debt on them, and provided that the school could still be a church Sunday school on Sundays. But the Privy Council Committee would not allow the debt to be transferred. In the end, the managers raised enough to pay it off, transferred the premises, and sold the books and furniture at a valuation. The board's first attempt to engage a teacher was not successful; they advertised for a certificated woman, who was to be paid not more than £50 p.a., though her coals would be found. In the end they had to engage a man at £85 p.a., and he objected to being expected to take evening school without extra remuneration.

Sometimes a voluntary school handed over to the board when it got into difficulties. Such was Houghton Conquest, where the managers found themselves with an unsatisfactory teacher. Mr. and Mrs. Walker had been engaged in June 1877, as the result of an advertisement for a good churchman, organist, choirtrainer, who for a salary of £90 would take school, Sunday school, and night school (for which he could retain the fees); while his wife would take the infants and the sewing. Unfortunately on 23 June Mr. Walker was intoxicated at choir practice and was instantly dismissed. He refused to give up the keys of school, church and organ, and also the music, and demanded 3 months' salary. In September the managers resolved that the school be carried on in future on the school board system.[18]

Sometimes, though there was a voluntary school, it was not sufficient for the growing needs of the parish, and an additional school had to be built. Thus

[18] C.R.O., P. 11/25/29. The remaining references in records in C.R.O.
this section on school boards are from school board

at Arlesey the National school dated from 1856; but there was a growing population, especially in the neighbourhood of the brickworks; so the board continued
the former National school for girls and infants, and built a new school at the
Siding.

In towns there was special scope for extension, and the Luton board built
several new schools, beginning with a higher grade school in Waller St. in 1876;[19]
though it is worth noting that at one of Luton's National schools, that in Queen
Square, there was from 1885 a notable headmaster, T. B. Ellery, who was President of the National Union of Teachers. Bedford was a special case, for here
education was almost entirely in the hands of the Harpur Trust, which had
set up a school for poor boys as long ago as 1815, and built further schools in
1875 and 1893; so a board was not even initiated in Bedford till 1897.

Over 50 school boards were set up in the county. What they did was to
equalise provision, to stop the gaps, and to take over the minority of voluntary
schools which were running into difficulties. But there was still much vigour in the
voluntary movement as a whole, and at the end of the period nearly half the
parishes in the county still had one or more voluntary schools.

THE SHIRE HALL

The Sessions House was inadequate. As early as 1831 Matthiason noted that
the courts were too much confined, and that there was no waiting accommodation
for the friends and relatives of the accused, who were found weeping and lament-
ing in nearby public-houses.[20] Some justices, including T. C. Higgins and Henry
Littledale, began to urge that a new building was required. Economy prevailed,
probably because of all the other development that was going on at the time, and
only minor alterations were made in 1858. By 1877, when Mr. Justice Denman
complained of "the foetid and unwholesome state of the courts" the county
population had trebled since the Sessions House was built in 1752. Denman
engaged a room elsewhere to serve as indictment office, presenting the justices
with a bill. Even then the new building came about by two stages. At first the
progressive justices, led by C. Magniac and W. B. Higgins, were only able to
get authority for building new courts at the back of the existing Sessions House.
The architect engaged, Alfred Waterhouse, had Gothic tastes, and new Gothic
courts rose behind the Georgian front. Meanwhile W. B. Higgins died, but opinion had been won over, and at Michaelmas sessions 1880 a resolution was carried
that the building was still inadequate. The old Sessions House was swept away,
and its rubble used for foundations. In front of his new courts, Waterhouse built
as a waiting area a Gothic hall, with subsidiary rooms opening off it, one of which
was for the use of the clerk of the peace. The new Shire Hall thus completed would
have functioned splendidly in 1830. But for the new era in local government which
was about to begin it had no provision at all.

[19] Dyer–Stygall–Dony, *Luton*, p.155.   [20] J. H. Matthiason, *Bedford and its environs*, p.101.

BOUNDARIES

A clearer conception was emerging of a form of local government adapted to the changes which had taken place. First some small anomalies which had existed for centuries were cleared away. Already in 1844 detached parts of counties were annexed to the counties in which they were situated, so the fragment of Meppershall which had belonged to Herts. became Beds. The newly-set up national Local Government Board dealt with detached parts of parishes, and tidied up Pertenhall in 1878 and Westoning in 1888; in 1884 it adjusted the boundary with Northants. in the north and in 1885 with Bucks. in the west; then in 1896 it transferred Swineshead from Hunts. to Beds. in exchange for Tilbrook; and in 1897 it adjusted the Herts. boundary, of which the main result was that Bedfordshire gained Kensworth and lost some parts of other southern parishes.

THE NEW SET-UP

The chief change was the setting up of the county council by the local government act of 1888. The number of county councillors was 68. The electoral campaign was conducted in a dignified manner. The electoral address of E. T. Leeds Smith, the Sandy solicitor, read as follows: "It will devolve upon you in January to elect someone to represent you in the new authority . . . Should you confer upon me the honour I seek at your hands, it will be my duty and endeavour to bring the best abilities I have to the impartial consideration of the important matters which will come before the council."[21] Leeds Smith was a considerable figure in Sandy and beyond – he was treasurer of Sandy show, and secretary of the building society and the gas committee – but another candidate had the temerity to oppose him on the first occasion. After 3 years, over a hundred electors signed a request to him to stand again.[22] This time his address ran "When you conferred upon me the honour of sending me to represent you in the first county council for Bedfordshire, you asked no pledges and I gave none . . . You reposed in me a trust to which I hope I have not been unfaithful."[23] This time he was unopposed.

The first county council showed only a slight change from the social composition of quarter sessions. Most councillors were already justices of the peace, but not all, especially the farmers. Councillors included Lord St. John, and gentry like J. H. Brooks, J. S. Crawley, W. F. Higgins, C. Magniac, R. Orlebar, F. Shuttleworth, W. Stuart, and S. Whitbread, all justices. Besides Leeds Smith there were other solicitors, Henry Trethewy who was a justice, and Henry Pettit of Leighton who was not. There were farmers, like John Pedley of Gt. Barford, William Inskip of Shefford, James Crouch of Ridgmont, and George Cook of Flitwick, none of them on the commission. There was A. Hucklesby, future mayor of Luton, already a county justice; and there was J. H. Limbrey, a Dunstable

[21] C.R.O., LS 586.
[22] C.R.O., LS 603.
[23] C.R.O., LS 607.

ironmonger, who was not on the county commission.

The duties of this first county council were not in fact very important. They had nothing whatever to do with education. They had to administer 254 miles of main roads taken over from the highway boards (grass was growing between the tracks on Watling St., so much had traffic decreased); they were responsible for weights and measures; and in 1893 they appointed a part-time medical officer who was to inform himself respecting influences affecting the public health. A joint committee of the county council and quarter sessions administered police. T. W. Pearse was the first clerk of the council. As their first chairman, the council appointed Charles Magniac of Colworth; for Hastings, 9th Duke of Bedford, was nearing the end of his life and died in 1891. In 1892 they appointed as chairman Sackville, 10th Duke of Bedford. The room in which they met was that which had been designed for the grand jury.

County property listed at the take-over comprised the Shire Hall (that is to say, the new courts, waiting-hall and auxiliary rooms), in which Bedford town council had a right to share on payment of rent; the courthouses at Luton and Sharnbrook; and the police stations at Ampthill, Bedford, Biggleswade, Leighton and Woburn.[24] (It will be recalled that Bedford town council took over the old school premises as town hall in 1891.)

Just as the smaller urban centres became urban districts (ch. 42), so the rural areas in 1894 became rural districts with sanitary powers and with authority to administer the remaining roads, also with elective councils. The rural districts followed the area of the poor law unions, for they were in fact the rural residue after the boroughs and the urban districts had been taken out. To some extent these were reasonable areas, the rural districts of Ampthill, Bedford, Biggleswade and Luton.

But in the remaining cases there was trouble. The poor law of 1834 had ignored county boundaries, while the local government act of 1894 respected them. The area of a poor law union which bestrode the county boundary was truncated in the 1894 rural district; and the severed remnant was not large enough to work satisfactorily. Thus six northern Beds. parishes, of which Eaton Socon was the chief, formed part of St. Neots Union; they now constituted the perilously small rural district of Eaton Socon. Still smaller was the rural district of Eaton Bray, for this was the Bedfordshire remnant of parishes in Leighton Union, severed, both from Bucks. parishes in this union, and from Leighton itself. To act thus with Wellingborough Union would have been a *reductio ad absurdum*; Podington and Wymington could hardly form a rural district by themselves; so that they were added to Bedford rural district. But the unsatisfactory rural districts of Eaton Socon and Eaton Bray struggled on for some years.

The parish had by degrees lost nearly all its former responsibilities – for poor,

[24] C.R.O., QSM 48, pp.336-9.

for police, and for roads. In some parishes attendance at the vestry meeting sank low, and about 1840 a Dunton churchwarden, when summoning the vestry, added to his notice "If none attends, I shall proceed as I think proper."[25] Even church rates, the original responsibility of the parish, were no longer obligatory after 1868. Surviving vestry minutes for some parishes however still show activity. Any civil powers the vestry still possessed were transferred by the local government act of 1894 to newly-set up civil parish councils, or (in the smallest parishes) to parish meetings. Such is the contrariety of human nature that at least one parish council resolved at its inaugural meeting that a parish council was not required.

Thus by the end of the period the electoral framework of local government by county and district councils which was to last to the present day was in being. Those survivals of the Victorian system, the poor law boards and the school boards, were to linger for some years. Quarter sessions continued for purposes of justice and as part of the joint police authority. And of course the venerable shrievalty and lieutenancy remained also.

25 C.R.O., P 51/8/1.

Epilogue

47 – MODERN BEDFORDSHIRE, 1888–1968
(With military material contributed by Brigadier Peter Young, D.S.O., M.C.)

IN THE main the trends in Bedfordshire history ran almost undeflected through three wars, and were indeed partly accelerated by them. But since when modern war occurs it increasingly affects all our lives, it will be taken first.

WAR

Viewed from the regimental angle, we see the Bedfordshire Regiment becoming merged in one associated with a much larger area. Its association with Hertfordshire began in 1881 when Bedford became the official centre for The Hertfordshire Militia as well as the Bedfordshire Light Infantry Militia, which formed its 3rd and 4th Battalions. After the 1914–18 war its name was changed to The Bedfordshire and Hertfordshire Regiment. When the 1939–45 war was over, and the 2nd Battalion disbanded, the remaining battalion was absorbed into The East Anglian, afterwards The Royal Anglian Regiment.

In the three wars of the period, the Regiment has played a varied part. The South African War called for expansion; the 2nd Battalion was reinforced from the volunteer battalions; and 7 officers and 272 non-commissioned officers from these served in South Africa. The Regiment suffered from enteric, as did many others, at Bloemfontein in 1900; and in 1901 was part of a small force surprised by Boers, which held out till relief came. After this war Lord Haldane reorganised the army, cut down the Militia, and organized the Special Reserve to supply drafts for the Regular Army. Yeomanry and Volunteers were merged in the Territorial Army, and on mobilisation became operational units.

During the 1914–18 war the Regiment was greatly expanded, and sustained a total of 18,894 casualties. Many were lost in the mud and slaughter of the Flanders trenches; others at Gallipoli (the nickname of the "yellow devils" was gained at Suvla Bay in 1915); the Regiment was also in Italy; and one battalion was in Palestine when Allenby marched into Jerusalem in 1917.

In the 1939–45 war each Territorial battalion was split, forming cadres for four new units. The 2nd Battalion fought with great skill and success during the disastrous Dunkirk campaign, and, though continually in the front line, got home nearly 600 strong – a record equalled by few. Later this Battalion served with distinction in North Africa and Italy. One battalion landed at Singapore in 1940 just in time to be involved in its fall and to spend the rest of the war in Japanese prison camps. The 1st Battalion, after taking part in the successful defence of

Tobruk, was with the Chindits in Burma.

However, regimental history does not cover all the county's involvement, for under conscription The Bedfordshire (later Bedfordshire and Hertfordshire) Regiment included many men from other counties, while many Bedfordshire men served in other regiments or in the Royal Navy or the Royal Air Force. In fact, the county's total losses in the 1914–18 war were nearly 5,000 men. In terms of total county population, this was about $2\frac{1}{2}\%$; but in terms of one generation of young men, it was the majority. Often several were killed in one family; thus at Arlesey 4 Albones, 2 Browns, 2 Crawleys, 2 Devereux, 2 Pikes, 3 Rainbows, 3 Streets, 2 Thompsons, 4 Tophams, 2 Walkers and 2 Watertons were lost. In the 1939–45 war losses were much fewer; for instance, Sharnbrook's war memorial shows 21 men for 1914–18, 13 for 1939–45; while Barton, with a growing population, lost 25 men in the earlier war but only 8 in the later one.

The increasing importance of the air involved the county in another way. It began on a small scale at Cardington and Henlow in the 1914–18 war (between the wars the former was associated with the ill-fated construction of airships). In the 1939–45 war Cardington was a reception centre for recruits. From Tempsford, R.A.F. aircraft dropped agents and equipment in German-occupied Europe. At Leighton Buzzard was the headquarters of the R.A.F. Signals organisation, and another R.A.F. station was formed at Chicksands. New stations were created with long runways for the R.A.F./U.S.A.A.F. in their pitiless bombing offensive against Germany and German-occupied territory; these were at Cranfield, Thurleigh and Little Staughton – the creation of this last base involved the destruction of 3 inns, the 18th cent. Baptist chapel, and more than half the village. Most of these lapsed after the war, but Cranfield became the home of the College of Aeronautical Engineering (equipped partly with plant and instruments taken from the Germans); Thurleigh became the nucleus of the Royal Aircraft Establishment (Bedford); while Henlow remains a large unit; and Chicksands is manned almost entirely by the U.S.A.F.

What was practically a new factor in the two latter wars was the tremendous involvement of the civilian population. These suffered in the 1914–18 war from strain resulting from the loss of key men in agriculture and industry before conscription was introduced; and from food shortages till rationing was devised; while country houses like Ampthill Park became hospitals. Post-war revival here as elsewhere was hampered by the loss of able young men. Though in the 1939–45 war casualties were much fewer, other effects at home were felt still more. Evacuation of school-children from London and from the south coast to this county put a strain both on evacuees in strange surroundings and on their hosts; many soon drifted back, though in some cases lifelong friendships were formed. Rationing was prompt and efficient. Civil defence against air attack was organised; 1,000 high explosive and 8,000 incendiaries fell on the county, the chief damage being at Bedford, and at Luton (Skefko works); while a landmine fell near Kempston barracks. The Home Guard was organised in 8 battalions, which were based on Ampthill, Bedford, Biggleswade, Dunstable and Luton. An immense amount of voluntary work was done, mainly through the Women's Voluntary Services.

After both world wars, but particularly after the latter, the pent-up forces of change gained added strength; and these must now be traced throughout the period.

COUNTRYSIDE

Agriculture was an exception to the other long-term trends of the period, for after a long decline it was successfully revived. Apart from 1916–18,[1] when war-time food shortages temporarily attracted government attention, there were 50 years of agricultural depression, with few gleams of light. One of these latter was progress in education and experiment. There was a farm school at Ridgmont from 1896 to 1913, one of the first in England (the farm was leased by the Duke to the county council at a nominal rent). At Woburn experimental work continued (since 1926 the experimental station here has been run by Rothamsted). In 1908 a Liberal government thought to help farm workers to progress by means of smallholdings rented from county councils, and Bedfordshire county council bought its first smallholdings land and rented more from the Whitbread estate. Lloyd George in 1913 in a speech at Bedford[2] attacked the big estates, but the Liberals' diagnosis was wrong: the cause of depression was not the large size of estates but unrestricted imports. After the 1914–18 war the smallholdings move-ment was stepped up for ex-service men, some of whom lacked experience, and falling post-war prices brought many to bankruptcy. Copyhold tenure which still lingered, for instance in the manors of Luton, Leighton Buzzard and Stevington, was brought to a gradual end by an act passed in 1925.

During this bad time for farming, market-gardeners in east Bedfordshire, for whose fresh vegetables the demand was continually growing, operated on an increasing scale, as for instance did Mark Young and Frank Davison. To reach markets, the railways in the early 20th cent. were their main form of transport; and in the 1920's they began to use lorries to reach the big midland towns also. Their onions were famed.

A small glasshouse and nursery industry developed. A pioneer was W. E. Wallace, who was growing carnations at Eaton Bray in the 1890's – years after-wards, when he had a wide reputation, Wallace told how his wife once made him a suit by cutting out a pattern from an old one – "the best suit I ever had", he added with a twinkle. The Bedford firm of Laxton was known for 50 years for the breeding of fruit-trees.

---

[1] R. Prothero, who had been agent-in-chief to the Duke of Bedford since 1898, became President of the Board of Agriculture in 1916.
[2] C.R.O., X 67/829.

Meanwhile, with the depression and with war taxation, the old estates began to break up, and this happened earlier in Bedfordshire than in many other counties. The Haynes Park estate was sold in 1914; the Wrest Park estate about 1919; and others followed between the wars and subsequently. The majority of landowners sold before 1939, but there have been large sales from the Woburn estate since the death of Herbrand, 11th Duke, in 1940 (and greater ones from the same estate in Devon). The two largest privately owned estates are those of Woburn (12,620 a.) and Southill (10,850 a.); the county council's smallholdings estate is about 12,000 a. The remaining estates are few and small compared with those of 1873 (ch. 41). Frequently farms were bought by the occupying tenant-farmers.

The great houses came into use for other purposes, even where the estate – or some of it – remained; some are schools or colleges, like Haynes, Sandye Place, and Old Warden; some are occupied by institutions, like Wrest, Colworth and Hasells; one is in military occupation (Chicksands); and a few have been pulled down, like Stockwood and Pavenham Bury. Stately homes and parks are shared: there is public access to Hinwick House, Wrest Park, Woburn Abbey and Luton Hoo.

With the 1939–45 war agricultural recovery began. The War Agricultural Executive Committee took in hand about 5,000 a. of scrub-covered or otherwise unproductive land. Government-assisted mechanised land drainage, together with powerful crawler tractors, made possible arable cropping on extensive clay areas. Prisoners of war and the Women's Land Army supplemented the depleted labour force on the farms. Ploughing-up grants encouraged the bringing back of land into cultivation. After the war, help with buildings and equipment continued, and a system of support prices annually reviewed.

Thus there has been a technical advance on a scale greater than in any period of recorded history. Tractors, combine harvesters and milking machines are in general use. Apart from their greater efficiency (one man can reap and thresh 100 a. with a combine harvester in the time that it would take him merely to reap 25 a. with a horse-reaper), they were essential to save labour. The use of fertilisers, pesticides, hormone weedkillers and improved crop varieties increased production. Whereas the average estimated wheat yield for Bedfordshire 1929–38 was 17·7 cwt. per acre, for 1951–60 it was 25·5 cwt. per acre; and in 1965 it was 35·2 cwt. per acre. It is still rising, and the most progressive farmers reach much higher figures.

Landholding is never static; the tide ebbs and flows. Since the Victorian estates broke up, the process has begun again, for modern production requires larger farming units. Farming firms are being formed, while small farms are amalgamated. The fragmented market-garden holdings in the east are gradually being consolidated, and traditional part-time holdings are declining, although in 1966 Bedfordshire Growers Ltd. was formed to help the smaller man with packing and marketing. General market-gardening, as it was known at its peak in Bedfordshire between the wars, is giving way to contracting on a big scale.

Education, cooperation and advisory facilities have improved. There is now an agricultural college of high reputation in the county (Shuttleworth College, Old Warden). Mander College has a farm at Silsoe. Help and direction are given by the County Agricultural Committee and by the National Agricultural Advisory Service established after the 1939–45 war. The Beds. and Hunts. branch of the National Farmers' Union celebrated its 50th anniversary in 1968. The National Institute of Agricultural Engineering has its headquarters in the county, and the National College for Agricultural Engineering is near it at Silsoe.

Modern agriculture requires a very few skilled men: 3·5% of our population work on the land. These farm-workers are protected by their union and by national wage-awards; they are key-men and sometimes skilled mechanics.

However, the car and the bus, which give the countryman speedier access to urban areas for shopping and entertainment, have brought to many villages commuters, who go to an urban centre to work. Some are birds of passage, making little contribution to rural life, but others have brought new ideas and a less parochial outlook. In addition, a London overspill estate has come to Houghton Regis.

Hence the downward trend in rural population, except in remote villages like Battlesden and Astwick, has been reversed. Here are some examples:

parish	peak	nadir	1961 census
Oakley	(1831) 516	(1891) 250	624
Sutton	(1851) 449	(1921) 189	292
Westoning	(1861) 784	(1911) 494	792
Husborne	(1831) 680	(1951) 317	382

Today, if we take as our unit of calculation the geographical county (which includes Luton county borough,) more than half the population are townsmen; but if we take the administrative county, country-dwellers, their ranks swollen by the commuters, still outnumber town-dwellers by 2 : 1.

The self-contained village community has gone, and villagers are in touch with many organisations. The first village Women's Institute was formed in 1917 at Shelton; now nearly every village has one. The work of the national Rural Industries Bureau is carried on by the Rural Community Council, set up in 1953, which also deals with the Playing Fields Association (1946), Parish Councils Association (1947), and Old People's Welfare Council (1952). Very few villages are without some form of communal premises; the standard varies tremendously, but more and more local committees are either replacing older buildings or improving them. The county library serves all villages.

INDUSTRY

In 1891 in Bedfordshire townsmen formed the minority, and even in 1911 they did not quite equal countrymen. In Edwardian Bedford country shoppers could leave a pony and trap standing in High Street while they made their purchases; Clarke, the Harpur Street grocer, gave customers' children penny bars of chocolate; and in the Town and County Club (1885) retired army officers and Indian civil servants refought the Afghan wars and readministered their Indian districts. In Edwardian Luton there were still a few hat factories in George Street and many more in the neighbouring streets. Edwardian Dunstable was almost rural.

The small scale of affairs is instanced by a reminiscence of the late Walter Peacock. When , a young man returning from the South African war, he set up in Bedford as an auctioneer, he omitted to secure his in-payments before paying out, and had only 10s. left. "It was a lesson to me", he used to say.

With the agricultural depression, most firms in the small towns producing agricultural implements gave up by degrees (the larger Britannia Ironworks in the general depression of 1932).

But there was a new factor. While in north England the old industries found increasing foreign competition, southeast England began to expand, and Bedfordshire with it. As the advent of electrical power (provided by both Bedford and Luton corporations) lessened dependence on coal, new industries found space in our towns within easy reach of London. The wave broke most strongly on Luton, partly because there was male labour available (the hat trade depended mainly on women), and also because there was little trade unionism (again because of the many small firms in the hat trade). Dunstable began once more to go ahead, and Bedford was able to diversify its economy. Outside the towns, the industries of brick, cement and sand grew in scale. The process began before 1914. The industrial depression of the 1930's hit Bedfordshire less severely than the north of England; (in fact, it had the curious result that the Land Settlement Association established estates at Chawston and Potton in a not altogether successful attempt to relieve unemployment in the depressed areas of the north). Apart from this check, and from the 1939–45 war, industrial development has steadily continued.

The following are instances of the kind of thing that happened in the early days. In 1894 W. H. Allen, who wanted a site for engineering works, perhaps at Derby, saw from the train at Bedford that 13 a. near the railway were for sale; he stopped and bought the site. W. H. A. Robertson, who in 1907 was working with a Birmingham firm, wanted to set up his own works for making rolling mills and auxiliary machinery, and aimed at a site midway between Birmingham and a port; as he knew Bedford, from being at one time on Allen's staff, he tried Bedford first, and found a small factory for sale. The Igranic Electric Co. came to Bedford in 1913 and so did Meltis.

Dunstable's first break came with the arrival of the printing firm of Waterlow in 1891, followed by the engineer J. Harrison Carter in 1894. Then Luton and Dunstable actively tried to promote development. In 1900 Luton town council and chamber of commerce secured a special supplement to the periodical *Engineering*, advertising Luton; it was written by young Thomas Keens, and one object was to increase the demand for electricity. Vauxhall Motors came in 1906; Commer Cars in the same year; Davis Gas Stove Co. in 1907; George Kent (meters) in 1908; and Skefko Ball-Bearing Co. in 1910. Meanwhile Dunstable had appointed a new industries committee, and Arthur Bagshawe, who was looking for a site for engineering works within reach of his London offices, was persuaded to set up his chain manufactory in Dunstable in 1906.

Brewing, one of the old stand-bys, continued to concentrate in bigger units: J. W. Green in Luton and Charles Wells in Bedford.

Since there was almost a new dimension in industrial and commercial life, private banks were no longer viable. Bassett's was taken over by Barclay, and Barnard's by the Westminster Bank.

Between the wars development continued in all towns, and fortunately employers (like Sir Charles Bartlett at Vauxhall) were concerned to maintain good labour relations. Perhaps it has helped that in this rural county there were no bitter memories of early days in industry. (The bitter memories were in the countryside, and time assuaged them, for the countryman's centuries-old response to intolerable pressure has been to leave the village for the town.)

The geographical areas of towns expanded by successive boundary alterations; Dunstable has drawn on surrounding parishes; Bedford absorbed Goldington; and Luton progressively recovered all its former hamlets except Hyde. By 1961 Luton's population was over one-third of the county total. Now, if we exclude Luton county borough, Bedford and Dunstable comprise one-third of the total of the administrative county. Manufacturing industries employ 54·7% of our population.

	Luton	Bedford	Dunstable	geographical county
1891	30,053	28,023	4,513	160,621
1911	49,978	39,183	8,057	194,588
1961	131,583	63,334	25,645	380,837

Town clearance and redevelopment, multi-storied buildings, and tower blocks of flats have made Bedfordshire towns almost unrecognisable to anyone returning after an absence of years. Big new housing estates, like Brickhill at Bedford, form semi-suburban areas. At the same time, a number who might have otherwise been active townsmen have gone to live in the villages.

An organisation like the Townswomen's Guild has to form many branches, and is less able to bring together all classes than is its sister organisation in rural areas, the Women's Institute; while special clubs like Rotary, Round Table, Soroptimists, and Business and Professional Women, cater for a limited range.

In libraries Luton has led the way, having rebuilt its library twice (in 1910 with a Carnegie grant and recently), while Bedford did not adopt the public libraries act till 1935. But Bedford has continued to develop parks and gardens with the Embankment, Longholme and Putnoe; while it was after some hesitation that Luton acquired Wardown Park in 1903 and Stockwood Park in 1945.

Brickmaking, which had been able to expand in scale as soon as the railway provided a ready means of transporting bricks to distant areas, had been growing at Arlesey since 1852 (ch. 44). At Westoning B. J. H. Forder of Luton opened works near Harlington station in 1894, and a few years later further works at Wootton Pillinge and Elstow; and when the company of B. J. Forder and Son was formed in 1900, Halley Stewart became chairman.[3] After the 1914–18 war, this company either amalgamated with or took over other companies, including in 1923 the London Brick Co., which was making bricks at Fletton, and in 1928 the Arlesey company and several brickworks in other counties. Meanwhile lorries became available to provide long-distance road transport. Since 1936 the whole concern has been known as the London Brick Co. The Westoning works have long ceased (1906), but the Pillinge works have grown, and here the village has been converted into a model one; under the name of Stewartby (after Sir Halley Stewart, who had been succeeded by his son, Sir Malcolm Stewart) it became a separate parish in 1937. Now the London Brick Co. produces over 2,500,000,000 bricks p.a., of which about 2/5 come from Bedfordshire. It has been calculated that they make enough bricks to produce a house every 5 minutes day and night.

Cement and lime were also produced by B. J. Forder & Son in their early days, cement at Arlesey and lime at Sewell and Blow's Down near Dunstable; but in 1912 they sold these interests to British Portland Cement Manufacturers (now Blue Circle Group). Operations at Arlesey ceased before 1939. The cement plant at Sundon is still operating; and a major cement plant was built at Dunstable in the 1920's. In 1967 over 16 million tons were produced by the Blue Circle Group at home and overseas, of which some 650,000 tons came from Bedfordshire.

Sand is extensively excavated at Leighton Buzzard; one use of it is for Marley tiles, made by a firm of Kentish origin which acquired a factory at Leighton by 1928 and now produce a wide range of plastic products.

PUBLIC SERVICE

Society, which was expanding both in population and wealth, expected a higher standard; and that standard necessitated an expanded public service, local and national, operating in bigger units. The school boards were dropped in 1903, when the county council and town councils took over education. Since 1890 in boroughs and since 1919 in rural areas the district councils have improved housing to a more uniform standard than the landowner could provide; they have also

---

[3] *B. Mag.* i, 150; ix, 18.

supplied piped water, and are completing rural sewerage schemes (the over small rural districts of Eaton Bray and Eaton Socon were absorbed by larger neighbours in 1933 and 1934). The last trace of the honour of Ampthill disappeared when it ceased to have its own coroner in 1929. The subsidiary roads were transferred from the district councils to the county council in 1930; and the motorway from London to Birmingham was built nationally.

Services previously voluntary have become public, like the nursing services under the health act of 1946, and the fire services in 1947. New ones like planning (first foreshadowed in 1909 but made really effective in 1943 and 1947) have been called into being. Some services have required cooperation, such as the regional crime squad set up in 1964; or the Gt. Ouse Water authority in 1961, which created a reservoir at Grafham Water. Public corporations have taken over gas and electricity. Inevitably the state is bearing an increasing share; old age pensions (1908) and national insurance (1911) were from the first organised nationally; hospitals, physical and mental, were taken over by the government in 1946; while the old poor law, first revised in 1930 and then entrusted to the county council, came to an end in 1948, since when destitution has been relieved nationally. The growth of Luton was recognised by its becoming a county borough in 1964.

Though much of this development has been nationally inspired or controlled, local initiative has still been possible. Prompted by G. H. Fowler, the county council from 1913 onwards led the way in the development of local record offices.

Personnel in county affairs has changed. There has been a decrease in the part played by aristocracy and gentry, many of whom have left the county. The lieutenancy has been affected least; after Earl Cowper of Wrest (d. 1905), came Lord St. John and then S. H. Whitbread; who was followed by the 1st Lord Luke. The office of high sheriff, since it changes annually, responds more quickly to change, and is now held from time to time by a prominent Luton business man. The chairman of the county council from 1895 to 1927 was Herbrand, 11th Duke of Bedford; but from 1935 to 1952 Sir Thomas Keens, a Luton accountant. Since Luton became a county borough, the Lutonian element is lacking from the county council; now the two main groups are farmers and business men, with a sprinkling of professional men, workers, retired people, and women.

When W.W. Marks was clerk of the county council 1891–1925, he himself paid and appointed such few assistants as he required. He was a notable figure, able and highly irascible; the words "You're fired!" sprang readily to his lips; and one member of the staff who retired recently at a mature age said that after his last dismissal Mr. Marks had forgotten to reinstate him. When the county council took over education, the question of staff accommodation in the subsidiary rooms of the lawcourts became desperate. In 1906 the director of education begged that he might have at least two rooms, one for himself and one for his clerks; while the chief constable, F. I. Josselyn, stated "I have the use of a small cupboard in the lavatory room, and two more rooms in the passage, one . . . used by the inspector of food and drugs." A council chamber was then built, with some offices; and subsequently council staff spread into adjoining buildings and others scattered in the town. A projected county hall was quashed by war in 1939. Greatly increased responsibilities made a new start necessary, and the first planned premises for the council's staff were completed in 1969. Now, to take the county council alone (i.e., excluding district councils), those in the public service, including teachers and nurses, number about 8,000.

A spotlight on one or two aspects will instance the great developments of the present century.

For instance, in education a report in 1904 shows that several primary schools then had no water, others had defective drains, and many were inadequately heated. For secondary education there were only the four Harpur Trust schools in Bedford, Ashton Grammar School in Dunstable, and some private schools; and even in 1944 these had been extended only to the extent of two grammar schools in Luton and one in Leighton Buzzard. There were however in Bedford a Froebel and a Physical Training college, both private.

The education act of 1944 proved a watershed. Though many old school buildings still exist (with improvements), 69 primary and 35 secondary schools have been built in the geographical county since 1944. There are modern colleges of further education at Bedford, Luton and Dunstable, catering for nearly 20,000 students; Luton, which adopted comprehensive education in 1966, has also a Sixth Form College. There are two teacher-training colleges: one at Luton, and the former Froebel college in Bedford, which was taken over in 1950 and is now housed in new buildings; while the facilities at Bedford Physical Education college (taken over in 1952) have been enlarged out of recognition; these three colleges cater for over a thousand students. In the villages there are 38 further education centres; there is a craft centre at Elstow; and there are residential courses for Luton at Luton and for the county at Woburn. There are also 3 special schools for the sub-normal; and 3 nursery schools.

While in 1888 a small minority of boys had the hope of being educated to the full extent of their capacity, now such education should be within the reach of every child; and the adult can follow up intellectual, artistic or practical interests throughout life.

Communications in 1968 show a great change as compared with 1888. Then villagers not served by a railway had to walk to their nearest town or go by carrier. Now buses serve most villages. The mileage of all vehicles is over 300 million p.a. – in the rush-hour in towns a doubtful blessing. The closure of some of the railways which were a Victorian triumph causes misgiving. Air transport is here: there is an airport at Luton. Telephones, first introduced at Bedford and

Luton in 1896 and Dunstable in 1897 now number 52,500; in fact the Bedford exchange controls in all 107,000 lines, the remainder being outside the county.

In health too there have been immense changes. For instance, in 1888 environmental hygiene was poor owing to bad housing and lack of piped water supply in rural areas. Slum clearance, large-scale building and improvement of homes, and the making of new reservoirs have made a vastly different picture.

Personal health too has improved. In 1888, infectious diseases, including pulmonary tuberculosis, were rife. Medical care at home had to be paid for, except by the poor who were attended by a district medical officer employed by a board of guardians. Nursing care at home was limited to a few areas where it was provided by voluntary associations. Midwifery was in the hands of women not subject to supervision and often untrained. Admission to the voluntary hospitals (the County Hospital in Bedford and the Bute Hospital in Luton) was on the recommendation of a subscribing association or individual; while to a hospital run by a board of guardians (St. Peter's in Bedford and St. Mary's in Luton) admission of the medically destitute was by order of the relieving officer. There were also several fever hospitals provided by the local authority, including one for smallpox.

Some of the improvement since then was due to local initiative. As early as 1893 the county council appointed a medical officer "to inform himself respecting influences affecting injuriously the public health in the county";[4] later Luton built a maternity hospital, and more recently the borough of Bedford has done research into the diseases of diabetes and glaucoma.

Now infectious diseases are neither so prevalent nor so dangerous as in 1888. The hospital once provided by the county council for tuberculosis treatment is now used almost entirely for other purposes. The dreaded diphtheria has virtually disappeared, and the rare occurrence of a case of typhoid fever makes national news. There is only one fever hospital in the county and no smallpox hospital at all. Every person, whether resident in town or country, has his own doctor, and the services (when required) of a fully-trained nurse. There is a complete service of domiciliary midwives, all fully trained and supervised. The welfare of mothers and children is promoted by a service of health visitors, by child welfare centres and ante-natal clinics. The hospital service was improved even between 1929 (when the guardians' responsibility terminated) and 1947 when the Ministry of Health took over: at Bedford there was a considerable extension of beds and facilities, while at Luton the committee provided an entirely new hospital (as it happens within a stone's throw of a junction with the later M.1). Ambulances provide transfer to hospital. Infant mortality is now only one-tenth of what it was in the year 1900. Generally the figures for Bedfordshire compare very favourably

---

[4] The second medical officer became chief medical officer of the Ministry of Health; and the present holder of the latter post is of Bedfordshire origin.

with those of the rest of the country, but the incidence of cancer of the lung continues to increase, and much remains to be done in the prevention of heart disease. Auxiliary services play their part: there are home helps and care for children available in case of need; while the aged can find comfort and security in eventide homes.

POLITICS

The long process of equalising parliamentary representation has continued. A Bedford Society for Women's Suffrage was formed in 1908 – among its members were Miss A. Walmsley of the Froebel College and Miss M. Stansfeld of the Physical Training College. A young doctor, Dora Mason, was sent by headquarters to help them in 1913 – she used to recall that once she escaped from the police by way of the Shire Hall roof, and that friends revived her afterwards with cherry brandy.[5] The vote was granted to women in 1918.

At the same time, constituency boundaries were revised on the basis of the geographical county. The separate status of Bedford disappeared in 1918, when the three constituencies were equalised. In 1950 readjustment was carried a stage further by making four constituencies: Bedford (with the north), Mid-Beds., South Beds., and Luton.

The centuries-old dominance of both county and county town by local aristocracy and gentry ended when C. G. Pym was elected for the last time for Bedford in 1900. Since then party organisations have increasingly controlled the choice of candidates, often from a distance, though in 1922 local feeling revolted, and S. R. Wells of the brewing firm stood for Bedford and continued to represent this constituency till 1945. The independence of the Victorian M.P., who largely paid his own expenses, has given way to increasing party regimentation. The possession of only moderate means is no longer an obstacle to parliamentary candidature, but the party organisation necessary for this sometimes frustrates the member, and public interest flags.

The traditional support of this county, at first for the Whigs, then for their successors the Liberals, lessened slowly. The last Liberal member for a county area was E. L. Burgin, a National Liberal, elected for the last time for South Beds. in 1935. Luton returned Charles Hill as National Liberal for the last time in 1959. In the north and centre, as Liberals declined, Conservatives strengthened, with S. R. Wells and A. Lennox-Boyd.

Nationally, the great fact in politics has been the emergence of a new factor, organised Labour, but this has been slow in gaining ground here. Labour gained its first victories in the Bedford and South Beds. divisions in 1945, and in Luton in 1964; but has never won Mid-Beds.

LIFE IN GENERAL

The pattern of entertainment has changed. At first through films, then

[5] C.R.O., X 114.

through television, standards have become national or even international. Cinemas proliferated in Bedford and Luton, and even reached Ampthill and Sandy; now only large modern ones continue. Luton's theatre has given way to a super-market, and Bedford's is given up to bingo.

In sport specialisation attains a high standard. The County Cricket Club was re-formed in 1899. Football matches, like those of the Luton Town Club which 1955–9 was in the First Division and reached the Cup Final, draw spectators. Overseas crews compete at Bedford regatta, which is now highly organised.

Yet there are many people doing things for themselves. There are amateur theatricals and operatical societies and choirs. The Bedfordshire Natural History Society has revived and goes bird-watching (incidentally the Zoological Society between the wars opened a zoo at Whipsnade and the Royal Society for the Protection of Birds has its headquarters at Sandy). A county flora has been produced by a Luton schoolmaster. Vauxhall works has an angling club. Amateur archaeologists excavate at Bedford, Luton and Dunstable. Museums, since 1928 at Luton, more recently at Bedford (Cecil Higgins 1949, Bedford Museum in present premises 1962),[6] and at Elstow since 1951 attract thousands of visitors. Historical talent finds an outlet in the *Bedfordshire Magazine* and the publications of the *Record Society*. While in 1888 facilities for reading were minimal, in 1968 the book issue from public libraries in the geographical county was nearly six million. There is a county *Bibliography*.

The incidence of crime, however, has not fallen, even taking into account greatly increased population. Man's endeavour to be at peace with himself and his fellows, or his failure to do so, takes on new forms as society changes, but is always there. In 1967 there were 8,894 indictable offences and 2,440 road accidents in which 63 persons were killed. Housebreaking and larceny are still frequent. Two advances are the provision of legal aid for those who cannot afford it; and the increasing use of probation for first offenders.

Perhaps one of the best-known cases of this period was the Luton riot of 1919. The ex-service men concerned had some provocation; the town council had not planned a thanksgiving service as part of the peace celebrations, and refused the use of Wardown Park when one was organised. Luton's old restless spirit stirred again – perhaps for the last time – and the town hall was burnt down. I was spending the weekend in Luton with a school-friend; we found George St. jammed with a sullen, silent crowd, and watched a man in front of the town hall (which was already smouldering) throw a stone through one of its windows. The other notorious case was the A6 murder of 1961 – the longest trial of the century to date.

---

[6] This museum originated at Bedford Modern School in 1884 with Charles Prichard's collection and was transferred to the corporation in 1959.

THE CHURCHES

The churches have been faced by two problems. One is that of redeployment in view of inflation and town expansion. Again diocesan boundaries were adjusted; since 1914 the archdeaconry has been in St. Albans diocese, latterly with a suffragan Bishop of Bedford. In Bedford and Luton new Anglican parishes have been formed, while country parishes are linked, and lay-readers are more in evidence. Several of the free churches have built or are building new churches in the towns, often on new housing estates, while closing central and smaller buildings. Roman Catholic churches were opened in the remaining urban centres between 1897 and 1935 (7 in Luton). The Society of Friends reopened a meeting in Bedford. The other is the national tendency to withdraw from organised religion, while paying homage to the Christian ethic (not the same thing as attempting to make it the basis of life).

One growing-point seems to be the ecumenical movement, noticeable not only in councils of churches in the towns, but in joint services and discussions in many villages. Another is the way in which the churches are joining with secular organisations and individuals in a drive for a juster allocation of the world's resources, and the care for misfits and deprived. One thing is certain: new growth always appears in unexpected places and in an unexpected form, and is seldom if ever at first recognised for what it is. Some of us may think we see signs of it now.

THE WIDER WORLD

The old song said:

> Go north or south or east or west –
> Wherever you roam o'er the earth's wide breast
> You'll find the boys of the eagle crest,
> From Bedford by the river.

Now both boys and girls, not only from Bedford but from all over the county, are probably to be found throughout the commonwealth and elsewhere; and it seems likely that there is now no village without some overseas connections – probably many villages have several (Willington is connected with at least ten countries).

A far greater change is that the wider world has come to southeast England, and in this immigration Bedfordshire has a prominent share. The largest immigrant group is that of the Italians (who came mainly for the brickworks but have since spread into other walks of life); but Caribbeans, Indians and Pakistanis amounted in 1968 to 4·6% of Bedford's population,[7] and at one school there was a form with only one white child. The last census (1961) showed in the county over 2,000 Poles; 8,000 Italians; over 3,000 Caribbeans; and over 3,000 Indians and Pakistanis. The Pakistanis work mainly in the brickworks; the Caribbeans

[7] Institute of Race Relations, *Colour and immigration in the United Kingdom*, 1968. The highest percentage was Brent with 7·4%; Wolverhampton had 4·8%

and Indians in engineering; and many Caribbean girls have been recruited for local nursing. A recent study has shown that the prime factor in this immigration is the shortage of white labour; conditions in the immigrants' home countries merely create a favourable atmosphere for response to the demand here.[8]

Some recent developments continue the tradition of Howard and Whitbread. In 1968 Bedford International Friendship Association appointed an Asian woman graduate to act as liaison officer and help the newcomers. In 1967–68 a Bedford-shire Lord Mayor of London instituted the Absent Guest Fund, which collected £102,000 to help alleviate poverty in the developing countries overseas. The President of the Save the Children Fund is a former M.P. for Mid-Beds.

World trends of today may cause us to under-estimate the supreme impor-tance of the individual in the vast and intricate processes of history. Such trends are the product of innumerable individual choices, and the pattern that is being created is only apparent subsequently.

The unknown man who was Bunyan's father-in-law made a choice on the day he bought *The plain man's pathway to Heaven*. The girl who became Bunyan's wife absorbed her father's teaching. The women whose conversation Bunyan heard in Bedford had made moral choices. Thomas and Elizabeth Bunyan made such a choice when they decided to spare the money for little John to be taught to read and write – they could have spent it on beer, or a new gown, or betting at cockfighting. Bunyan himself made many choices, from the day he got bored with tipcat (he could have sought excitement in poaching), to the day when he overcame his reluctance to preach. So on that November afternoon in 1660 when he was confronted with the choice between home and prison, the right decision came naturally. There was one more: that to rise above imprisonment instead of being defeated by it. So came *The Pilgrim's Progress*, now obtainable in almost every language in the world. When today the inhabitants of Borneo, or of the Gilbert Islands, or Red Indians, or Kikuyu, read the story of Christian and Faithful, they form a link in a chain of events which goes back to an unknown 17th cent. man buying a book.

Meanwhile, change comes ever more swiftly. Which of the changes since 1888 would cause greatest astonishment to the residents of that day? Would it be our affluence? our social services? our technical know-how? our appalling congestion? our egalitarianism? our materialism? our ecumenism? our cos-mopolitanism?

And (supposing man to overcome the great challenges of today posed by his fear – armaments leading to war, and by his selfish greed – material acquisitiveness which runs counter to world justice) how will Bedfordshire residents of a century hence view us, and what will they conclude to have been our main problems? Certainly they will see us in quite another light than that in which we see ourselves.

[8] C. Peach, *West Indian immigration.*

Their outlook will probably be global. They may be as shocked at the present difference between the have and the have-not countries as we are at the old difference between have and have-not classes. Possibly they will take a world police-force for granted, as we now do our comparatively recent professional constabulary. Perhaps the dwindling differences between creeds and denominations will have almost merged in world understanding. One thing is certain: future generations will have problems of their own – problems of a nature and on a scale which we cannot even envisage, for each generation has its own struggle to face and its own glory to achieve.

A READING LIST

REFERENCE   Publications of the Bedfordshire Historical Record Society, from 1913.
 Victoria County History, 4 vols., 1904–14.
 Harvey, W. M. *The history and antiquities of the hundred of Willey*, 1878.
 Blaydes, F. A. *Bedfordshire notes and queries*, 3 vols., 1886–93.

PRELIMINARY READING   Hamson, J. *Bedford town and townsmen*, 1896.
 Smith, Worthington G. *Dunstable and its surroundings*, 1904.
 Blundell, J. H. *Toddington*, 1925.
 Farrar, C. F. *Ouse's silent tide*, 1921; *Old Bedford*, 1926.
 Austin, W. *The history of Luton and its hamlets*, 2 vols., 1928.
 Dyer, J., Stygall, F., Dony, J. *The Story of Luton*, 1964.
 Carnell, H. A., Booth, T., Tibbutt, H. G., *A Kempston history*, 1966.
 [Elstow] *Moot Hall Leaflets* (from 1952). *The Bedfordshire Magazine* (from 1947). *The Lock Gate* (from 1961).

ARCHAEOLOGICAL   Smith, Worthington G. *Man the primeval savage*, 1894.
 Wadmore, Beauchamp. *The earthworks of Bedfordshire*, 1920.
 Dyer, J. Bedfordshire earthworks (in *B. Mag.*, 1961–3).
 Bedfordshire Archaeologist (from 1955).
 Bedfordshire Archaeological Journal (from 1962).
 Manshead Magazine (from 1958).

RELIGIOUS LIFE   Sister Elspeth. The religious houses (in *V.C.H.* i).
 Monastic cartularies (in *B.H.R.S.* x, xiii, xvii, xxii, xliii).
 Tibbutt, H. G. Histories of nonconformist churches, e.g. *Bunyan Meeting*.
 Wigfield, W. M. Recusancy and nonconformity (in *B.H.R.S.* xx).

THE SCHOOLS   Sargeaunt, J. *A history of Bedford School*, 1925.
 Kuhlicke, F. W. Chronicles of Bedford Modern (in *B.M.S. Eagle*, 1947–55).
 Farrar, C. F. *Harper's Bedford charity*, 1930.

BIOGRAPHY   Brown, J. *John Bunyan* (F. M. Harrison ed.), 1928.
 Brittain, V. *In the steps of John Bunyan*, 1950.
 Fulford, R. *Samuel Whitbread, 1764–1815*, 1967.
 (See also Bedfordshire Biographies in *B. Mag.*; and biographies in some vols. of *B.H.R.S.*)

TRADITIONAL CRAFTS   Dony, J. *A history of the straw hat industry*, 1942.
 Freeman, C. E. *Pillow lace in the East Midlands*, 1958 (Luton Museum).

ARCHITECTURE   Richardson, (Sir) A. E. and others. *Southill, a Regency house*, 1951.
 Bedfordshire County Council: *A Bedfordshire heritage*, 1961.

NATURAL HISTORY   Dony, J. *Flora of Bedfordshire*, 1953.
 Bedfordshire Naturalist (from 1947).

Further details may be found in L. R. Conisbee, *A Bedfordshire Bibliography*, 1962; supplt. 1967.

INDEX OF NAMES

A separate index of subjects appears on page 586.

Note: A hamlet is indexed under the parish of which it forms part; thus Ickwell will be found under Northill; but where the hamlet later became a parish it is given a separate entry; thus Silsoe will be found throughout under Silsoe, not under Flitton. Wrest, however, is given a separate entry. Bishops are found under their diocese; archdeacons under the Bedford archdeaconry; and monks under their monastery; but incumbents appear under their own names.

INDEX OF SUBJECTS